军号

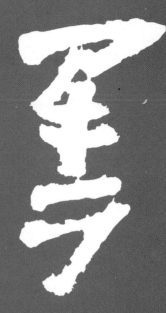

A Kodansha Comics Trade Paperback Original

AKIRA Volume 3 © 1986 MASH•ROOM. All rights reserved.
English translation copyright © 1986 MASH•ROOM /Kodansha Ltd.
First published in Japan in 1986 by Kodansha Ltd., Tokyo.
Publication rights for this English edition arranged through Kodansha Ltd., Tokyo.

Published in the United States by Kodansha Comics, an imprint of Kodansha USA Publishing, New York.

Kodansha Comics is a registered trademark of Kodansha Ltd.

ISBN 978-1-935429-04-3

First edition: July 2010
Printed in the United States of America

10 9 8 7 6 5 4

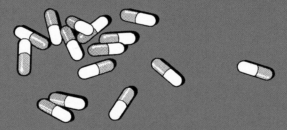

Translation and English-language adaptation:Yoko Umezawa, Linda M. York, Jo Duffy.
Graphics adaptation and sound effects lettering: David Schmit/ Digibox, Editions Glénat
Digital lettering and additional graphics adaptation: Digital Chameleon, Dark Horse Comics
English edition cover design and art direction: Lia Ribacchi, Mark Cox

MASH•ROOM staff: Makoto Shiosaki, Yasumitsu Suetake
Original series editor: Koichi Yuri
Original cover design: Akira Saito/Veia
Editor for this edition: Naoto Yasunaga, Takeshi Katsurada

AKIRA

KATSUHIRO OTOMO

**BOOK
THREE**

KODANSHA
COMICS

AKIRA
PART 3

アキラ II

Akira II

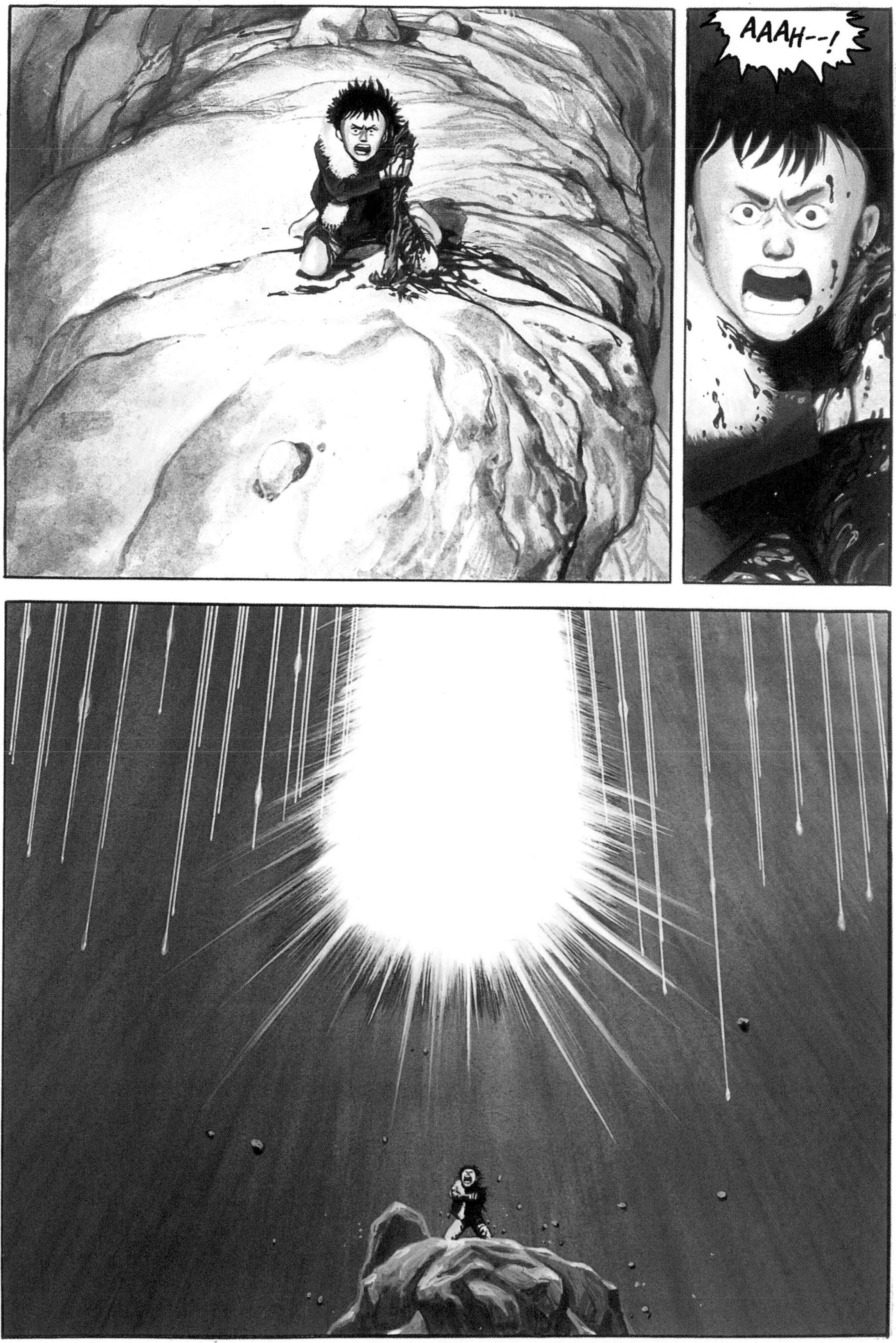
AAAH--!

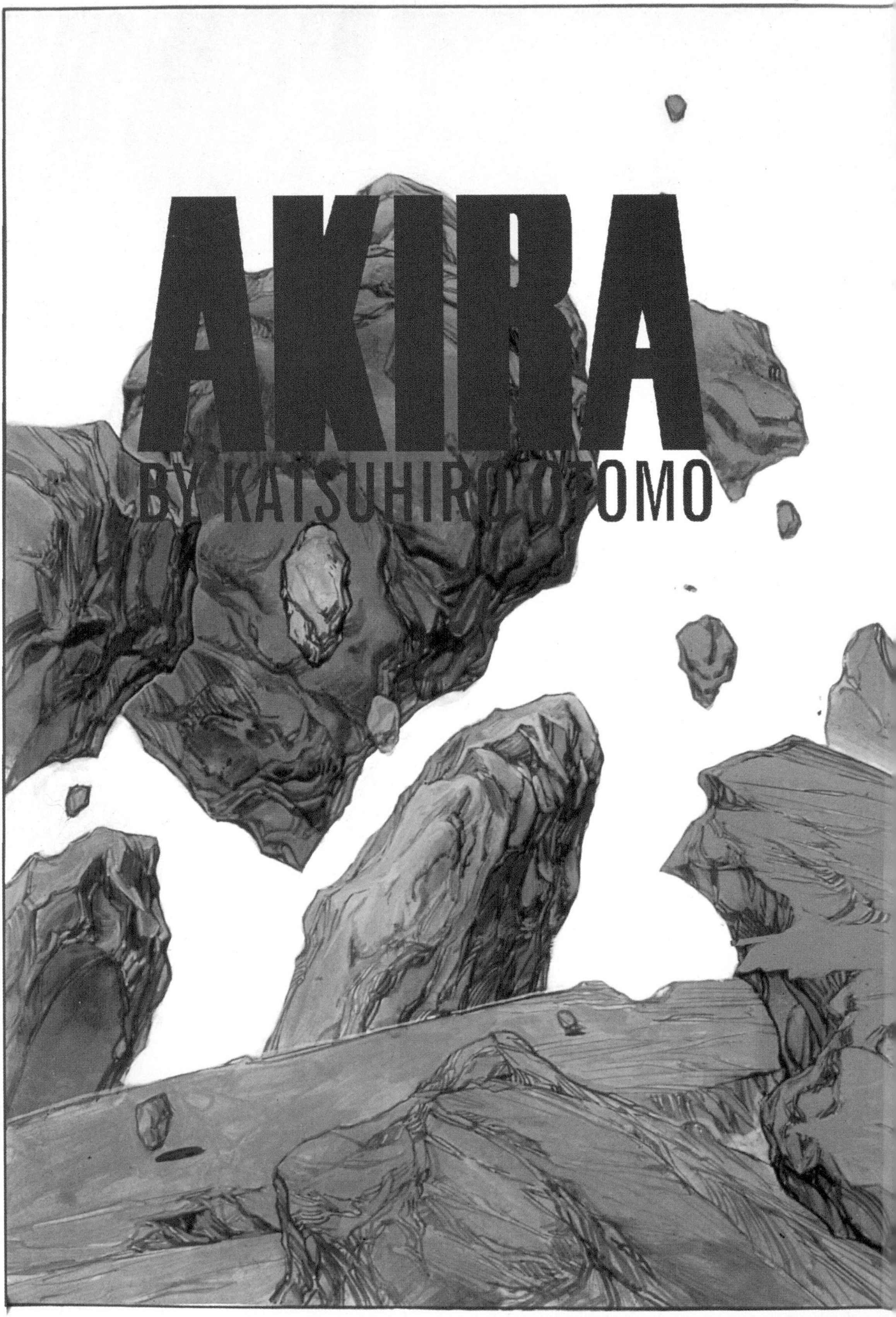
AKIRA
BY KATSUHIRO OTOMO

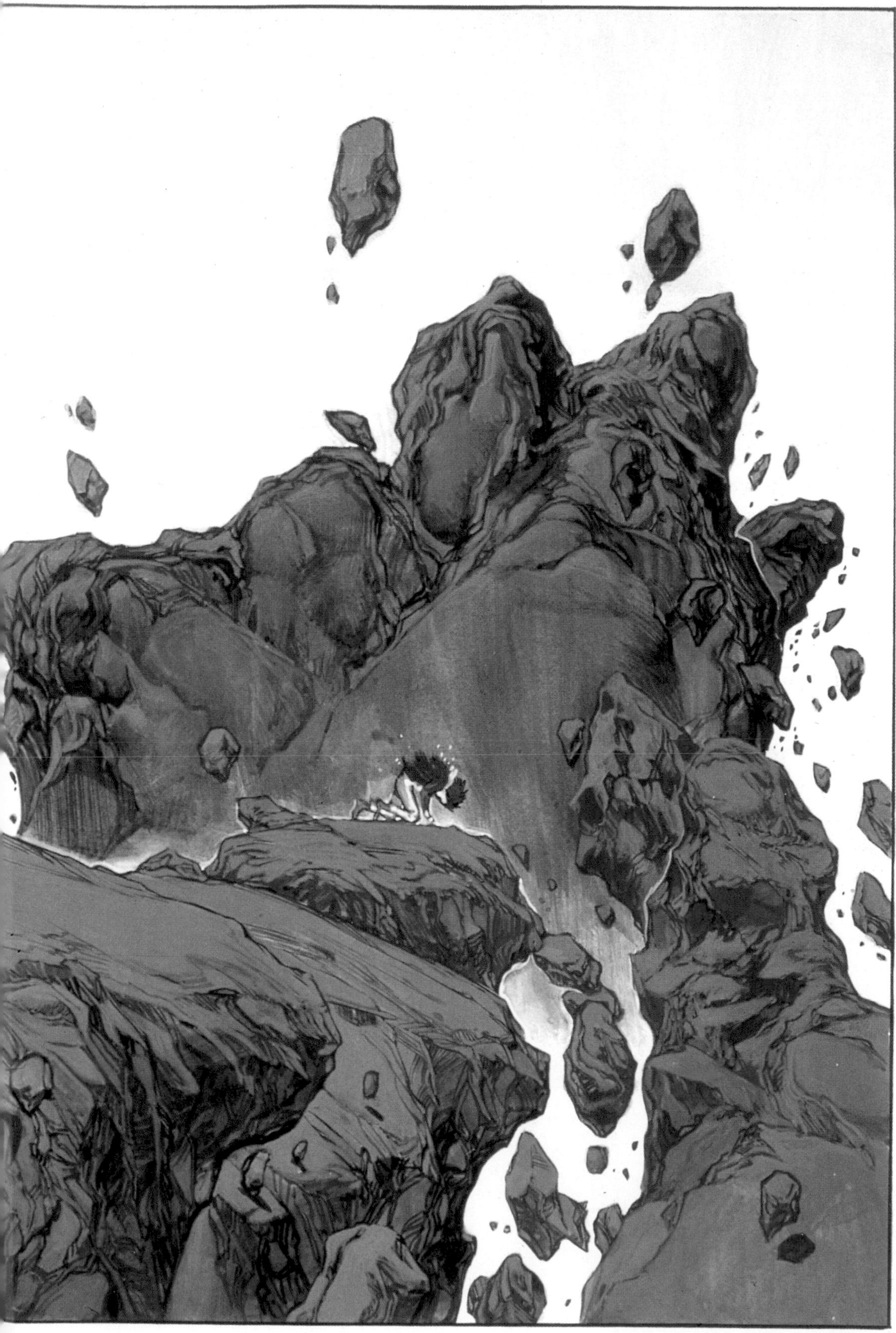

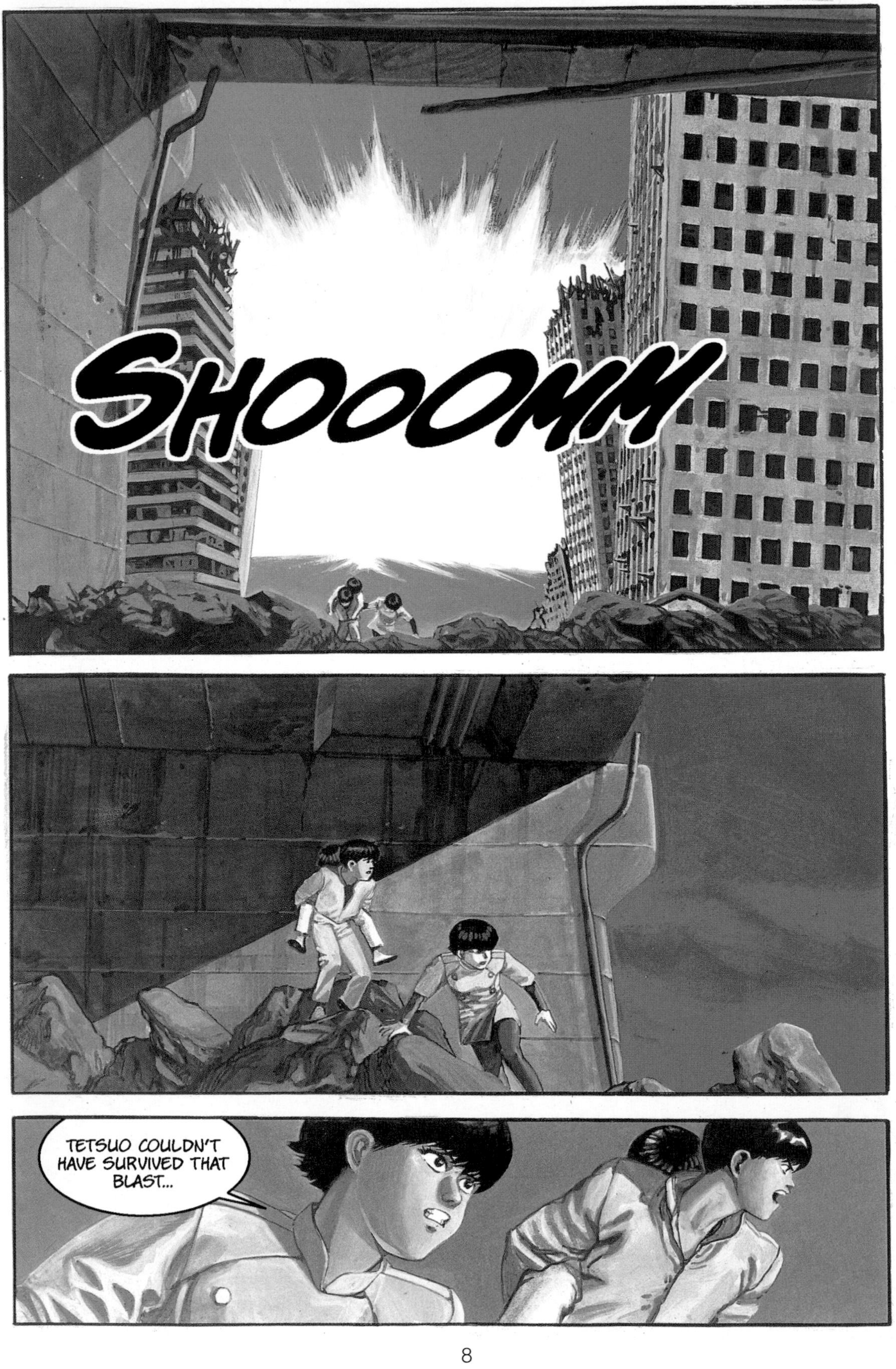
SHOOOMM
TETSUO COULDN'T HAVE SURVIVED THAT BLAST...

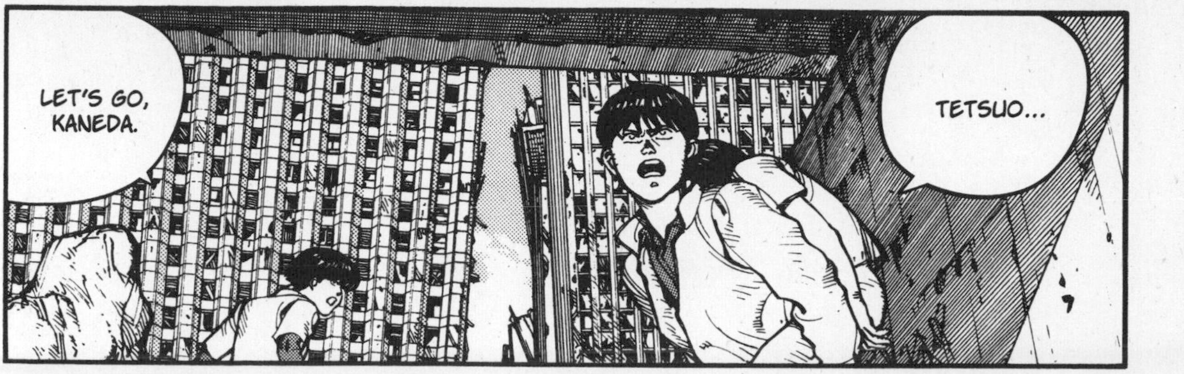
LET'S GO, KANEDA.
TETSUO...

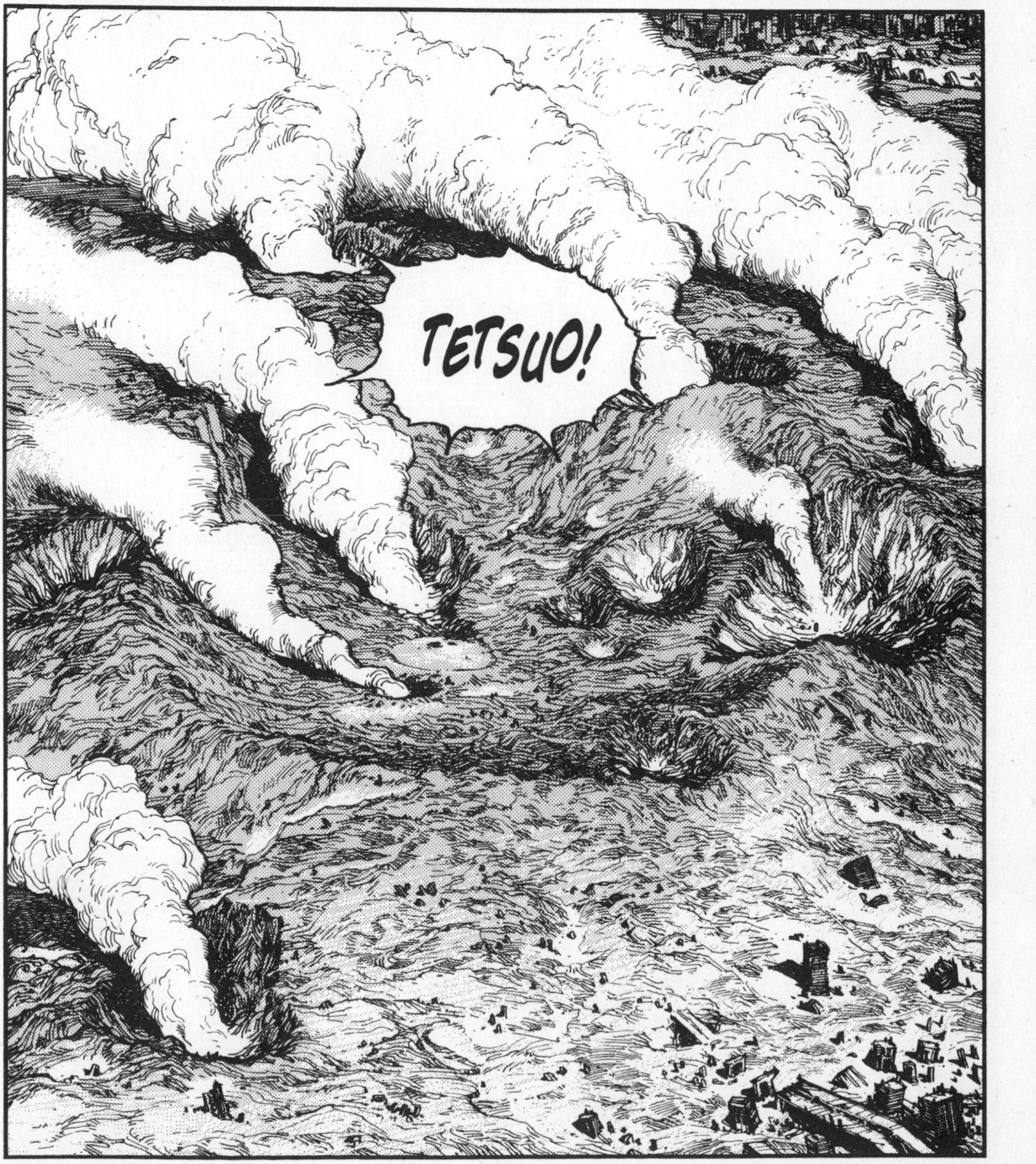
TETSUO!

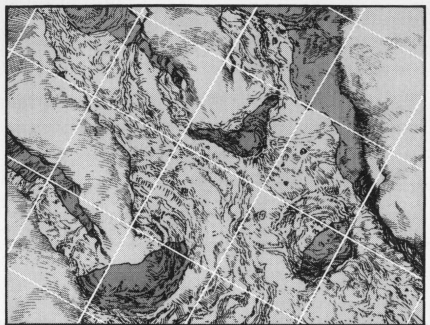

FOCUS ON THE AREA BETWEEN COORDINATES N-35 AND E-75 AND INCREASE MAGNIFICATION.

BEGIN SCANNING!

SIR, AT THIS ANGLE OUR ORBITAL VELOCITY IS CAUSING A DELAY IN THE SCANNING CALCULATIONS...

CORRECT FOR THE DELAY!

SCAN NEXT QUADRANT!

...

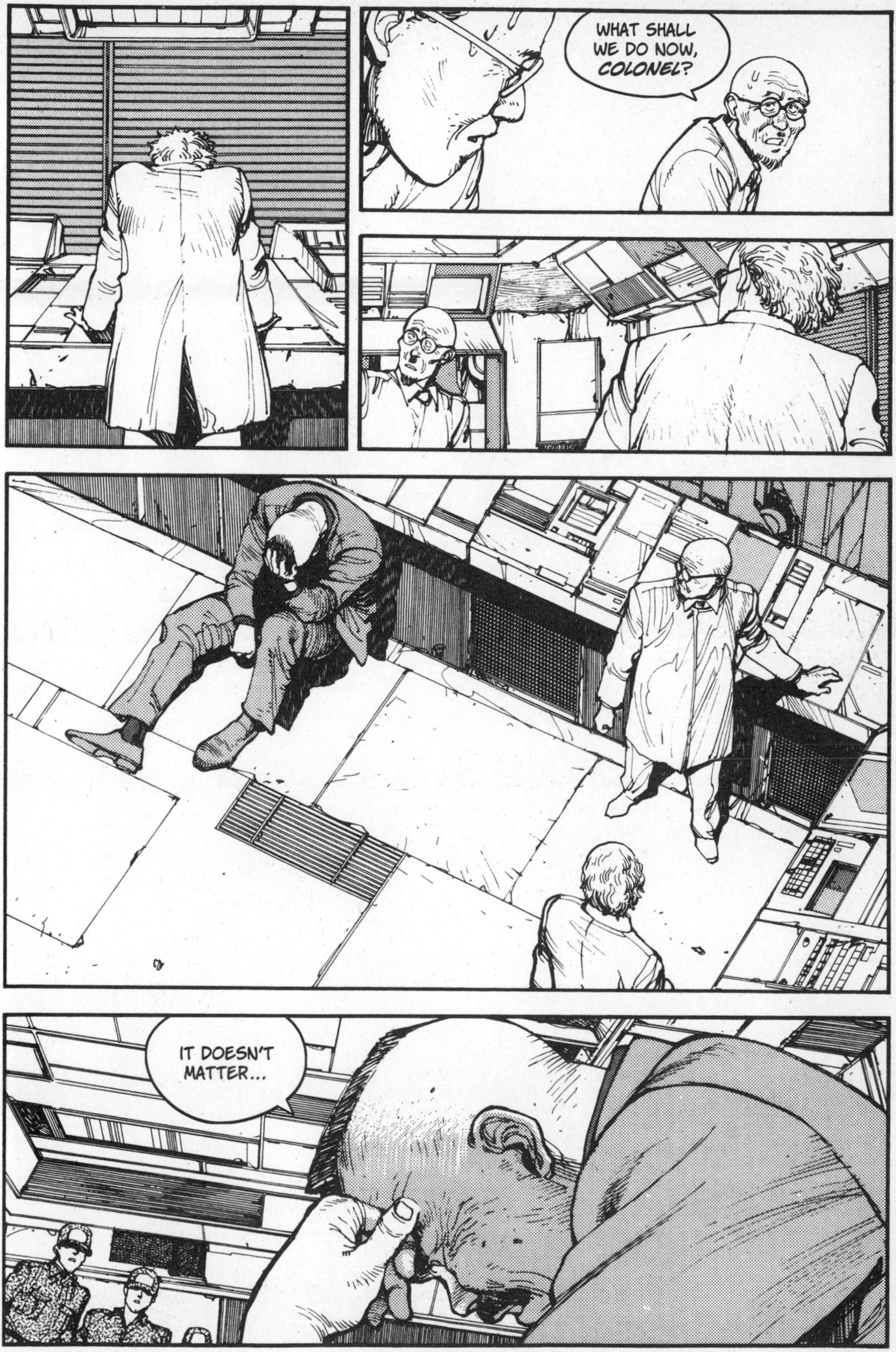
WHAT SHALL WE DO NOW, COLONEL?
IT DOESN'T MATTER...

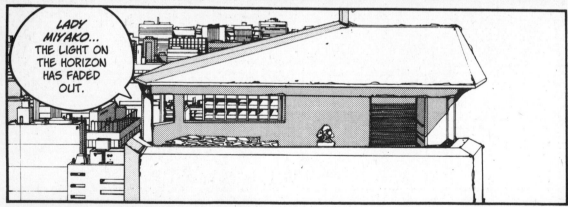

LADY MIYAKO... THE LIGHT ON THE HORIZON HAS FADED OUT.

FROM THE LOOK OF IT, I SUSPECT THE SOURCE WAS A MILITARY SATELLITE CALLED *SOL.* THE ARMY LAUNCHED IT THREE YEARS AGO, AND IT CARRIES A HUGE LASER CANNON.

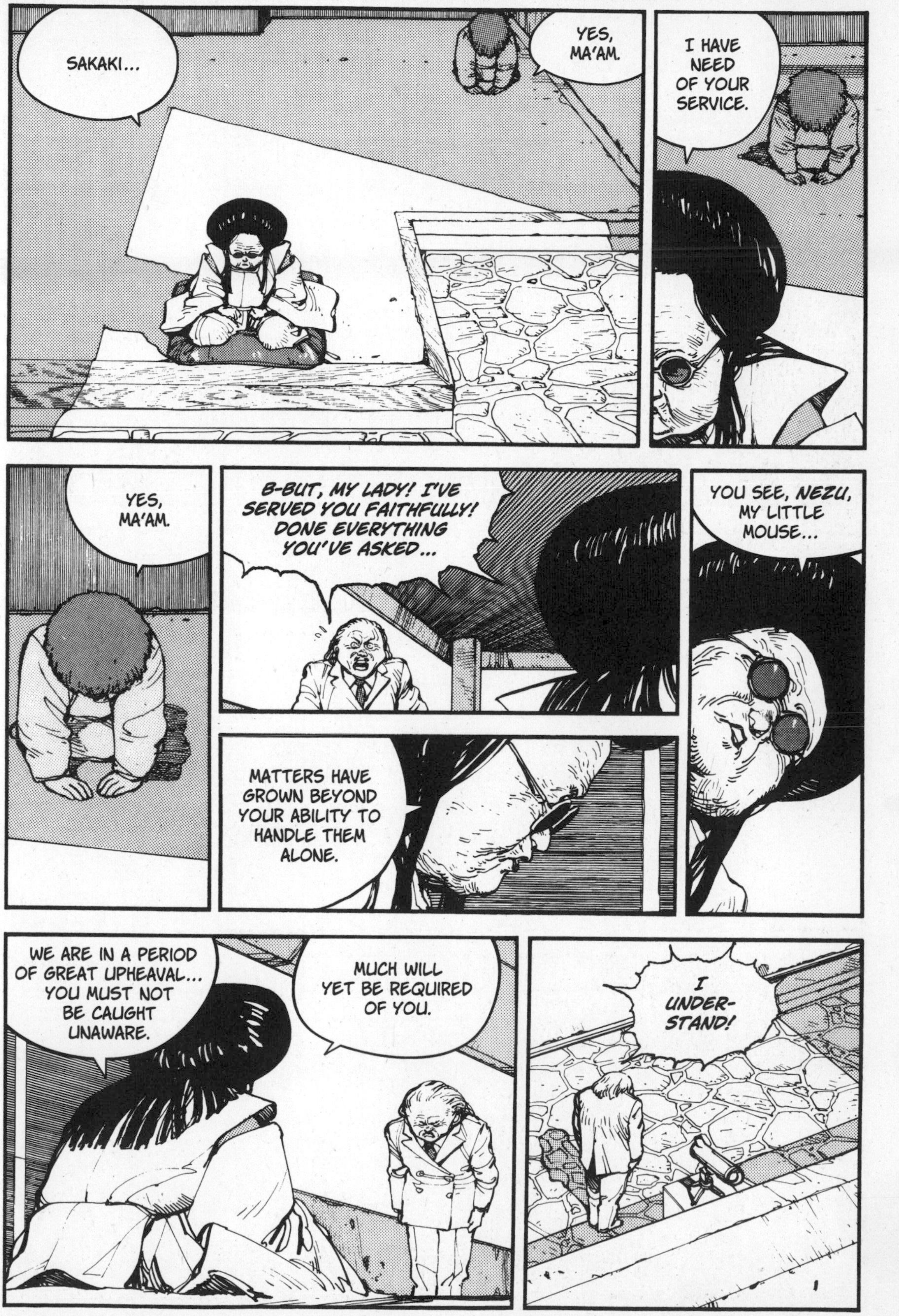
SAKAKI...
YES, MA'AM.
I HAVE NEED OF YOUR SERVICE.
YES, MA'AM.
B-BUT, MY LADY! I'VE SERVED YOU FAITHFULLY! DONE EVERYTHING YOU'VE ASKED...
MATTERS HAVE GROWN BEYOND YOUR ABILITY TO HANDLE THEM ALONE.
YOU SEE, NEZU, MY LITTLE MOUSE...
WE ARE IN A PERIOD OF GREAT UPHEAVAL... YOU MUST NOT BE CAUGHT UNAWARE.
MUCH WILL YET BE REQUIRED OF YOU.
I UNDER-STAND!

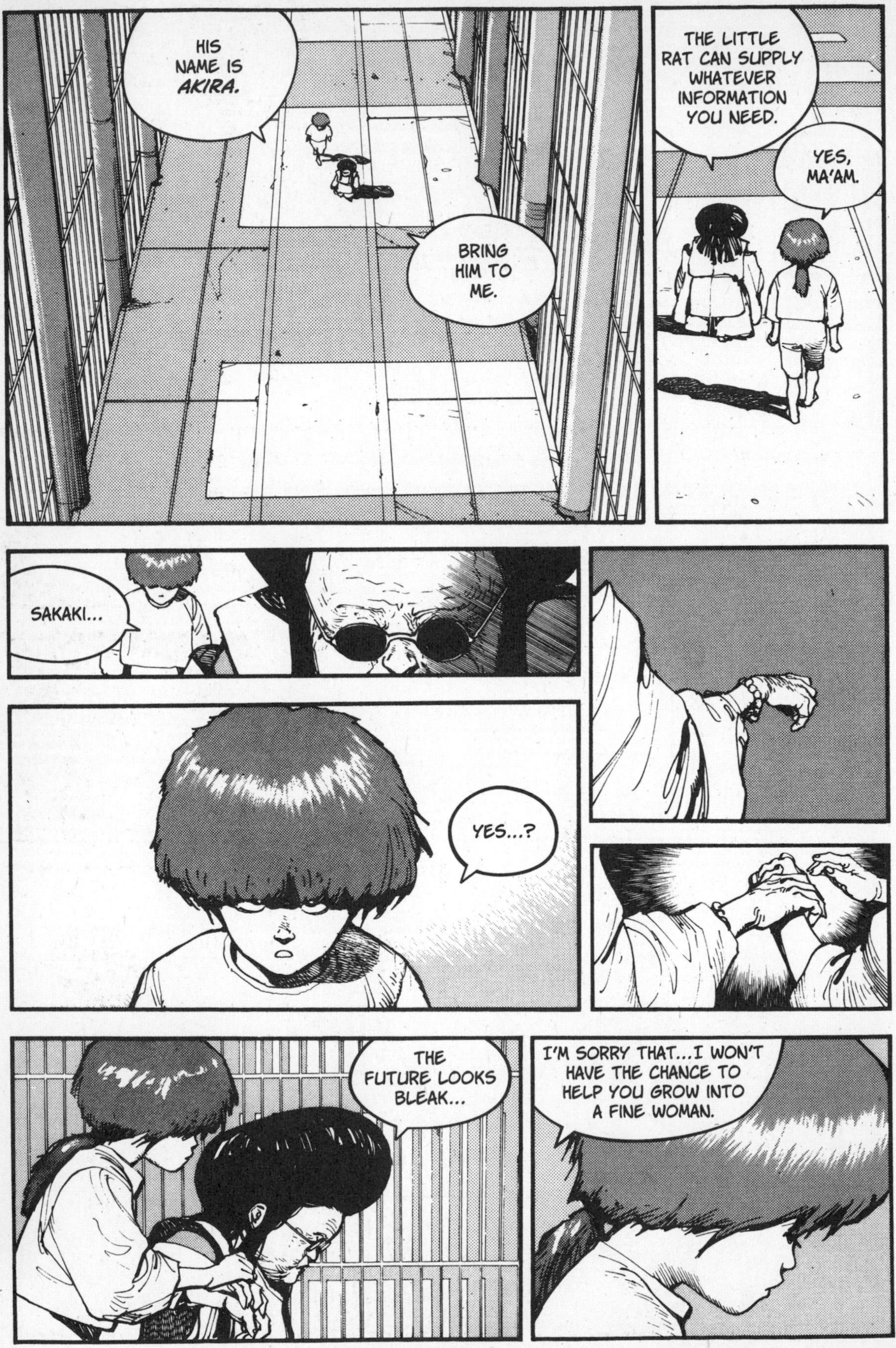
HIS NAME IS AKIRA.
BRING HIM TO ME.
THE LITTLE RAT CAN SUPPLY WHATEVER INFORMATION YOU NEED.
YES, MA'AM.
SAKAKI...
YES...?
THE FUTURE LOOKS BLEAK...
I'M SORRY THAT...I WON'T HAVE THE CHANCE TO HELP YOU GROW INTO A FINE WOMAN.

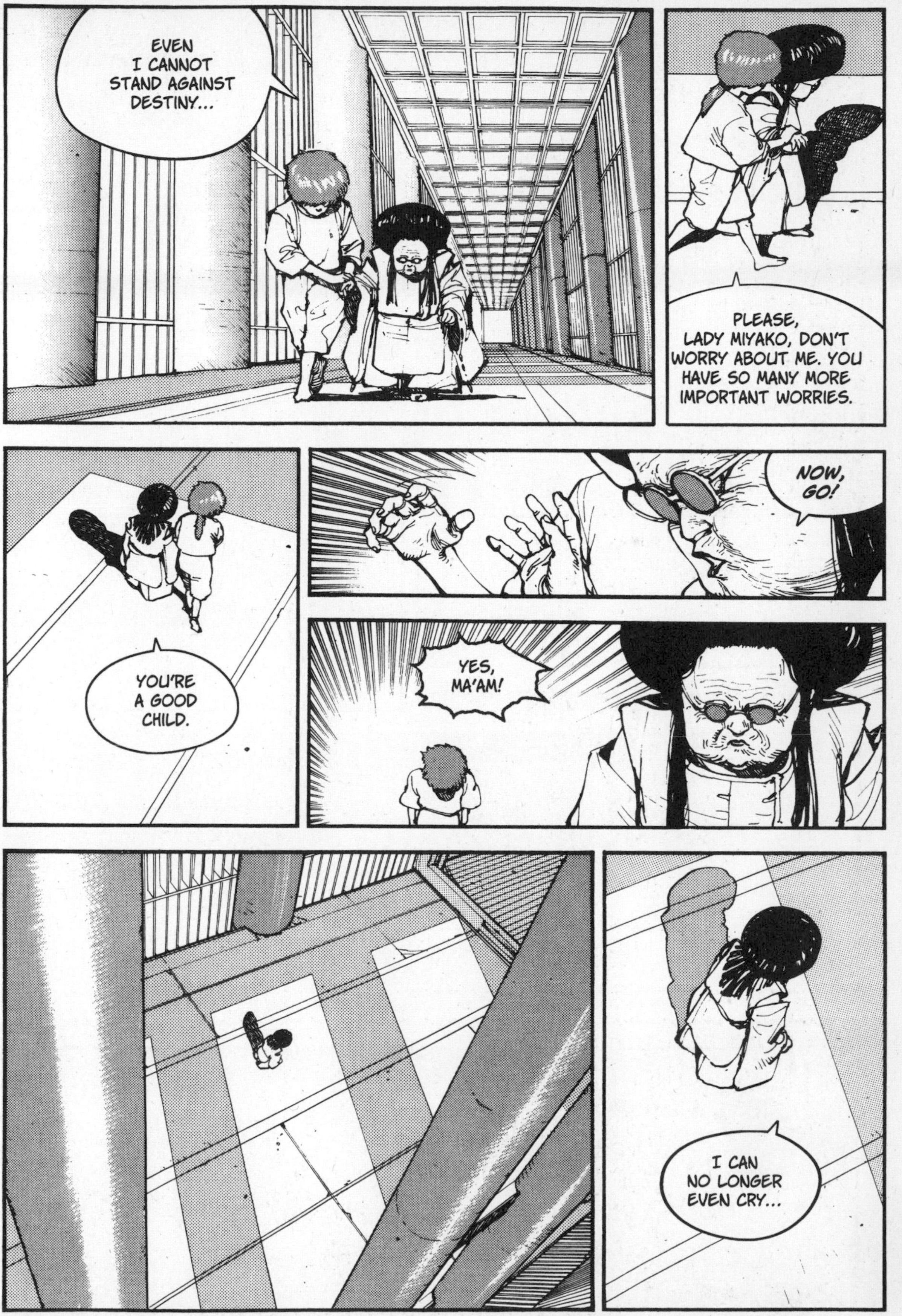
EVEN I CANNOT STAND AGAINST DESTINY...
PLEASE, LADY MIYAKO, DON'T WORRY ABOUT ME. YOU HAVE SO MANY MORE IMPORTANT WORRIES.
YOU'RE A GOOD CHILD.
NOW, GO!
YES, MA'AM!
I CAN NO LONGER EVEN CRY...

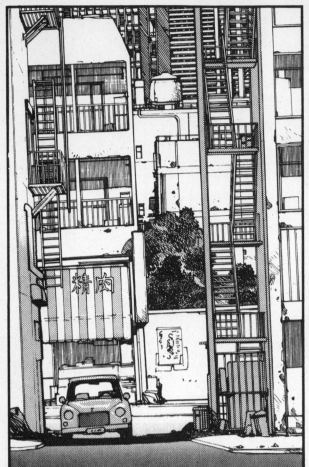

STOMP

GRROOO

TAP
TAP

SPOF

NOTHING...
NOT EVEN THE
SOUND OF
TRAFFIC.

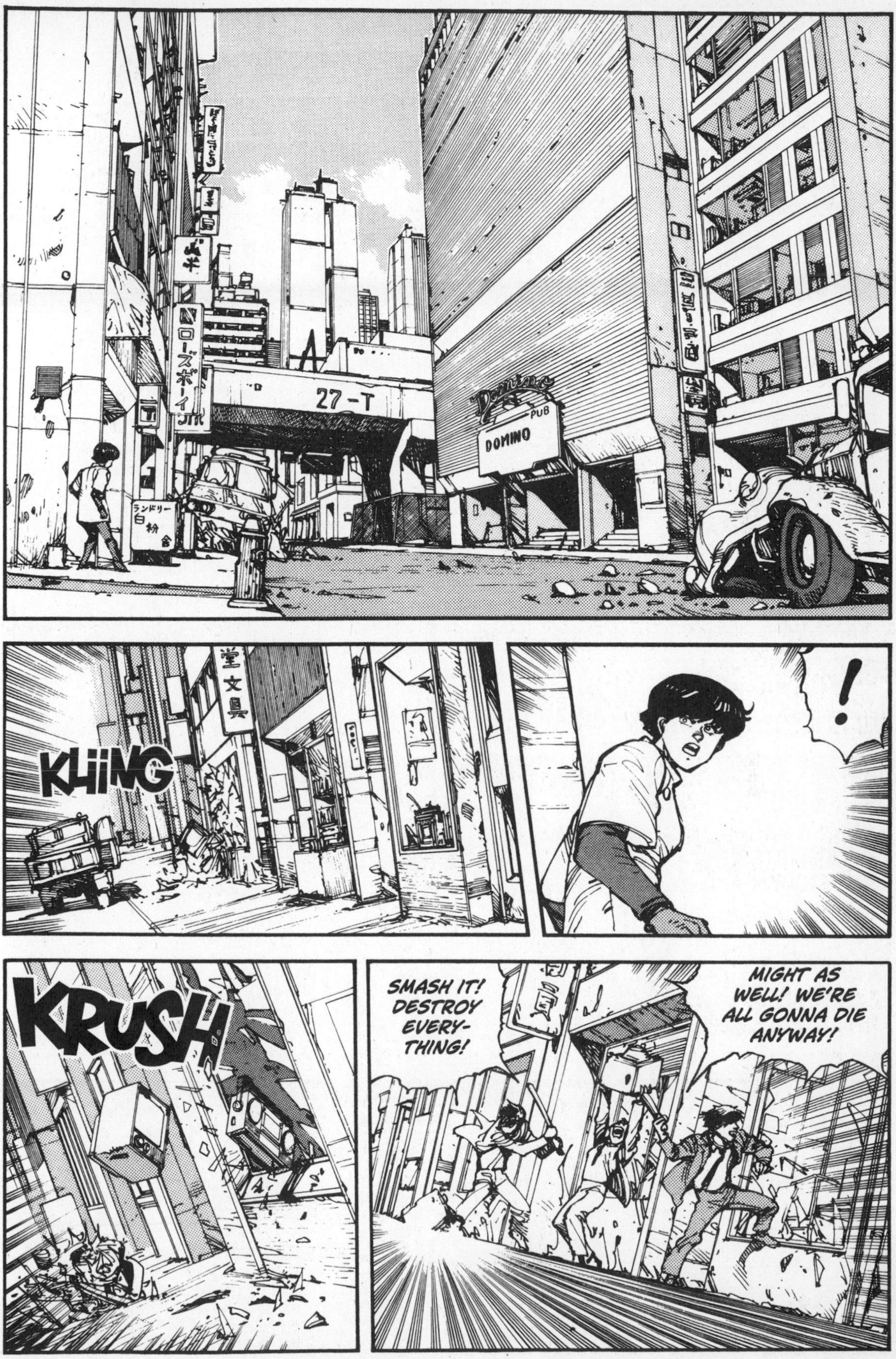
ローズボーイ
27-T
PUB
DOMINO
ランドリー
KLiiNG
!
KRUSH
SMASH IT! DESTROY EVERY-THING!
MIGHT AS WELL! WE'RE ALL GONNA DIE ANYWAY!

BONK

OW!

WHAT IDIOT PARKED THEIR CAR HERE?!

41-3617

KATCHA

KATCHA

KSHAK

≷WHEW...≷

≷NHH...≷

HMM?

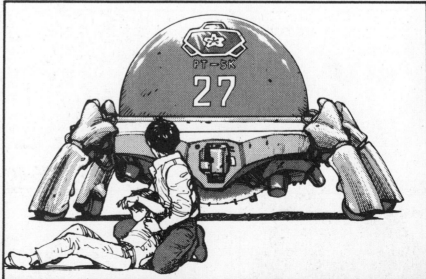

PT-5K
27

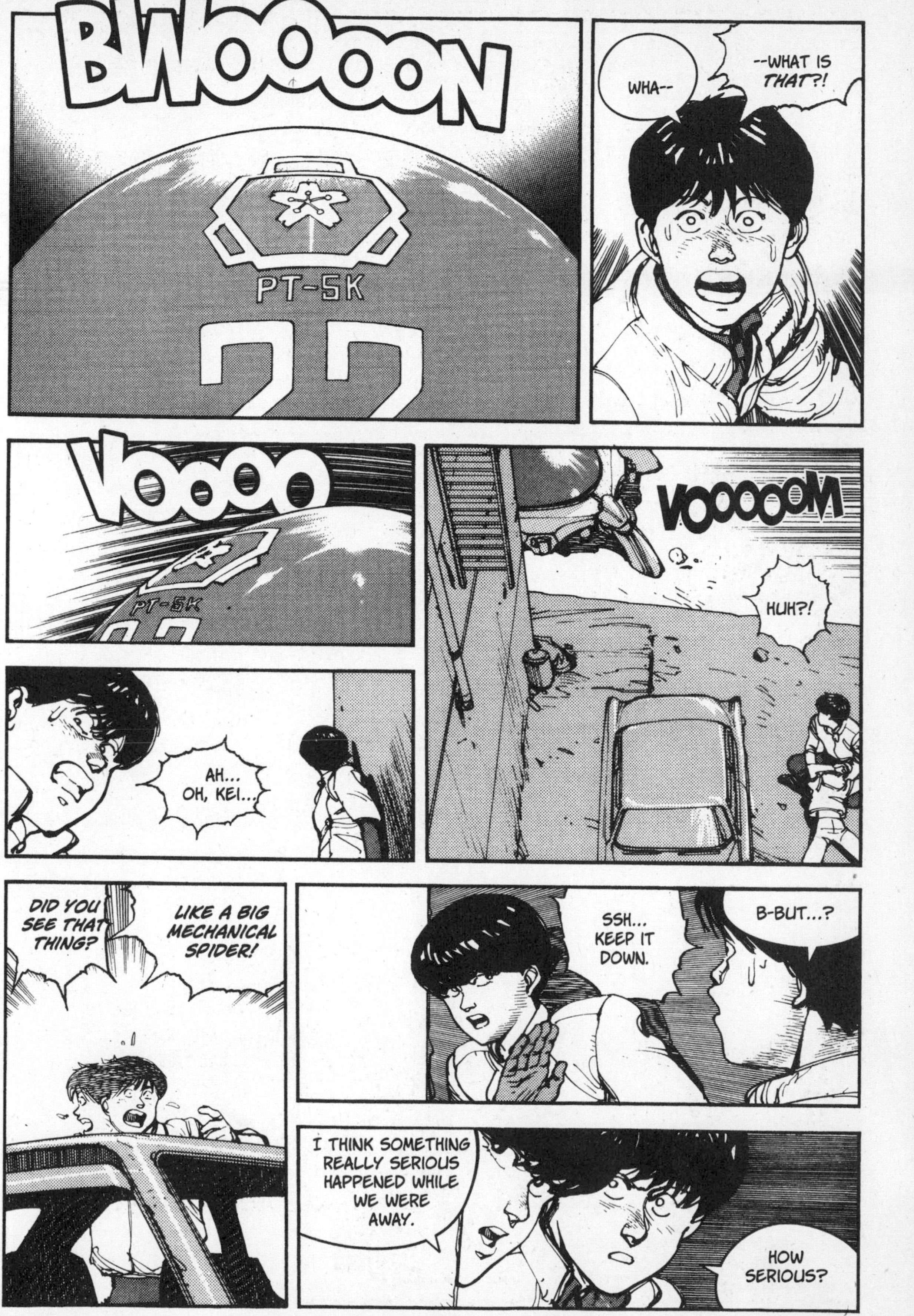
BWOOOOON
PT-5K
WHA--
--WHAT IS THAT?!
VOOOO
PT-5K
VOOOOOM
HUH?!
AH... OH, KEI...
DID YOU SEE THAT THING?
LIKE A BIG MECHANICAL SPIDER!
SSH... KEEP IT DOWN.
B-BUT...?
I THINK SOMETHING REALLY SERIOUS HAPPENED WHILE WE WERE AWAY.
HOW SERIOUS?

BAD ENOUGH TO MAKE PEOPLE ACT LIKE *THIS!*

OH!

HUNH?

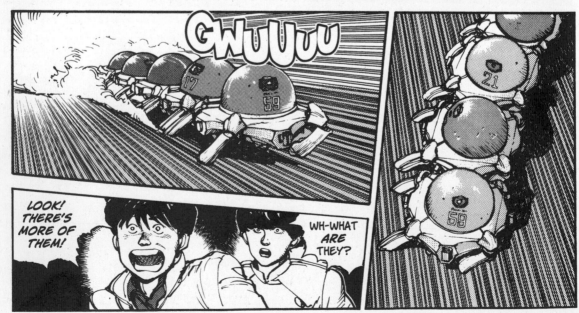

LOOK! THERE'S MORE OF THEM!

WH-WHAT ARE THEY?

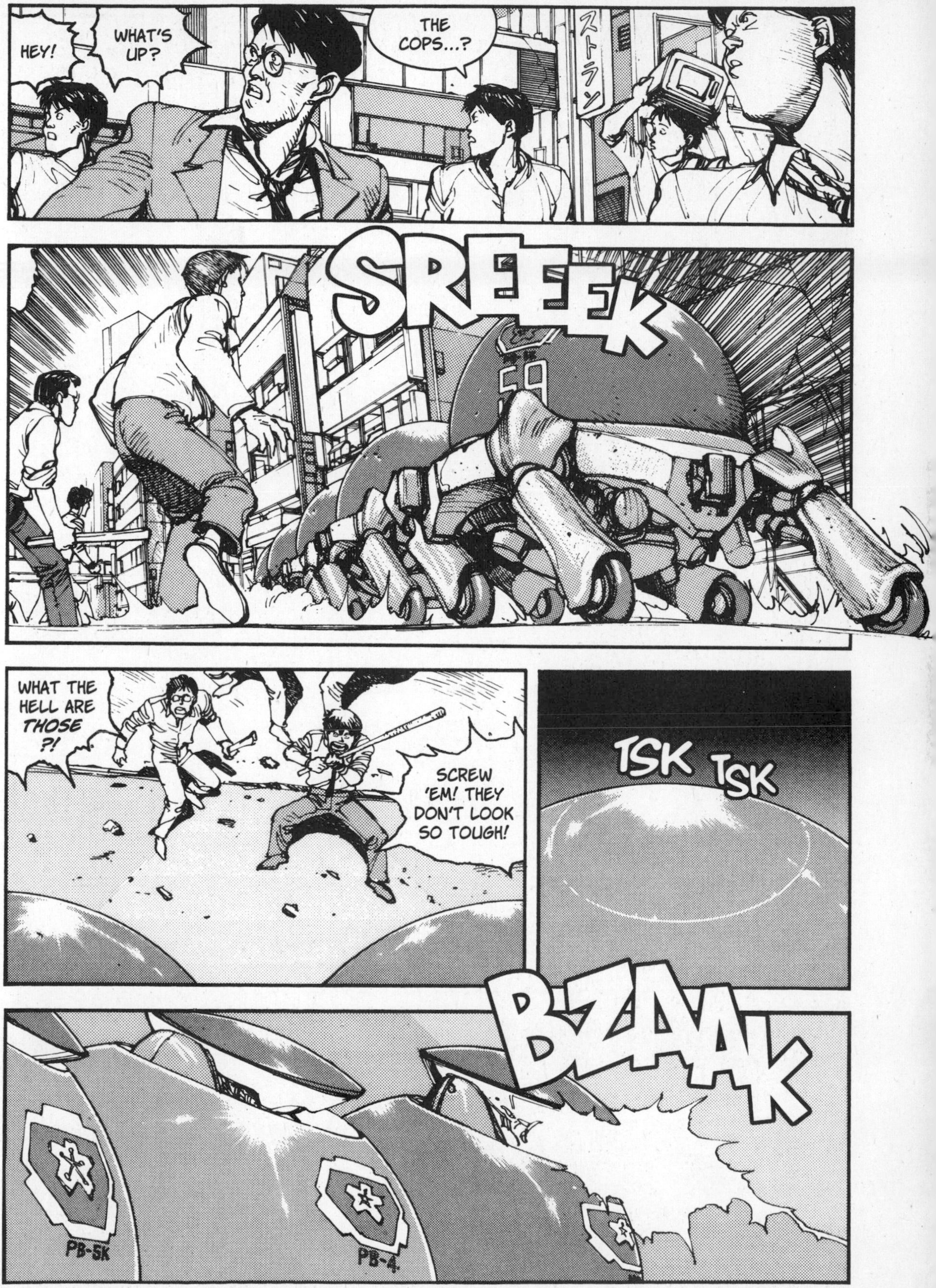
HEY!
WHAT'S UP?
THE COPS...?
ストラン
SREEEK
WHAT THE HELL ARE THOSE ?!
SCREW 'EM! THEY DON'T LOOK SO TOUGH!
TSK TSK
BZAAAK
PB-5K
PB-4

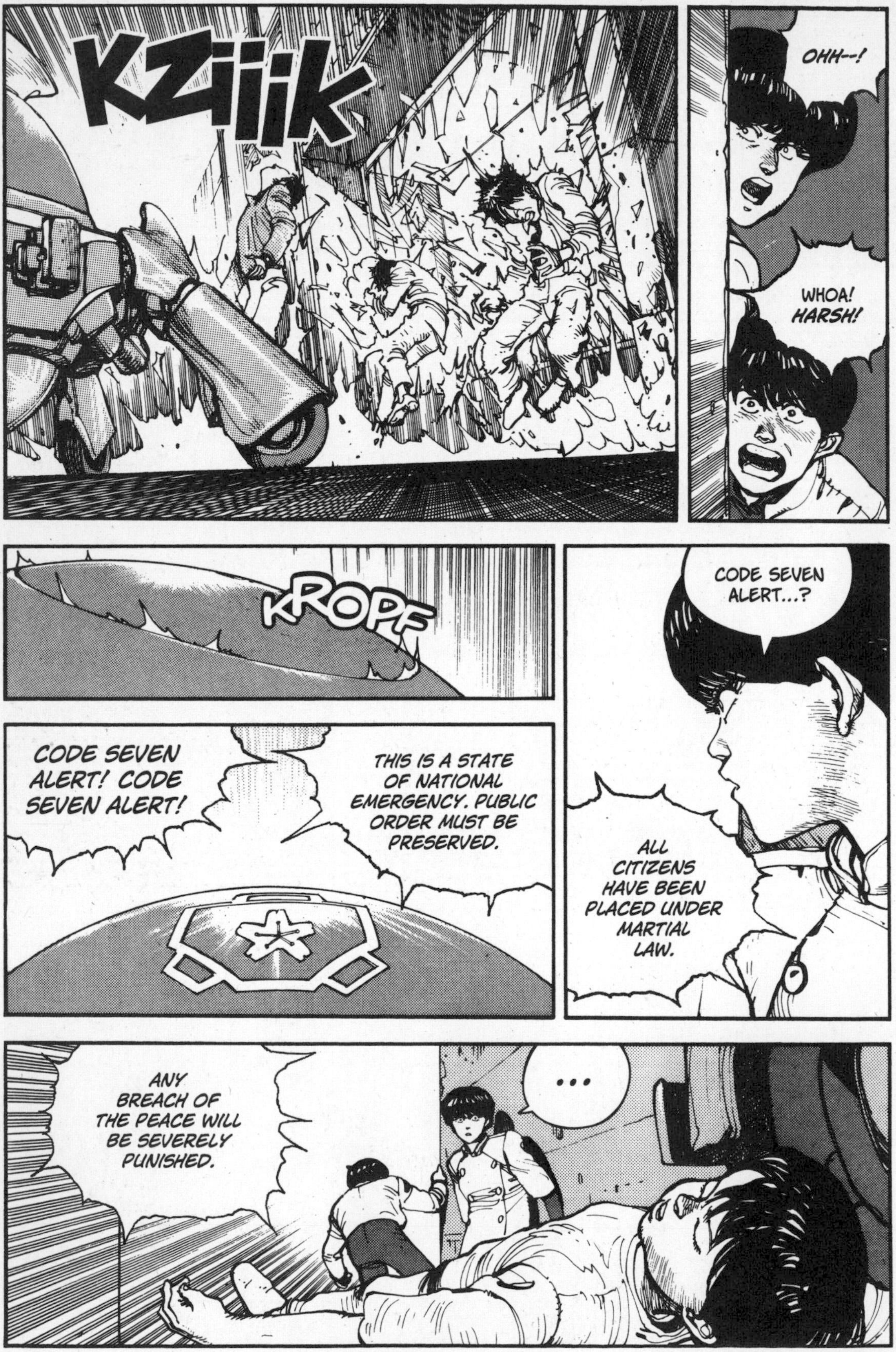

KZiiik
OHH--!
WHOA! HARSH!
kROPF
CODE SEVEN ALERT...?
CODE SEVEN ALERT! CODE SEVEN ALERT!
THIS IS A STATE OF NATIONAL EMERGENCY. PUBLIC ORDER MUST BE PRESERVED.
ALL CITIZENS HAVE BEEN PLACED UNDER MARTIAL LAW.
ANY BREACH OF THE PEACE WILL BE SEVERELY PUNISHED.
...

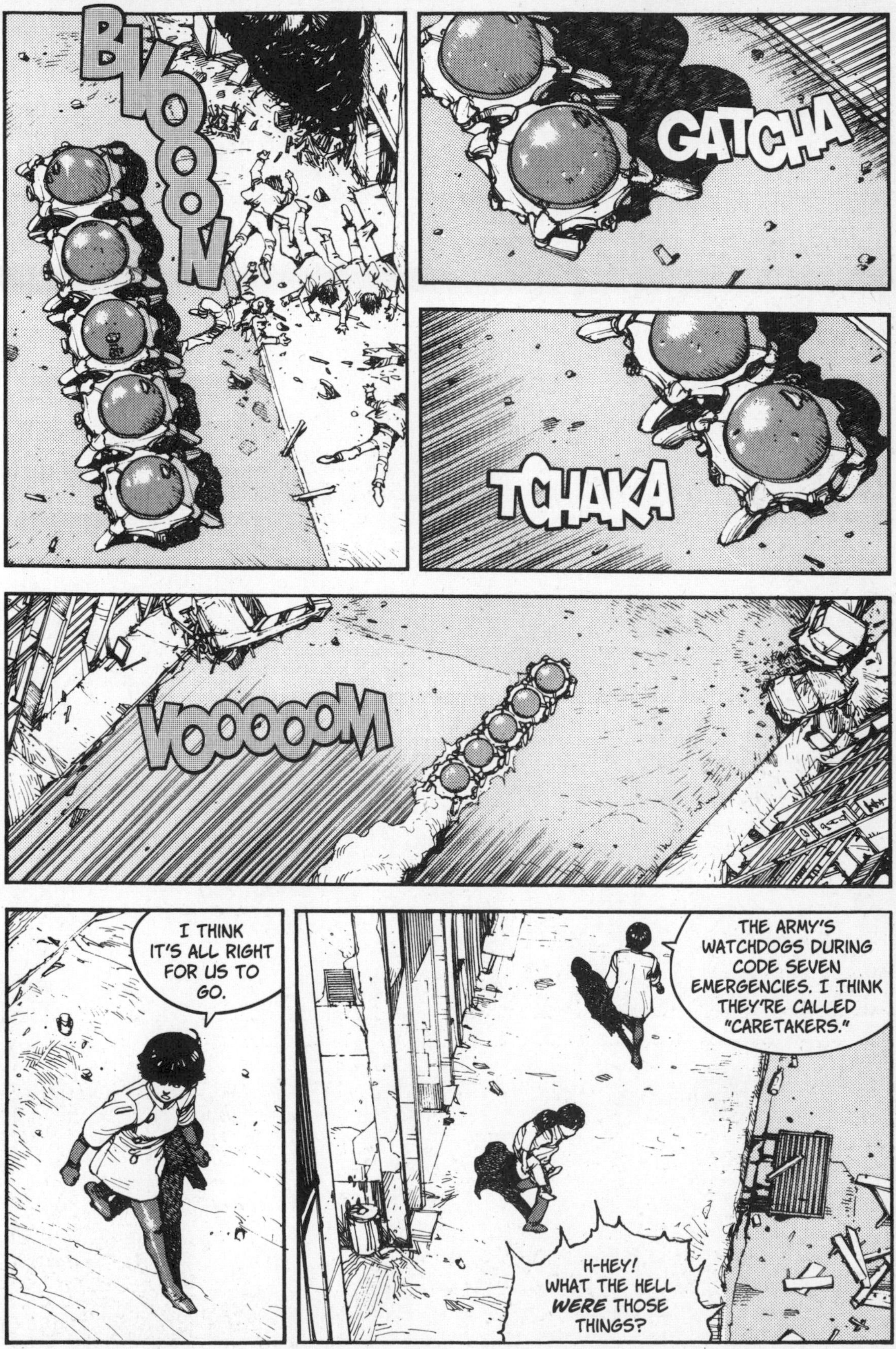
BWOOON
GATCHA
TCHAKA
VOOOOOM
I THINK IT'S ALL RIGHT FOR US TO GO.
THE ARMY'S WATCHDOGS DURING CODE SEVEN EMERGENCIES. I THINK THEY'RE CALLED "CARETAKERS."
H-HEY! WHAT THE HELL *WERE* THOSE THINGS?

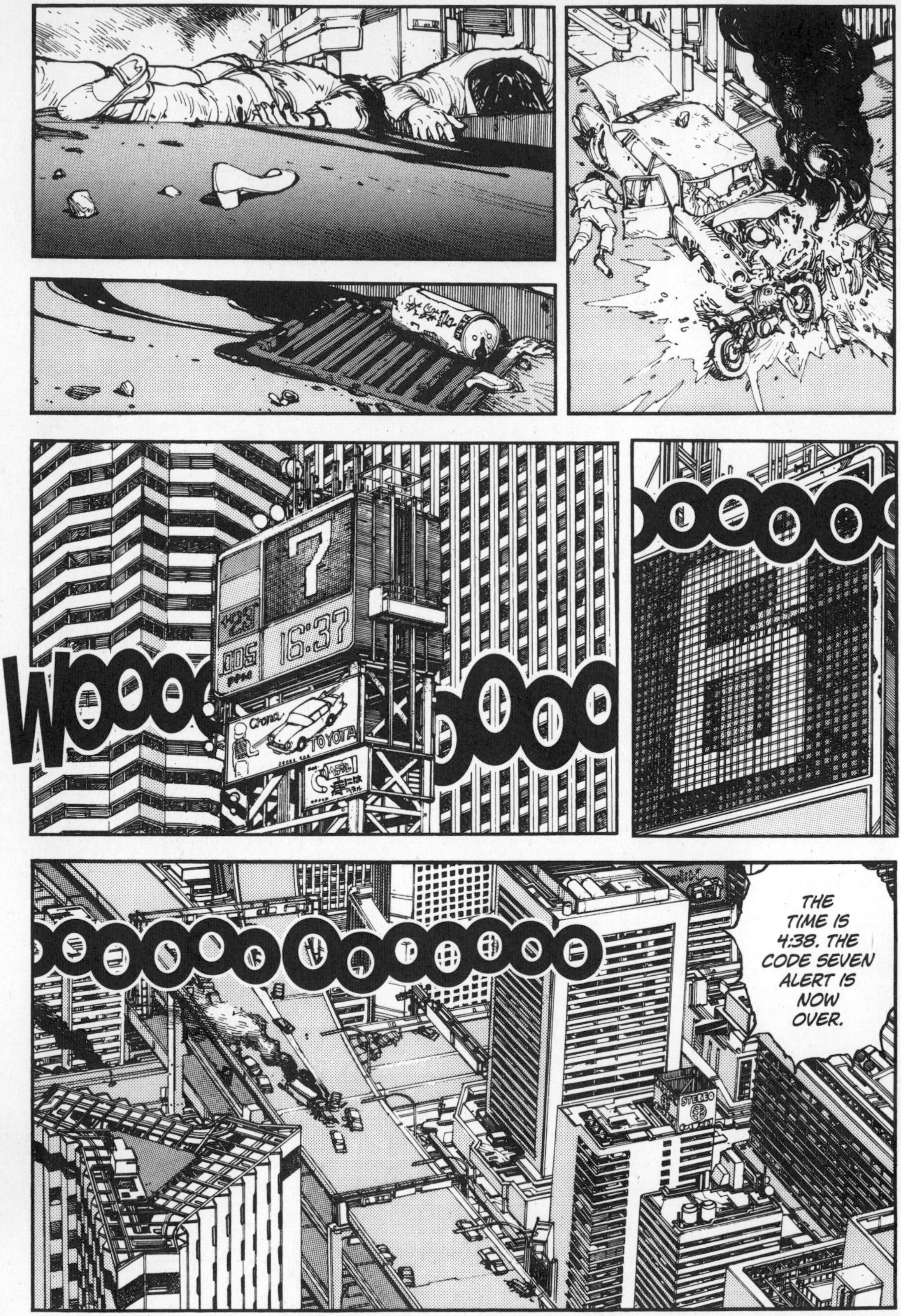
7
16:37
TOYOTA
STEREO
THE TIME IS 4:38. THE CODE SEVEN ALERT IS NOW OVER.

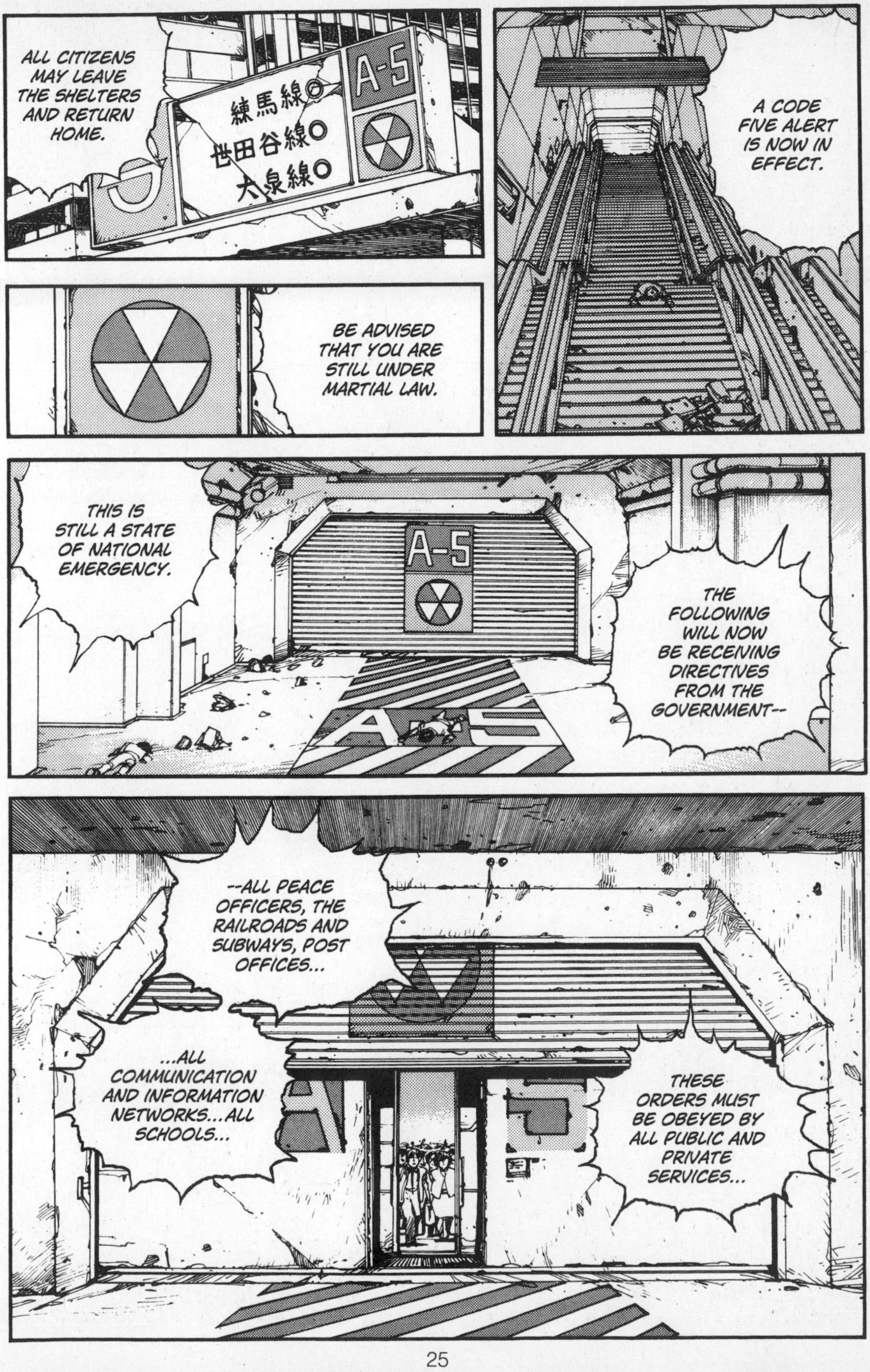
ALL CITIZENS MAY LEAVE THE SHELTERS AND RETURN HOME.
A-5
練馬線
世田谷線
大泉線
BE ADVISED THAT YOU ARE STILL UNDER MARTIAL LAW.
A CODE FIVE ALERT IS NOW IN EFFECT.
THIS IS STILL A STATE OF NATIONAL EMERGENCY.
A-5
THE FOLLOWING WILL NOW BE RECEIVING DIRECTIVES FROM THE GOVERNMENT--
A-5
--ALL PEACE OFFICERS, THE RAILROADS AND SUBWAYS, POST OFFICES...
...ALL COMMUNICATION AND INFORMATION NETWORKS...ALL SCHOOLS...
THESE ORDERS MUST BE OBEYED BY ALL PUBLIC AND PRIVATE SERVICES...

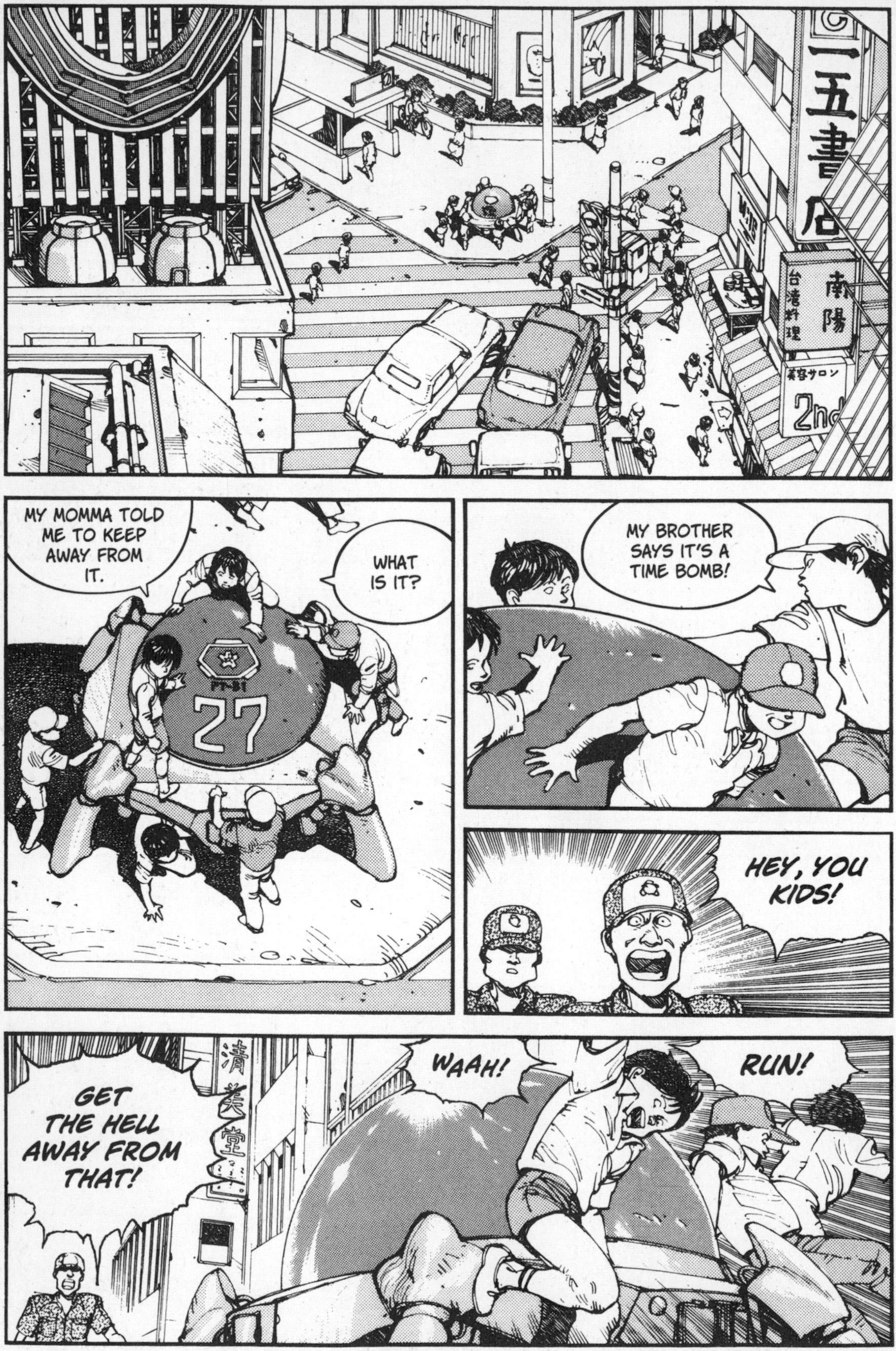
一五書店
南陽
美容サロン
2nd
MY MOMMA TOLD ME TO KEEP AWAY FROM IT.
WHAT IS IT?
27
MY BROTHER SAYS IT'S A TIME BOMB!
HEY, YOU KIDS!
清美堂
GET THE HELL AWAY FROM THAT!
WAAH!
RUN!

AW, SHUT UP! STUPID PIGS!

STUPID KIDS! THEY THINK THIS IS ALL SOME KINDA GAME!

HEY, KNOW WHAT I HEARD ABOUT THESE THINGS?

WHAT?

YESTERDAY AT THE ENLISTED MEN'S CLUB, SOMEONE SAID...

"...THE 'CARETAKERS' WERE BUILT TO WITHSTAND NUCLEAR ATTACK."

"IF WE HAVE TO TAKE SHELTER UNDERGROUND, THEY CAN STAY UP HERE IN ALL THE RADIATION..."

...AND FIGHT OFF ANYONE WHO TRIES TO INVADE.

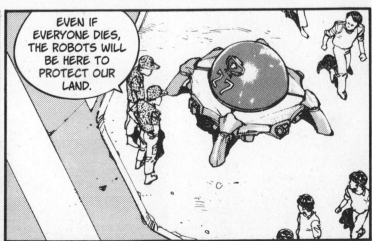

EVEN IF EVERYONE DIES, THE ROBOTS WILL BE HERE TO PROTECT OUR LAND.

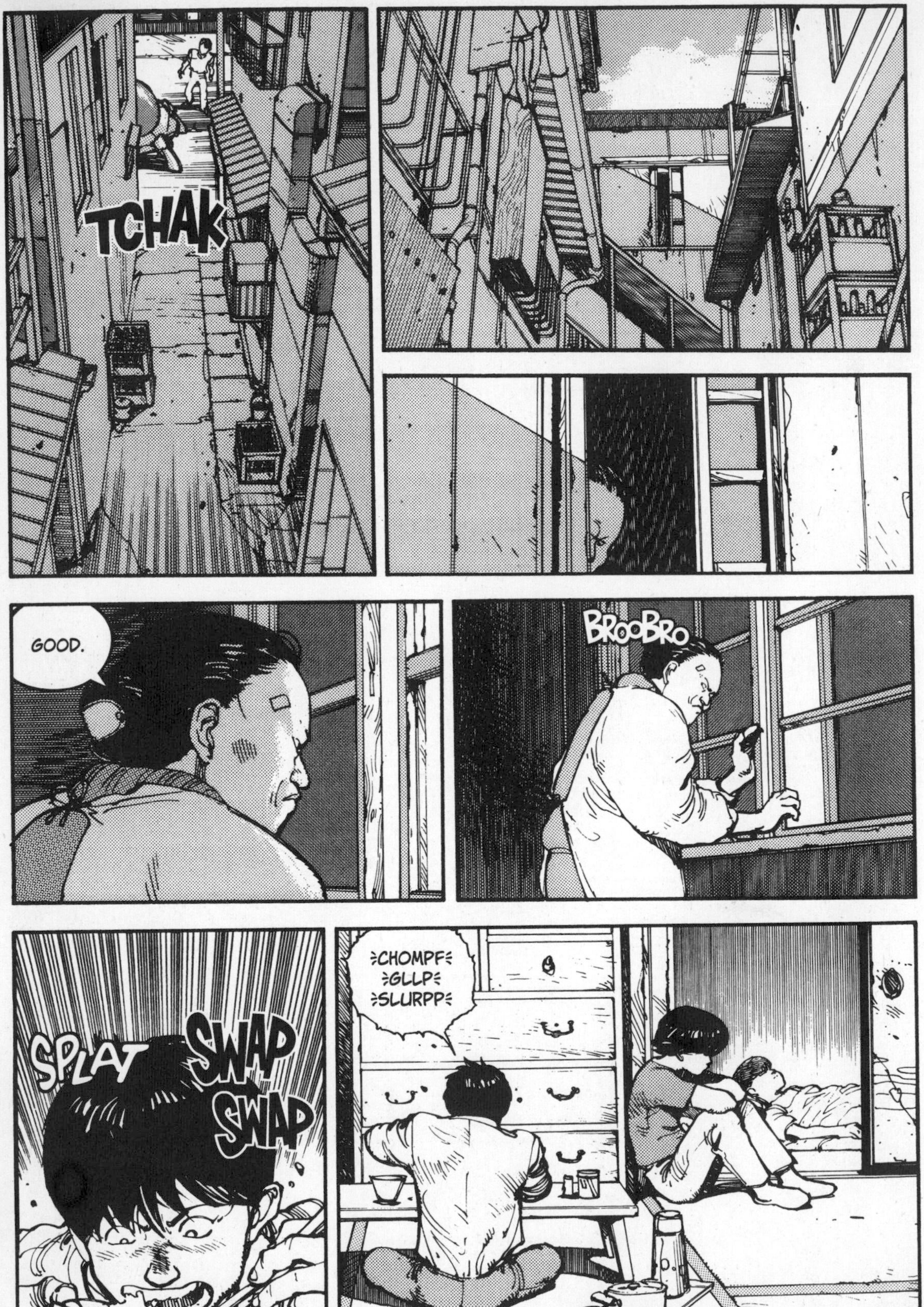
TCHAK
GOOD.
BROOBRO
SPLAT
SWAP
SWAP
CHOMPF
GLLP
SLURPP

CHLAM

THE PHONES ARE STILL OUT, AND OUR PEOPLE ARE IN HIDING.

NO.

ANY LUCK?

...

OH...

DON'T WORRY ABOUT *RYU*. HE CAN TAKE CARE OF HIMSELF.

YEAH... THAT'S TRUE.

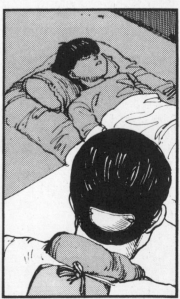

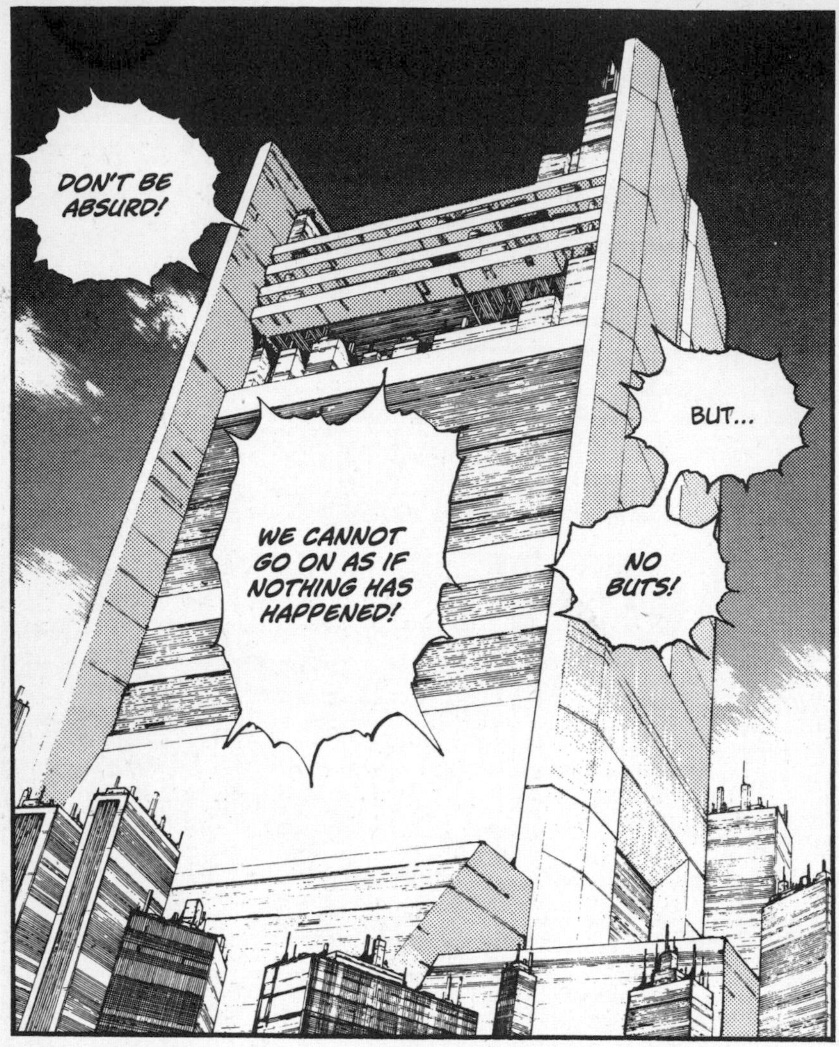
DON'T BE ABSURD!
WE CANNOT GO ON AS IF NOTHING HAS HAPPENED!
BUT...
NO BUTS!
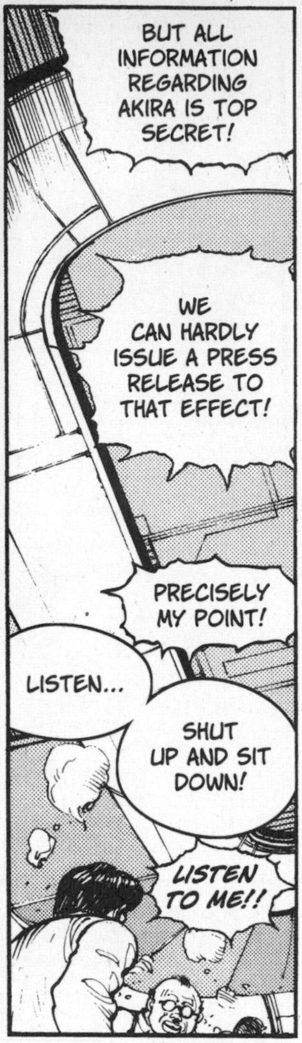
BUT ALL INFORMATION REGARDING AKIRA IS TOP SECRET!
WE CAN HARDLY ISSUE A PRESS RELEASE TO THAT EFFECT!
PRECISELY MY POINT!
LISTEN...
SHUT UP AND SIT DOWN!
LISTEN TO ME!!
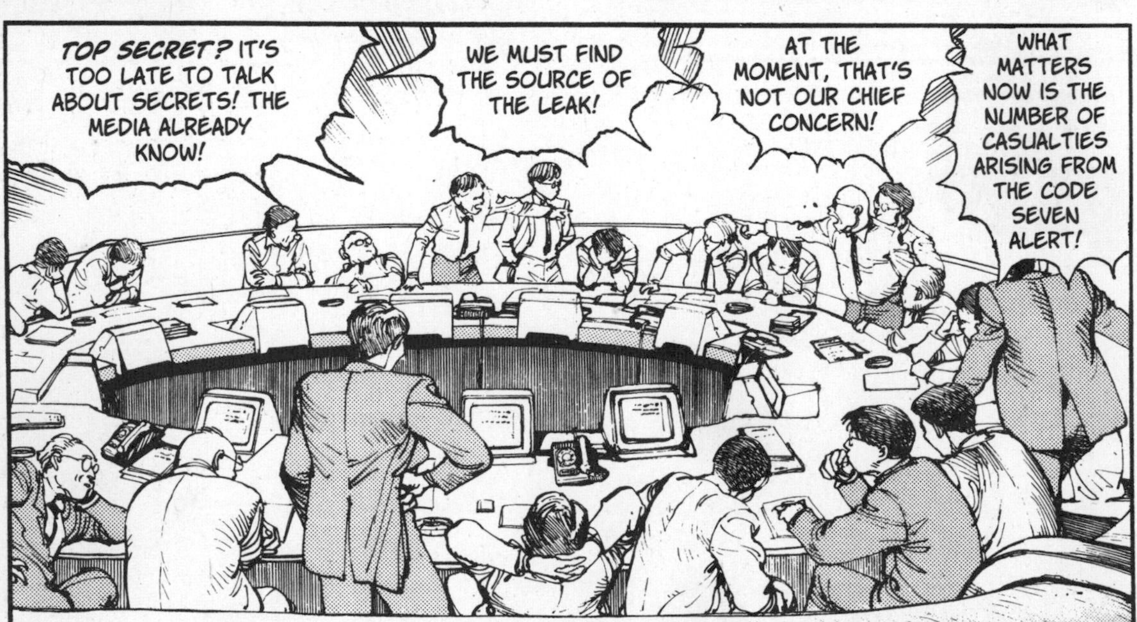
TOP SECRET? IT'S TOO LATE TO TALK ABOUT SECRETS! THE MEDIA ALREADY KNOW!
WE MUST FIND THE SOURCE OF THE LEAK!
AT THE MOMENT, THAT'S NOT OUR CHIEF CONCERN!
WHAT MATTERS NOW IS THE NUMBER OF CASUALTIES ARISING FROM THE CODE SEVEN ALERT!

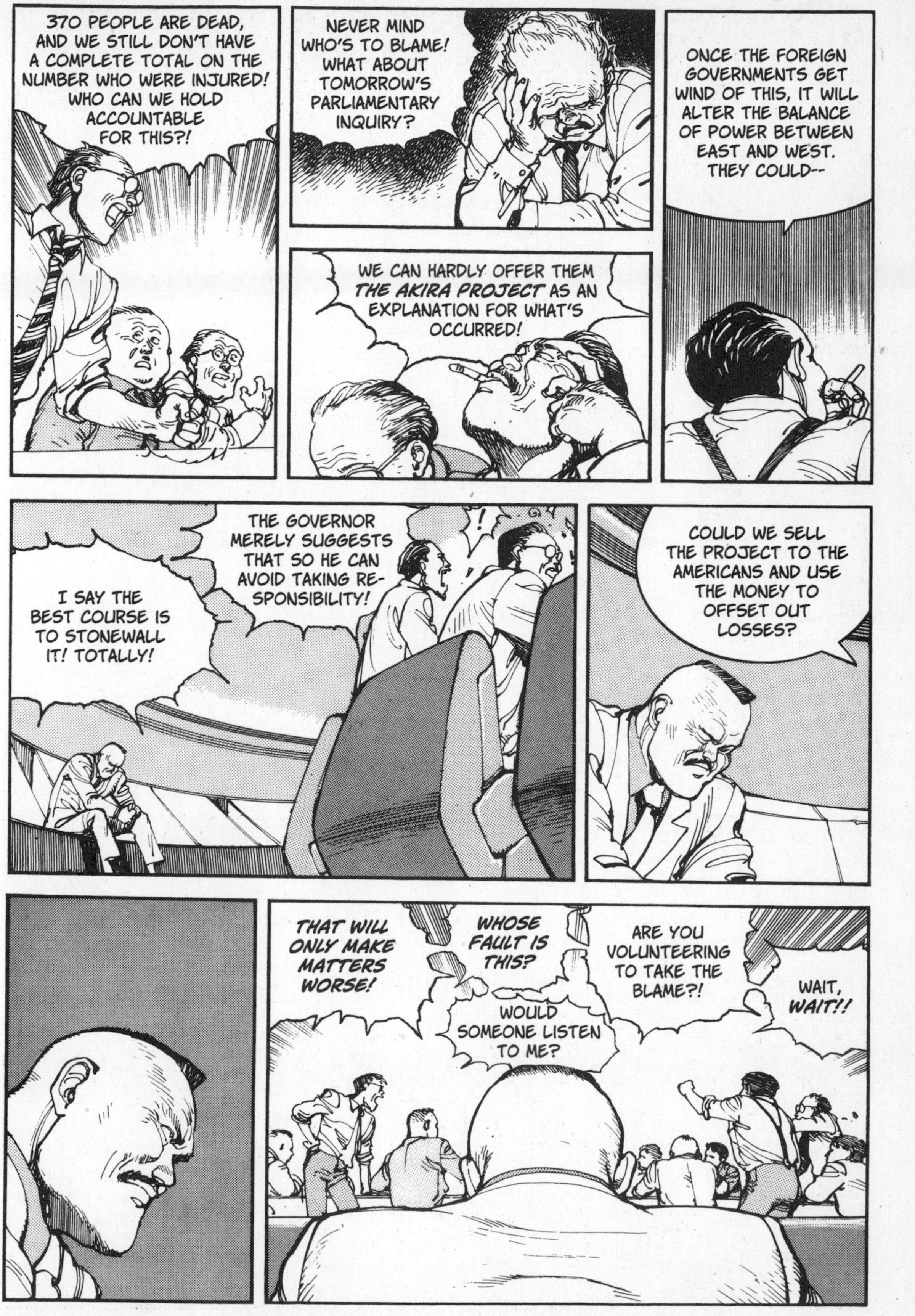
370 PEOPLE ARE DEAD, AND WE STILL DON'T HAVE A COMPLETE TOTAL ON THE NUMBER WHO WERE INJURED! WHO CAN WE HOLD ACCOUNTABLE FOR THIS?!
NEVER MIND WHO'S TO BLAME! WHAT ABOUT TOMORROW'S PARLIAMENTARY INQUIRY?
WE CAN HARDLY OFFER THEM *THE AKIRA PROJECT* AS AN EXPLANATION FOR WHAT'S OCCURRED!
ONCE THE FOREIGN GOVERNMENTS GET WIND OF THIS, IT WILL ALTER THE BALANCE OF POWER BETWEEN EAST AND WEST. THEY COULD--
I SAY THE BEST COURSE IS TO STONEWALL IT! TOTALLY!
THE GOVERNOR MERELY SUGGESTS THAT SO HE CAN AVOID TAKING RE-SPONSIBILITY!
!
COULD WE SELL THE PROJECT TO THE AMERICANS AND USE THE MONEY TO OFFSET OUT LOSSES?
THAT WILL ONLY MAKE MATTERS WORSE!
WHOSE FAULT IS THIS?
WOULD SOMEONE LISTEN TO ME?
ARE YOU VOLUNTEERING TO TAKE THE BLAME?!
WAIT, *WAIT!!*

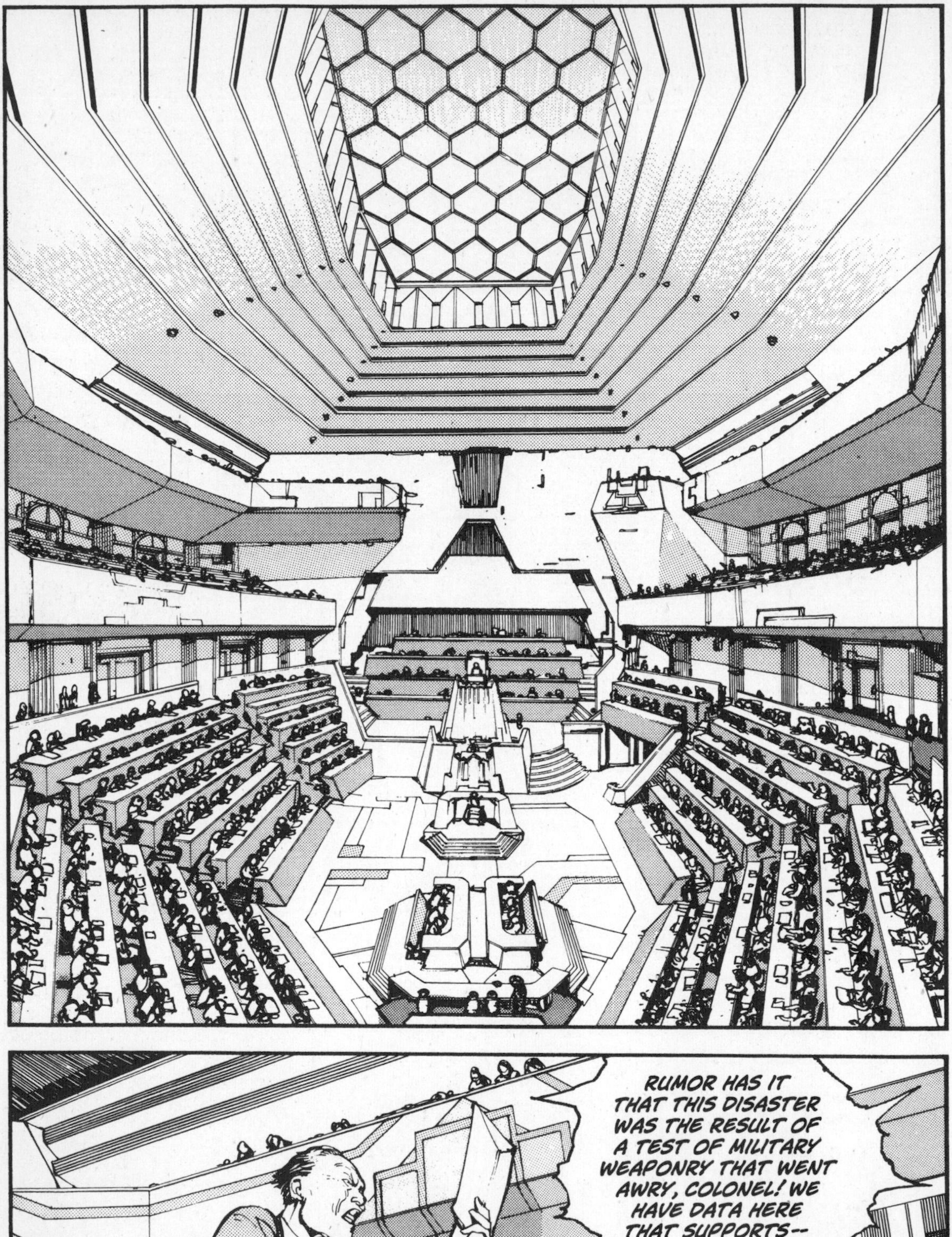

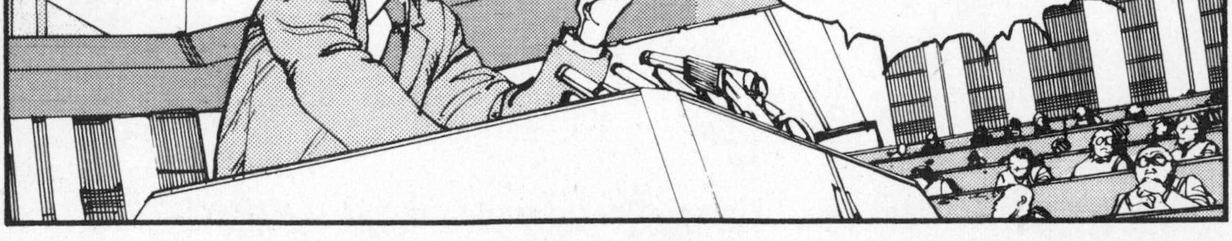
RUMOR HAS IT THAT THIS DISASTER WAS THE RESULT OF A TEST OF MILITARY WEAPONRY THAT WENT AWRY, COLONEL! WE HAVE DATA HERE THAT SUPPORTS--

THERE ARE ALWAYS RUMORS! RUMORS AND MISINFORMATION DISSEMINATED BY RADICAL FORCES TRYING TO CREATE A NATIONAL STATE OF PANIC!

THE CODE SEVEN ALERT WAS SET IN MOTION BY A *COMPUTER ERROR!* THERE WAS A MALFUNCTION IN THE DEFENSE SYSTEMS! THAT IS ALL IT EVER WAS!

AS TO THE QUESTION OF WHEN WE WILL BE LIFTING *MARTIAL LAW...*

AS I HAVE ALREADY STATED, THERE ARE CERTAIN *RADICAL FORCES* ATTEMPTING TO EXPLOIT THIS SITUATION AS IT NOW EXISTS...

THEREFORE, IN THE INTEREST OF MAINTAINING ORDER...

SHUT UP AND *LET THE COLONEL FINISH SPEAKING!*

BUT, MR. CHAIRMAN, THE DATA I HAVE HERE...

WE'LL NEED A RECESS IN WHICH TO REVIEW THE INFORMATION.

THIS SESSION IS ADJOURNED!

BUT HOW CAN YOU...?

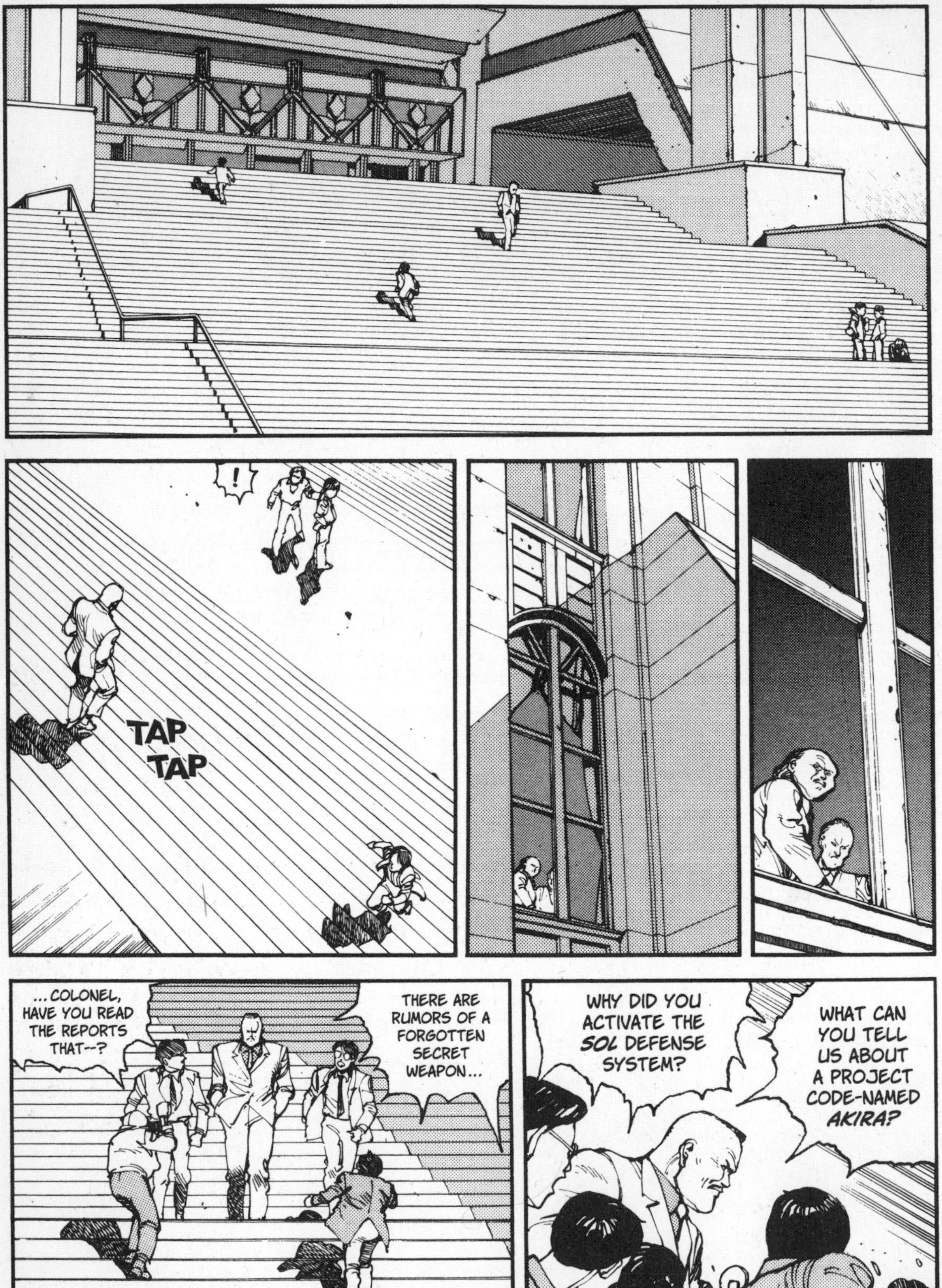
!
TAP
TAP
...COLONEL, HAVE YOU READ THE REPORTS THAT--?
THERE ARE RUMORS OF A FORGOTTEN SECRET WEAPON...
WHY DID YOU ACTIVATE THE SOL DEFENSE SYSTEM?
WHAT CAN YOU TELL US ABOUT A PROJECT CODE-NAMED AKIRA?

MR. NEZU'S OFFICE...

NO, I'M AFRAID MR. NEZU IS UNAVAILABLE AT THE MOMENT.

YES, I SEE... URGENT...

PERHAPS IF YOU WERE TO TELL ME...

WHO IS IT?

SHE INSISTS ON SPEAKING WITH YOU DIRECTLY, SIR.

SHE SAYS SHE'S RYUSAKU'S SISTER.

RYU'S SISTER... KEI?

VERY WELL.

THIS IS NEZU... YOU WERE TOLD NEVER TO CALL ME HE--

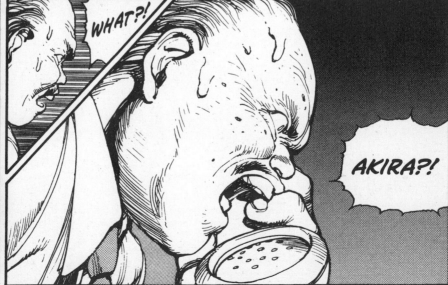

WHAT?!

AKIRA?!

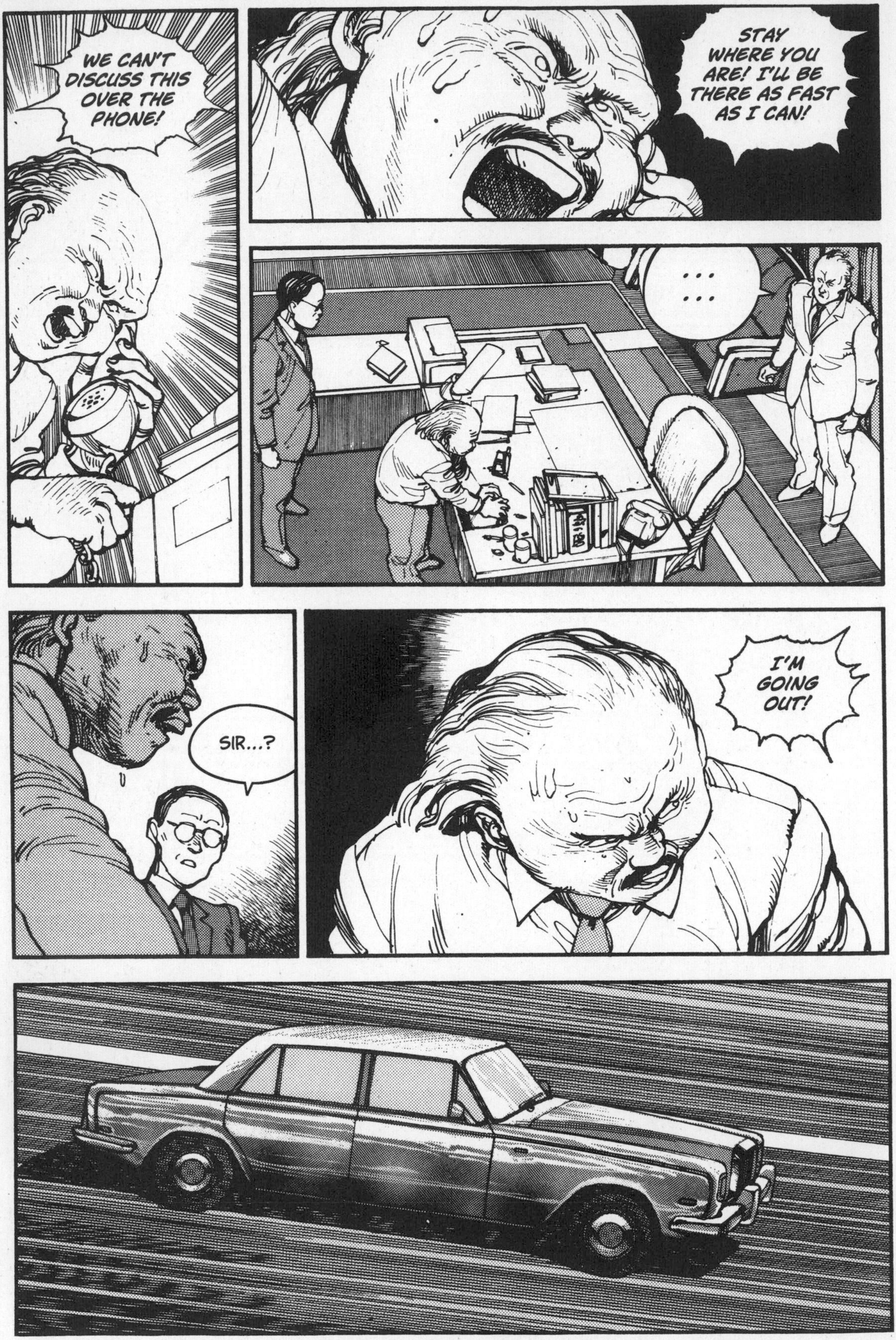

WE CAN'T DISCUSS THIS OVER THE PHONE!
STAY WHERE YOU ARE! I'LL BE THERE AS FAST AS I CAN!
... ...
SIR...?
I'M GOING OUT!

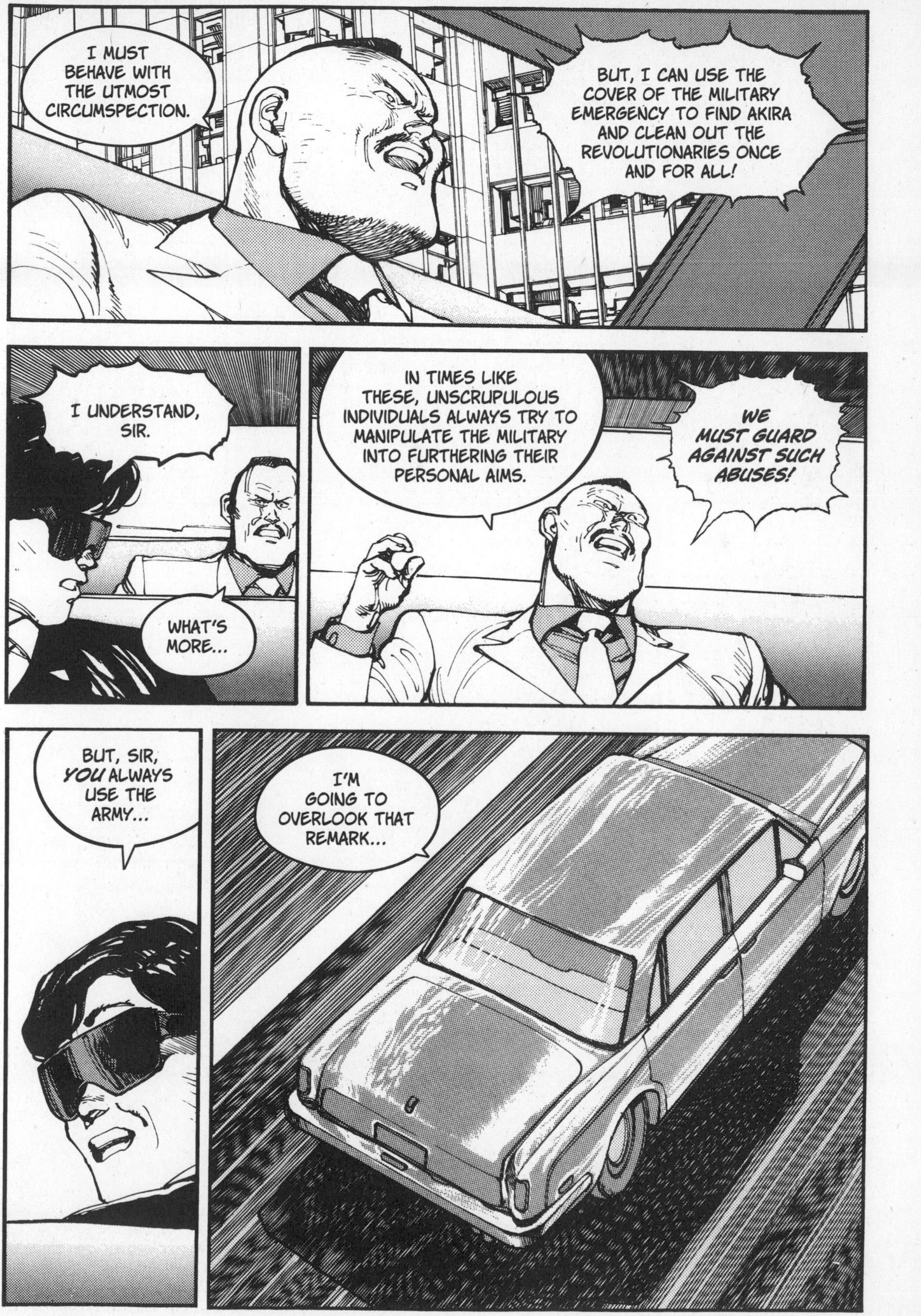
I MUST BEHAVE WITH THE UTMOST CIRCUMSPECTION.
BUT, I CAN USE THE COVER OF THE MILITARY EMERGENCY TO FIND AKIRA AND CLEAN OUT THE REVOLUTIONARIES ONCE AND FOR ALL!
I UNDERSTAND, SIR.
WHAT'S MORE...
IN TIMES LIKE THESE, UNSCRUPULOUS INDIVIDUALS ALWAYS TRY TO MANIPULATE THE MILITARY INTO FURTHERING THEIR PERSONAL AIMS.
WE MUST GUARD AGAINST SUCH ABUSES!
BUT, SIR, YOU ALWAYS USE THE ARMY...
I'M GOING TO OVERLOOK THAT REMARK...

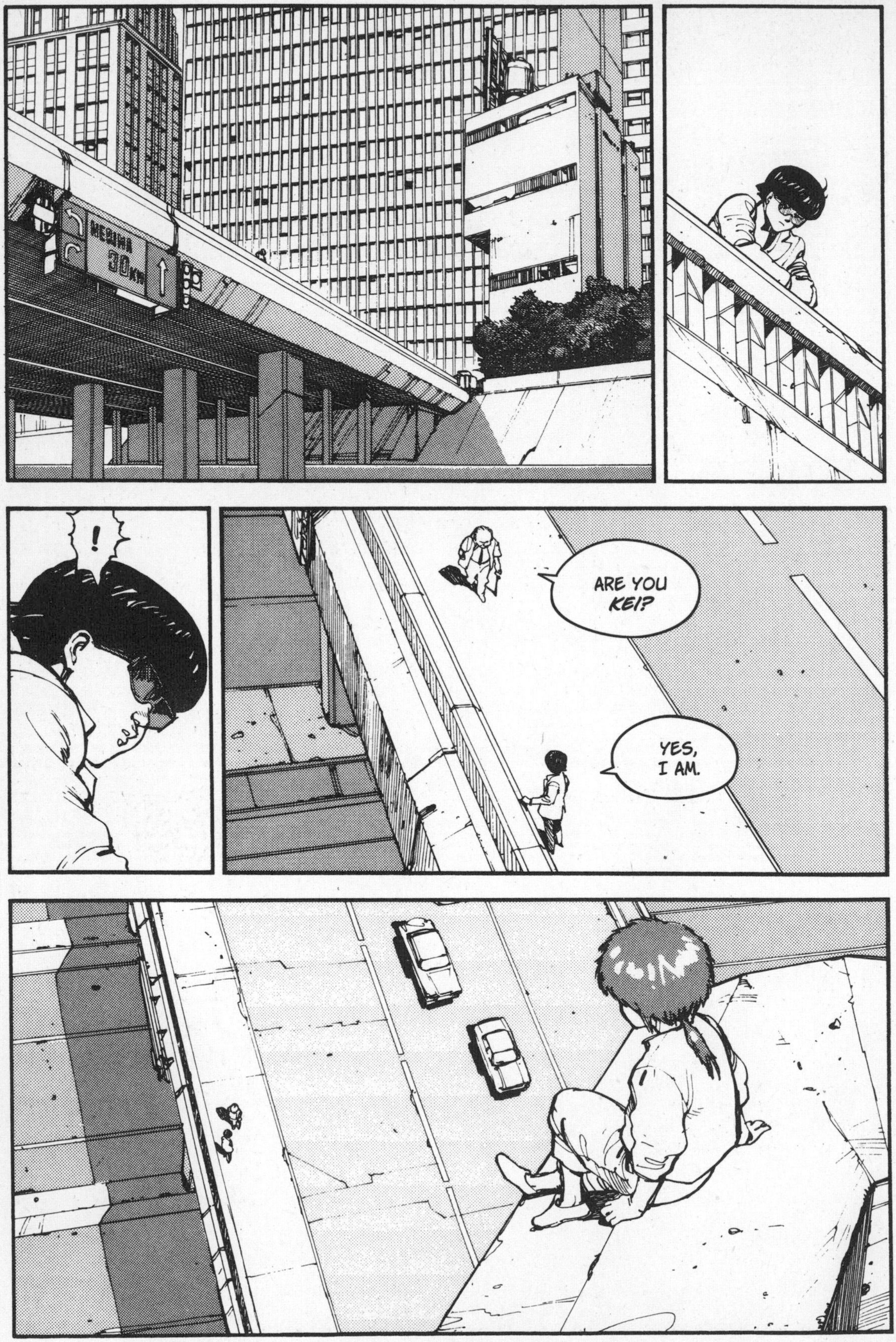
!
ARE YOU KEI?
YES, I AM.

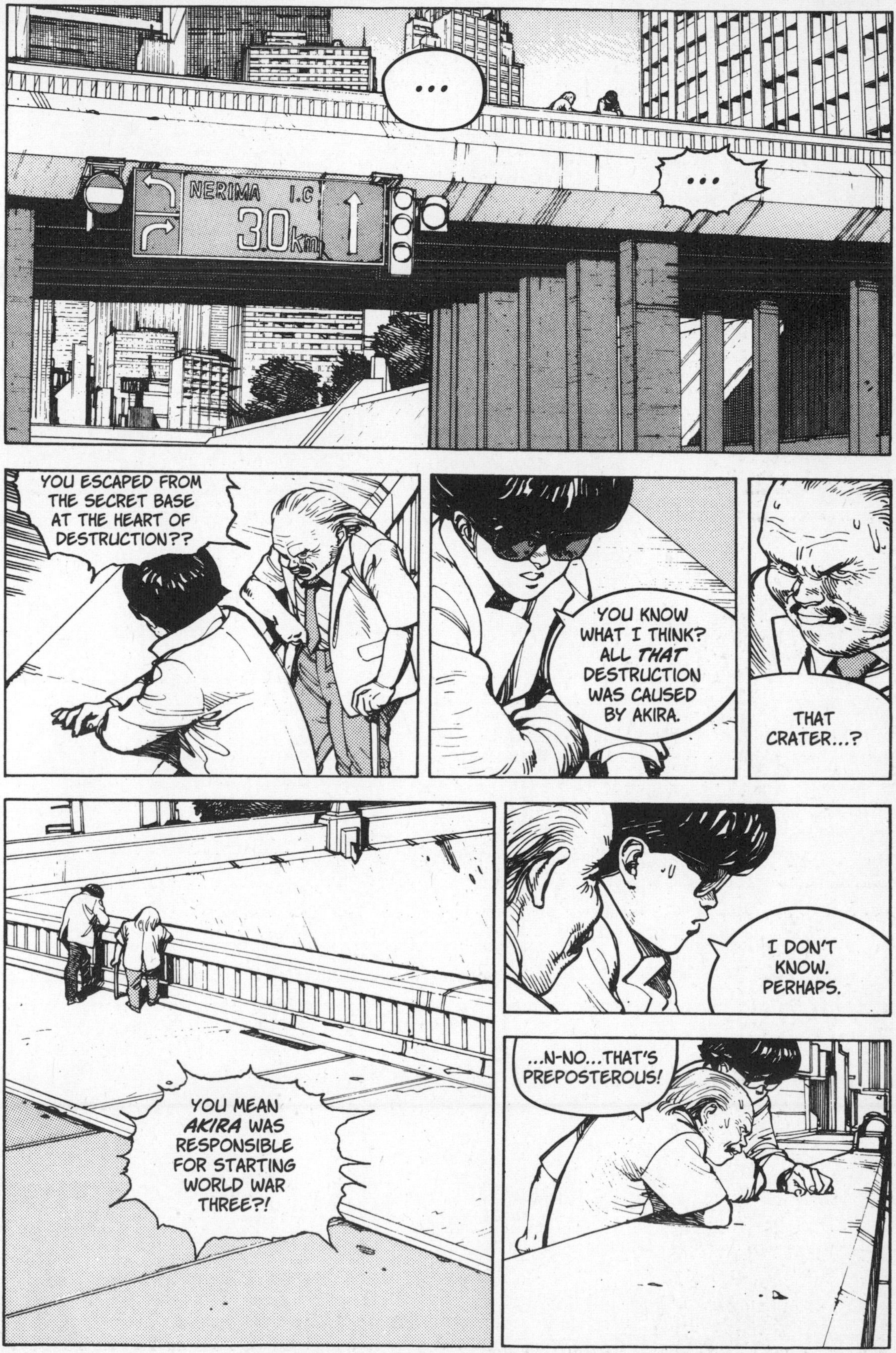

...
...
NERIMA I.C
30km
YOU ESCAPED FROM THE SECRET BASE AT THE HEART OF DESTRUCTION??
YOU KNOW WHAT I THINK? ALL *THAT* DESTRUCTION WAS CAUSED BY AKIRA.
THAT CRATER...?
YOU MEAN *AKIRA* WAS RESPONSIBLE FOR STARTING WORLD WAR THREE?!
I DON'T KNOW. PERHAPS.
...N-NO...THAT'S PREPOSTEROUS!

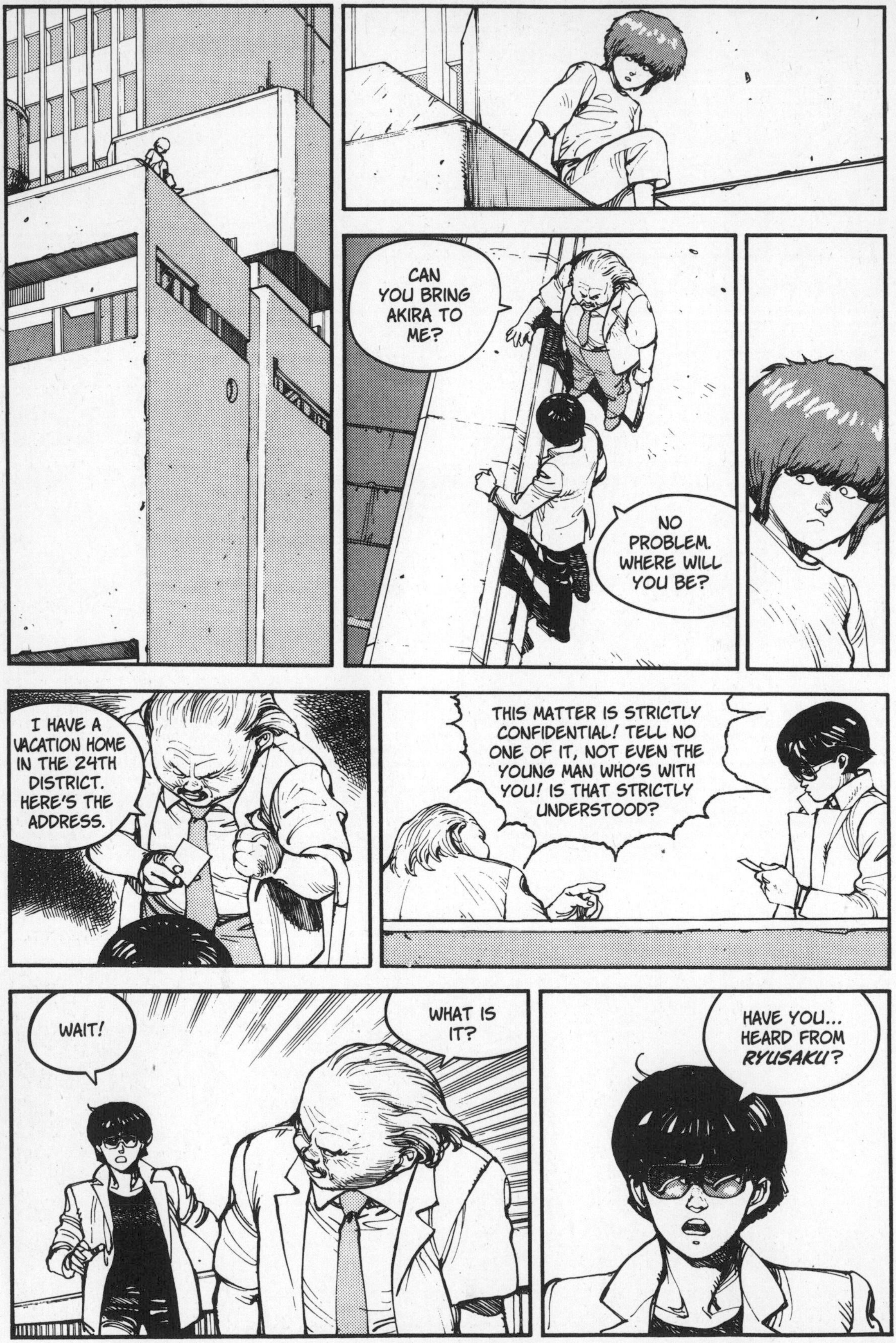
CAN YOU BRING AKIRA TO ME?
NO PROBLEM. WHERE WILL YOU BE?
I HAVE A VACATION HOME IN THE 24TH DISTRICT. HERE'S THE ADDRESS.
THIS MATTER IS STRICTLY CONFIDENTIAL! TELL NO ONE OF IT, NOT EVEN THE YOUNG MAN WHO'S WITH YOU! IS THAT STRICTLY UNDERSTOOD?
WAIT!
WHAT IS IT?
HAVE YOU... HEARD FROM *RYUSAKU*?

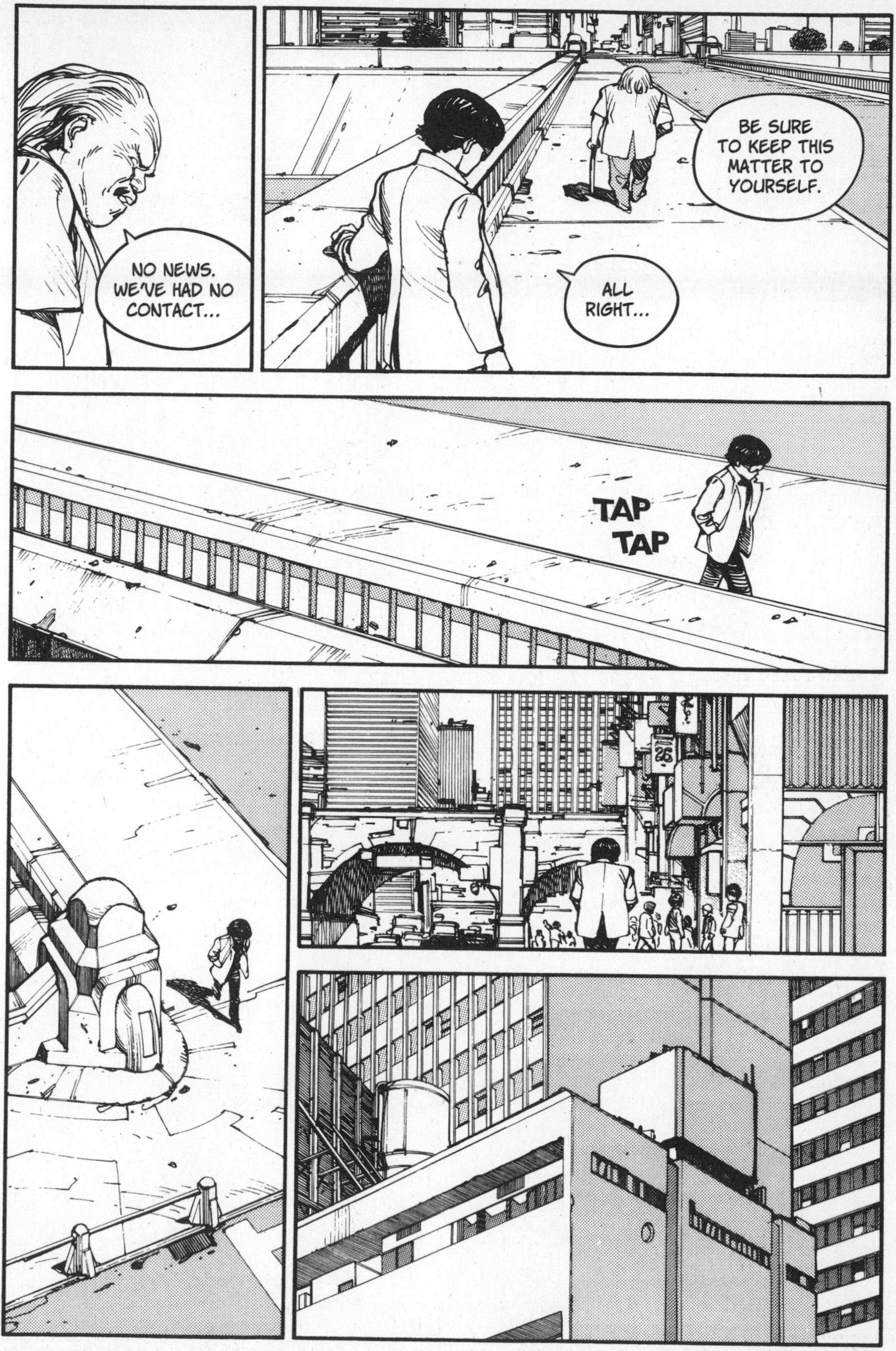
NO NEWS. WE'VE HAD NO CONTACT...
BE SURE TO KEEP THIS MATTER TO YOURSELF.
ALL RIGHT...
TAP TAP

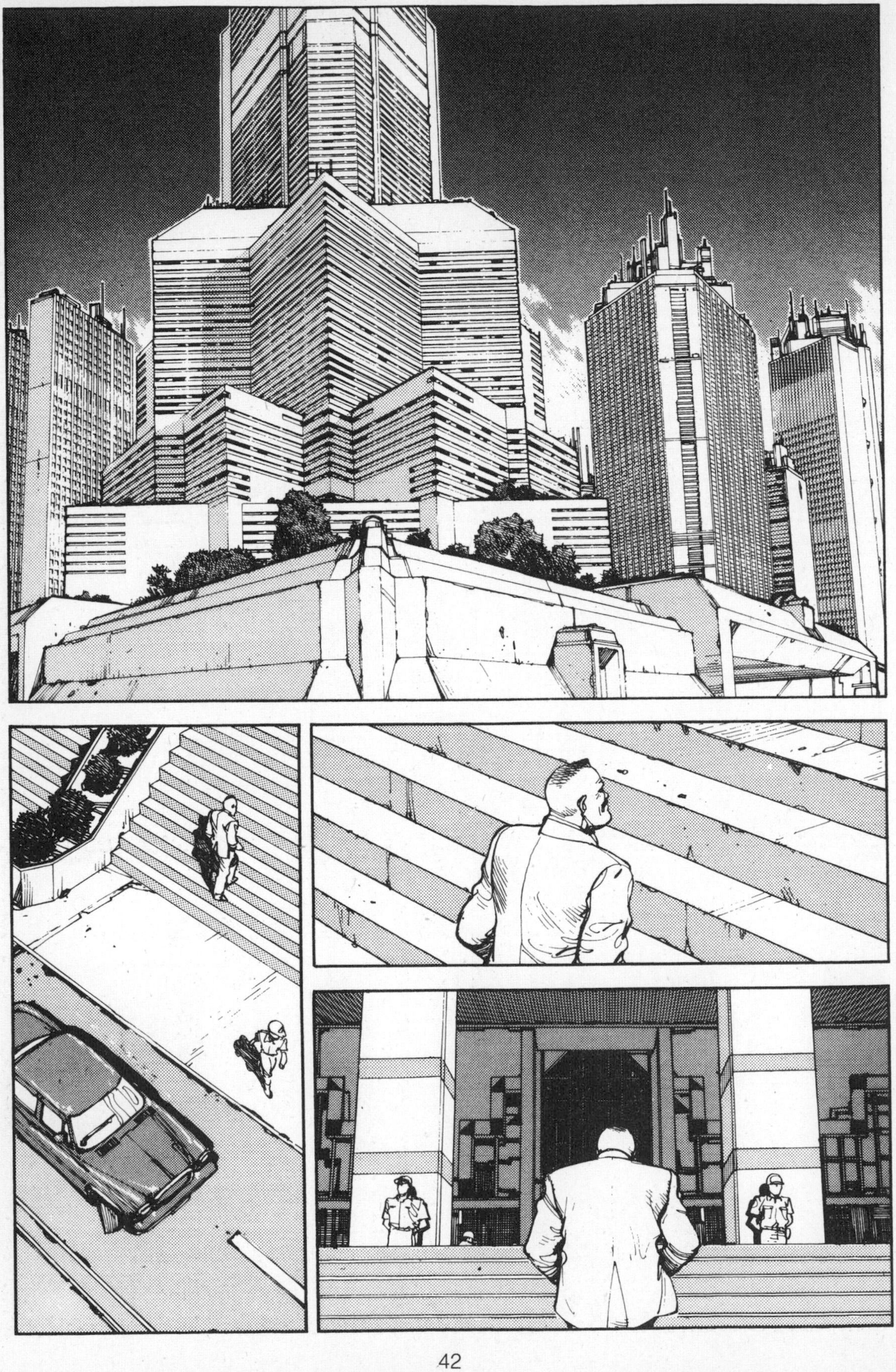

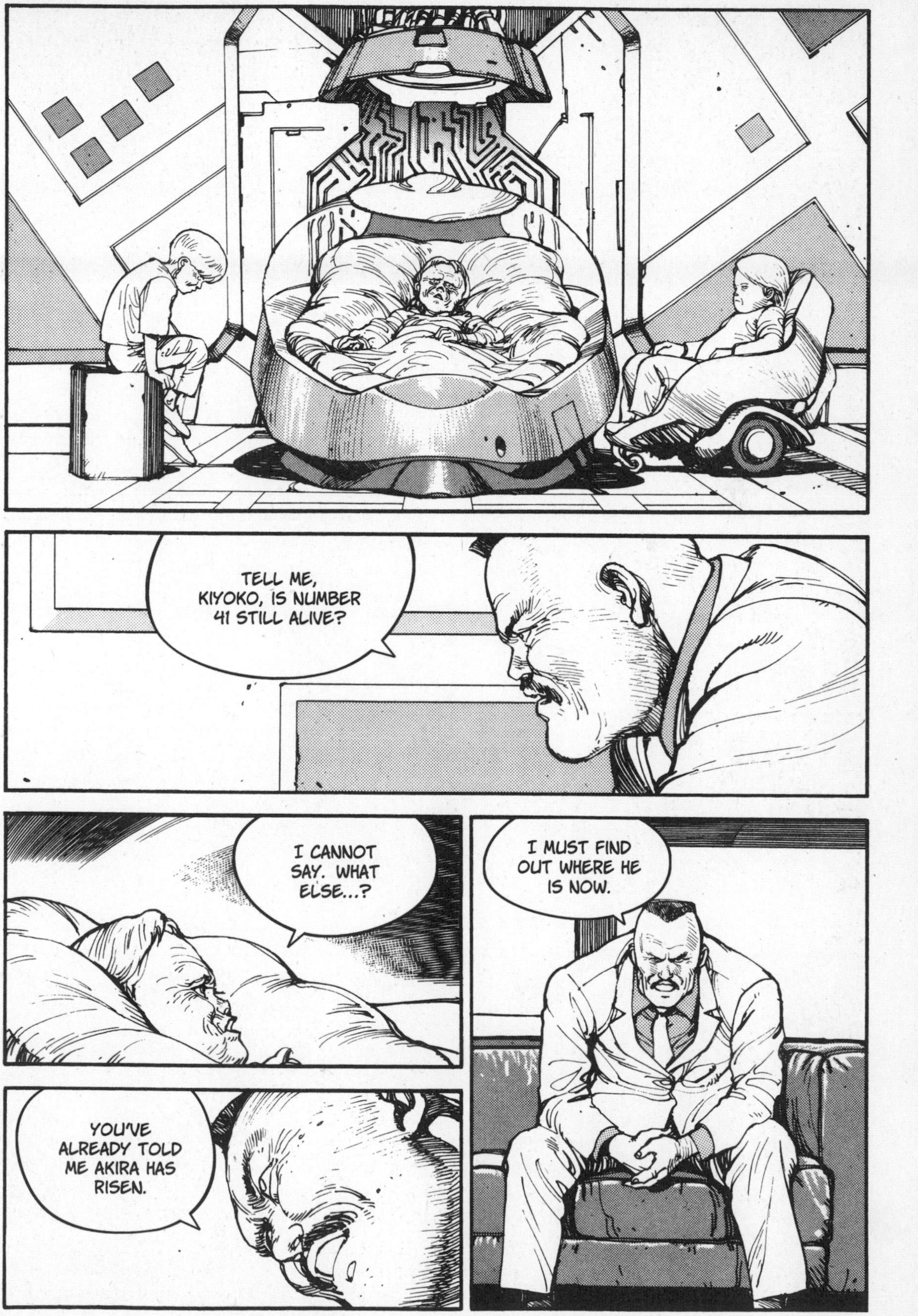
TELL ME, KIYOKO, IS NUMBER 41 STILL ALIVE?
I CANNOT SAY. WHAT ELSE...?
YOU'VE ALREADY TOLD ME AKIRA HAS RISEN.
I MUST FIND OUT WHERE HE IS NOW.

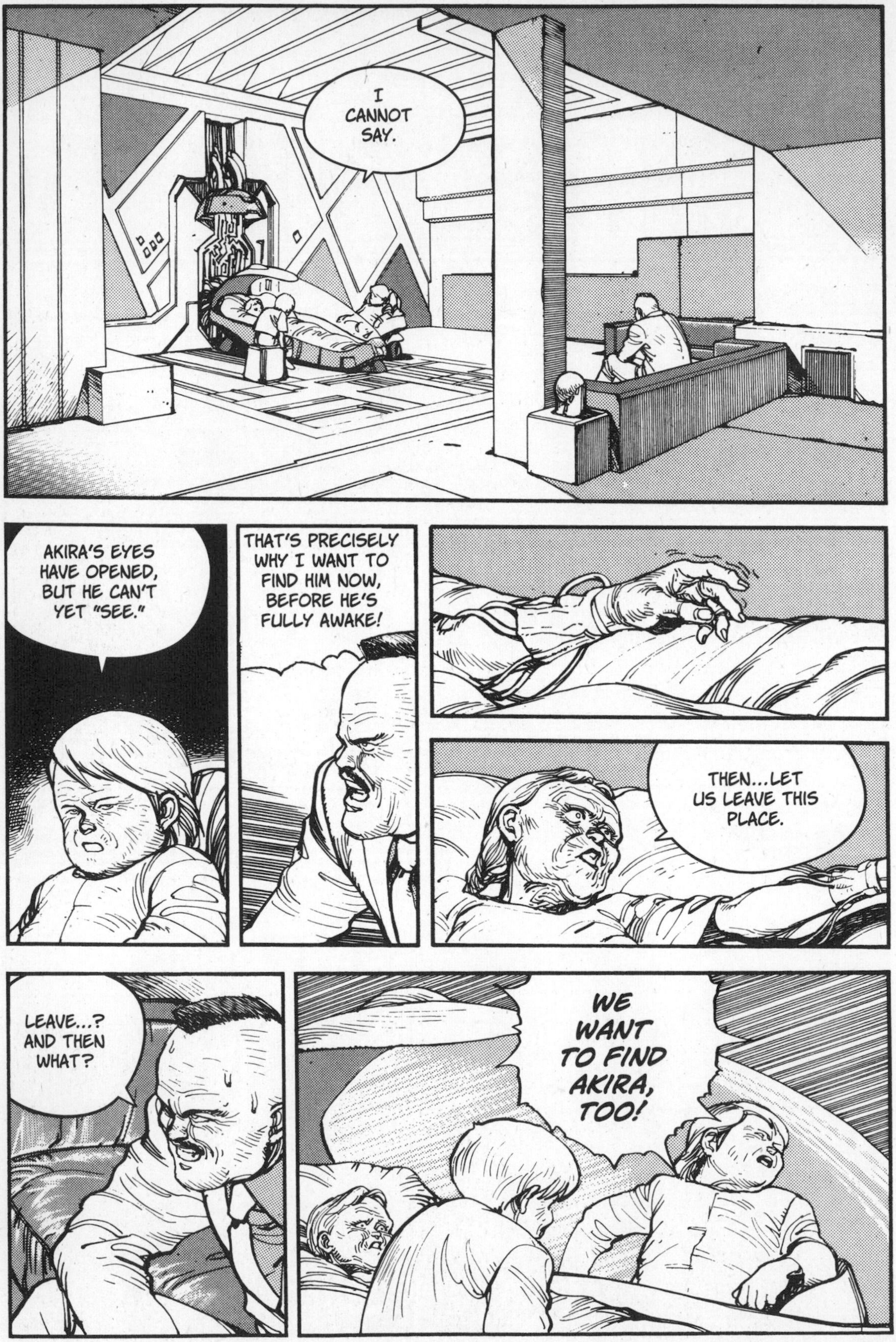
I CANNOT SAY.
AKIRA'S EYES HAVE OPENED, BUT HE CAN'T YET "SEE."
THAT'S PRECISELY WHY I WANT TO FIND HIM NOW, BEFORE HE'S FULLY AWAKE!
THEN...LET US LEAVE THIS PLACE.
LEAVE...? AND THEN WHAT?
WE WANT TO FIND AKIRA, TOO!

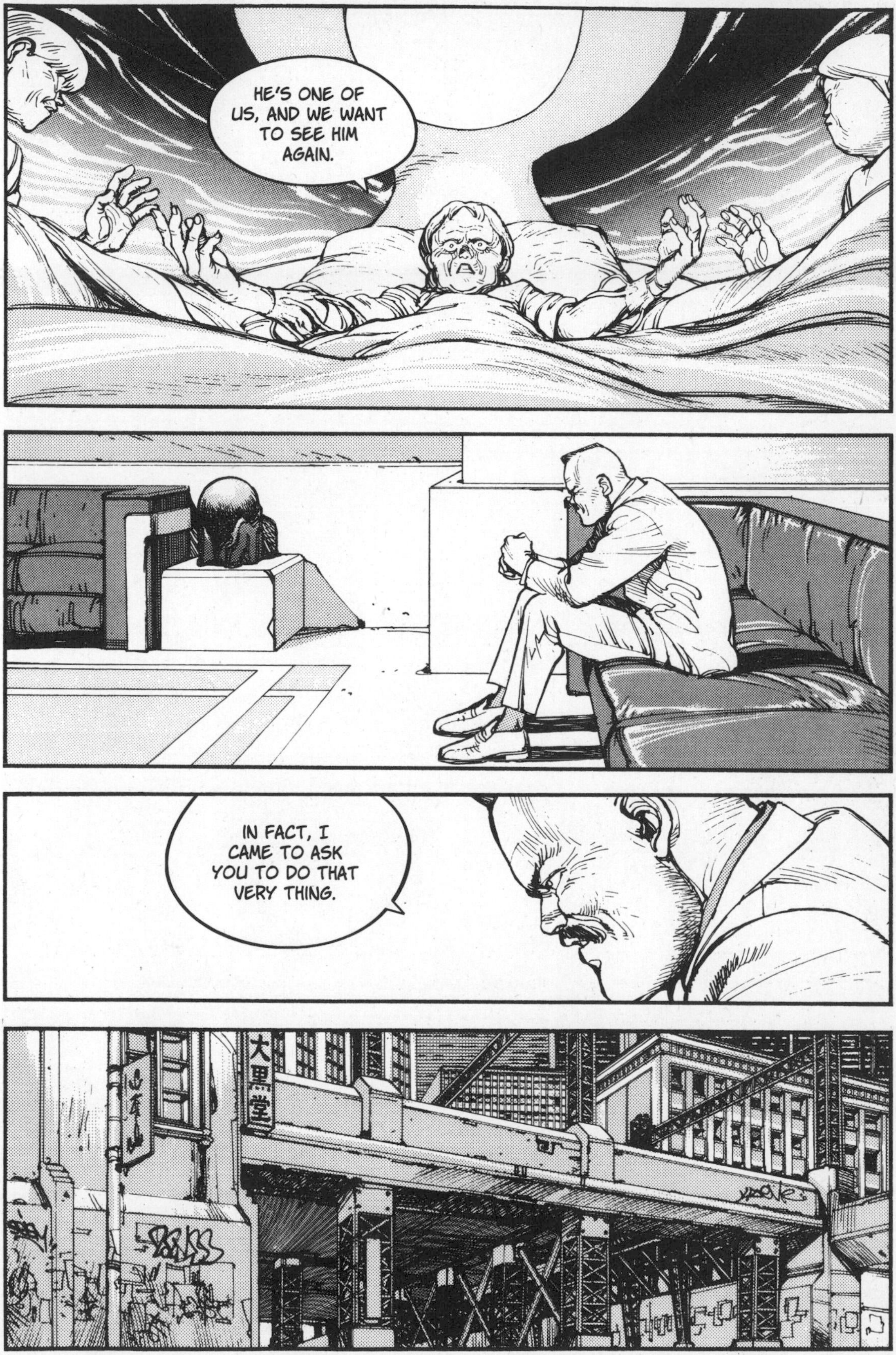
HE'S ONE OF US, AND WE WANT TO SEE HIM AGAIN.
IN FACT, I CAME TO ASK YOU TO DO THAT VERY THING.
大黒堂

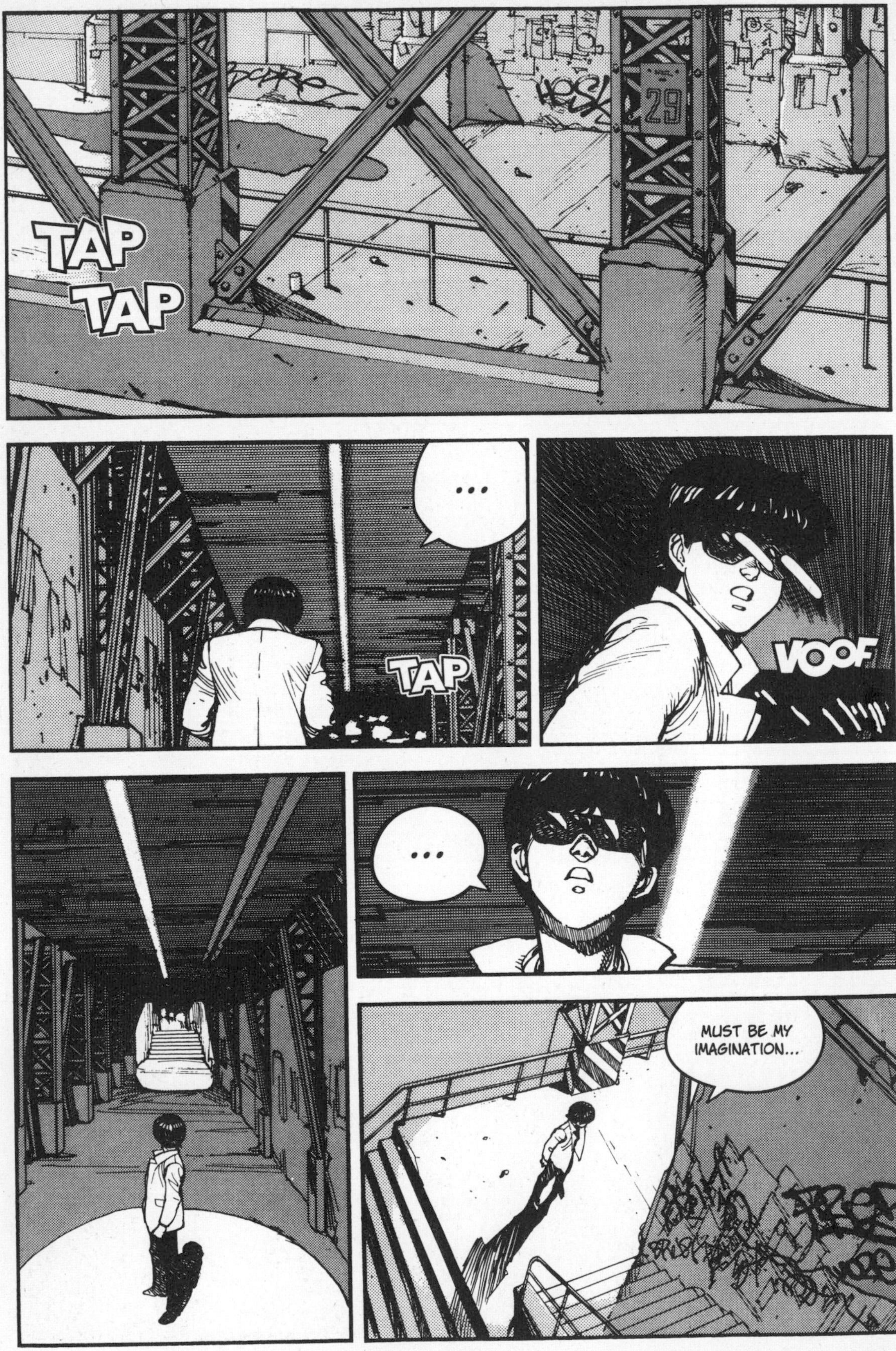
TAP
TAP
...
TAP
VOOF
...
MUST BE MY IMAGINATION...

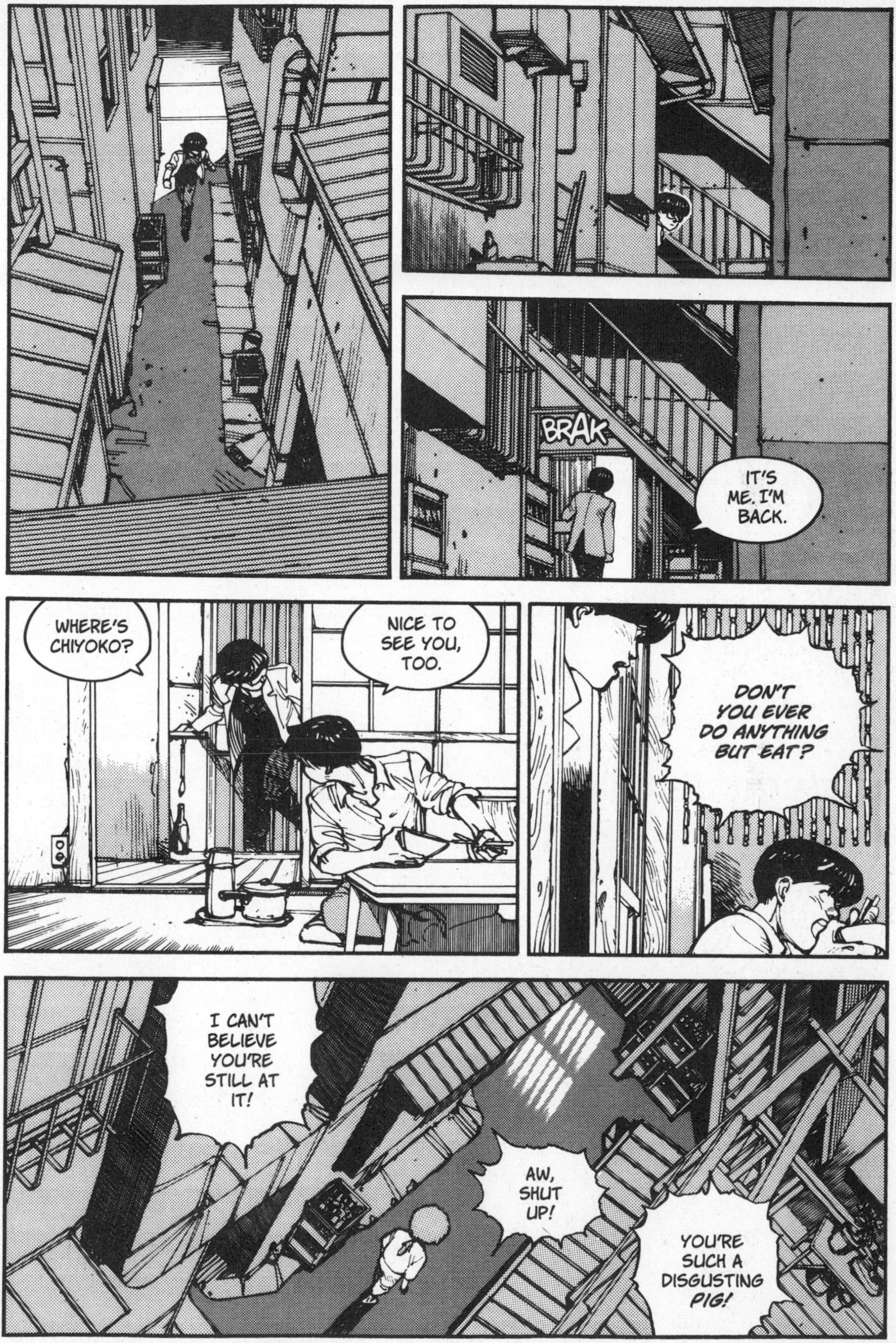
BRAK
IT'S ME. I'M BACK.
WHERE'S CHIYOKO?
NICE TO SEE YOU, TOO.
DON'T YOU EVER DO ANYTHING BUT EAT?
I CAN'T BELIEVE YOU'RE STILL AT IT!
AW, SHUT UP!
YOU'RE SUCH A DISGUSTING *PIG!*

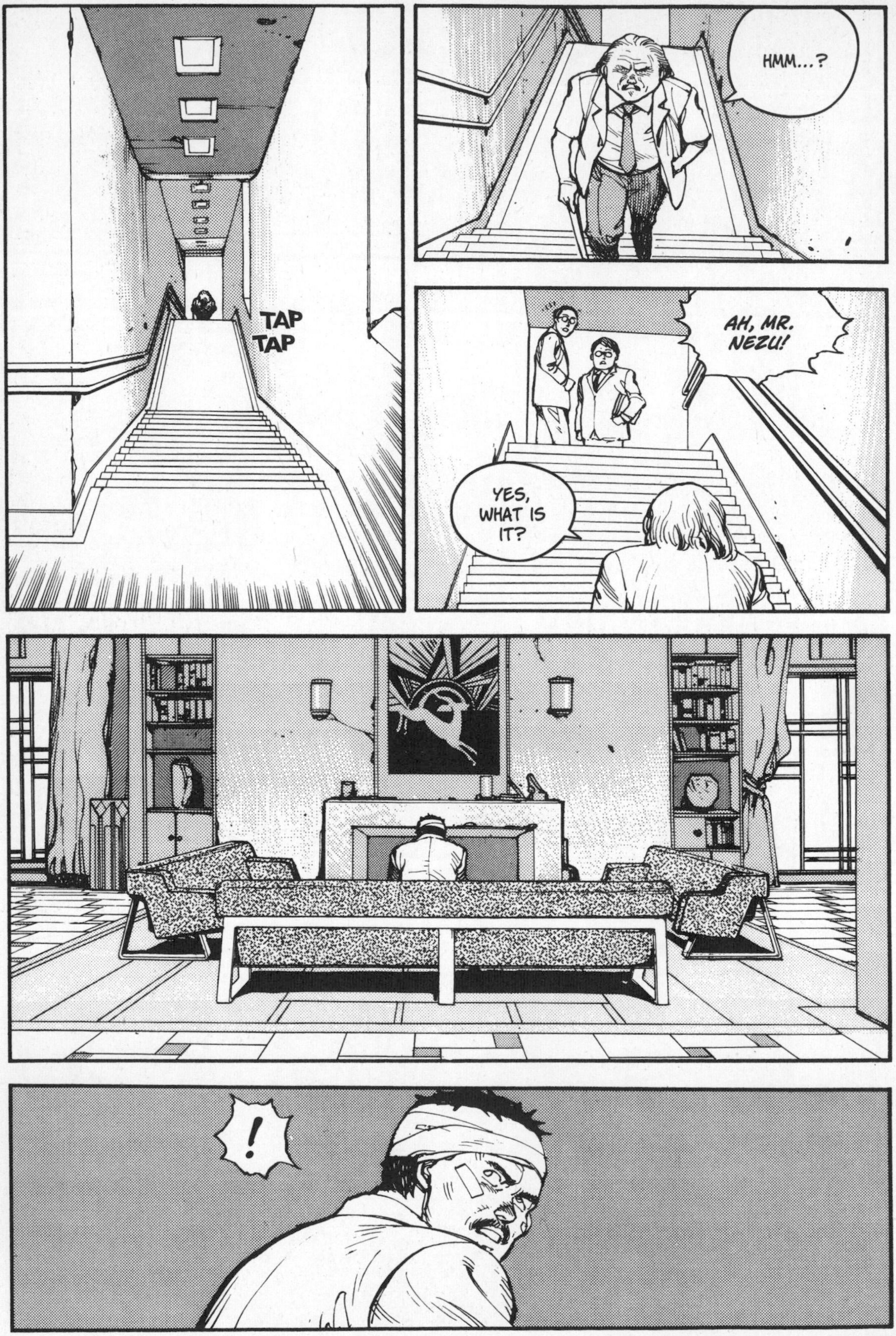
TAP
TAP
HMM...?
AH, MR. NEZU!
YES, WHAT IS IT?
!

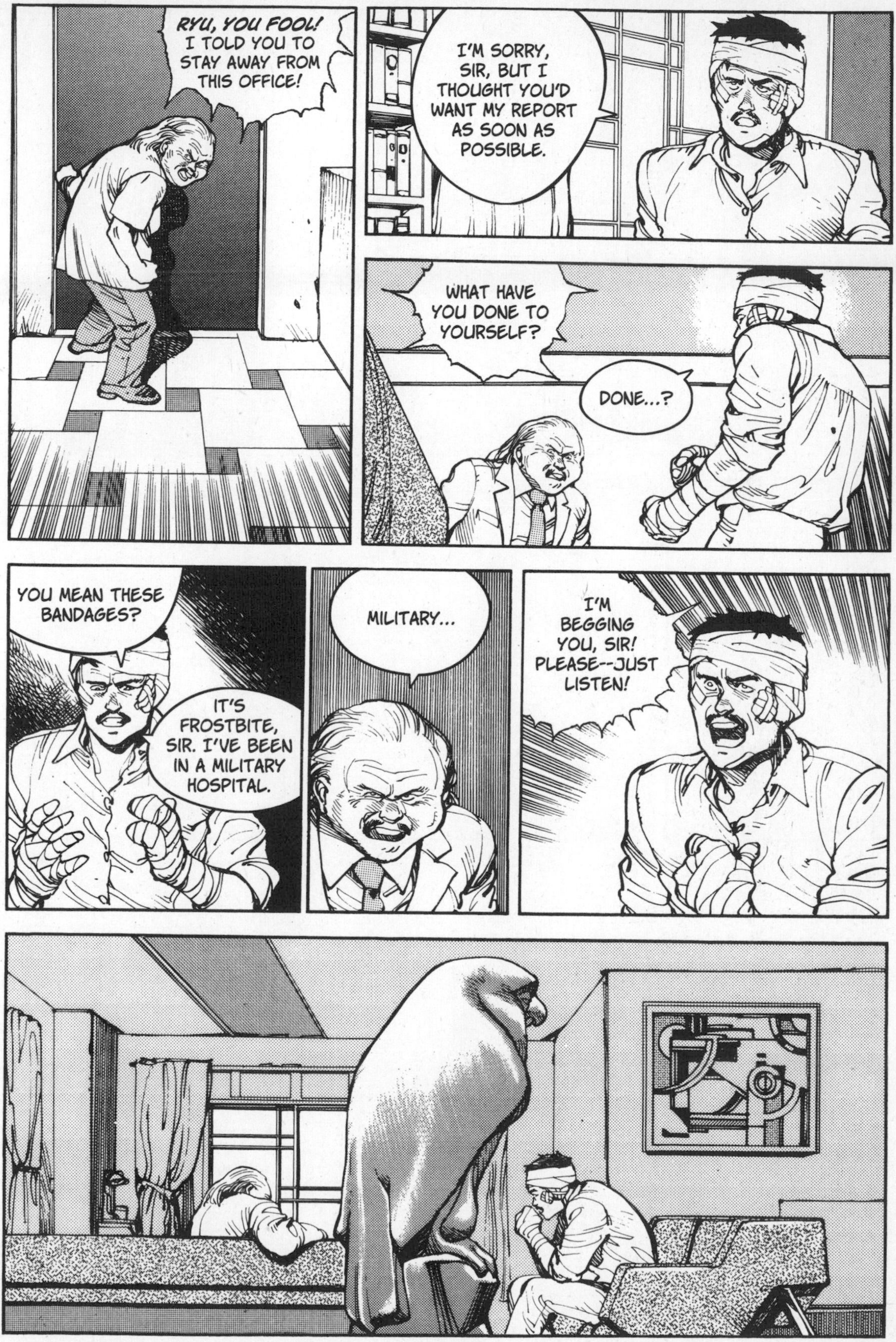
RYU, YOU FOOL! I TOLD YOU TO STAY AWAY FROM THIS OFFICE!
I'M SORRY, SIR, BUT I THOUGHT YOU'D WANT MY REPORT AS SOON AS POSSIBLE.
WHAT HAVE YOU DONE TO YOURSELF?
DONE...?
YOU MEAN THESE BANDAGES?
IT'S FROSTBITE, SIR. I'VE BEEN IN A MILITARY HOSPITAL.
MILITARY...
I'M BEGGING YOU, SIR! PLEASE--JUST LISTEN!

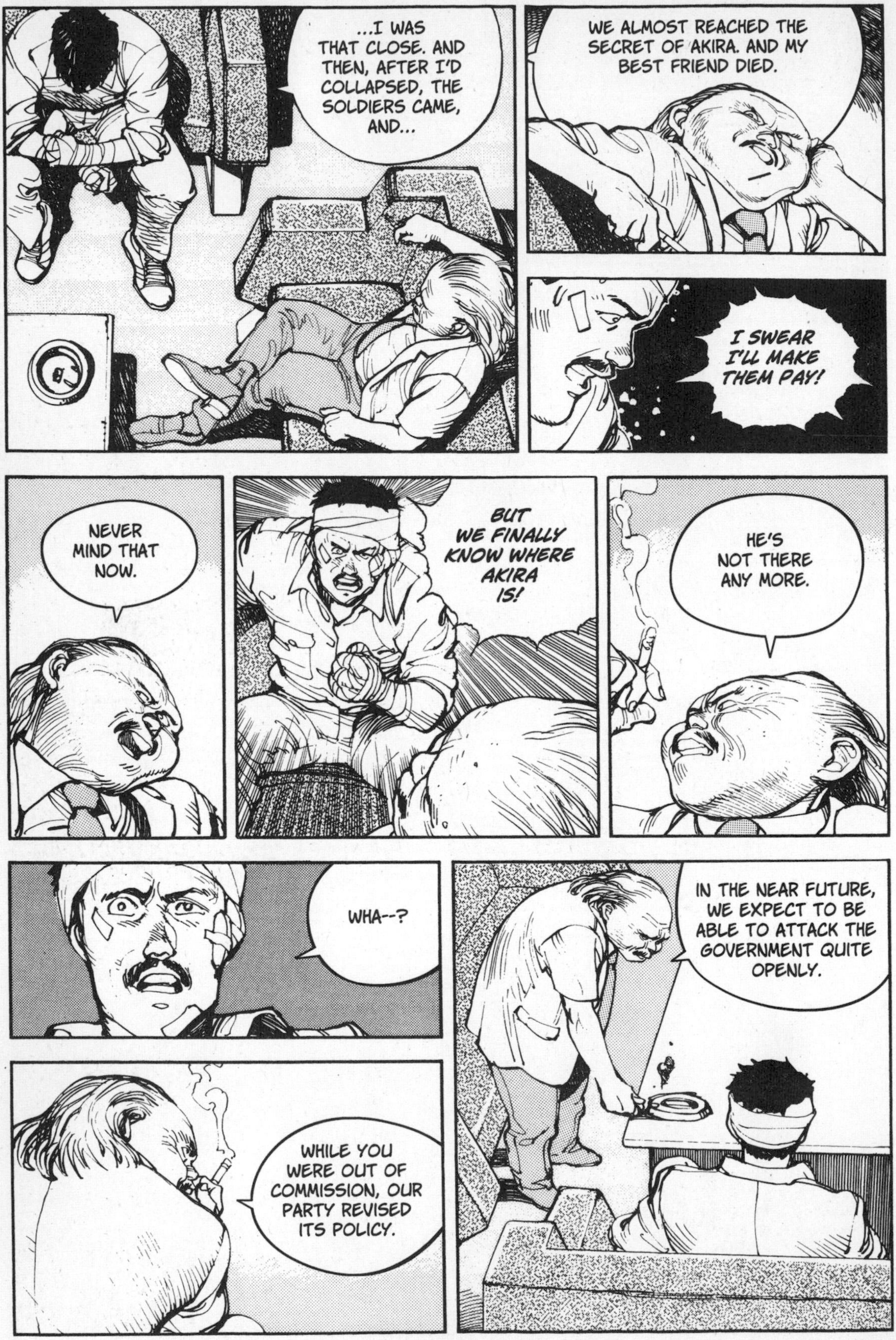
...I WAS THAT CLOSE. AND THEN, AFTER I'D COLLAPSED, THE SOLDIERS CAME, AND...
WE ALMOST REACHED THE SECRET OF AKIRA. AND MY BEST FRIEND DIED.
I SWEAR I'LL MAKE THEM PAY!
NEVER MIND THAT NOW.
BUT WE FINALLY KNOW WHERE AKIRA IS!
HE'S NOT THERE ANY MORE.
WHA--?
WHILE YOU WERE OUT OF COMMISSION, OUR PARTY REVISED ITS POLICY.
IN THE NEAR FUTURE, WE EXPECT TO BE ABLE TO ATTACK THE GOVERNMENT QUITE OPENLY.

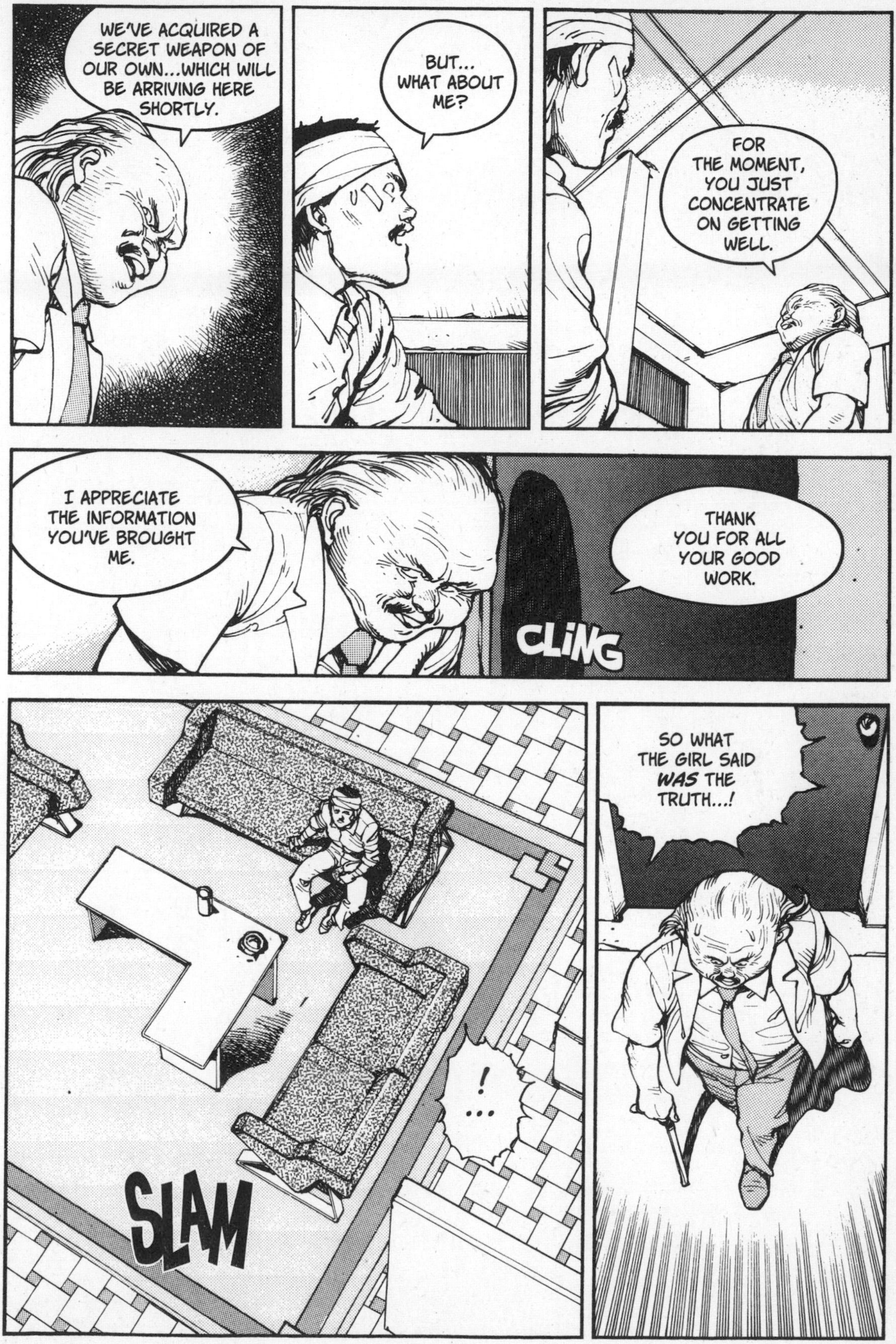
WE'VE ACQUIRED A SECRET WEAPON OF OUR OWN...WHICH WILL BE ARRIVING HERE SHORTLY.
BUT... WHAT ABOUT ME?
FOR THE MOMENT, YOU JUST CONCENTRATE ON GETTING WELL.
I APPRECIATE THE INFORMATION YOU'VE BROUGHT ME.
THANK YOU FOR ALL YOUR GOOD WORK.
CLING
SLAM
!...
SO WHAT THE GIRL SAID ***WAS*** THE TRUTH...!

AS I SEE IT...

...IT DOESN'T PAY TO BE TOO CLEVER. YOU MIGHT AS WELL WALK RIGHT IN, BUSINESS AS USUAL.

I THINK YOU'RE RIGHT.

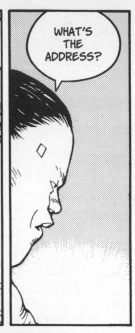

WHAT'S THE ADDRESS?

THE ADDRESS?

...

OH, I SEE...

...THEY WILL CONTACT YOU LATER.

52

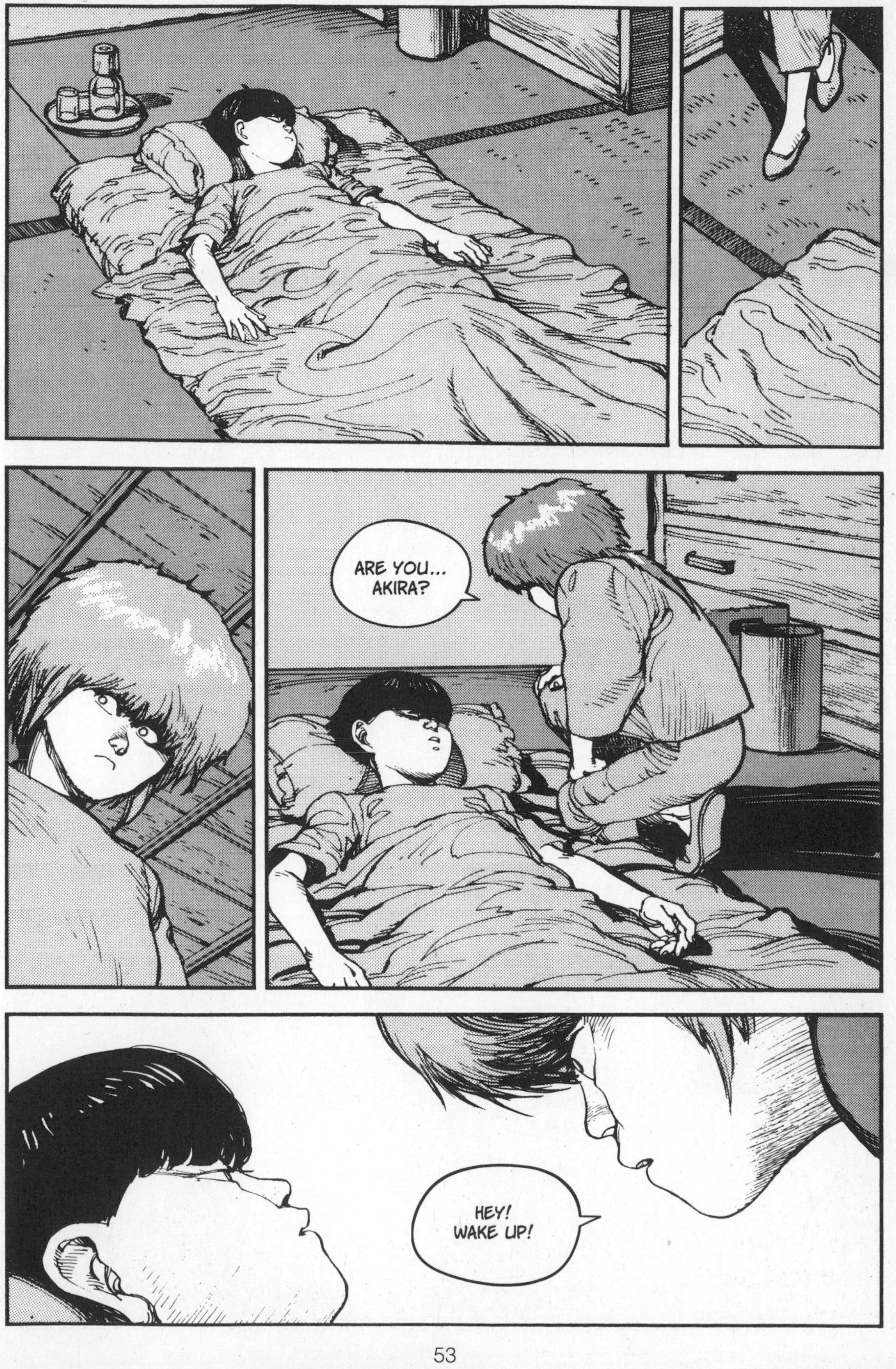
ARE YOU... AKIRA?
HEY! WAKE UP!

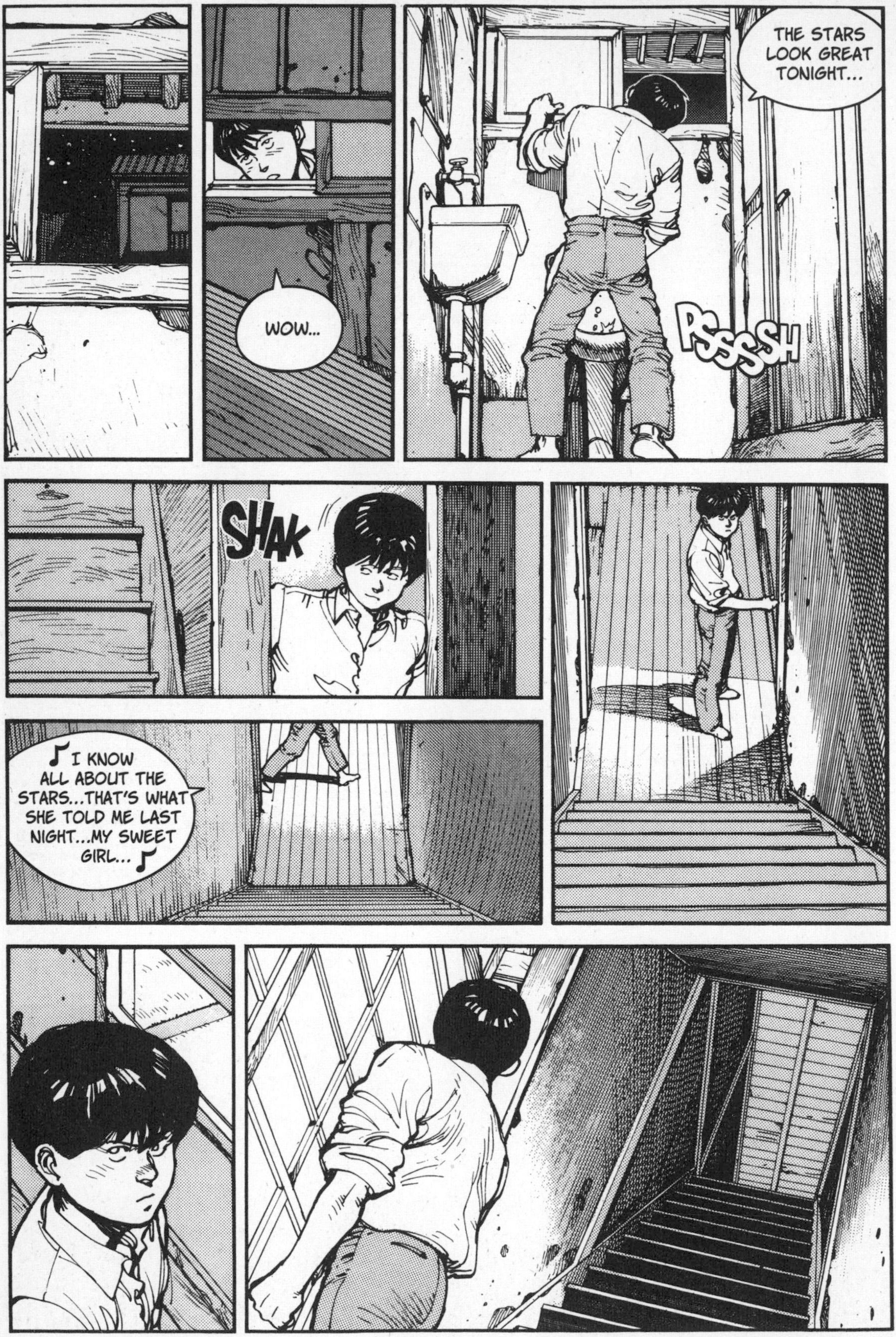
WOW...
THE STARS LOOK GREAT TONIGHT...
PSSSSH
SHAK
♪ I KNOW ALL ABOUT THE STARS...THAT'S WHAT SHE TOLD ME LAST NIGHT...MY SWEET GIRL... ♪

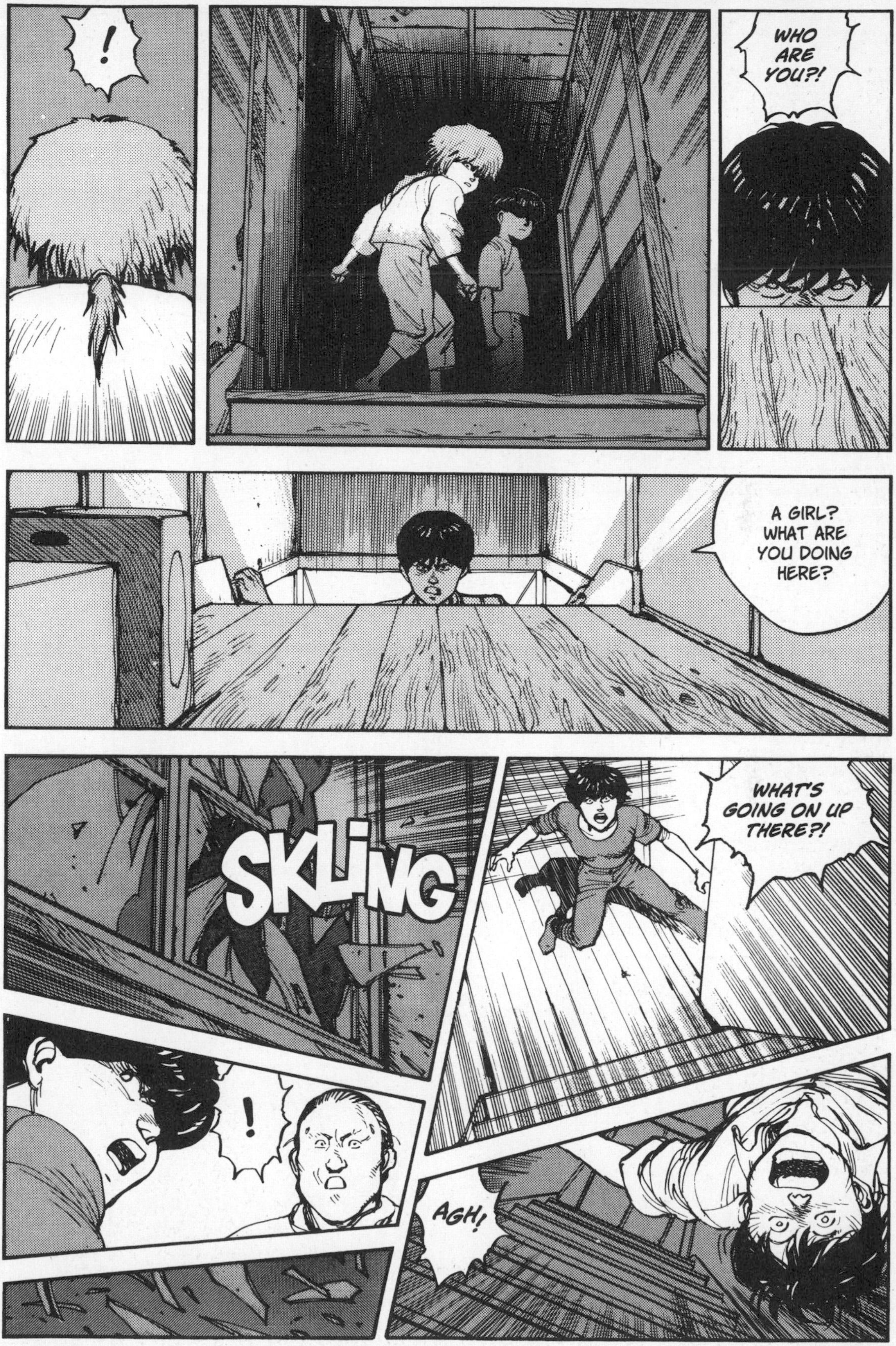
!
WHO ARE YOU?!
A GIRL? WHAT ARE YOU DOING HERE?
SKLING
WHAT'S GOING ON UP THERE?!
!
AGH!

BROOO
DOOM

BLOM
BRR
OW... OWWW!

YOU IDIOT! WHAT ARE YOU DOING?

THE KID-- AKIRA...

WHAT ABOUT AKIRA?!

THERE'S SOME- ONE UPSTAIRS KIDNAPPING HIM!

SOMEONE TAILED YOU, AND YOU NEVER NOTICED!

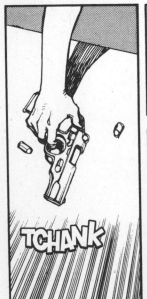
TCHANK

WE'LL DISCUSS IT LATER!

HOW MANY OF THEM ARE THERE? ARE THEY ARMED?

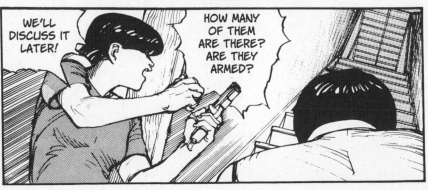

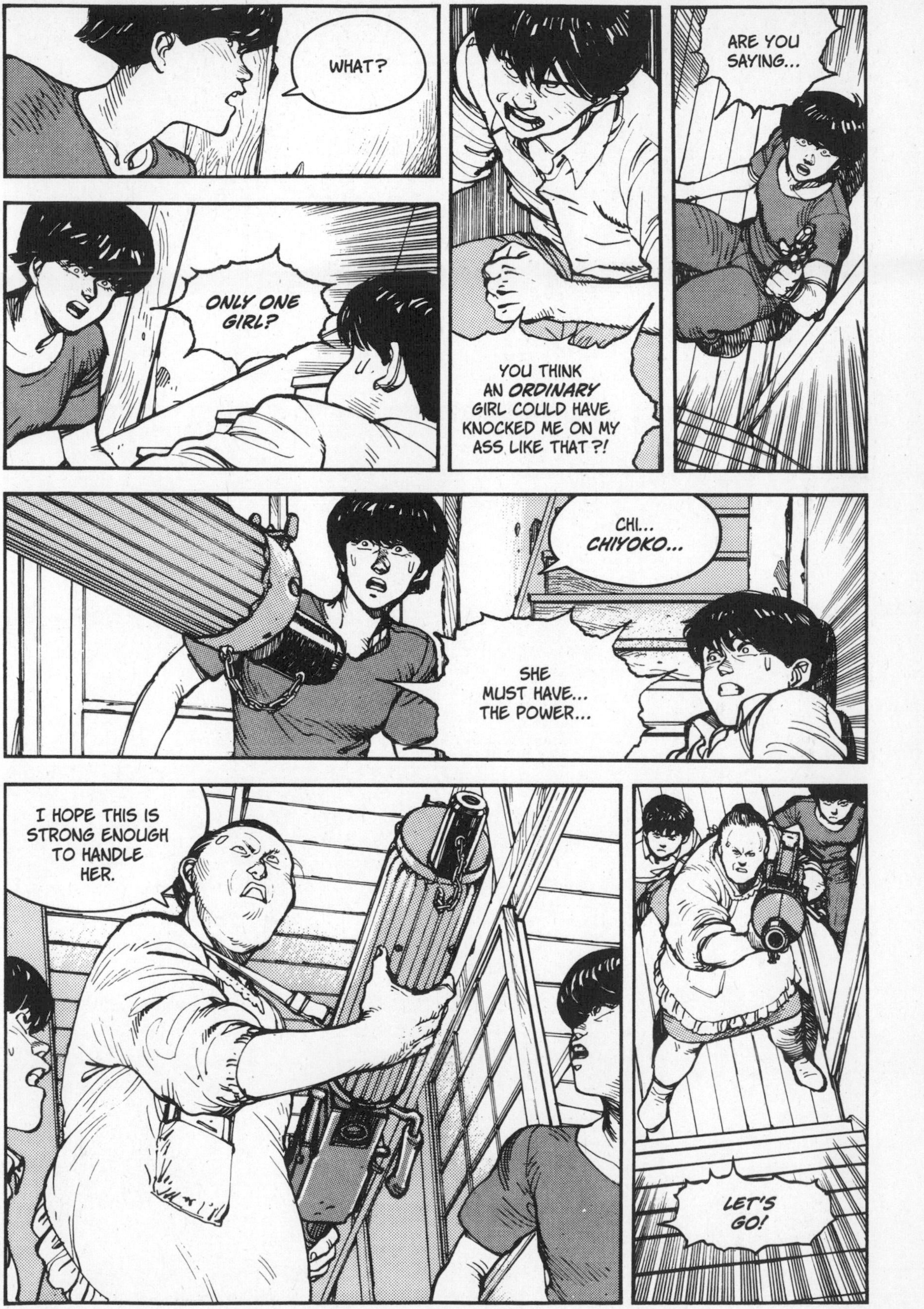
WHAT?
ONLY ONE GIRL?
YOU THINK AN ORDINARY GIRL COULD HAVE KNOCKED ME ON MY ASS LIKE THAT?!
ARE YOU SAYING...
CHI... CHIYOKO...
SHE MUST HAVE... THE POWER...
I HOPE THIS IS STRONG ENOUGH TO HANDLE HER.
LET'S GO!

71
GASP
GWOOON
THIS IS A CODE FIVE ALERT.
PK-2G
ZWOOO
A CURFEW IS IN EFFECT. IT IS FORBIDDEN TO GO OUT AT NIGHT.
I REPEAT, THIS IS A CODE FIVE ALERT!
PK 2G
95

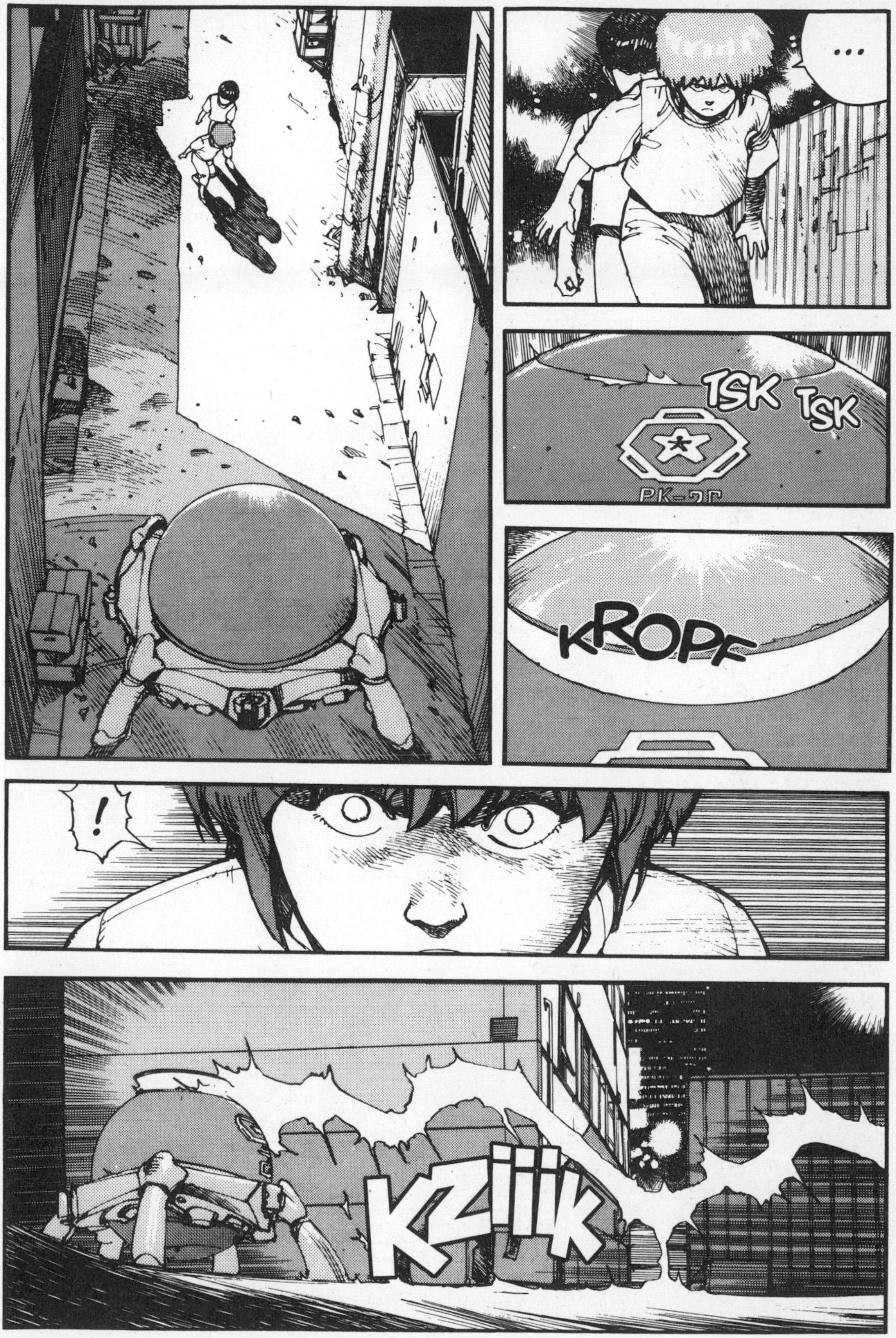
...
TSK TSK
KROPF
!
KZIIIK

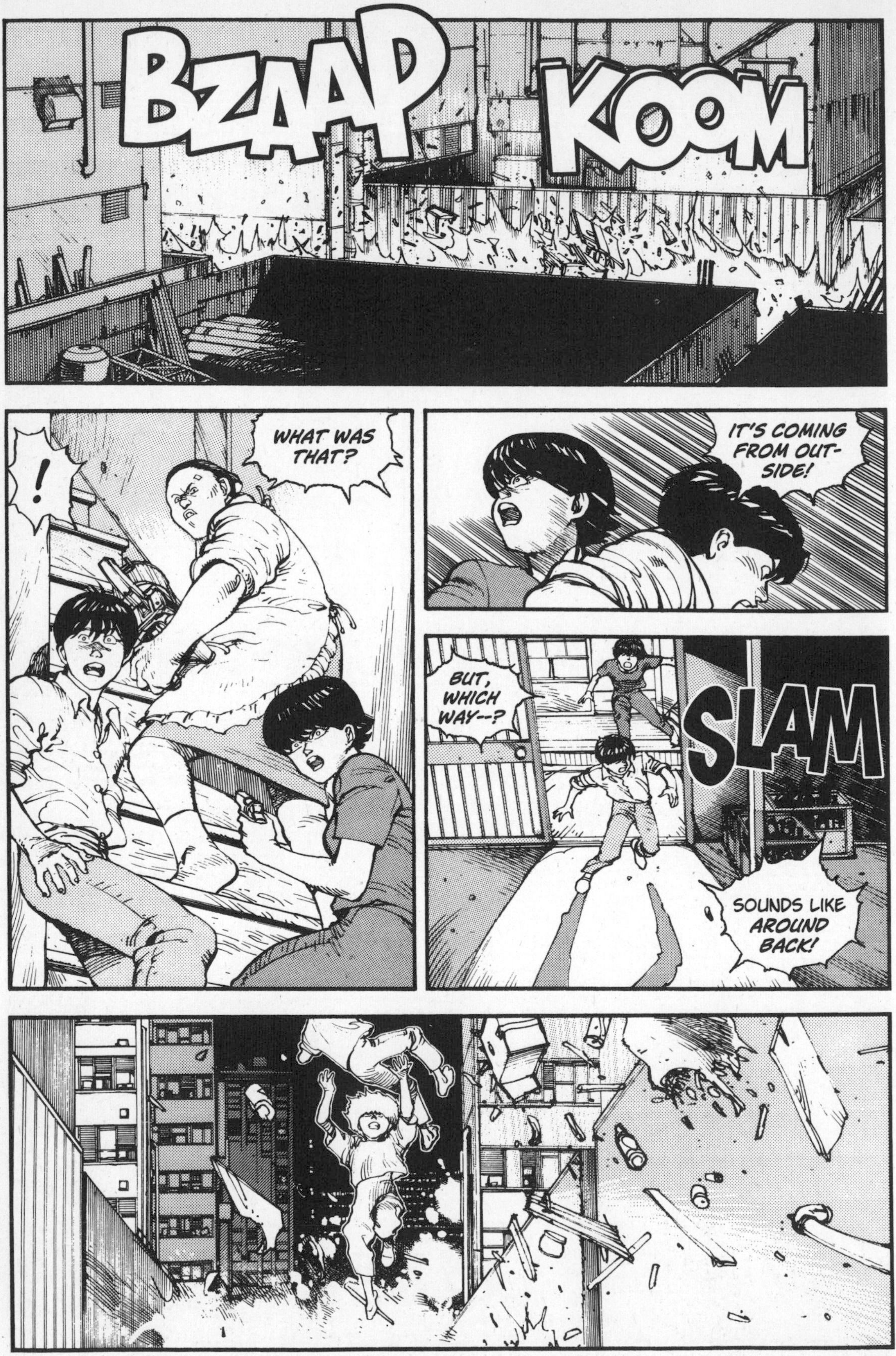

BZAAP
KOOM
!
WHAT WAS THAT?
IT'S COMING FROM OUT-SIDE!
BUT, WHICH WAY--?
SLAM
SOUNDS LIKE AROUND BACK!

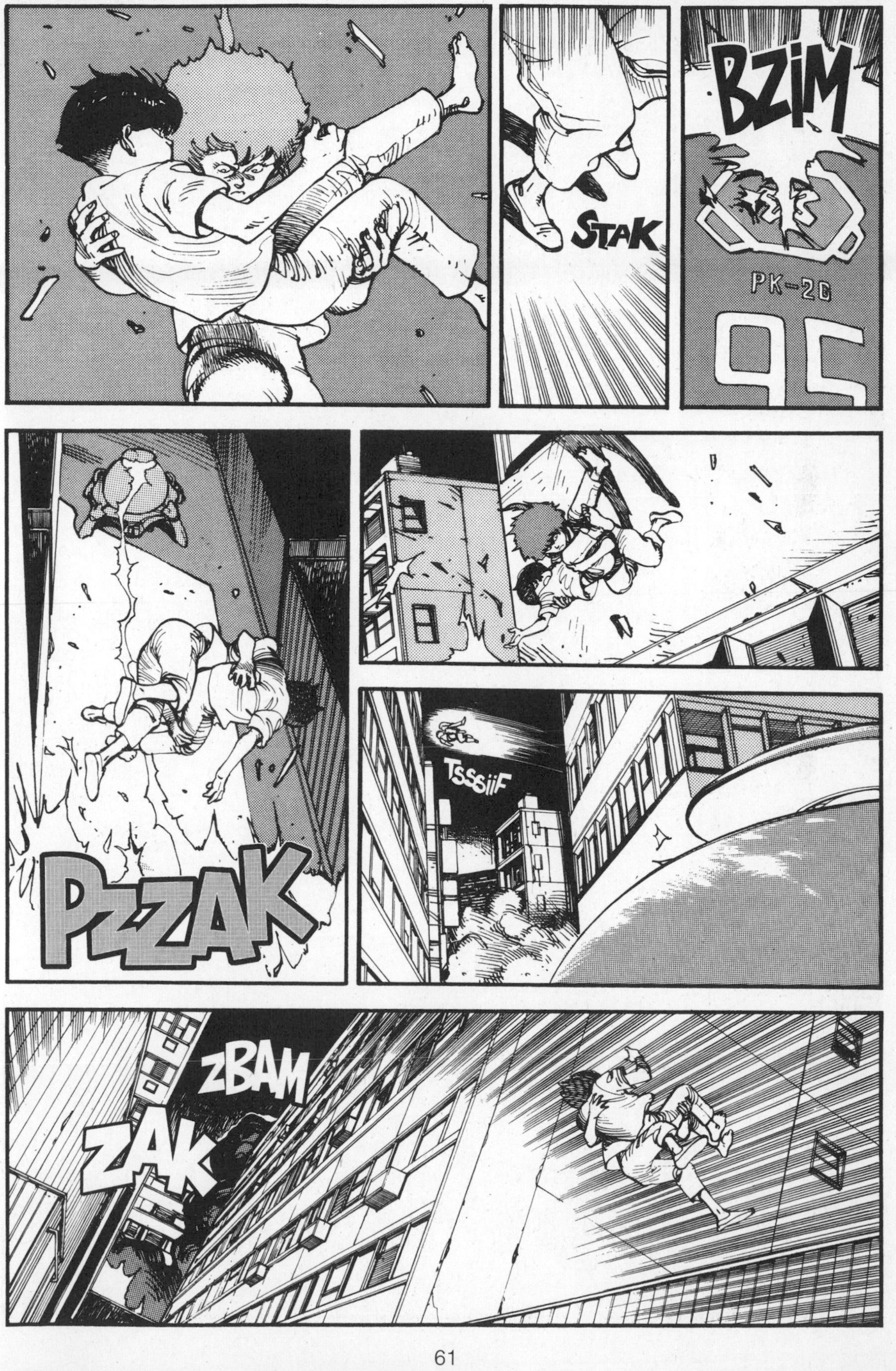
STAK
BZIM
PK-2G
95
PZZAK
TSSSIIF
ZBAM
ZAK

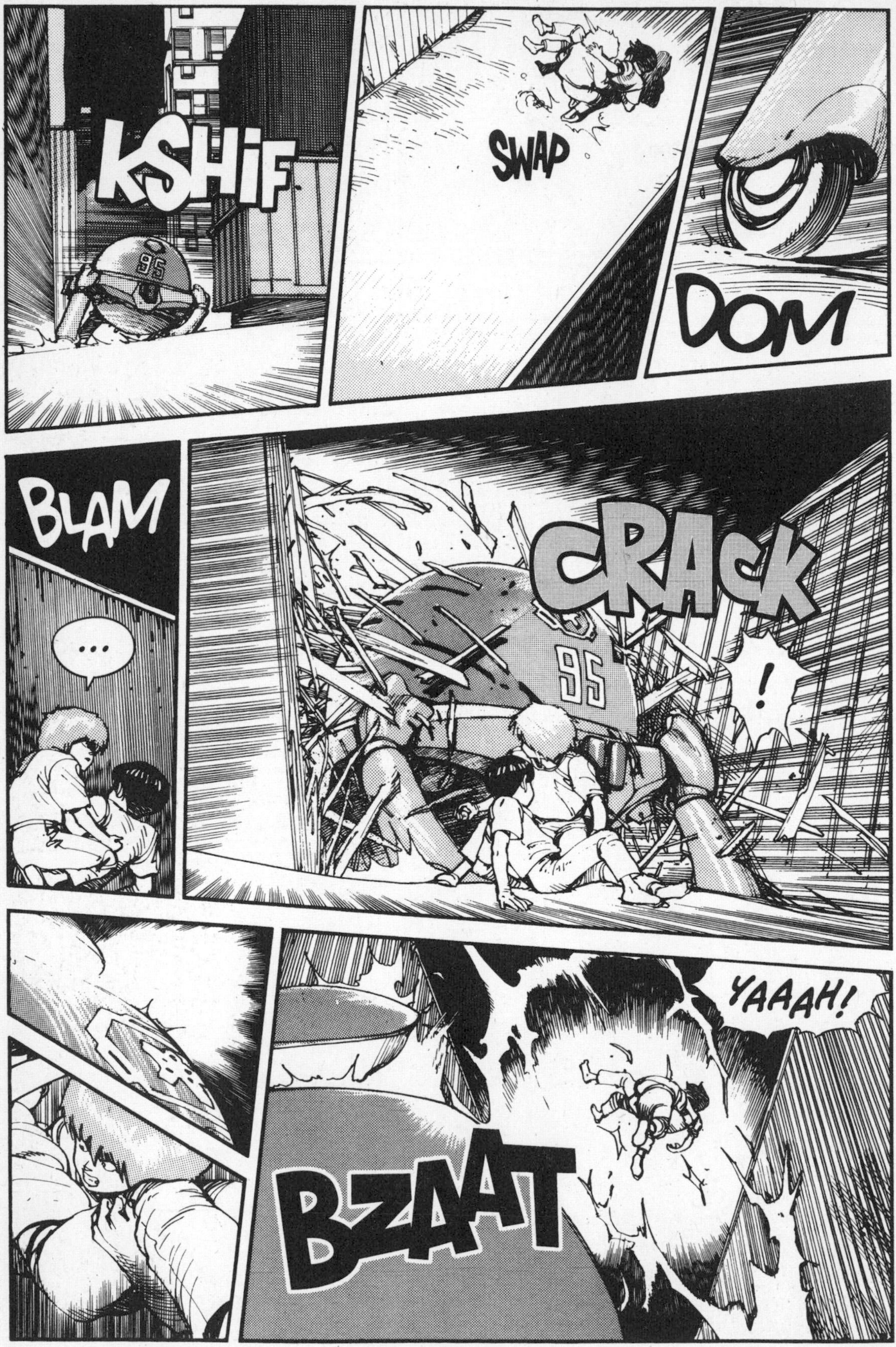
KSHIF
SWAP
DOM
BLAM
...
CRACK
!
YAAAH!
BZAAT

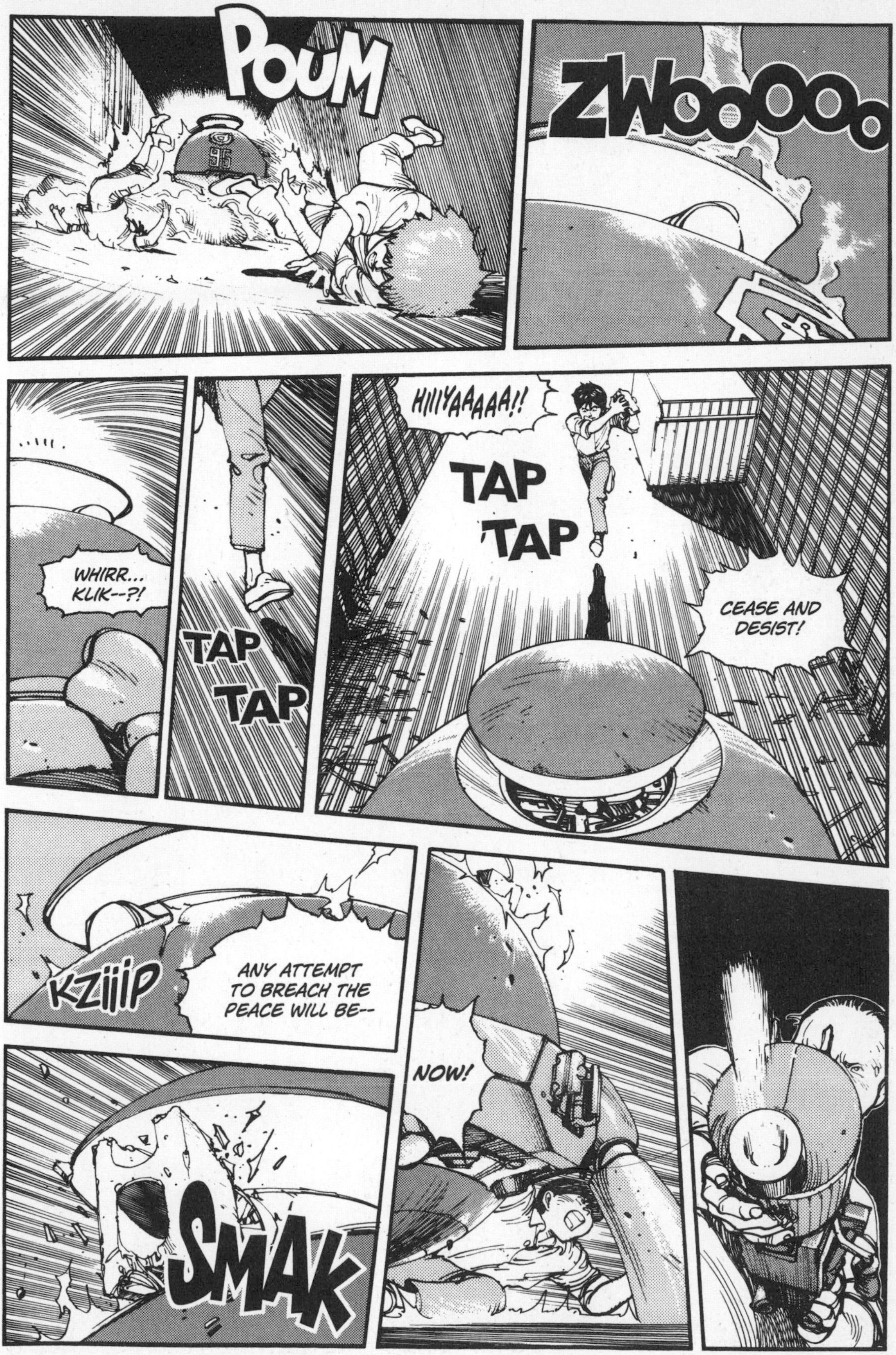
POUM
ZWOOOOOo
...
WHIRR... KLIK--?!
TAP
TAP
HIIIYAAAAA!!
TAP
TAP
CEASE AND DESIST!
KZIIIP
ANY ATTEMPT TO BREACH THE PEACE WILL BE--
SMAK
NOW!

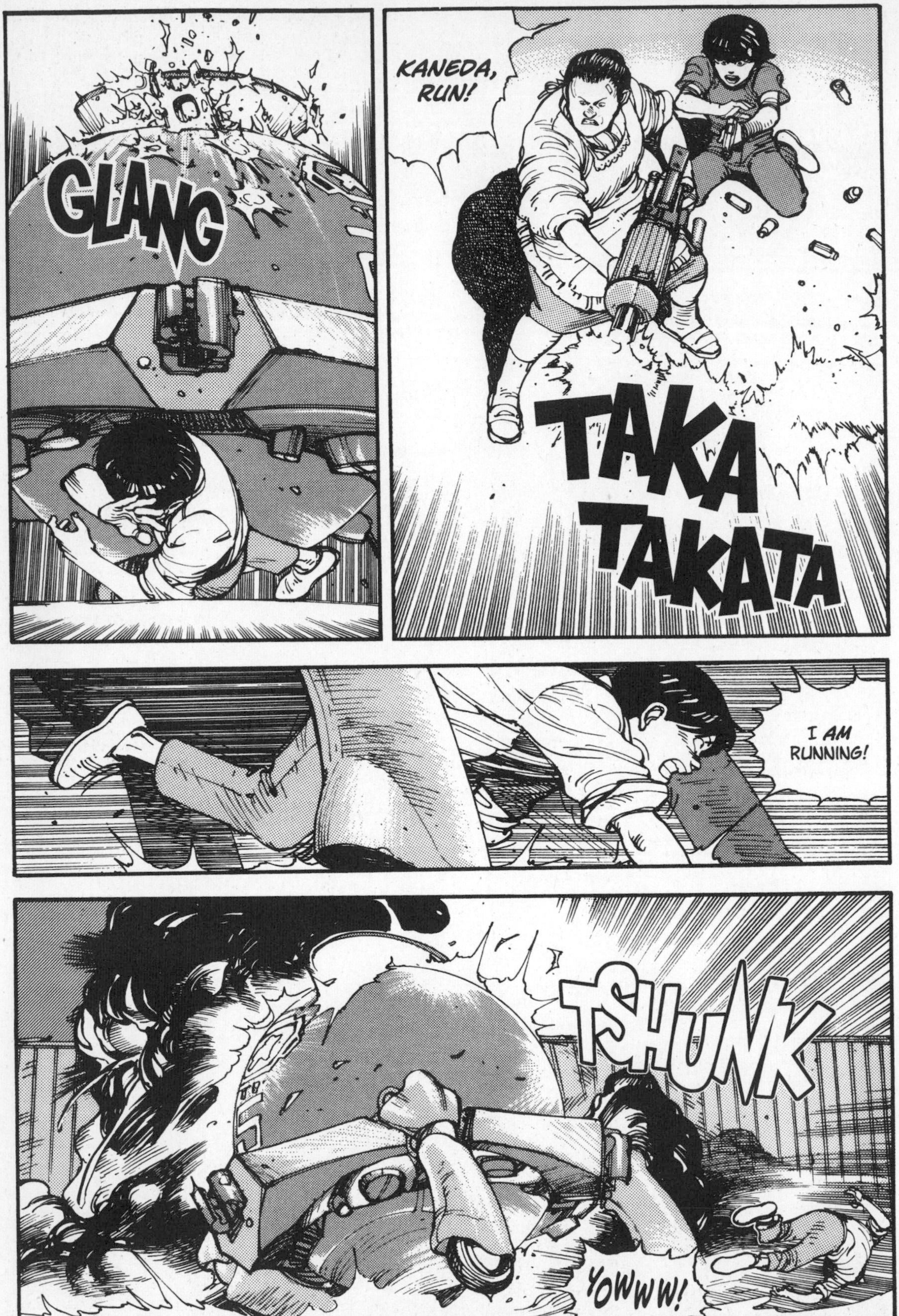
GLANG
KANEDA, RUN!
TAKA TAKATA
I AM RUNNING!
TSHUNK
YOWWW!

WHOOPS... TIME TO CHECK IN.

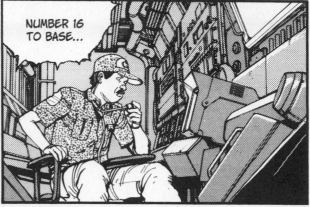

NUMBER 16 TO BASE...

TWIP

BASE HERE. EVERYTHING OKAY?

BIP

YEAH...JUST A BUNCH OF THE USUAL CRAP.

GIVE ME A RUN-DOWN.

OKAY...UH...29 DRUNKEN BRAWLS, 18 MISSING PERSONS, 43 CURFEW VIOLATIONS...

...AND ONE REPORT THAT SOUNDED KIND OF STRANGE.

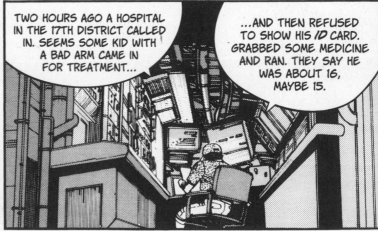

TWO HOURS AGO A HOSPITAL IN THE 17TH DISTRICT CALLED IN. SEEMS SOME KID WITH A BAD ARM CAME IN FOR TREATMENT...

...AND THEN REFUSED TO SHOW HIS *ID* CARD. GRABBED SOME MEDICINE AND RAN. THEY SAY HE WAS ABOUT 16, MAYBE 15.

65

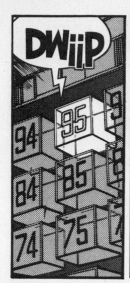

DWiiP

HOLD ON A MINUTE.

KLic

THERE'S A SIGNAL COMING IN FROM SPHERE #95, PATROLLING THE NINTH DISTRICT.

WHAT ...?!

PWiP

I'M GETTING A RED LIGHT ON IT! IT'S BEEN DESTROYED!

ALL SPHERES ARE BEING DIVERTED TO THE NINTH DISTRICT AT ONCE!

Pshhh

WONDER IF IT'S DEAD FOR SURE...?

HEY ...!?

HEY, GUYS... THEY'RE GONE.

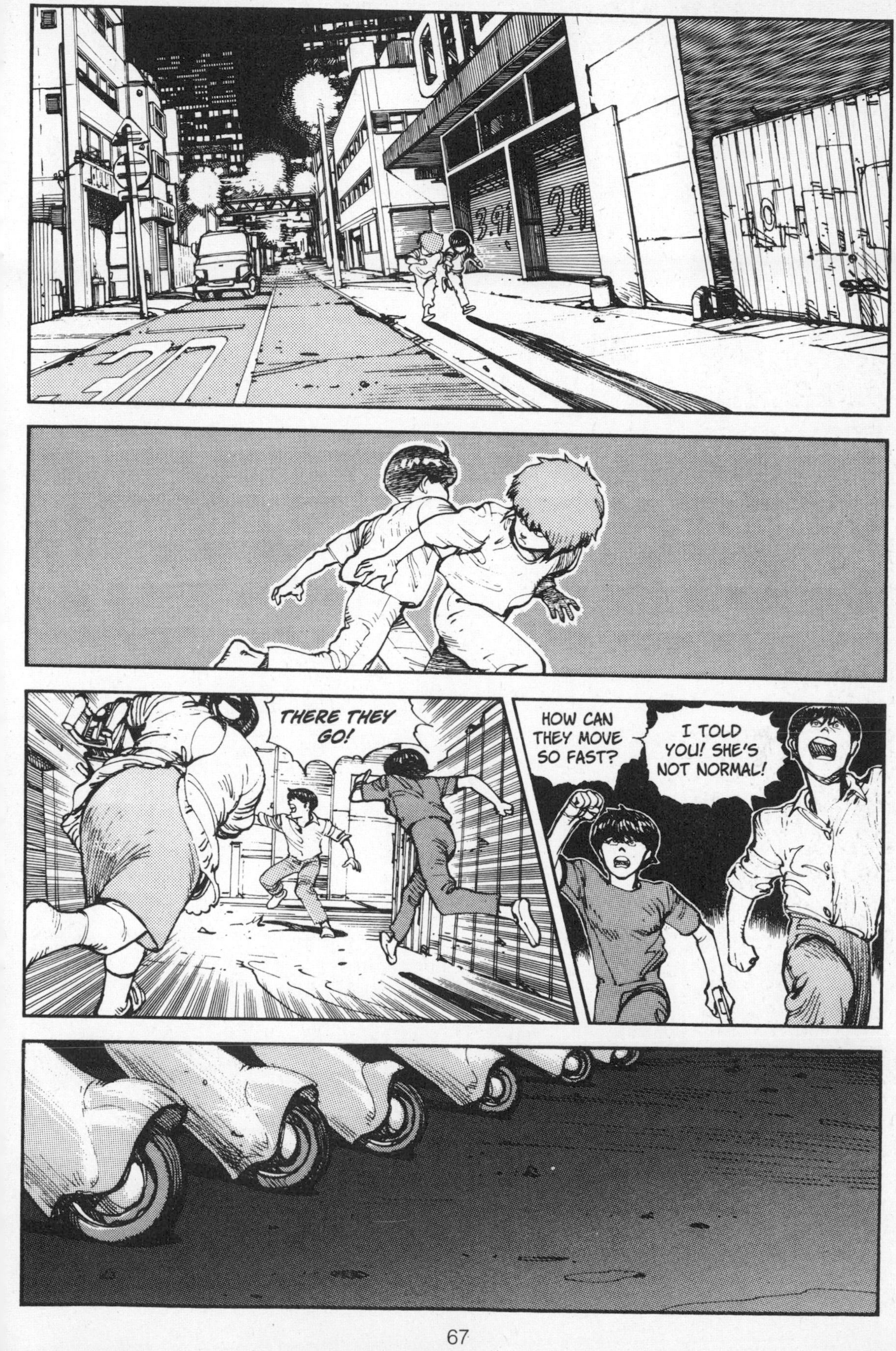
THERE THEY GO!
HOW CAN THEY MOVE SO FAST?
I TOLD YOU! SHE'S NOT NORMAL!

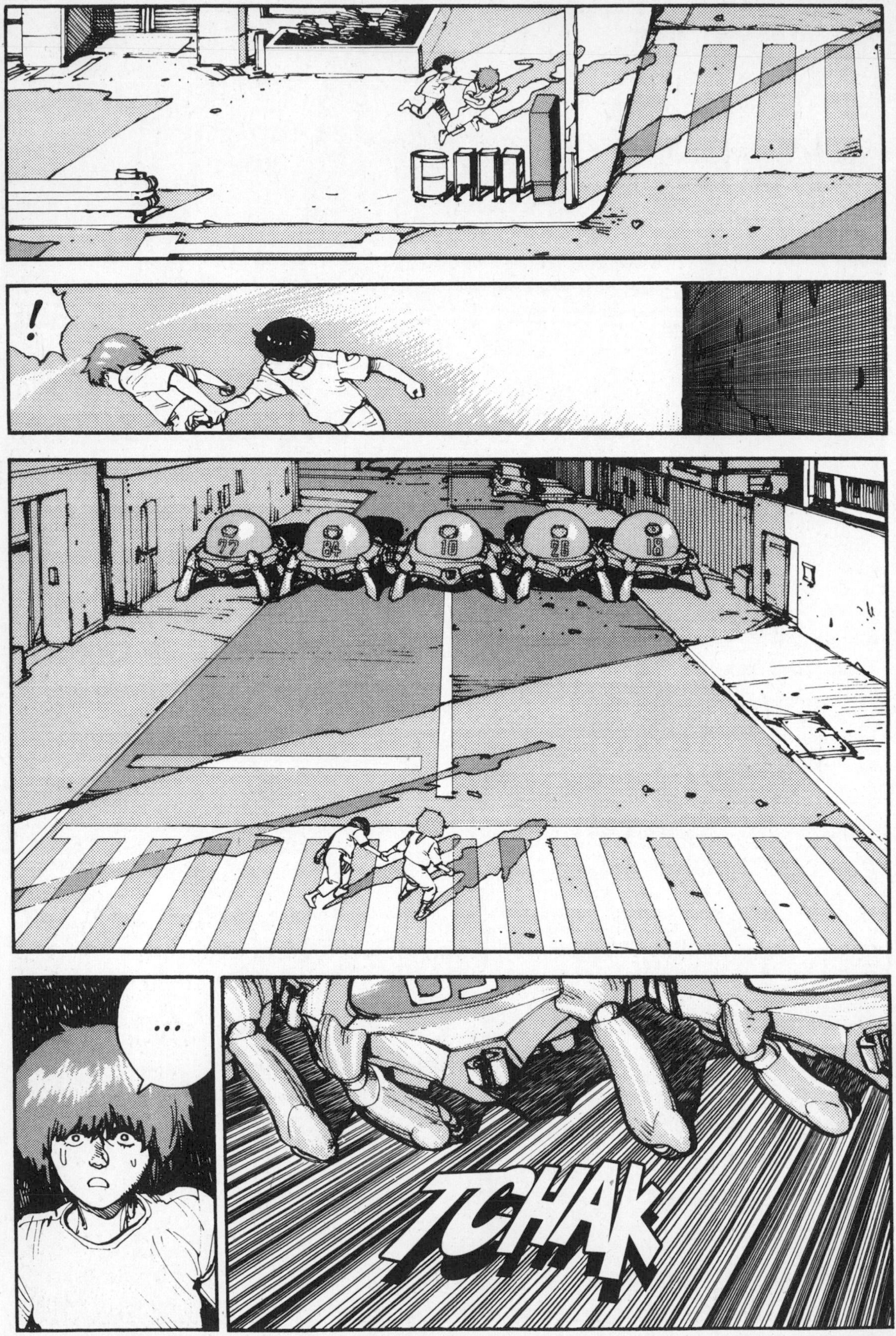
!
...
TCHAK

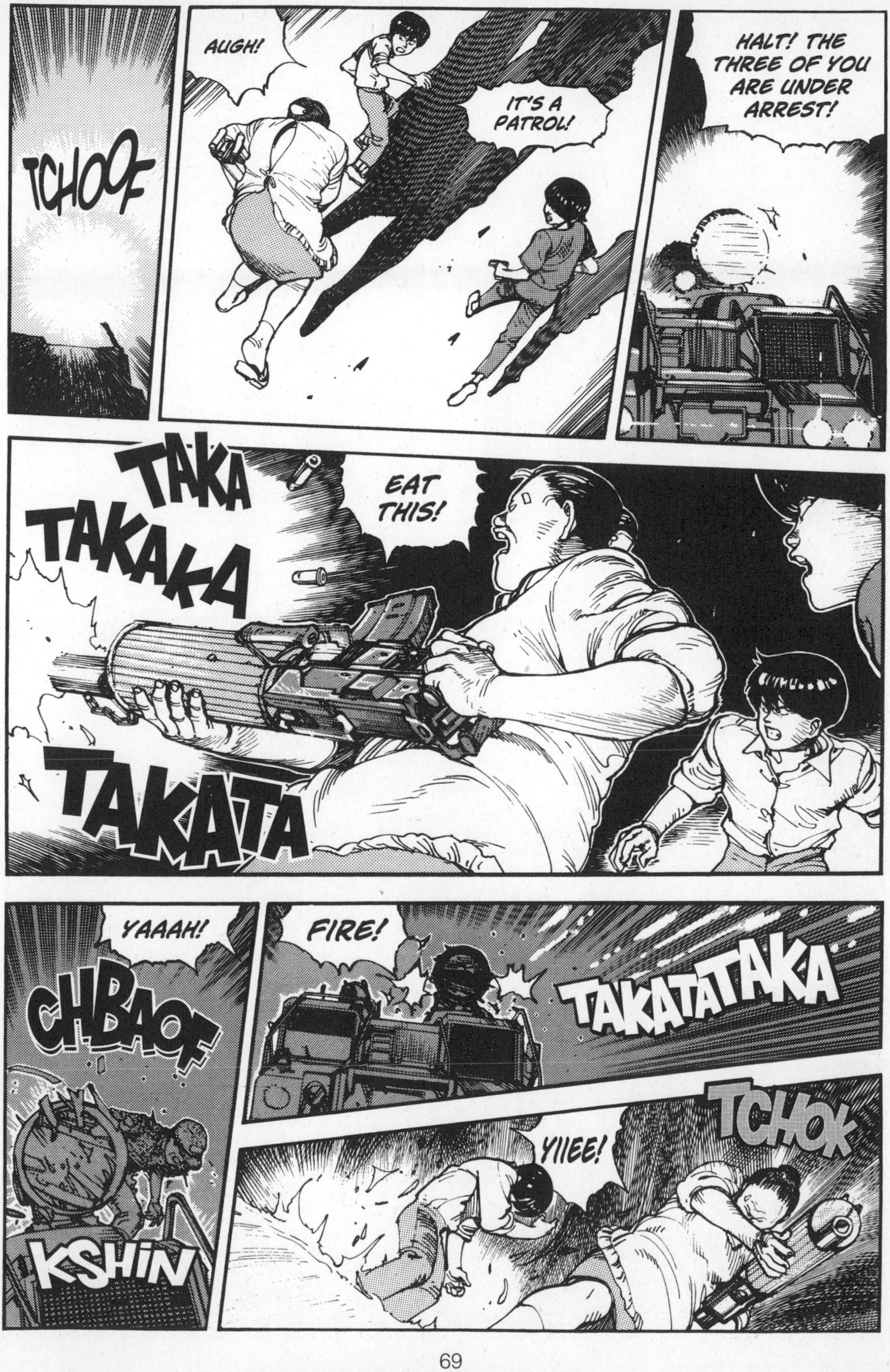
TCHOOF
AUGH!
IT'S A PATROL!
HALT! THE THREE OF YOU ARE UNDER ARREST!
TAKA TAKAKA
EAT THIS!
TAKATA
YAAAH!
CHBAOF
KSHIN
FIRE!
TAKATATAKA
TCHOK
YIIEE!

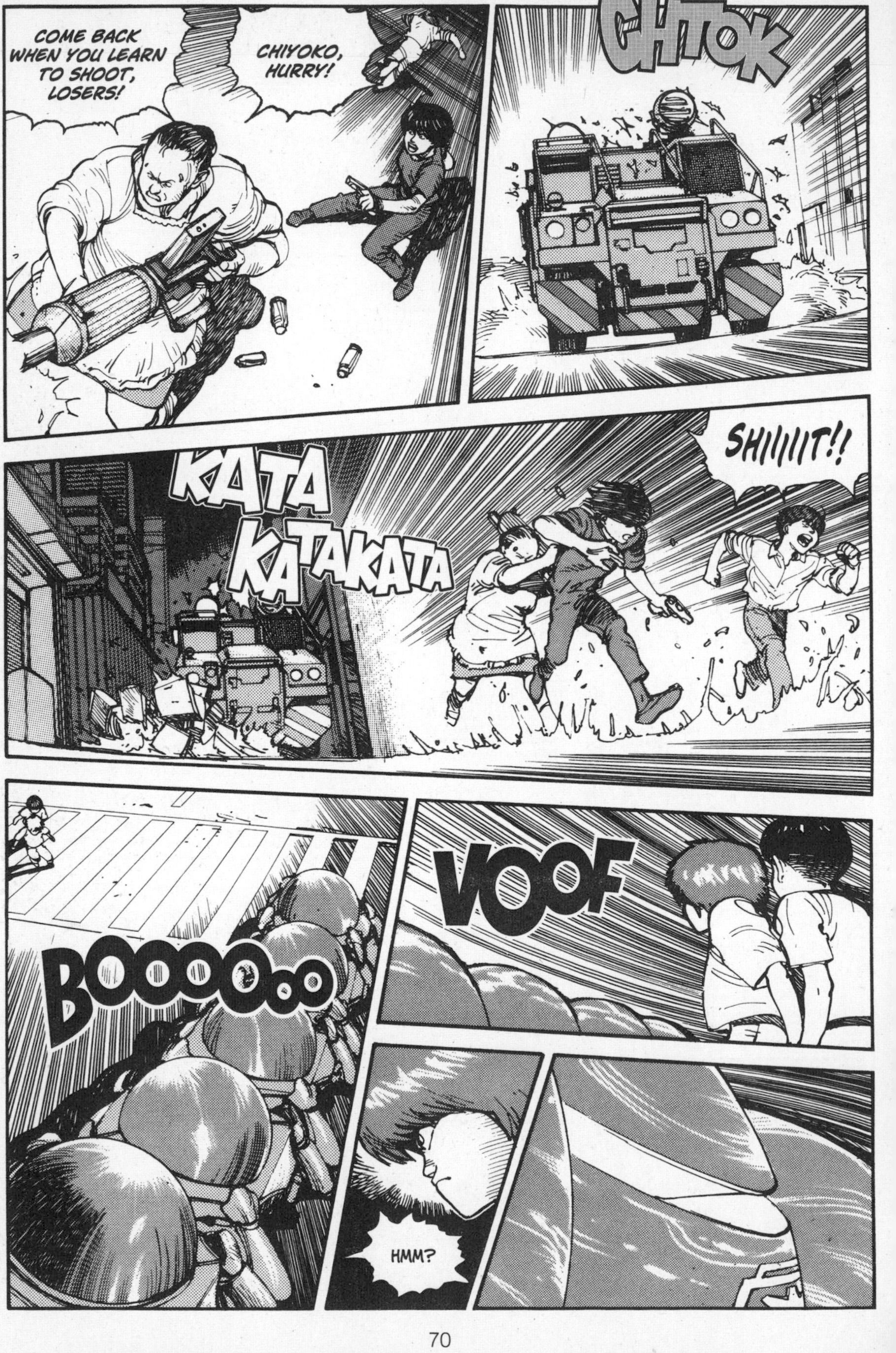

COME BACK WHEN YOU LEARN TO SHOOT, LOSERS!
CHIYOKO, HURRY!
CHTOK
KATA KATAKATA
SHI||||IT!!
BOOOOO..O
VOOF
HMM?

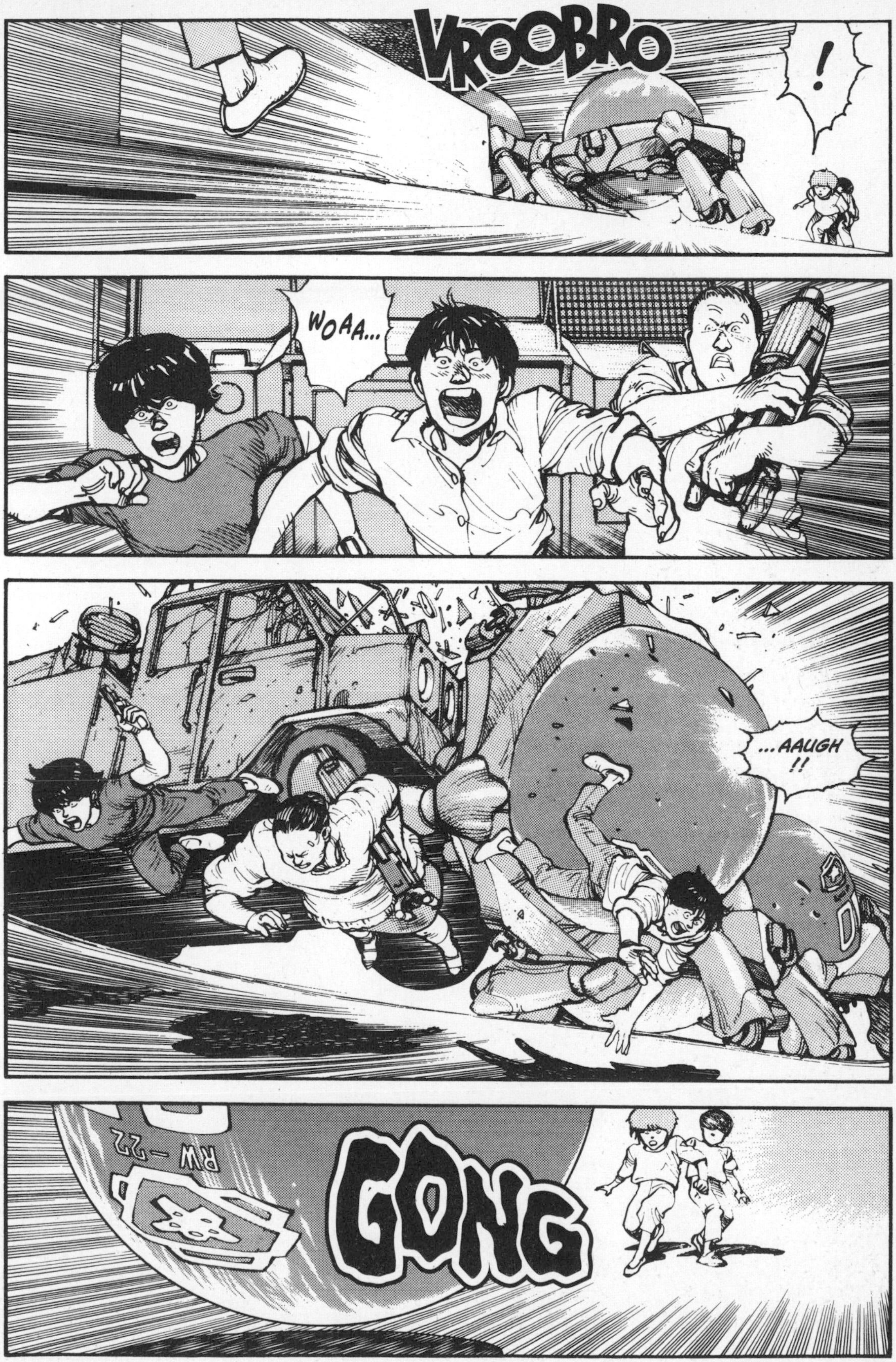
VROOBRO
!
WOAA...
...AAUGH !!
RW-22
GONG

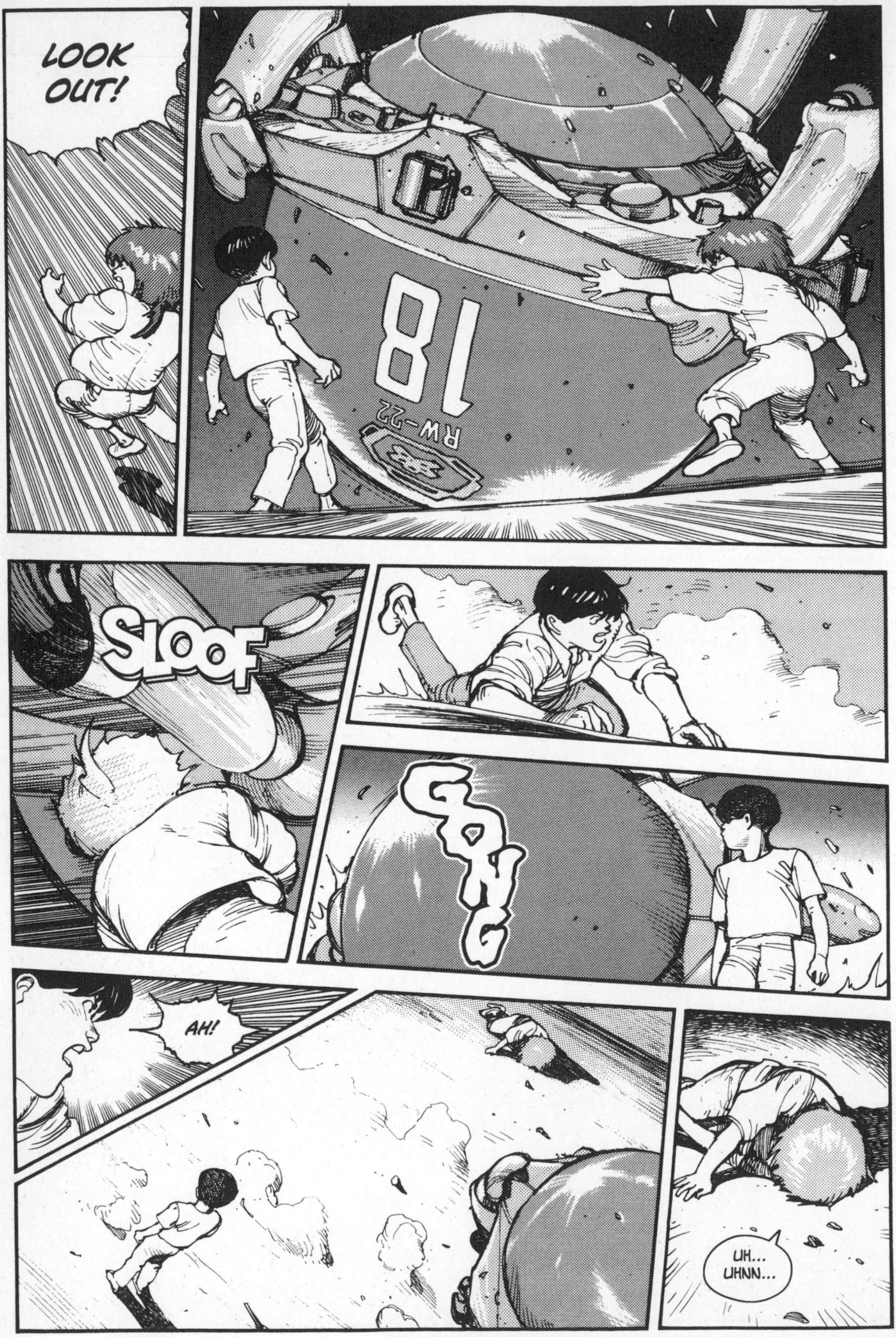
LOOK OUT!
18
RW-22
SLOOF
GONG
AH!
UH... UHNN...

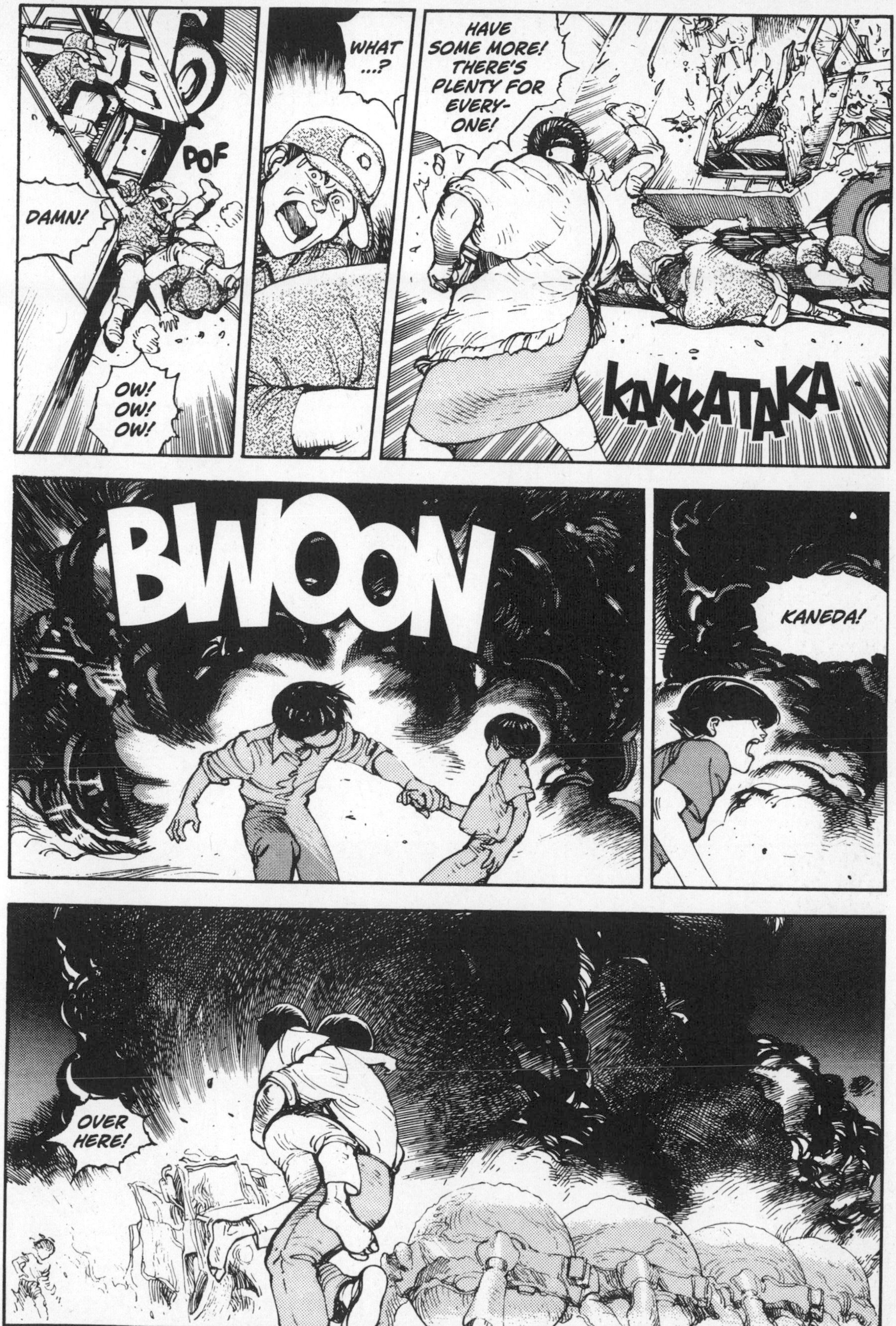
POF
DAMN!
OW! OW! OW!
WHAT ...?
HAVE SOME MORE! THERE'S PLENTY FOR EVERY-ONE!
KAKKATAKA
BWOON
KANEDA!
OVER HERE!

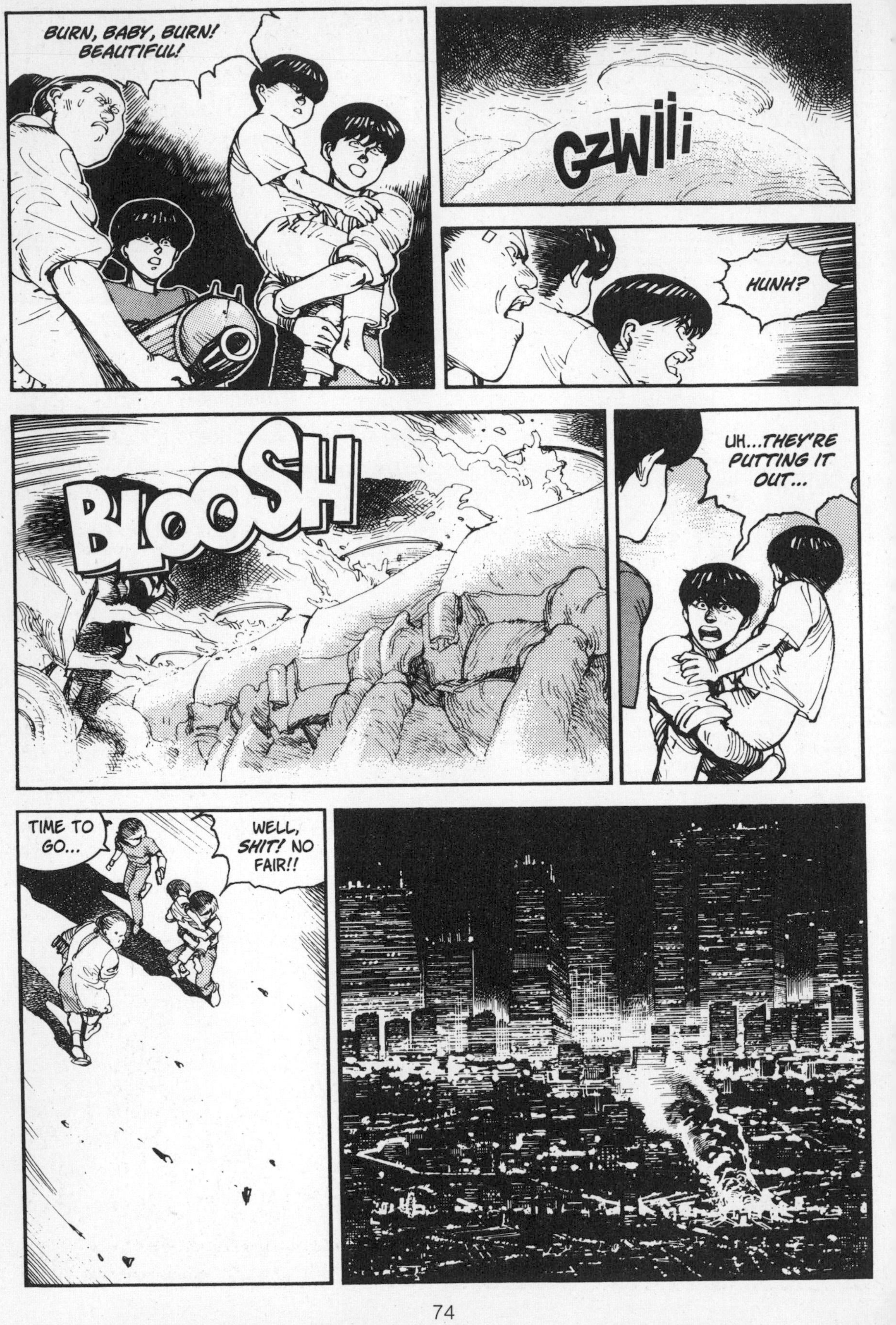
BURN, BABY, BURN! BEAUTIFUL!
GZWIII
HUNH?
BLOOSH
UH...THEY'RE PUTTING IT OUT...
TIME TO GO...
WELL, SHIT! NO FAIR!!

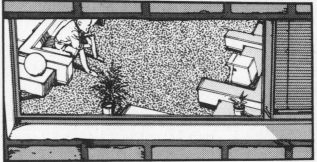

HIIYAAAA!

RAAK

SHiiiiiiz

75

THIS WAS THE LAST IMAGE WE GOT FROM #95 BEFORE IT WAS DESTROYED.

COLONEL...

I WANT TO SEE PART OF IT AGAIN. TAKE IT BACK TO FIVE MINUTES BEFORE THE END.

Y-YESSIR. RIGHT AWAY.

TZZAKK

KSIIIF

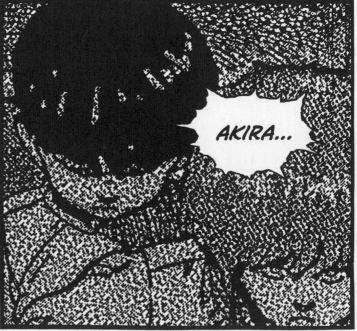

AKIRA...

BiiiP

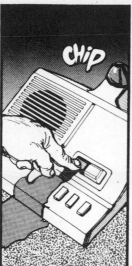

CHiP

WHAT IS IT?

MR. NEZU, THERE'S A CALL FROM A WOMAN NAMED *KEI*. SHE INSISTS ON SPEAKING WITH YOU DIRECTLY... SAYS IT'S URGENT.

PUT HER THROUGH.

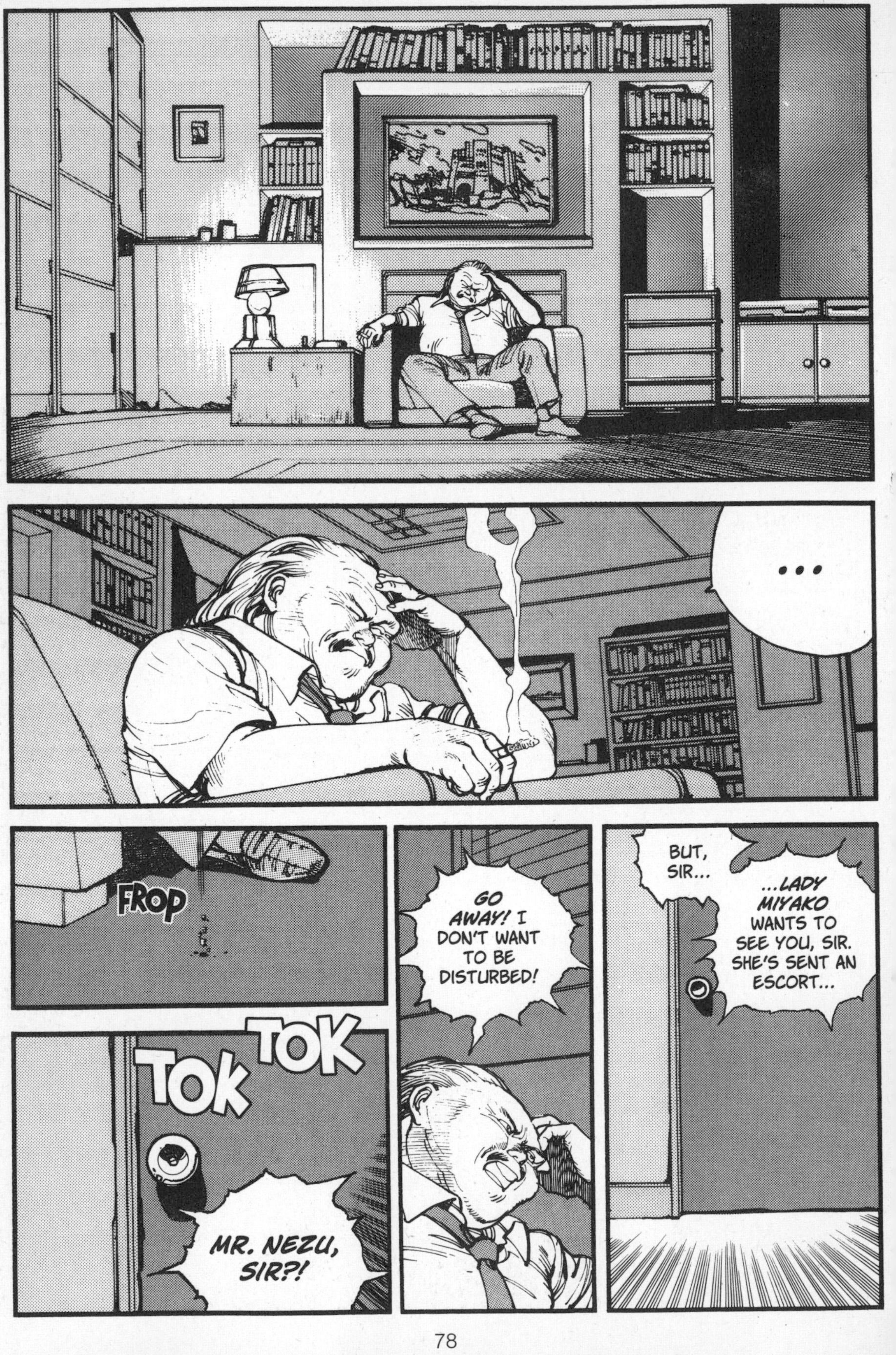
...
FROP
TOK TOK
MR. NEZU, SIR?!
GO AWAY! I DON'T WANT TO BE DISTURBED!
BUT, SIR...
...LADY MIYAKO WANTS TO SEE YOU, SIR. SHE'S SENT AN ESCORT...

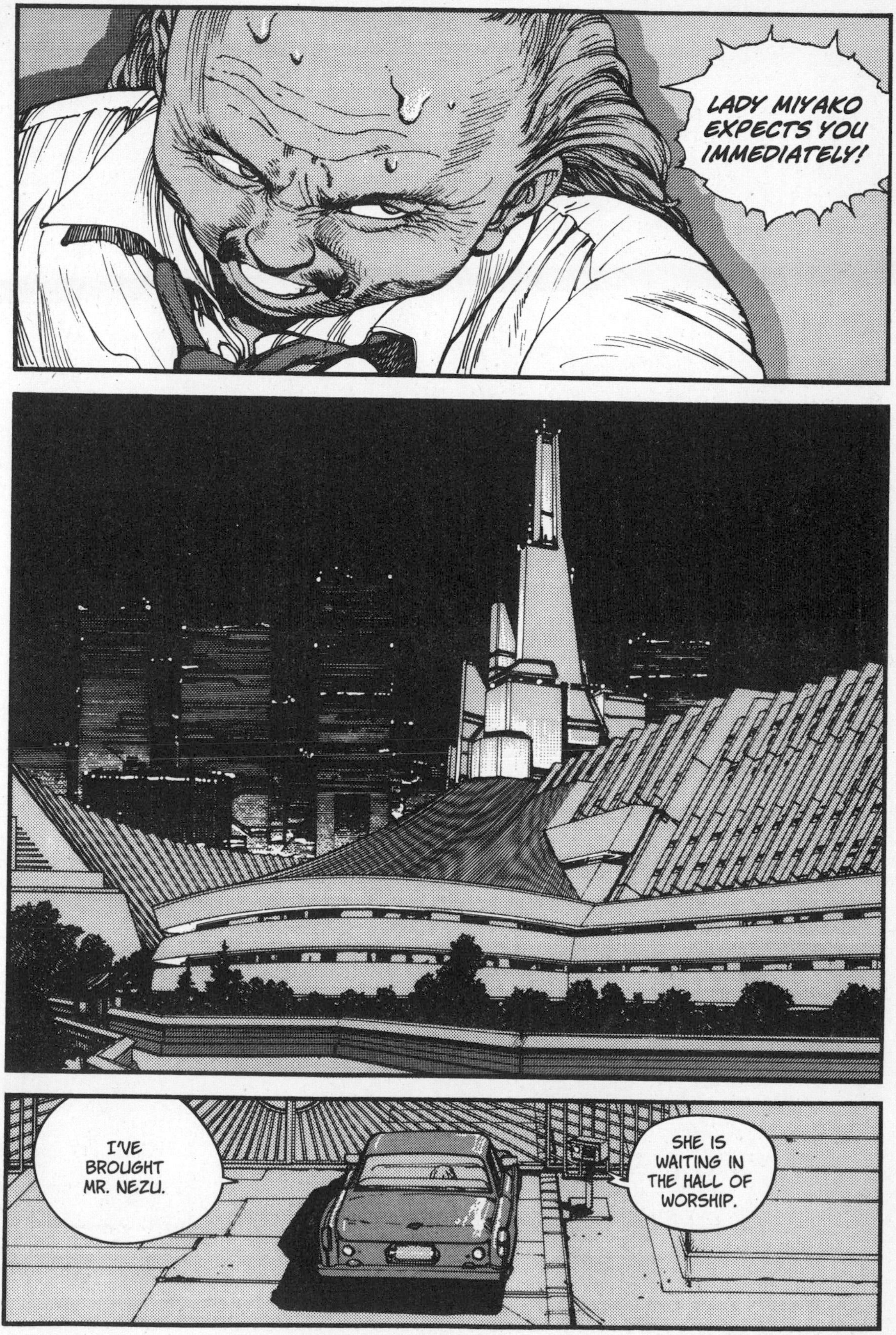
LADY MIYAKO EXPECTS YOU IMMEDIATELY!
I'VE BROUGHT MR. NEZU.
SHE IS WAITING IN THE HALL OF WORSHIP.

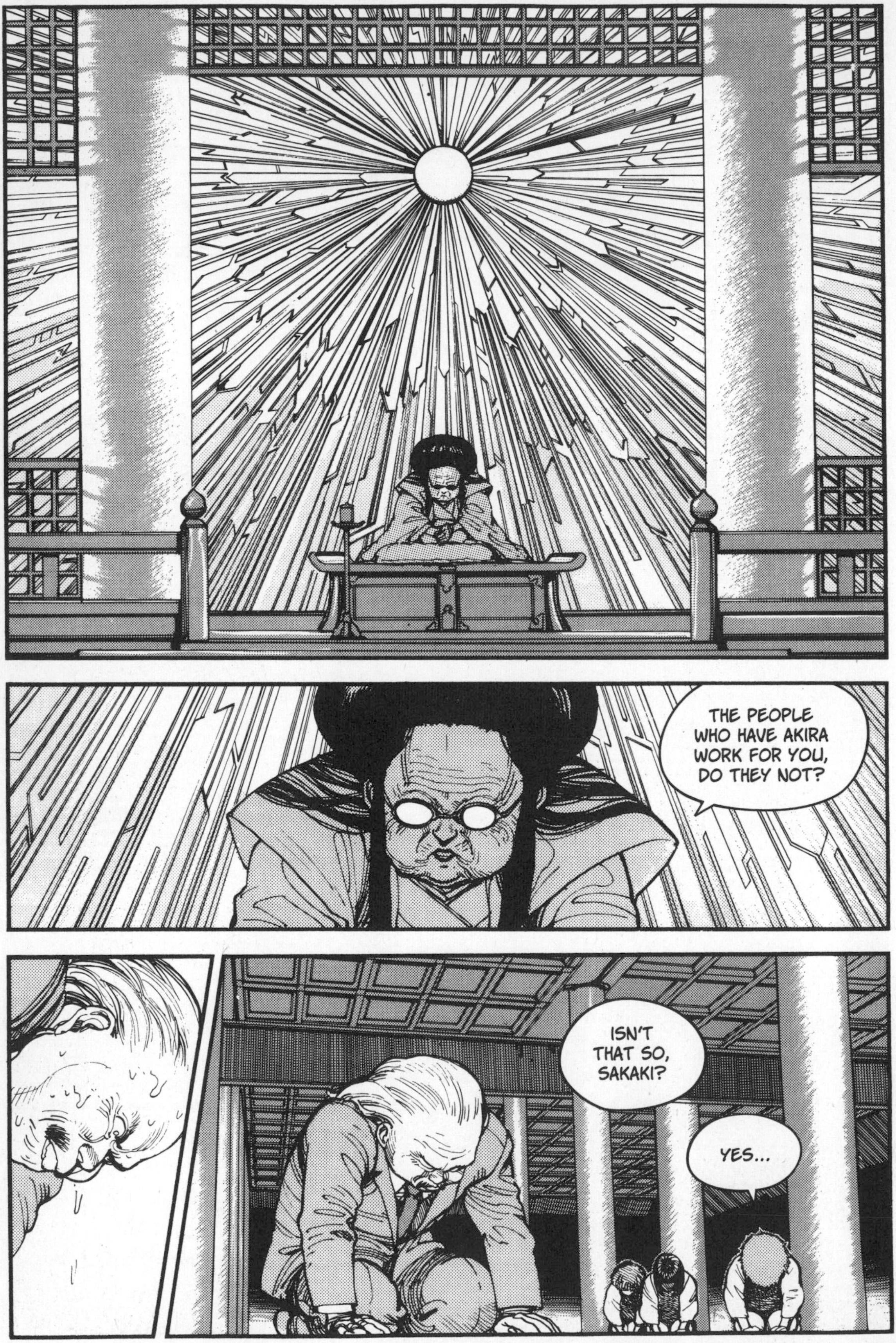
THE PEOPLE WHO HAVE AKIRA WORK FOR YOU, DO THEY NOT?
ISN'T THAT SO, SAKAKI?
YES...

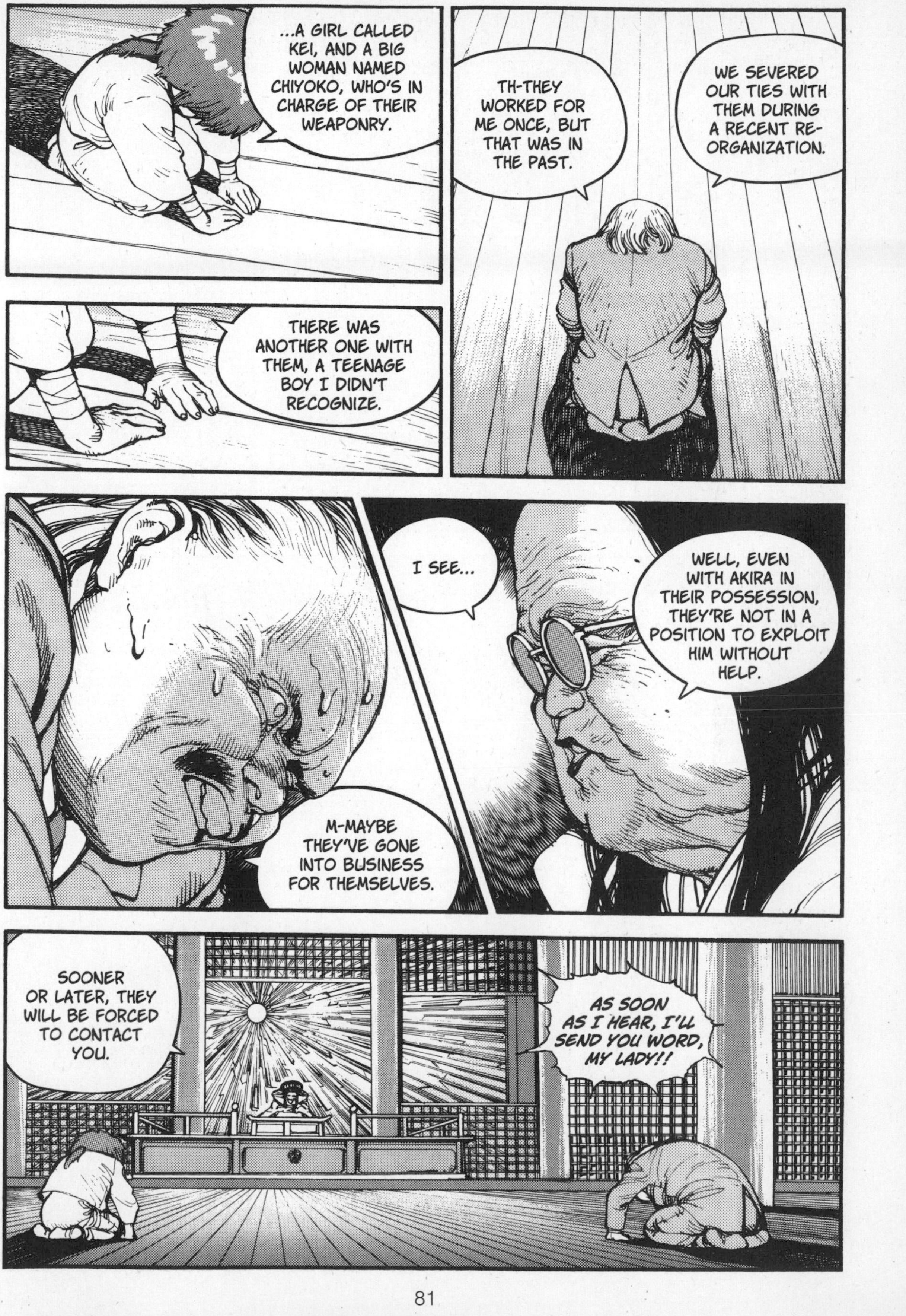

...A GIRL CALLED KEI, AND A BIG WOMAN NAMED CHIYOKO, WHO'S IN CHARGE OF THEIR WEAPONRY.
THERE WAS ANOTHER ONE WITH THEM, A TEENAGE BOY I DIDN'T RECOGNIZE.
TH-THEY WORKED FOR ME ONCE, BUT THAT WAS IN THE PAST.
WE SEVERED OUR TIES WITH THEM DURING A RECENT RE-ORGANIZATION.
M-MAYBE THEY'VE GONE INTO BUSINESS FOR THEMSELVES.
I SEE...
WELL, EVEN WITH AKIRA IN THEIR POSSESSION, THEY'RE NOT IN A POSITION TO EXPLOIT HIM WITHOUT HELP.
SOONER OR LATER, THEY WILL BE FORCED TO CONTACT YOU.
AS SOON AS I HEAR, I'LL SEND YOU WORD, MY LADY!!

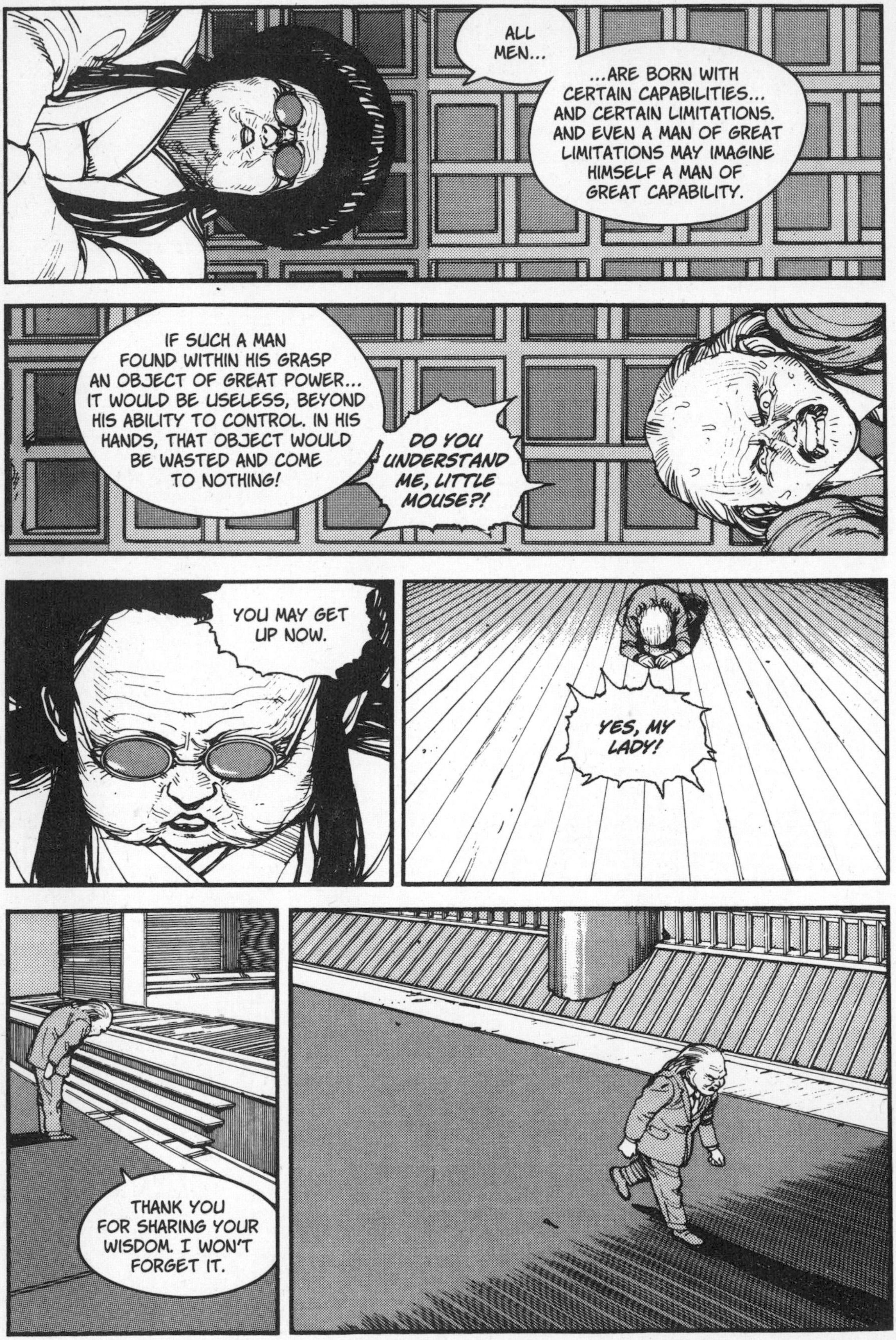

ALL MEN...
...ARE BORN WITH CERTAIN CAPABILITIES... AND CERTAIN LIMITATIONS. AND EVEN A MAN OF GREAT LIMITATIONS MAY IMAGINE HIMSELF A MAN OF GREAT CAPABILITY.
IF SUCH A MAN FOUND WITHIN HIS GRASP AN OBJECT OF GREAT POWER... IT WOULD BE USELESS, BEYOND HIS ABILITY TO CONTROL. IN HIS HANDS, THAT OBJECT WOULD BE WASTED AND COME TO NOTHING!
DO YOU UNDERSTAND ME, LITTLE MOUSE?!
YOU MAY GET UP NOW.
YES, MY LADY!
THANK YOU FOR SHARING YOUR WISDOM. I WON'T FORGET IT.

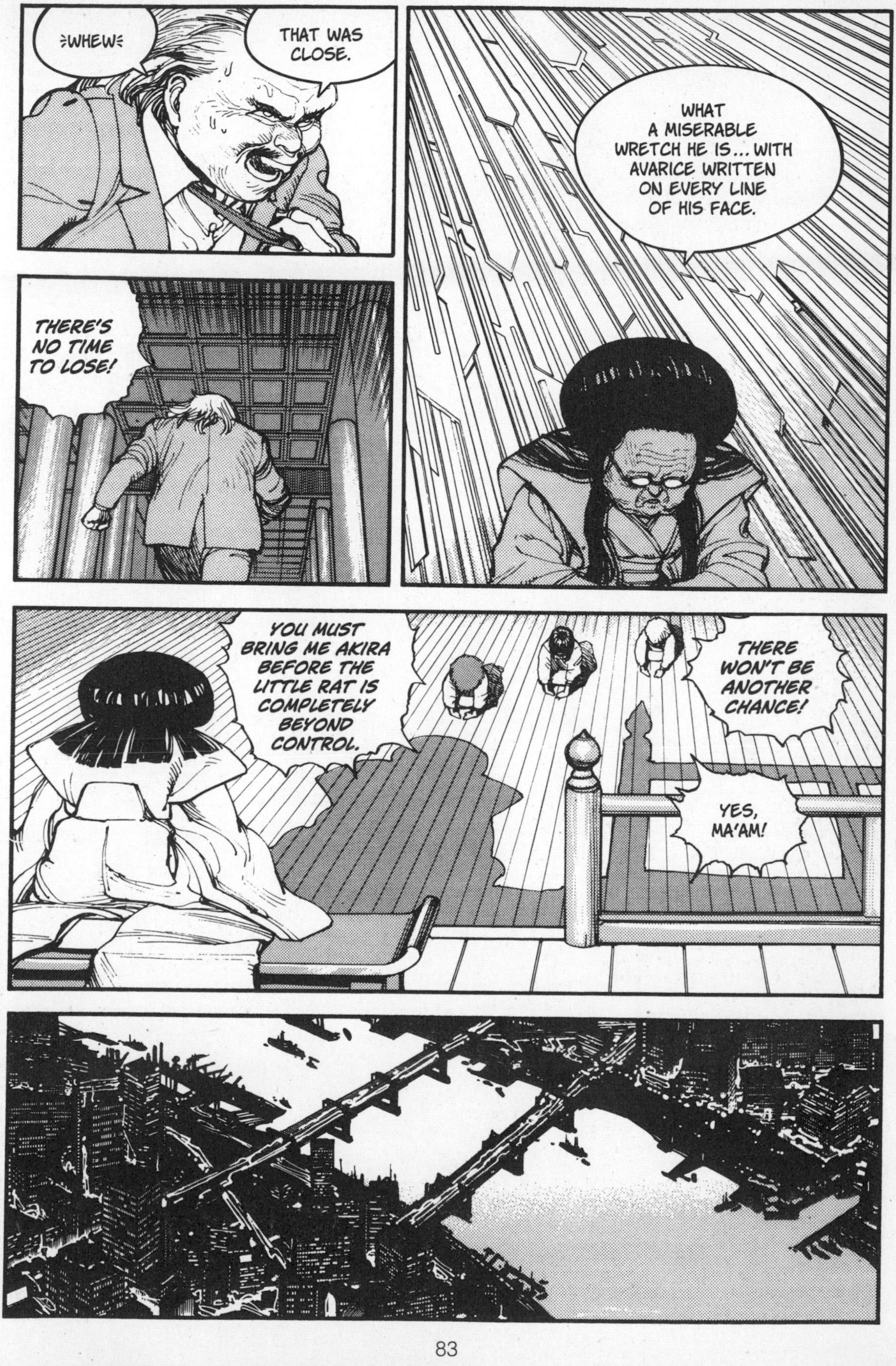

WHEW
THAT WAS CLOSE.
THERE'S NO TIME TO LOSE!
WHAT A MISERABLE WRETCH HE IS... WITH AVARICE WRITTEN ON EVERY LINE OF HIS FACE.
YOU MUST BRING ME AKIRA BEFORE THE LITTLE RAT IS COMPLETELY BEYOND CONTROL.
THERE WON'T BE ANOTHER CHANCE!
YES, MA'AM!

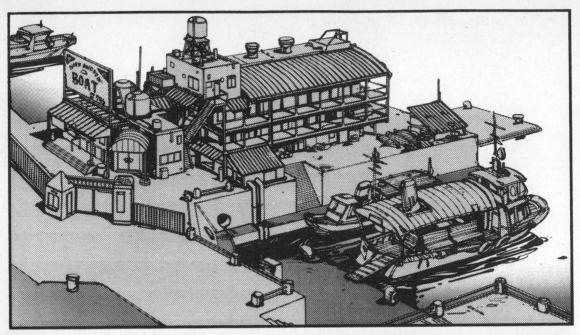

WE MUST HAVE COME TO THE WRONG PLACE.

WHEN HE SAID HIS VACATION HOME, I WAS EXPECTING SOMETHING A LITTLE MORE THAN A CHEAP CONDO ON THE CANAL.

YEAH, WELL, I GUESS YOU COULD CALL THIS DUMP A "VACATION HOME"... TECHNICALLY.

HEY!

TSHIF

SHIT!

DON'T SHOOT!

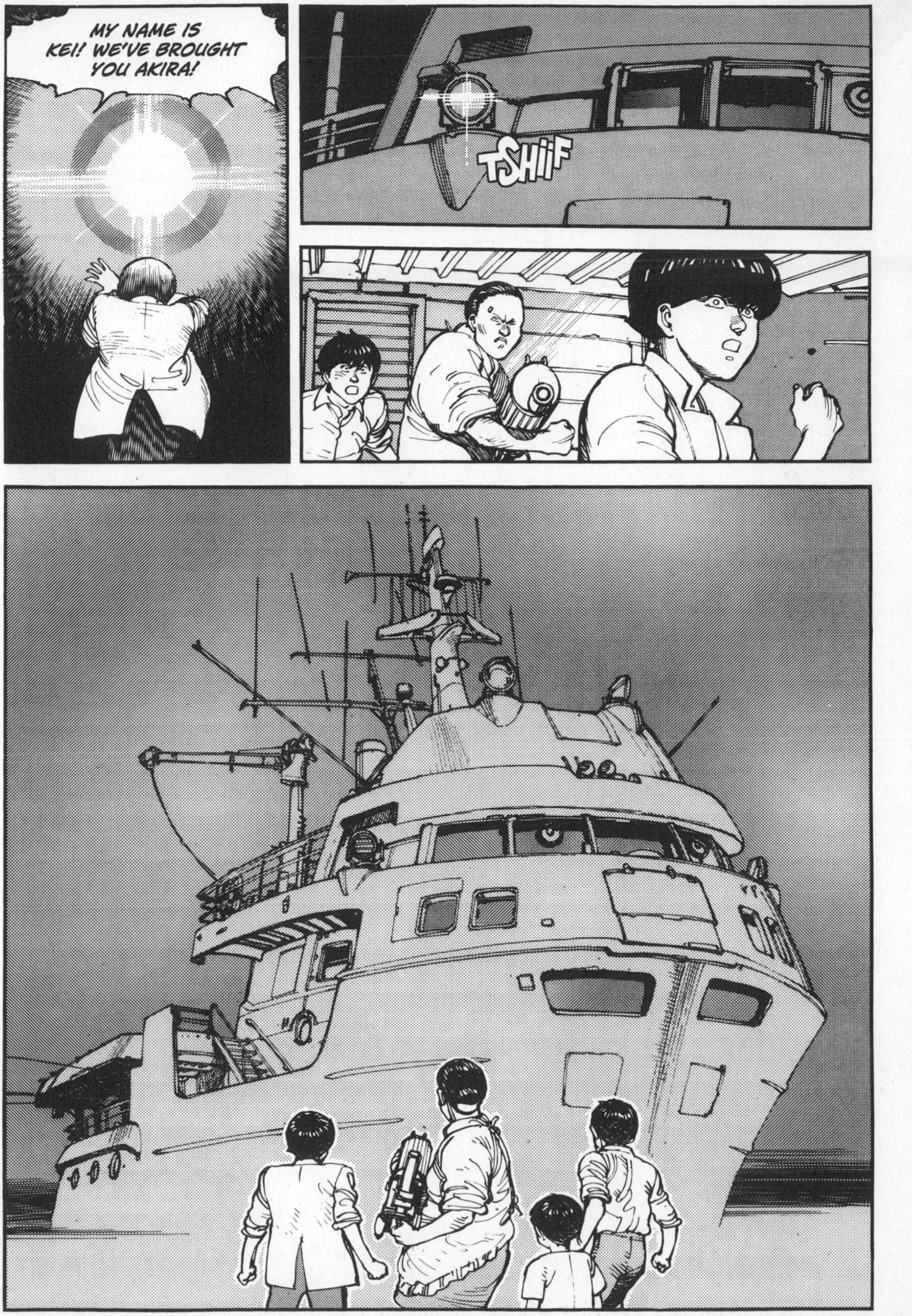
MY NAME IS KEI! WE'VE BROUGHT YOU AKIRA!
TSHIiF

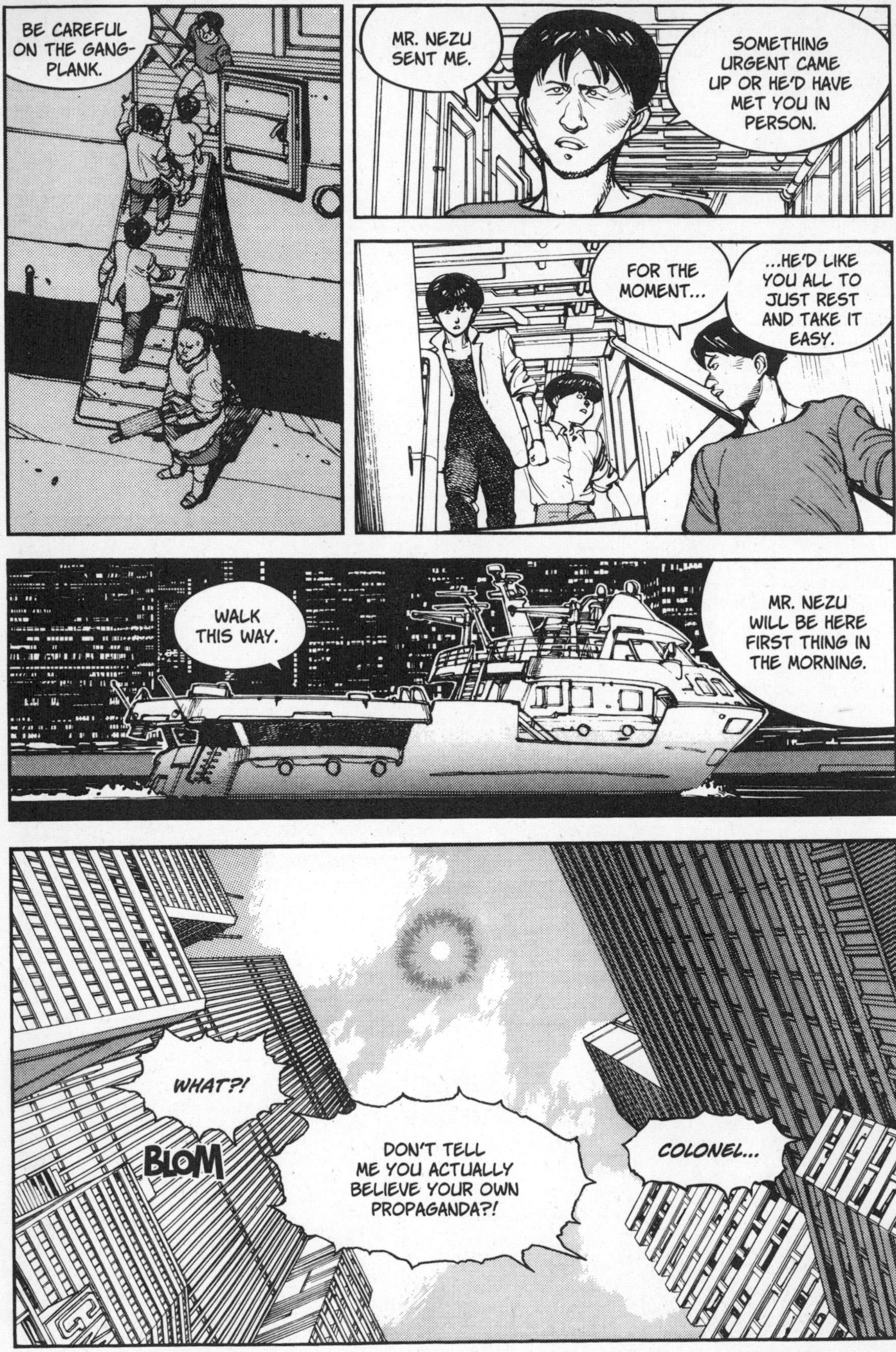

BE CAREFUL ON THE GANG-PLANK.
MR. NEZU SENT ME.
SOMETHING URGENT CAME UP OR HE'D HAVE MET YOU IN PERSON.
FOR THE MOMENT...
...HE'D LIKE YOU ALL TO JUST REST AND TAKE IT EASY.
WALK THIS WAY.
MR. NEZU WILL BE HERE FIRST THING IN THE MORNING.
WHAT?!
BLOM
DON'T TELL ME YOU ACTUALLY BELIEVE YOUR OWN PROPAGANDA?!
COLONEL...

AKIRA HAS BEEN KIDNAPPED! YOU'VE ALL SEEN THE VIDEO!

BY *CHILDREN!* ARE WE EXPECTED TO BELIEVE THAT THOSE TWO KIDS ARE PART OF SOME GROUP THAT POSES A THREAT TO NATIONAL SECURITY?!

I KNOW WHAT I'M TALKING ABOUT! I KNOW AKIRA, AND I KNOW THE PEOPLE WHO HAVE HIM!

IF WE DON'T ACT QUICKLY, IT WILL BE TOO LATE! GIVE ME BACK MY COMMAND!

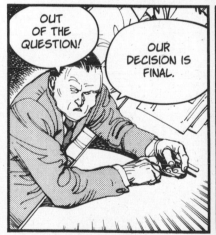

OUT OF THE QUESTION!

OUR DECISION IS FINAL.

AKIRA IS OFFICIALLY DEAD, KILLED BY *SOL.*

ALL THAT REMAINS IS FOR US TO LAY THE BLAME FOR THIS FIASCO. YOU'VE BEEN CHOSEN TO TAKE THE FALL, COLONEL, AND THAT ELIMINATES ANY CHANCE OF YOUR REGAINING COMMAND.

AKIRA IS ALIVE, AND SOMEWHERE IN NEO-TOKYO! DON'T YOU REALIZE WHAT THAT MEANS?! WE'RE ON THE BRINK OF CATASTROPHE!

YOU MUST REINSTATE THE CODE SEVEN EMERGENCY ALERT! FIND AKIRA WHILE THERE'S STILL TIME!

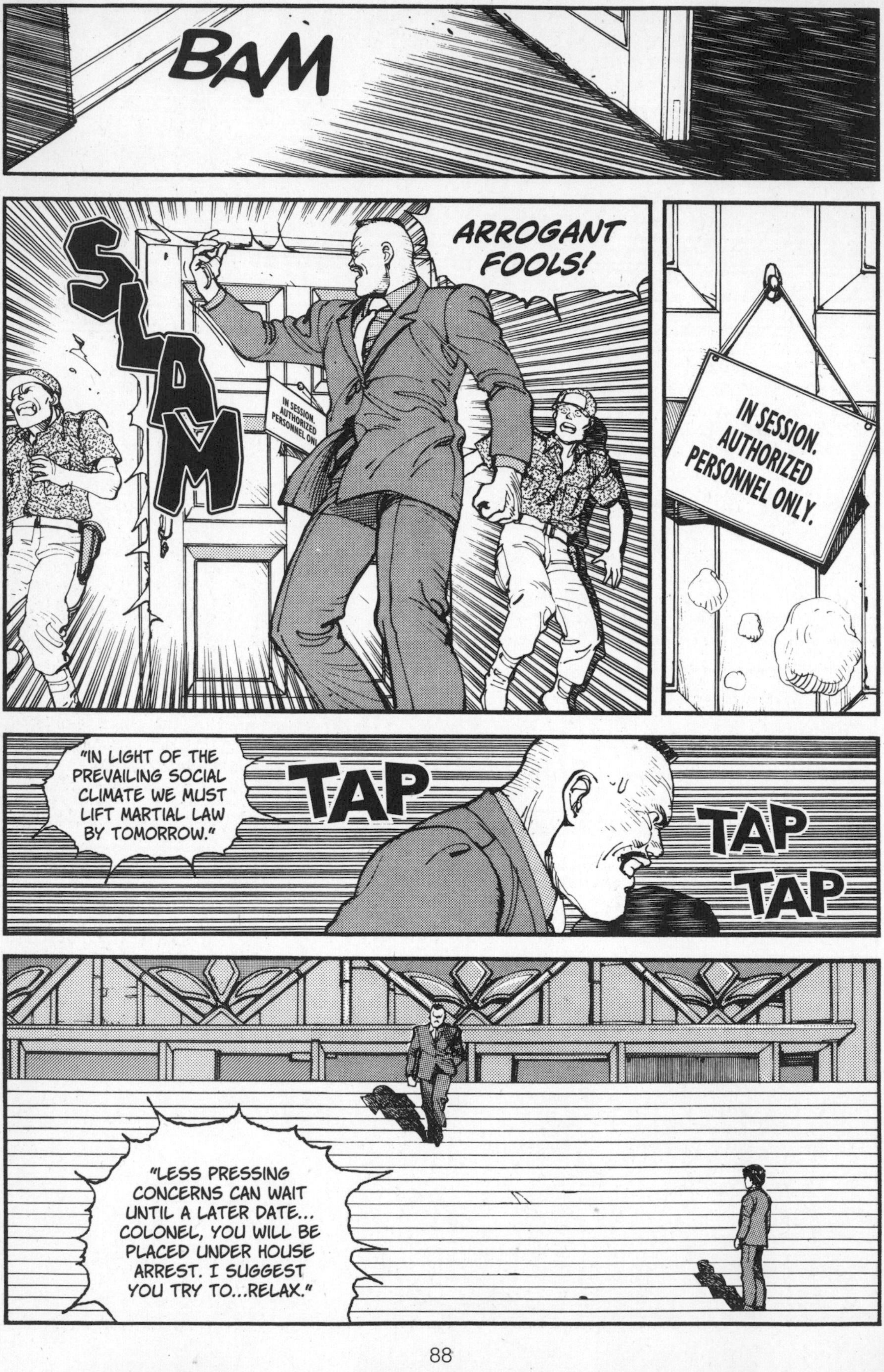
BAM
SLAM
ARROGANT FOOLS!
IN SESSION. AUTHORIZED PERSONNEL ONLY.
"IN LIGHT OF THE PREVAILING SOCIAL CLIMATE WE MUST LIFT MARTIAL LAW BY TOMORROW."
TAP
TAP TAP
"LESS PRESSING CONCERNS CAN WAIT UNTIL A LATER DATE... COLONEL, YOU WILL BE PLACED UNDER HOUSE ARREST. I SUGGEST YOU TRY TO...RELAX."

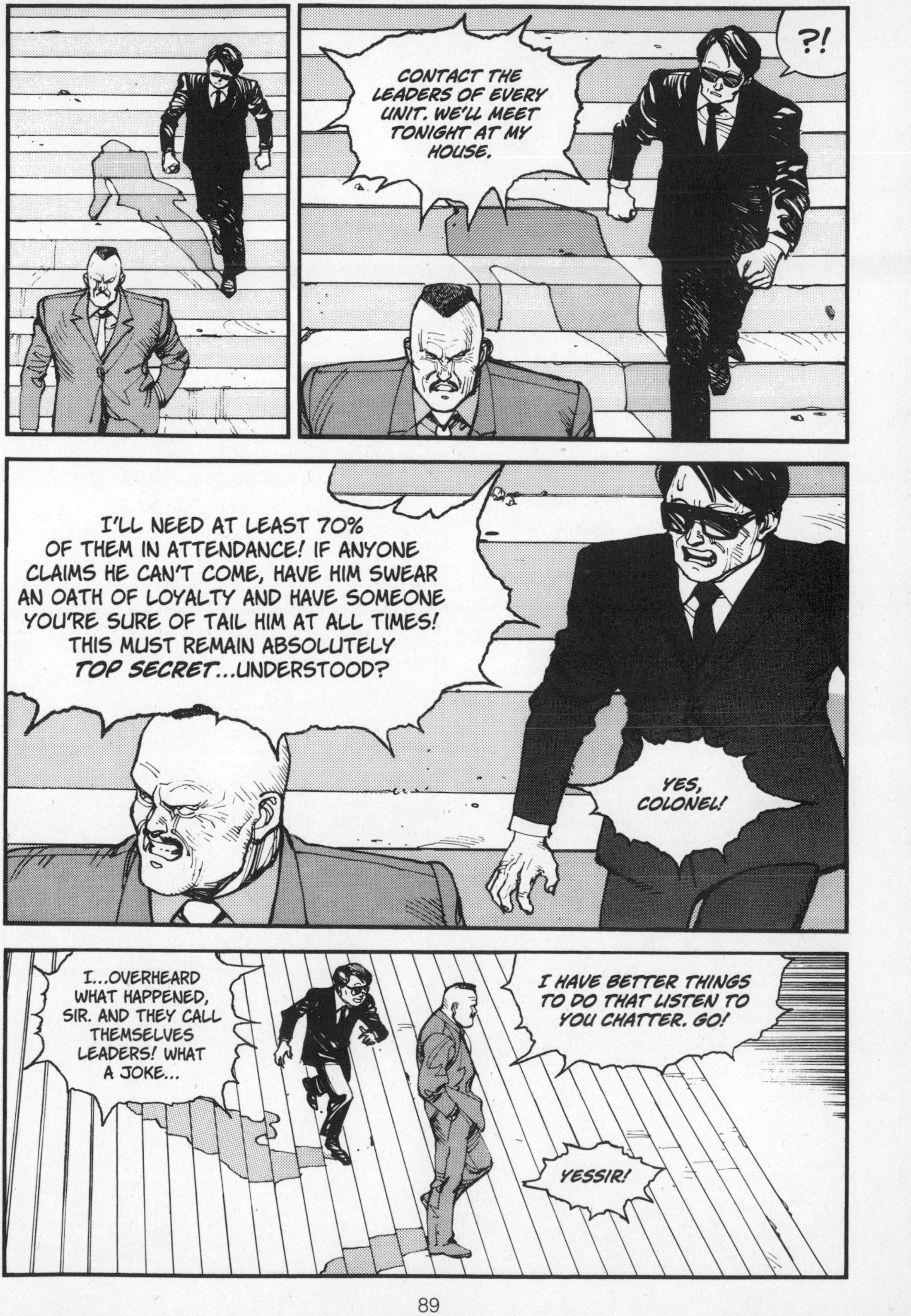
CONTACT THE LEADERS OF EVERY UNIT. WE'LL MEET TONIGHT AT MY HOUSE.
?!
I'LL NEED AT LEAST 70% OF THEM IN ATTENDANCE! IF ANYONE CLAIMS HE CAN'T COME, HAVE HIM SWEAR AN OATH OF LOYALTY AND HAVE SOMEONE YOU'RE SURE OF TAIL HIM AT ALL TIMES! THIS MUST REMAIN ABSOLUTELY TOP SECRET...UNDERSTOOD?
YES, COLONEL!
I...OVERHEARD WHAT HAPPENED, SIR. AND THEY CALL THEMSELVES LEADERS! WHAT A JOKE...
I HAVE BETTER THINGS TO DO THAT LISTEN TO YOU CHATTER. GO!
YESSIR!

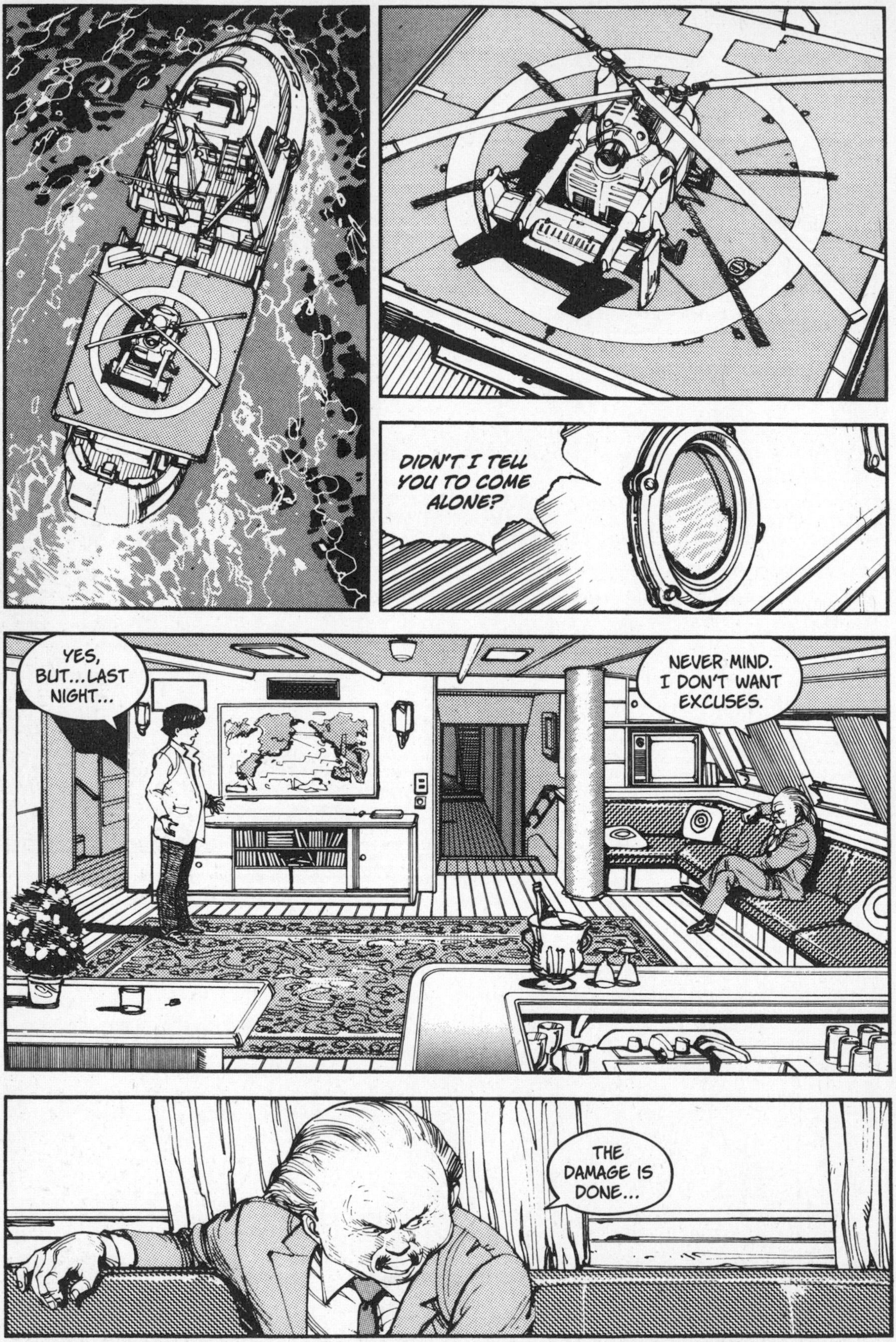
DIDN'T I TELL YOU TO COME ALONE?
YES, BUT...LAST NIGHT...
NEVER MIND. I DON'T WANT EXCUSES.
THE DAMAGE IS DONE...

...MM-HMM...

I WAS SURPRISED HE IS A CHILD, TOO, BUT HE IS AKIRA. I'M SURE.

WELL...

UNTIL WE EXAMINE HIM THOROUGHLY WE CAN'T BE CERTAIN.

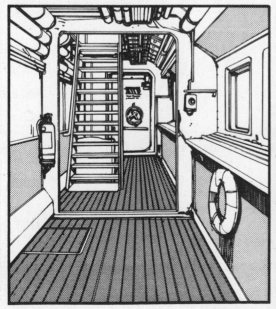

...ANYTHING TO *EAT* AROUND HERE?

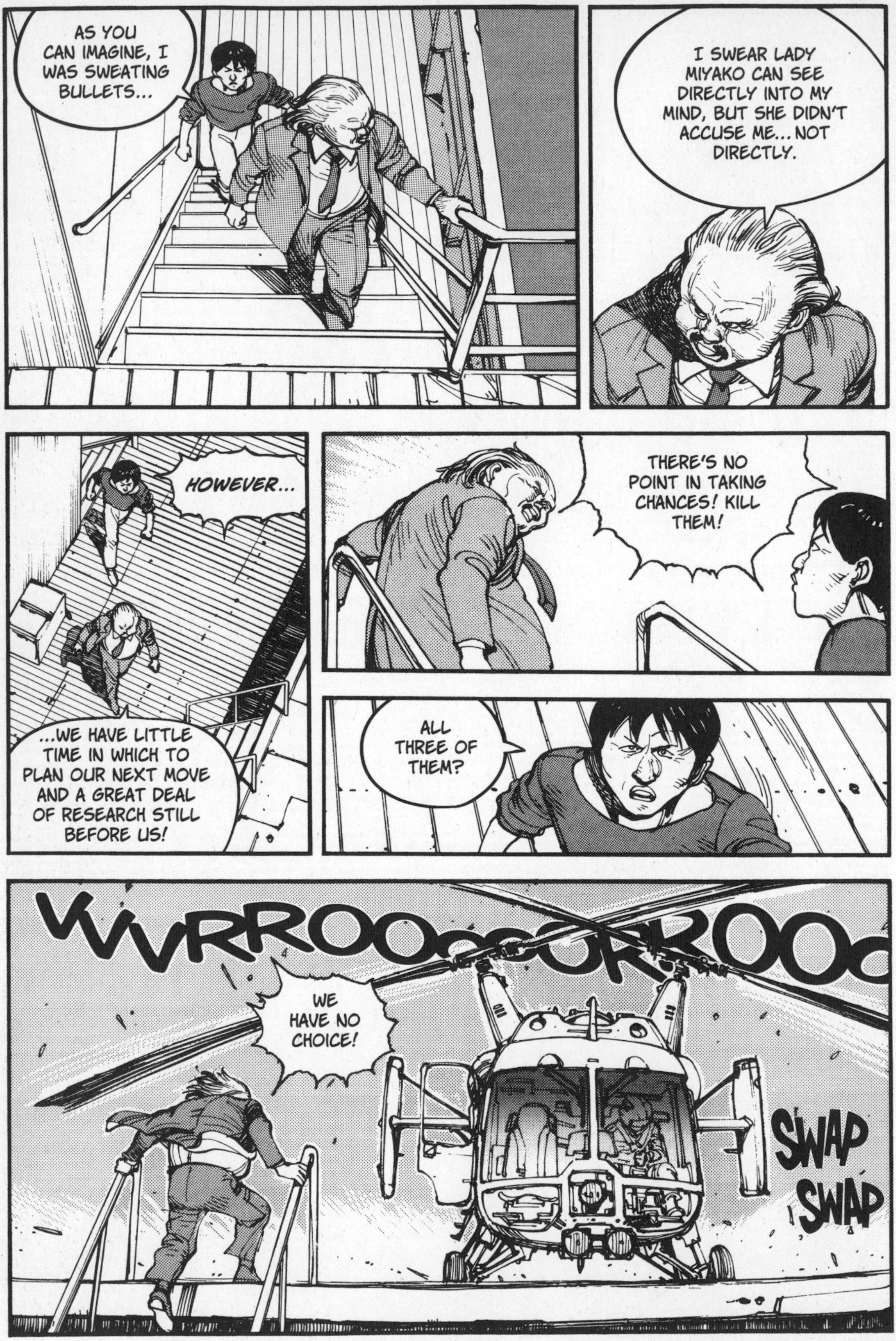
AS YOU CAN IMAGINE, I WAS SWEATING BULLETS...
I SWEAR LADY MIYAKO CAN SEE DIRECTLY INTO MY MIND, BUT SHE DIDN'T ACCUSE ME... NOT DIRECTLY.
HOWEVER...
...WE HAVE LITTLE TIME IN WHICH TO PLAN OUR NEXT MOVE AND A GREAT DEAL OF RESEARCH STILL BEFORE US!
THERE'S NO POINT IN TAKING CHANCES! KILL THEM!
ALL THREE OF THEM?
VVVRROOooOORROOo
WE HAVE NO CHOICE!
SWAP
SWAP

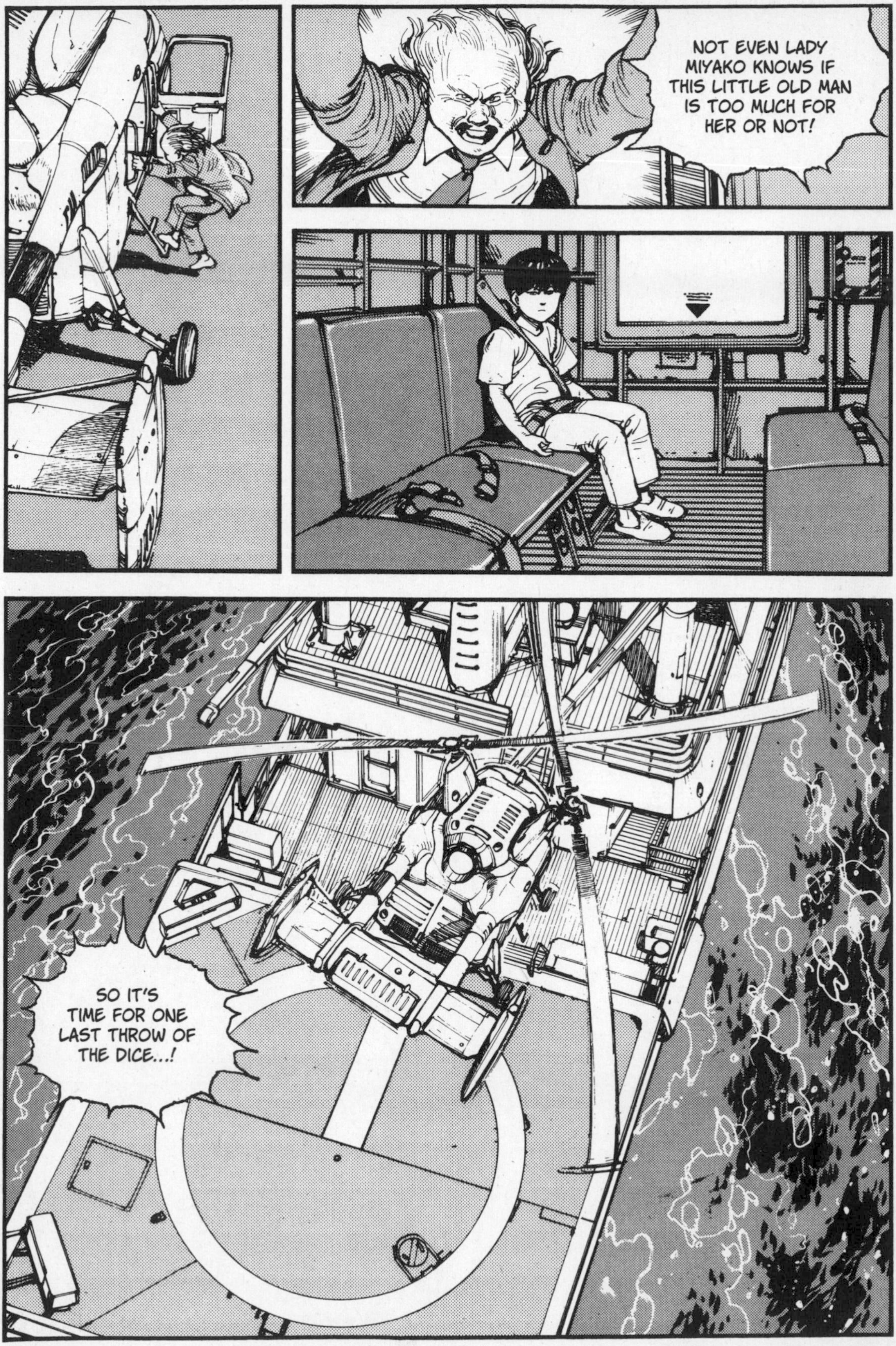

NOT EVEN LADY MIYAKO KNOWS IF THIS LITTLE OLD MAN IS TOO MUCH FOR HER OR NOT!
SO IT'S TIME FOR ONE LAST THROW OF THE DICE...!

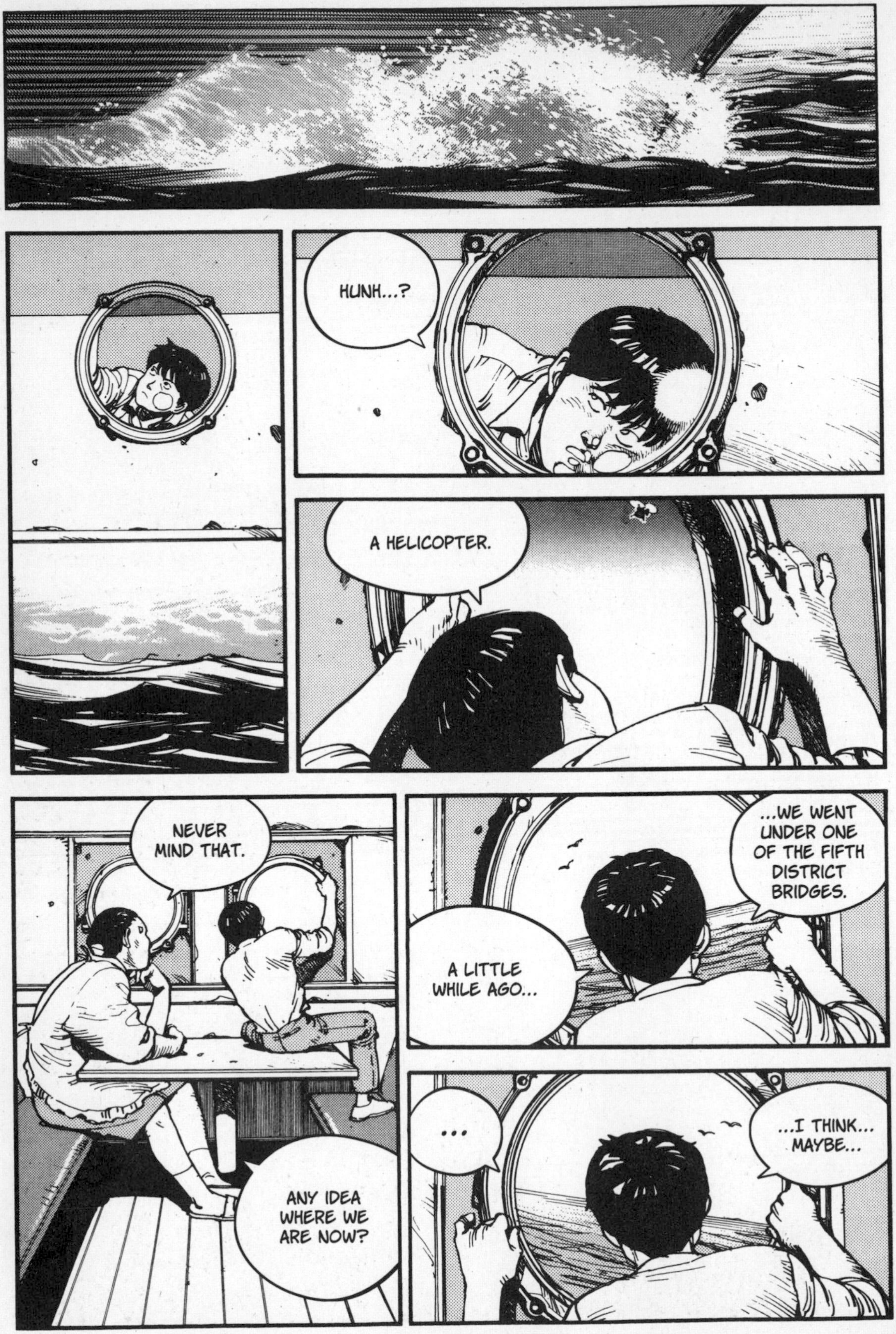
HUNH...?
A HELICOPTER.
NEVER MIND THAT.
ANY IDEA WHERE WE ARE NOW?
A LITTLE WHILE AGO...
...WE WENT UNDER ONE OF THE FIFTH DISTRICT BRIDGES.
...
...I THINK... MAYBE...

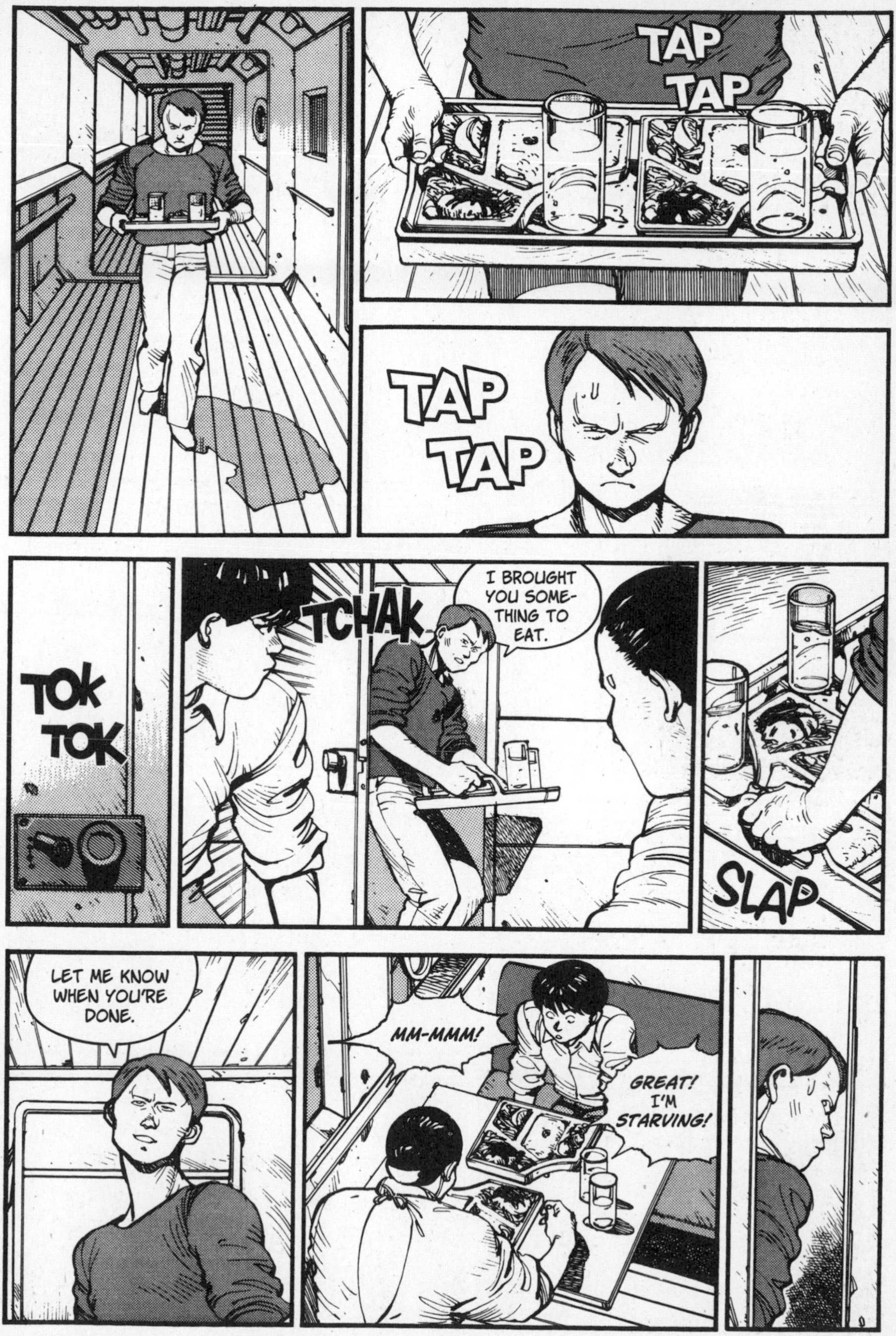
TAP
TAP
TAP
TAP
TOK
TOK
TCHAK
I BROUGHT YOU SOME-THING TO EAT.
SLAP
LET ME KNOW WHEN YOU'RE DONE.
MM-MMM!
GREAT! I'M STARVING!

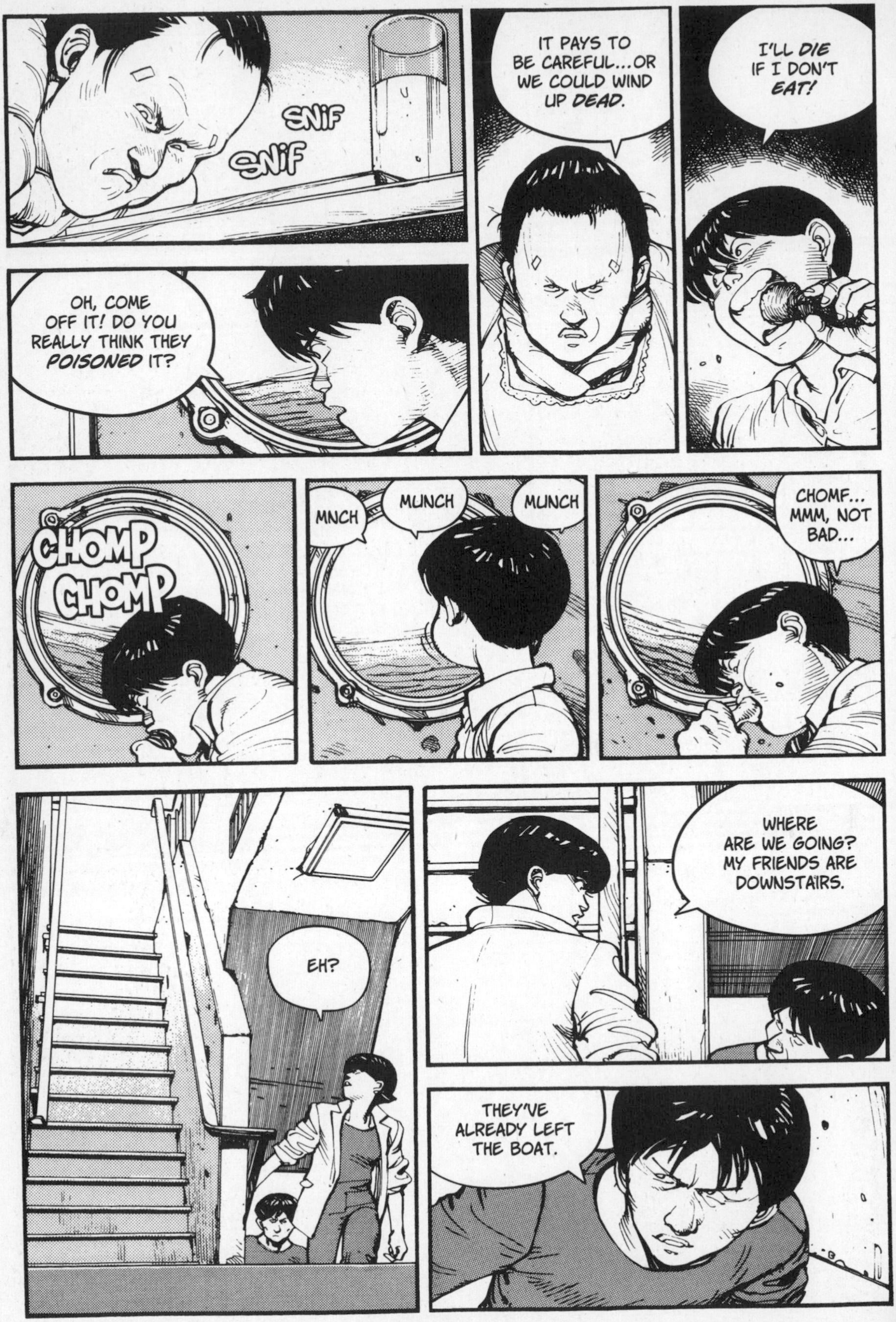
SNIF
SNIF
IT PAYS TO BE CAREFUL...OR WE COULD WIND UP DEAD.
I'LL DIE IF I DON'T EAT!
OH, COME OFF IT! DO YOU REALLY THINK THEY POISONED IT?
CHOMP
CHOMP
MNCH
MUNCH
MUNCH
CHOMF... MMM, NOT BAD...
EH?
WHERE ARE WE GOING? MY FRIENDS ARE DOWNSTAIRS.
THEY'VE ALREADY LEFT THE BOAT.

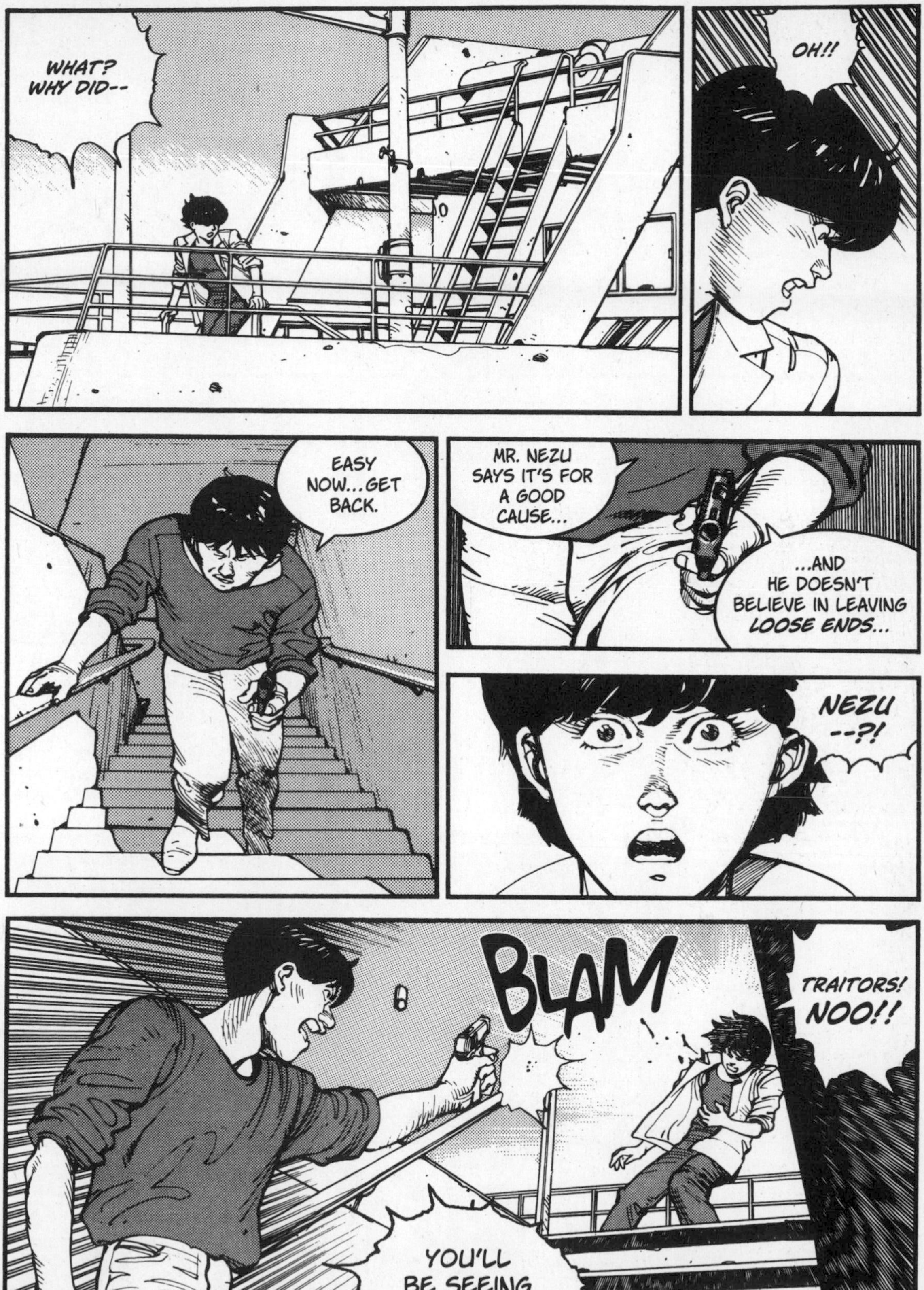
WHAT?
WHY DID--
OH!!
EASY NOW...GET BACK.
MR. NEZU SAYS IT'S FOR A GOOD CAUSE...
...AND HE DOESN'T BELIEVE IN LEAVING LOOSE ENDS...
NEZU --?!
BLAM
TRAITORS! NOO!!
YOU'LL BE SEEING YOUR FRIENDS IN HELL!

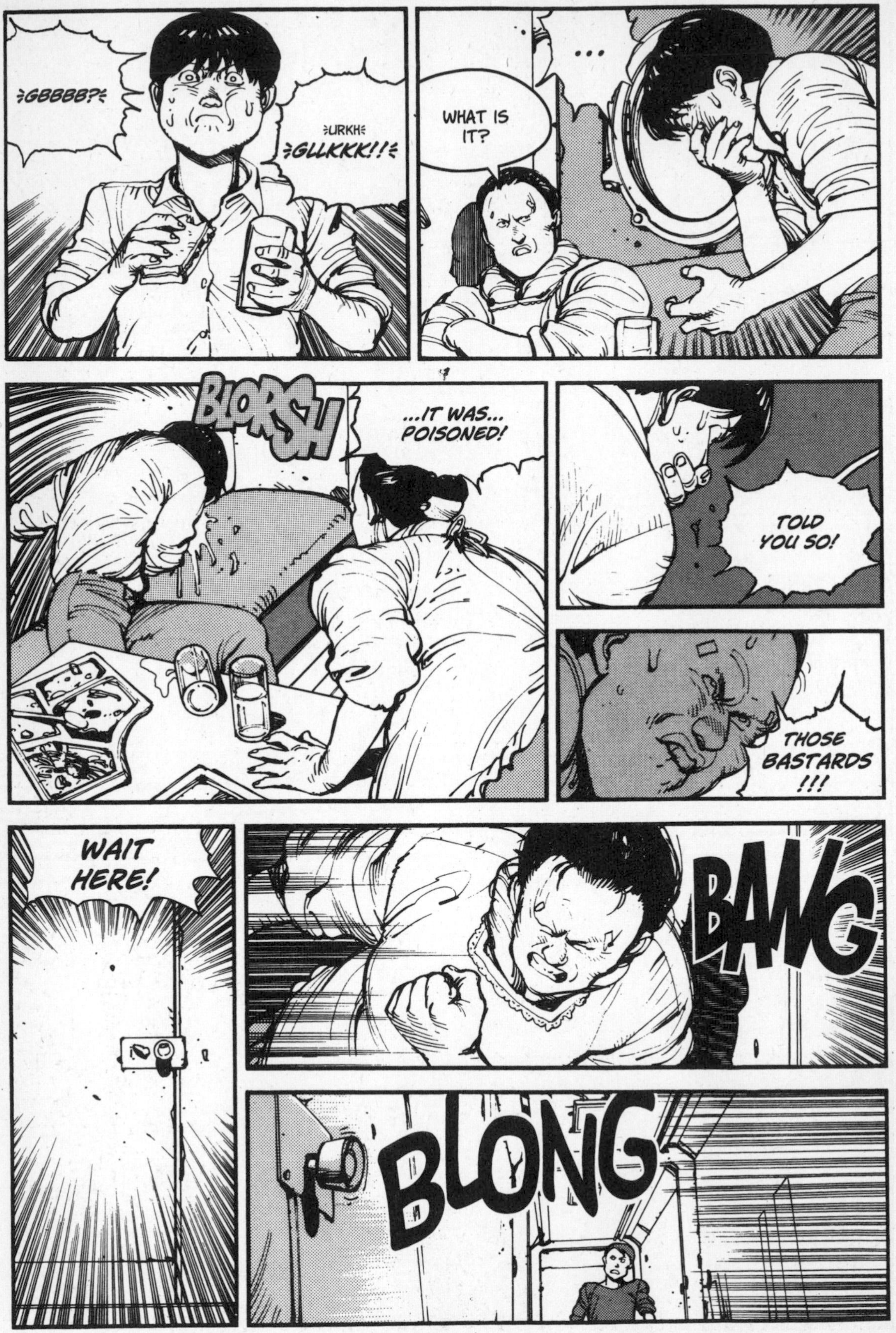

GBBBB?
URKH
GLLKKK!!
WHAT IS IT?
...
BLORSH
...IT WAS... POISONED!
TOLD YOU SO!
THOSE BASTARDS !!!
WAIT HERE!
BANG
BLONG

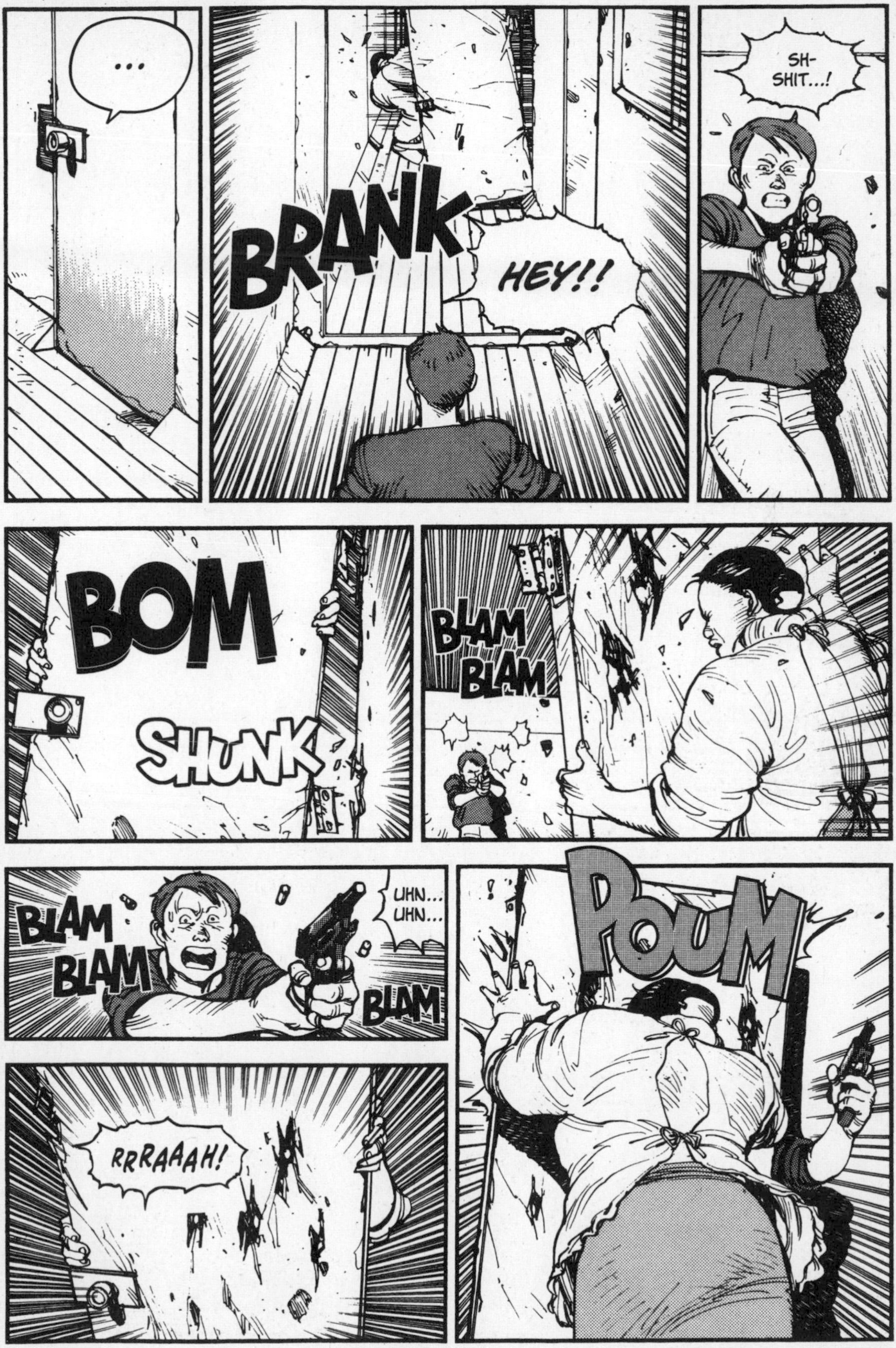
...
BRANK
HEY!!
SH-SHIT...!
BOM
SHUNK
BLAM BLAM
BLAM BLAM
UHN... UHN...
BLAM
POUM
RRRAAAH!

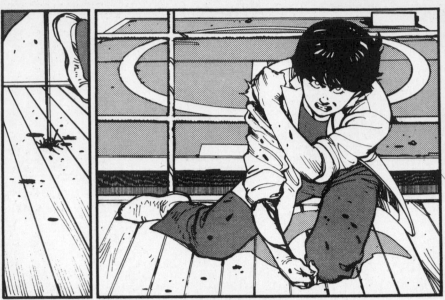

SORRY ABOUT THAT. DON'T WORRY, I WON'T MISS AGAIN.

KPOW

KRASH

KEI! CAN YOU HEAR ME? WHERE ARE YOU?

SHIT!

BLAM

CHIYOKO, RUN FOR IT!

BLAM

KIIN KZIING

≥NGH≤

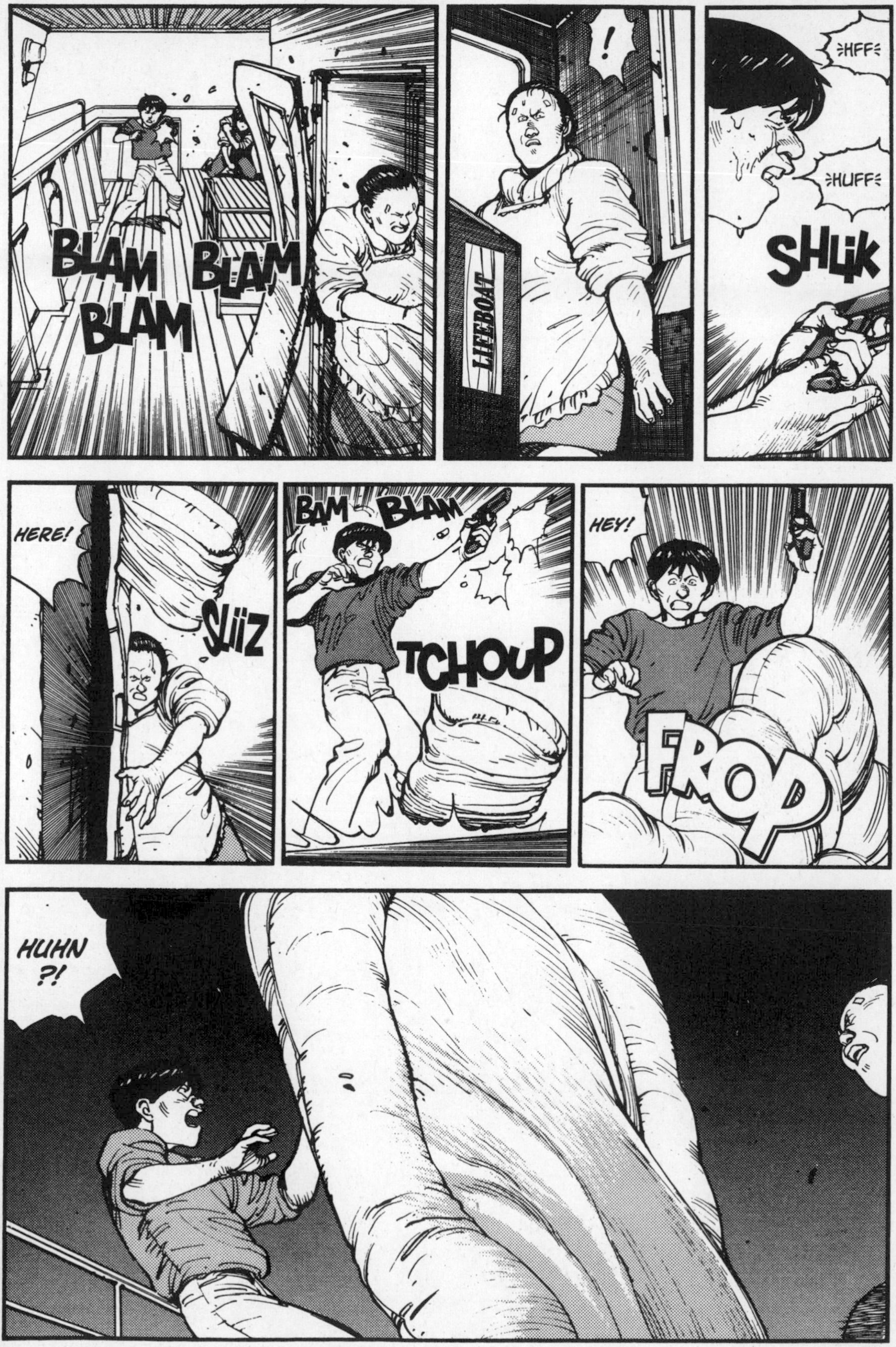
BLAM BLAM
BLAM
!
HFF
HUFF
SHLIK
HERE!
SLIIZ
BAM BLAM
TCHOUP
HEY!
FROP
HUHN ?!

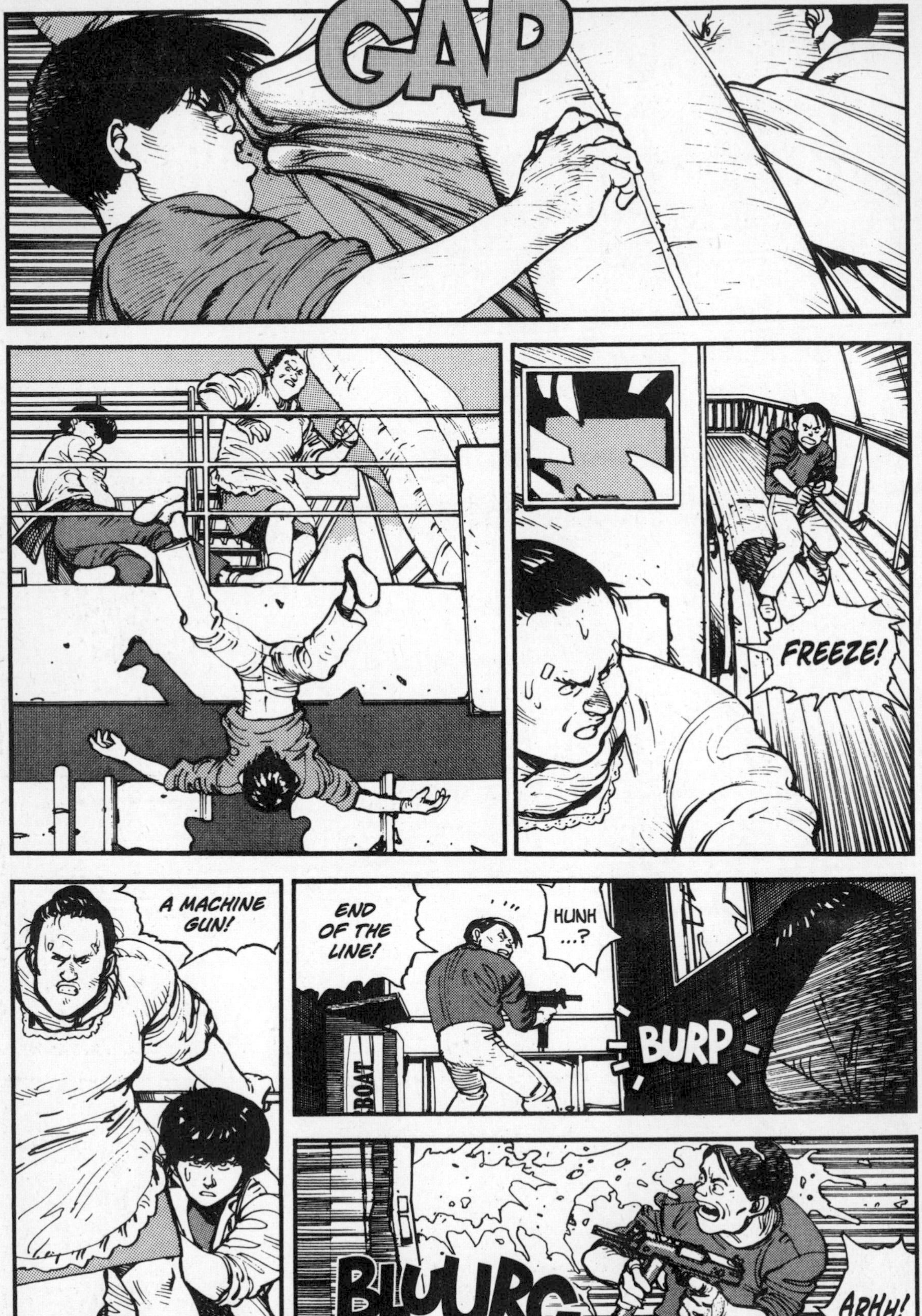
GAP
FREEZE!
A MACHINE GUN!
END OF THE LINE!
HUNH ...?
BOAT
BURP
BLUURG
ARHH!

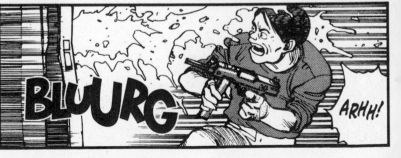

GYAAHHH!?

WAK

≥UHHN!≤

KA--

--KANEDA!

≥KOF≤
≥SPLUTT≤

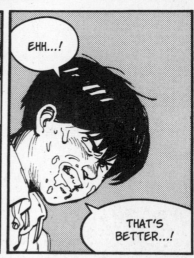

EHH...!

THAT'S BETTER...!

ARE YOU OKAY?

≥BLURGH≤...

I DON'T KNOW WHETHER THEY POISONED ME...

...OR I'M JUST SEASICK.

THIS SUUUCKS!

BLAARGHH!

≥HRNN≤

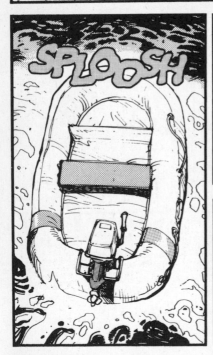

SPLOOSH

LESSEE NOW...

GOT IT!

VROOBRO

VVVRROOOOOOO

...OH SHIT!!

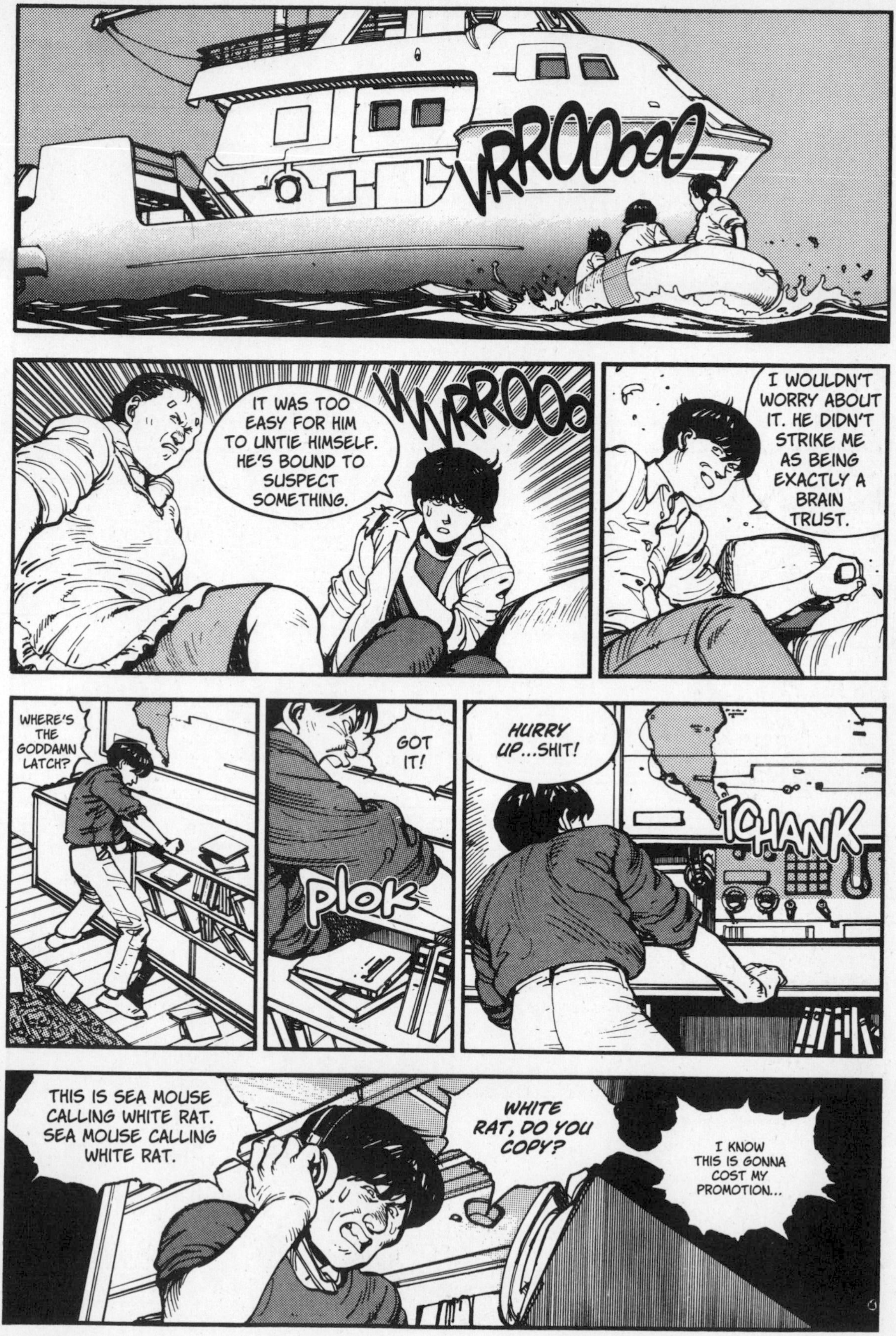
VRROOooO
IT WAS TOO EASY FOR HIM TO UNTIE HIMSELF. HE'S BOUND TO SUSPECT SOMETHING.
WVRROOOo
I WOULDN'T WORRY ABOUT IT. HE DIDN'T STRIKE ME AS BEING EXACTLY A BRAIN TRUST.
WHERE'S THE GODDAMN LATCH?
GOT IT!
plok
HURRY UP...SHIT!
TCHANK
THIS IS SEA MOUSE CALLING WHITE RAT. SEA MOUSE CALLING WHITE RAT.
WHITE RAT, DO YOU COPY?
I KNOW THIS IS GONNA COST MY PROMOTION...

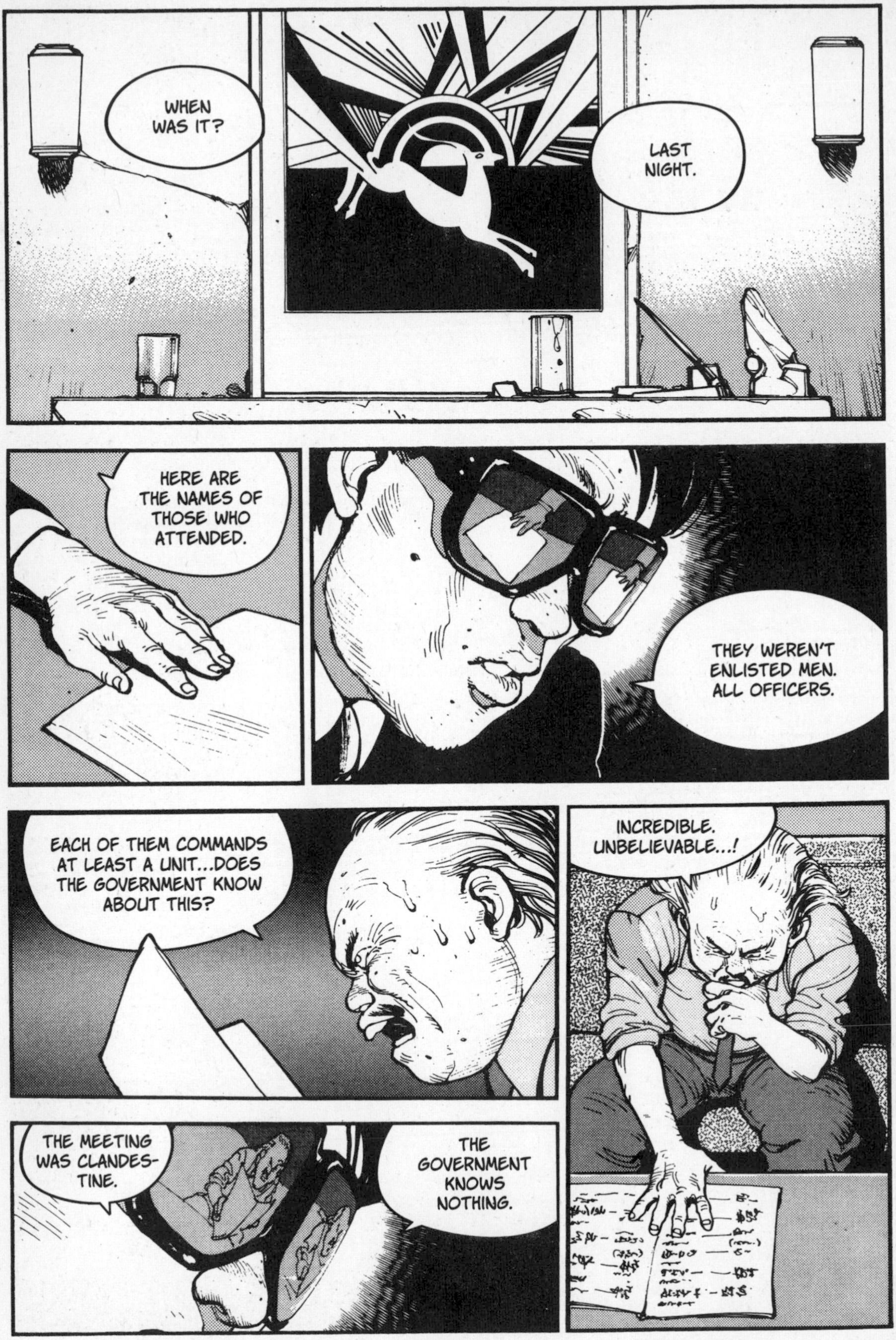
WHEN WAS IT?
LAST NIGHT.
HERE ARE THE NAMES OF THOSE WHO ATTENDED.
THEY WEREN'T ENLISTED MEN. ALL OFFICERS.
EACH OF THEM COMMANDS AT LEAST A UNIT...DOES THE GOVERNMENT KNOW ABOUT THIS?
THE MEETING WAS CLANDES-TINE.
THE GOVERNMENT KNOWS NOTHING.
INCREDIBLE. UNBELIEVABLE...!

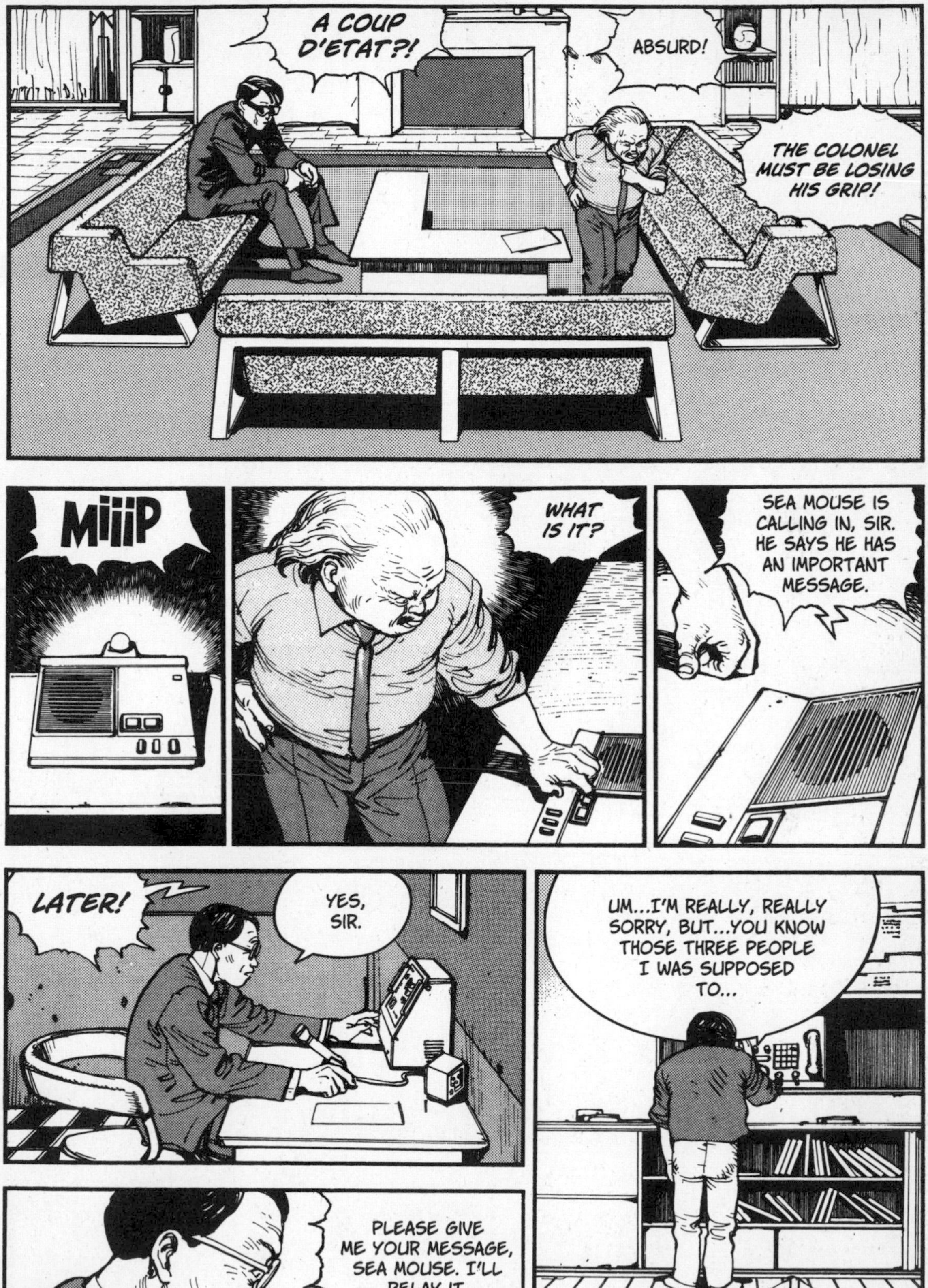
A COUP D'ETAT?!
ABSURD!
THE COLONEL MUST BE LOSING HIS GRIP!
MIIIP
WHAT IS IT?
SEA MOUSE IS CALLING IN, SIR. HE SAYS HE HAS AN IMPORTANT MESSAGE.
LATER!
YES, SIR.
PLEASE GIVE ME YOUR MESSAGE, SEA MOUSE. I'LL RELAY IT.
UM...I'M REALLY, REALLY SORRY, BUT...YOU KNOW THOSE THREE PEOPLE I WAS SUPPOSED TO...

WHAT?! YOU LET THEM GET AWAY?!?

YES, SIR!

I'M REALLY REALLY REALLY REALLY SORRY, SIR!!

YOU MORON! CAN'T YOU EVEN TAKE CARE OF A WOMAN AND TWO KIDS?!

UM...I WAS SUPPOSED TO TAKE CARE OF AKIRA AFTER I FINISHED UP HERE.

SO, UM... WHERE IS HE?

NRRGH! YOU IDIOT!

HE'S AT MR. NEZU'S PLACE, OF COURSE!

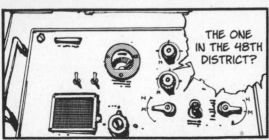

THE ONE IN THE 48TH DISTRICT?

THE 11TH!

...?

108

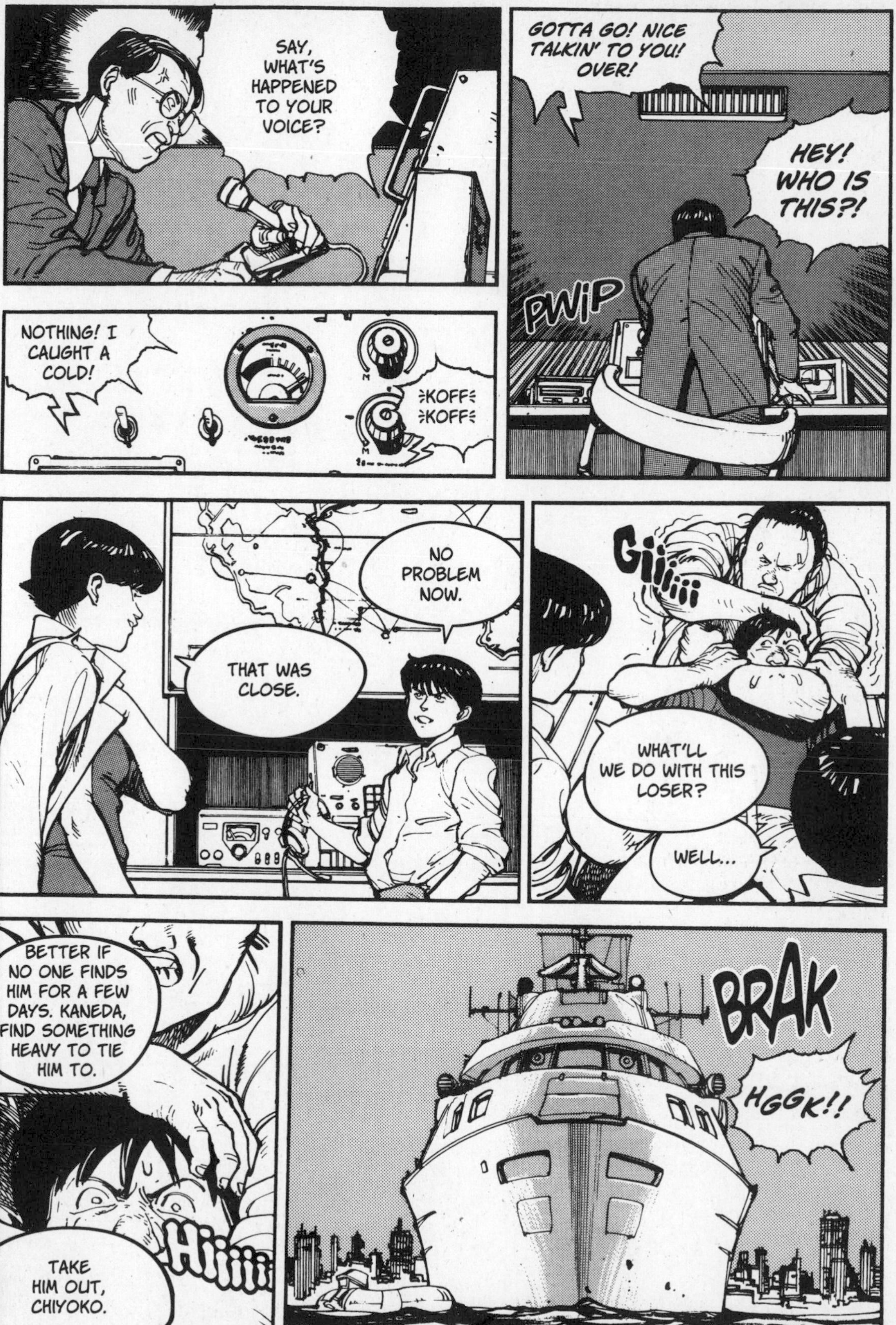
SAY, WHAT'S HAPPENED TO YOUR VOICE?
NOTHING! I CAUGHT A COLD!
KOFF KOFF
GOTTA GO! NICE TALKIN' TO YOU! OVER!
HEY! WHO IS THIS?!
PWIP
NO PROBLEM NOW.
THAT WAS CLOSE.
Giiiiii
WHAT'LL WE DO WITH THIS LOSER?
WELL...
BETTER IF NO ONE FINDS HIM FOR A FEW DAYS. KANEDA, FIND SOMETHING HEAVY TO TIE HIM TO.
Hiiiiii
TAKE HIM OUT, CHIYOKO.
BRAK
HGGK!!

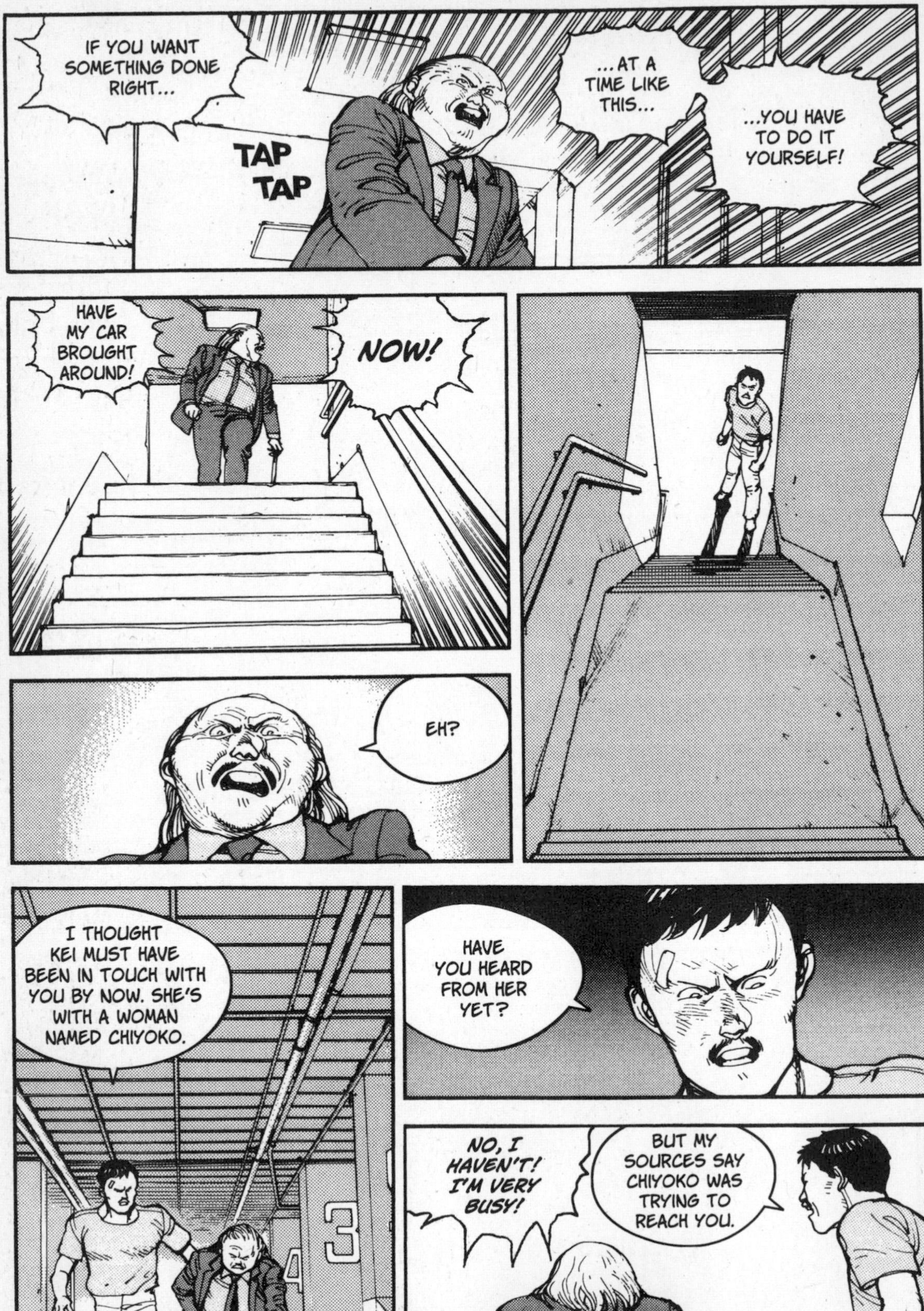
IF YOU WANT SOMETHING DONE RIGHT...
TAP TAP
...AT A TIME LIKE THIS...
...YOU HAVE TO DO IT YOURSELF!
HAVE MY CAR BROUGHT AROUND!
NOW!
EH?
I THOUGHT KEI MUST HAVE BEEN IN TOUCH WITH YOU BY NOW. SHE'S WITH A WOMAN NAMED CHIYOKO.
HAVE YOU HEARD FROM HER YET?
NO, I HAVEN'T! I'M VERY BUSY!
BUT MY SOURCES SAY CHIYOKO WAS TRYING TO REACH YOU.

SWIIIP
ARHH!
SMAK
DIDN'T I JUST TELL YOU HOW BUSY I AM?!
IDIOT...
SLAM
VRAOOOM
ROOM
ROOM

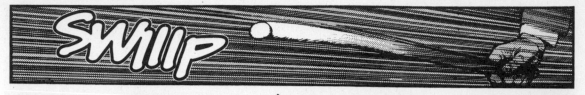

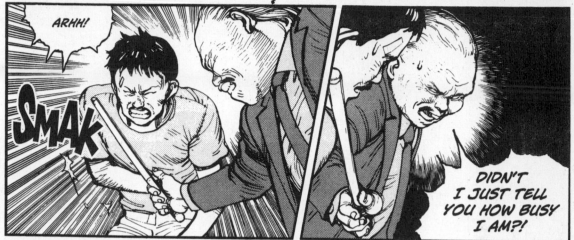

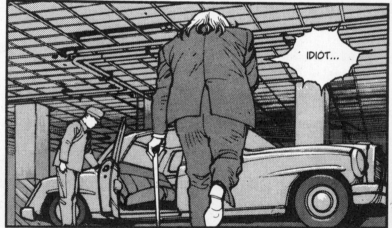

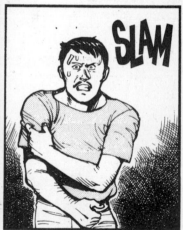

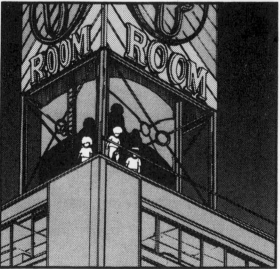

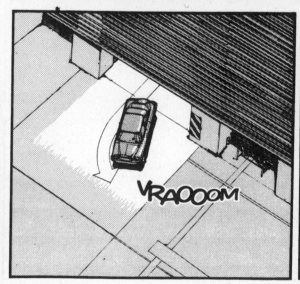

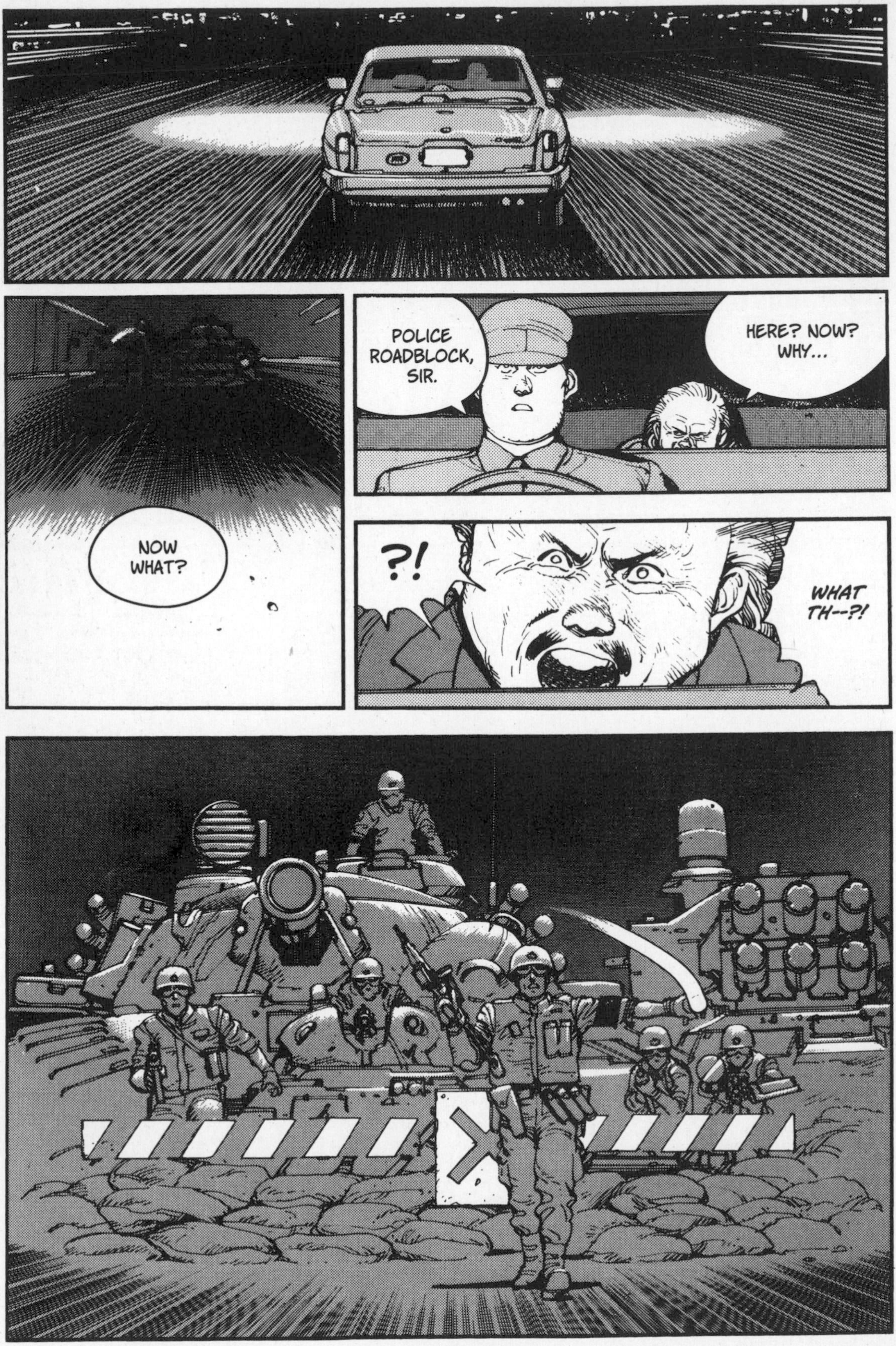
NOW WHAT?
POLICE ROADBLOCK, SIR.
HERE? NOW? WHY...
?!
WHAT TH--?!

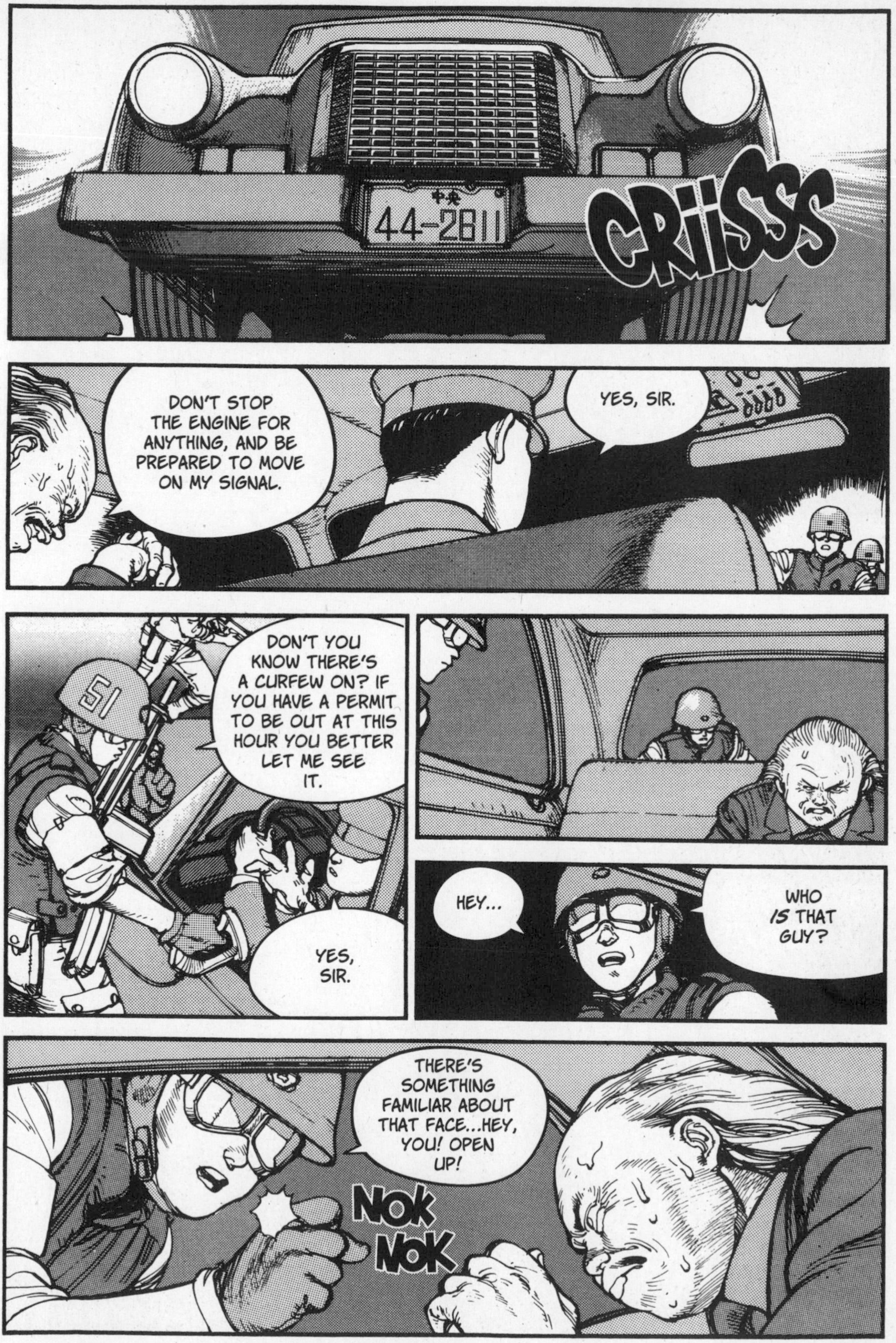
44-28 11
CRiiSSS
DON'T STOP THE ENGINE FOR ANYTHING, AND BE PREPARED TO MOVE ON MY SIGNAL.
YES, SIR.
DON'T YOU KNOW THERE'S A CURFEW ON? IF YOU HAVE A PERMIT TO BE OUT AT THIS HOUR YOU BETTER LET ME SEE IT.
YES, SIR.
HEY...
WHO *IS* THAT GUY?
THERE'S SOMETHING FAMILIAR ABOUT THAT FACE...HEY, YOU! OPEN UP!
NOK NOK

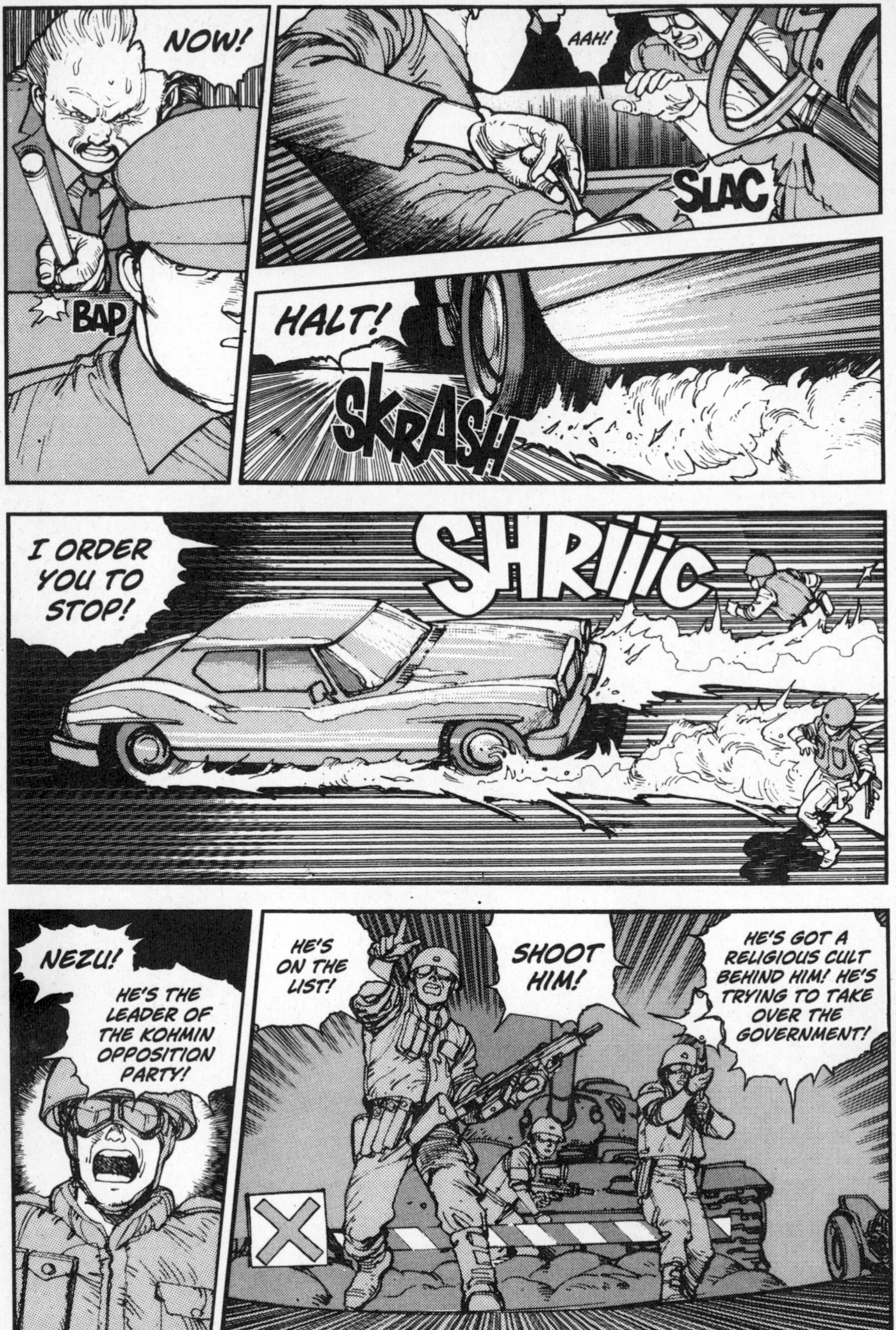
NOW!
BAP
AAH!
SLAC
HALT!
SKRASH
I ORDER YOU TO STOP!
SHRIiiC
NEZU!
HE'S THE LEADER OF THE KOHMIN OPPOSITION PARTY!
HE'S ON THE LIST!
SHOOT HIM!
HE'S GOT A RELIGIOUS CULT BEHIND HIM! HE'S TRYING TO TAKE OVER THE GOVERNMENT!

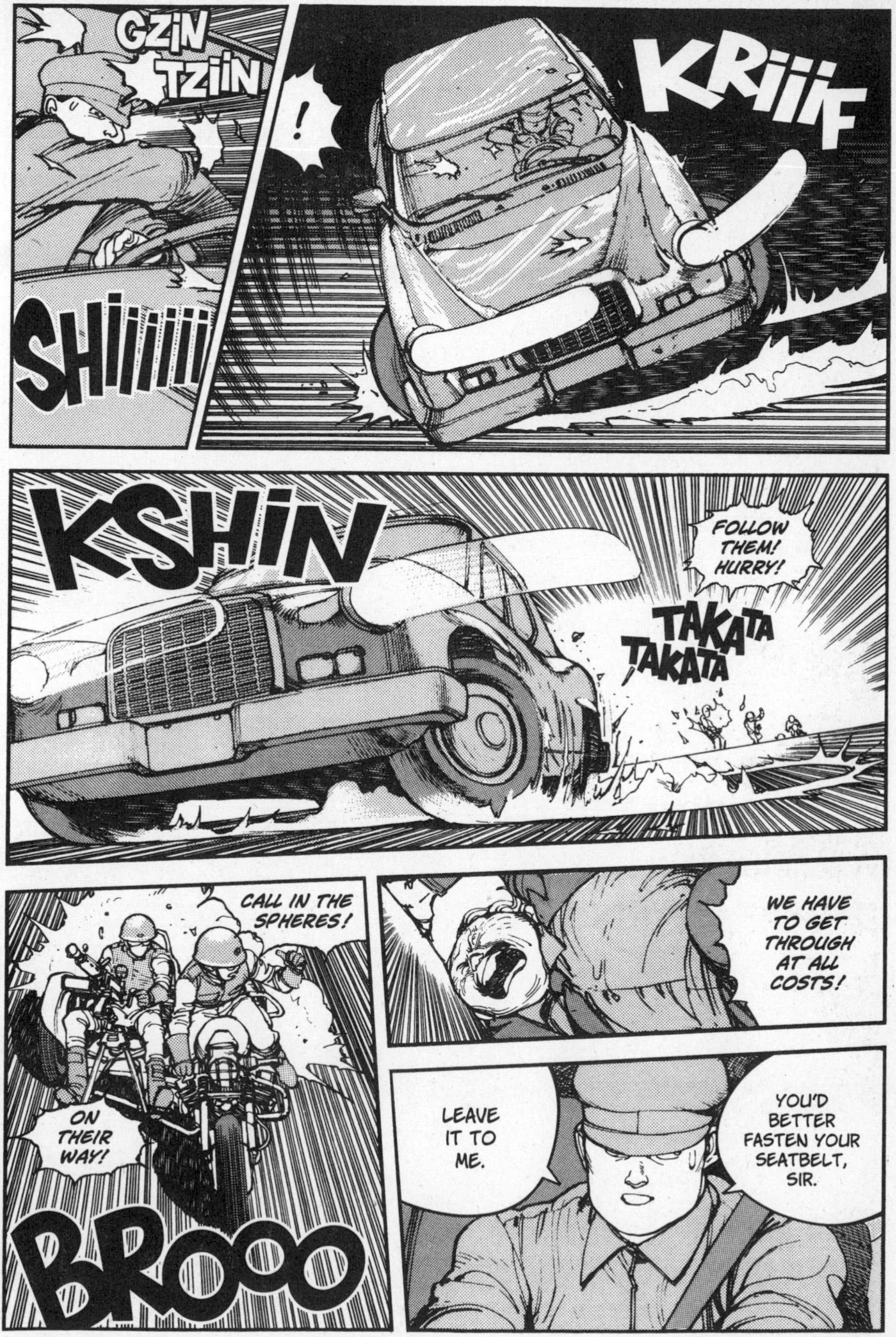

GZIN
TZIIN
SHIIIIIII
!
KRIIIF
KSHIN
FOLLOW THEM! HURRY!
TAKATA TAKATA
CALL IN THE SPHERES!
ON THEIR WAY!
BROOO
WE HAVE TO GET THROUGH AT ALL COSTS!
LEAVE IT TO ME.
YOU'D BETTER FASTEN YOUR SEATBELT, SIR.

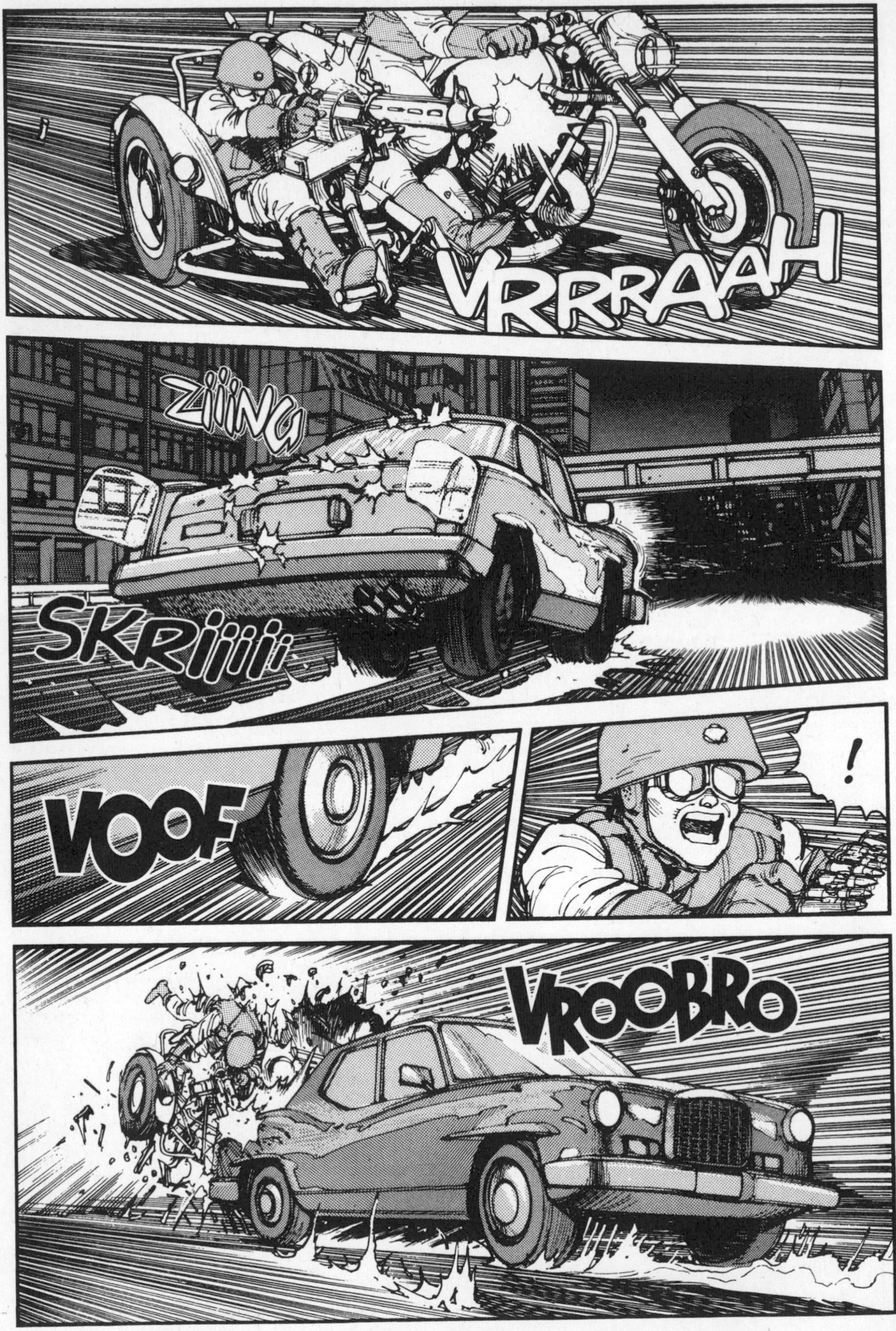
VRRRAAH
ZiiNG
SKRiiiii
VOOF
!
VROOBRO

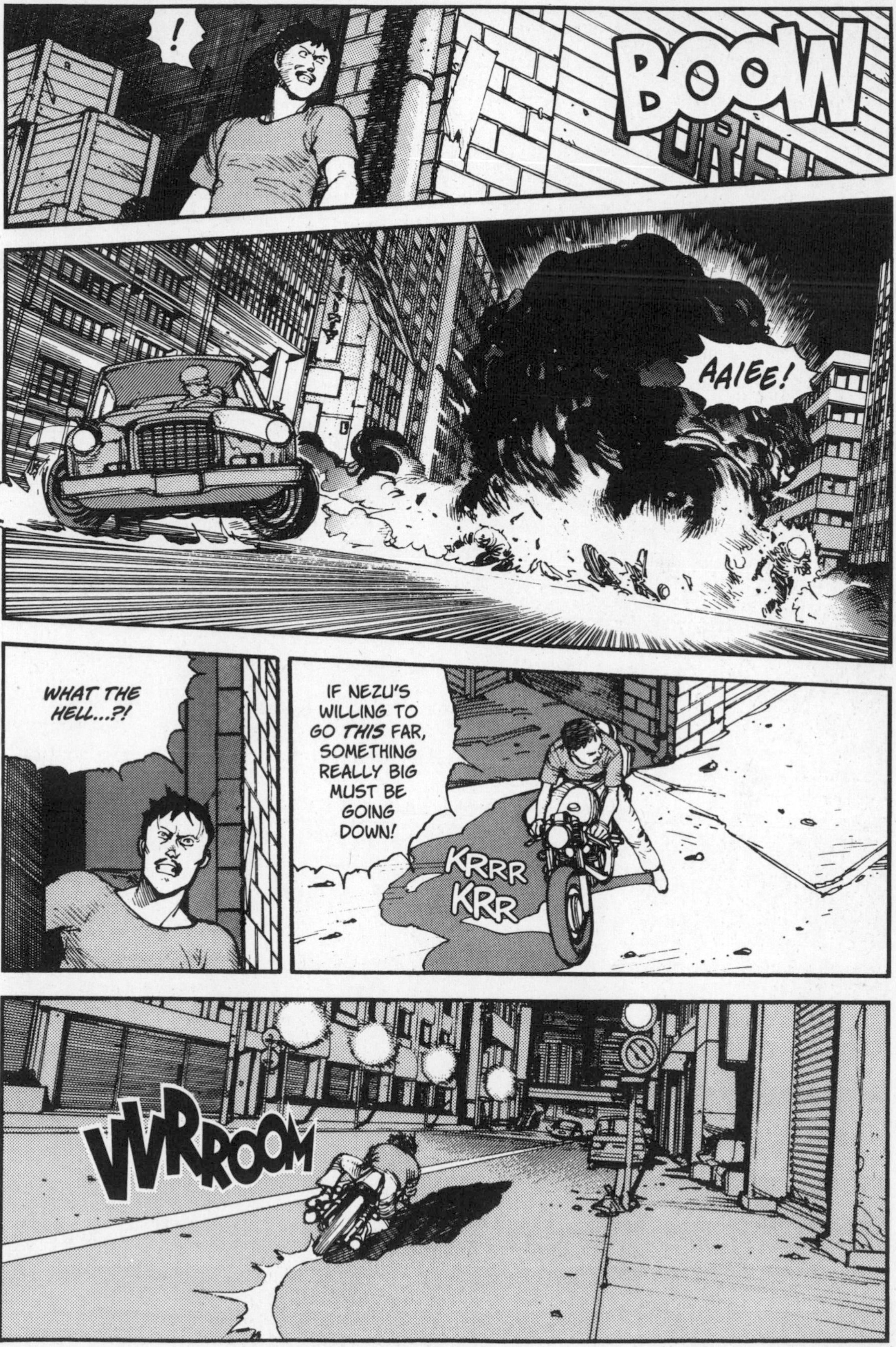
!
BOOW
AAIEE!
WHAT THE HELL...?!
IF NEZU'S WILLING TO GO THIS FAR, SOMETHING REALLY BIG MUST BE GOING DOWN!
KRRR KRR
VVRROOM

VOOOOOM

WHAT DO YOU THINK, SAKAKI?

CURIOUS THAT THE ARMY'S GETTING INVOLVED.

LOOKS LIKE THEY'RE HEADING FOR NEZU'S HOME! LET'S GO.

HMM...

TSUF

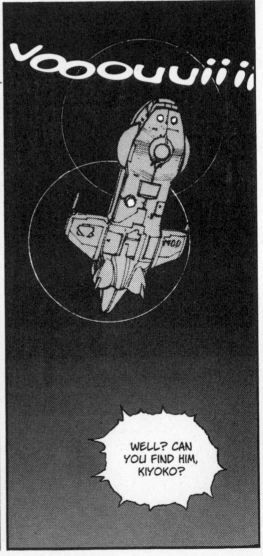

VOOOUiiii

WELL? CAN YOU FIND HIM, KIYOKO?

FOR A MOMENT, I SENSED A PRESENCE. IT WAS HE...

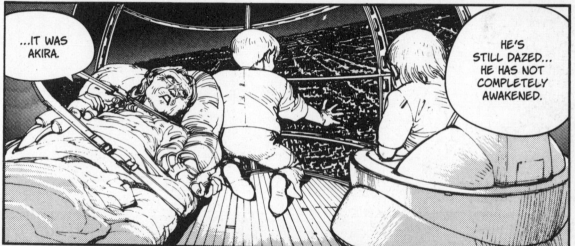

...IT WAS AKIRA.

HE'S STILL DAZED... HE HAS NOT COMPLETELY AWAKENED.

GOOD!

WE MUST HURRY! THERE'S STILL TIME TO STOP HIM!

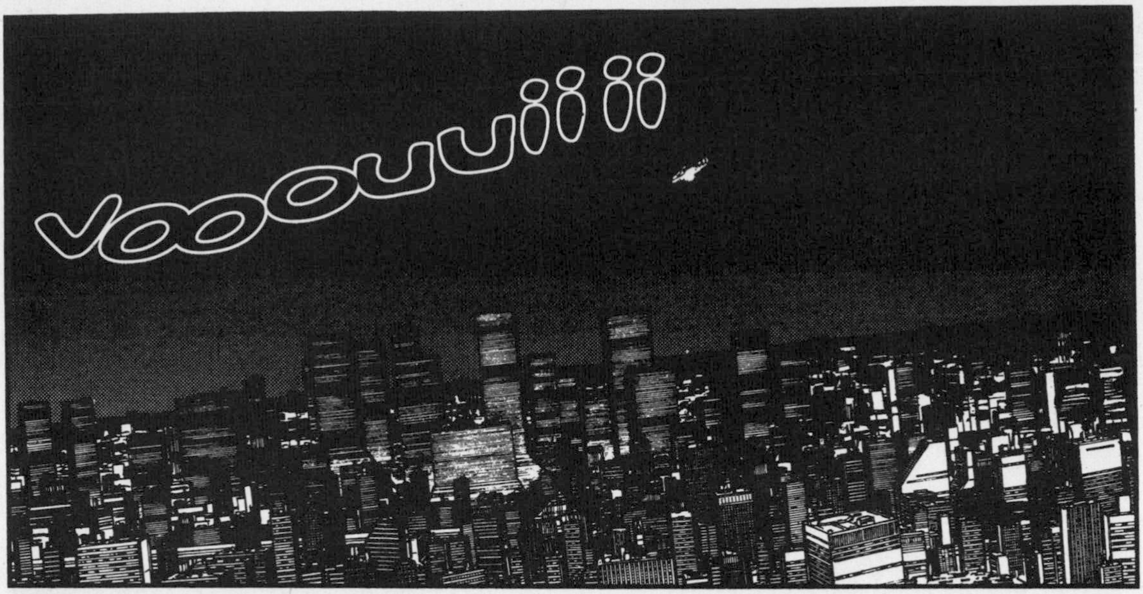
vooouuiiii

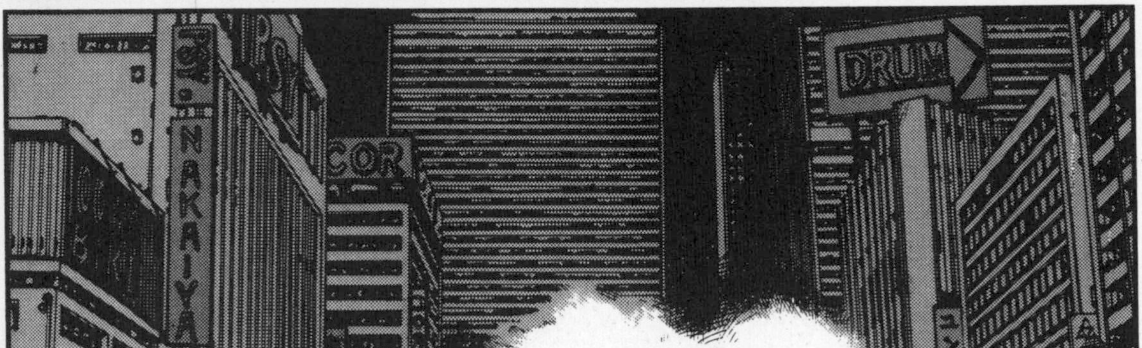
DRUM
COR
NAKAIYA
GRiiik

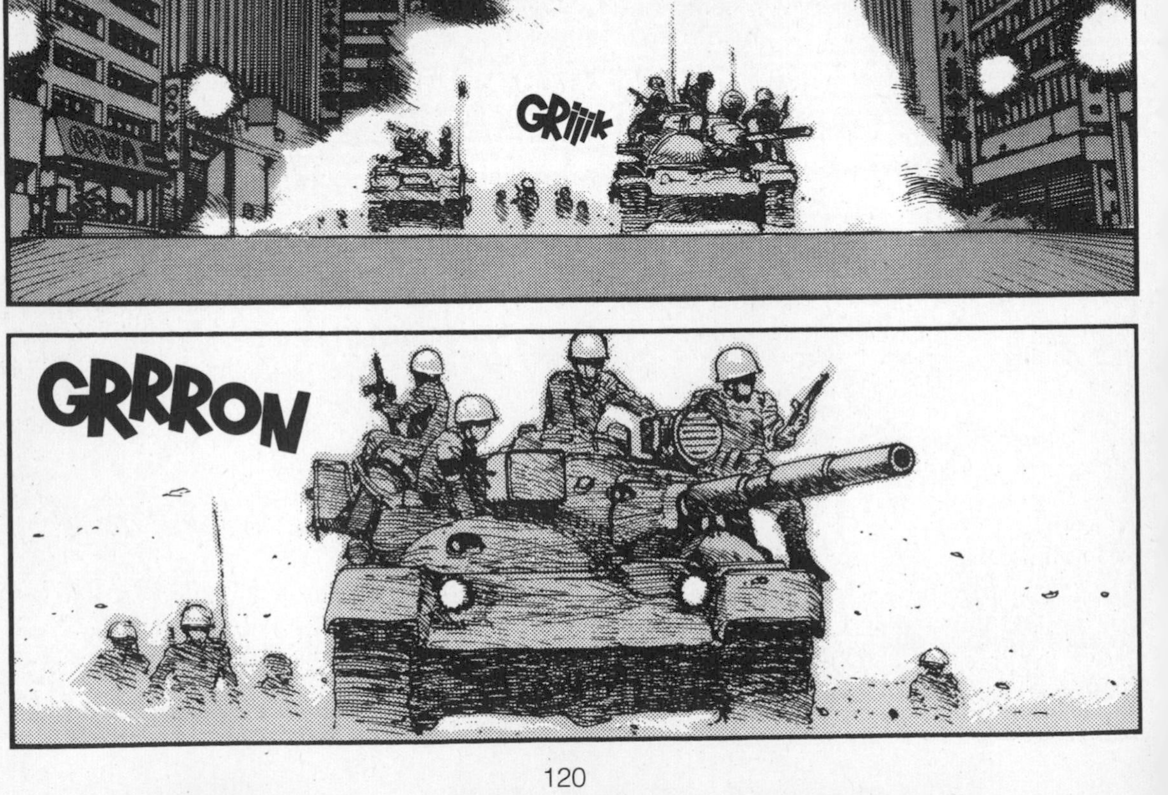
GRRRON

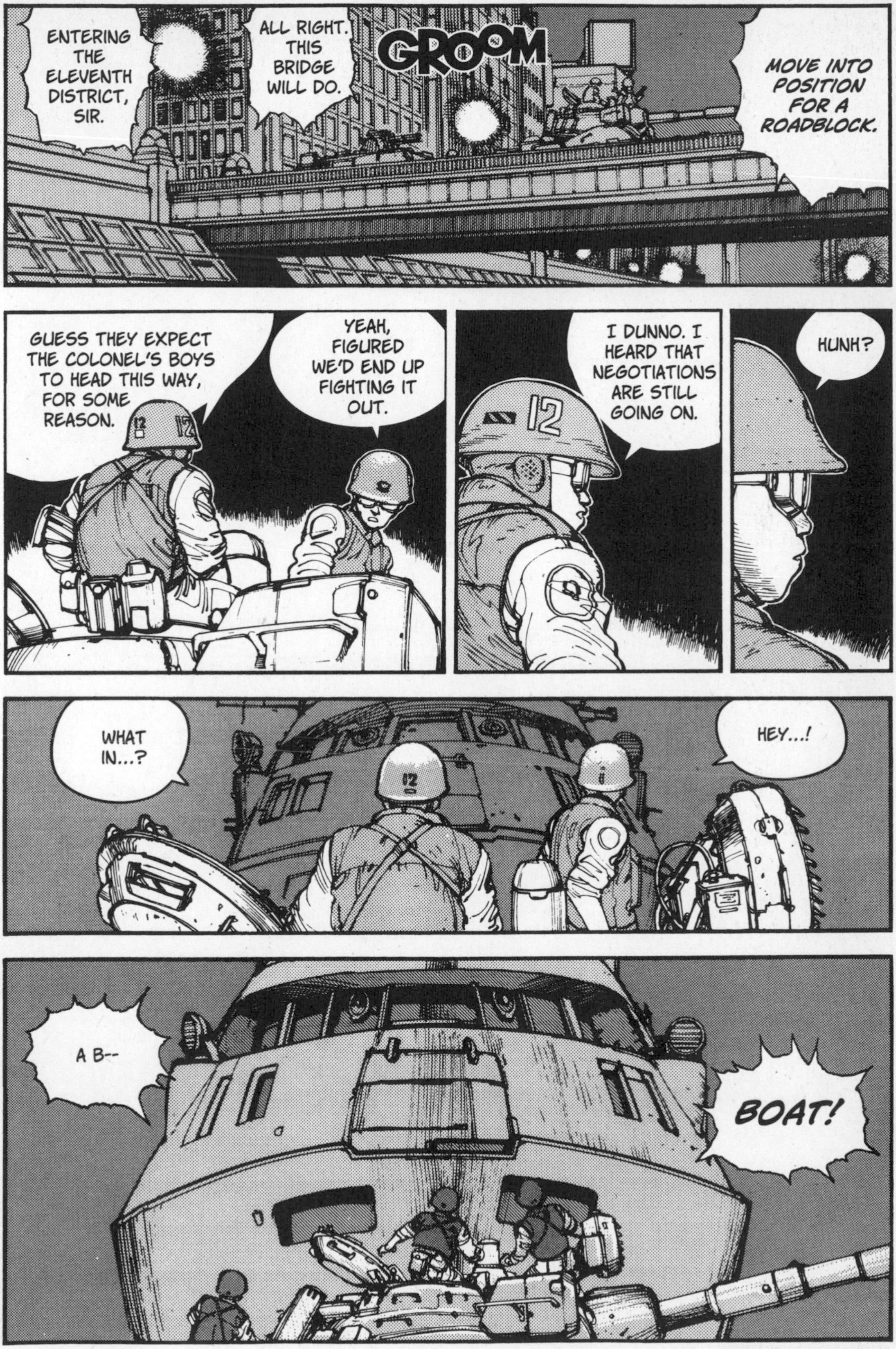

ENTERING THE ELEVENTH DISTRICT, SIR.
ALL RIGHT. THIS BRIDGE WILL DO.
GROOM
MOVE INTO POSITION FOR A ROADBLOCK.
GUESS THEY EXPECT THE COLONEL'S BOYS TO HEAD THIS WAY, FOR SOME REASON.
YEAH, FIGURED WE'D END UP FIGHTING IT OUT.
I DUNNO. I HEARD THAT NEGOTIATIONS ARE STILL GOING ON.
HUNH?
WHAT IN...?
HEY...!
A B--
BOAT!

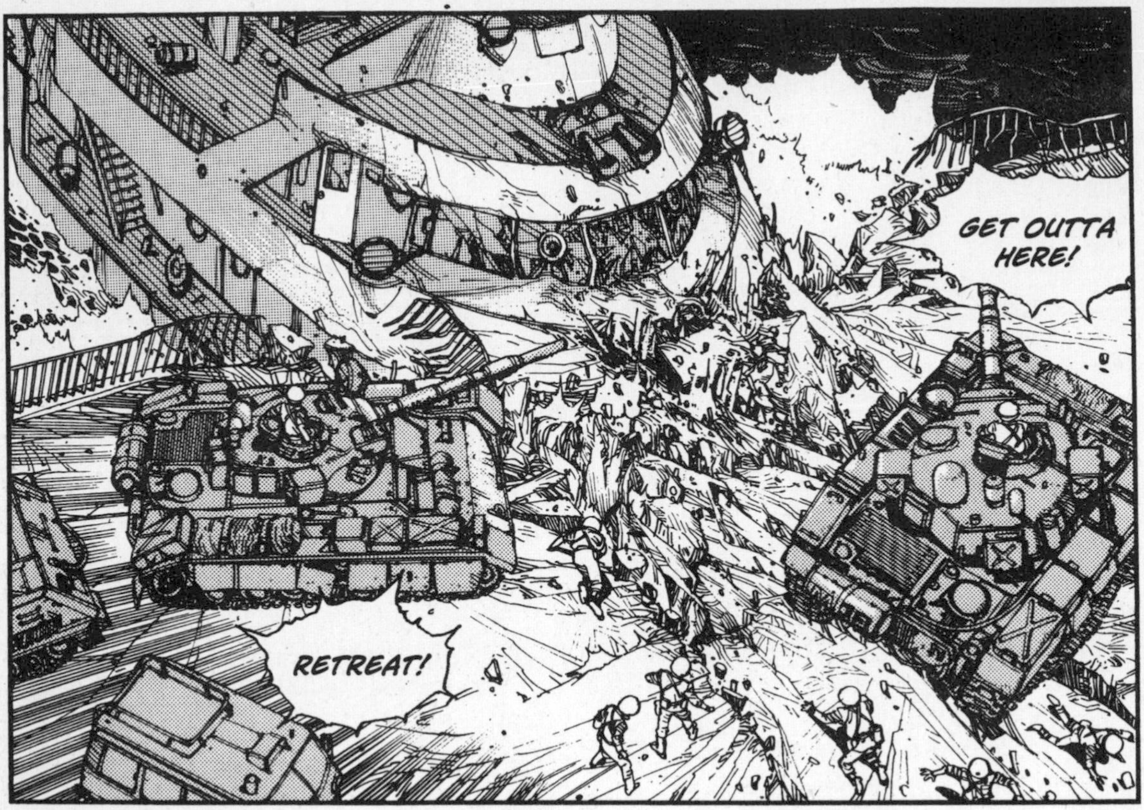
GET OUTTA HERE!
RETREAT!

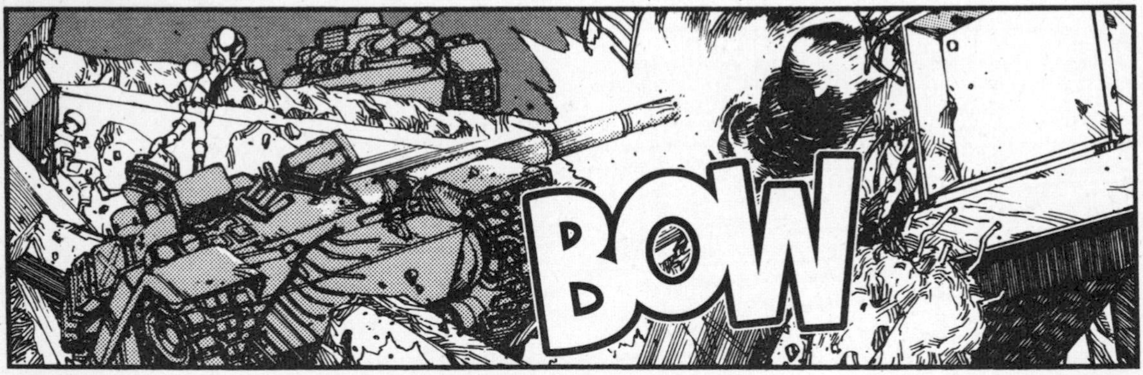
BOW

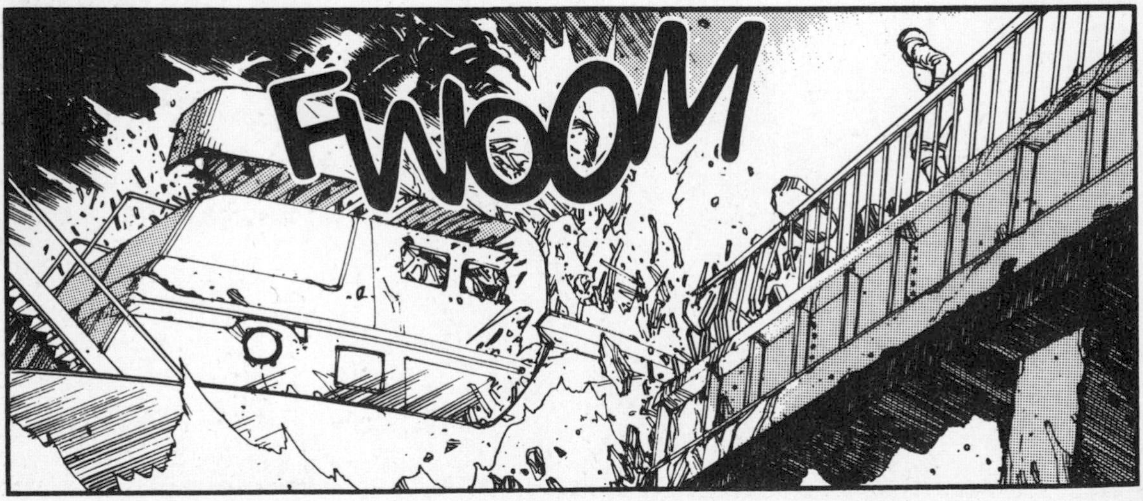
FWOOM

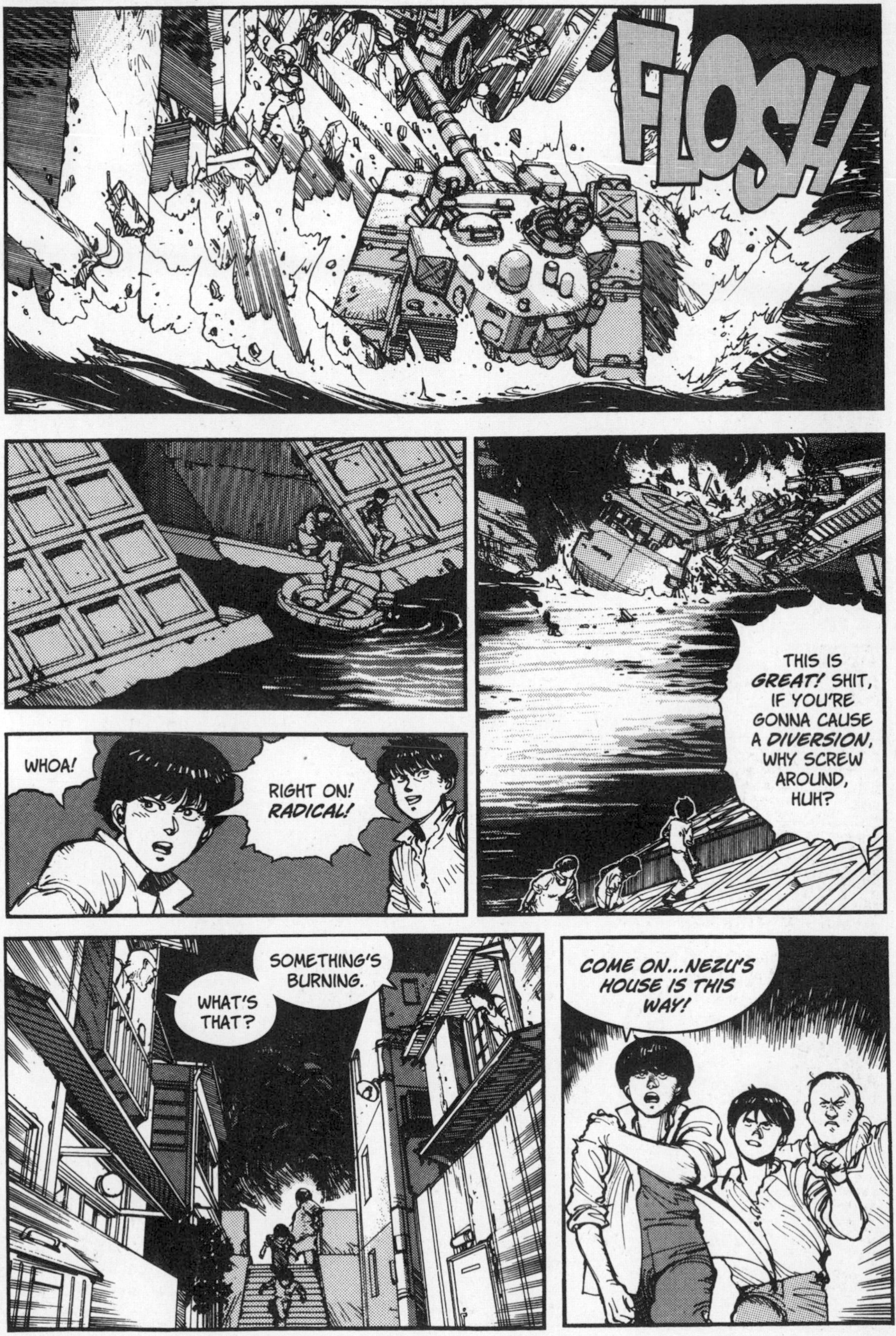
FLOSH
WHOA!
RIGHT ON! RADICAL!
THIS IS GREAT! SHIT, IF YOU'RE GONNA CAUSE A DIVERSION, WHY SCREW AROUND, HUH?
SOMETHING'S BURNING.
WHAT'S THAT?
COME ON...NEZU'S HOUSE IS THIS WAY!

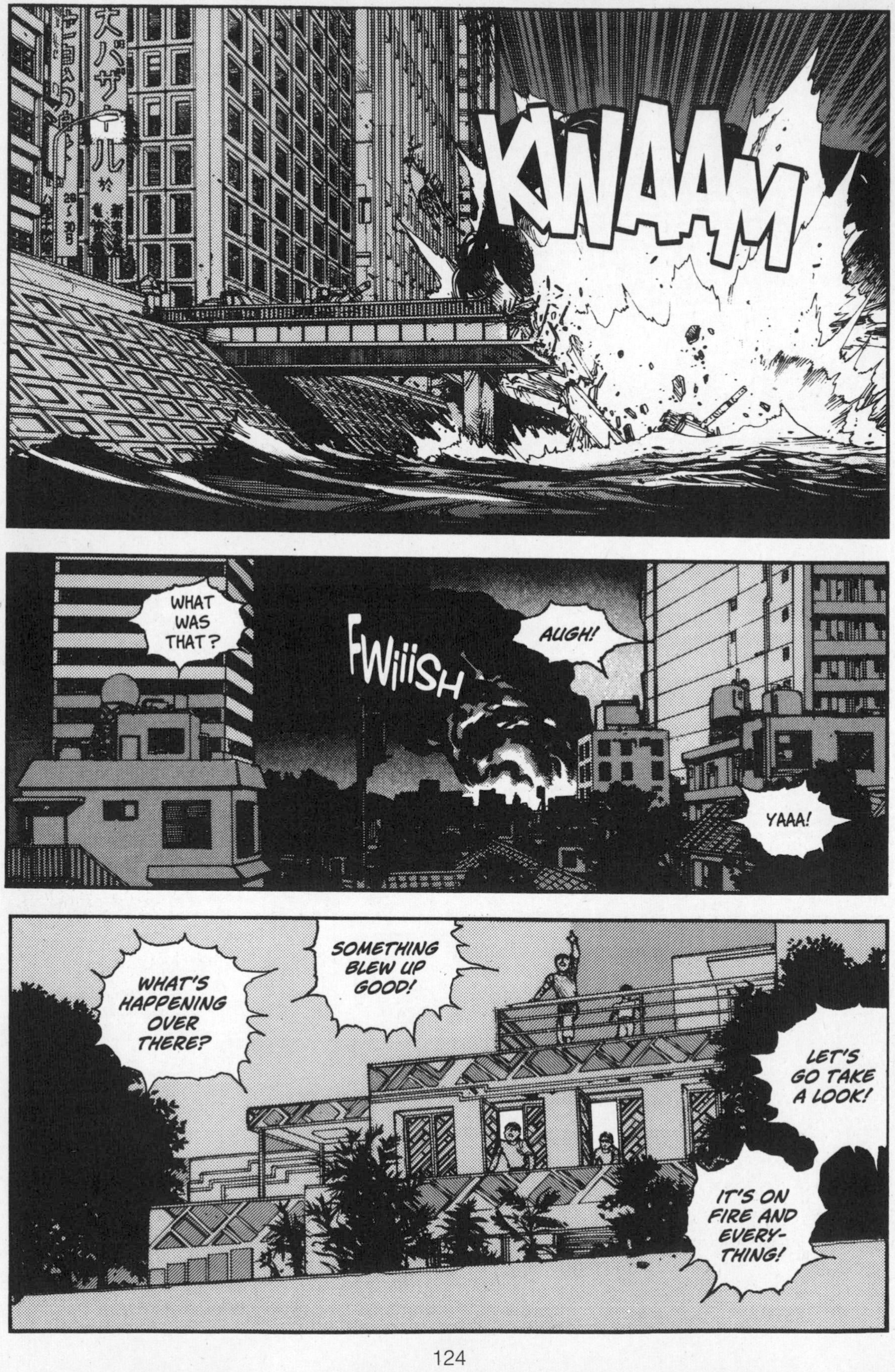
KWAAM
WHAT WAS THAT?
FWiiiSH
AUGH!
YAAA!
WHAT'S HAPPENING OVER THERE?
SOMETHING BLEW UP GOOD!
LET'S GO TAKE A LOOK!
IT'S ON FIRE AND EVERY-THING!

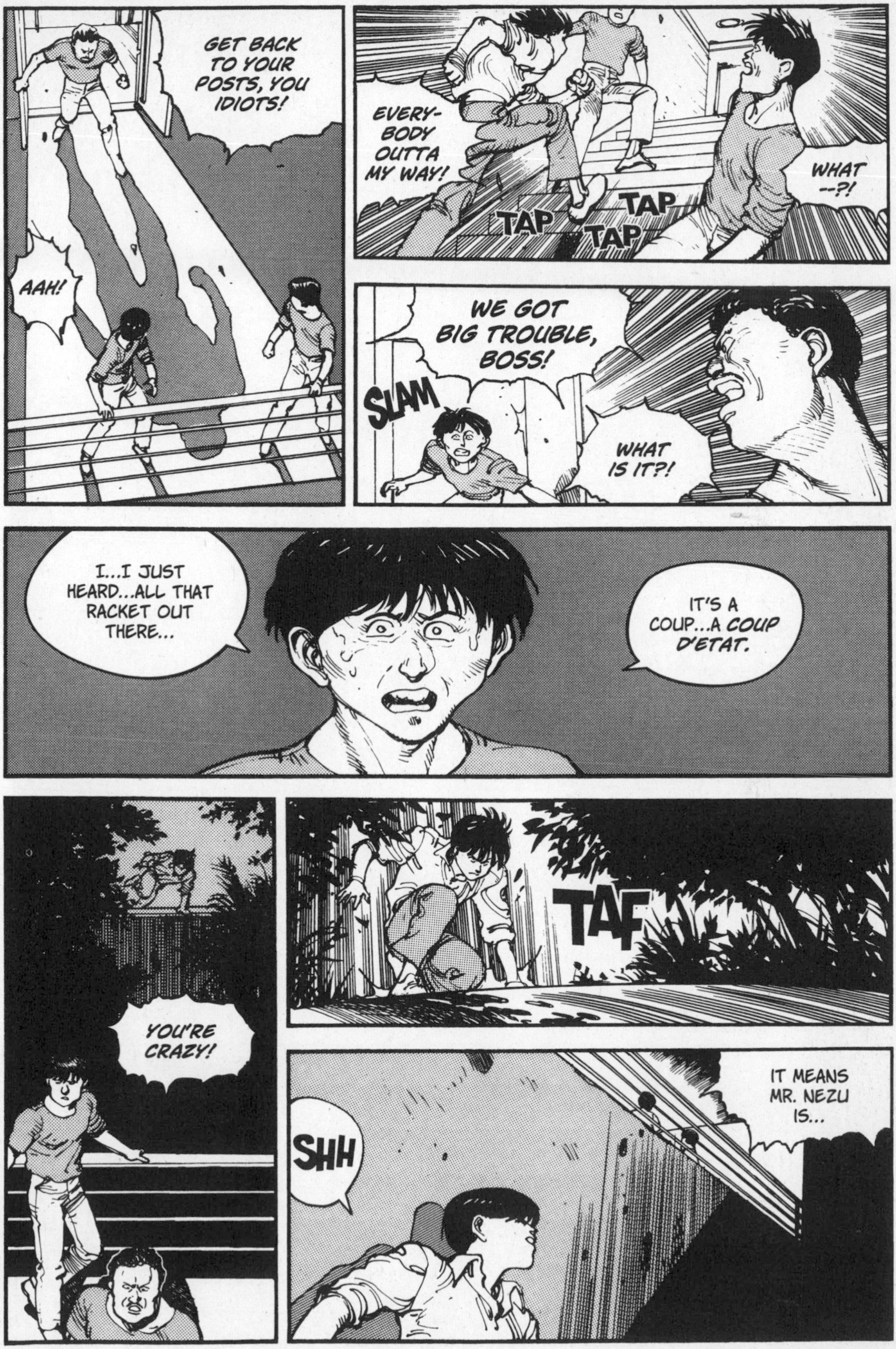
GET BACK TO YOUR POSTS, YOU IDIOTS!
AAH!
EVERY-BODY OUTTA MY WAY!
TAP TAP TAP
WHAT --?!
WE GOT BIG TROUBLE, BOSS!
SLAM
WHAT IS IT?!
I...I JUST HEARD...ALL THAT RACKET OUT THERE...
IT'S A COUP...A COUP D'ETAT.
YOU'RE CRAZY!
TAF
SHH
IT MEANS MR. NEZU IS...

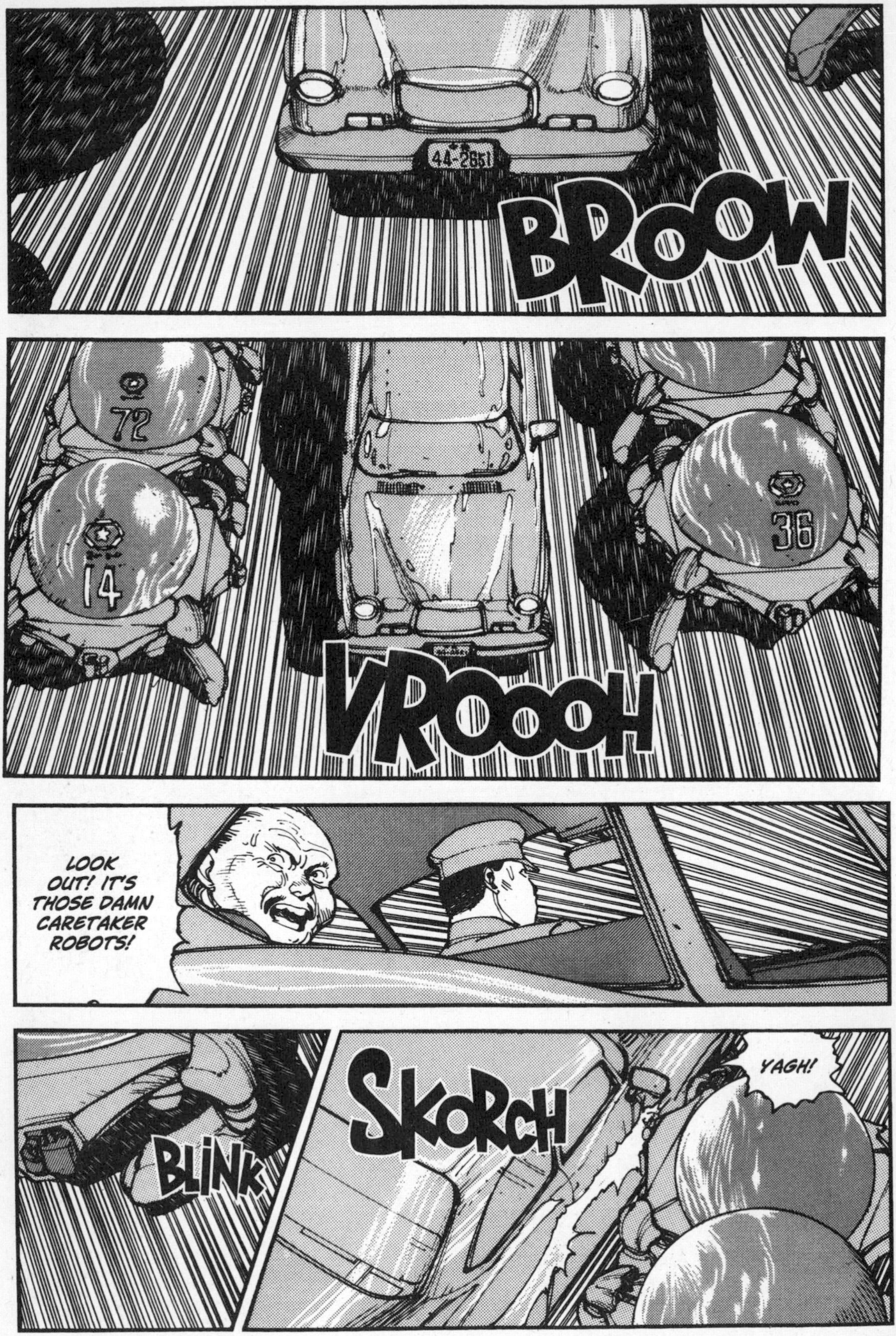
44-2651
BROOW
72
14
36
VROOOH
LOOK OUT! IT'S THOSE DAMN CARETAKER ROBOTS!
BLINK
SKORCH
YAGH!

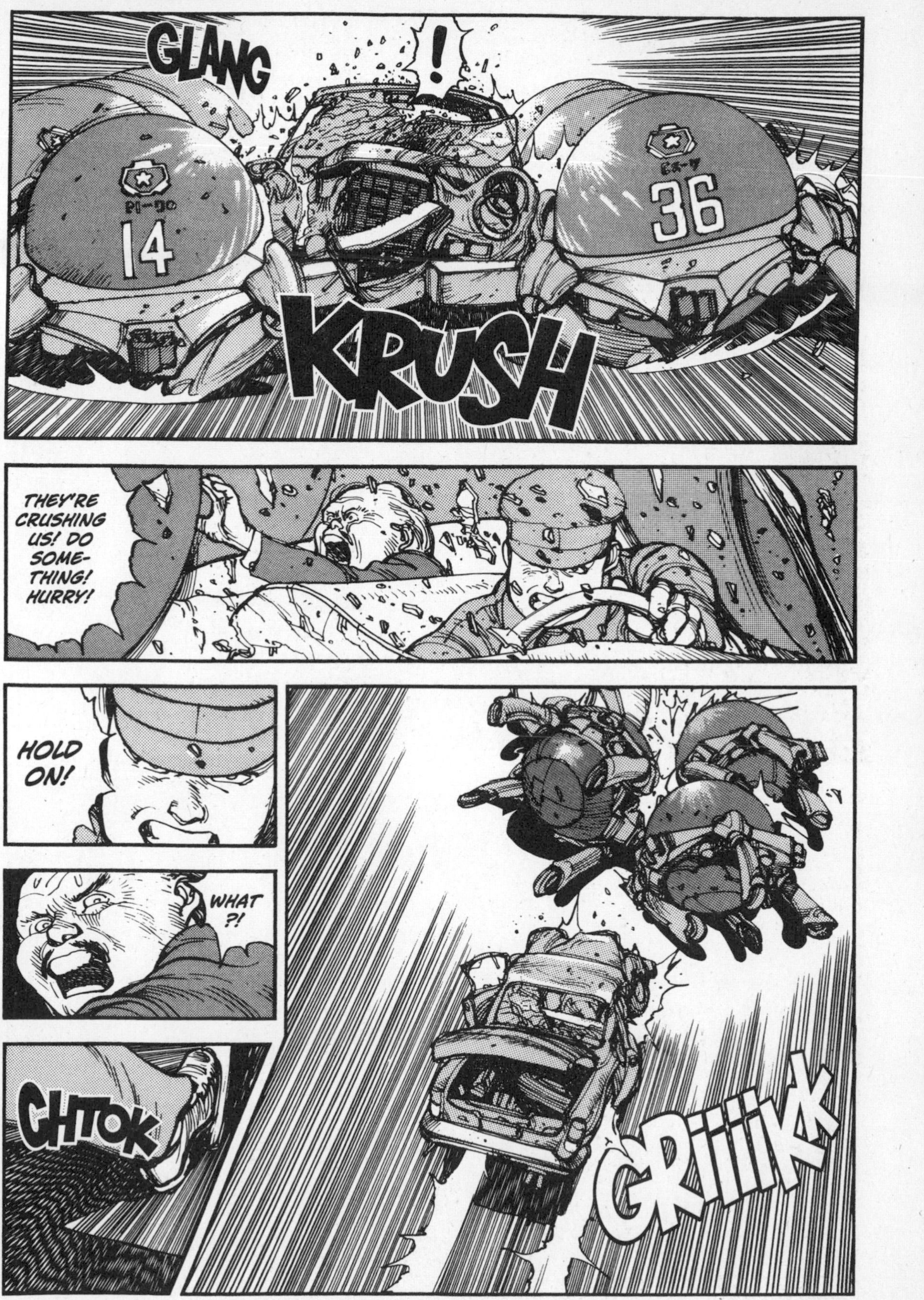
GLANG
!
14
36
KRUSH
THEY'RE CRUSHING US! DO SOMETHING! HURRY!
HOLD ON!
WHAT ?!
CHTOK
GRIiiiKK

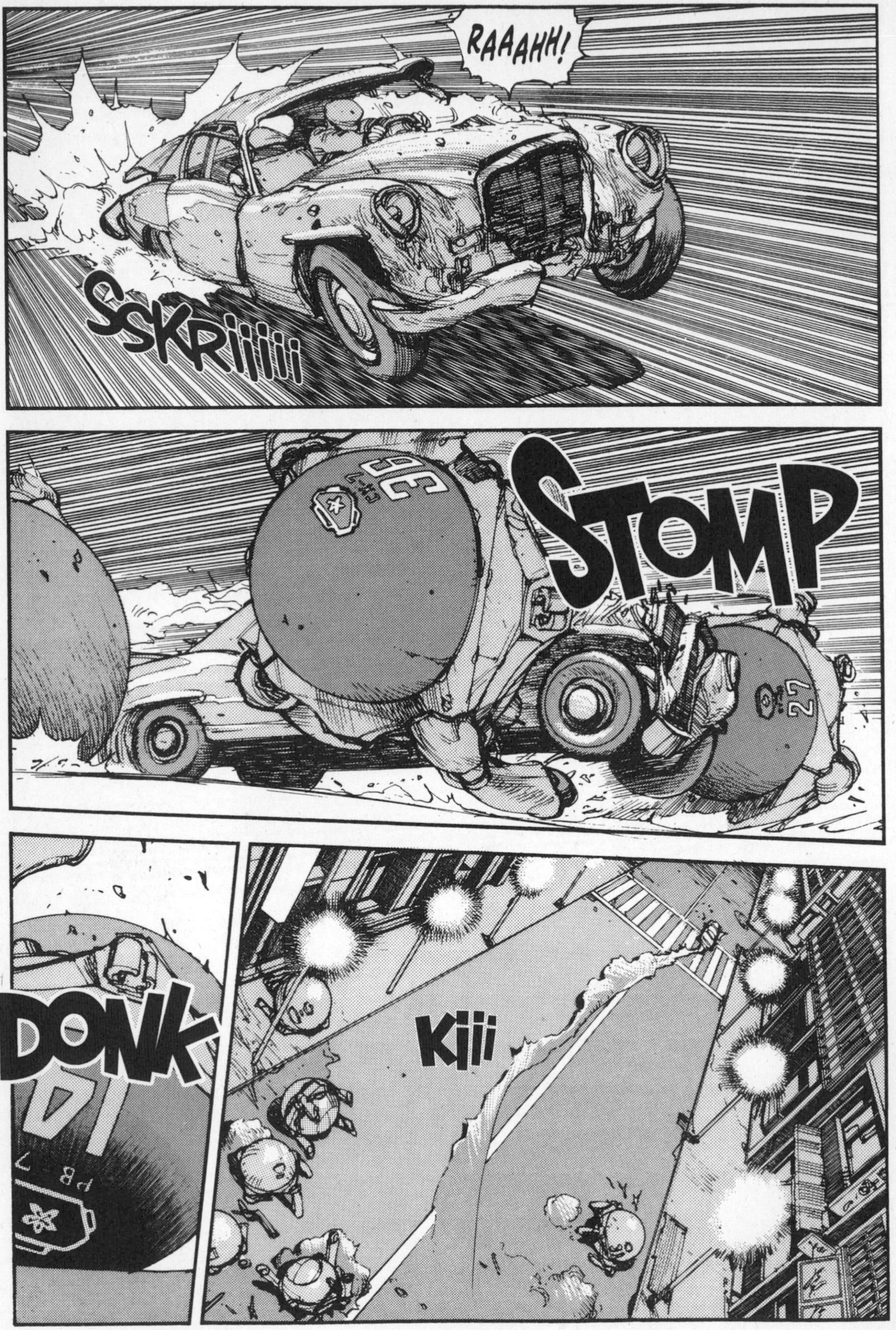
RAAAHH!
SSKRiiiiii
STOMP
DONK
Kiii

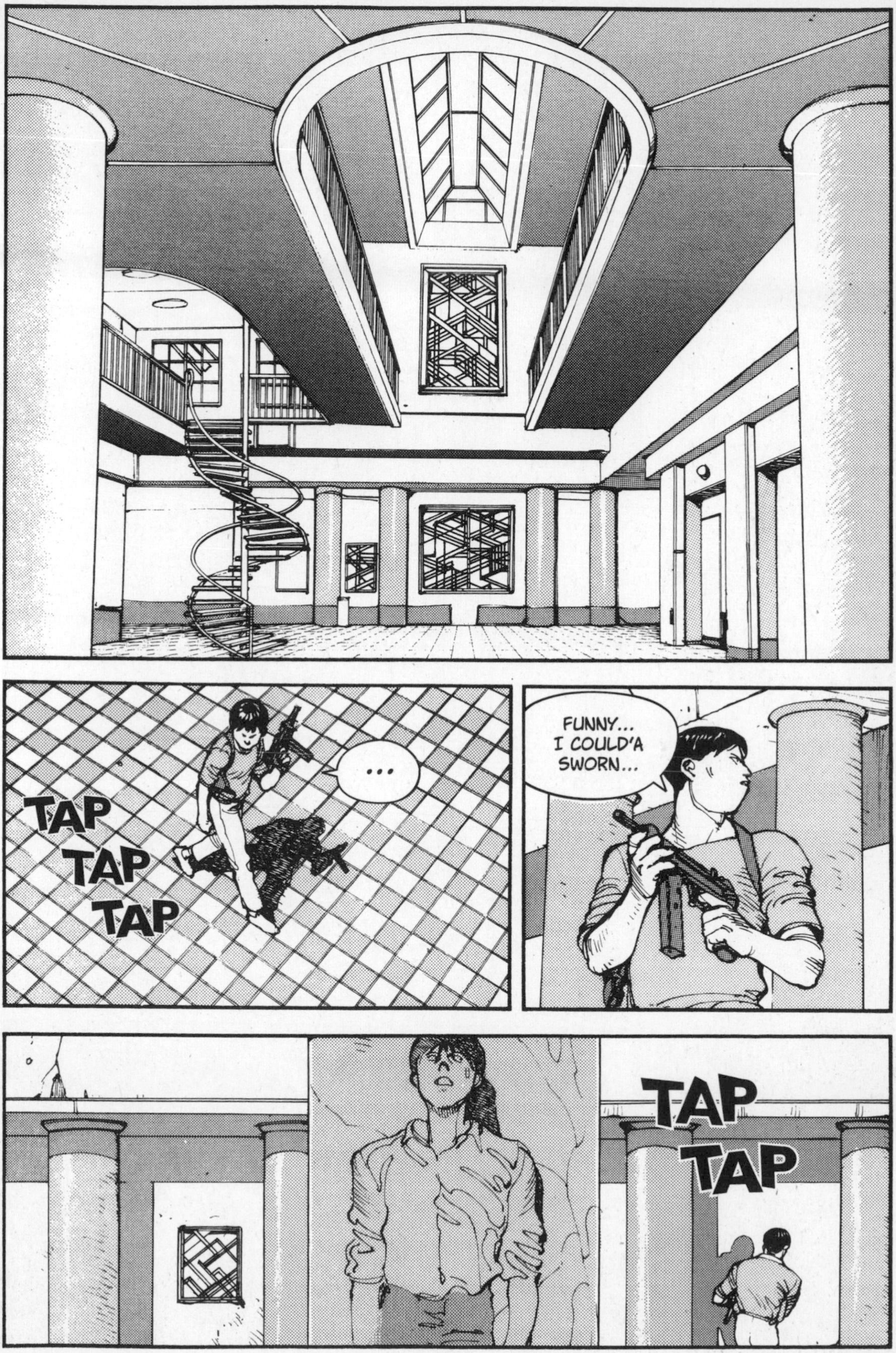
TAP
TAP
TAP
...
FUNNY... I COULD'A SWORN...
TAP
TAP

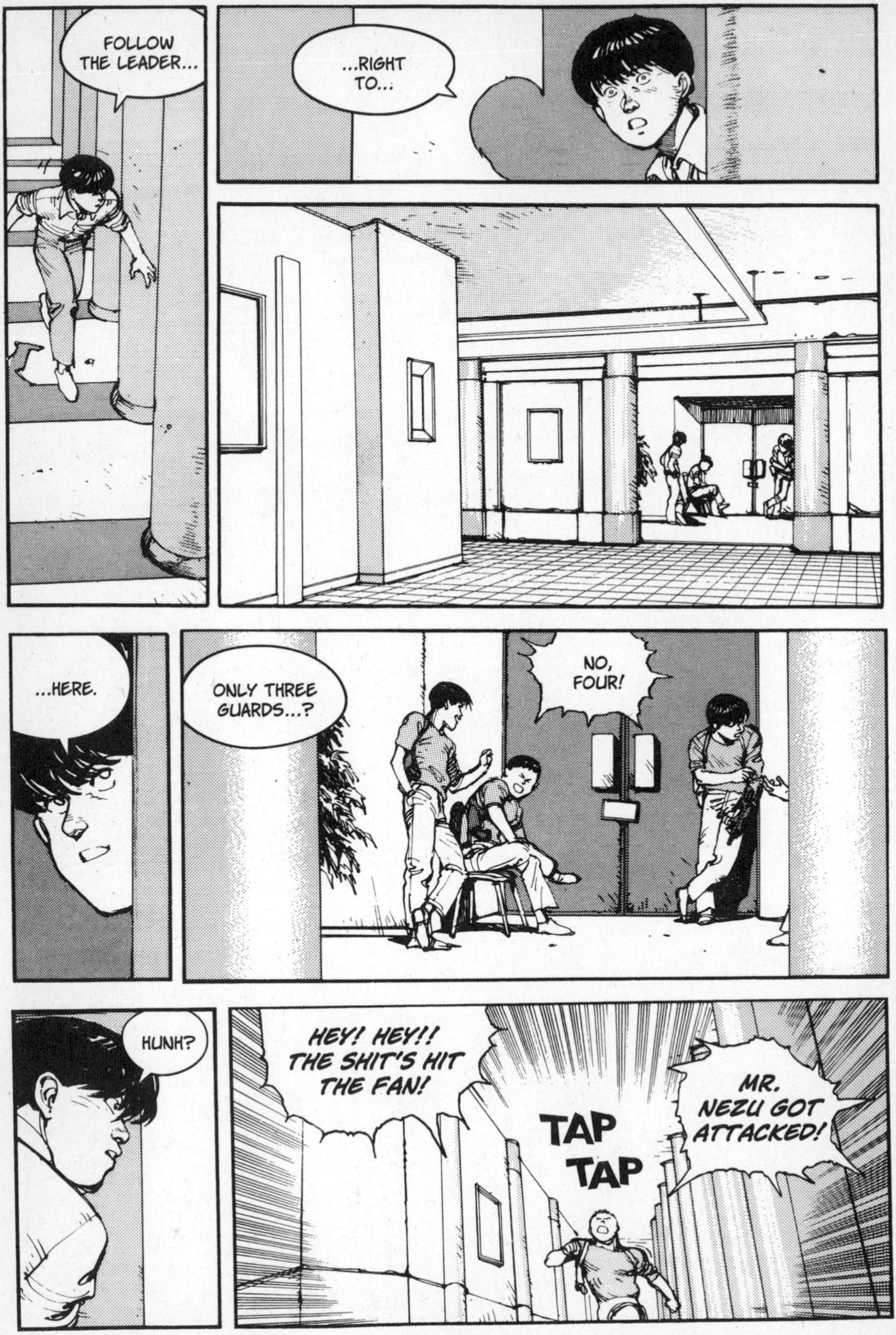

FOLLOW THE LEADER...
...RIGHT TO...
...HERE.
ONLY THREE GUARDS...?
NO, FOUR!
HUNH?
HEY! HEY!! THE SHIT'S HIT THE FAN!
TAP TAP
MR. NEZU GOT ATTACKED!

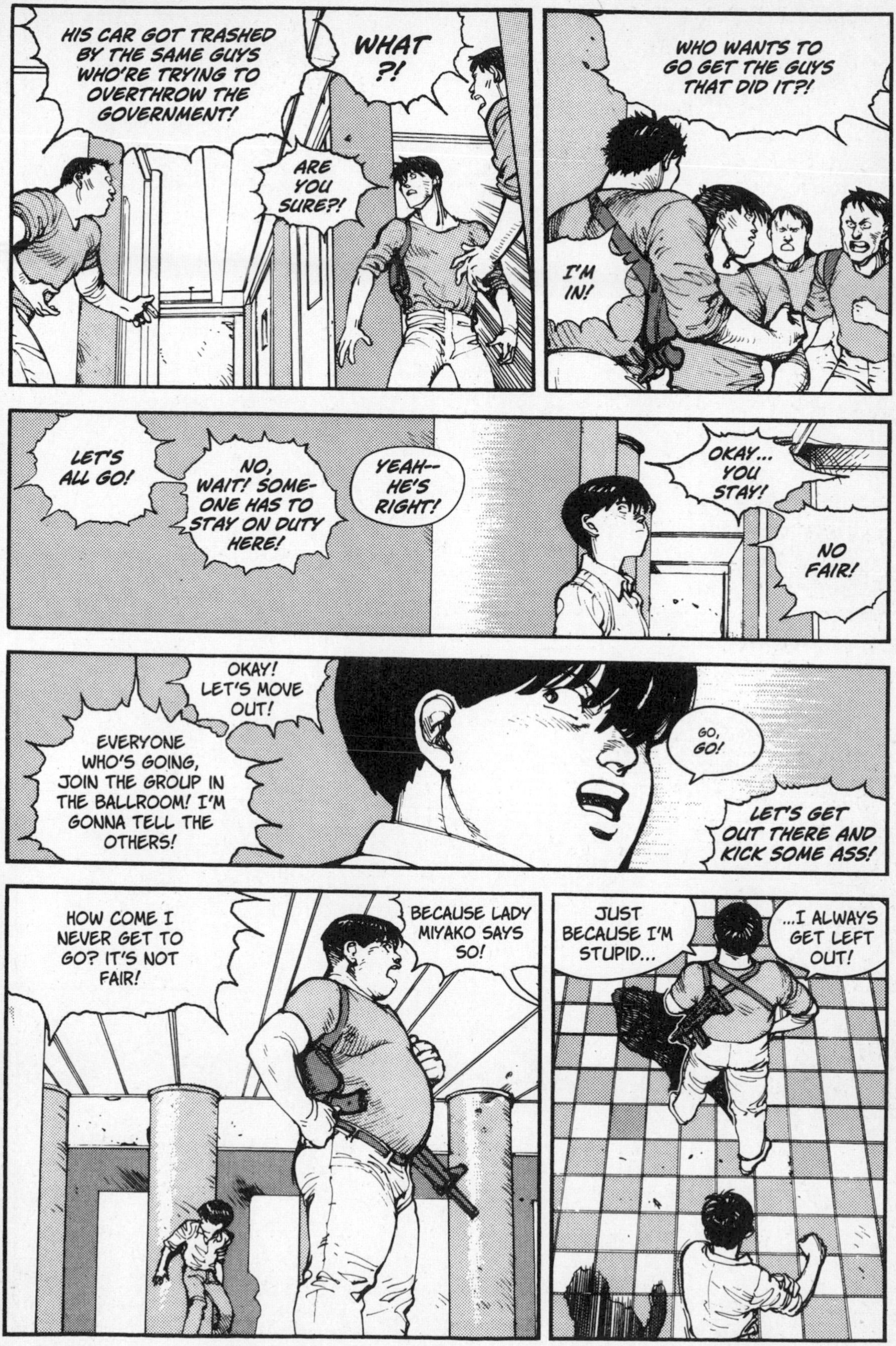

HIS CAR GOT TRASHED BY THE SAME GUYS WHO'RE TRYING TO OVERTHROW THE GOVERNMENT!
WHAT ?!
ARE YOU SURE?!
WHO WANTS TO GO GET THE GUYS THAT DID IT?!
I'M IN!
LET'S ALL GO!
NO, WAIT! SOME-ONE HAS TO STAY ON DUTY HERE!
YEAH-- HE'S RIGHT!
OKAY... YOU STAY!
NO FAIR!
OKAY! LET'S MOVE OUT!
EVERYONE WHO'S GOING, JOIN THE GROUP IN THE BALLROOM! I'M GONNA TELL THE OTHERS!
GO, GO!
LET'S GET OUT THERE AND KICK SOME ASS!
HOW COME I NEVER GET TO GO? IT'S NOT FAIR!
BECAUSE LADY MIYAKO SAYS SO!
JUST BECAUSE I'M STUPID...
...I ALWAYS GET LEFT OUT!

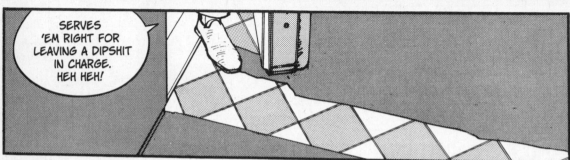

SERVES 'EM RIGHT FOR LEAVING A DIPSHIT IN CHARGE. HEH HEH!

HEY, LITTLE GUY...SORRY TO DISTURB YOUR SLEEP, BUT IT'S TIME TO GO FOR A LITTLE WALK...

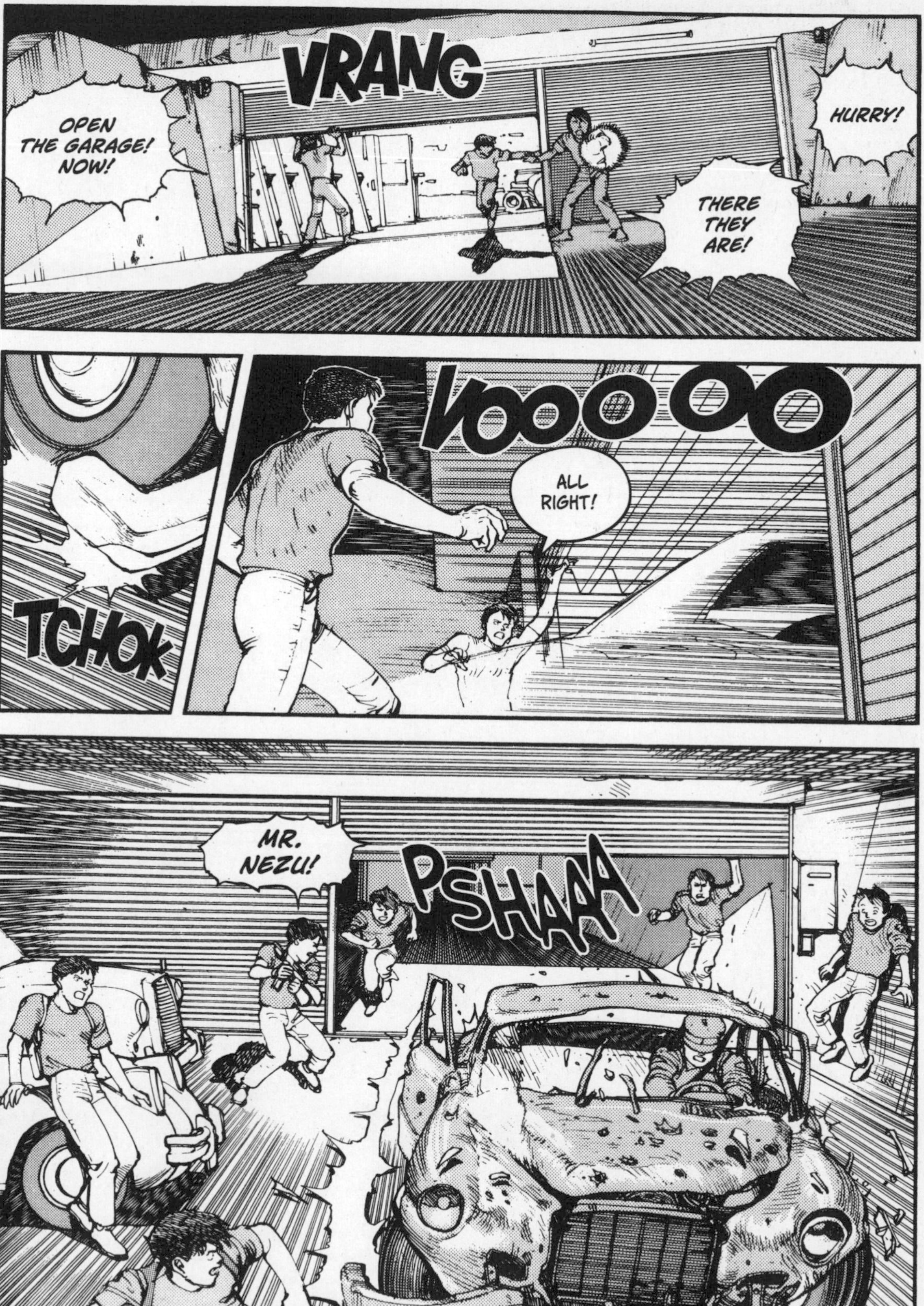
OPEN THE GARAGE! NOW!
VRANG
HURRY!
THERE THEY ARE!
TCHOK
VOOOOO
ALL RIGHT!
MR. NEZU!
PSHAAA

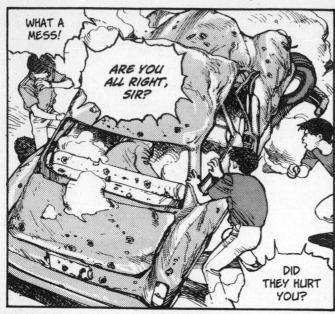

WHAT A MESS!

ARE YOU ALL RIGHT, SIR?

DID THEY HURT YOU?

KRANG

AH... AHN...

WE MUST... TRANSFER AKIRA... IMMEDIATELY!

YESSIR!

GET THE CHOPPER!

AT ONCE!

TCHAK

AUGH!

POOM

WHOA!

134

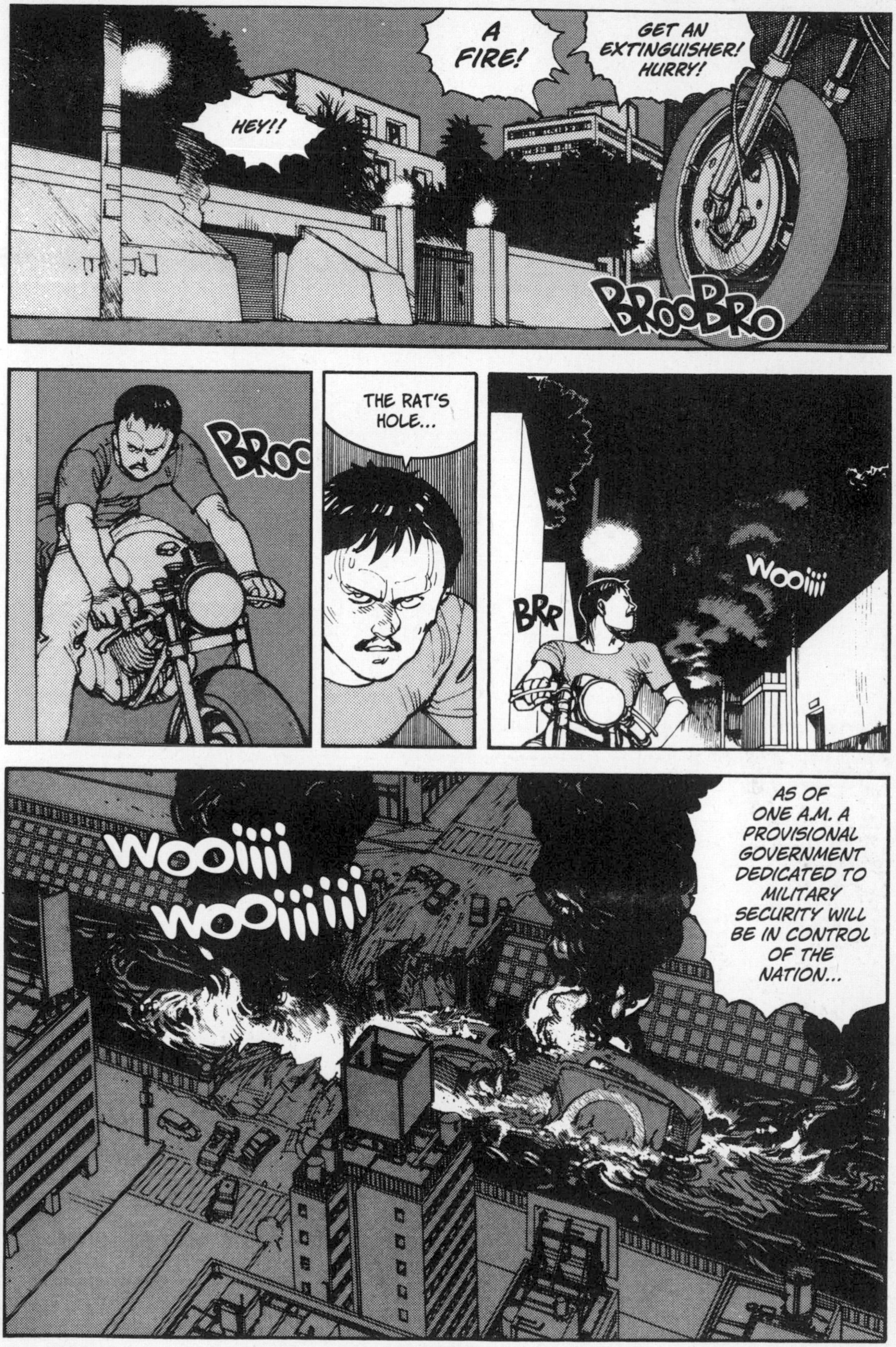
HEY!!
A FIRE!
GET AN EXTINGUISHER! HURRY!
BROOBRO
BROO
THE RAT'S HOLE...
BRR
Wooiiii
WOOiiii
WOOiiiiiii
AS OF ONE A.M. A PROVISIONAL GOVERNMENT DEDICATED TO MILITARY SECURITY WILL BE IN CONTROL OF THE NATION...

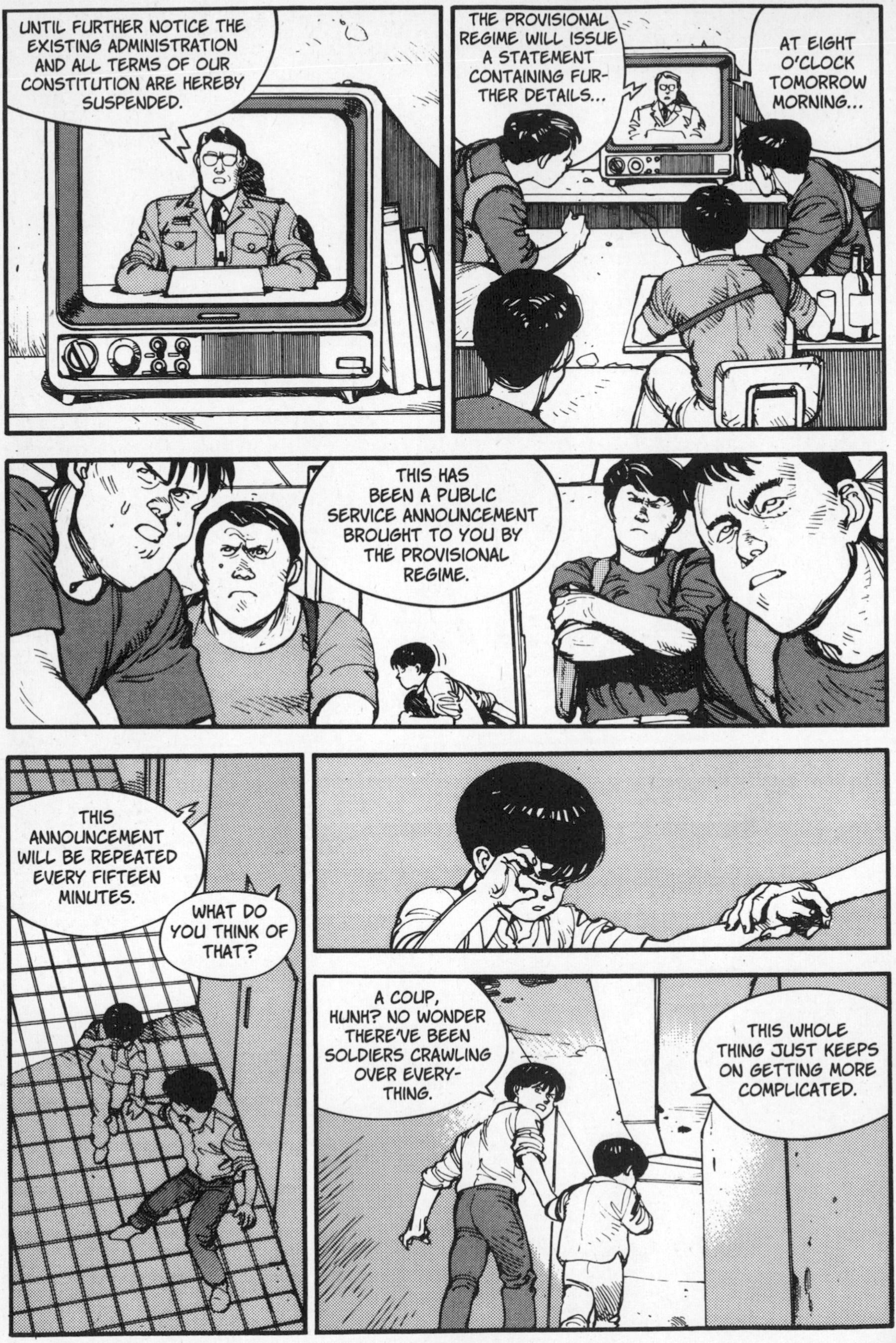
UNTIL FURTHER NOTICE THE EXISTING ADMINISTRATION AND ALL TERMS OF OUR CONSTITUTION ARE HEREBY SUSPENDED.
THE PROVISIONAL REGIME WILL ISSUE A STATEMENT CONTAINING FURTHER DETAILS...
AT EIGHT O'CLOCK TOMORROW MORNING...
THIS HAS BEEN A PUBLIC SERVICE ANNOUNCEMENT BROUGHT TO YOU BY THE PROVISIONAL REGIME.
THIS ANNOUNCEMENT WILL BE REPEATED EVERY FIFTEEN MINUTES.
WHAT DO YOU THINK OF THAT?
A COUP, HUNH? NO WONDER THERE'VE BEEN SOLDIERS CRAWLING OVER EVERYTHING.
THIS WHOLE THING JUST KEEPS ON GETTING MORE COMPLICATED.

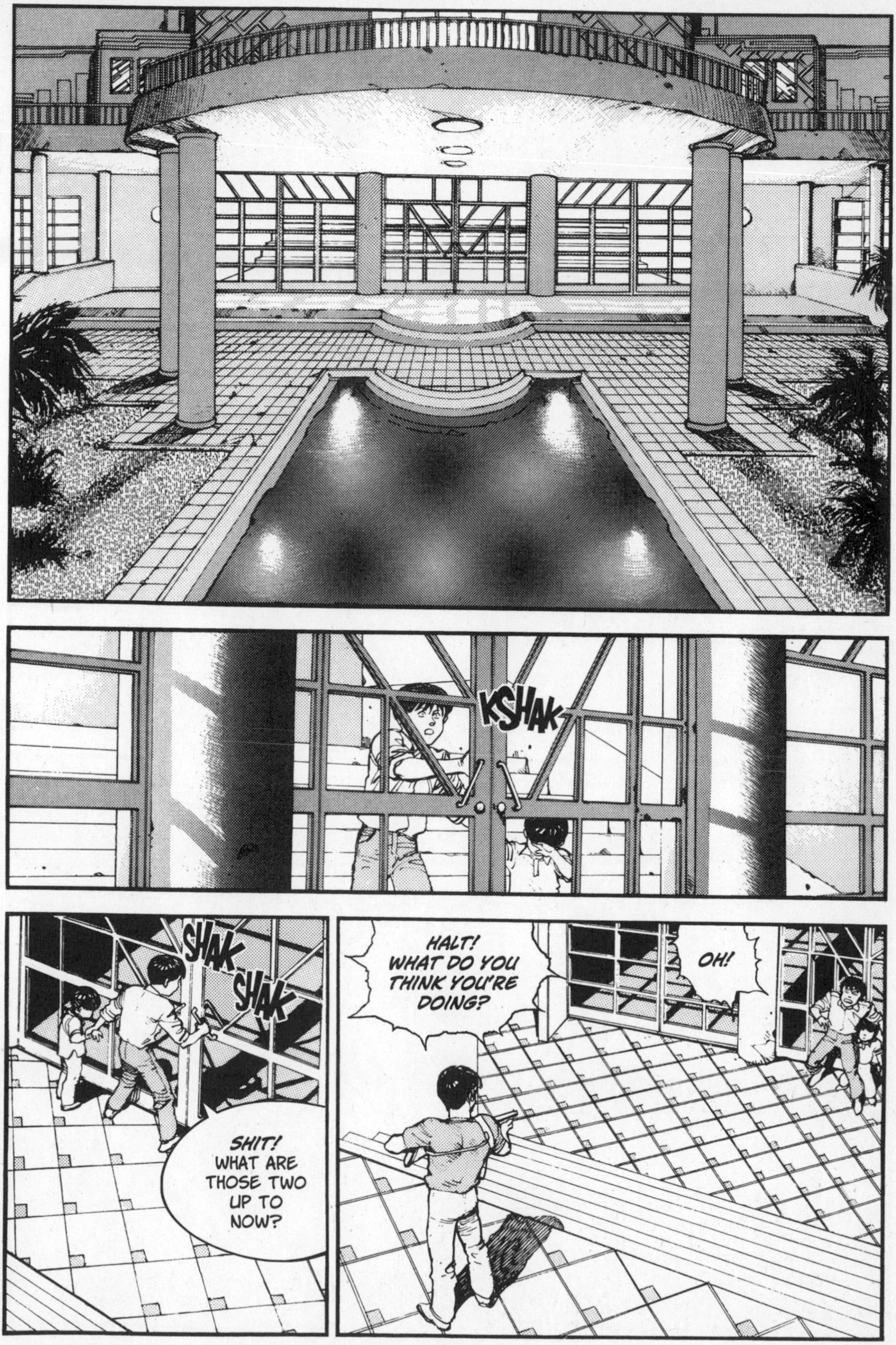
KSHAK
SHAK
SHAK
SHIT! WHAT ARE THOSE TWO UP TO NOW?
HALT! WHAT DO YOU THINK YOU'RE DOING?
OH!

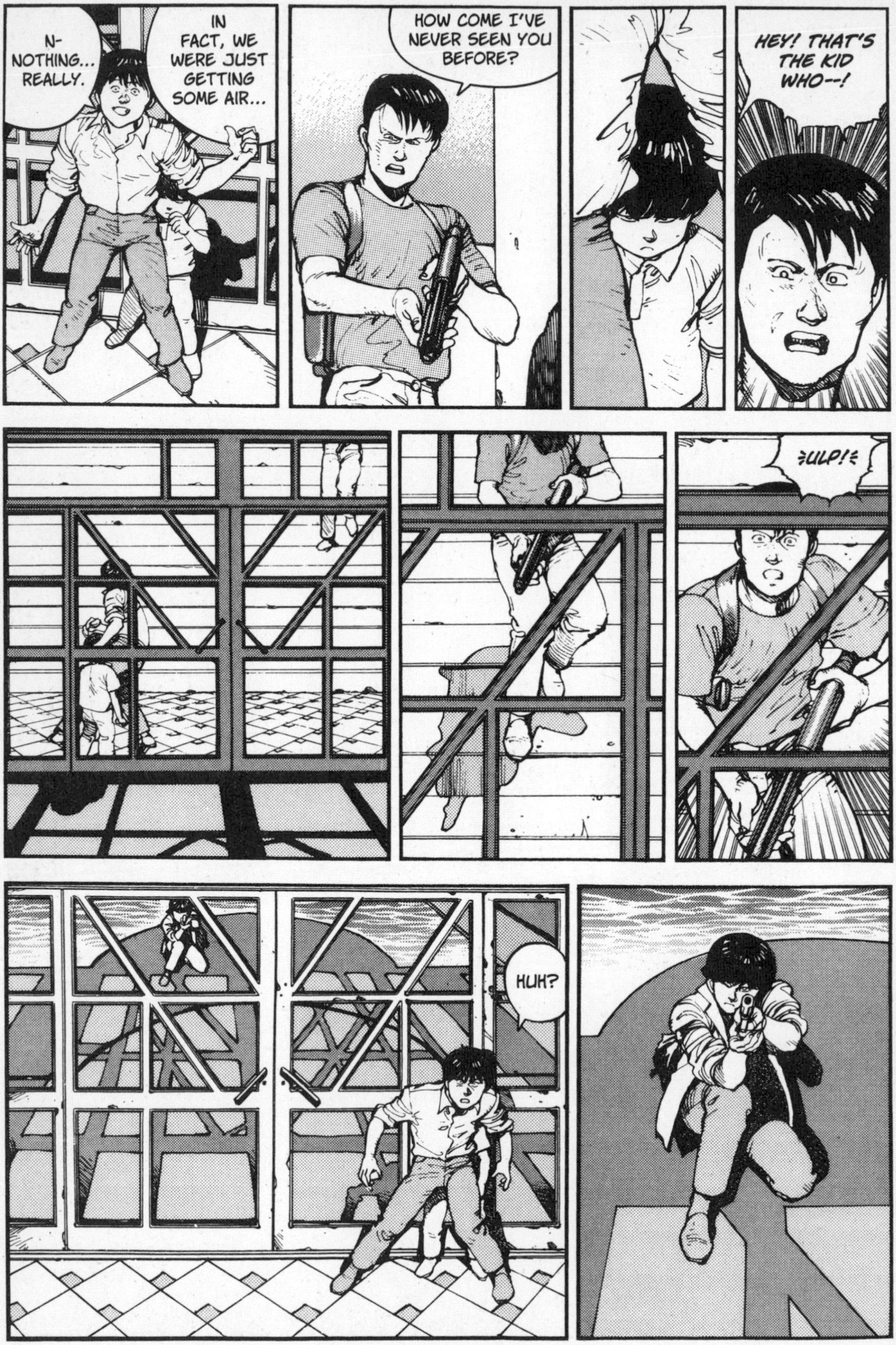
N-NOTHING... REALLY.
IN FACT, WE WERE JUST GETTING SOME AIR...
HOW COME I'VE NEVER SEEN YOU BEFORE?
HEY! THAT'S THE KID WHO--!
ULP!
HUH?

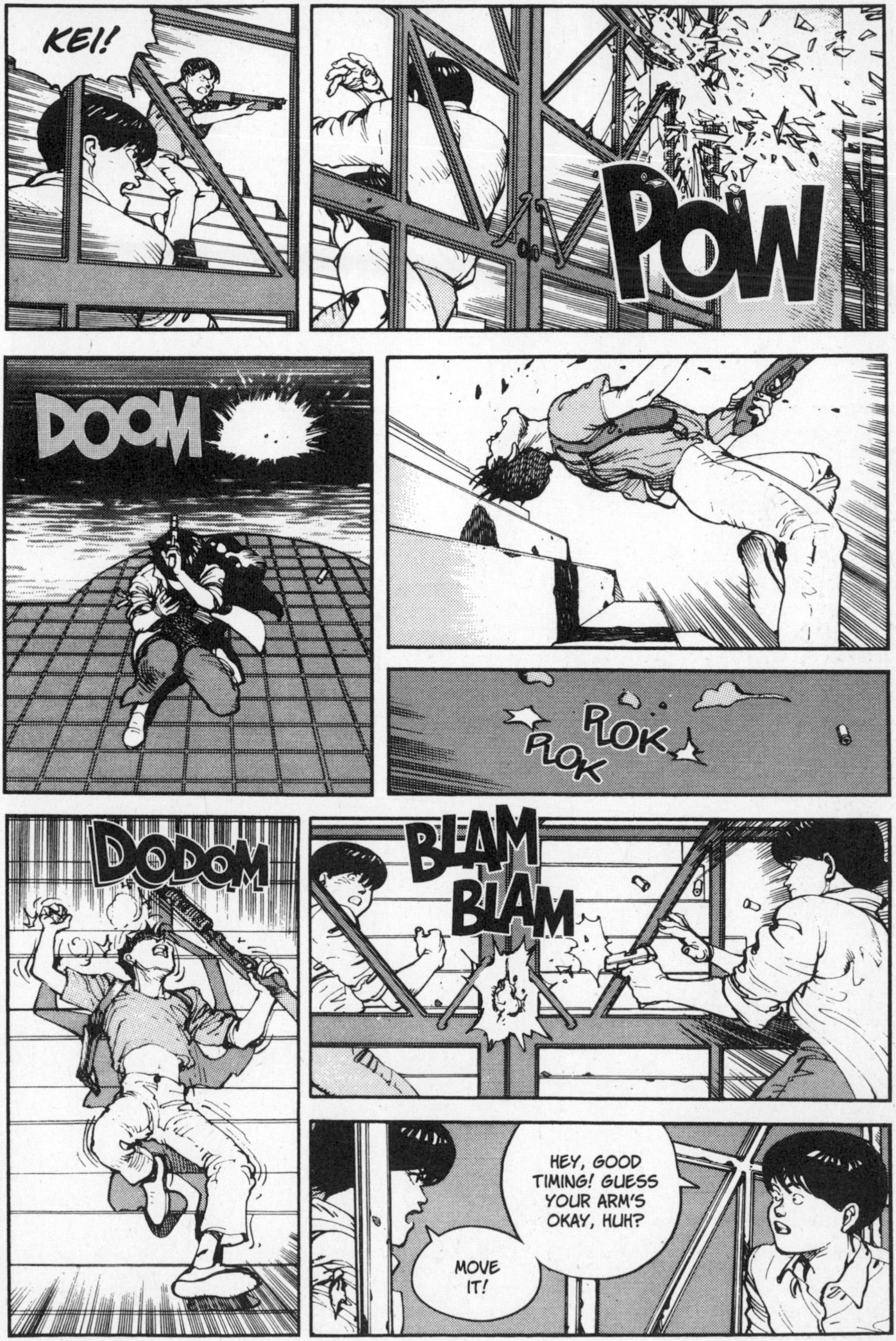
KEI!
POW
DOOM
PLOK
PLOK
DODOM
BLAM
BLAM
HEY, GOOD TIMING! GUESS YOUR ARM'S OKAY, HUH?
MOVE IT!

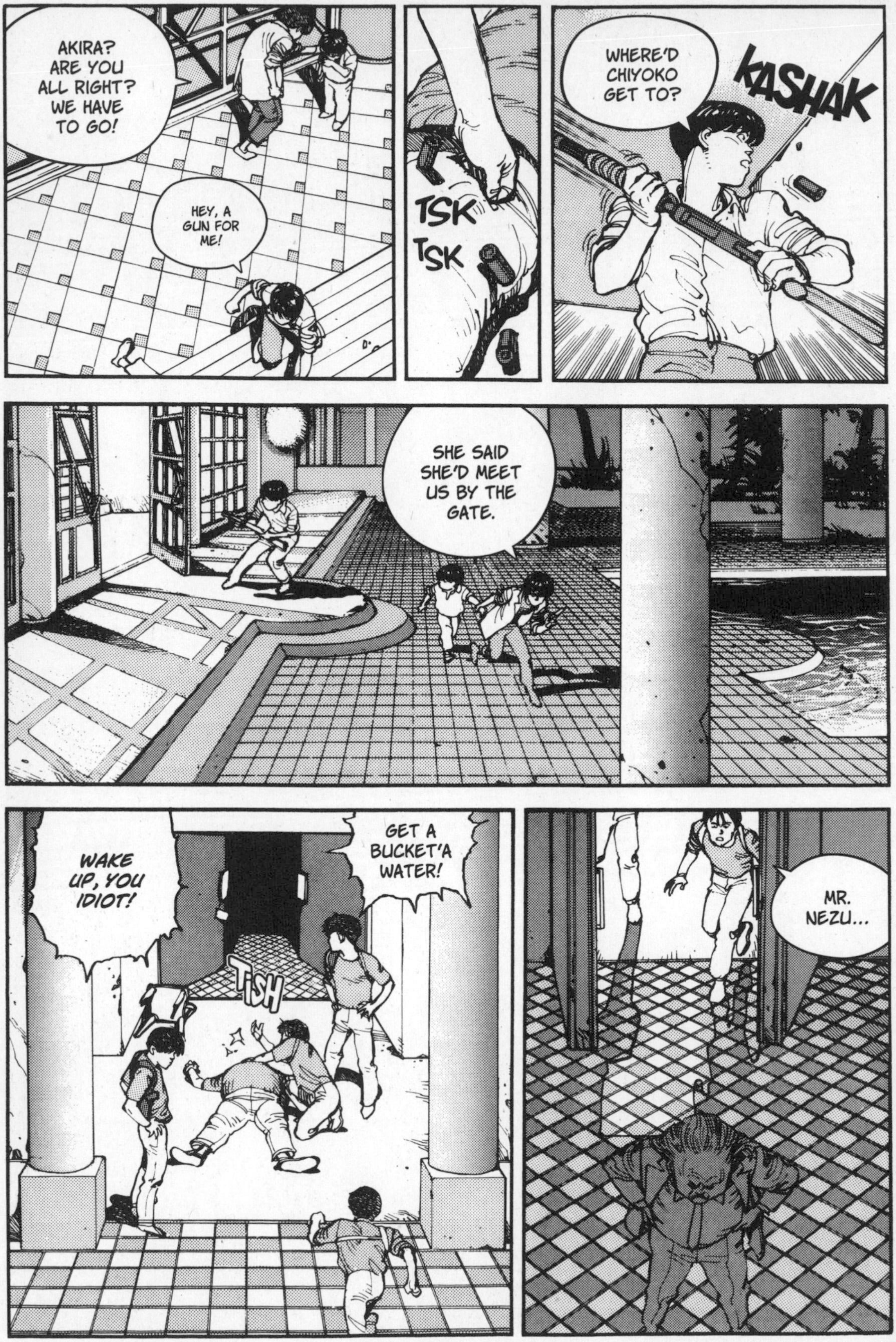
AKIRA? ARE YOU ALL RIGHT? WE HAVE TO GO!
HEY, A GUN FOR ME!
TSK
TSK
WHERE'D CHIYOKO GET TO?
KASHAK
SHE SAID SHE'D MEET US BY THE GATE.
WAKE UP, YOU IDIOT!
GET A BUCKET'A WATER!
TISH
MR. NEZU...

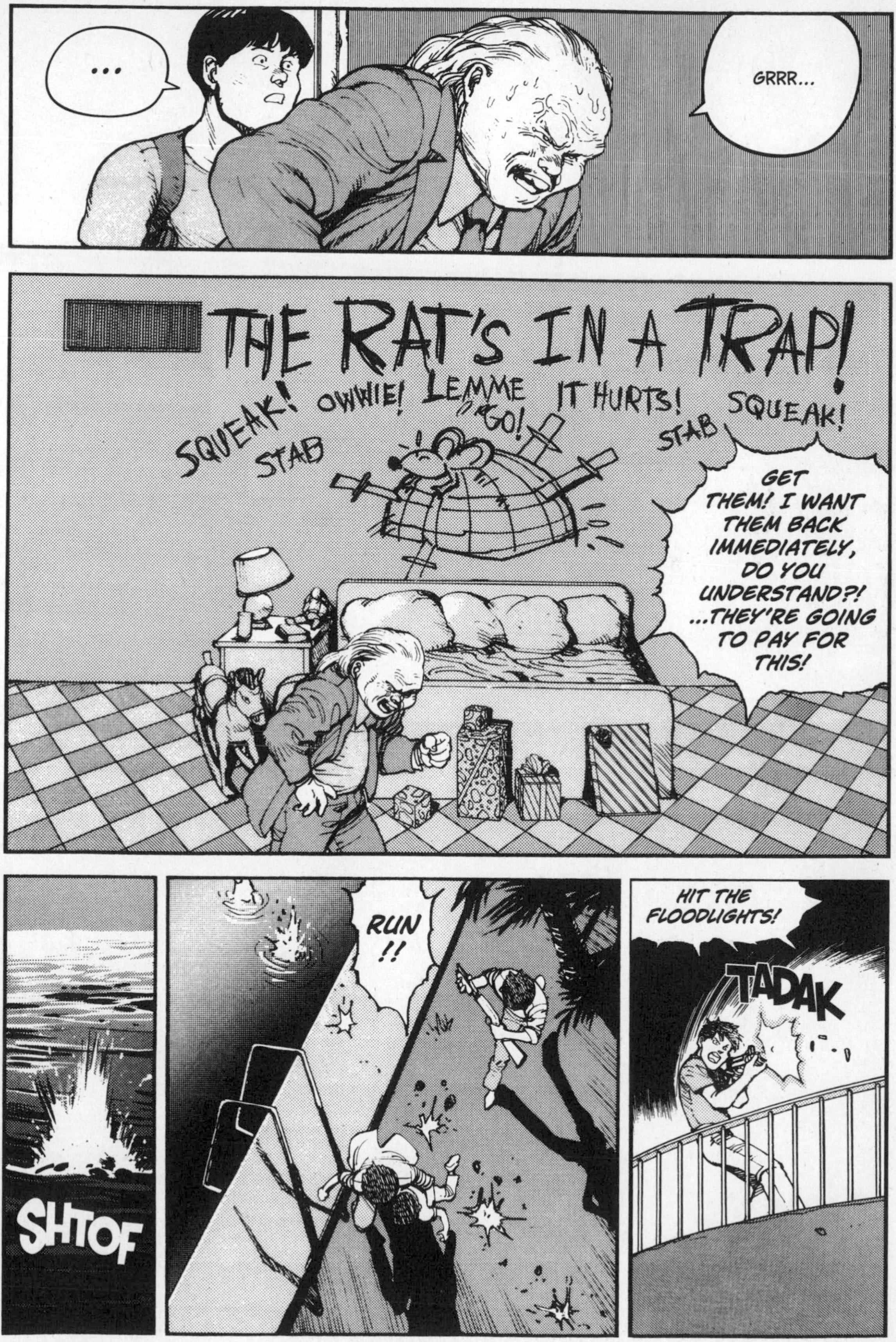
...
GRRR...
THE RAT'S IN A TRAP!
SQUEAK!
OWWIE!
LEMME GO!
STAB
IT HURTS!
STAB
SQUEAK!
GET THEM! I WANT THEM BACK IMMEDIATELY, DO YOU UNDERSTAND?! ...THEY'RE GOING TO PAY FOR THIS!
SHTOF
RUN !!
HIT THE FLOODLIGHTS!
TADAK

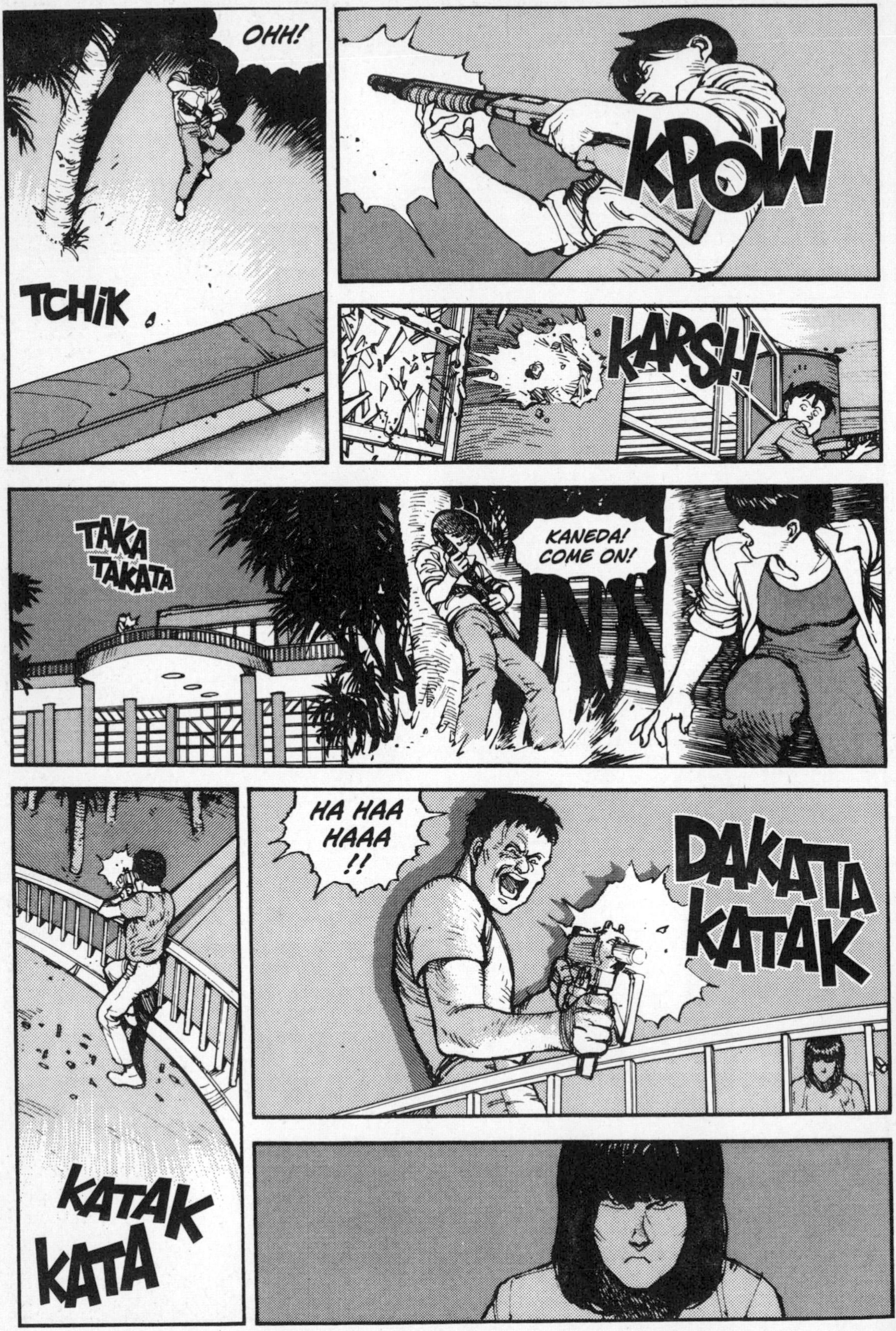
OHH!
TCHIK
KPOW
KARSH
TAKA TAKATA
KANEDA! COME ON!
KATAK KATA
HA HAA HAAA !!
DAKATA KATAK

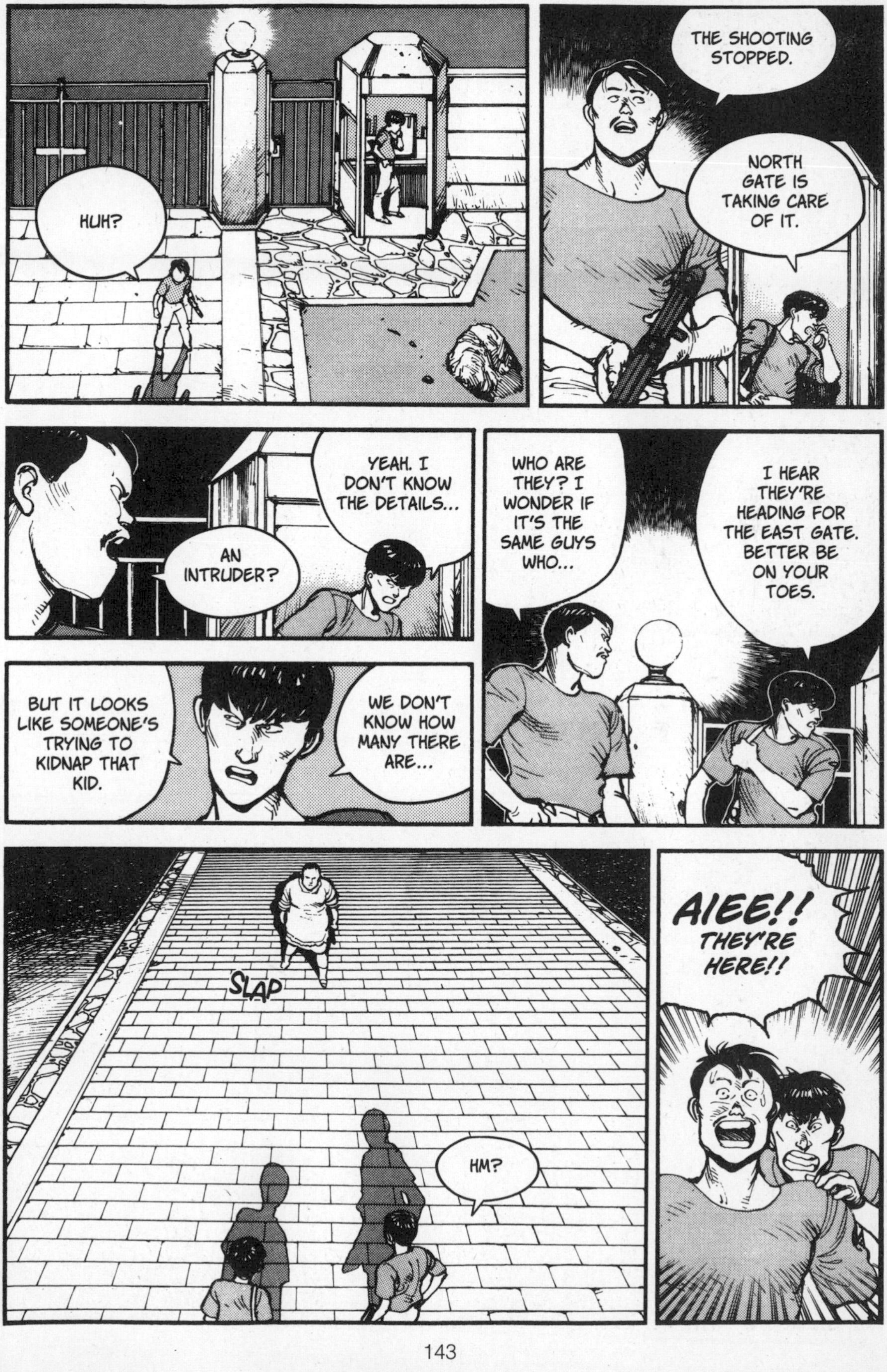
HUH?
THE SHOOTING STOPPED.
NORTH GATE IS TAKING CARE OF IT.
YEAH. I DON'T KNOW THE DETAILS...
AN INTRUDER?
WHO ARE THEY? I WONDER IF IT'S THE SAME GUYS WHO...
I HEAR THEY'RE HEADING FOR THE EAST GATE. BETTER BE ON YOUR TOES.
BUT IT LOOKS LIKE SOMEONE'S TRYING TO KIDNAP THAT KID.
WE DON'T KNOW HOW MANY THERE ARE...
SLAP
HM?
AIEE!! THEY'RE HERE!!

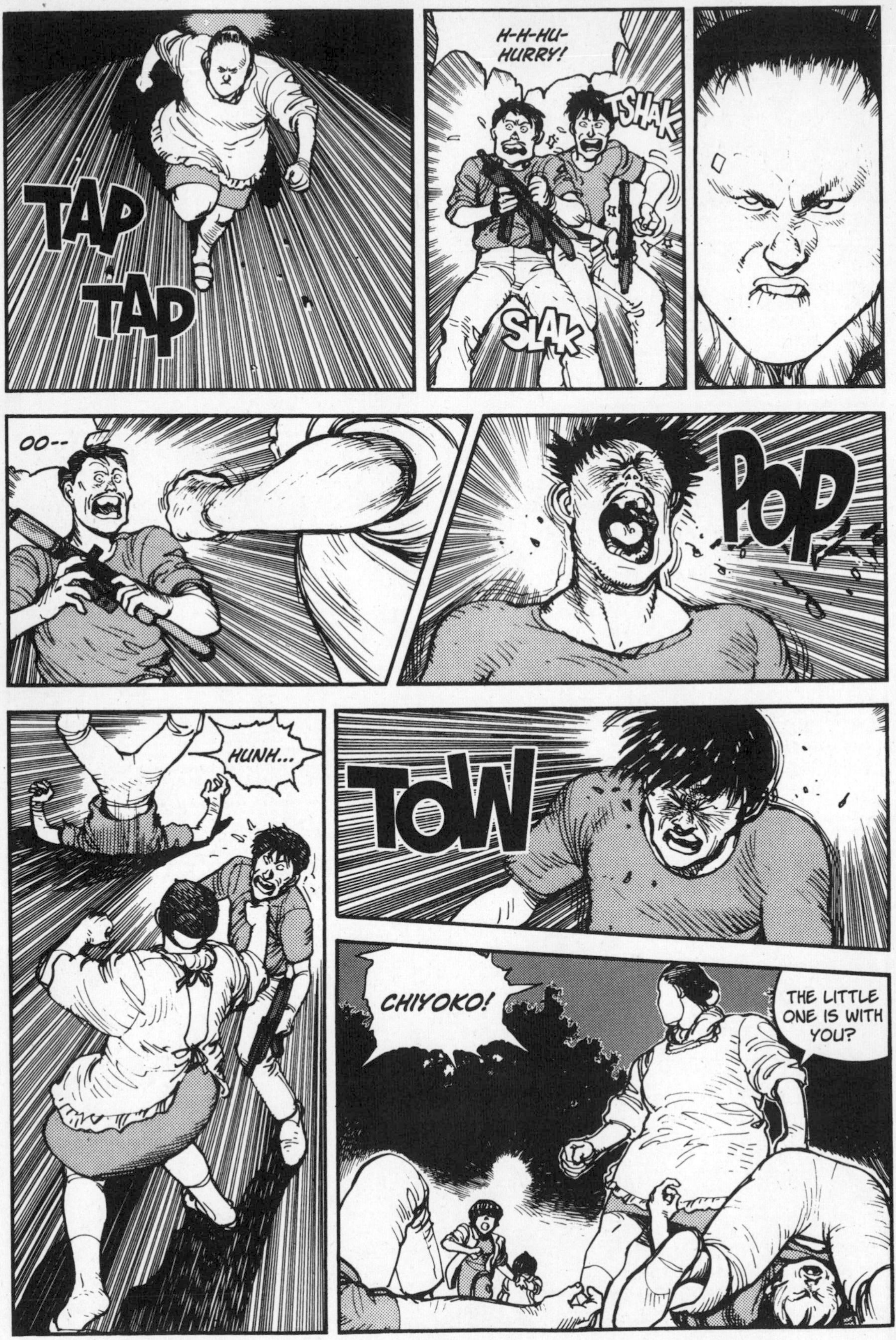
TAP
TAP
H-H-HU-
HURRY!
TSHAK
SLAK
OO--
POP
HUNH...
TOW
CHIYOKO!
THE LITTLE ONE IS WITH YOU?

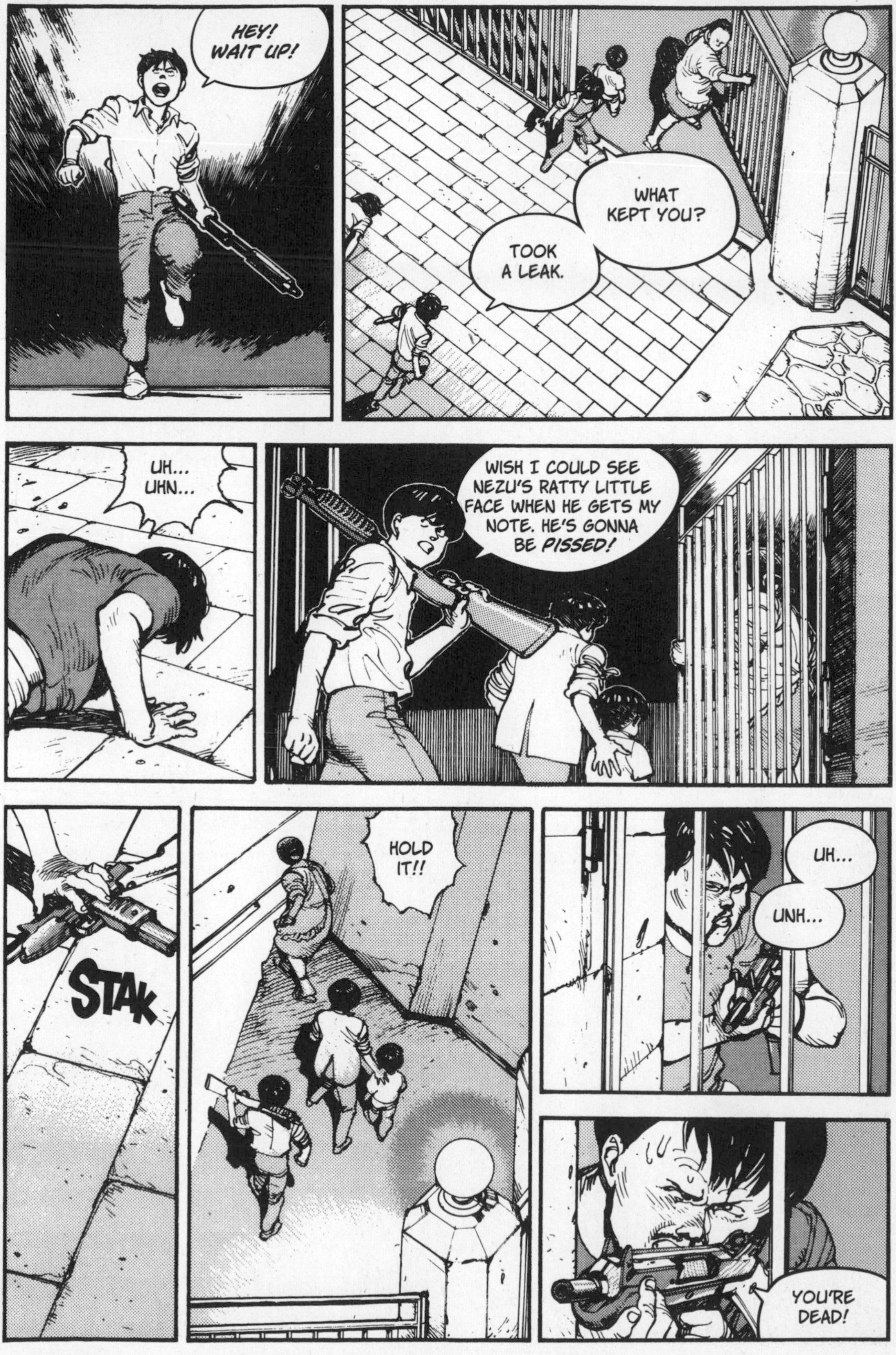
HEY! WAIT UP!
WHAT KEPT YOU?
TOOK A LEAK.
UH... UHN...
WISH I COULD SEE NEZU'S RATTY LITTLE FACE WHEN HE GETS MY NOTE. HE'S GONNA BE PISSED!
STAK
HOLD IT!!
UH...
UNH...
YOU'RE DEAD!

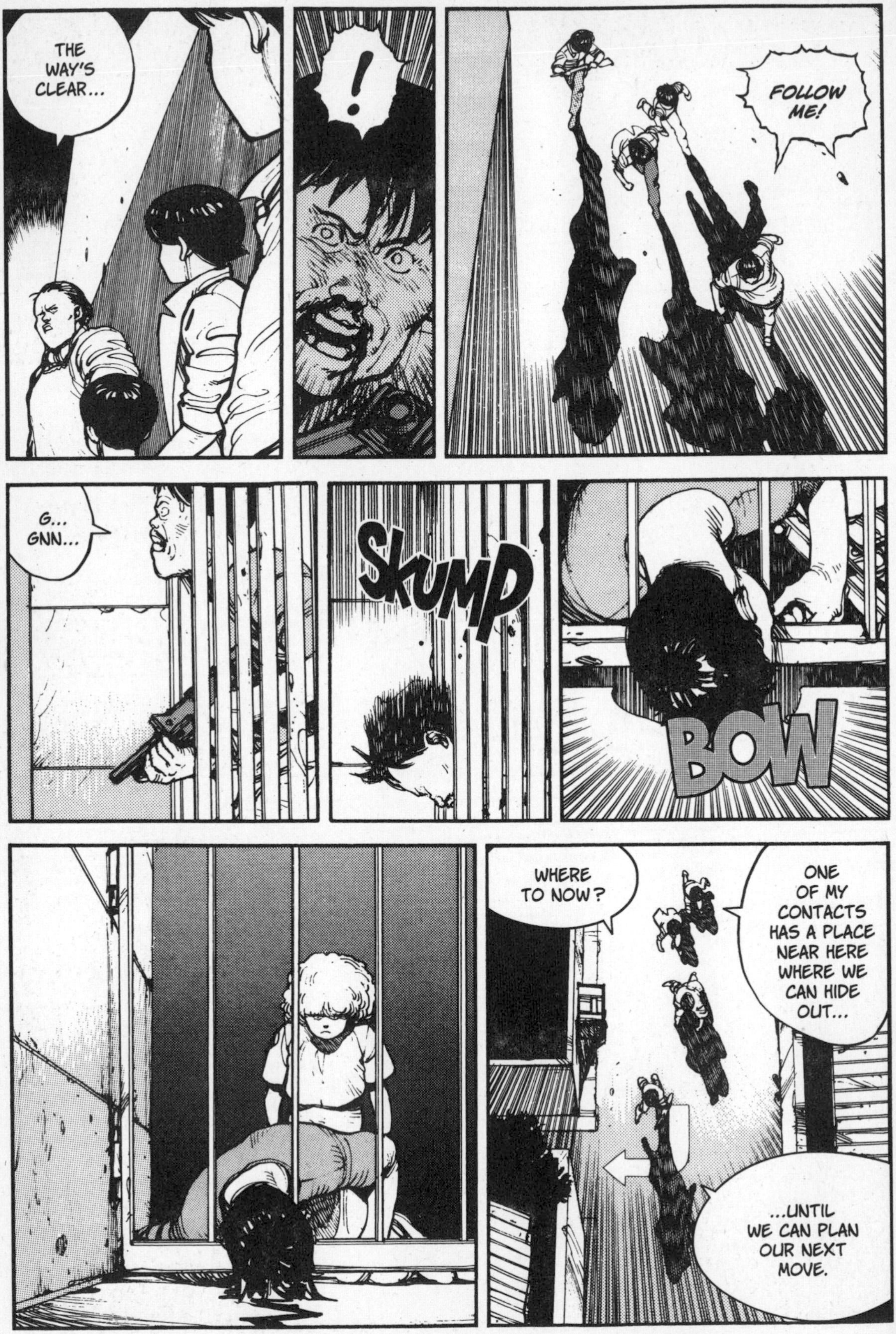
THE WAY'S CLEAR...
!
FOLLOW ME!
G... GNN...
SKUMP
BOW
WHERE TO NOW?
ONE OF MY CONTACTS HAS A PLACE NEAR HERE WHERE WE CAN HIDE OUT...
...UNTIL WE CAN PLAN OUR NEXT MOVE.

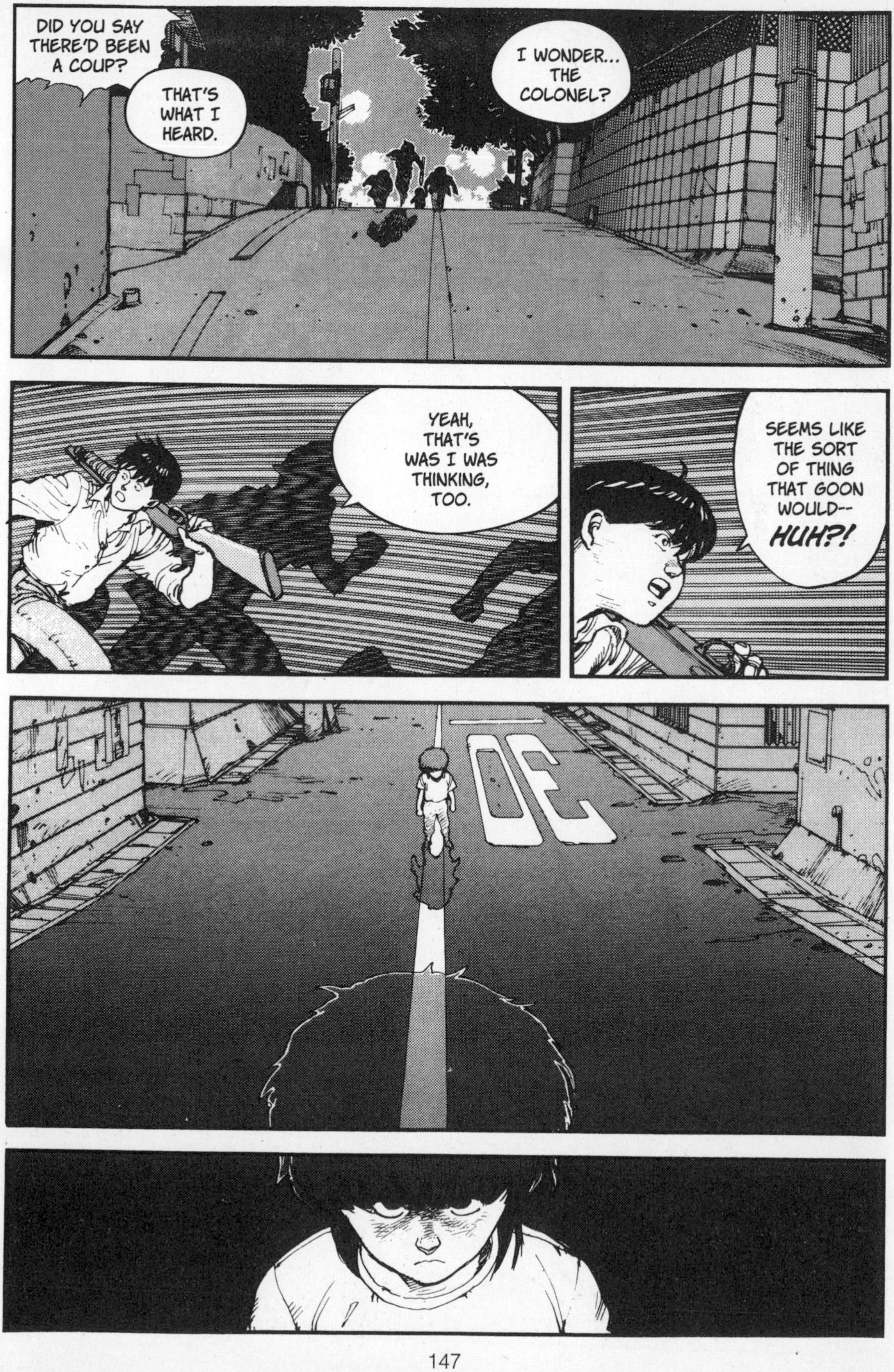
DID YOU SAY THERE'D BEEN A COUP?
THAT'S WHAT I HEARD.
I WONDER... THE COLONEL?
YEAH, THAT'S WAS I WAS THINKING, TOO.
SEEMS LIKE THE SORT OF THING THAT GOON WOULD-- HUH?!

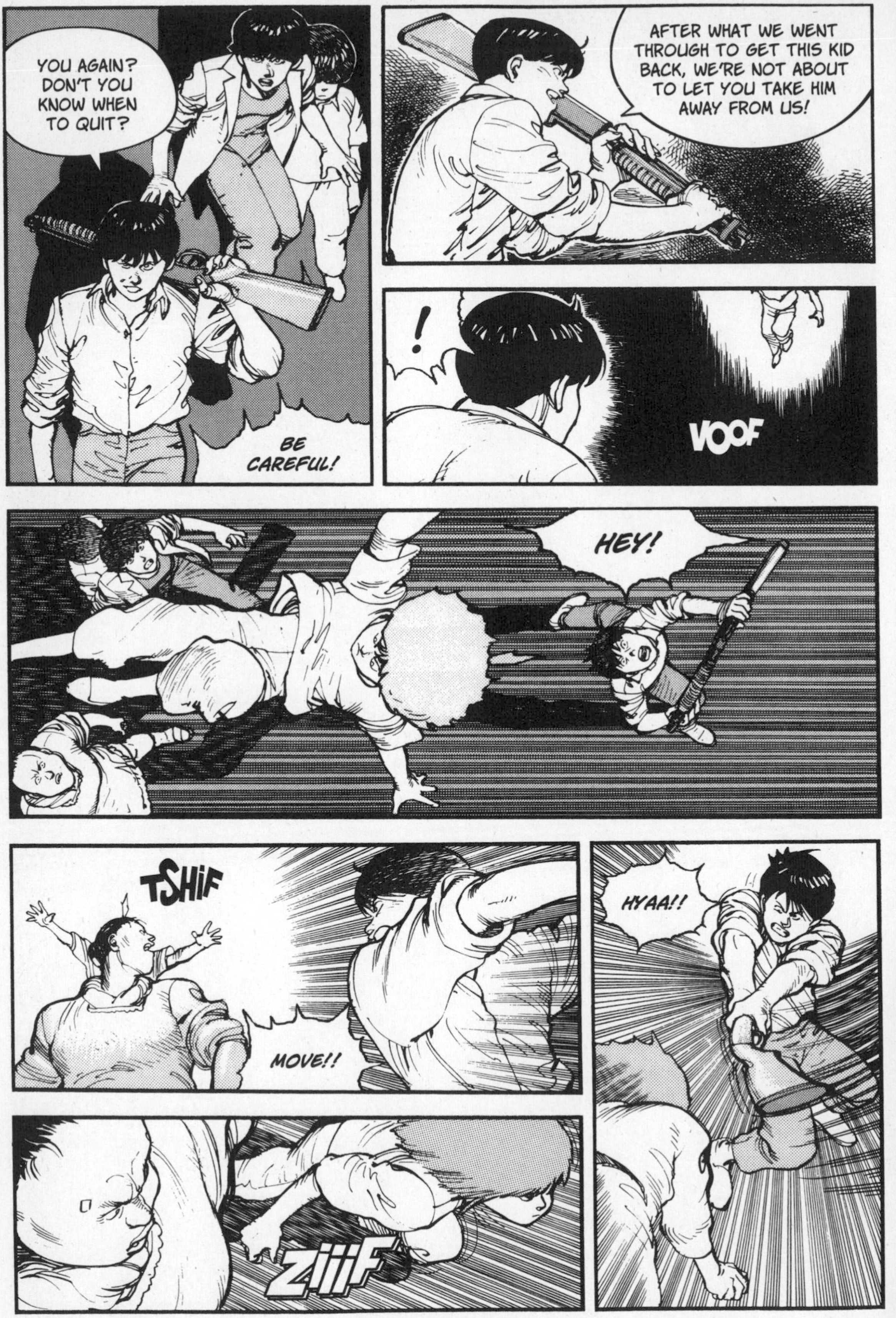

YOU AGAIN? DON'T YOU KNOW WHEN TO QUIT?
BE CAREFUL!
AFTER WHAT WE WENT THROUGH TO GET THIS KID BACK, WE'RE NOT ABOUT TO LET YOU TAKE HIM AWAY FROM US!
!
VOOF
HEY!
TSHIF
MOVE!!
HYAA!!
ZIIIF

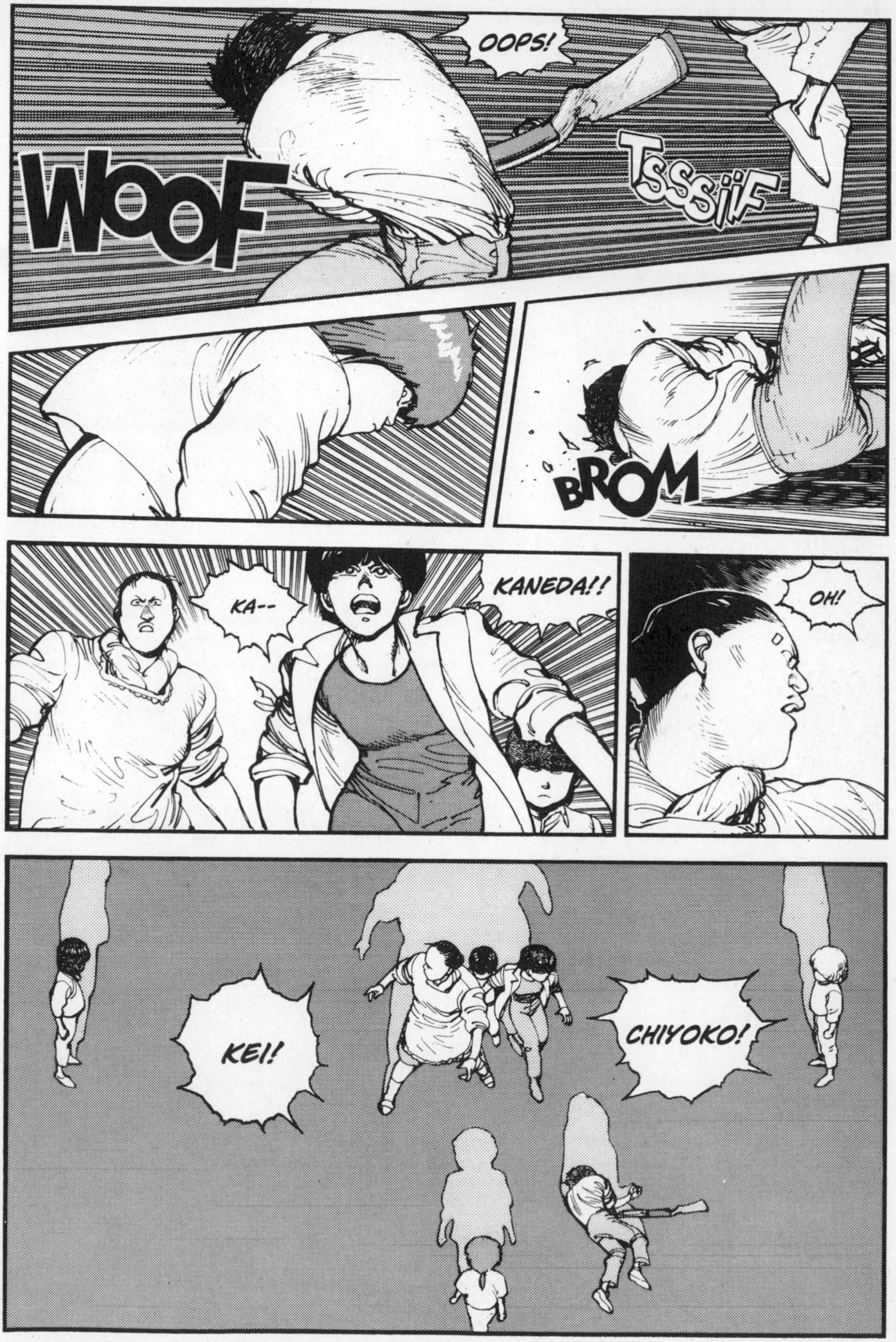
OOPS!
WOOF
TSSSIIF
BROM
KA--
KANEDA!!
OH!
KEI!
CHIYOKO!

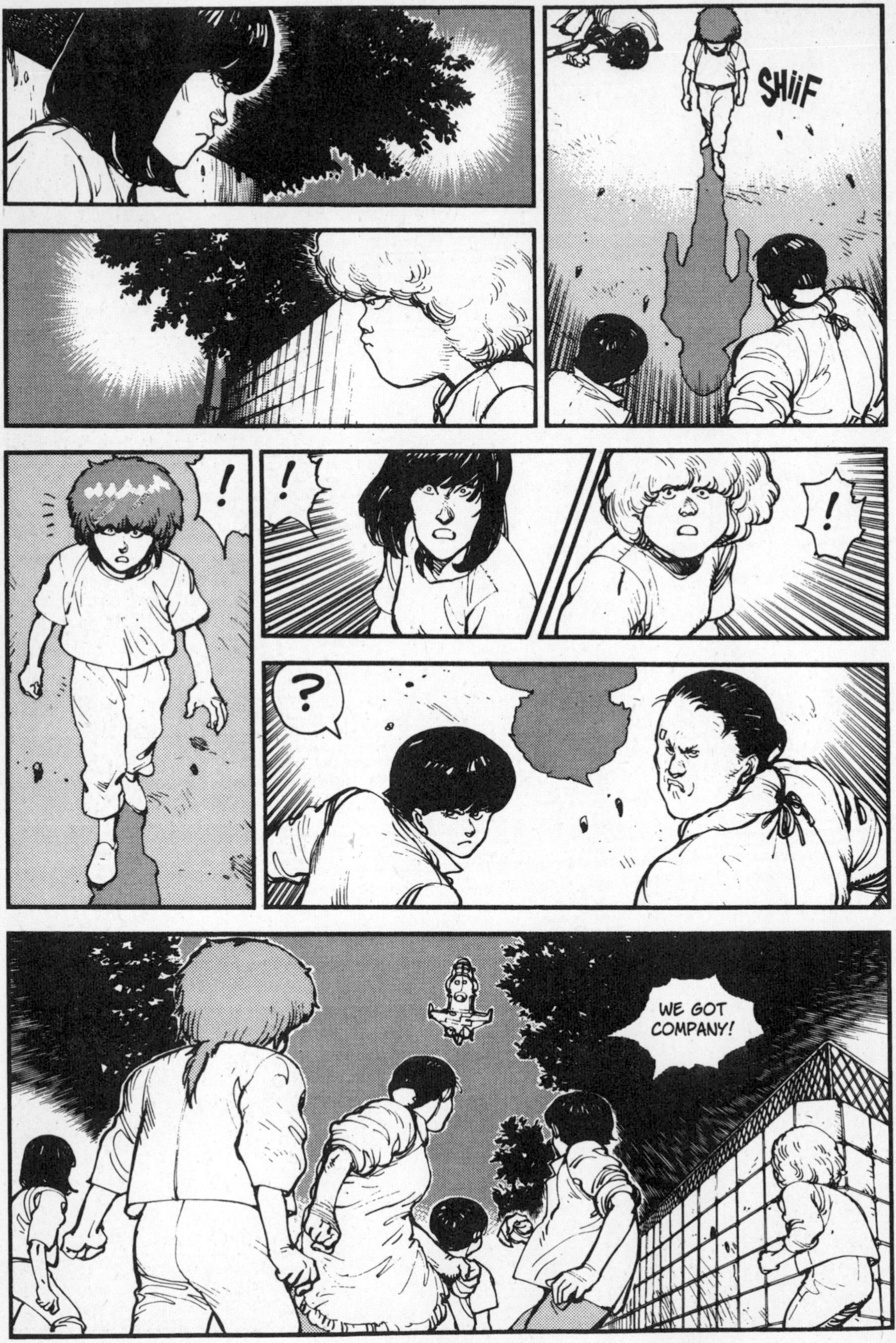
SHIIF
!
!
!
?
WE GOT COMPANY!

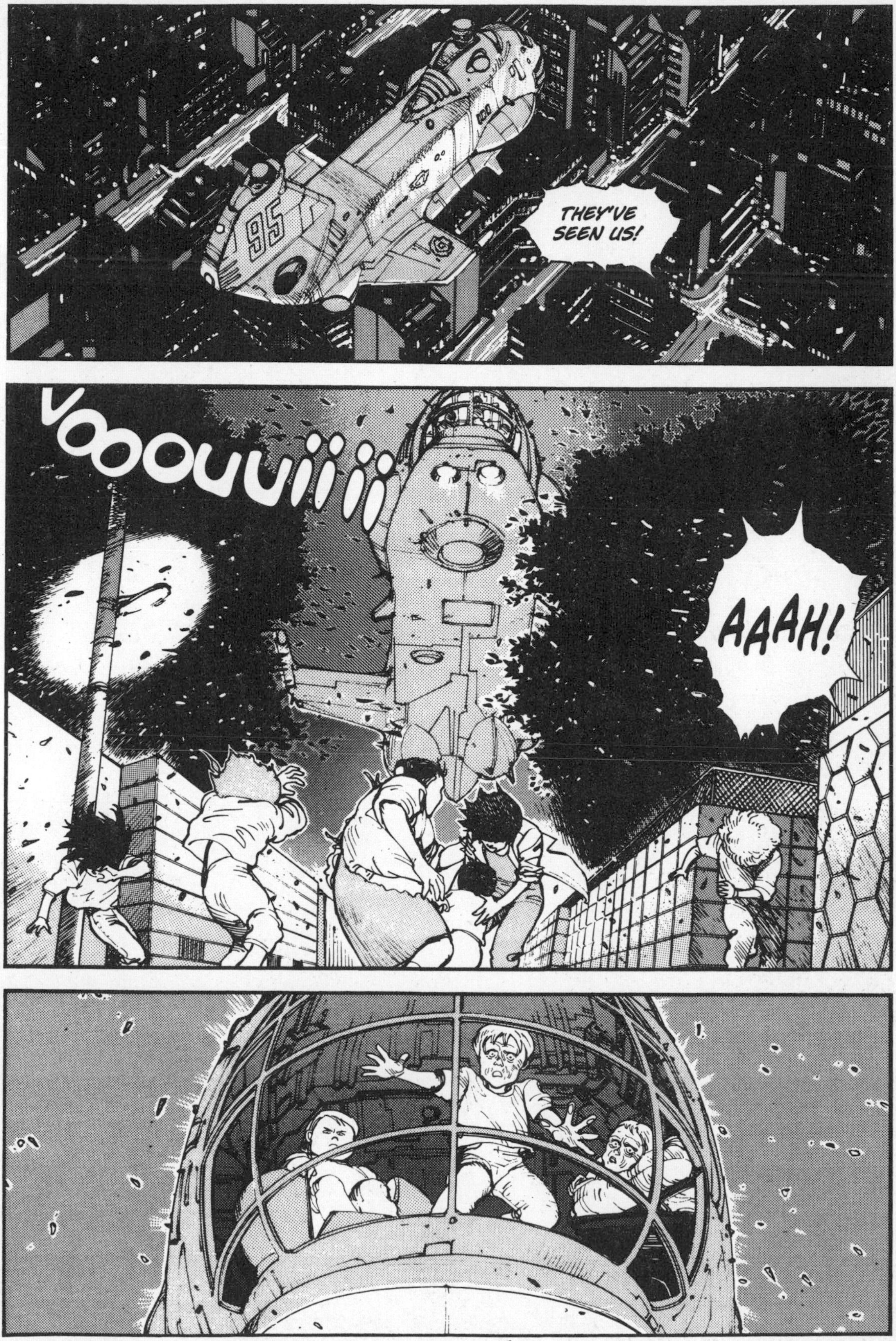
THEY'VE SEEN US!
VOOOUIIII
AAAH!

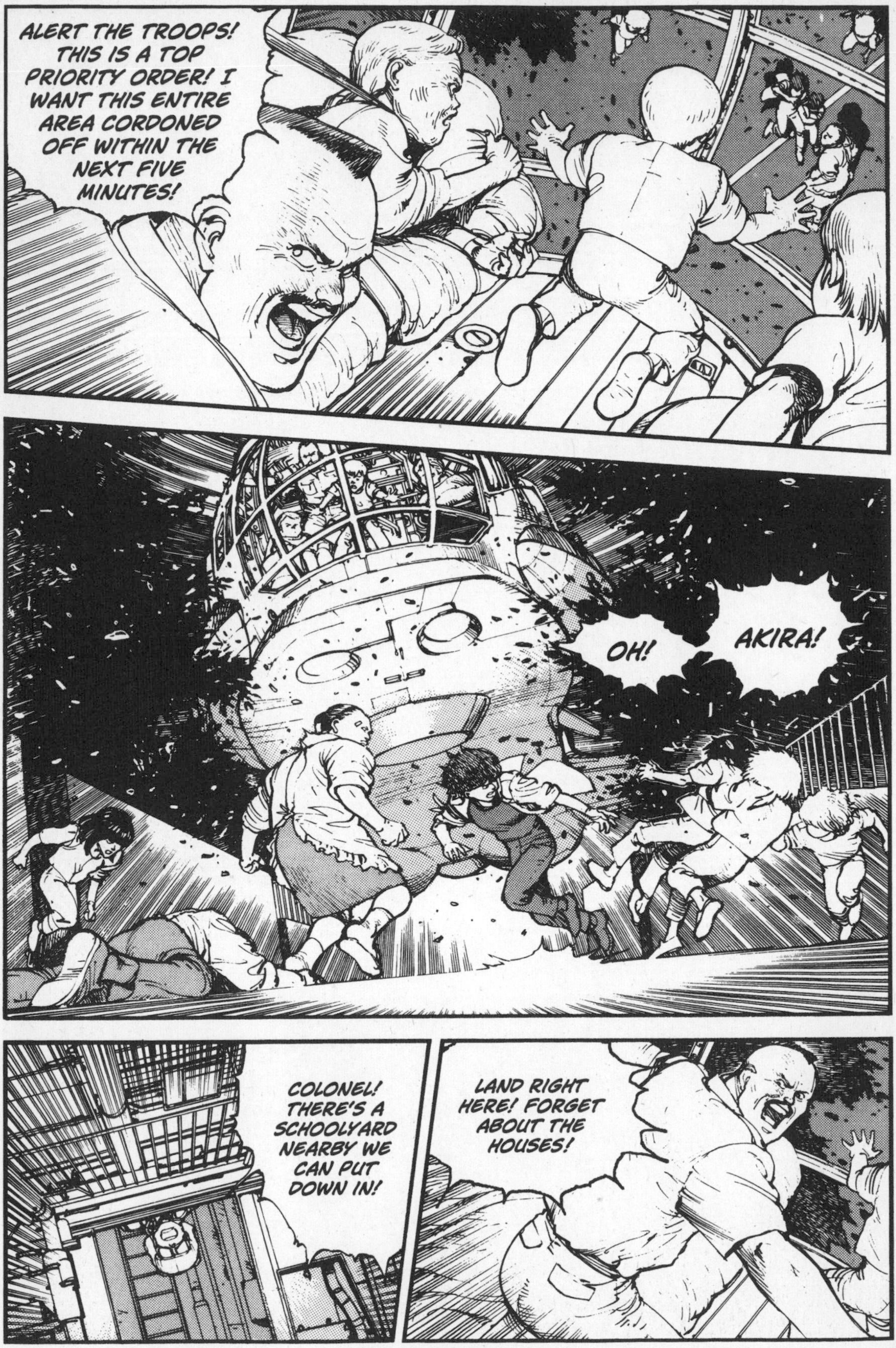
ALERT THE TROOPS! THIS IS A TOP PRIORITY ORDER! I WANT THIS ENTIRE AREA CORDONED OFF WITHIN THE NEXT FIVE MINUTES!
OH!
AKIRA!
COLONEL! THERE'S A SCHOOLYARD NEARBY WE CAN PUT DOWN IN!
LAND RIGHT HERE! FORGET ABOUT THE HOUSES!

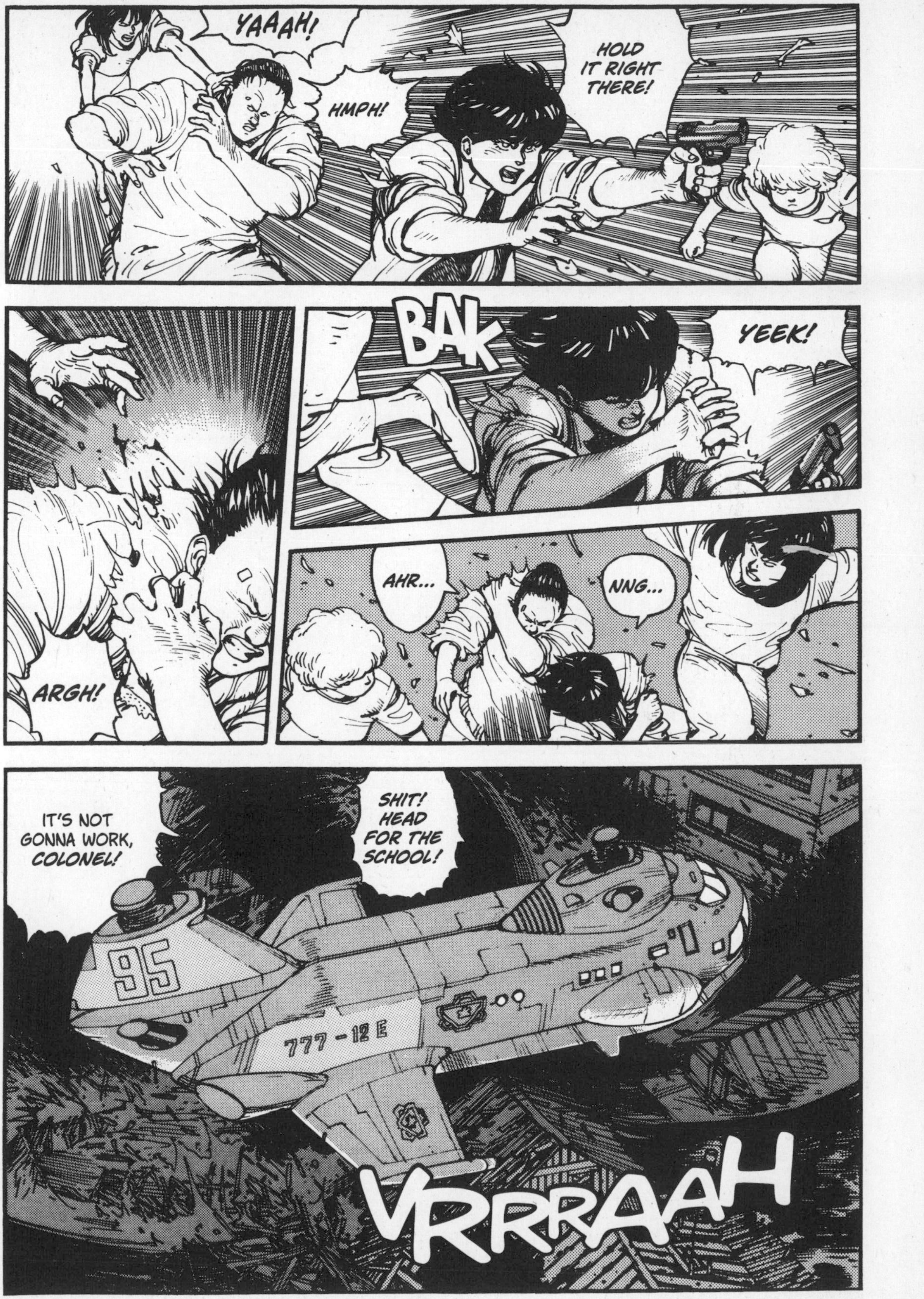
YAAAH!
HMPH!
HOLD IT RIGHT THERE!
ARGH!
BAK
YEEK!
AHR...
NNG...
IT'S NOT GONNA WORK, COLONEL!
SHIT! HEAD FOR THE SCHOOL!
95
777-12E
VRRRAAH

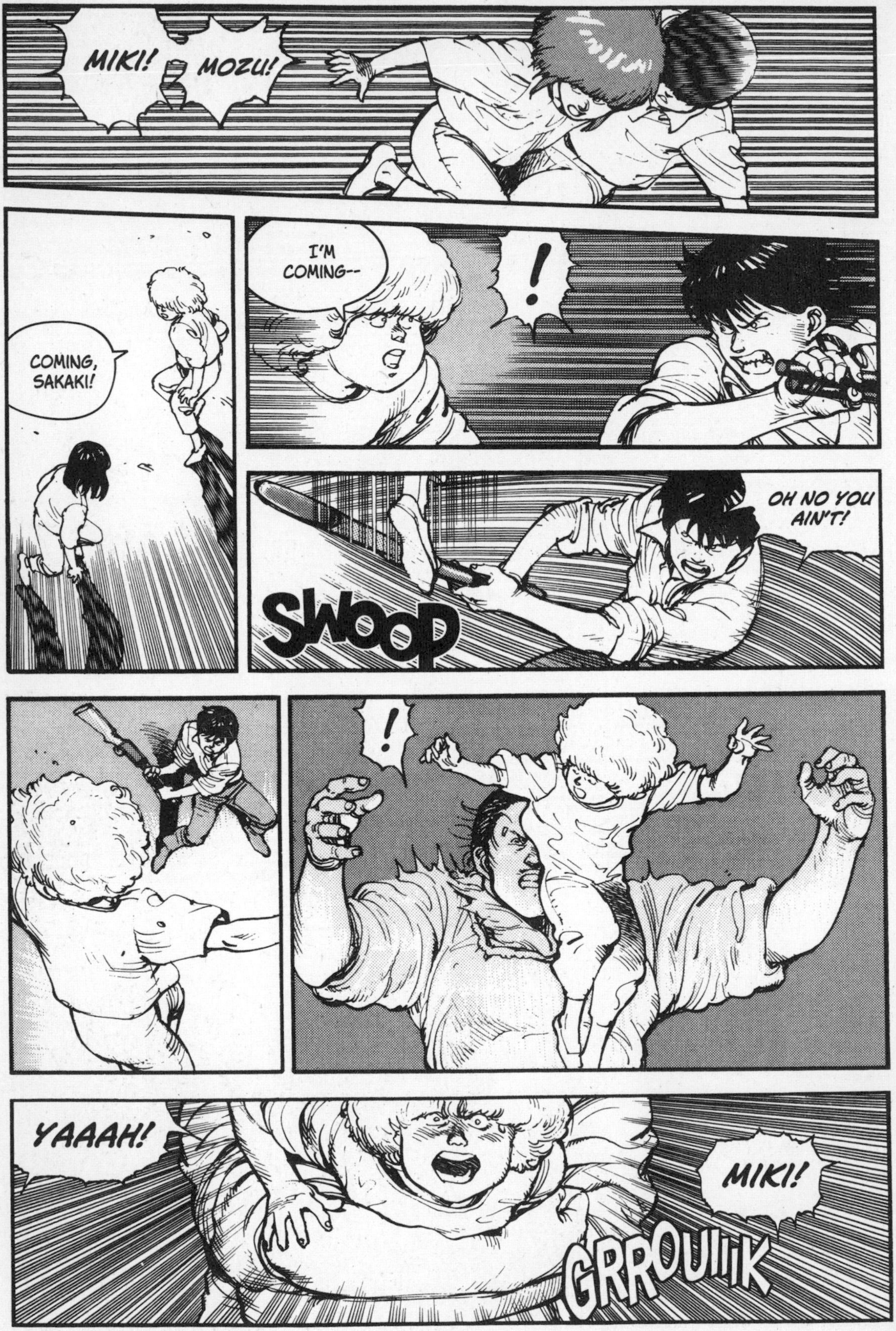

MIKI!
MOZU!
COMING, SAKAKI!
I'M COMING--
!
SWOOP
OH NO YOU AIN'T!
!
YAAAH!
MIKI!
GRROUIIIK

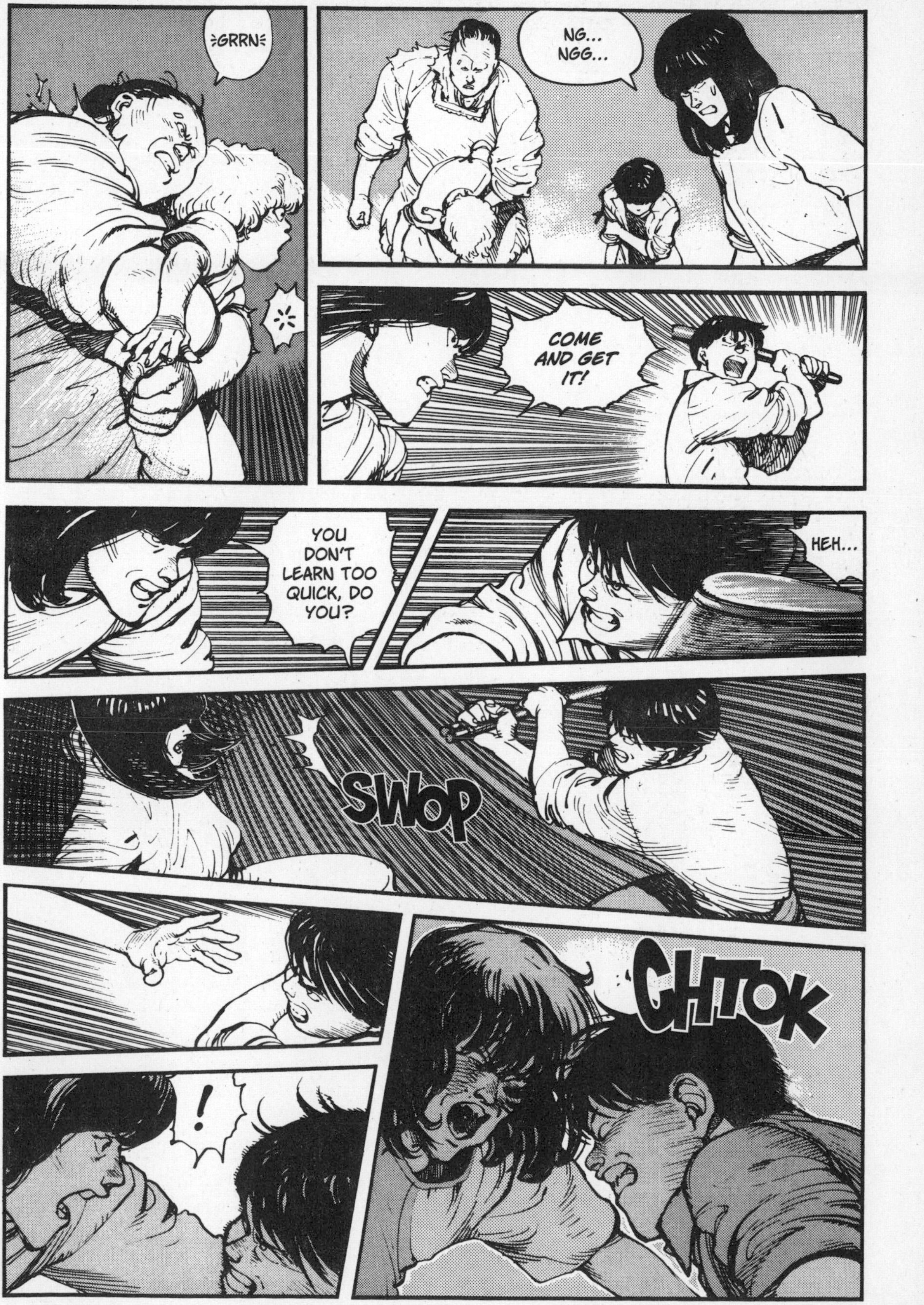
GRRN
NG... NGG...
COME AND GET IT!
YOU DON'T LEARN TOO QUICK, DO YOU?
HEH...
SWOP
CHTOK
!

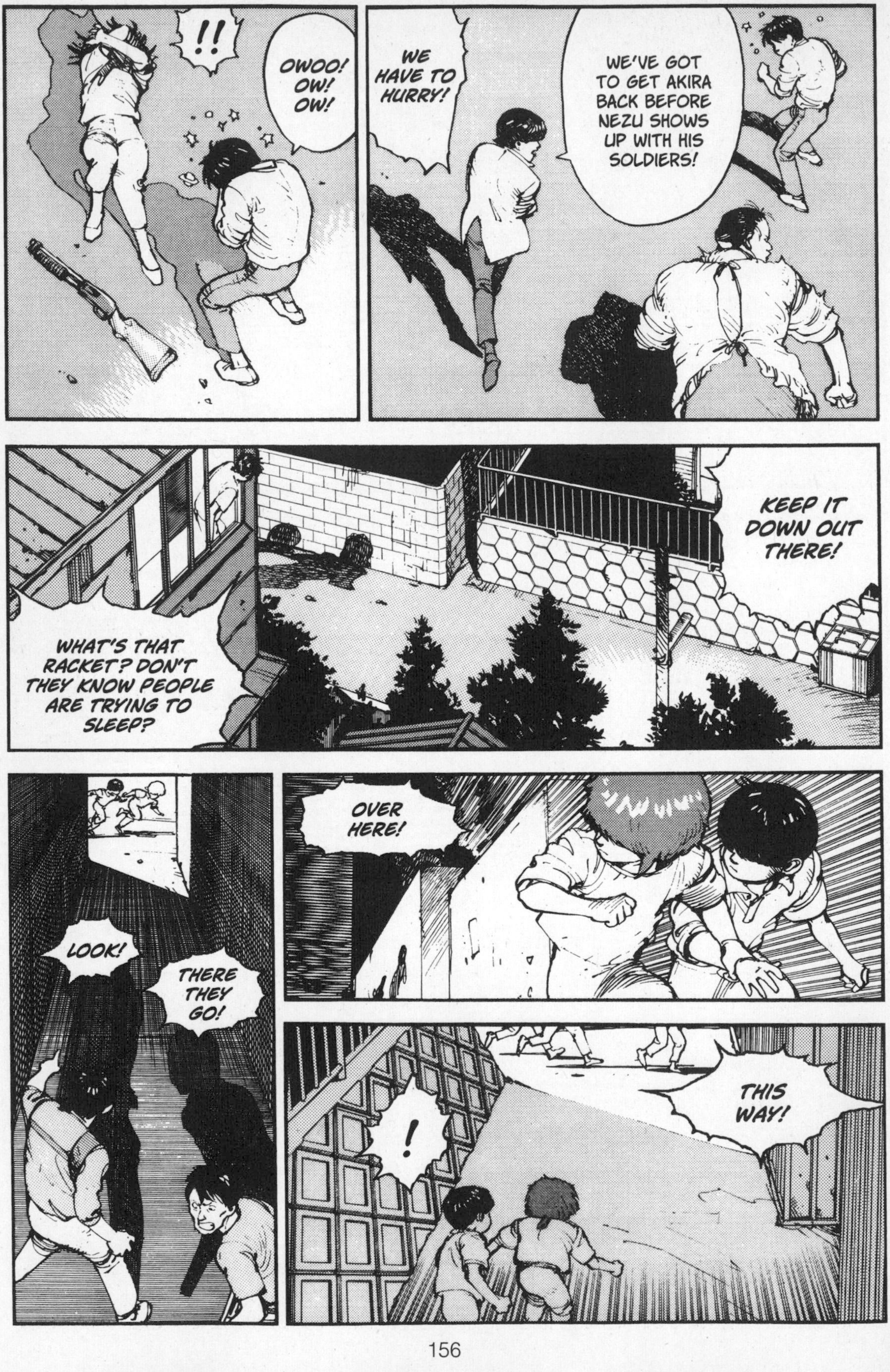
!!
OWOO! OW! OW!
WE HAVE TO HURRY!
WE'VE GOT TO GET AKIRA BACK BEFORE NEZU SHOWS UP WITH HIS SOLDIERS!
KEEP IT DOWN OUT THERE!
WHAT'S THAT RACKET? DON'T THEY KNOW PEOPLE ARE TRYING TO SLEEP?
LOOK!
THERE THEY GO!
OVER HERE!
!
THIS WAY!

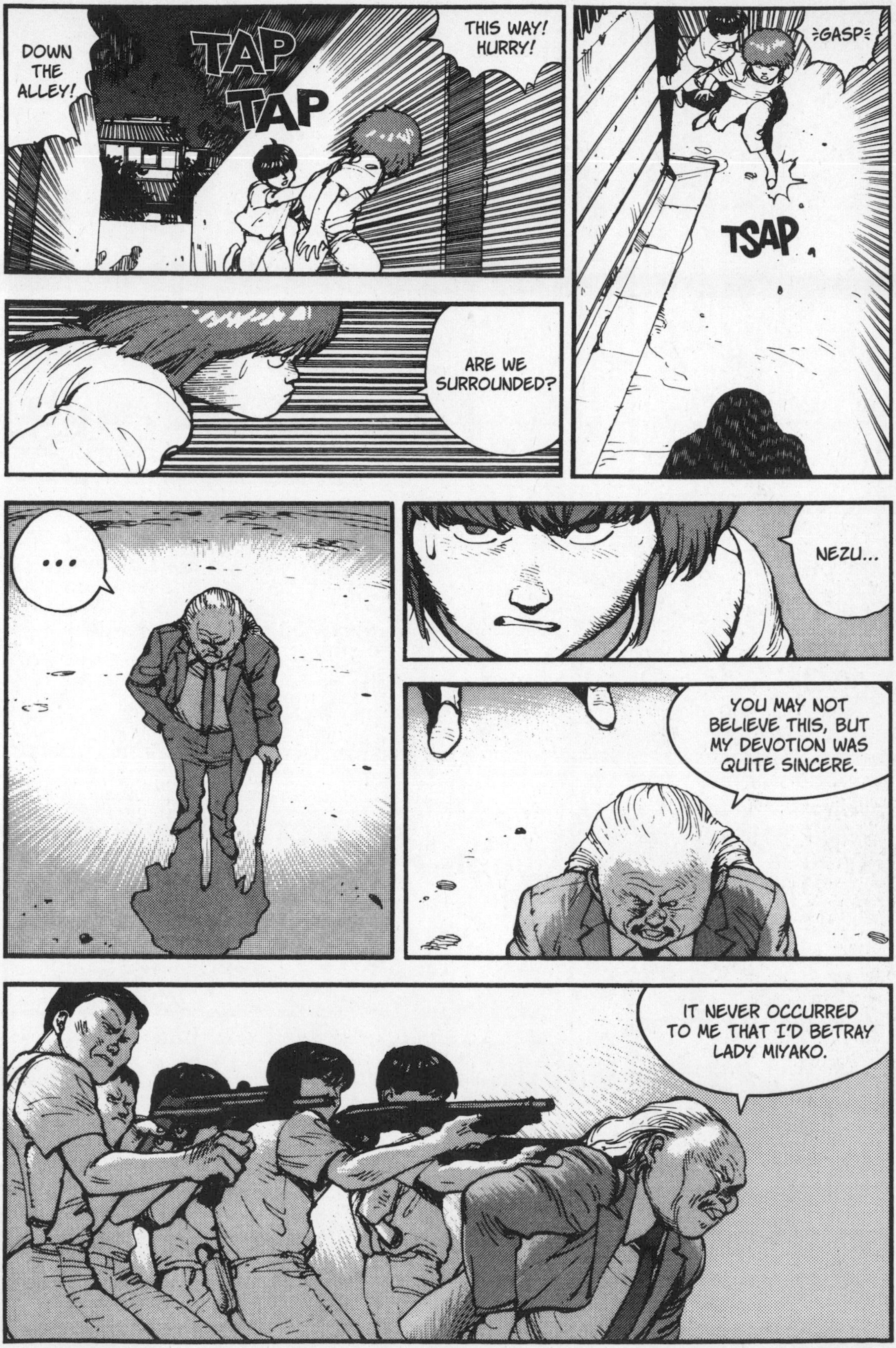
DOWN THE ALLEY!
TAP
TAP
THIS WAY! HURRY!
ARE WE SURROUNDED?
GASP
TSAP
...
NEZU...
YOU MAY NOT BELIEVE THIS, BUT MY DEVOTION WAS QUITE SINCERE.
IT NEVER OCCURRED TO ME THAT I'D BETRAY LADY MIYAKO.

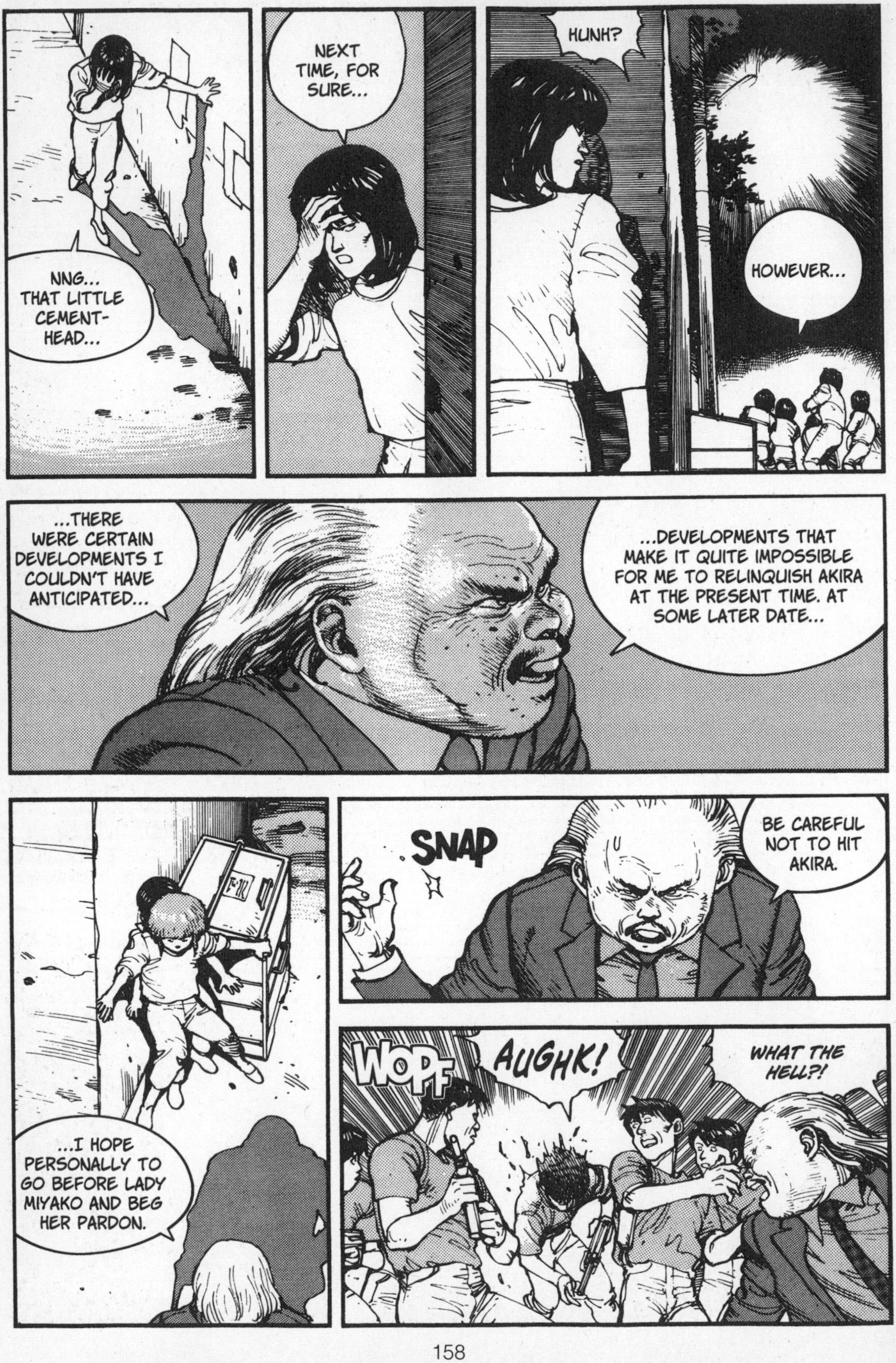
NNG... THAT LITTLE CEMENT-HEAD...
NEXT TIME, FOR SURE...
HUNH?
HOWEVER...
...THERE WERE CERTAIN DEVELOPMENTS I COULDN'T HAVE ANTICIPATED...
...DEVELOPMENTS THAT MAKE IT QUITE IMPOSSIBLE FOR ME TO RELINQUISH AKIRA AT THE PRESENT TIME. AT SOME LATER DATE...
...I HOPE PERSONALLY TO GO BEFORE LADY MIYAKO AND BEG HER PARDON.
SNAP
BE CAREFUL NOT TO HIT AKIRA.
WOPF
AUGHK!
WHAT THE HELL?!

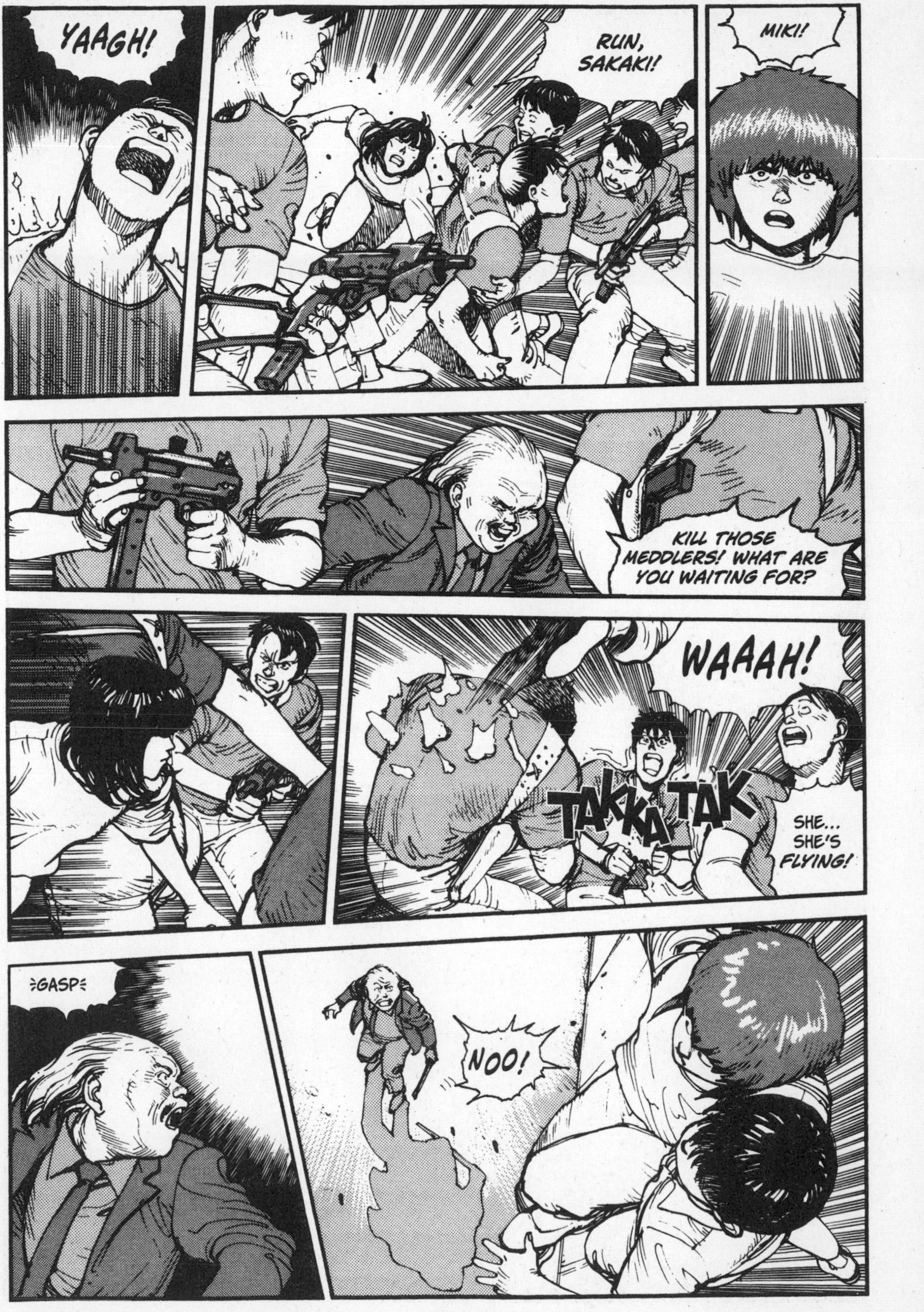
YAAGH!
RUN, SAKAKI!
MIKI!
KILL THOSE MEDDLERS! WHAT ARE YOU WAITING FOR?
WAAAH!
TAKKA TAK
SHE... SHE'S FLYING!
GASP
NOO!

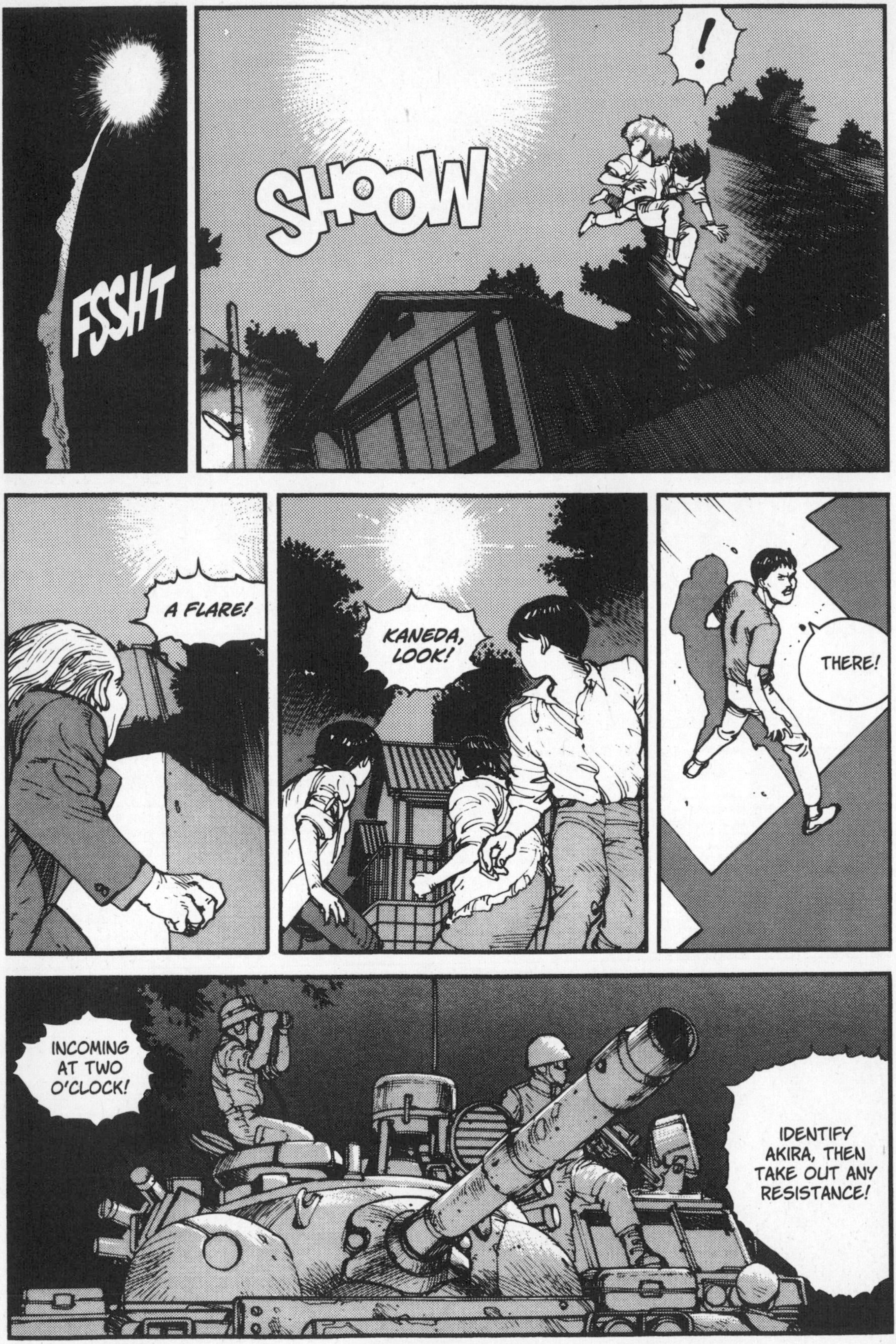
FSSHT
SHOOW
!
A FLARE!
KANEDA, LOOK!
THERE!
INCOMING AT TWO O'CLOCK!
IDENTIFY AKIRA, THEN TAKE OUT ANY RESISTANCE!

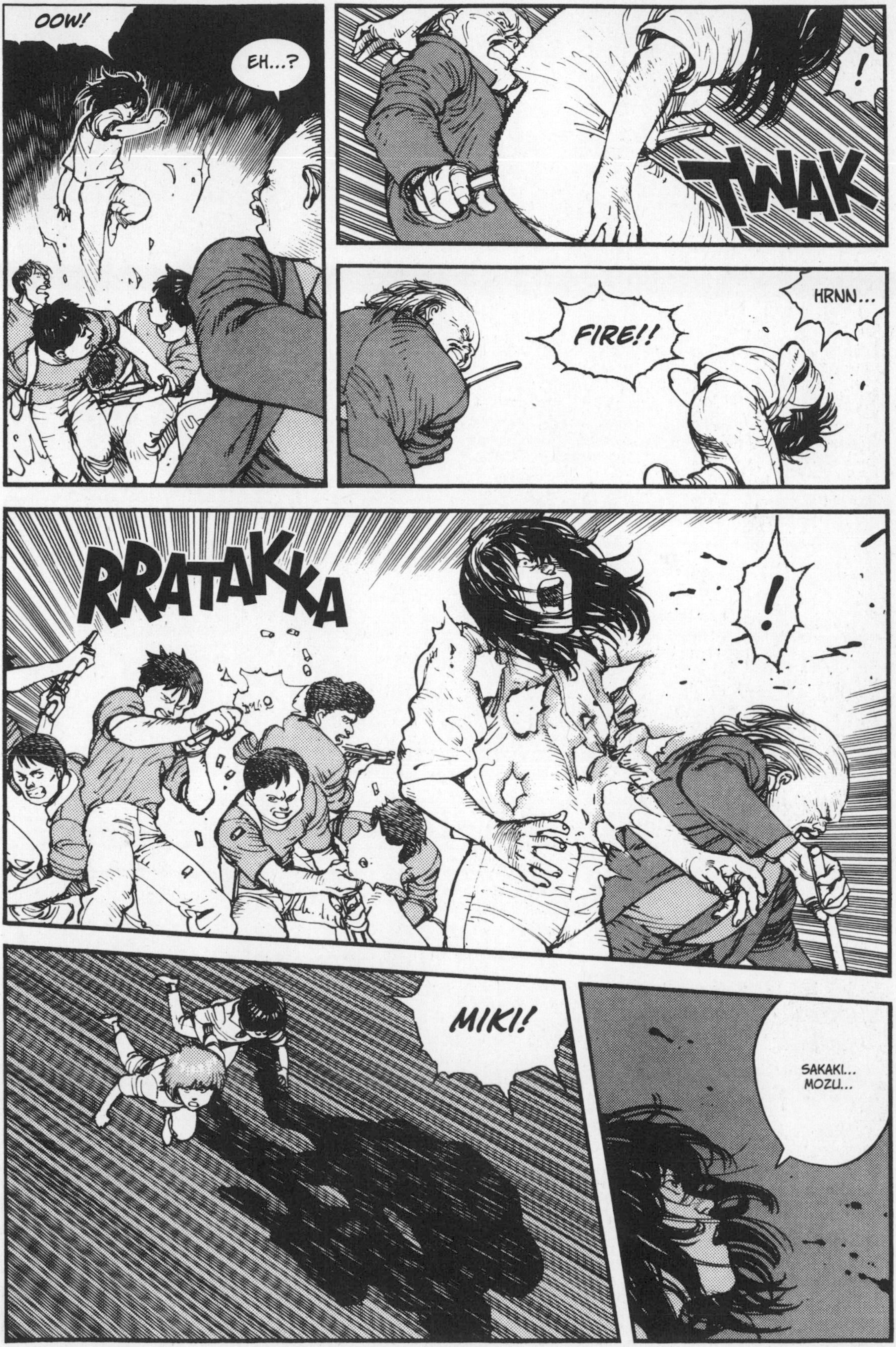

OOW!
EH...?
!
TWAK
FIRE!!
HRNN...
RRATAKKA
!
MIKI!
SAKAKI...
MOZU...

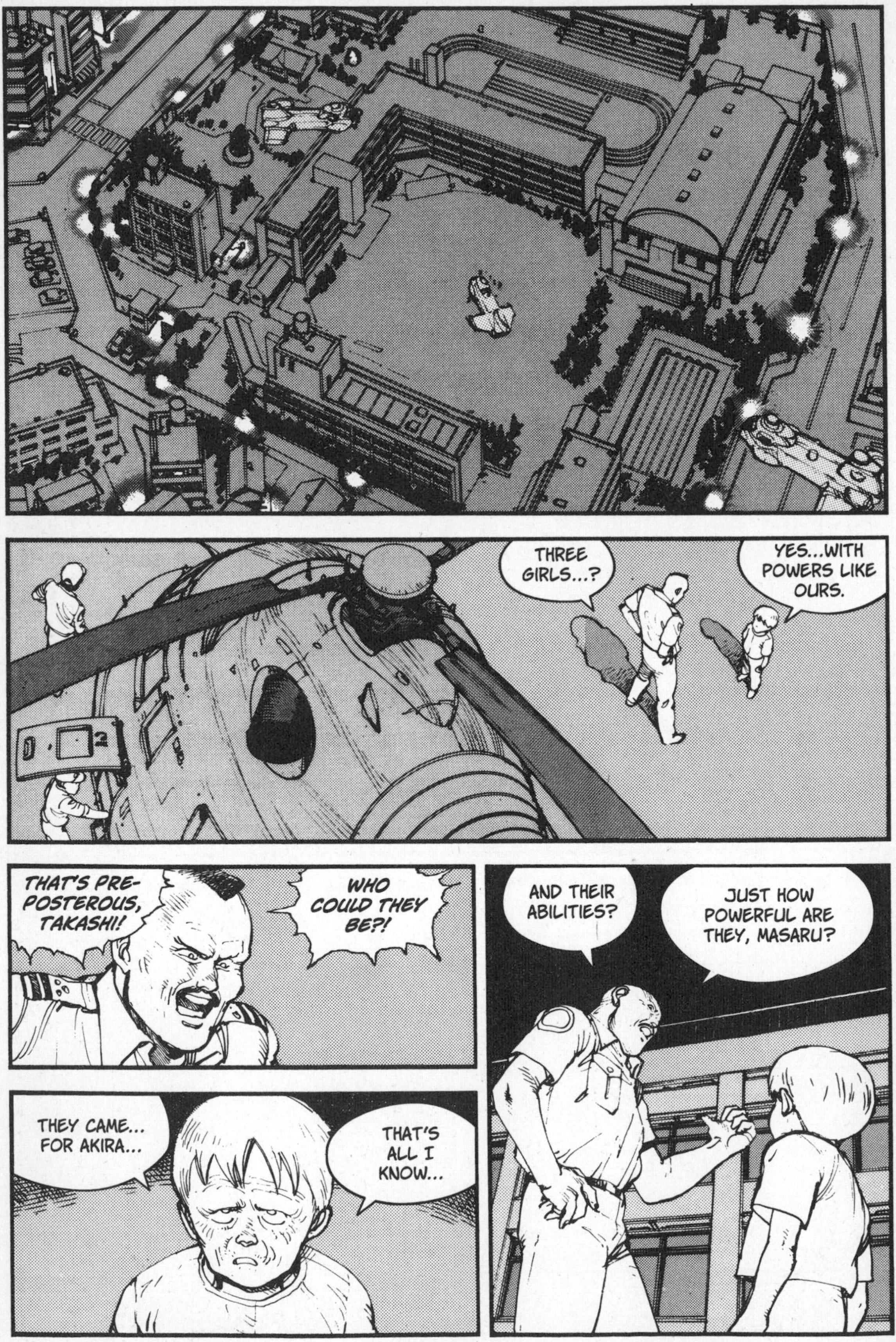
THREE GIRLS...?
YES...WITH POWERS LIKE OURS.
THAT'S PRE-POSTEROUS, TAKASHI!
WHO COULD THEY BE?!
THEY CAME... FOR AKIRA...
THAT'S ALL I KNOW...
AND THEIR ABILITIES?
JUST HOW POWERFUL ARE THEY, MASARU?

THEIR POWER IS... LIKE OURS...

...BUT VERY LIMITED.

EASY... THAT'S GOOD...

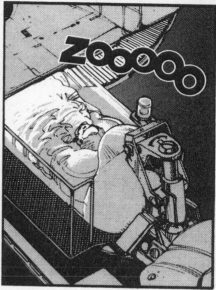

ZOOOOO

CORDONING OF THE AREA IS COMPLETE, SIR.

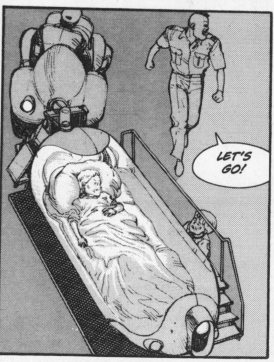

LET'S GO!

EXCELLENT! STAND BY.

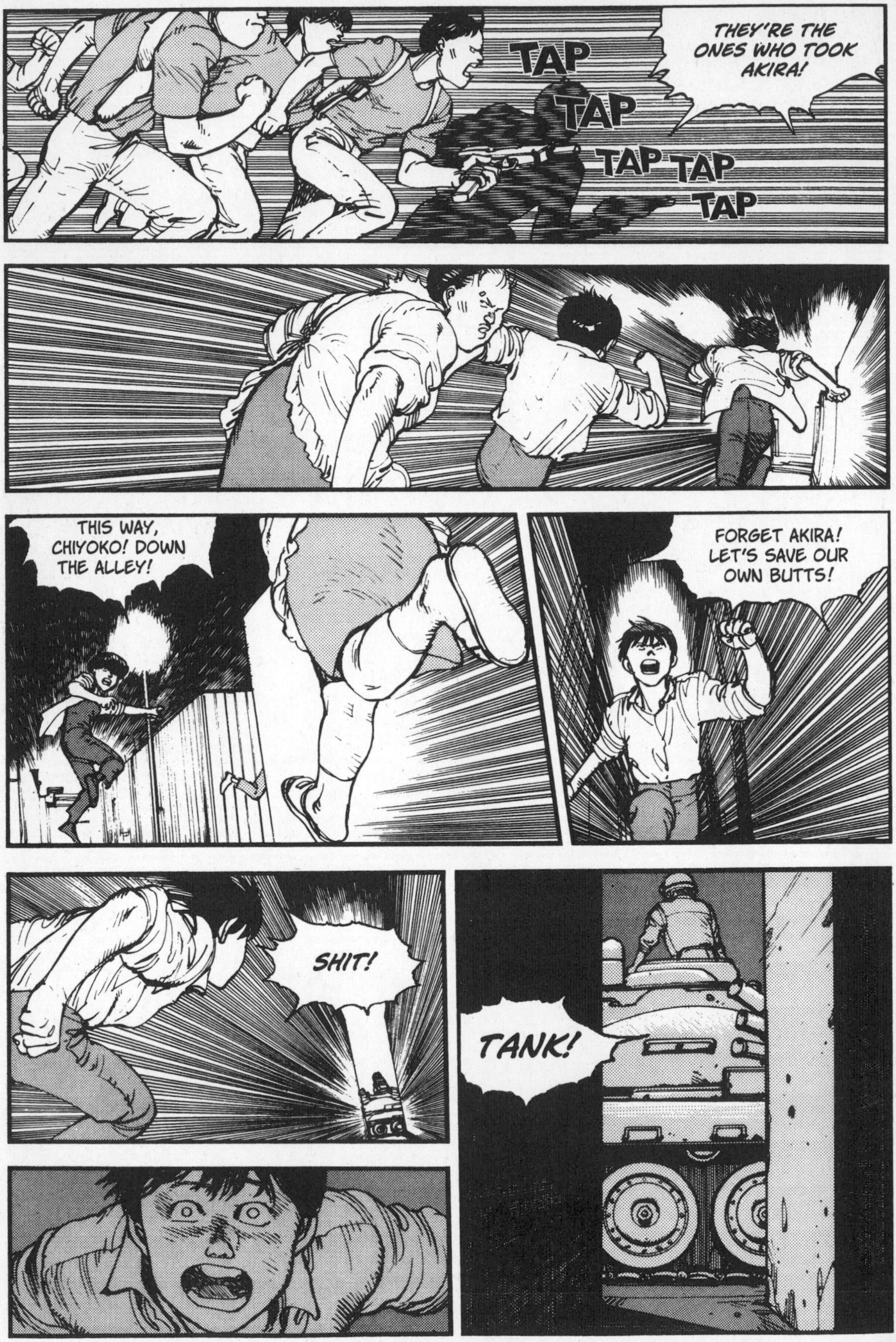
TAP
TAP
TAP TAP
TAP
THEY'RE THE ONES WHO TOOK AKIRA!
THIS WAY, CHIYOKO! DOWN THE ALLEY!
FORGET AKIRA! LET'S SAVE OUR OWN BUTTS!
SHIT!
TANK!

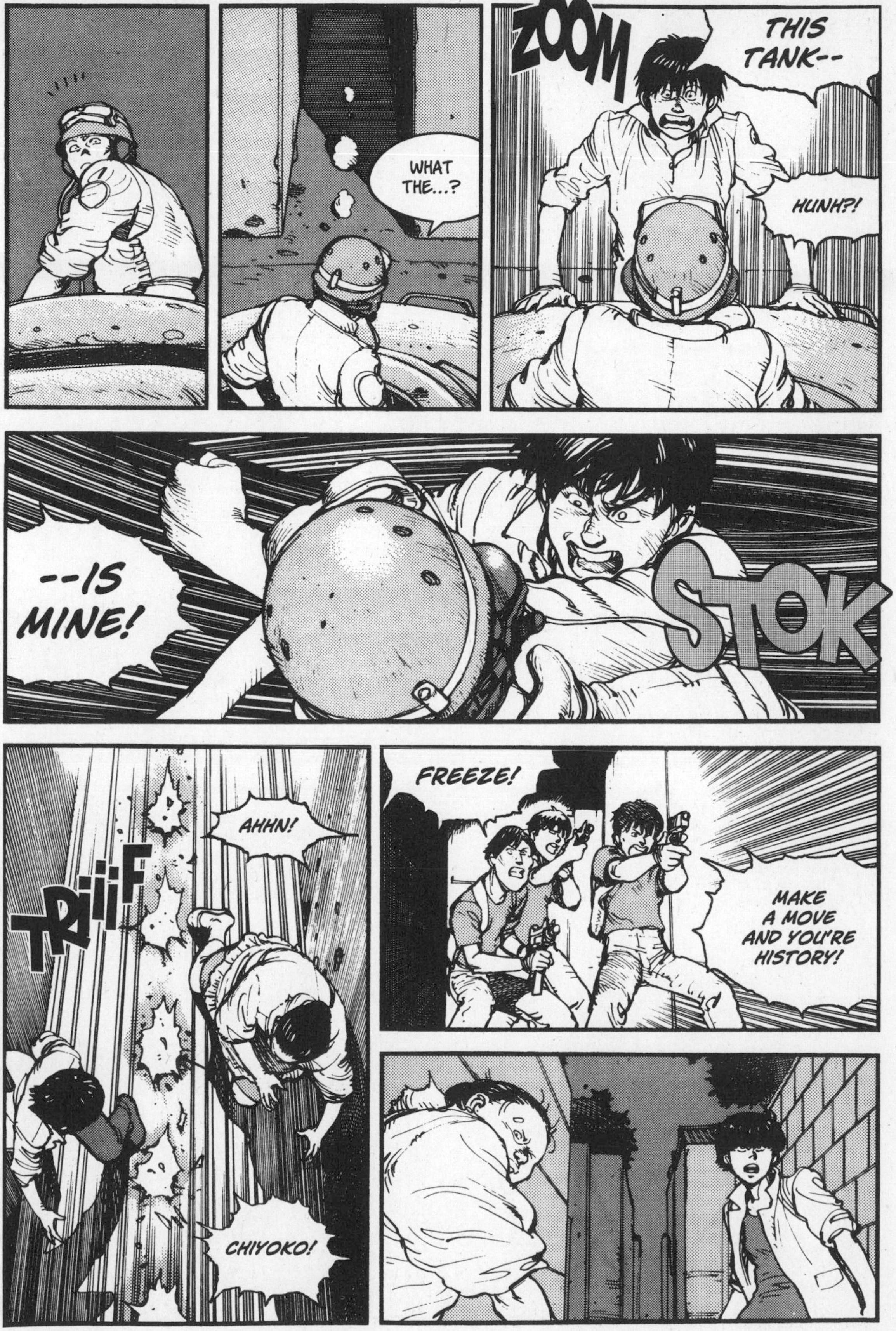
WHAT THE...?
ZOOM
THIS TANK--
HUNH?!
--IS MINE!
STOK
TRIIIF
AHHN!
CHIYOKO!
FREEZE!
MAKE A MOVE AND YOU'RE HISTORY!

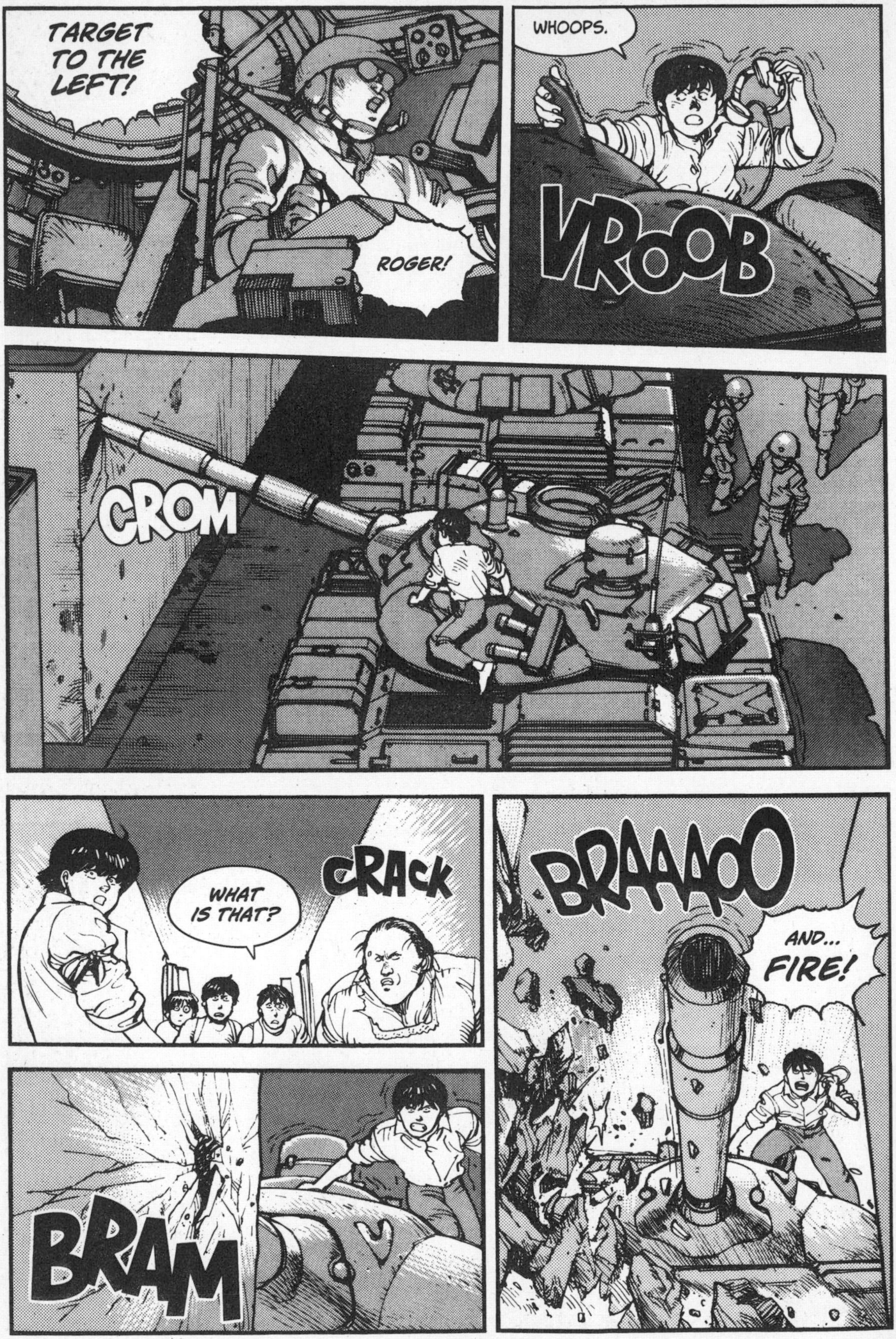
TARGET TO THE LEFT!
ROGER!
WHOOPS.
VROOB
CROM
WHAT IS THAT?
CRACK
BRAM
BRAAAOO
AND... FIRE!

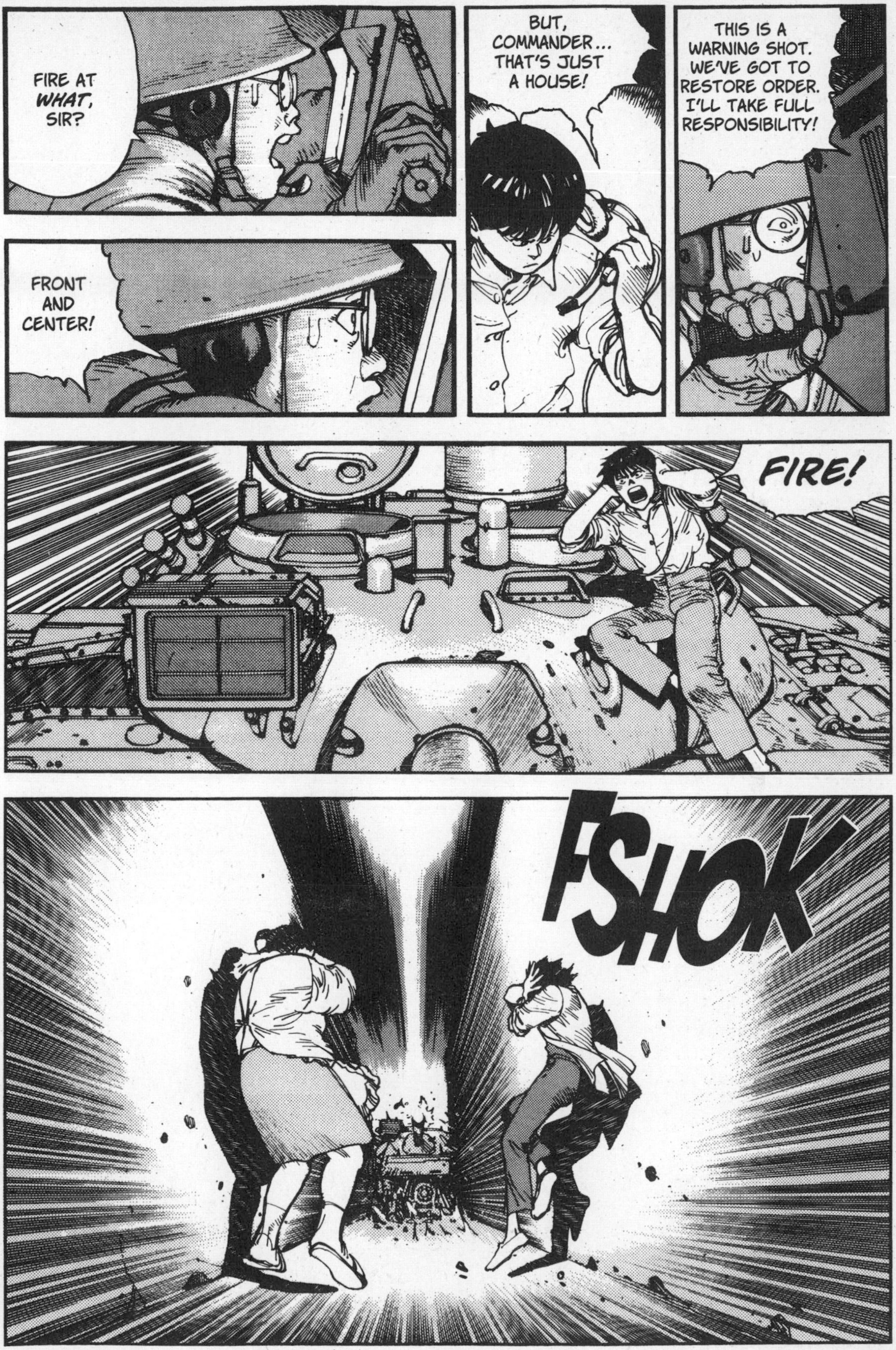
FIRE AT WHAT, SIR?
BUT, COMMANDER... THAT'S JUST A HOUSE!
THIS IS A WARNING SHOT. WE'VE GOT TO RESTORE ORDER. I'LL TAKE FULL RESPONSIBILITY!
FRONT AND CENTER!
FIRE!
FSHOK

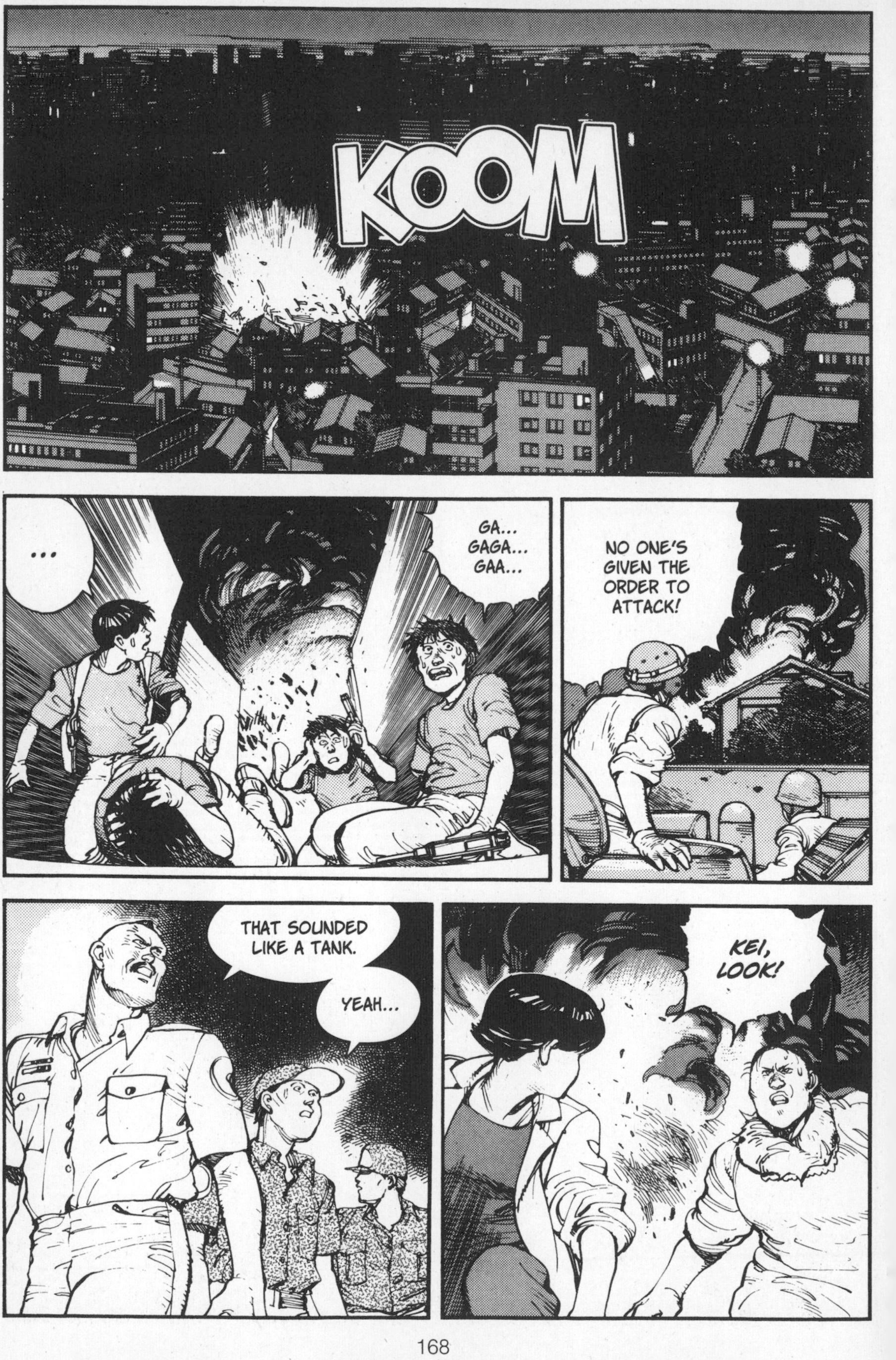
KOOM
...
GA... GAGA... GAA...
NO ONE'S GIVEN THE ORDER TO ATTACK!
THAT SOUNDED LIKE A TANK.
YEAH...
KEI, LOOK!

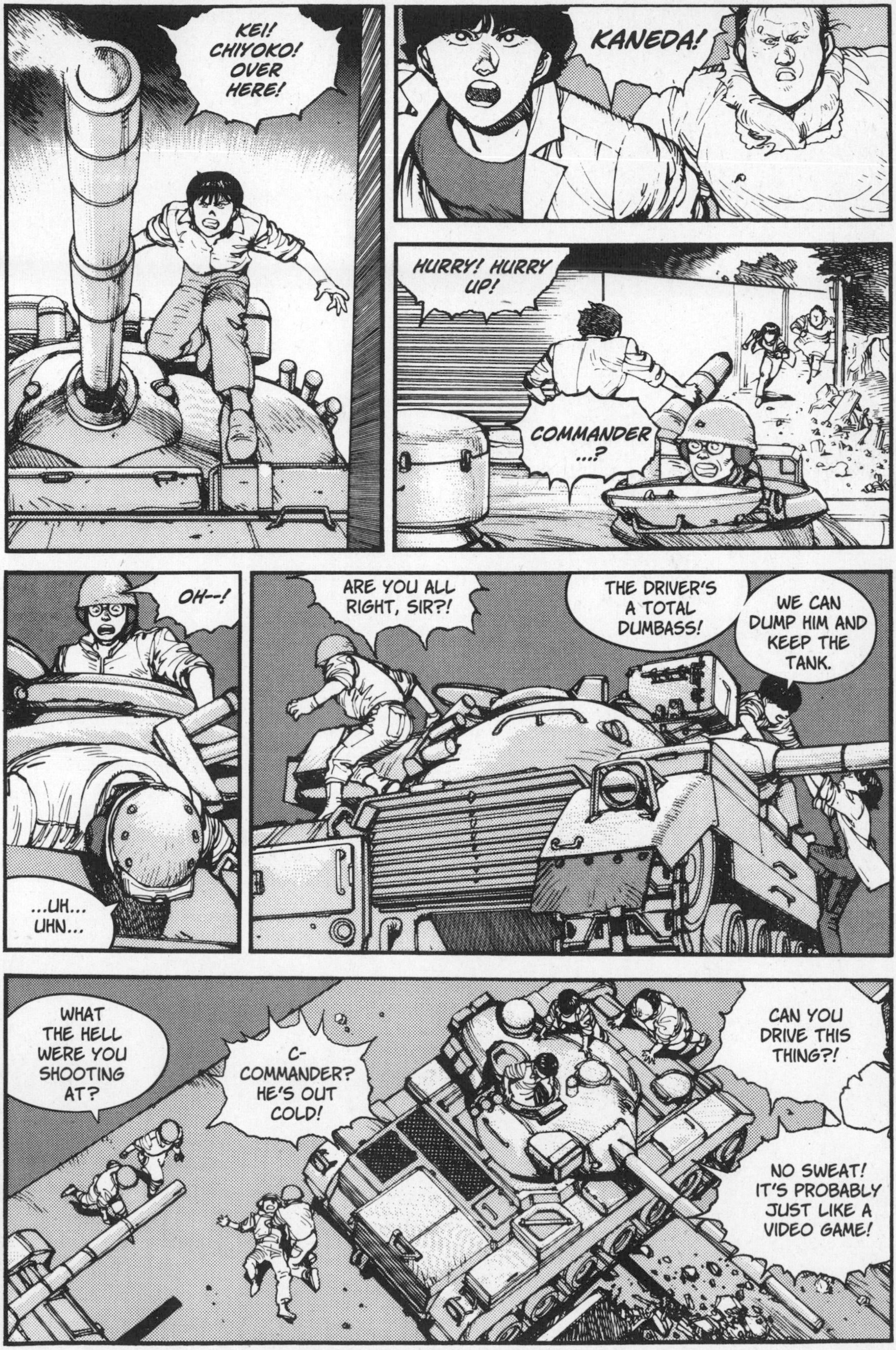
KEI! CHIYOKO! OVER HERE!
KANEDA!
HURRY! HURRY UP!
COMMANDER ...?
OH--!
...UH... UHN...
ARE YOU ALL RIGHT, SIR?!
THE DRIVER'S A TOTAL DUMBASS!
WE CAN DUMP HIM AND KEEP THE TANK.
WHAT THE HELL WERE YOU SHOOTING AT?
C-COMMANDER? HE'S OUT COLD!
CAN YOU DRIVE THIS THING?!
NO SWEAT! IT'S PROBABLY JUST LIKE A VIDEO GAME!

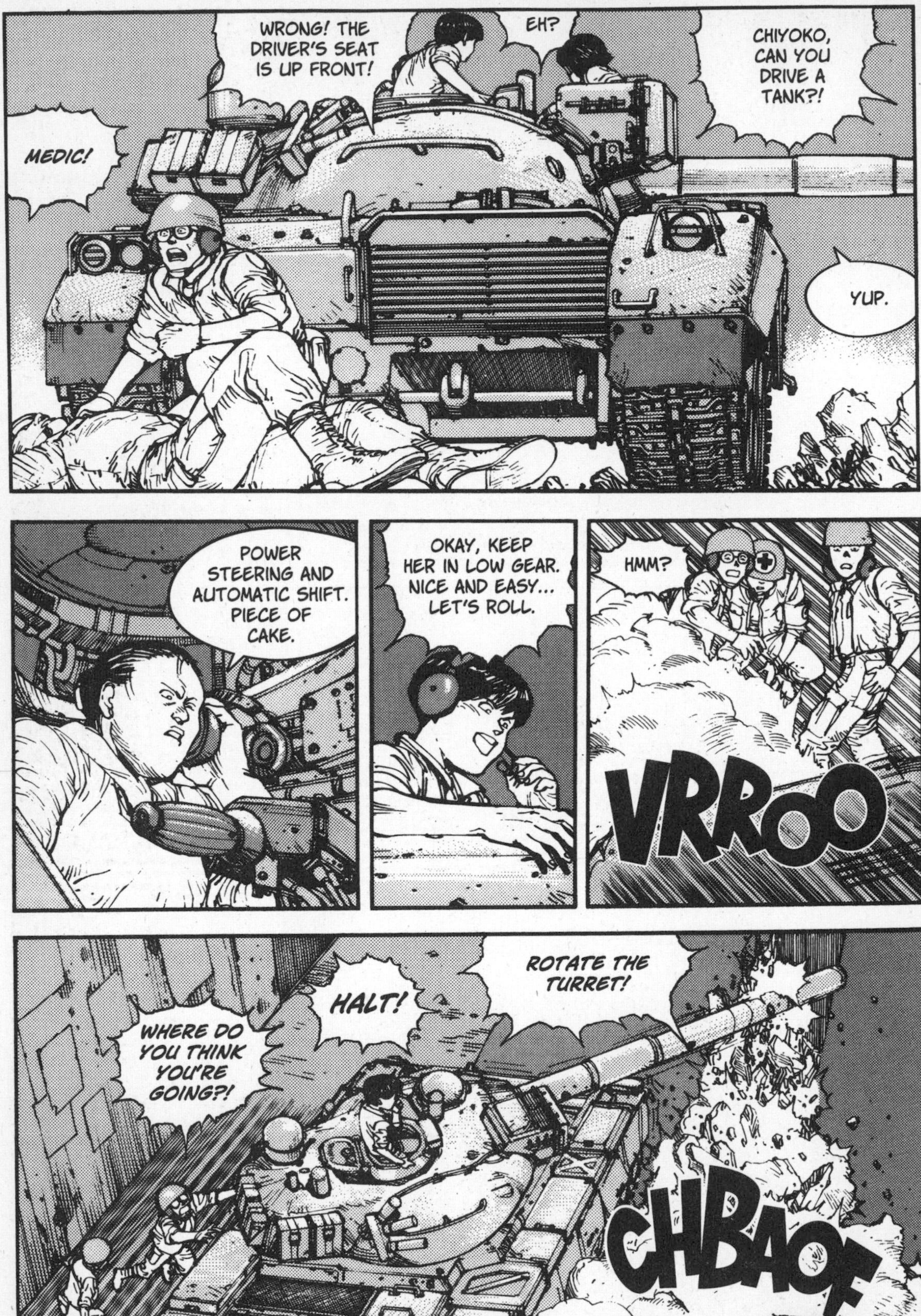
WRONG! THE DRIVER'S SEAT IS UP FRONT!
EH?
CHIYOKO, CAN YOU DRIVE A TANK?!
MEDIC!
YUP.
POWER STEERING AND AUTOMATIC SHIFT. PIECE OF CAKE.
OKAY, KEEP HER IN LOW GEAR. NICE AND EASY... LET'S ROLL.
HMM?
VRROOO
WHERE DO YOU THINK YOU'RE GOING?!
HALT!
ROTATE THE TURRET!
CHBAOF

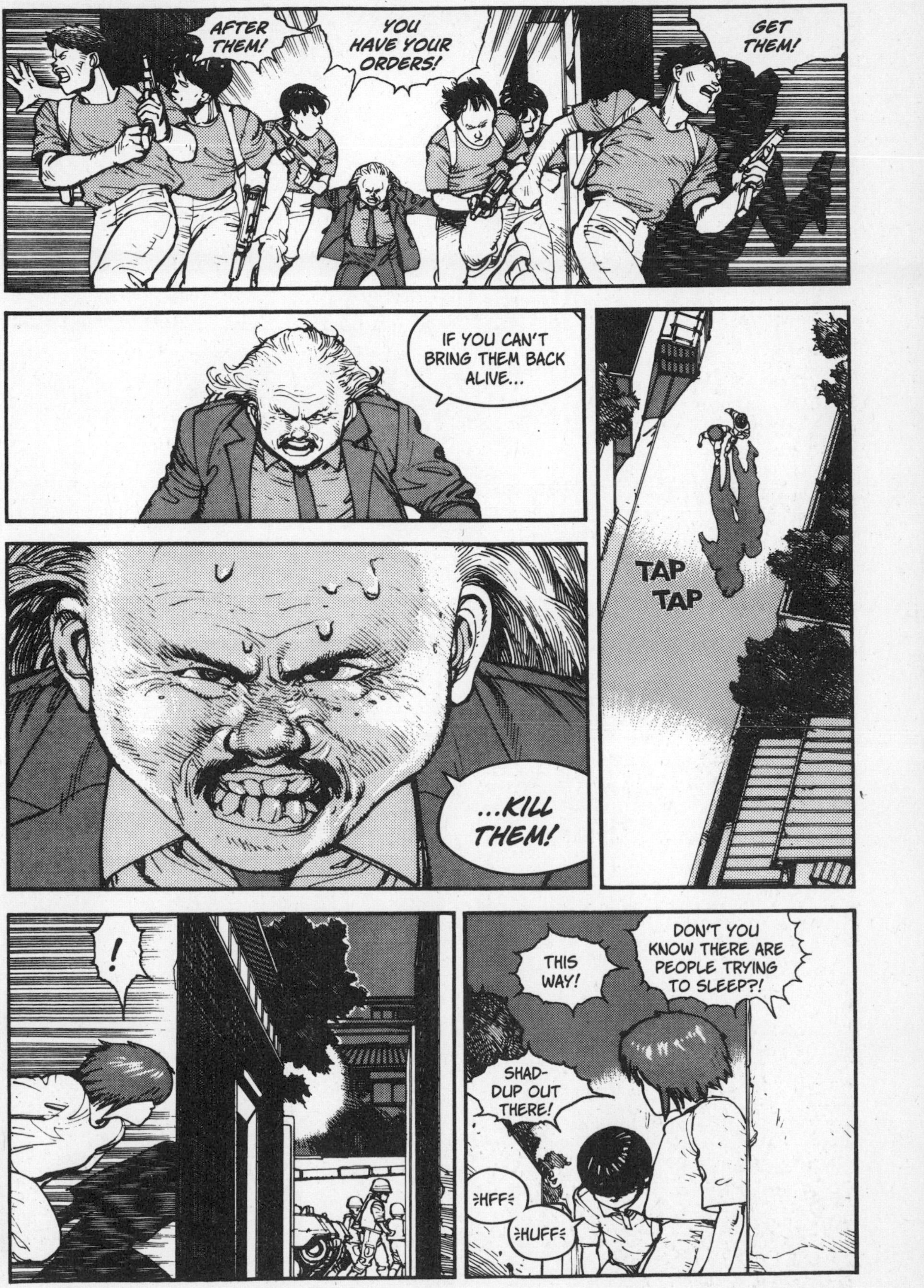
AFTER THEM!
YOU HAVE YOUR ORDERS!
GET THEM!
IF YOU CAN'T BRING THEM BACK ALIVE...
...KILL THEM!
TAP
TAP
!
THIS WAY!
DON'T YOU KNOW THERE ARE PEOPLE TRYING TO SLEEP?!
SHAD-DUP OUT THERE!
HFF
HUFF

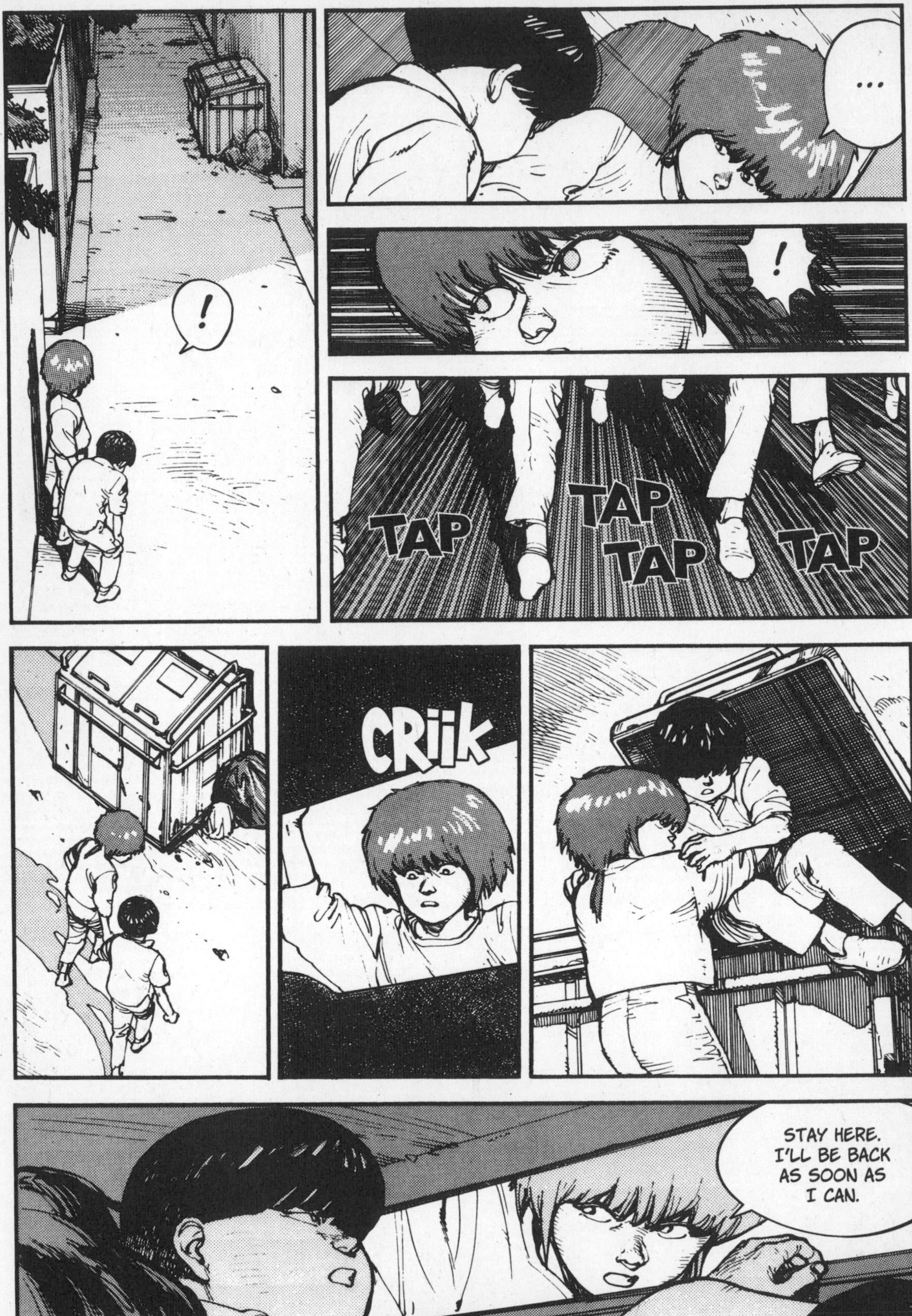
!
...
!
TAP
TAP
TAP
TAP
CRiik
STAY HERE. I'LL BE BACK AS SOON AS I CAN.

TAP
TAP
TAP

TAP

WE HAVE
TO HURRY,
IT'S ALMOST
DAWN.

HUMH!

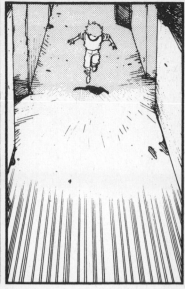

HyAA!!

OVER THERE!
IT'S HER!

BOK

HEY!!

SHE
CAN
FLY!

173

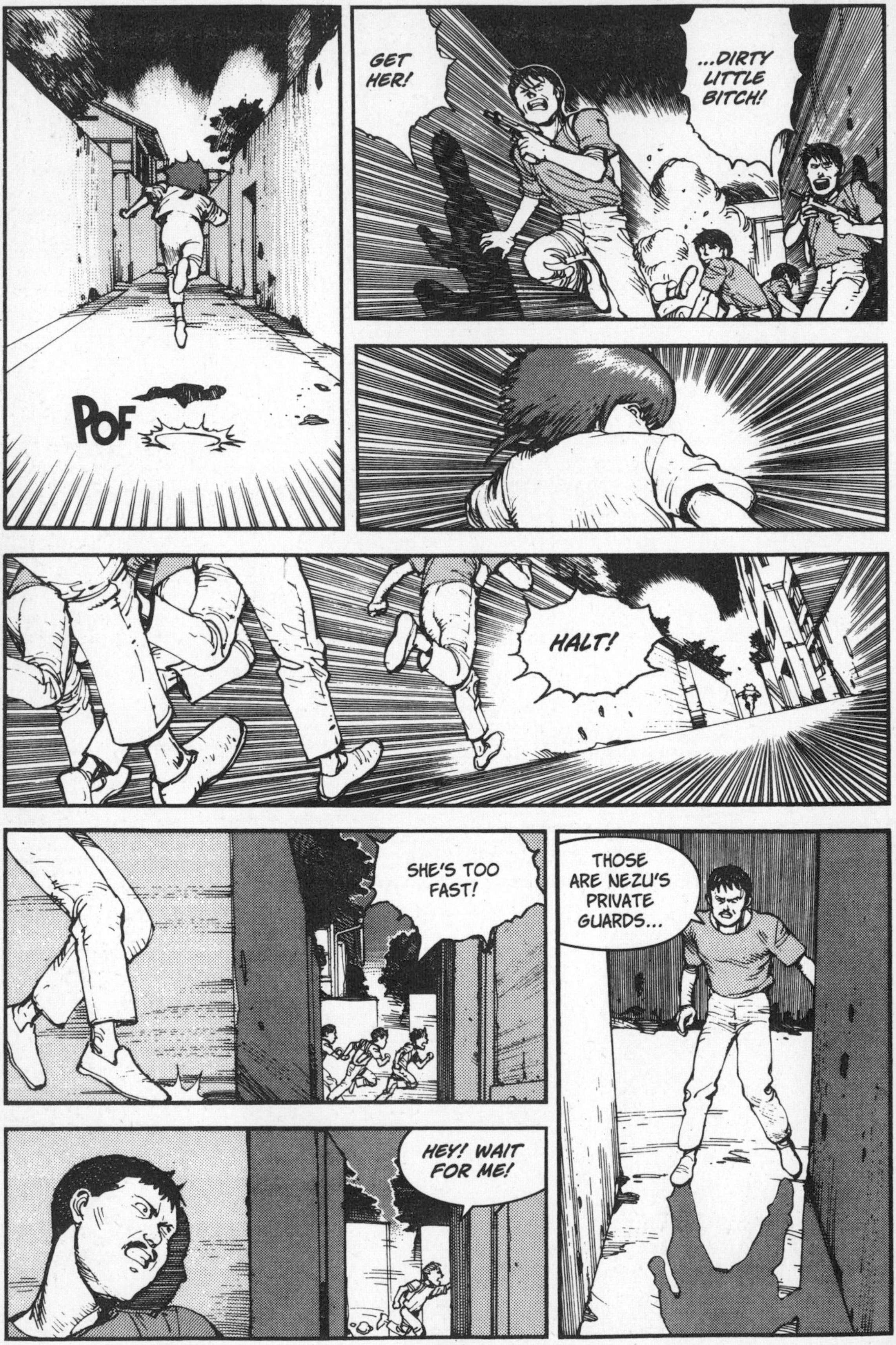
POF
GET HER!
...DIRTY LITTLE BITCH!
HALT!
SHE'S TOO FAST!
THOSE ARE NEZU'S PRIVATE GUARDS...
HEY! WAIT FOR ME!

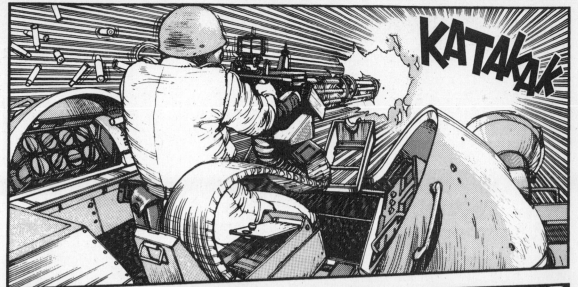

KATAKAK

ASSHOLE!

KAKAKKA

!

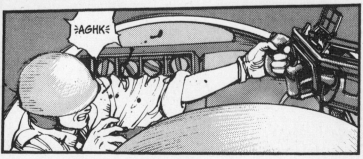

≡AGHK≡

175

HE'S HIT! GET A MEDIC! GIMME A HAND!

COME IN HEAD-QUARTERS! DO YOU READ ME?

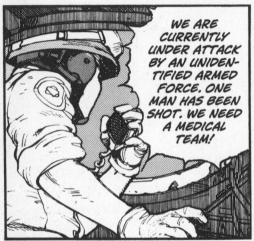

WE ARE CURRENTLY UNDER ATTACK BY AN UNIDEN-TIFIED ARMED FORCE. ONE MAN HAS BEEN SHOT. WE NEED A MEDICAL TEAM!

KATTA KATA

PREPARE TO FIRE!

GOT 'EM...

SRAAKK

AUGH!

FOLLOW THEM DOWN THAT ALLEY!

176

AAH --!

KRAMB

HEY, YOU IDIOTS! THAT'S OUR WALL!

MY GOD!

KEEP AWAY FROM THE HOUSE!

GROOM

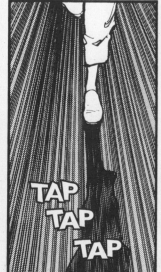

TAP
TAP
TAP

MOZU...WHERE ARE YOU NOW?

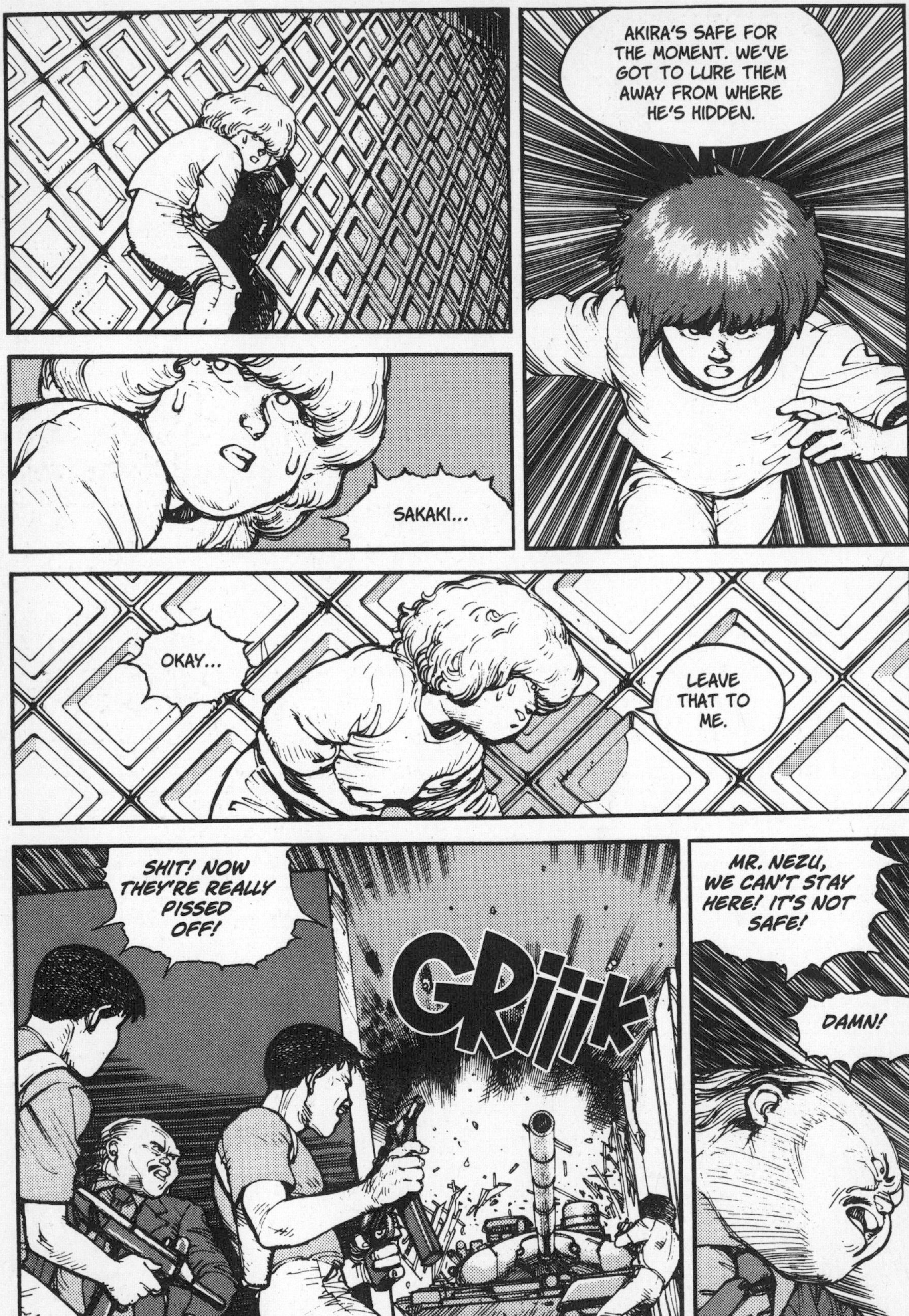
AKIRA'S SAFE FOR THE MOMENT. WE'VE GOT TO LURE THEM AWAY FROM WHERE HE'S HIDDEN.
SAKAKI...
OKAY...
LEAVE THAT TO ME.
SHIT! NOW THEY'RE REALLY PISSED OFF!
GRIIIK
MR. NEZU, WE CAN'T STAY HERE! IT'S NOT SAFE!
DAMN!

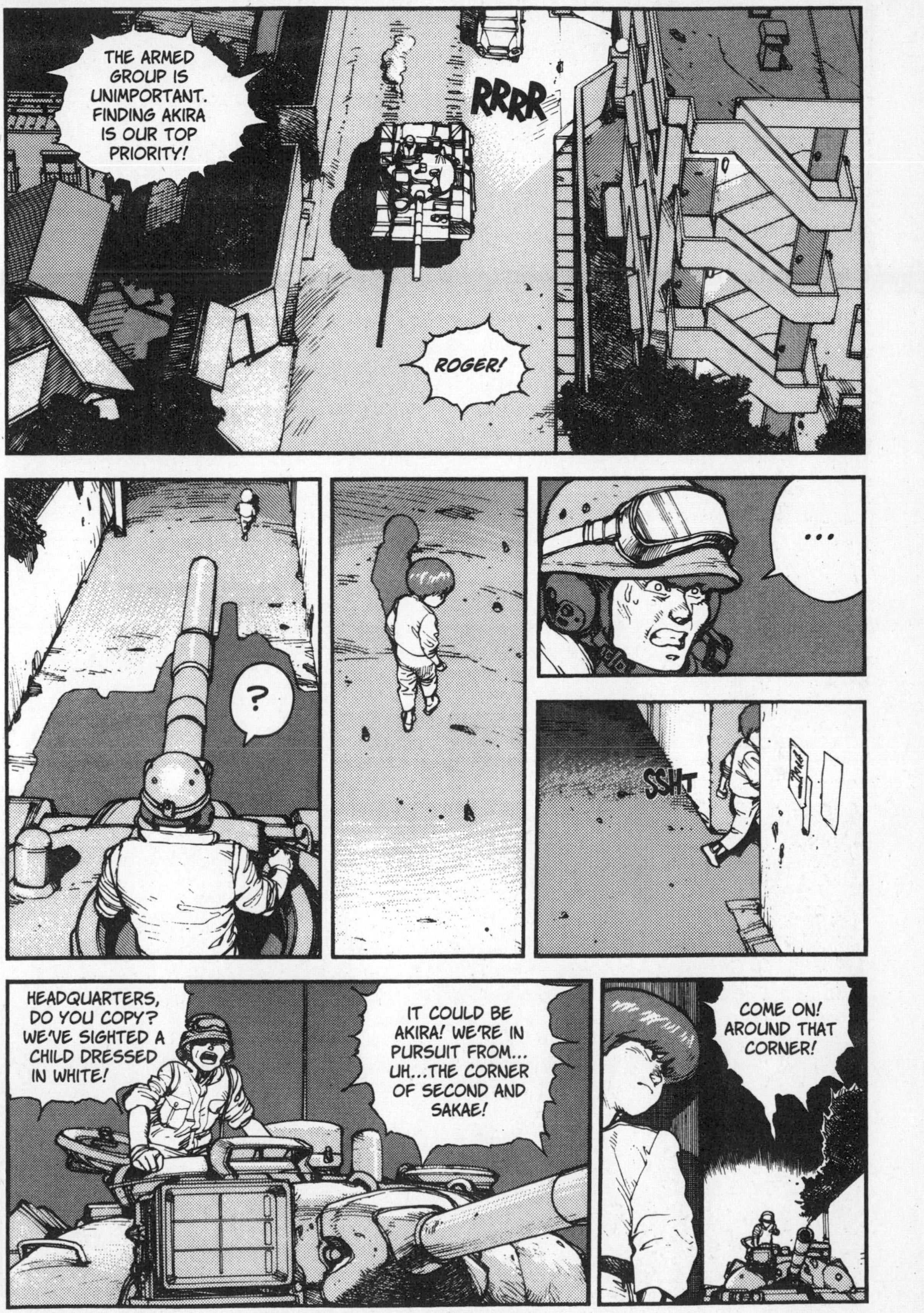
THE ARMED GROUP IS UNIMPORTANT. FINDING AKIRA IS OUR TOP PRIORITY!
RRRR
ROGER!
?
...
SSHT
HEADQUARTERS, DO YOU COPY? WE'VE SIGHTED A CHILD DRESSED IN WHITE!
IT COULD BE AKIRA! WE'RE IN PURSUIT FROM... UH...THE CORNER OF SECOND AND SAKAE!
COME ON! AROUND THAT CORNER!

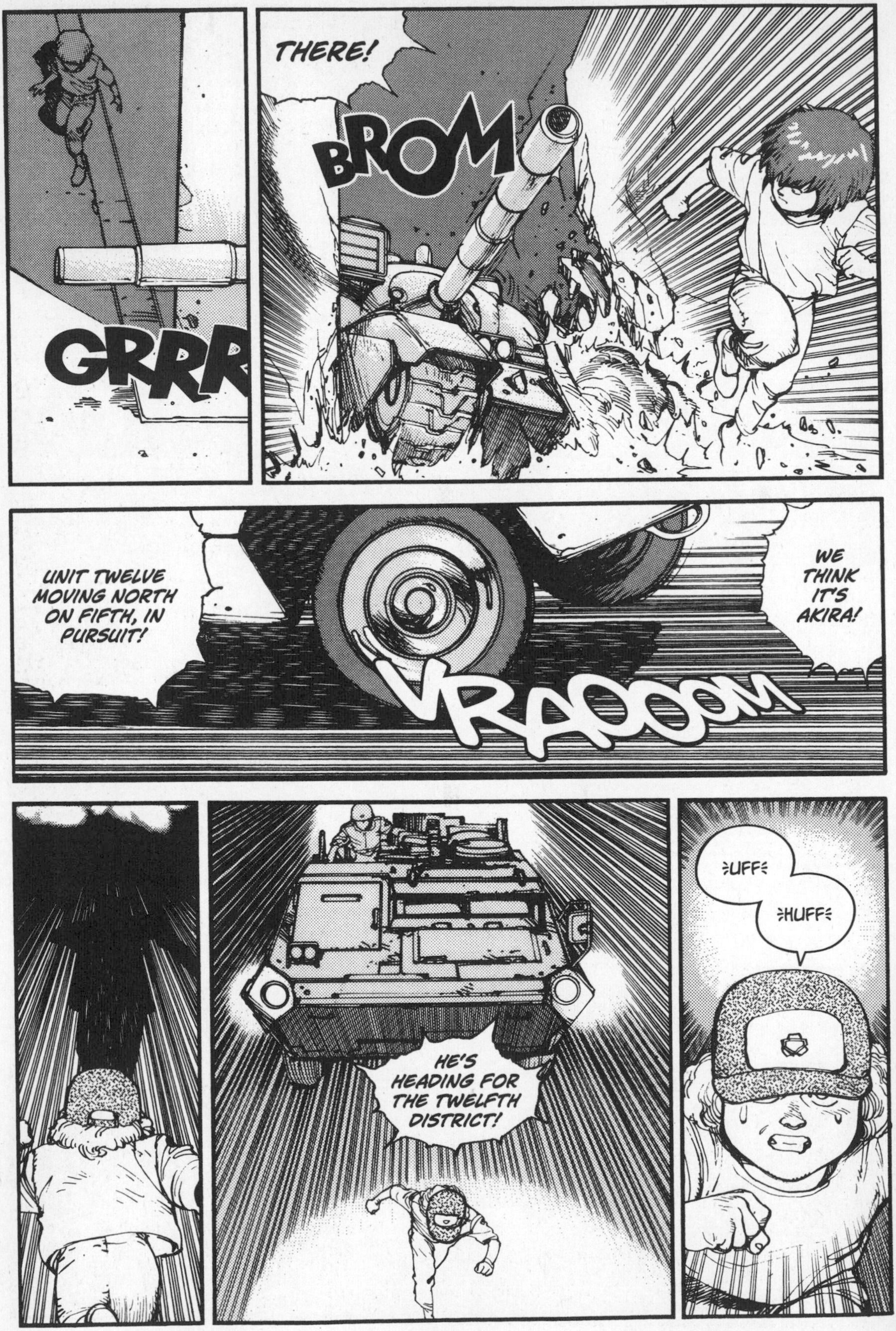
GRRR
THERE!
BROM
UNIT TWELVE MOVING NORTH ON FIFTH, IN PURSUIT!
WE THINK IT'S AKIRA!
VRAOOOM
HE'S HEADING FOR THE TWELFTH DISTRICT!
UFF
HUFF

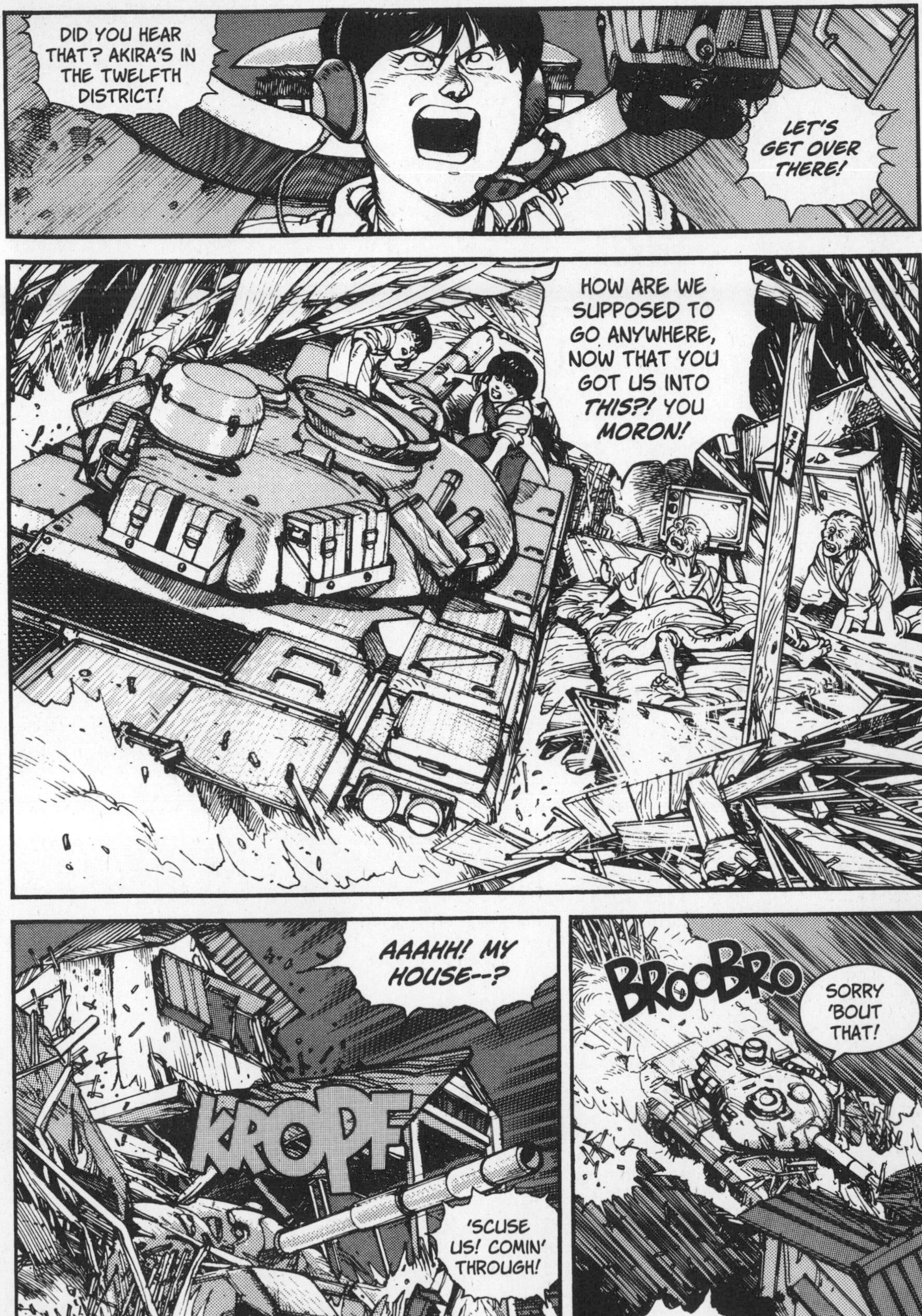
DID YOU HEAR THAT? AKIRA'S IN THE TWELFTH DISTRICT!
LET'S GET OVER THERE!
HOW ARE WE SUPPOSED TO GO ANYWHERE, NOW THAT YOU GOT US INTO THIS?! YOU MORON!
AAAHH! MY HOUSE--?
KROPF
'SCUSE US! COMIN' THROUGH!
BROOBRO
SORRY 'BOUT THAT!
DARLING! SPEAK TO ME!

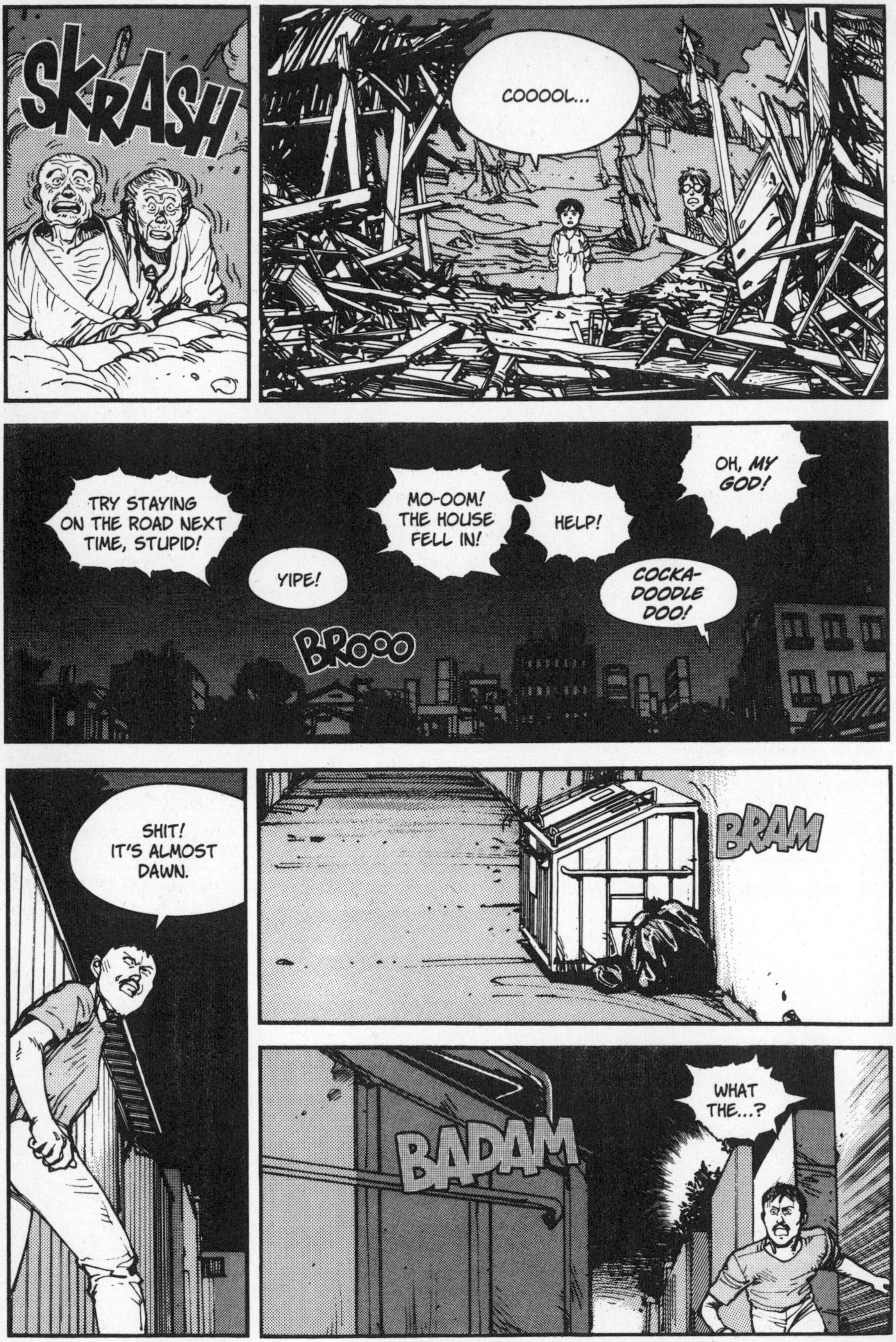
SKRASH
COOOOL...
TRY STAYING ON THE ROAD NEXT TIME, STUPID!
YIPE!
MO-OOM! THE HOUSE FELL IN!
HELP!
OH, MY GOD!
COCKA-DOODLE DOO!
BROOO
SHIT! IT'S ALMOST DAWN.
BRAM
BADAM
WHAT THE...?

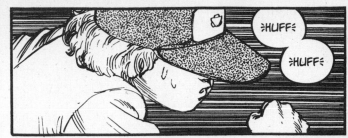

=HUFF=

=HUFF=

OHH--!

=HUFF=

=HFF=

=HUFF=

NOW WE'VE GOT 'ER!

ROOOOO

EASY, NOW...

=HFF=

=HUFF=

BE COOL, NOW. EVERYTHING'S OKAY. NO ONE'S GOING TO HURT YOU.

=HUFF=

=HUFF=

ZASH

183

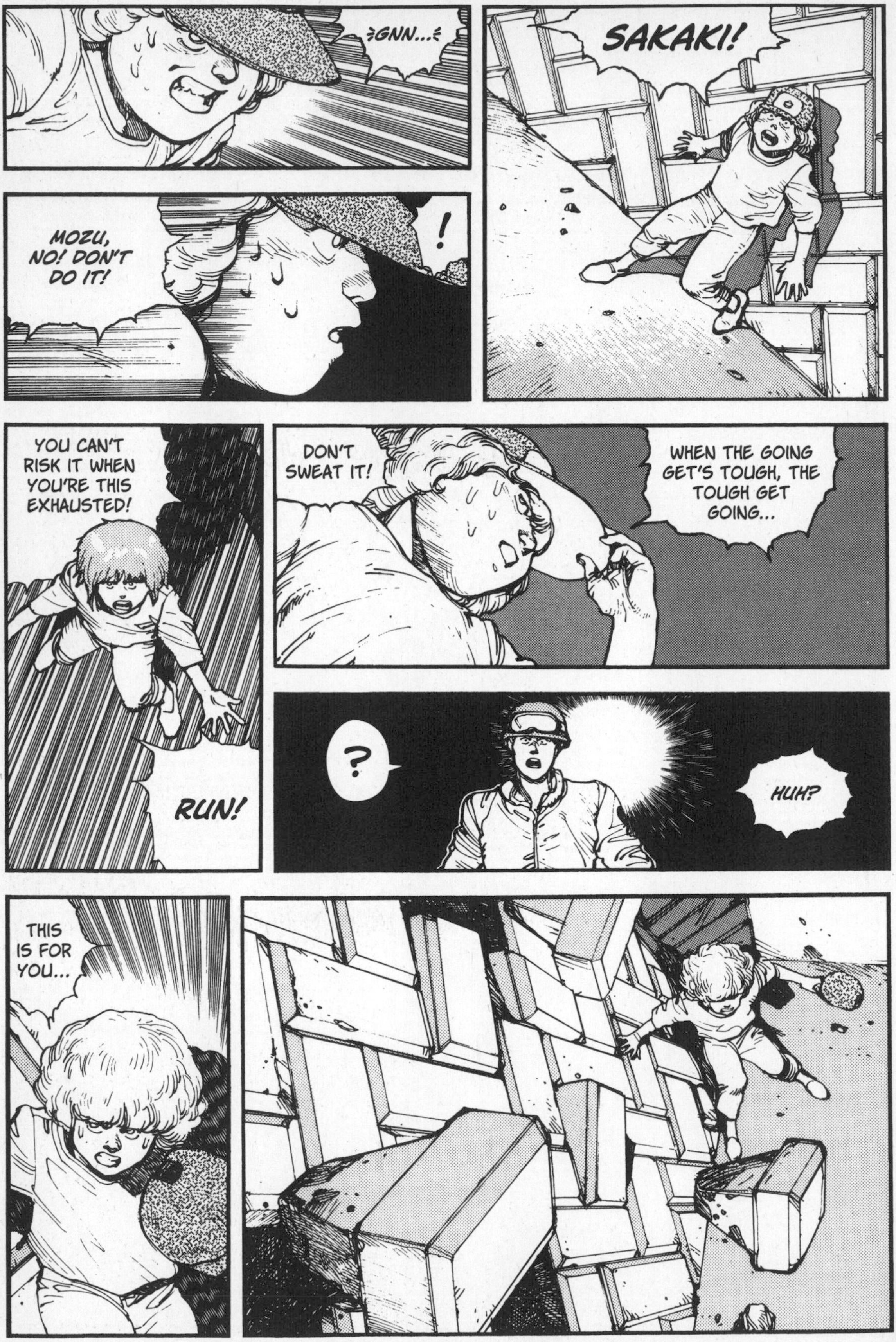
GNN...
SAKAKI!
MOZU, NO! DON'T DO IT!
!
YOU CAN'T RISK IT WHEN YOU'RE THIS EXHAUSTED!
RUN!
DON'T SWEAT IT!
WHEN THE GOING GET'S TOUGH, THE TOUGH GET GOING...
?
HUH?
THIS IS FOR YOU...

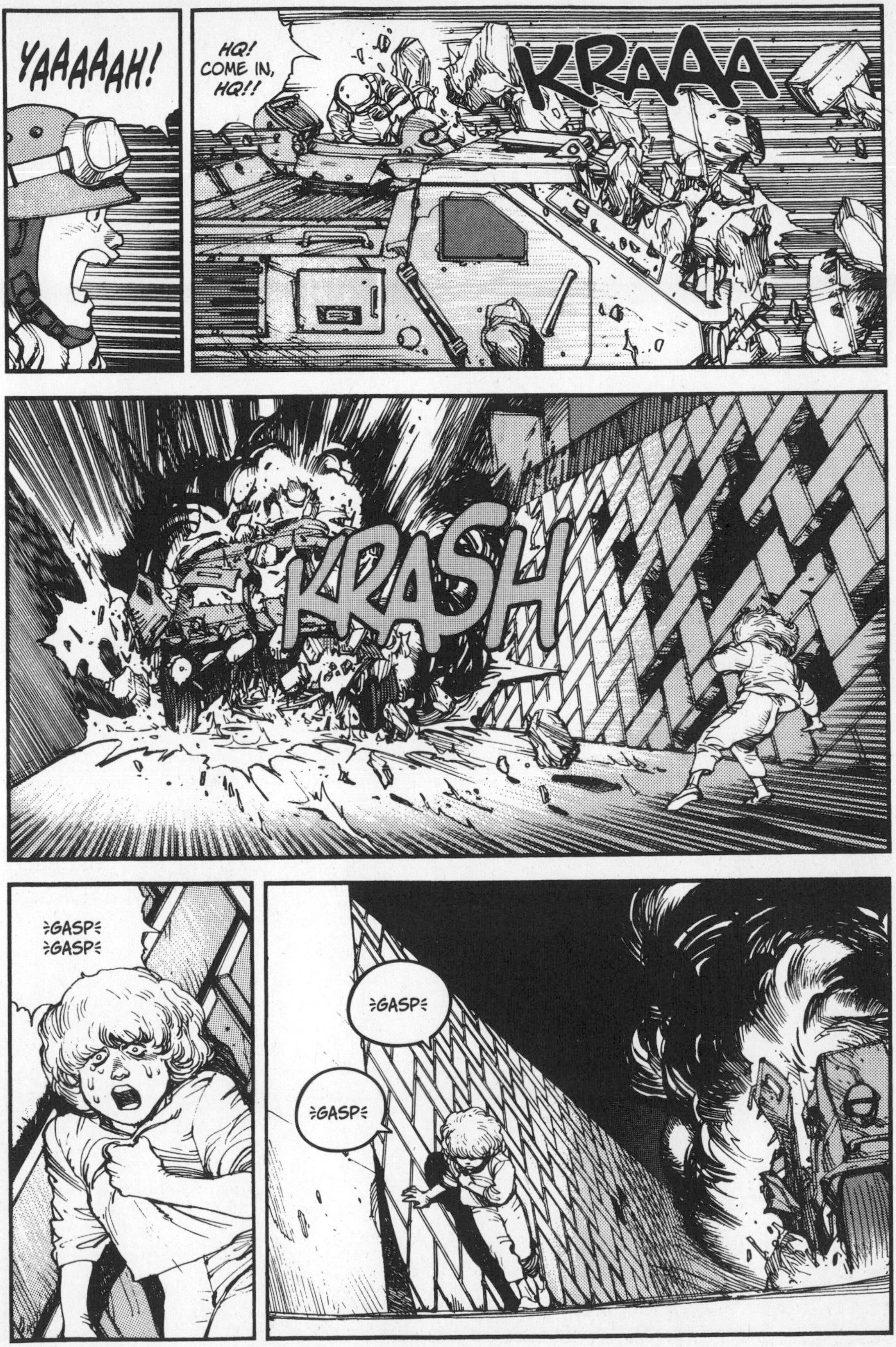
YAAAAAH!
HQ! COME IN, HQ!!
KRAAA
KRASH
GASP GASP
GASP
GASP

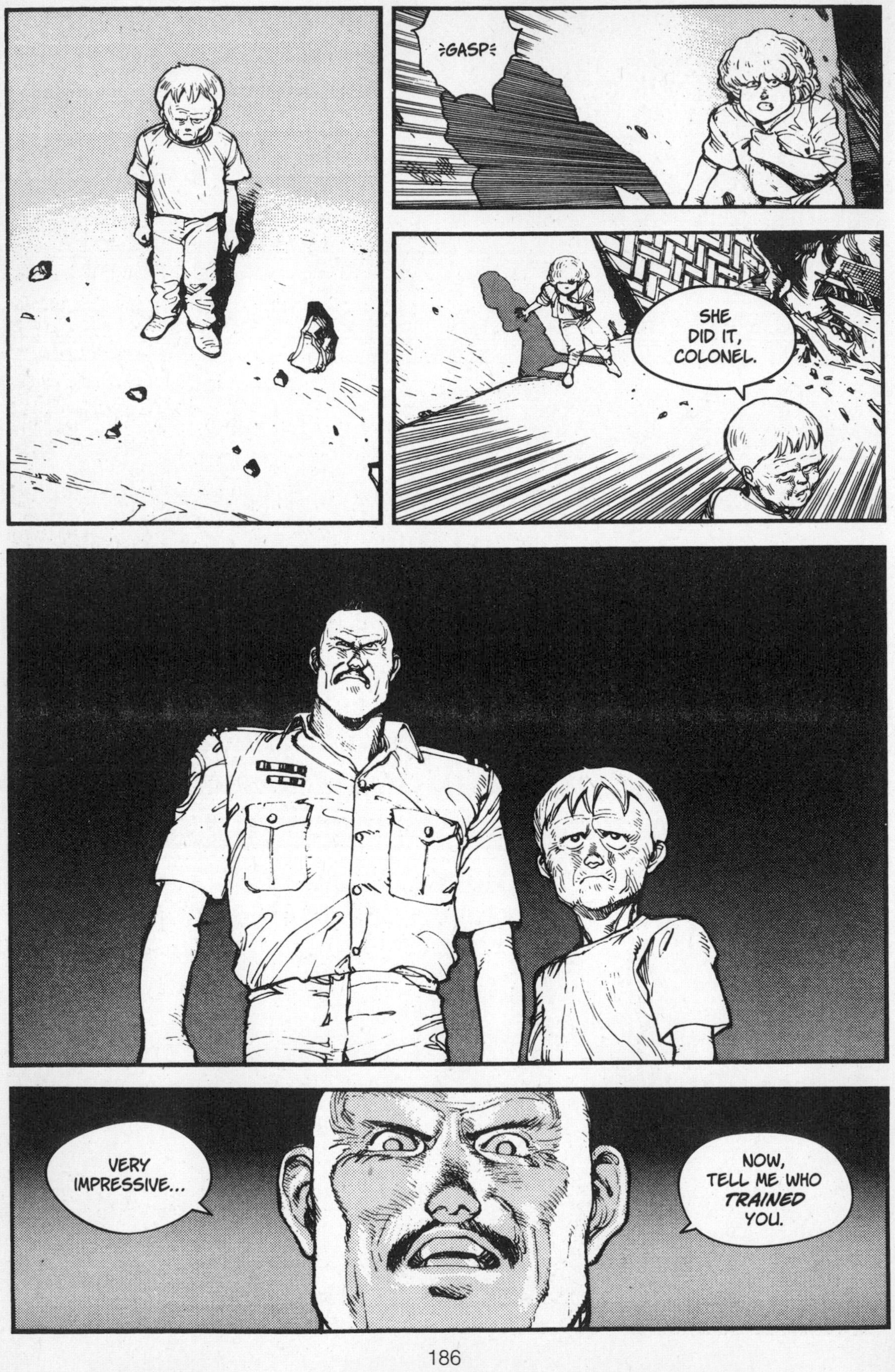
GASP
SHE DID IT, COLONEL.
VERY IMPRESSIVE...
NOW, TELL ME WHO *TRAINED* YOU.

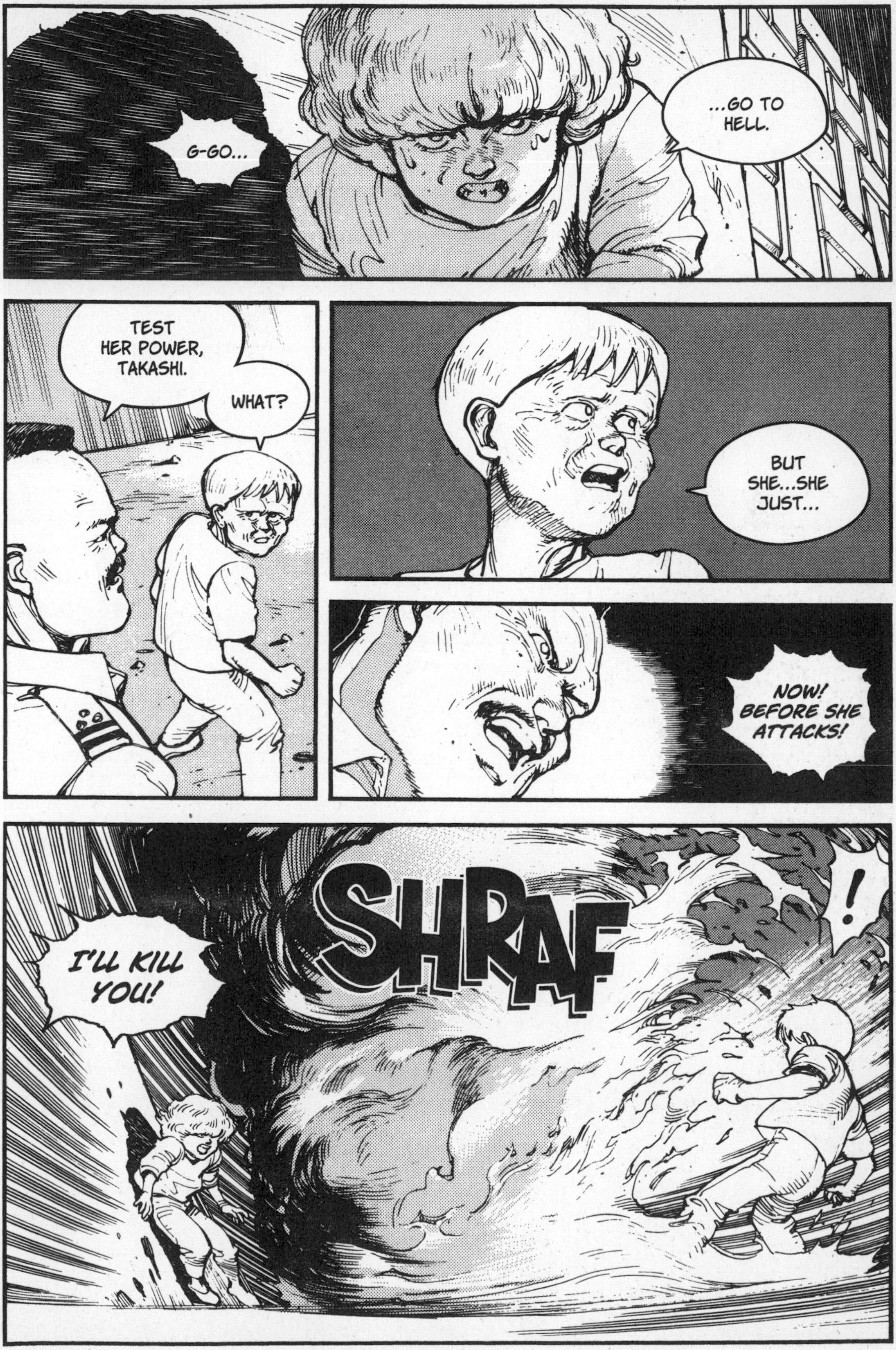
G-GO...
...GO TO HELL.
TEST HER POWER, TAKASHI.
WHAT?
BUT SHE...SHE JUST...
NOW! BEFORE SHE ATTACKS!
I'LL KILL YOU!
SHRAF
!

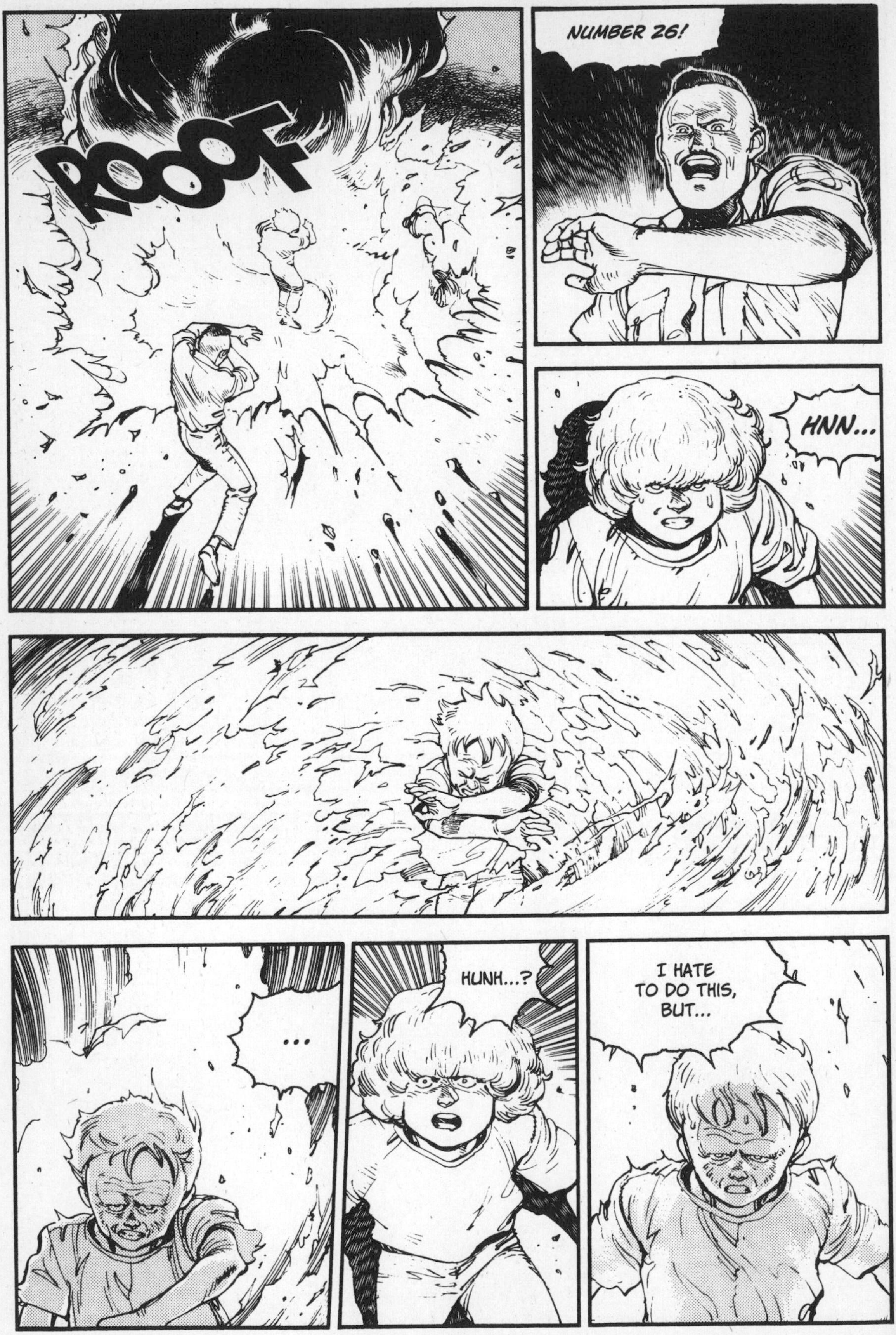
ROOF
NUMBER 26!
HNN...
...
HUNH...?
I HATE TO DO THIS, BUT...

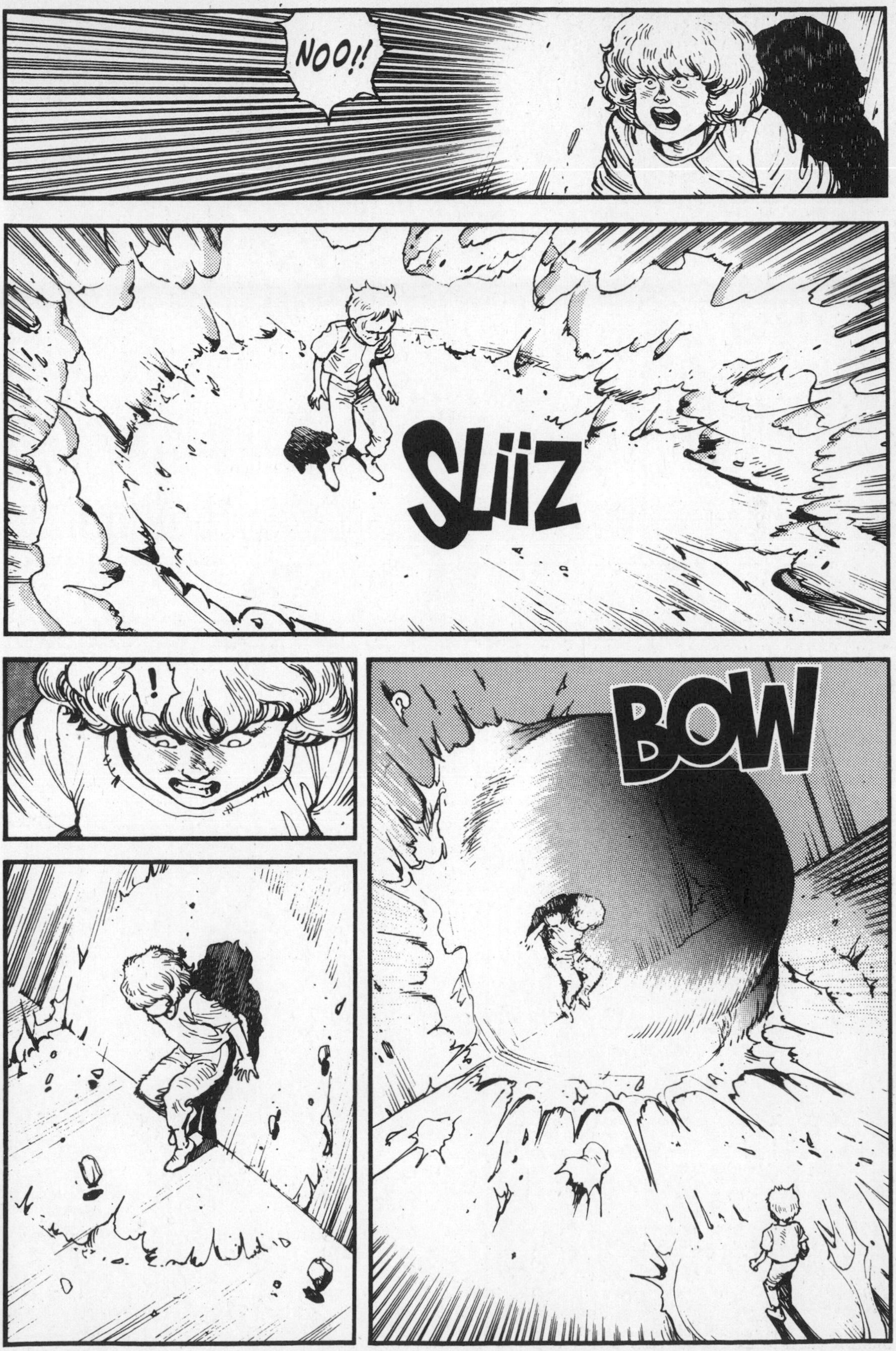
NOO!!
SUïZ
!
BOW

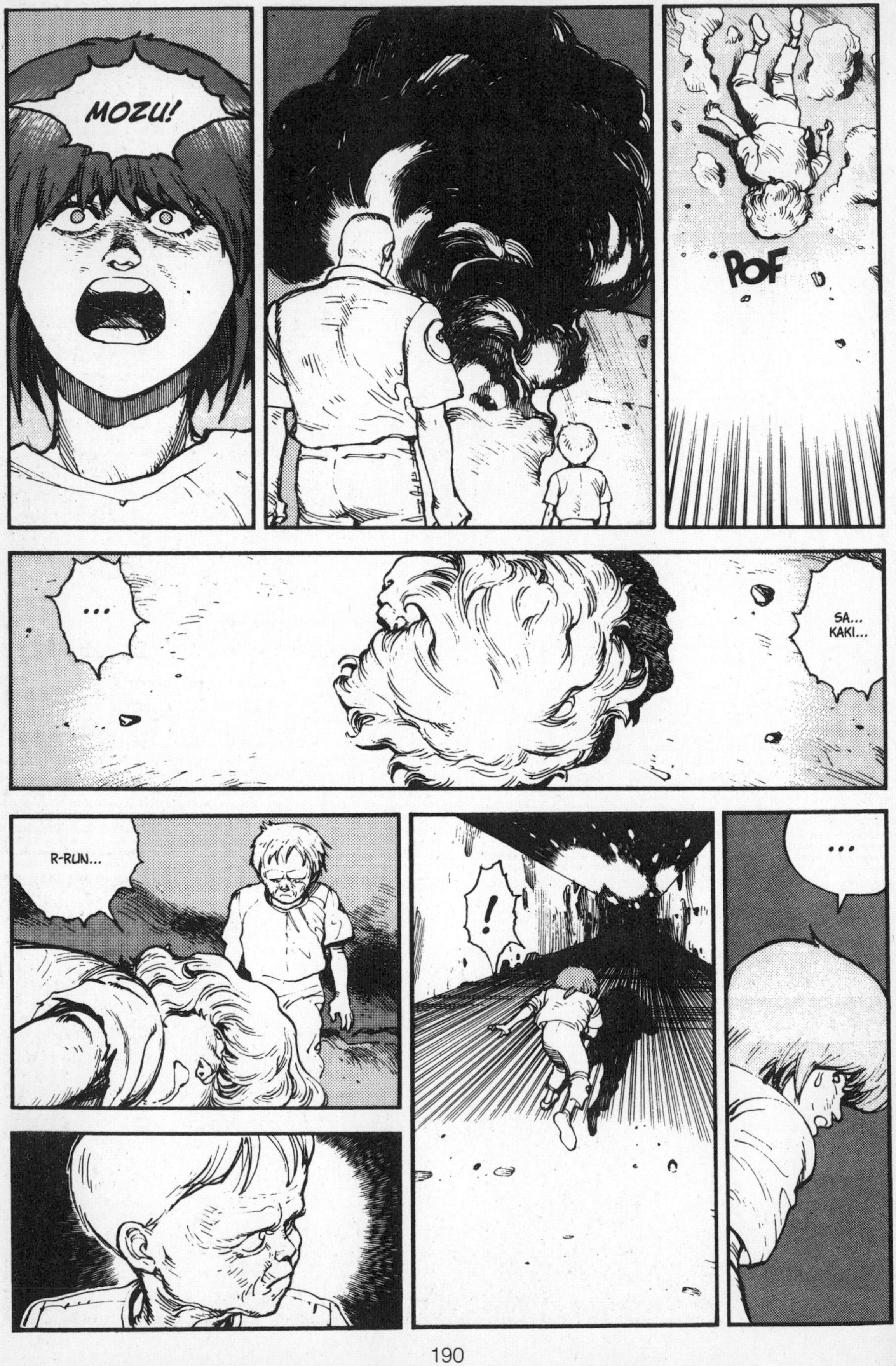
MOZU!
POF
...
SA... KAKI...
R-RUN...
!
...

...

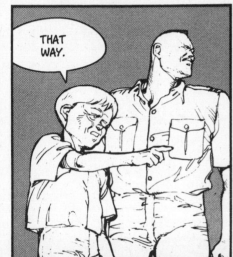

THAT WAY.

RIGHT.

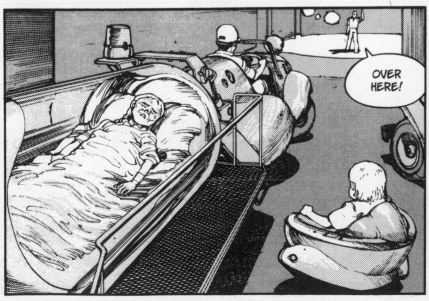

OVER HERE!

KIYOKO...

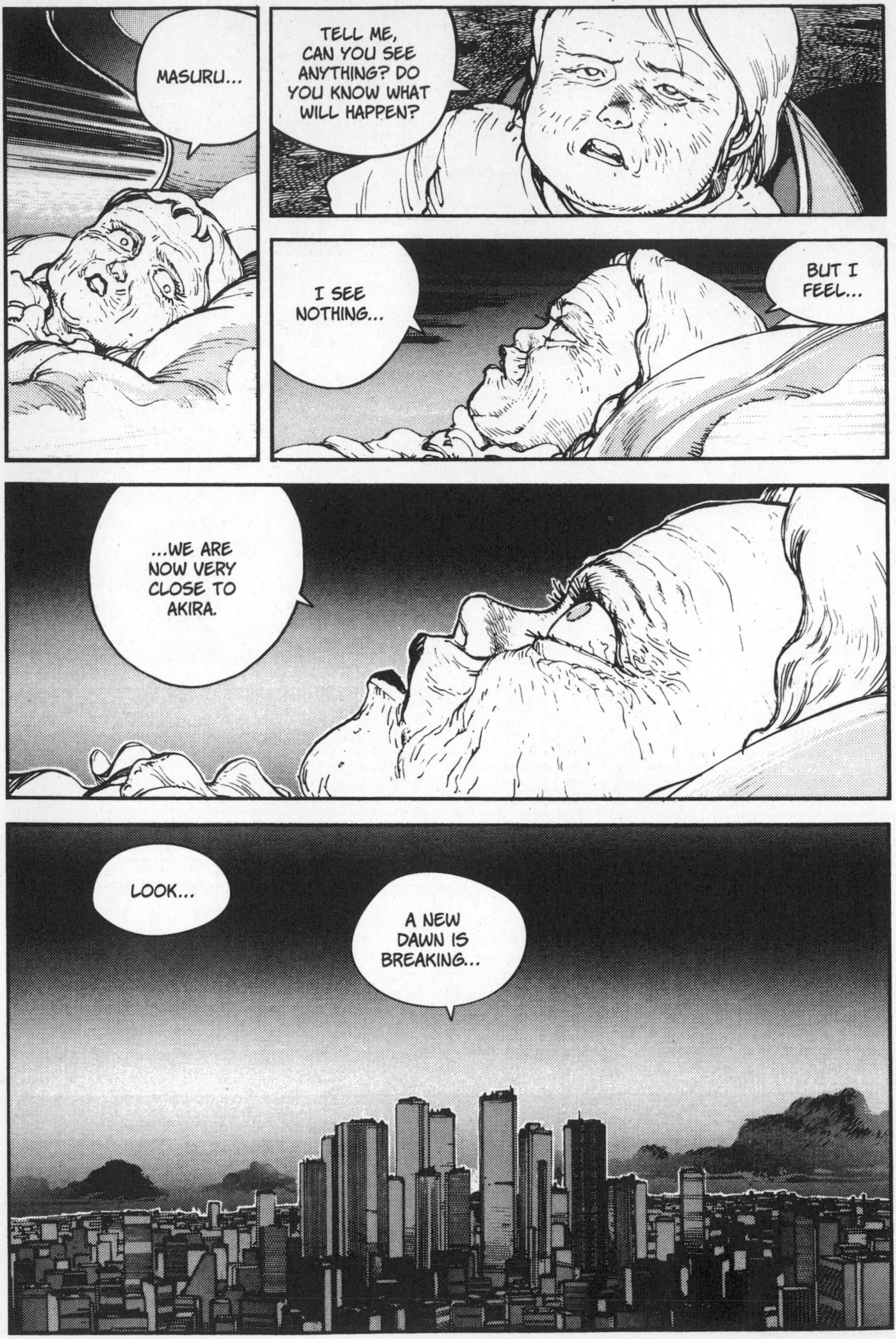
MASURU...
TELL ME, CAN YOU SEE ANYTHING? DO YOU KNOW WHAT WILL HAPPEN?
I SEE NOTHING...
BUT I FEEL...
...WE ARE NOW VERY CLOSE TO AKIRA.
LOOK...
A NEW DAWN IS BREAKING...

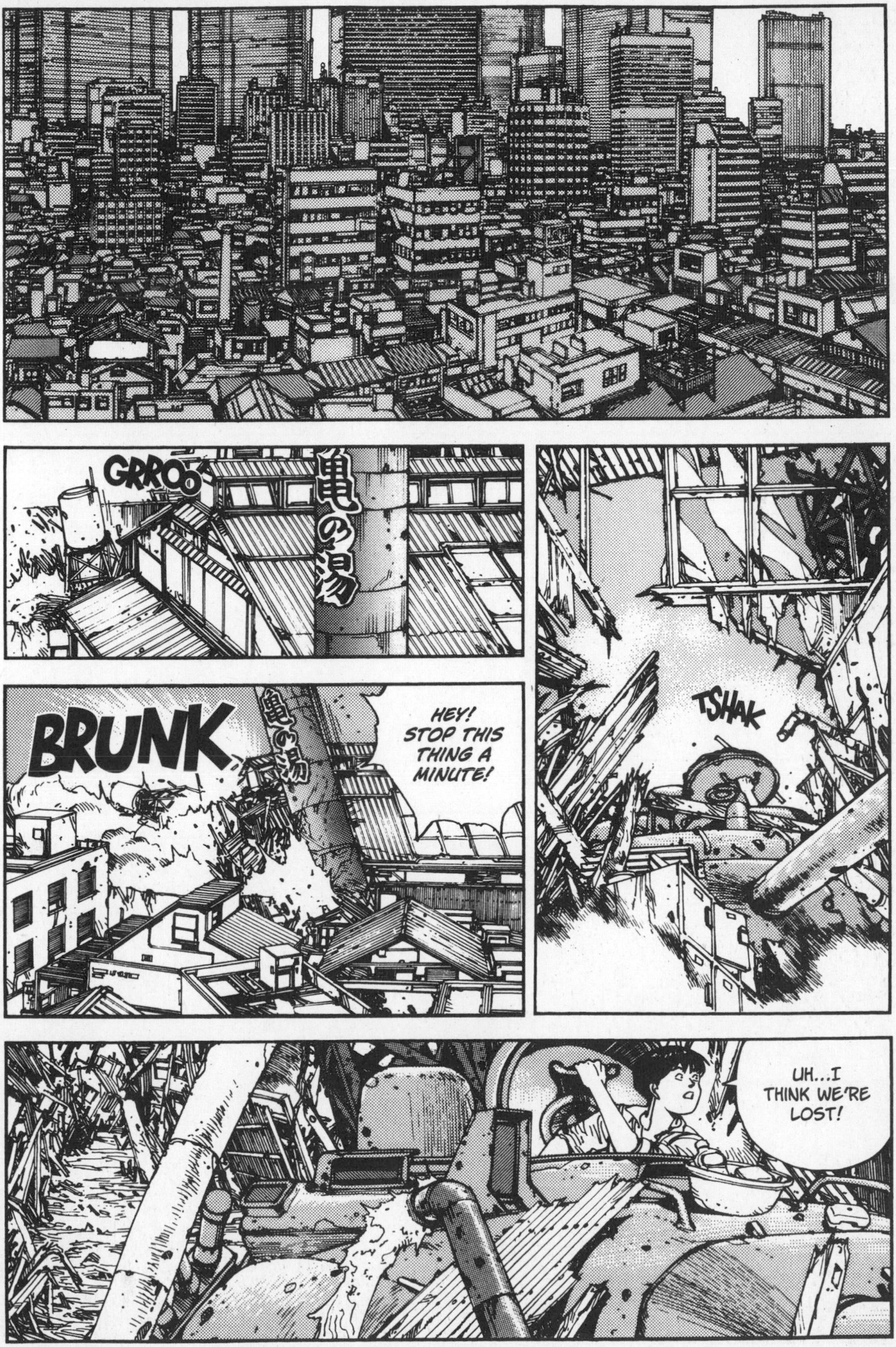
GRROO
亀の湯
BRUNK
亀の湯
HEY! STOP THIS THING A MINUTE!
TSHAK
UH...I THINK WE'RE LOST!

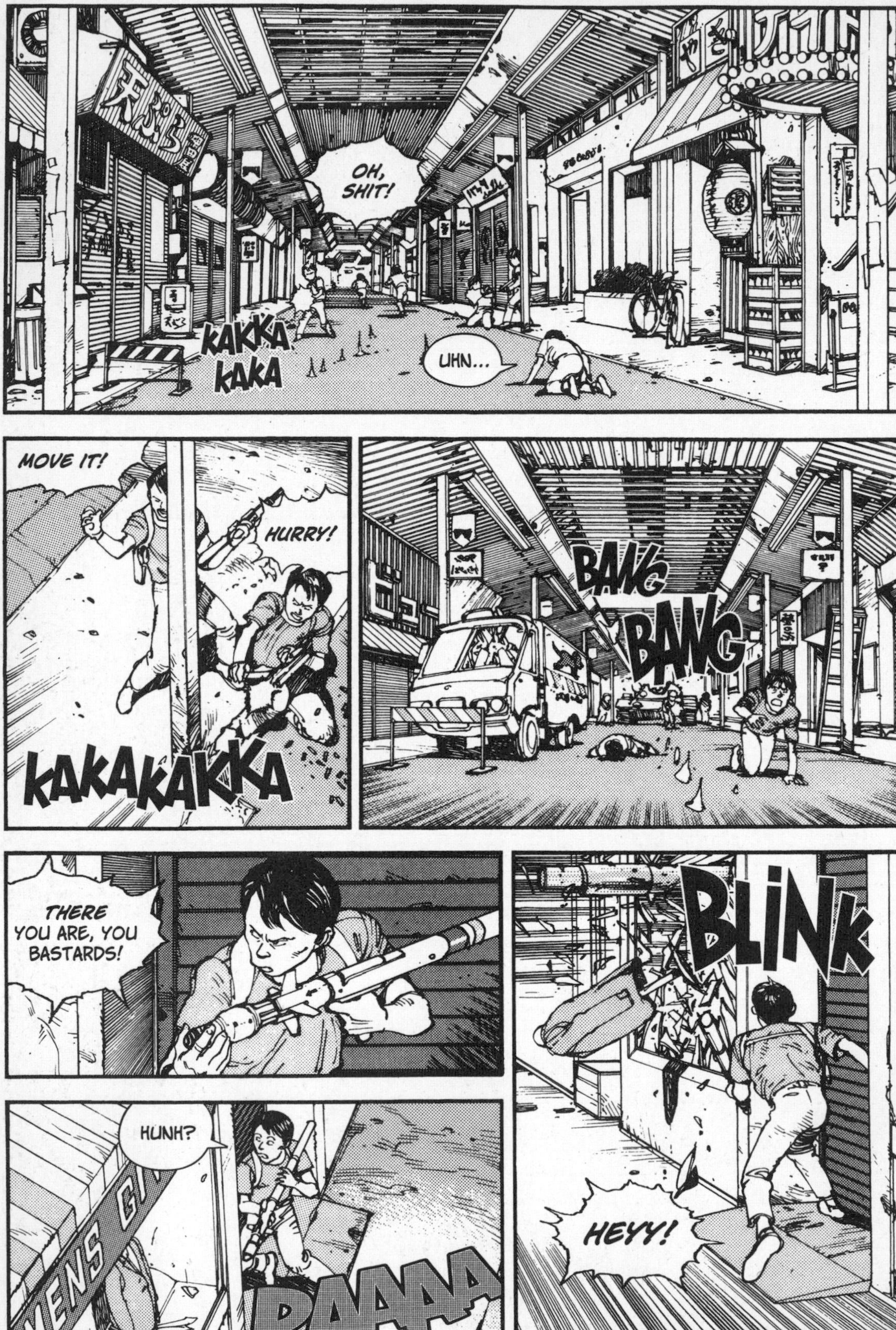
OH, SHIT!
KAKKA KAKA
UHN...
MOVE IT!
HURRY!
KAKAKAKKA
BANG
BANG
THERE YOU ARE, YOU BASTARDS!
HUNH?
RAAAA
BLINK
HEYY!

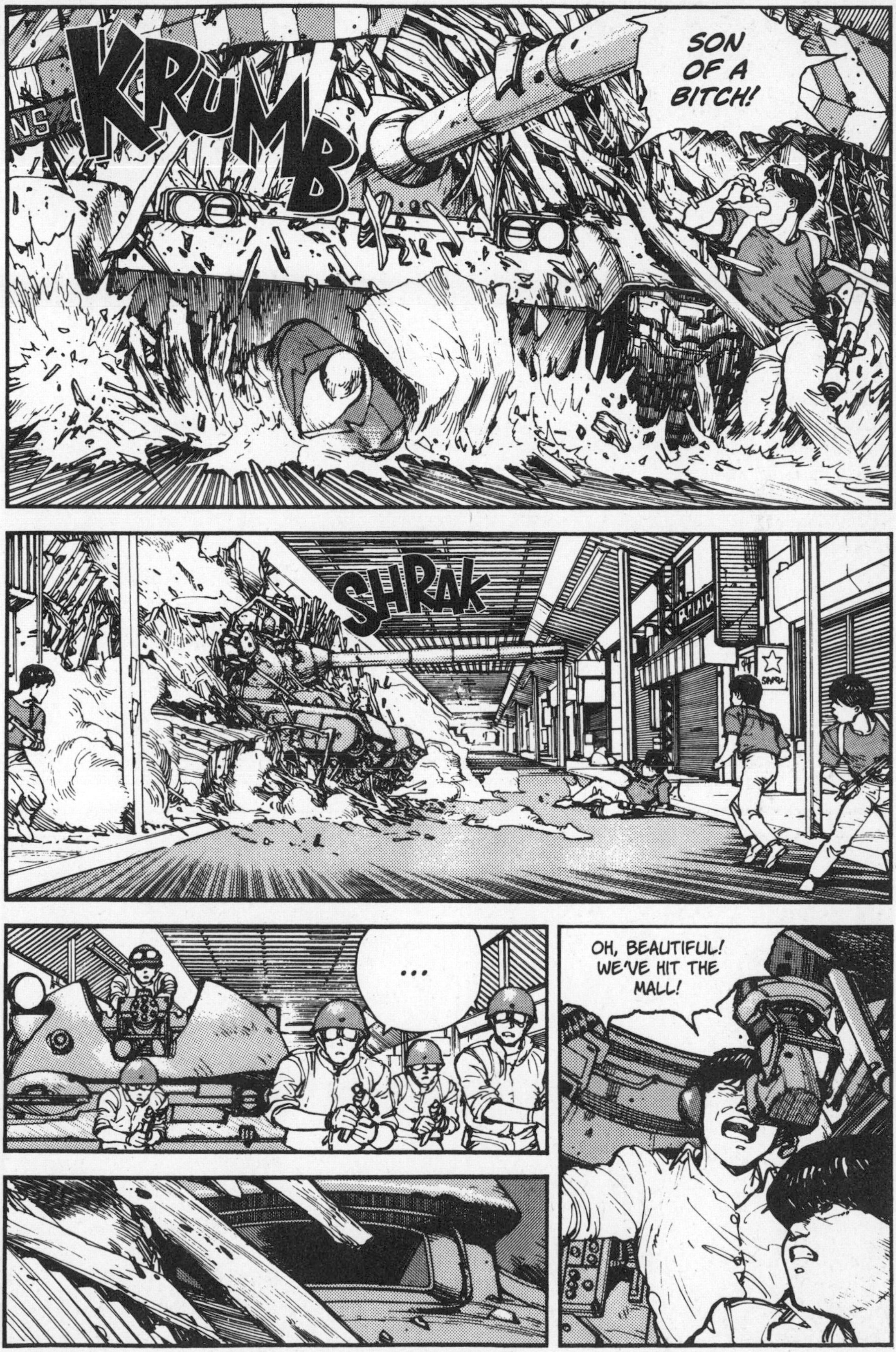
KRUMB
SON OF A BITCH!
SHRAK
...
OH, BEAUTIFUL! WE'VE HIT THE MALL!

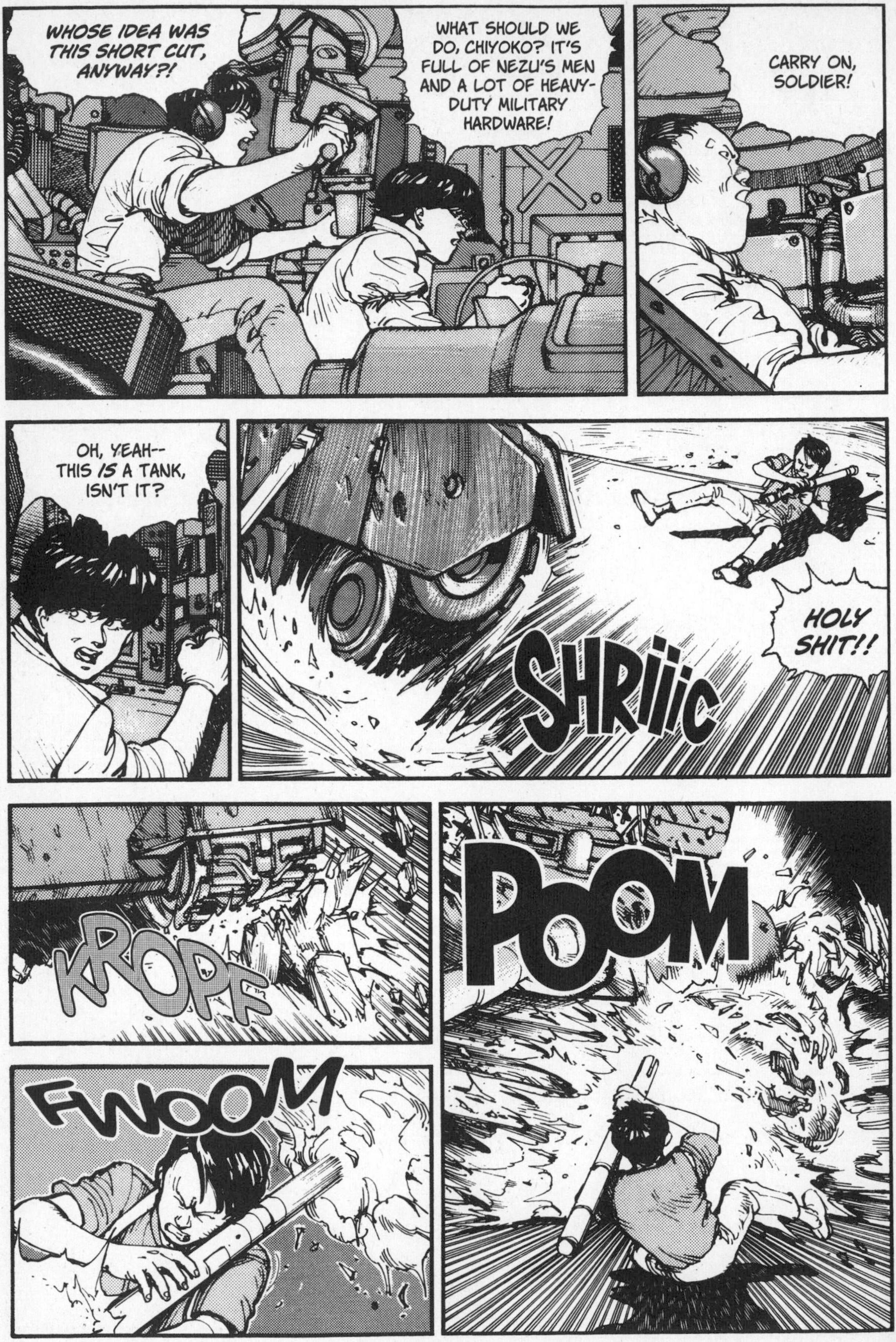
WHOSE IDEA WAS THIS SHORT CUT, ANYWAY?!
WHAT SHOULD WE DO, CHIYOKO? IT'S FULL OF NEZU'S MEN AND A LOT OF HEAVY-DUTY MILITARY HARDWARE!
CARRY ON, SOLDIER!
OH, YEAH-- THIS *IS* A TANK, ISN'T IT?
SHRIiic
HOLY SHIT!!
KROPF
FWOOM
POOM

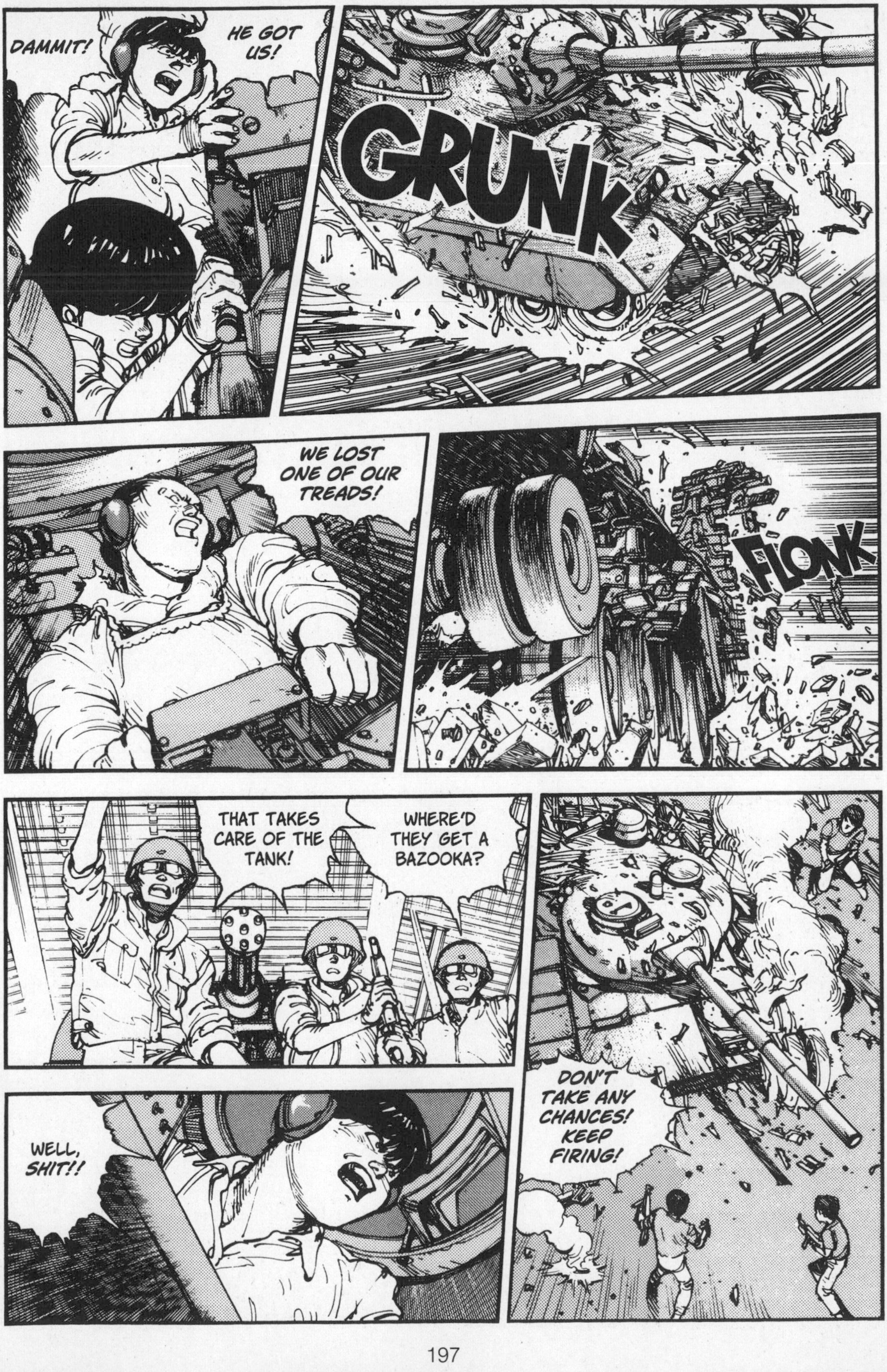

DAMMIT!
HE GOT US!
GRUNK
WE LOST ONE OF OUR TREADS!
FLONK
THAT TAKES CARE OF THE TANK!
WHERE'D THEY GET A BAZOOKA?
DON'T TAKE ANY CHANCES! KEEP FIRING!
WELL, SHIT!!

POOSH
POOOSH

?

HUH ?!

SHIT! SMOKE?! GAS?!

TAKA TAKATA

DAMN IT!

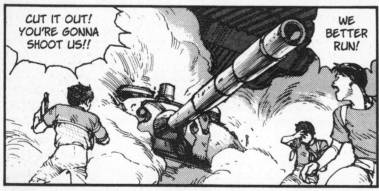

CUT IT OUT! YOU'RE GONNA SHOOT US!!

WE BETTER RUN!

WHOA!

QUICK! THE OTHER WAY!

KEI, HURRY!

OW! OW!

FASTER!

KANEDA, WHERE ARE YOU?

NOT THAT WAY! THIS WAY!

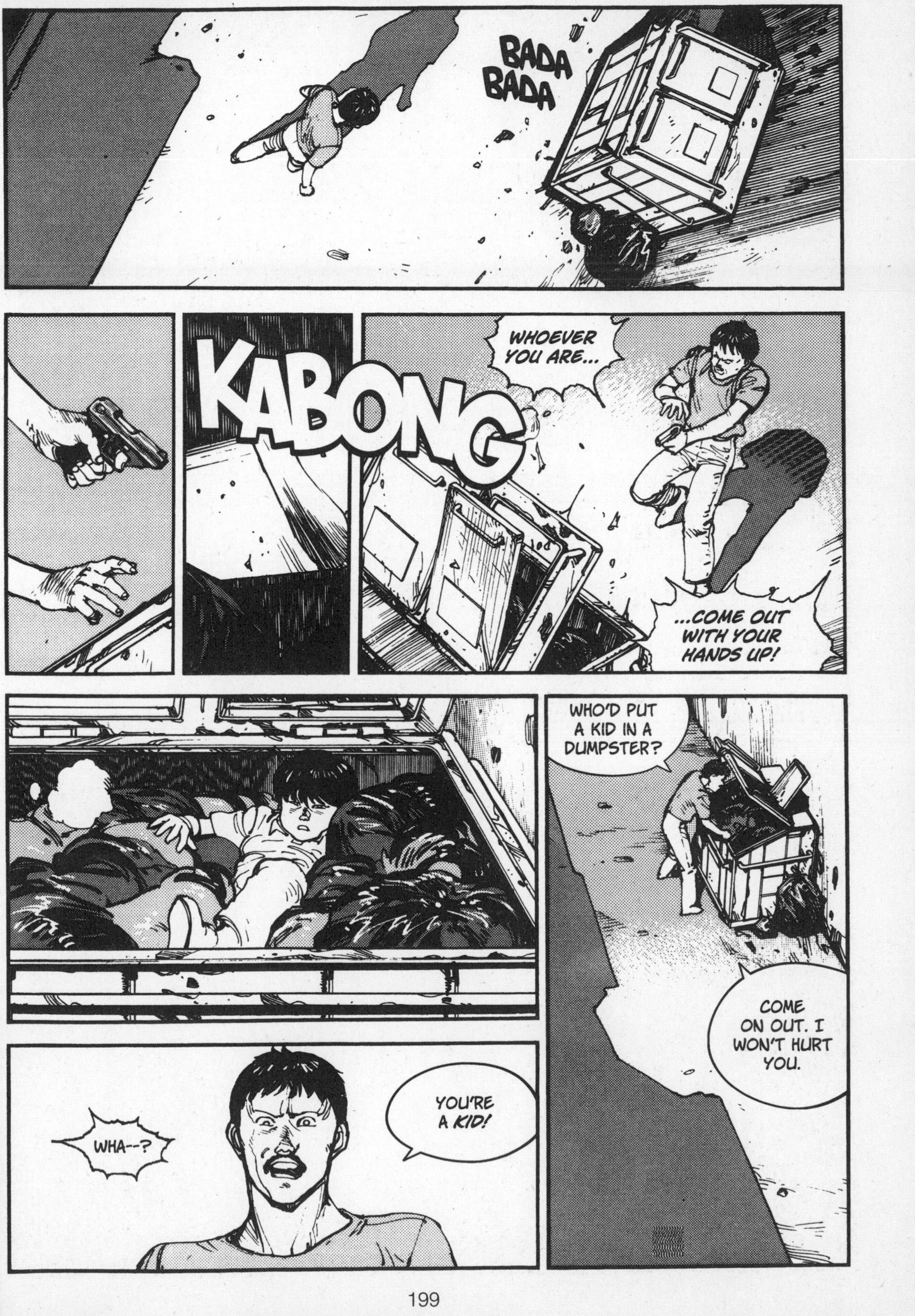
BADA BADA
KABONG
WHOEVER YOU ARE...
...COME OUT WITH YOUR HANDS UP!
WHO'D PUT A KID IN A DUMPSTER?
COME ON OUT. I WON'T HURT YOU.
WHA--?
YOU'RE A KID!

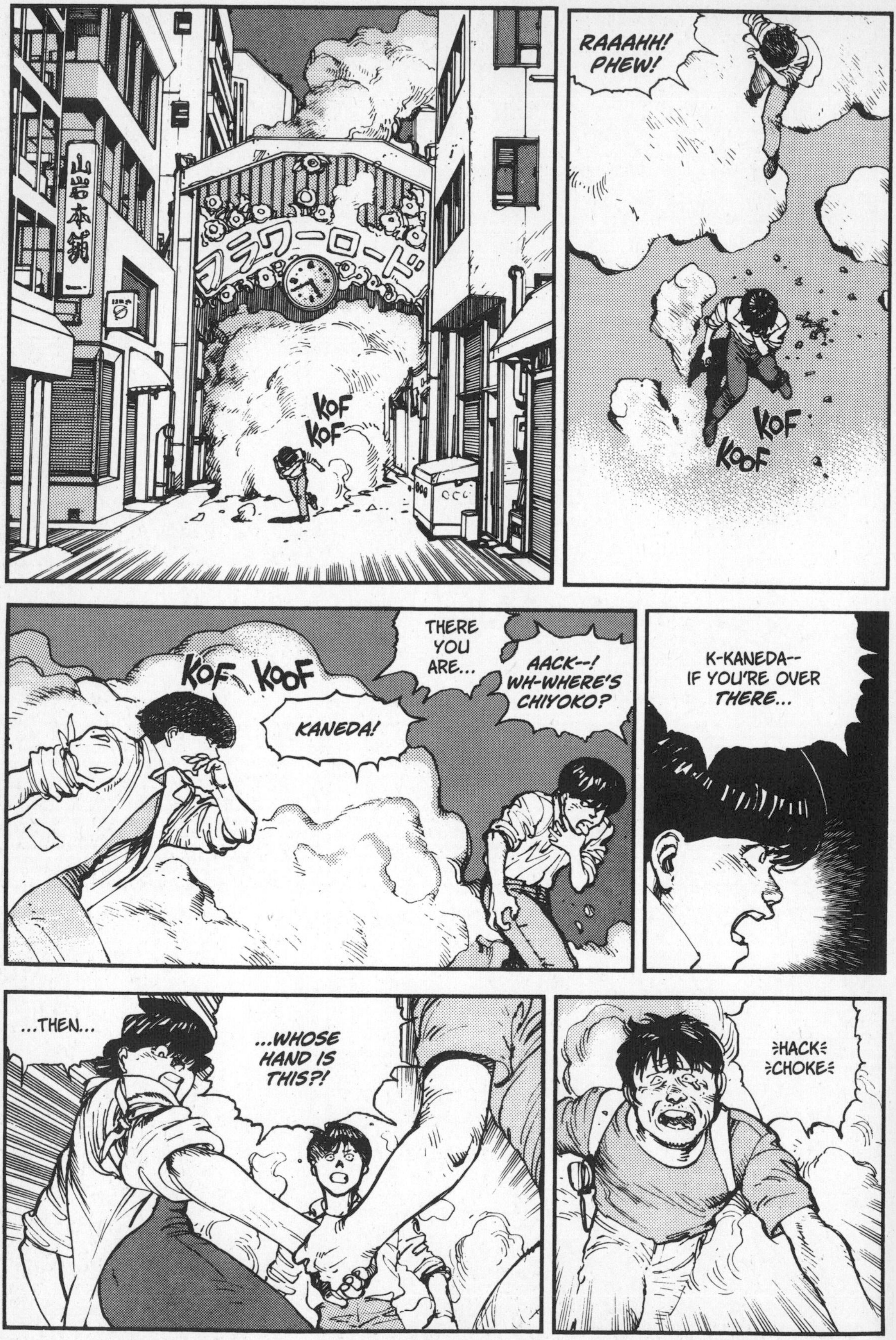
フラワーロード
KOF KOF
RAAAHH! PHEW!
KOF KOOF
KOF KOOF
KANEDA!
THERE YOU ARE...
AACK--! WH-WHERE'S CHIYOKO?
K-KANEDA-- IF YOU'RE OVER THERE...
...THEN...
...WHOSE HAND IS THIS?!
HACK CHOKE

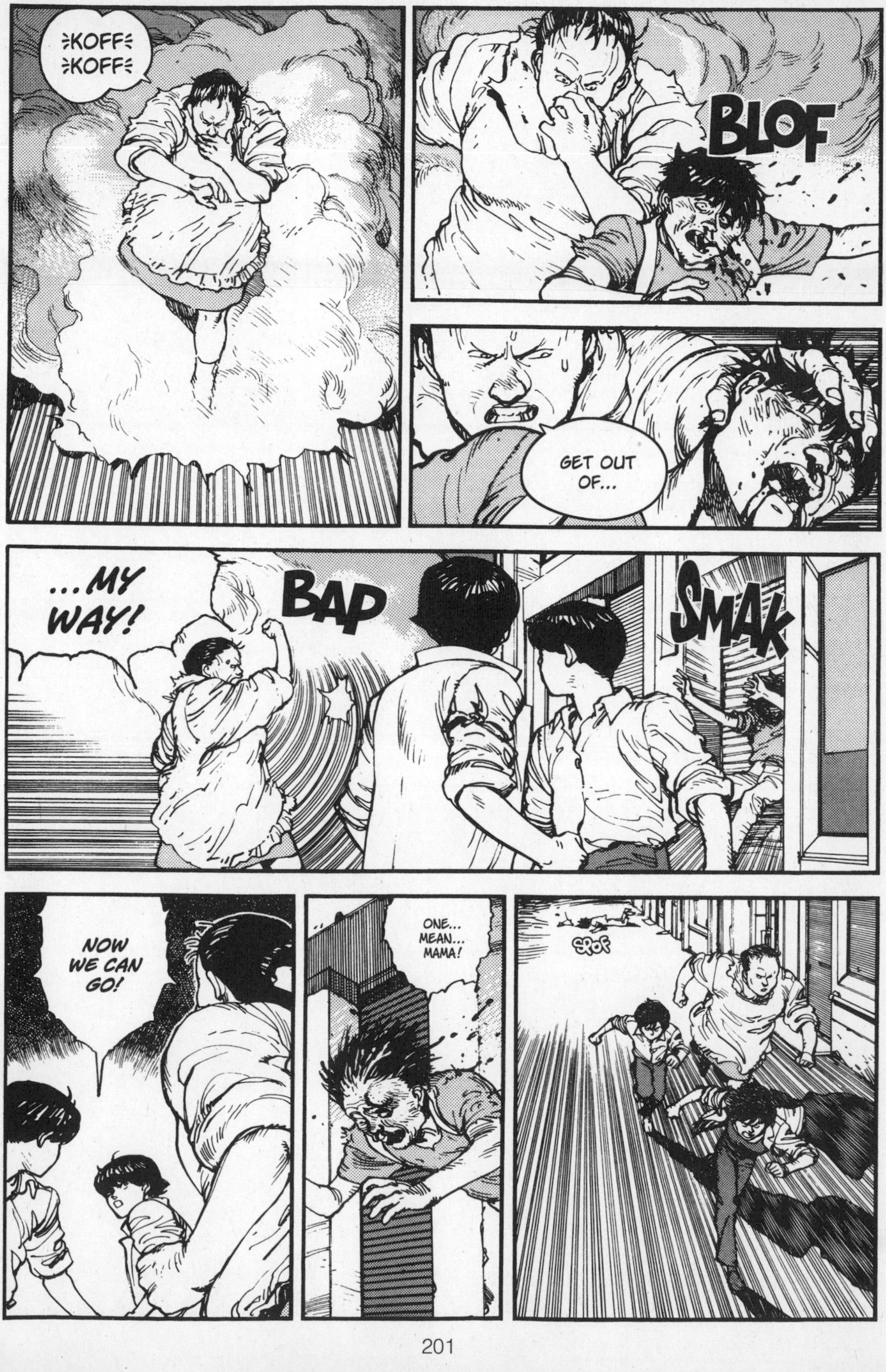

KOFF
KOFF
BLOF
GET OUT OF...
...MY WAY!
BAP
SMAK
NOW WE CAN GO!
ONE... MEAN... MAMA!
SPOF

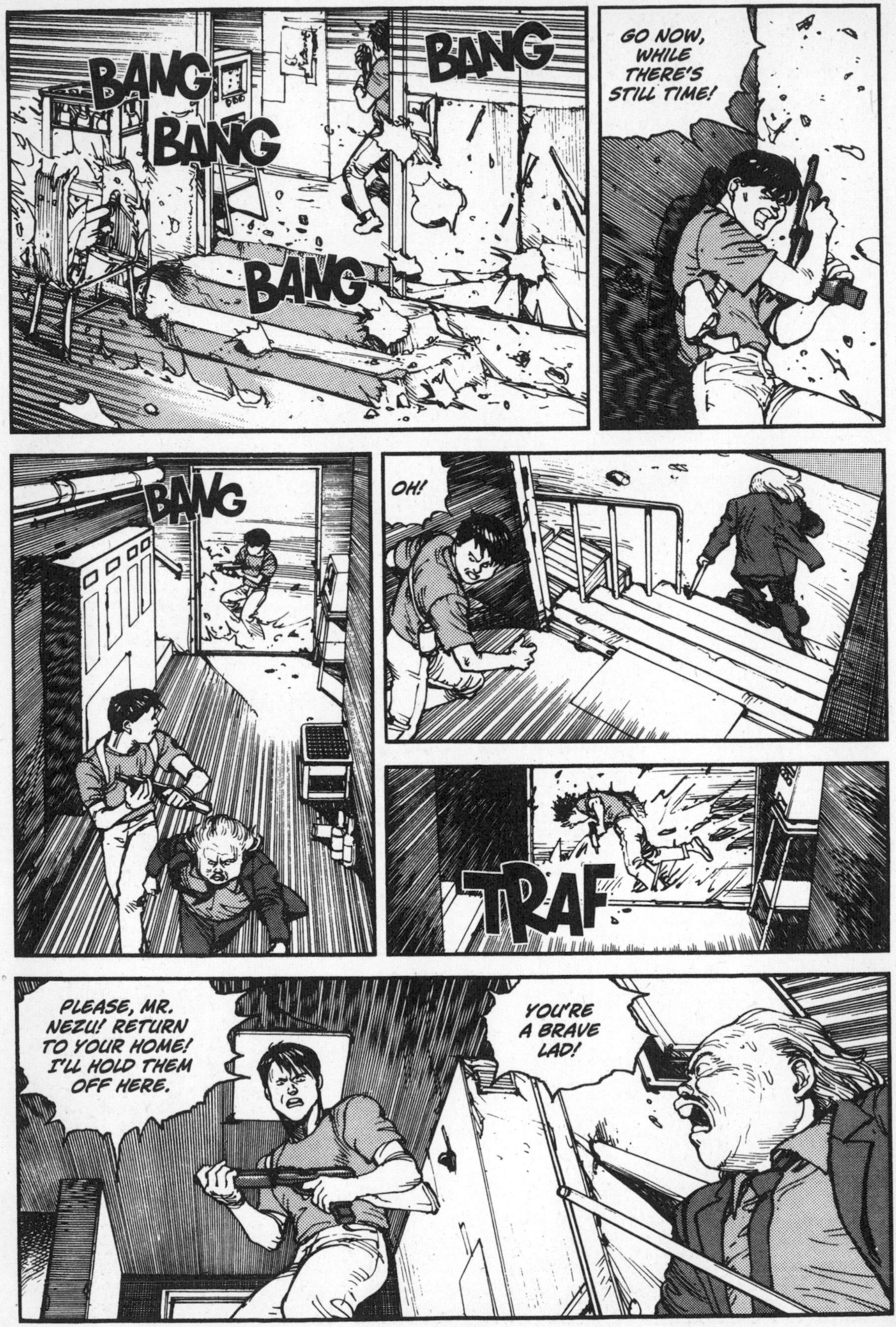
BANG
BANG
BANG
BANG
GO NOW, WHILE THERE'S STILL TIME!
BANG
OH!
TRAF
PLEASE, MR. NEZU! RETURN TO YOUR HOME! I'LL HOLD THEM OFF HERE.
YOU'RE A BRAVE LAD!

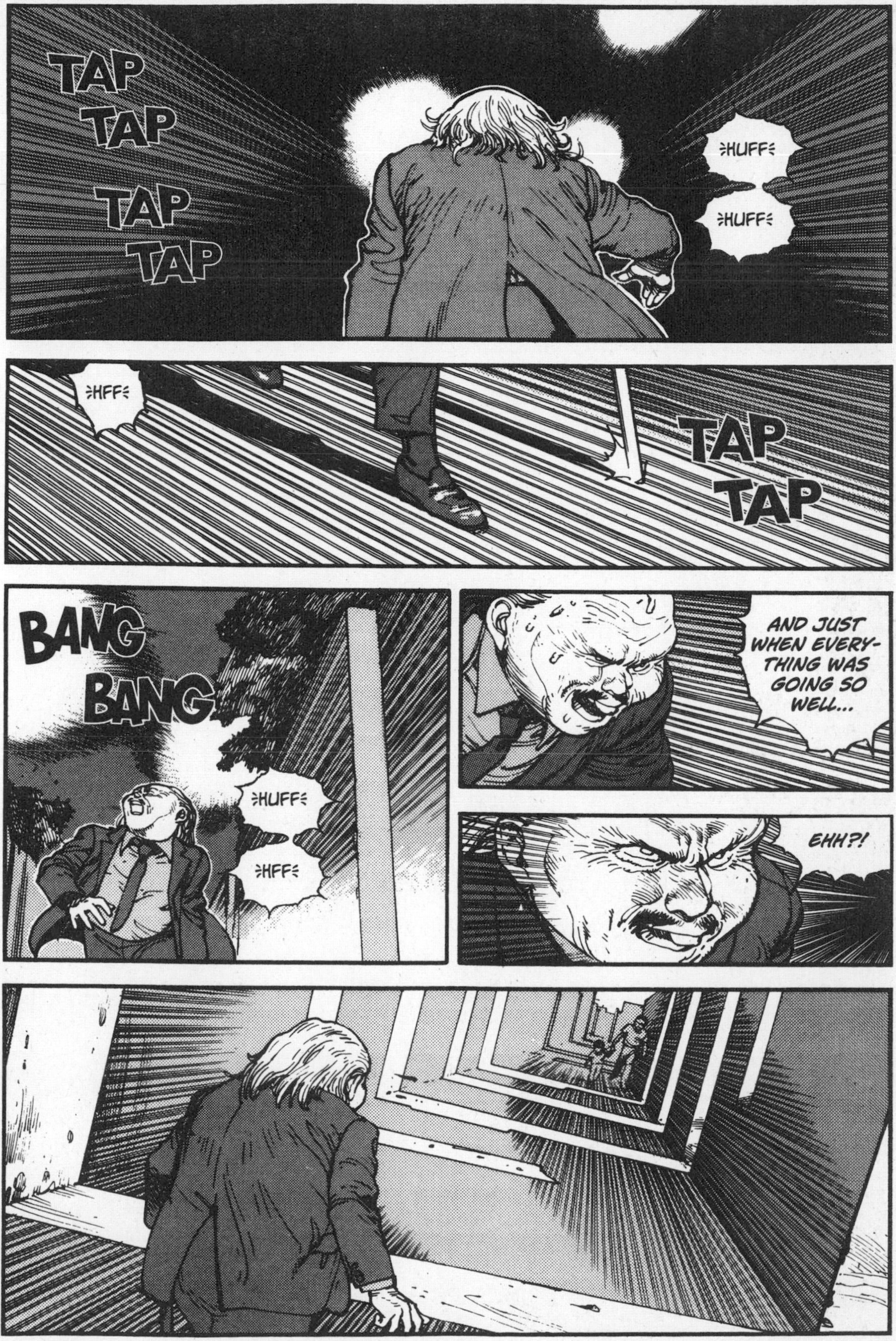
TAP
TAP
TAP
TAP
HUFF
HUFF
HFF
TAP
TAP
BANG
BANG
HUFF
HFF
AND JUST WHEN EVERY-THING WAS GOING SO WELL...
EHH?!

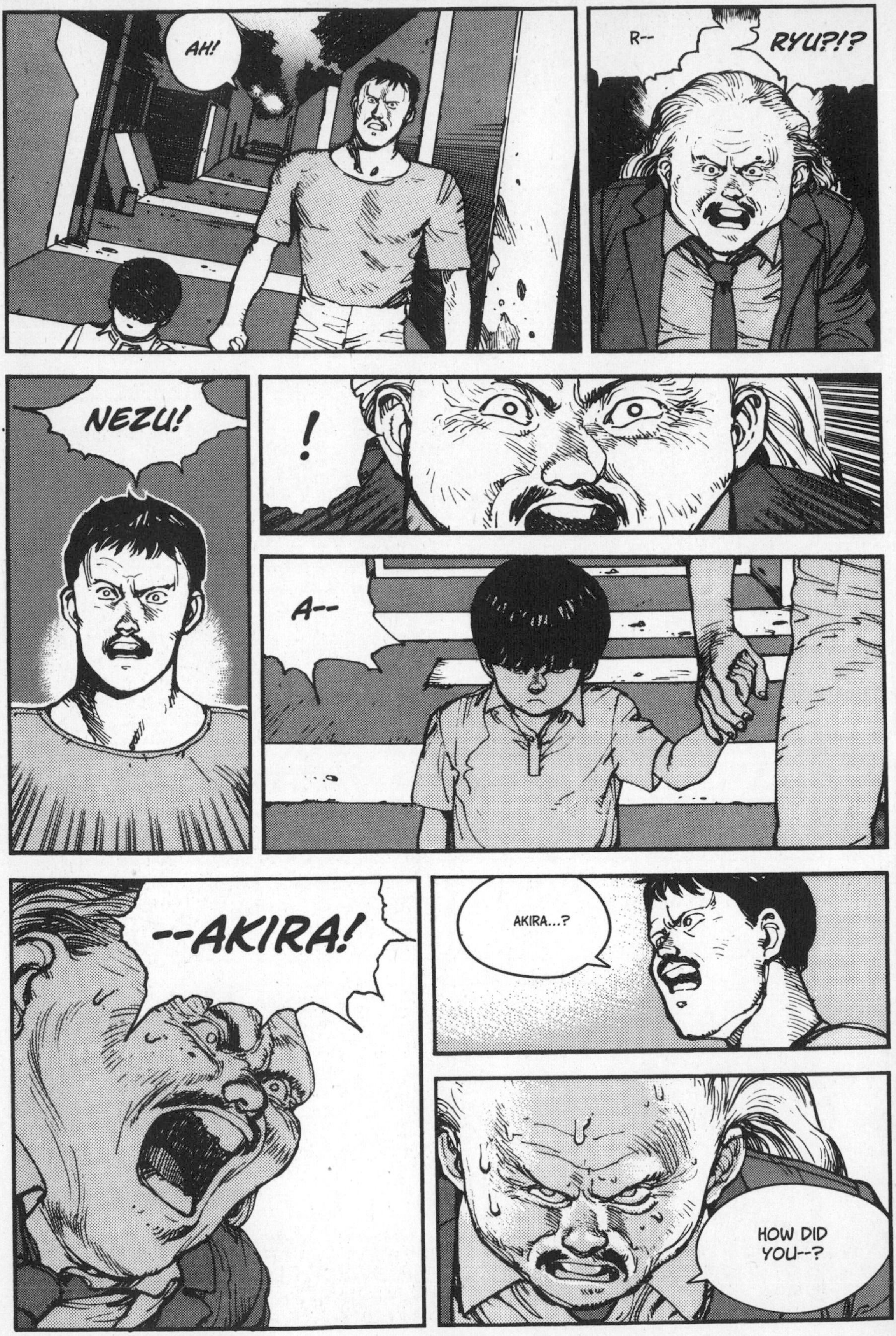
AH!
R--
RYU?!?
NEZU!
!
A--
--AKIRA!
AKIRA...?
HOW DID YOU--?

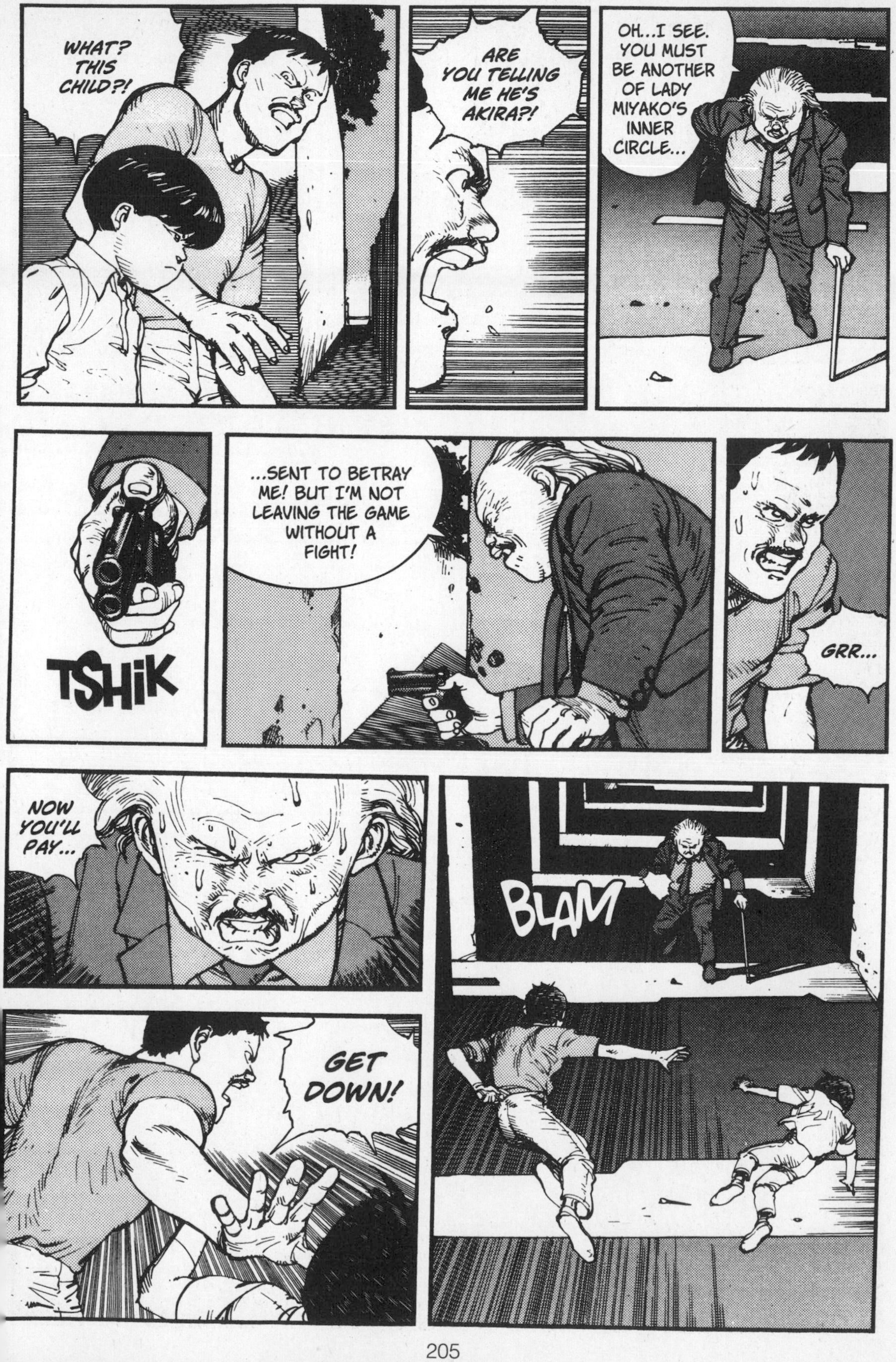
WHAT? THIS CHILD?!
ARE YOU TELLING ME HE'S AKIRA?!
OH...I SEE. YOU MUST BE ANOTHER OF LADY MIYAKO'S INNER CIRCLE...
TSHIK
...SENT TO BETRAY ME! BUT I'M NOT LEAVING THE GAME WITHOUT A FIGHT!
GRR...
NOW YOU'LL PAY...
BLAM
GET DOWN!

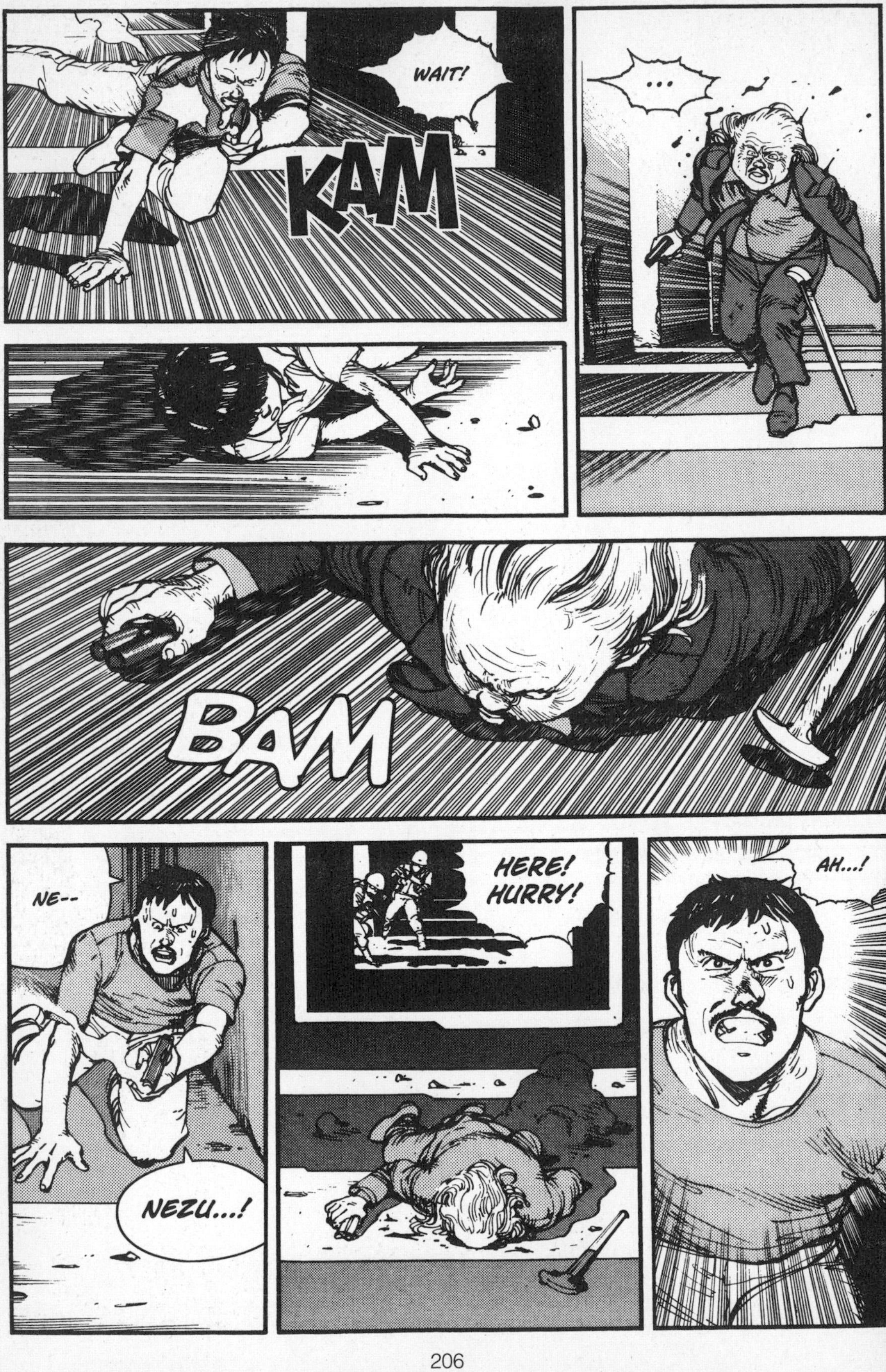
WAIT!
KAM
...
BAM
NE--
NEZU...!
HERE! HURRY!
AH...!

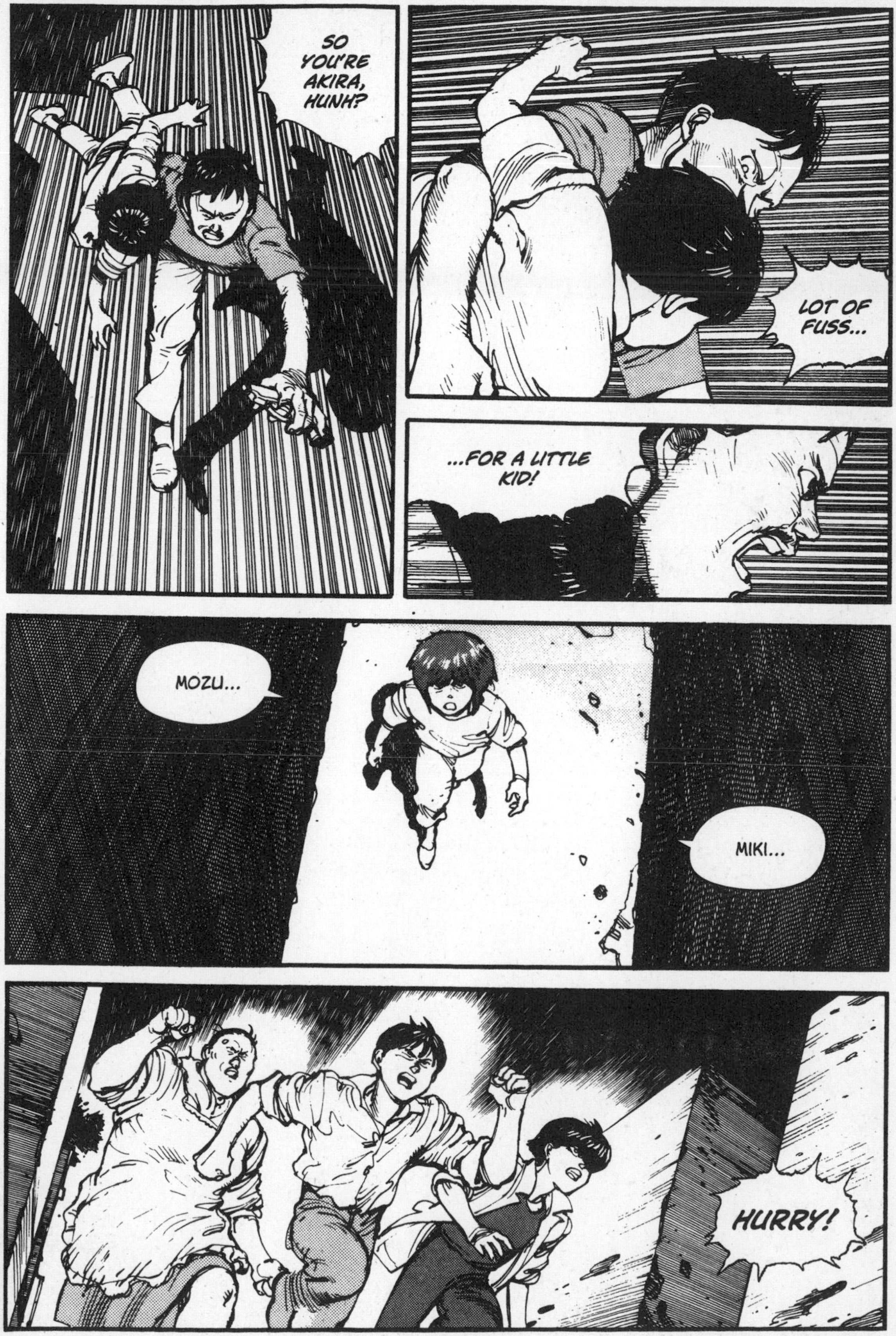
SO YOU'RE AKIRA, HUNH?
LOT OF FUSS...
...FOR A LITTLE KID!
MOZU...
MIKI...
HURRY!

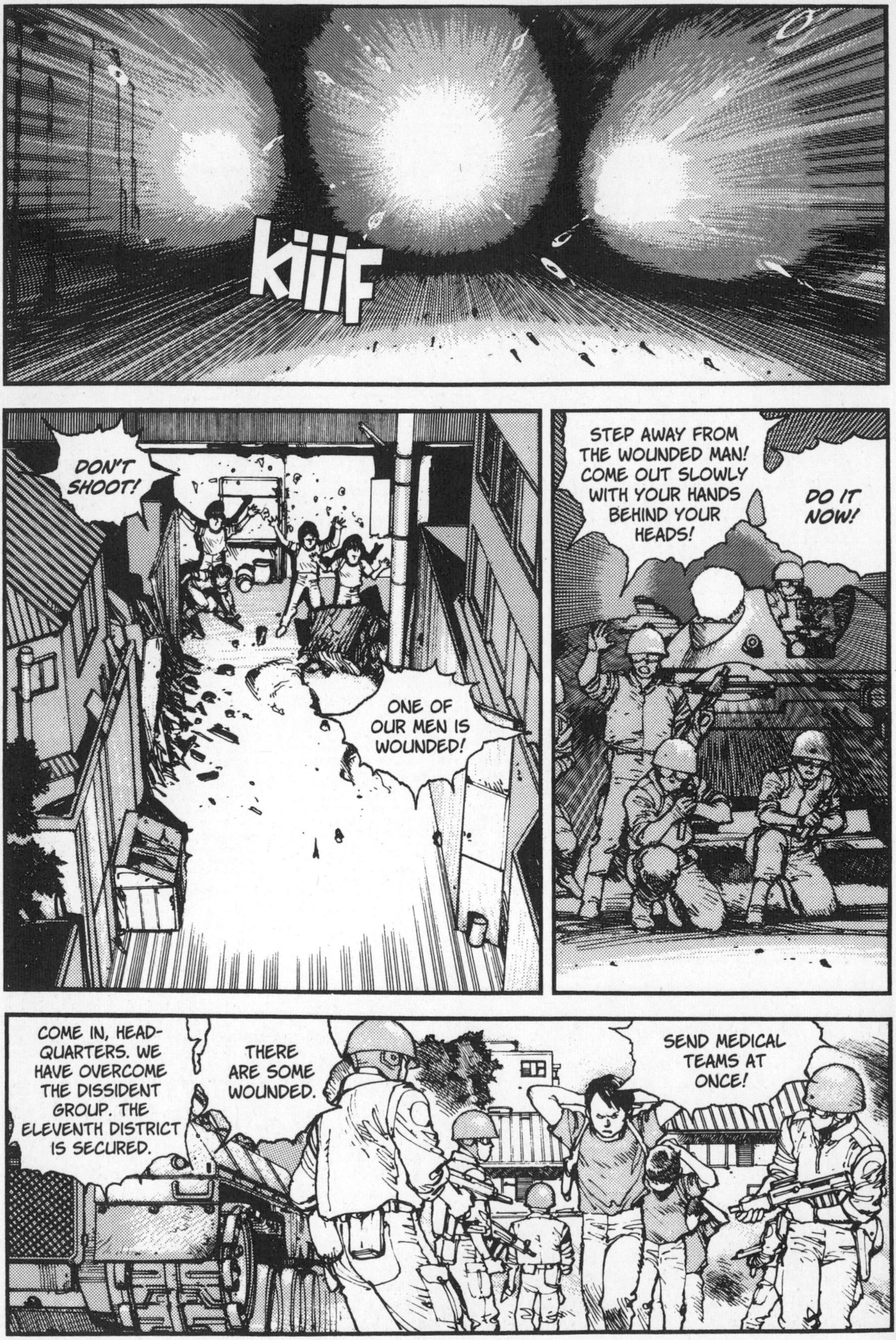

KIIIF
DON'T SHOOT!
ONE OF OUR MEN IS WOUNDED!
STEP AWAY FROM THE WOUNDED MAN! COME OUT SLOWLY WITH YOUR HANDS BEHIND YOUR HEADS!
DO IT NOW!
COME IN, HEAD-QUARTERS. WE HAVE OVERCOME THE DISSIDENT GROUP. THE ELEVENTH DISTRICT IS SECURED.
THERE ARE SOME WOUNDED.
SEND MEDICAL TEAMS AT ONCE!

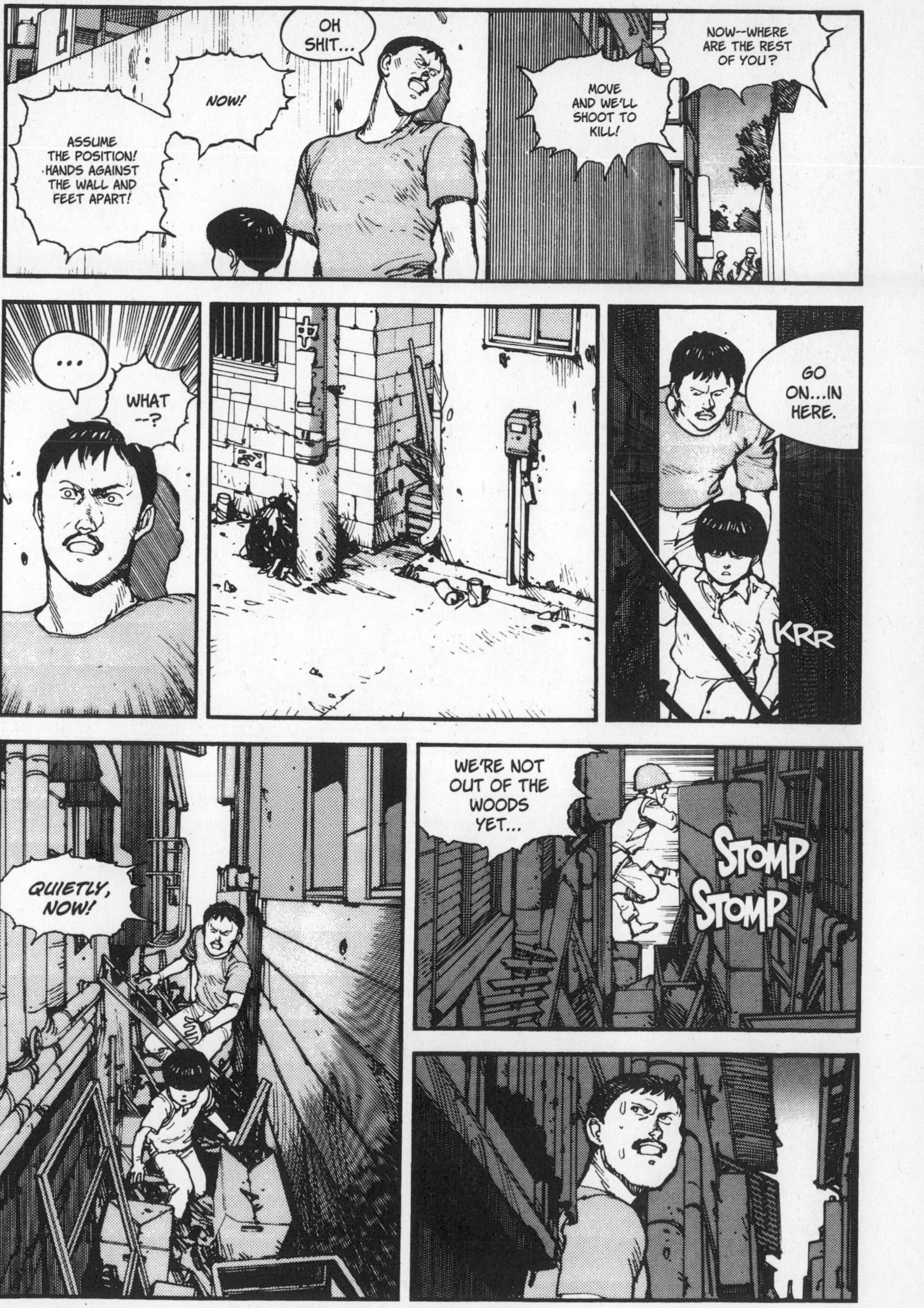

ASSUME THE POSITION! HANDS AGAINST THE WALL AND FEET APART!
NOW!
OH SHIT...
MOVE AND WE'LL SHOOT TO KILL!
NOW--WHERE ARE THE REST OF YOU?
...
WHAT --?
GO ON...IN HERE.
KRR
QUIETLY, NOW!
WE'RE NOT OUT OF THE WOODS YET...
STOMP
STOMP

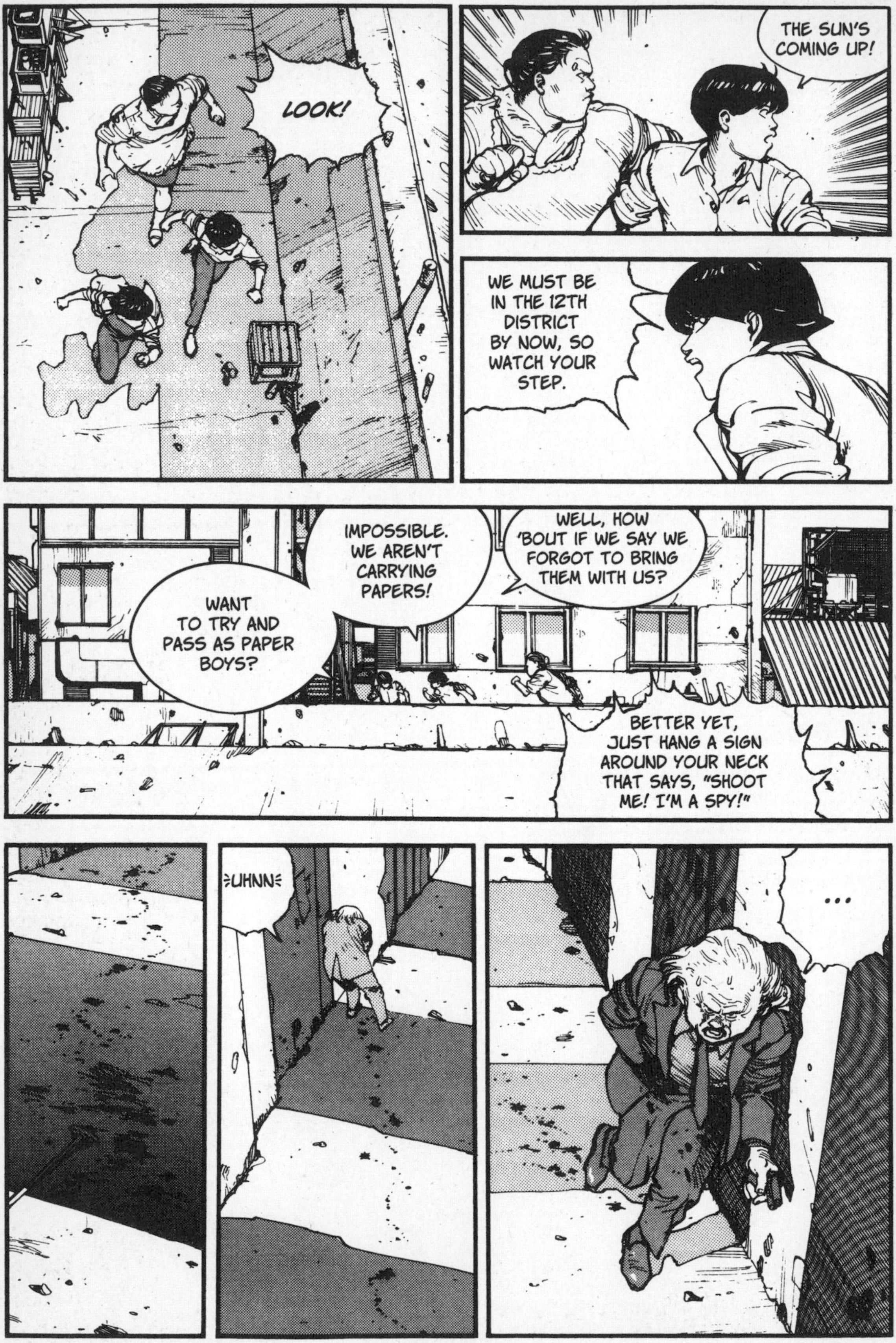
LOOK!
THE SUN'S COMING UP!
WE MUST BE IN THE 12TH DISTRICT BY NOW, SO WATCH YOUR STEP.
WANT TO TRY AND PASS AS PAPER BOYS?
IMPOSSIBLE. WE AREN'T CARRYING PAPERS!
WELL, HOW 'BOUT IF WE SAY WE FORGOT TO BRING THEM WITH US?
BETTER YET, JUST HANG A SIGN AROUND YOUR NECK THAT SAYS, "SHOOT ME! I'M A SPY!"
UHNN
...

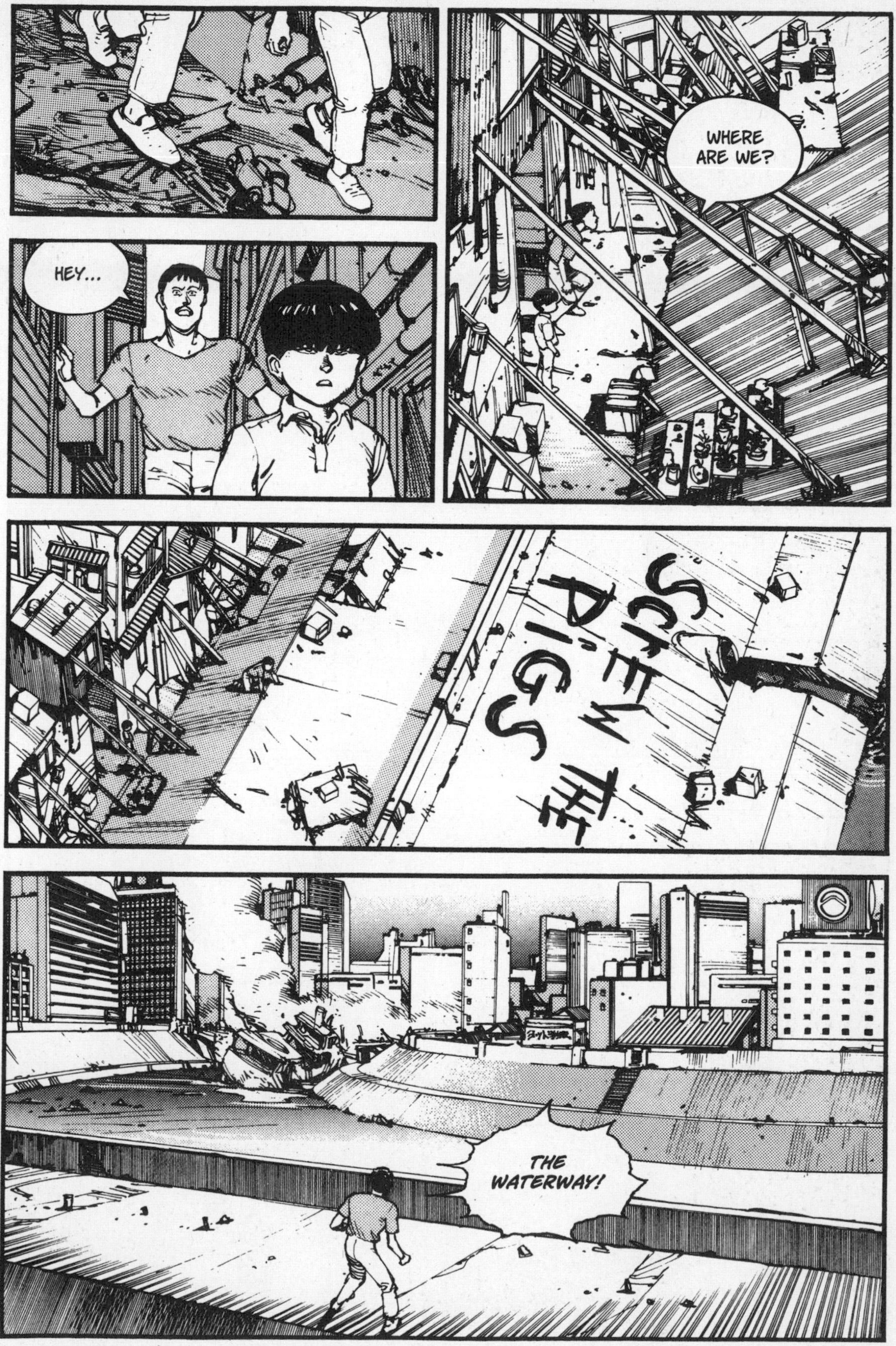
HEY...
WHERE ARE WE?
SCREW THE PIGS
THE WATERWAY!

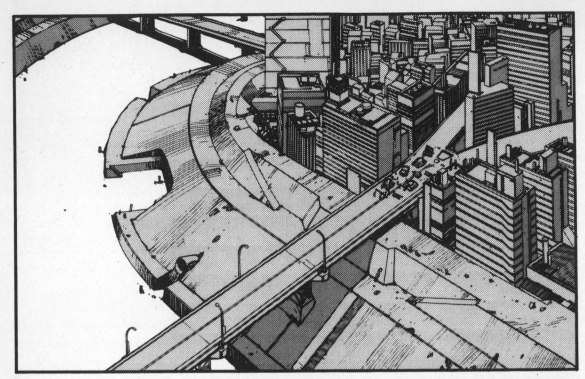

HUNH?

212

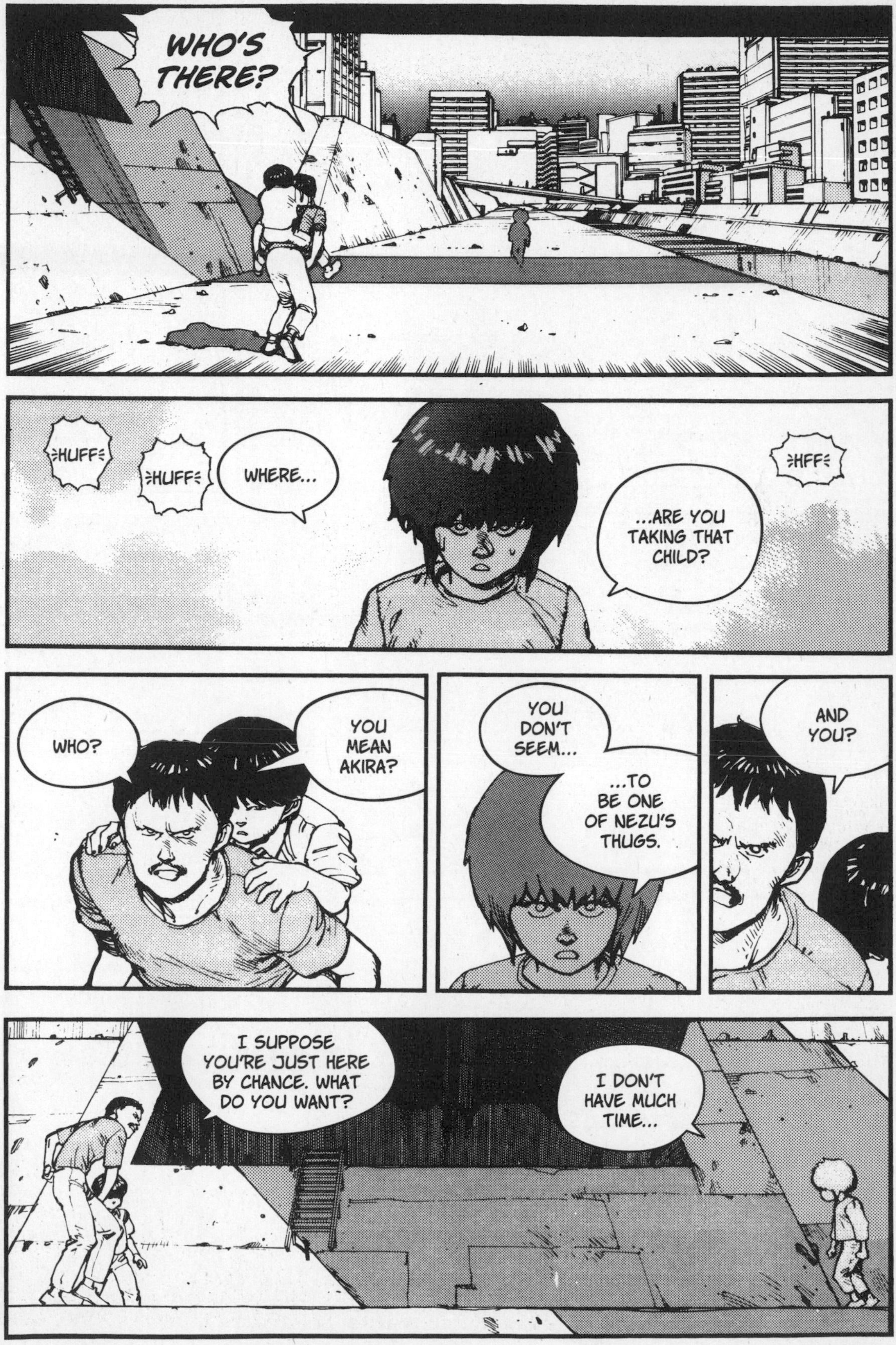
WHO'S THERE?
HUFF
HUFF
WHERE...
HFF
...ARE YOU TAKING THAT CHILD?
WHO?
YOU MEAN AKIRA?
YOU DON'T SEEM...
...TO BE ONE OF NEZU'S THUGS.
AND YOU?
I SUPPOSE YOU'RE JUST HERE BY CHANCE. WHAT DO YOU WANT?
I DON'T HAVE MUCH TIME...

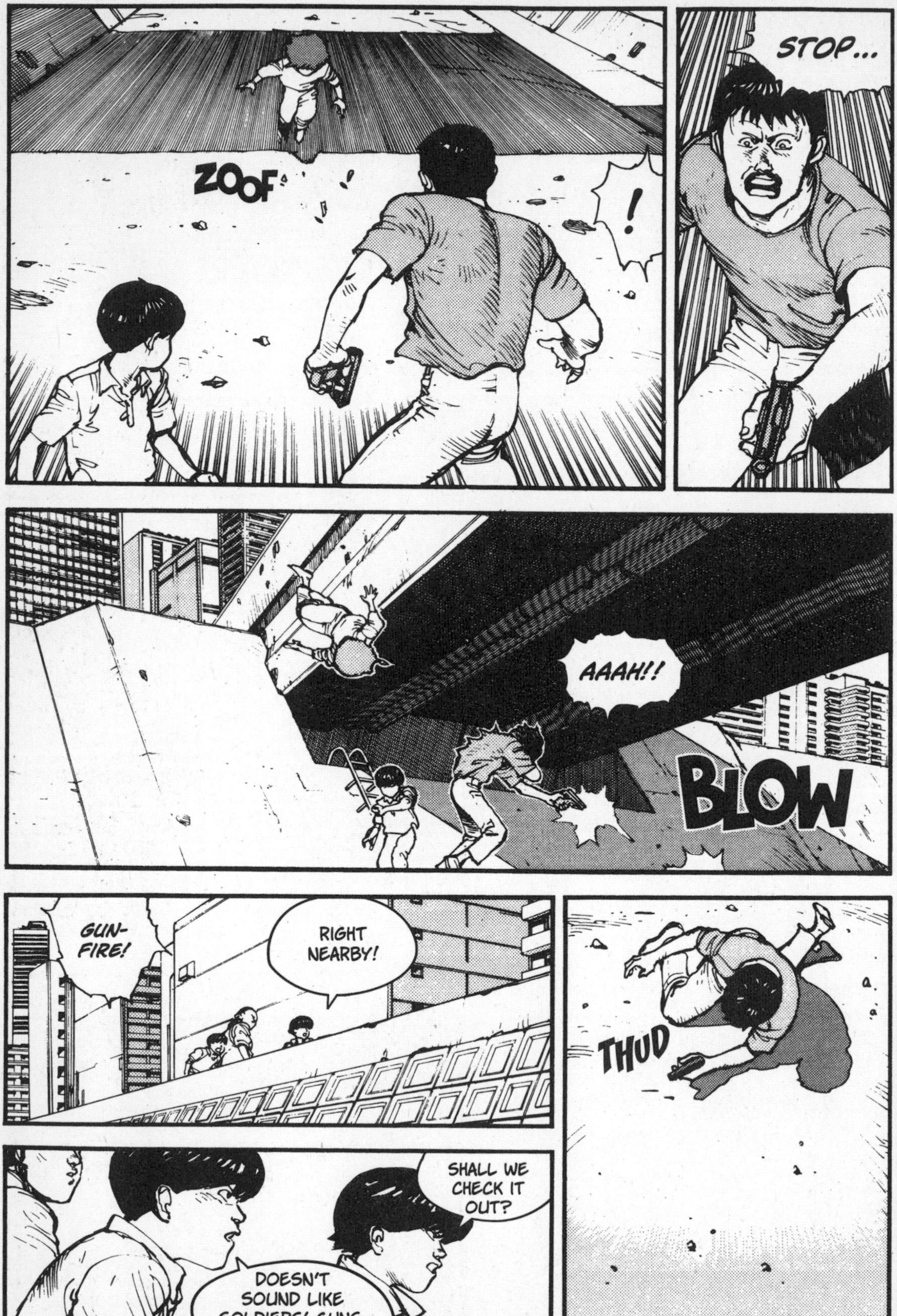
ZOOF
!
STOP...
AAAH!!
BLOW
GUN-
FIRE!
RIGHT
NEARBY!
THUD
SHALL WE
CHECK IT
OUT?
DOESN'T
SOUND LIKE
SOLDIERS' GUNS.

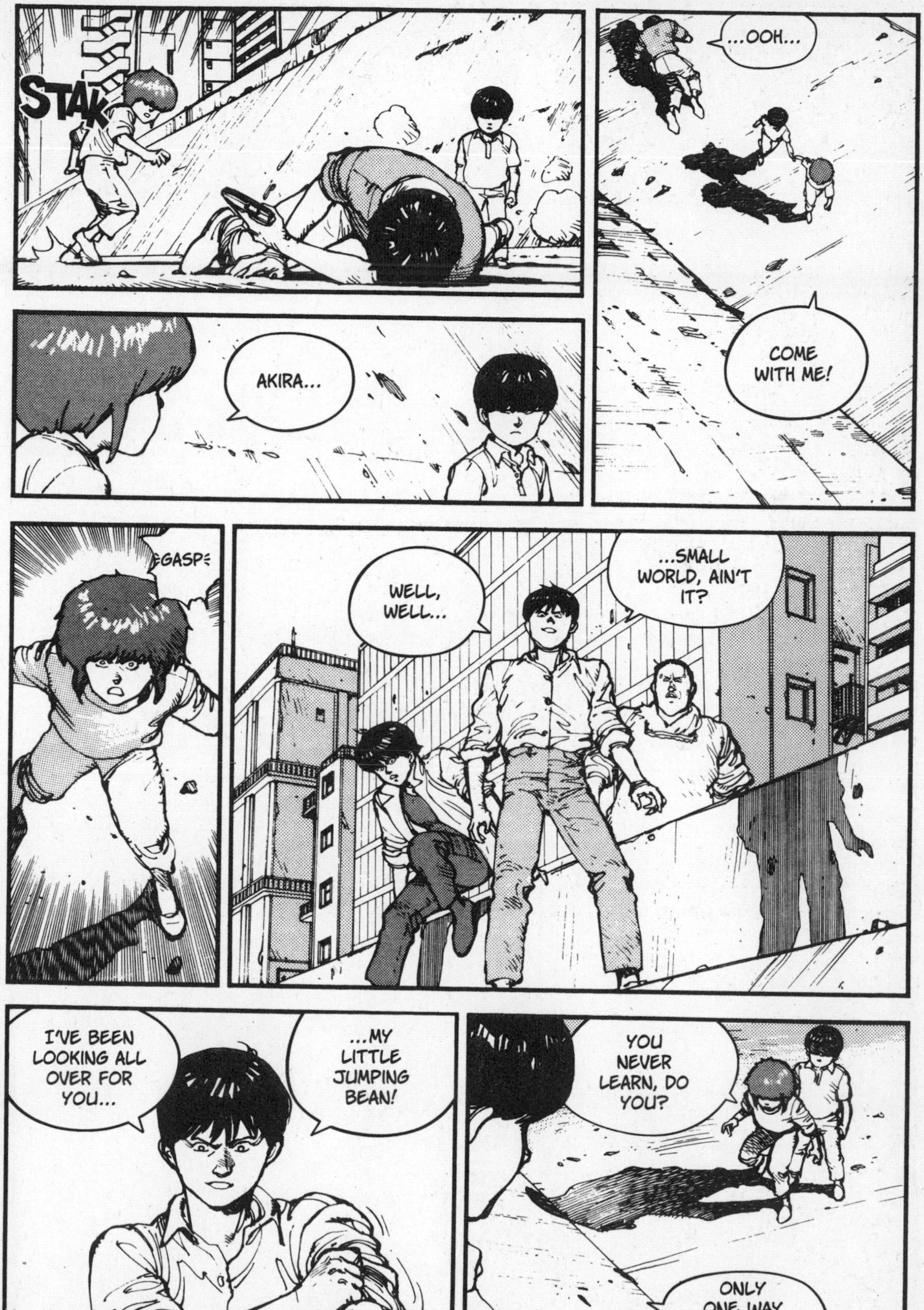
STAK
...OOH...
COME WITH ME!
AKIRA...
GASP
WELL, WELL...
...SMALL WORLD, AIN'T IT?
I'VE BEEN LOOKING ALL OVER FOR YOU...
...MY LITTLE JUMPING BEAN!
YOU NEVER LEARN, DO YOU?
ONLY ONE WAY TO FIND OUT.

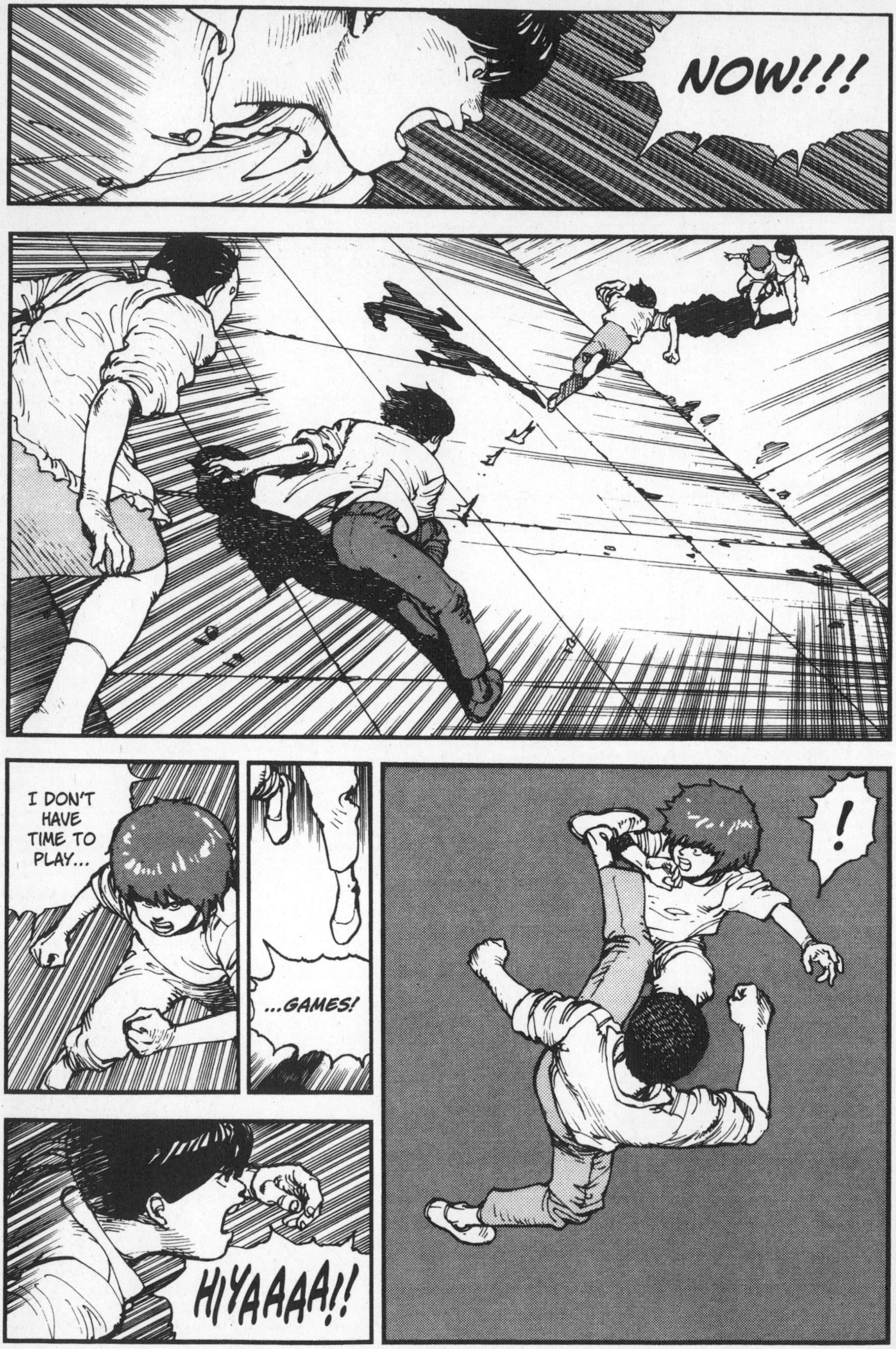
NOW!!!
I DON'T HAVE TIME TO PLAY...
...GAMES!
!
HIYAAAA!!

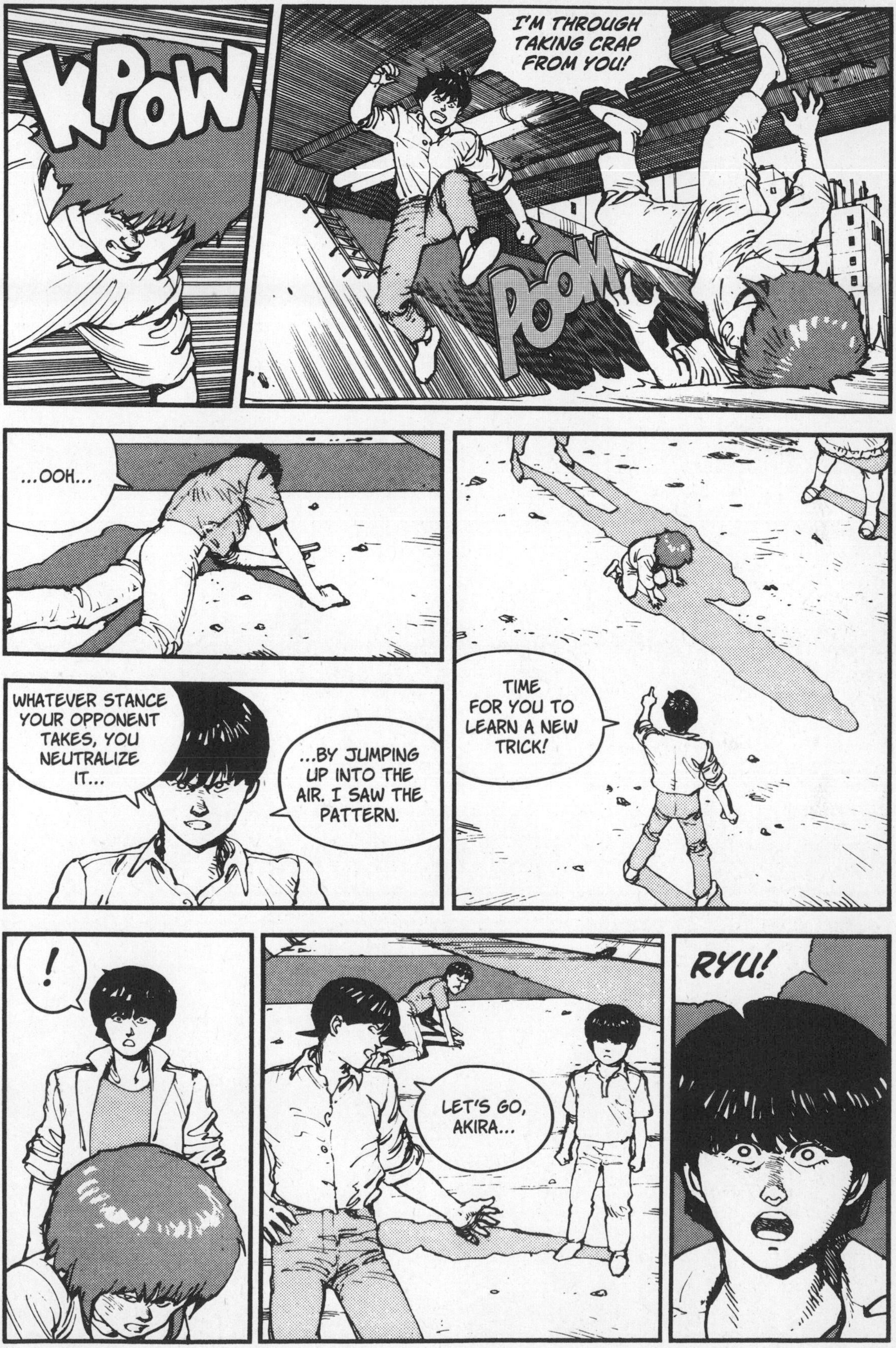
KPOW
I'M THROUGH TAKING CRAP FROM YOU!
POOM
...OOH...
WHATEVER STANCE YOUR OPPONENT TAKES, YOU NEUTRALIZE IT...
...BY JUMPING UP INTO THE AIR. I SAW THE PATTERN.
TIME FOR YOU TO LEARN A NEW TRICK!
!
LET'S GO, AKIRA...
RYU!

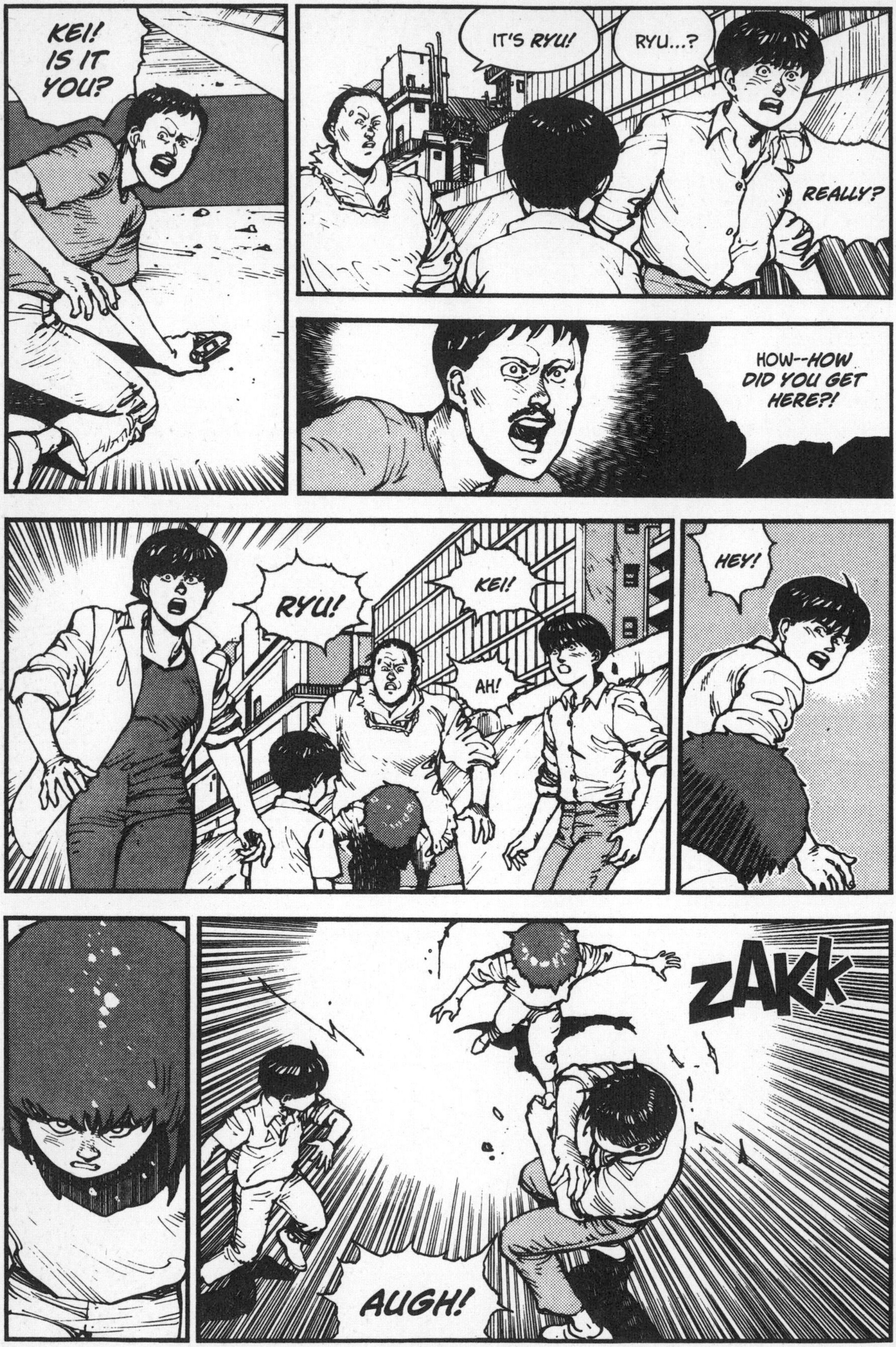
KEI! IS IT YOU?
IT'S *RYU!*
RYU...?
REALLY?
HOW--*HOW DID YOU GET HERE?!*
RYU!
KEI!
AH!
HEY!
ZAKK
AUGH!

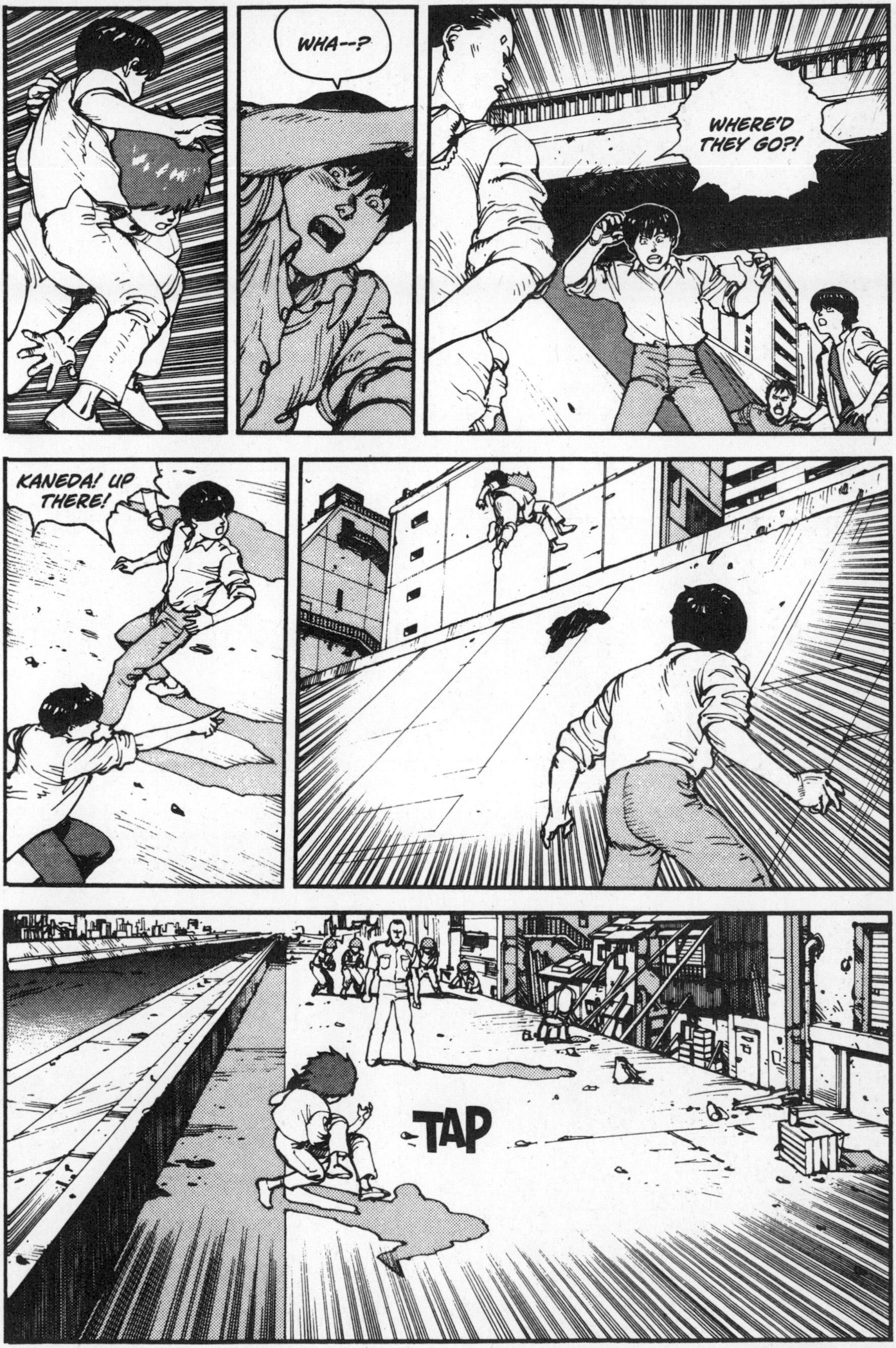
WHA--?
WHERE'D THEY GO?!
KANEDA! UP THERE!
TAP

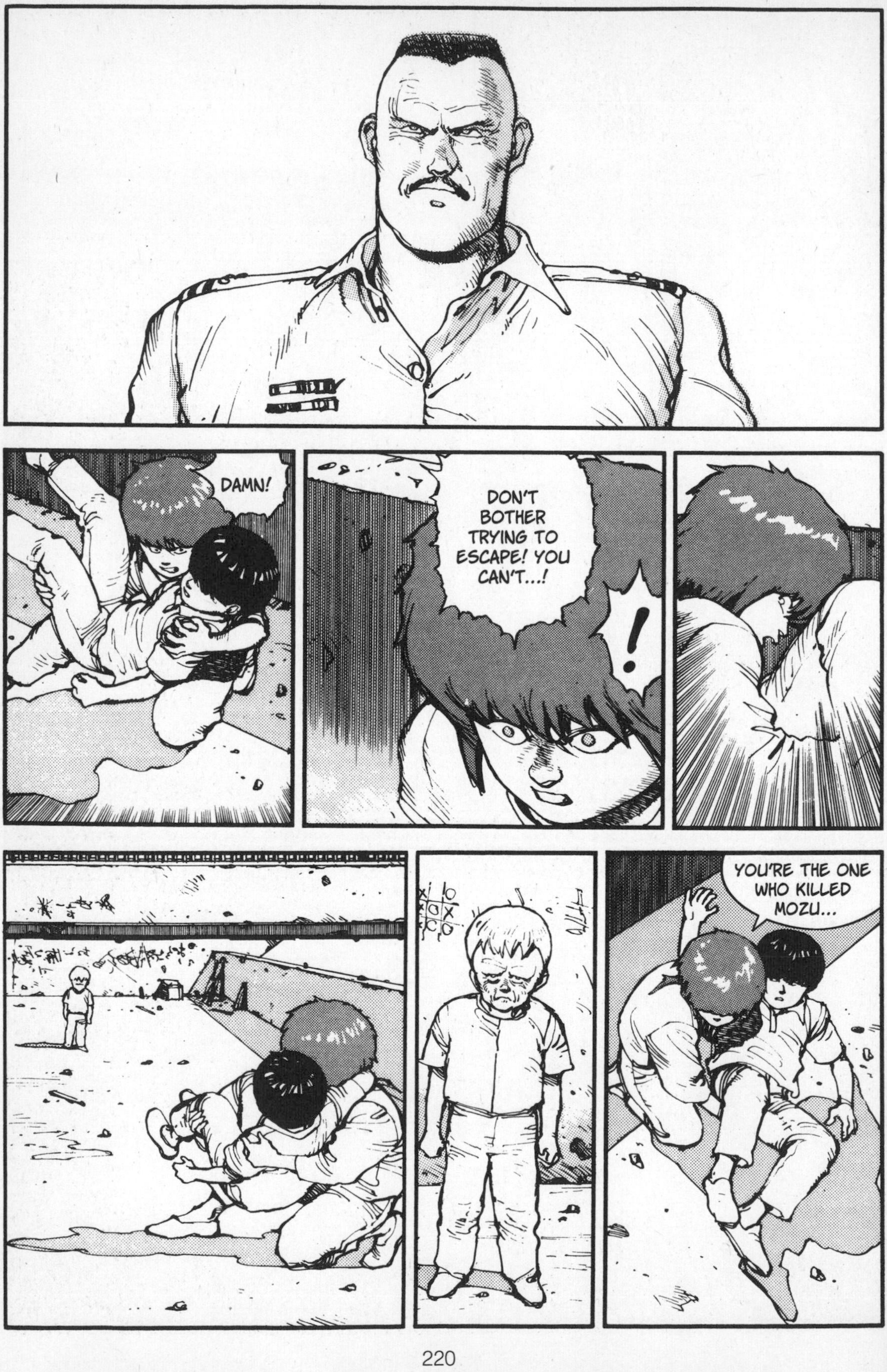
DAMN!
DON'T BOTHER TRYING TO ESCAPE! YOU CAN'T...!
!
YOU'RE THE ONE WHO KILLED MOZU...

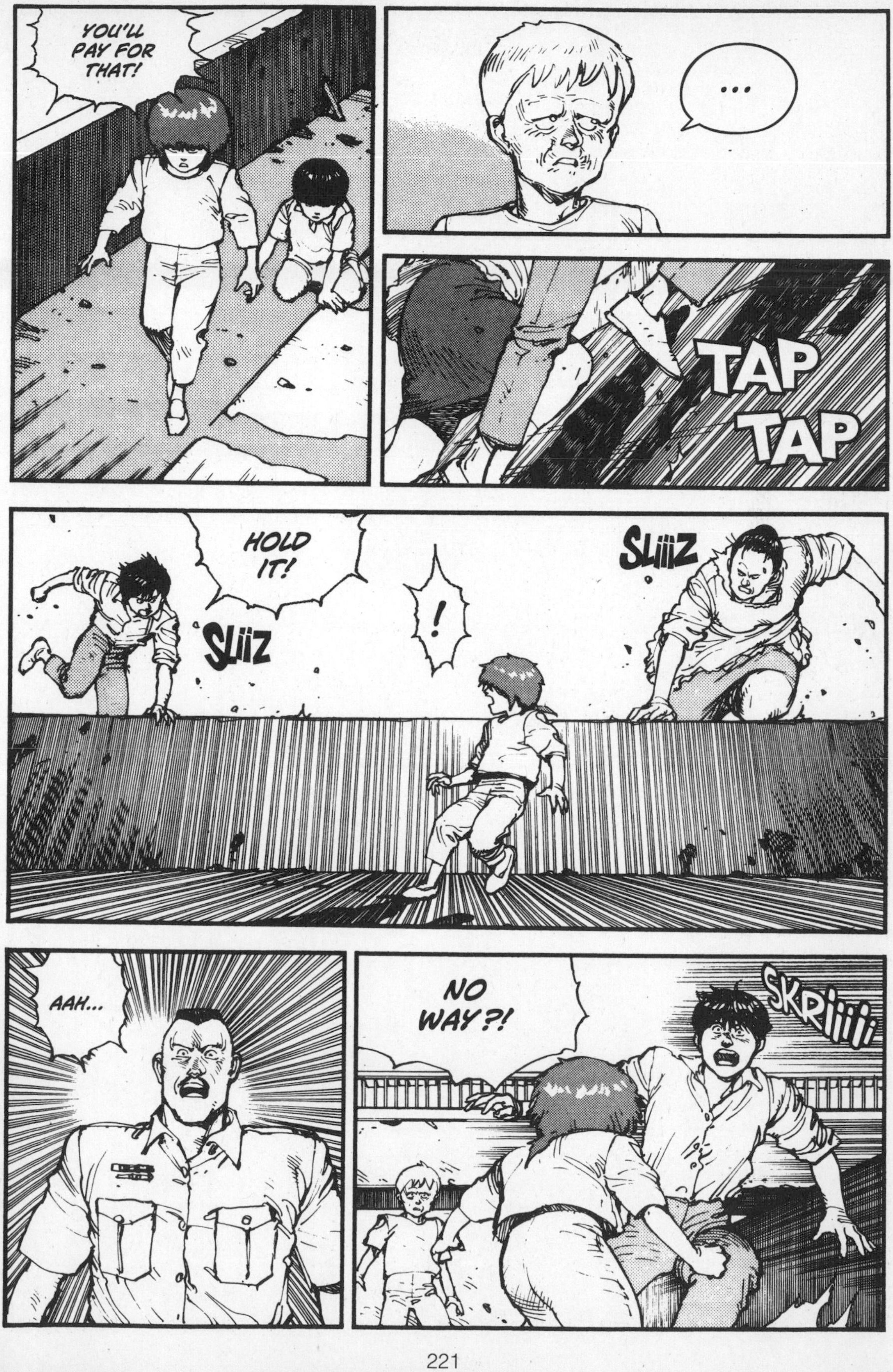
YOU'LL PAY FOR THAT!
...
TAP
TAP
HOLD IT!
SLIIZ
!
SLIIZ
AAH...
NO WAY?!
SKRIIIII

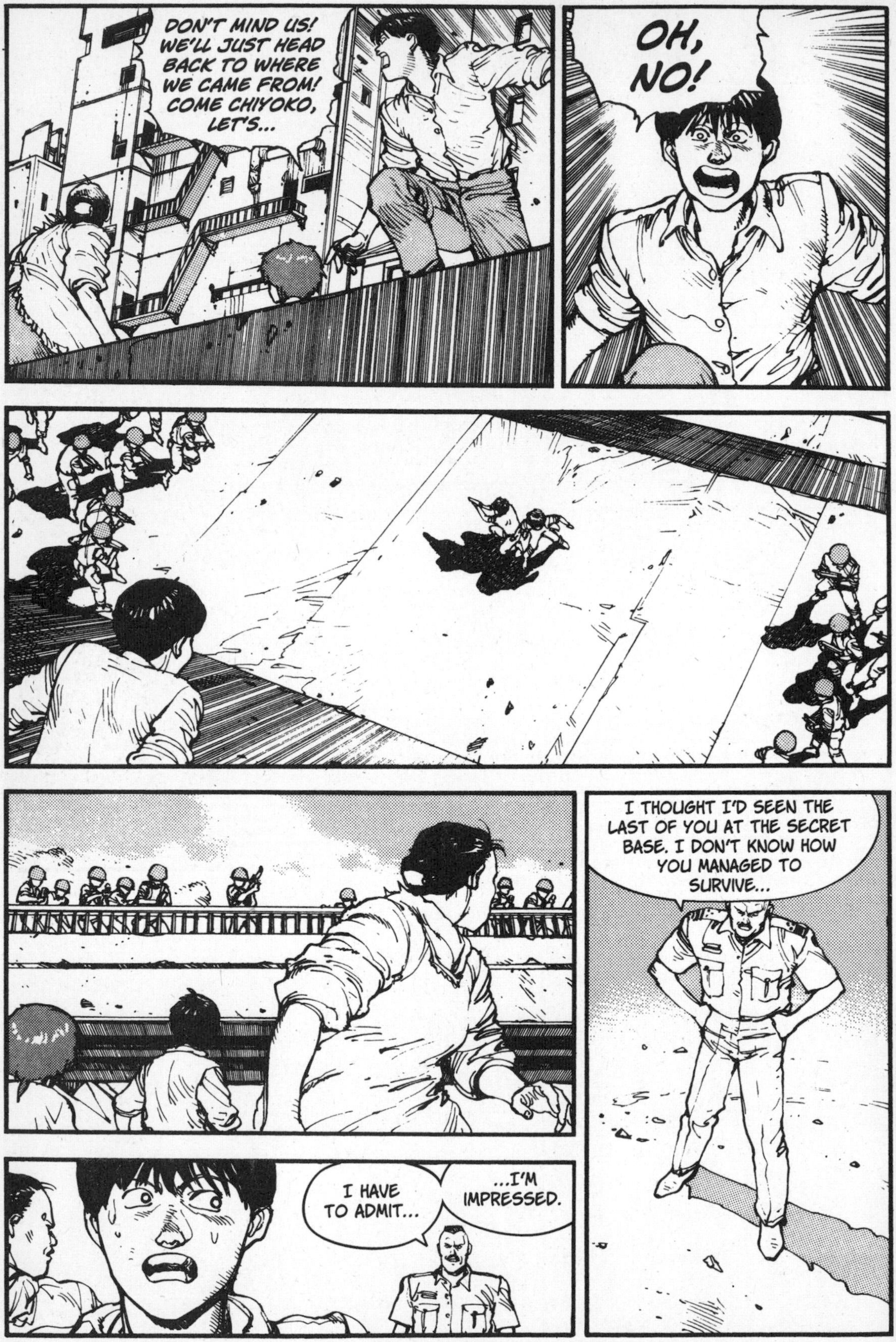
DON'T MIND US! WE'LL JUST HEAD BACK TO WHERE WE CAME FROM! COME CHIYOKO, LET'S...
OH, NO!
I THOUGHT I'D SEEN THE LAST OF YOU AT THE SECRET BASE. I DON'T KNOW HOW YOU MANAGED TO SURVIVE...
I HAVE TO ADMIT...
...I'M IMPRESSED.

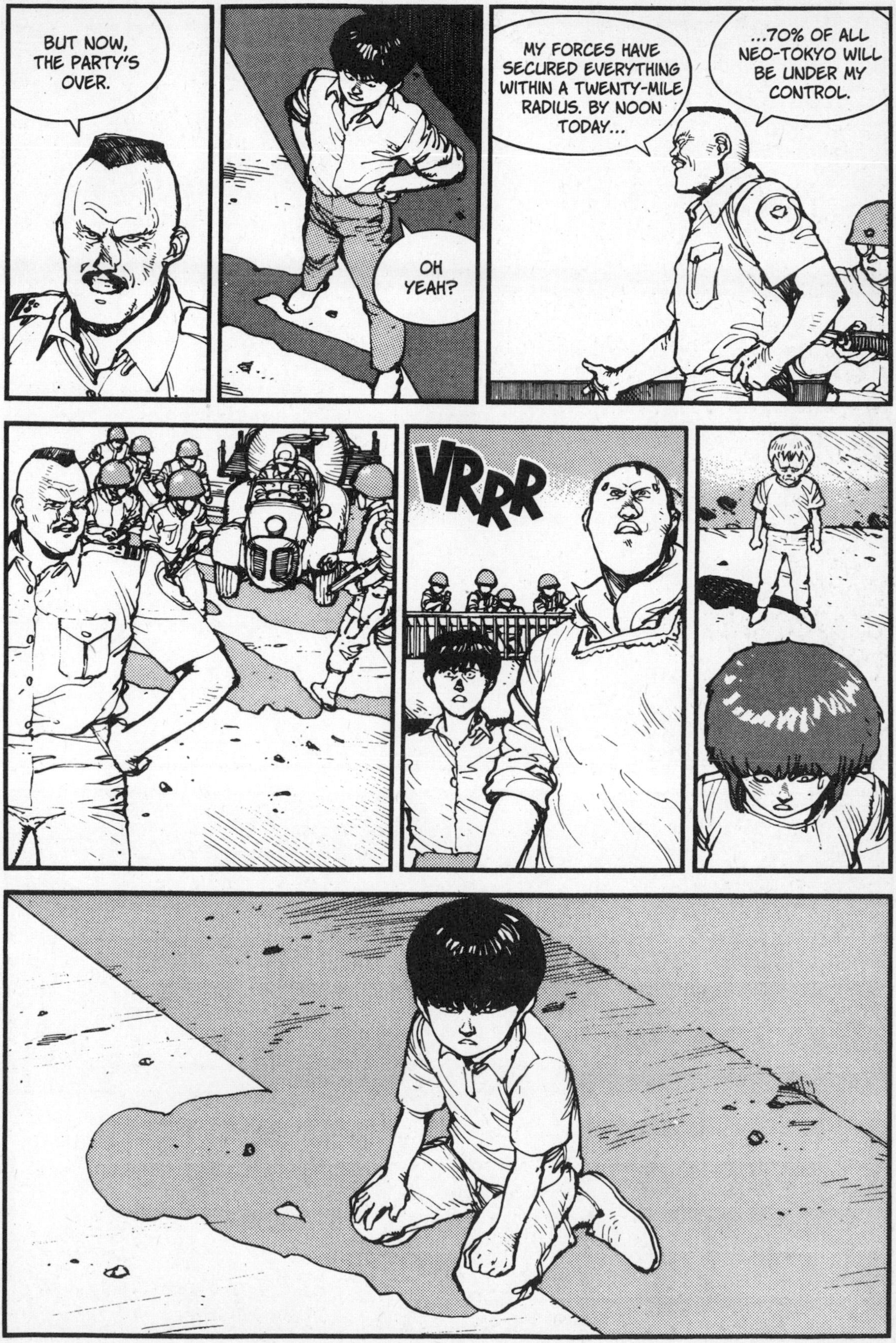
BUT NOW, THE PARTY'S OVER.
OH YEAH?
MY FORCES HAVE SECURED EVERYTHING WITHIN A TWENTY-MILE RADIUS. BY NOON TODAY...
...70% OF ALL NEO-TOKYO WILL BE UNDER MY CONTROL.
VRRR

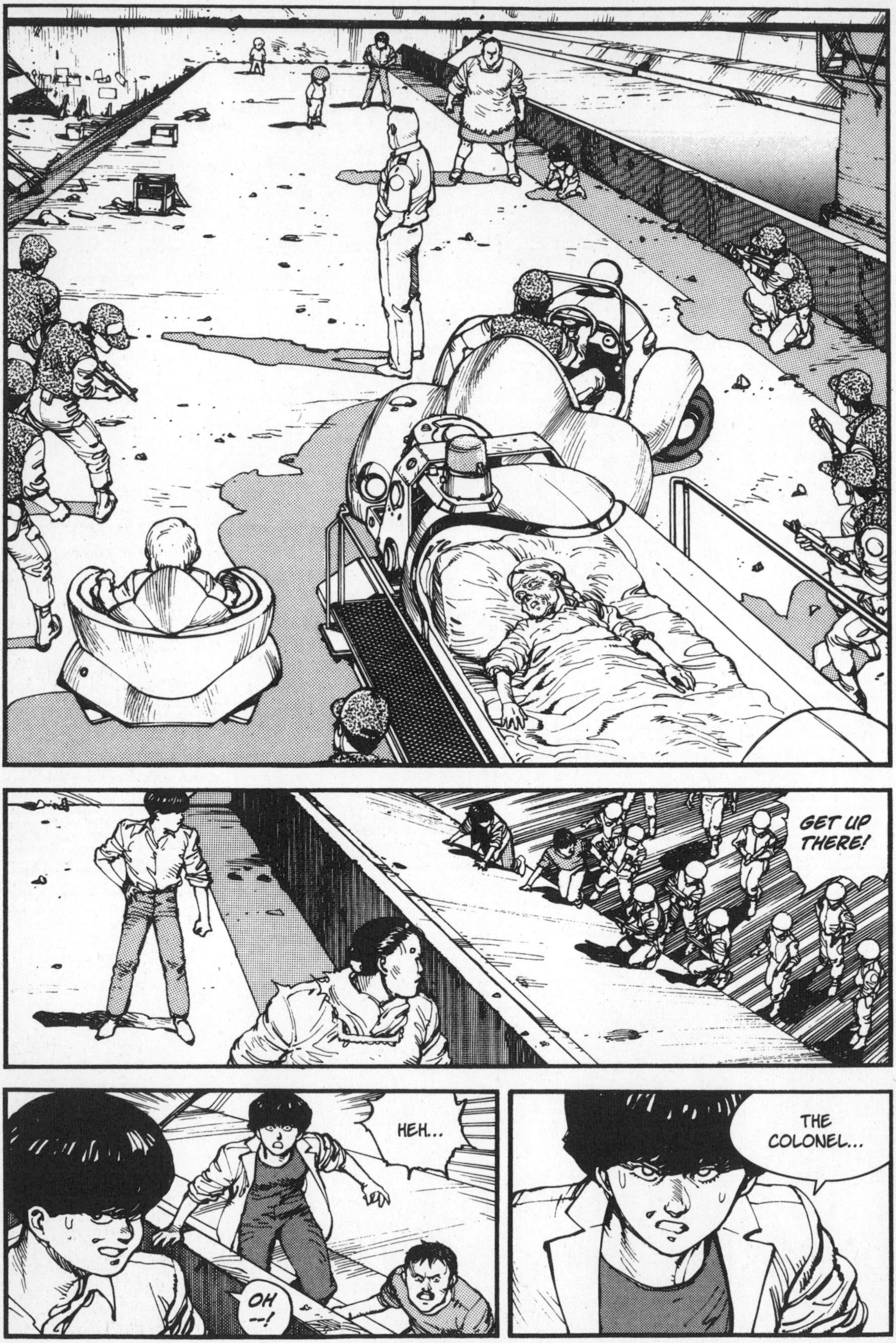
GET UP THERE!
HEH...
OH --!
THE COLONEL...

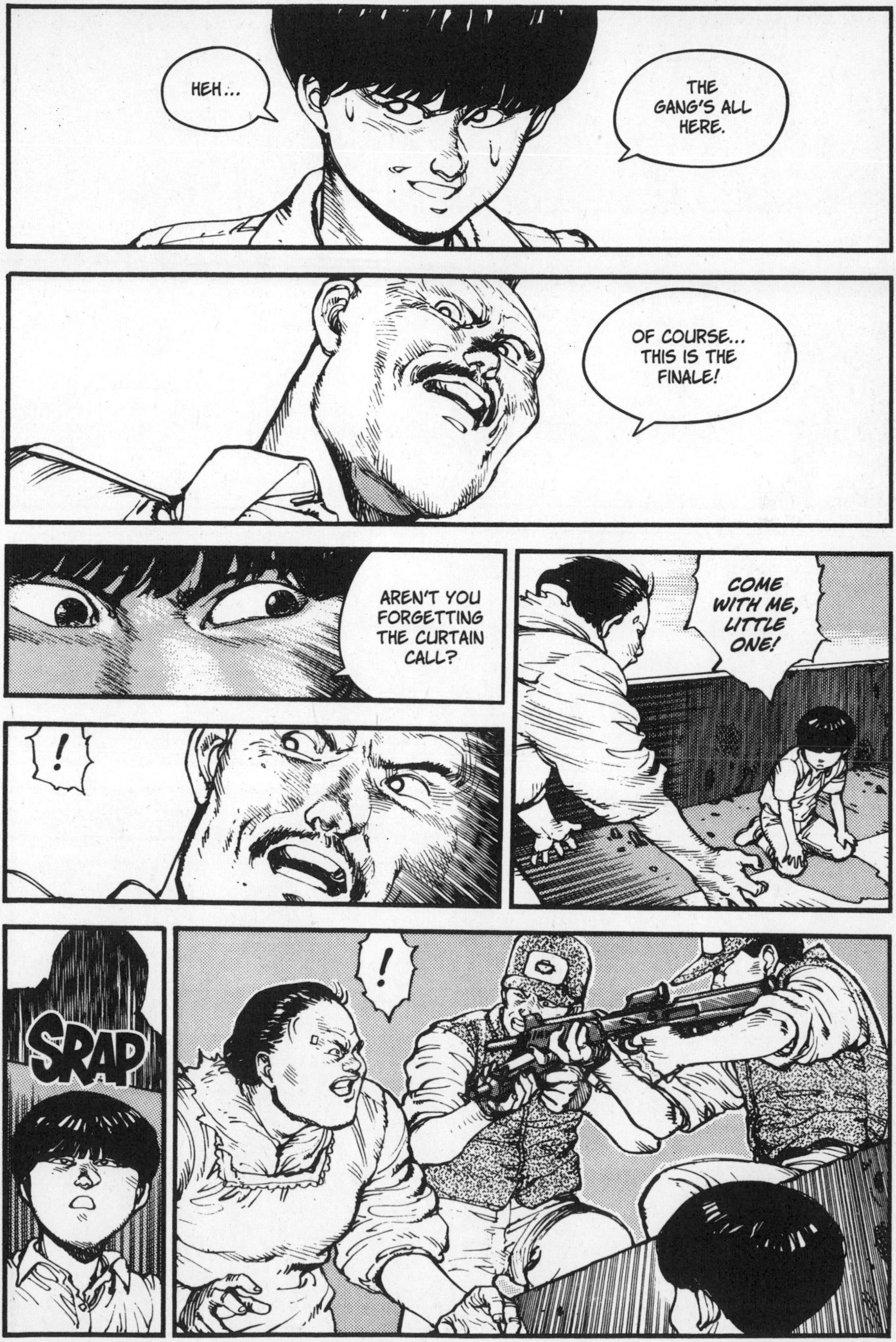
HEH...
THE GANG'S ALL HERE.
OF COURSE... THIS IS THE FINALE!
AREN'T YOU FORGETTING THE CURTAIN CALL?
!
COME WITH ME, LITTLE ONE!
SRAP
!

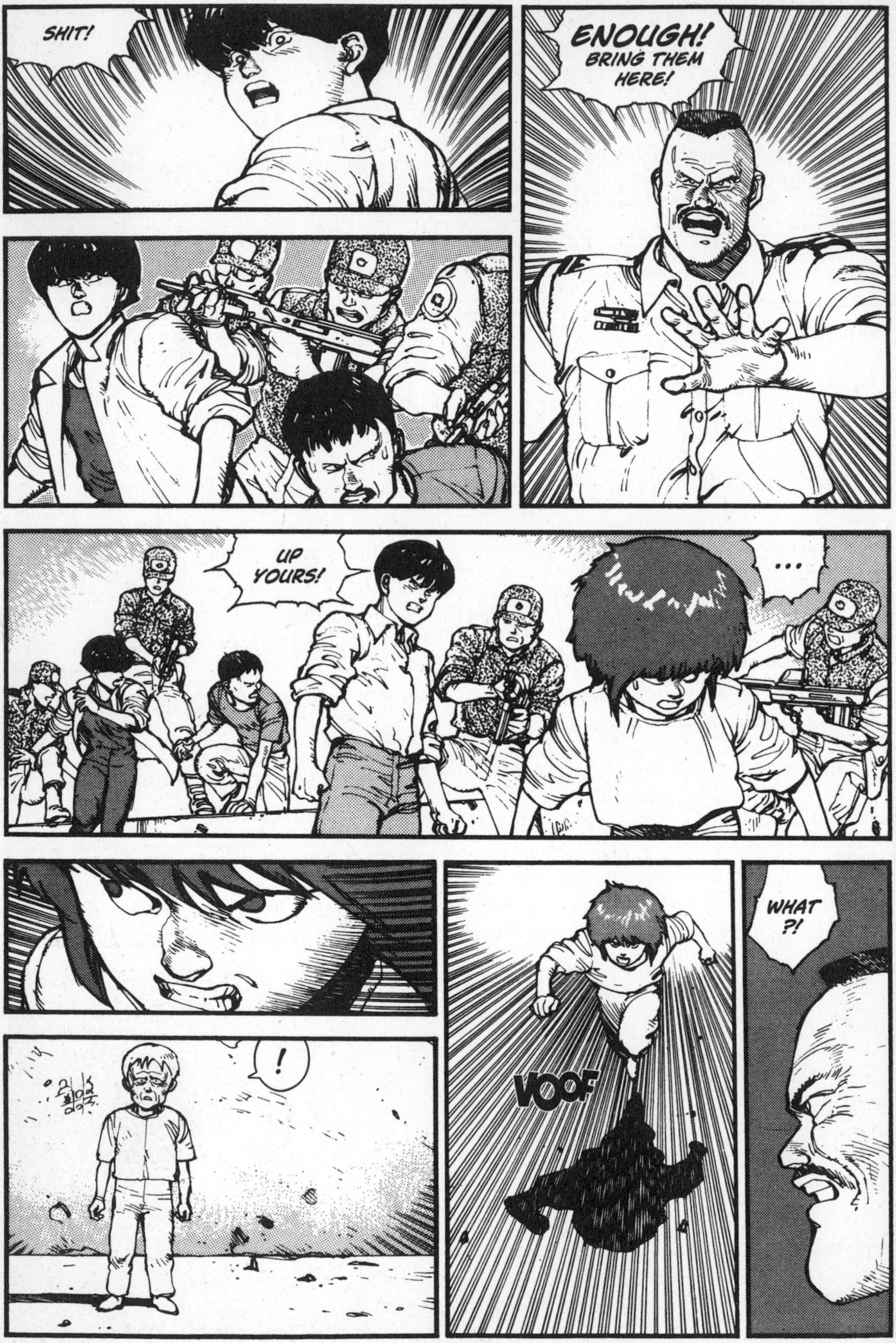
SHIT!
ENOUGH! BRING THEM HERE!
UP YOURS!
...
!
VOOF
WHAT ?!

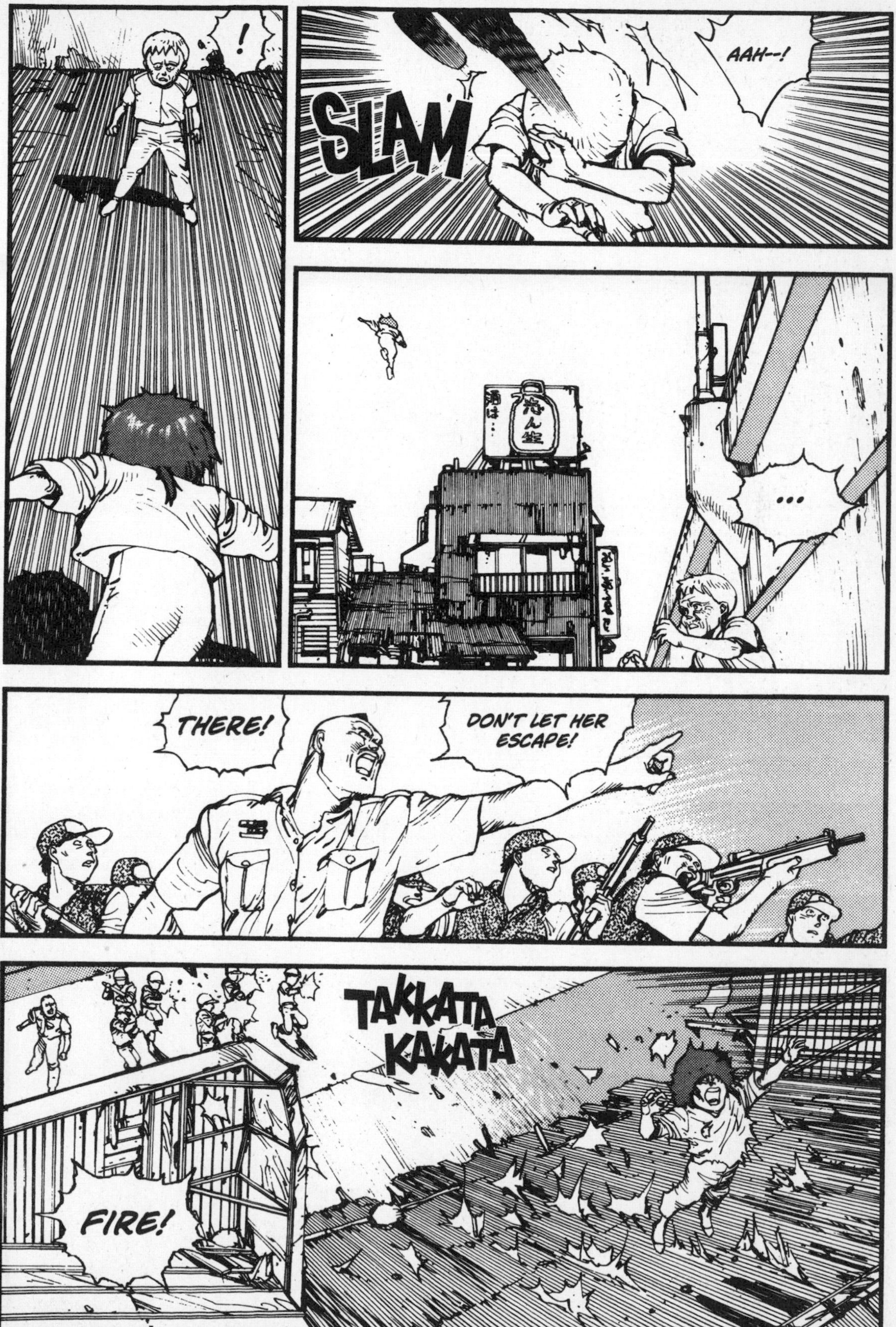
!
SLAM
AAH--!
...
THERE!
DON'T LET HER ESCAPE!
TAKKATA KAKATA
FIRE!

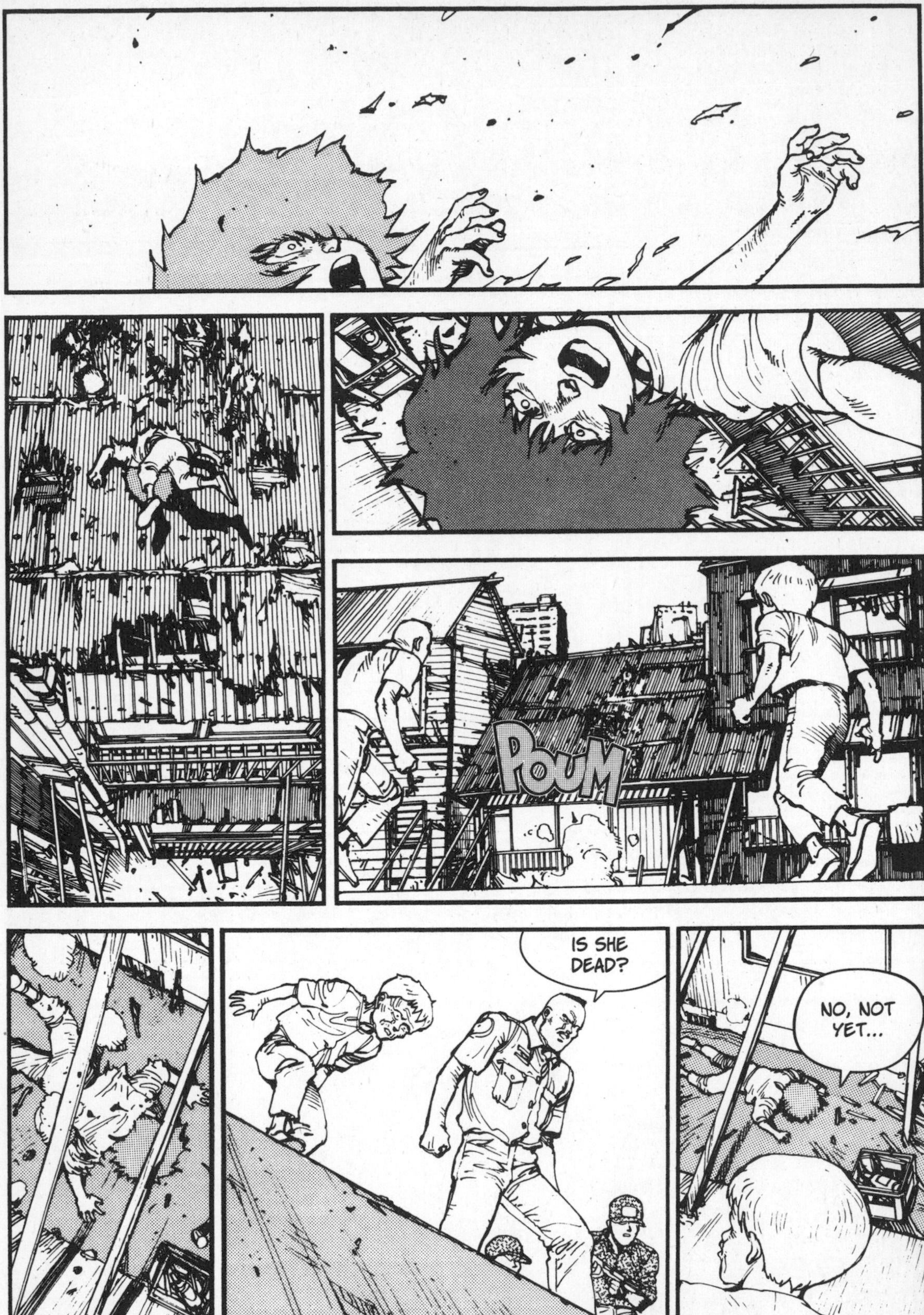
POUM
IS SHE DEAD?
NO, NOT YET...

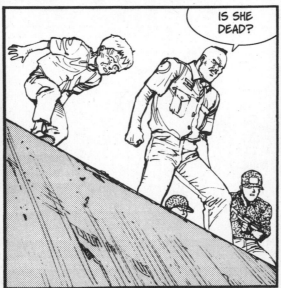

GO AND GET HER. THERE ARE SOME TESTS I WANT TO RUN ON HER LATER.

YES, COLONEL.

DZZiiiii

DZZZ DZZ

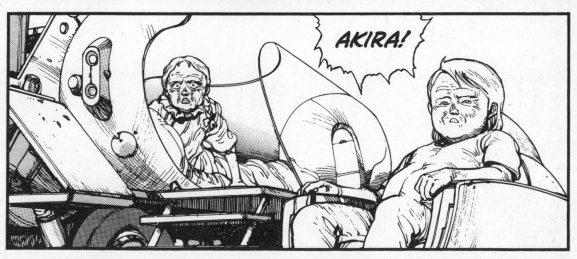

AKIRA!

OW! OW! THAT HURTS!! LEMME GO!

SHUT UP, PUNK!

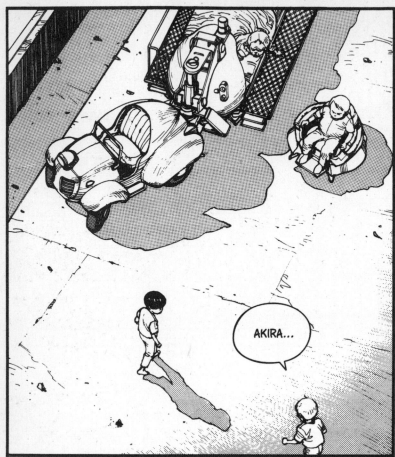

AKIRA...

IT'S YOU...

IT'S REALLY YOU!

YOU HAVEN'T CHANGED A BIT!

CRACK

YOU REMEMBER ME, DON'T YOU? I'M TAKASHI!

?!

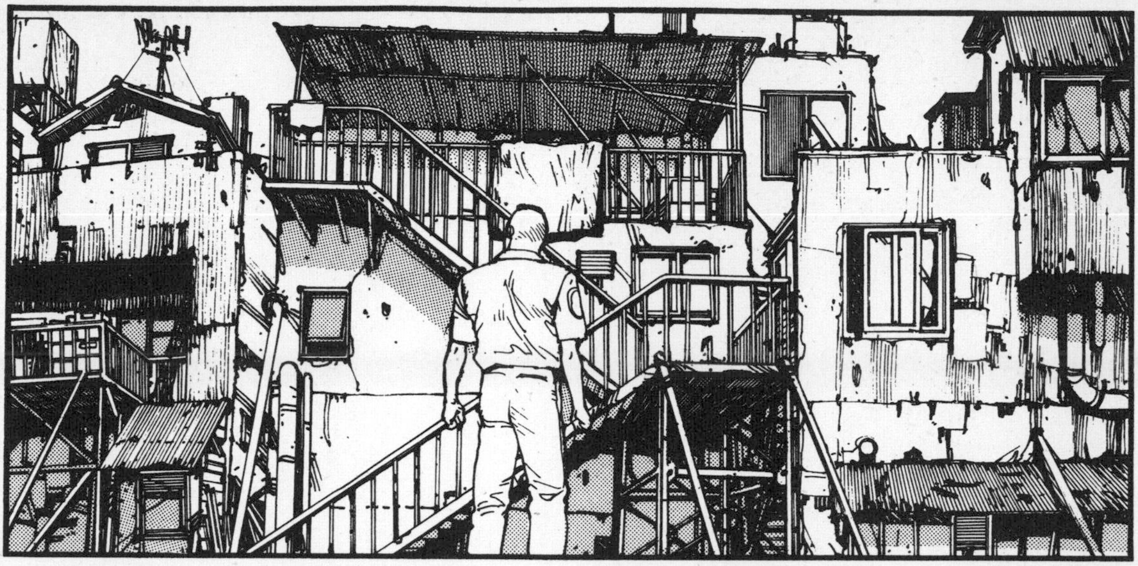

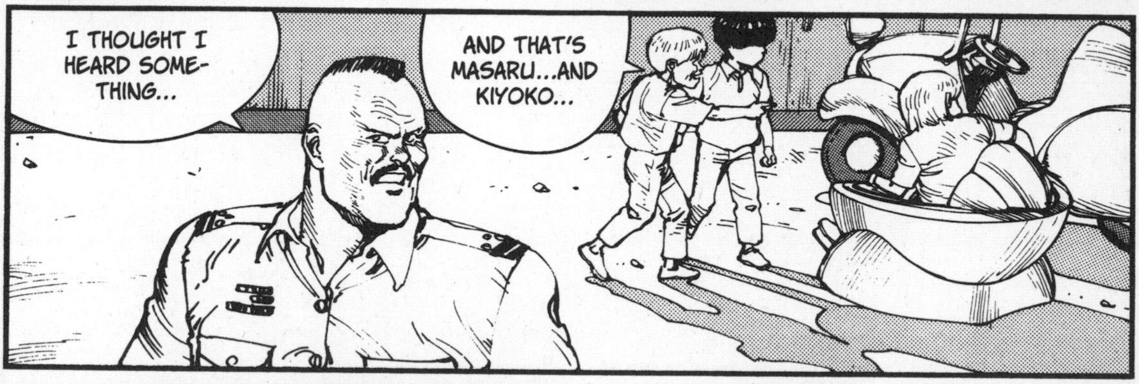
I THOUGHT I HEARD SOME-THING...
AND THAT'S MASARU...AND KIYOKO...

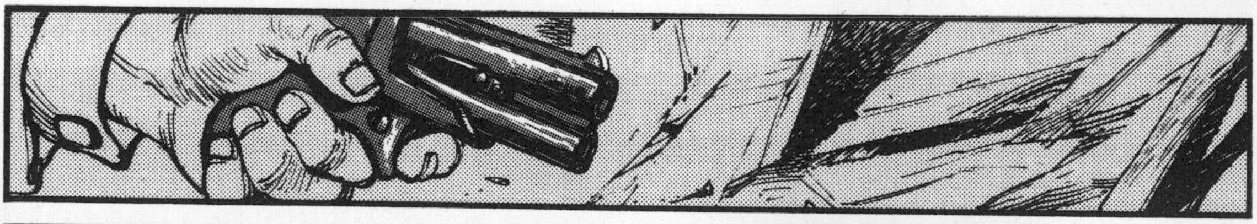

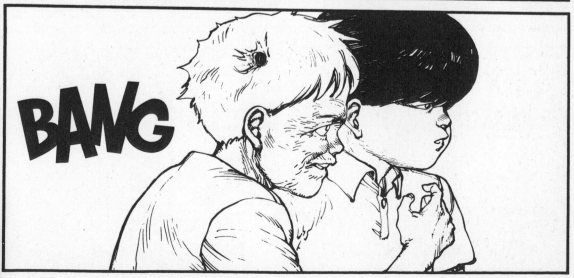

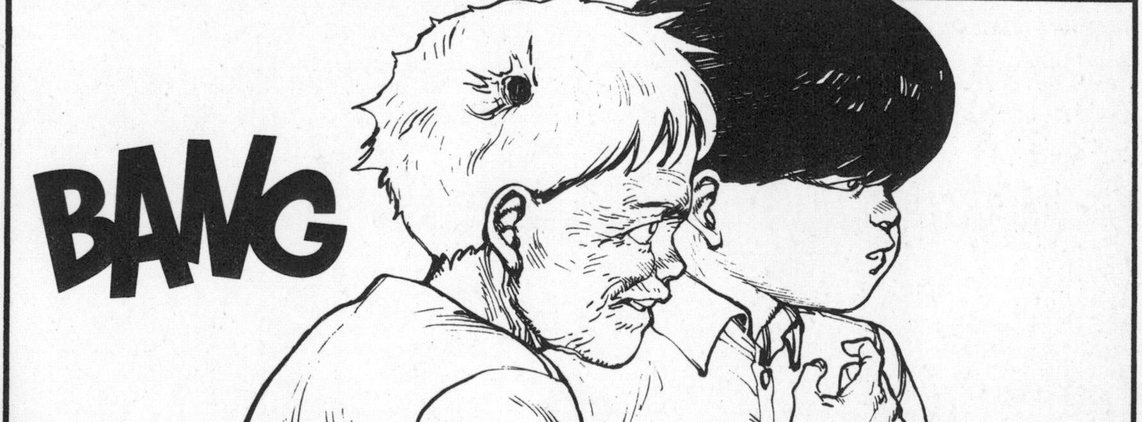
BANG

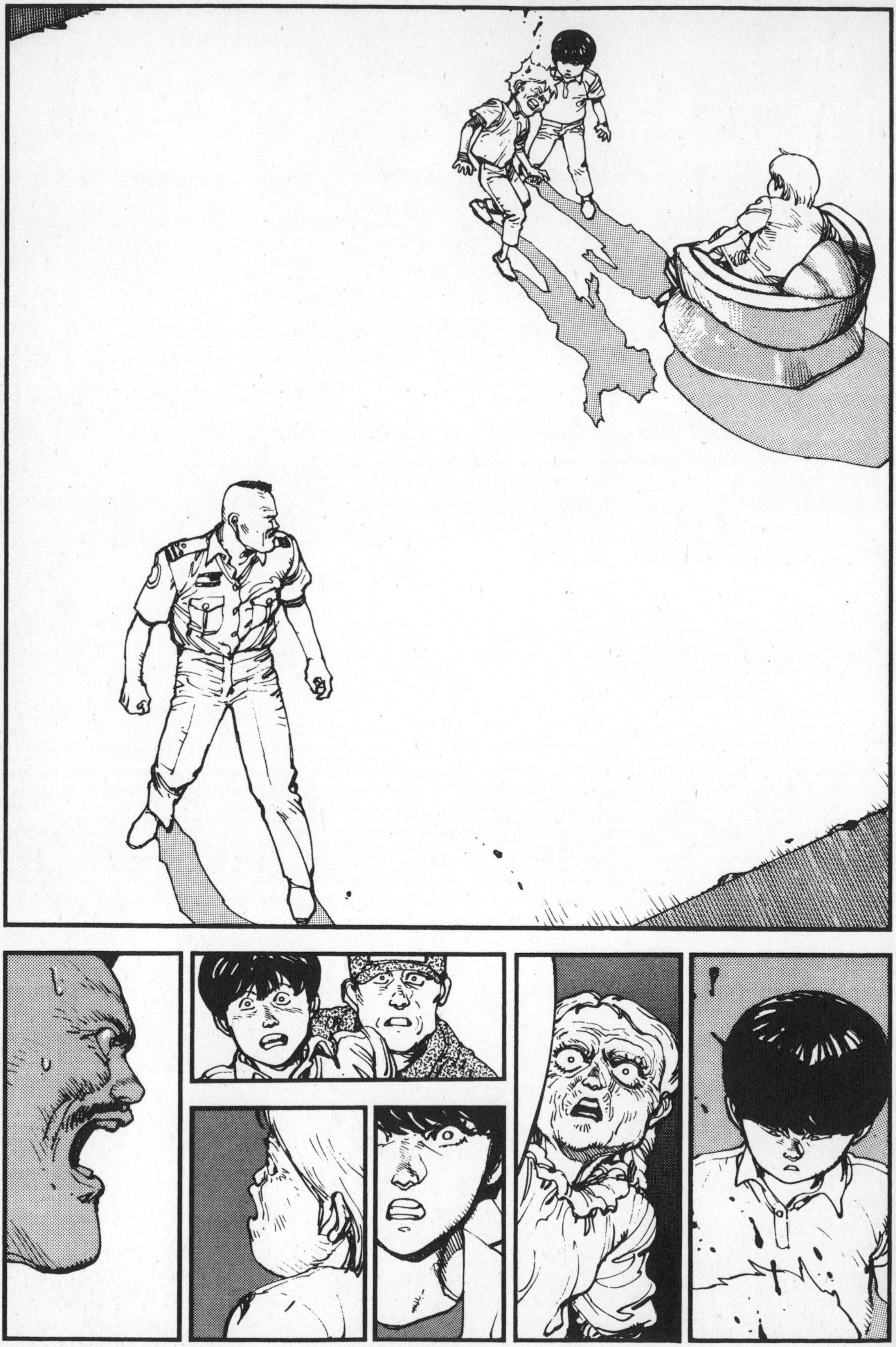

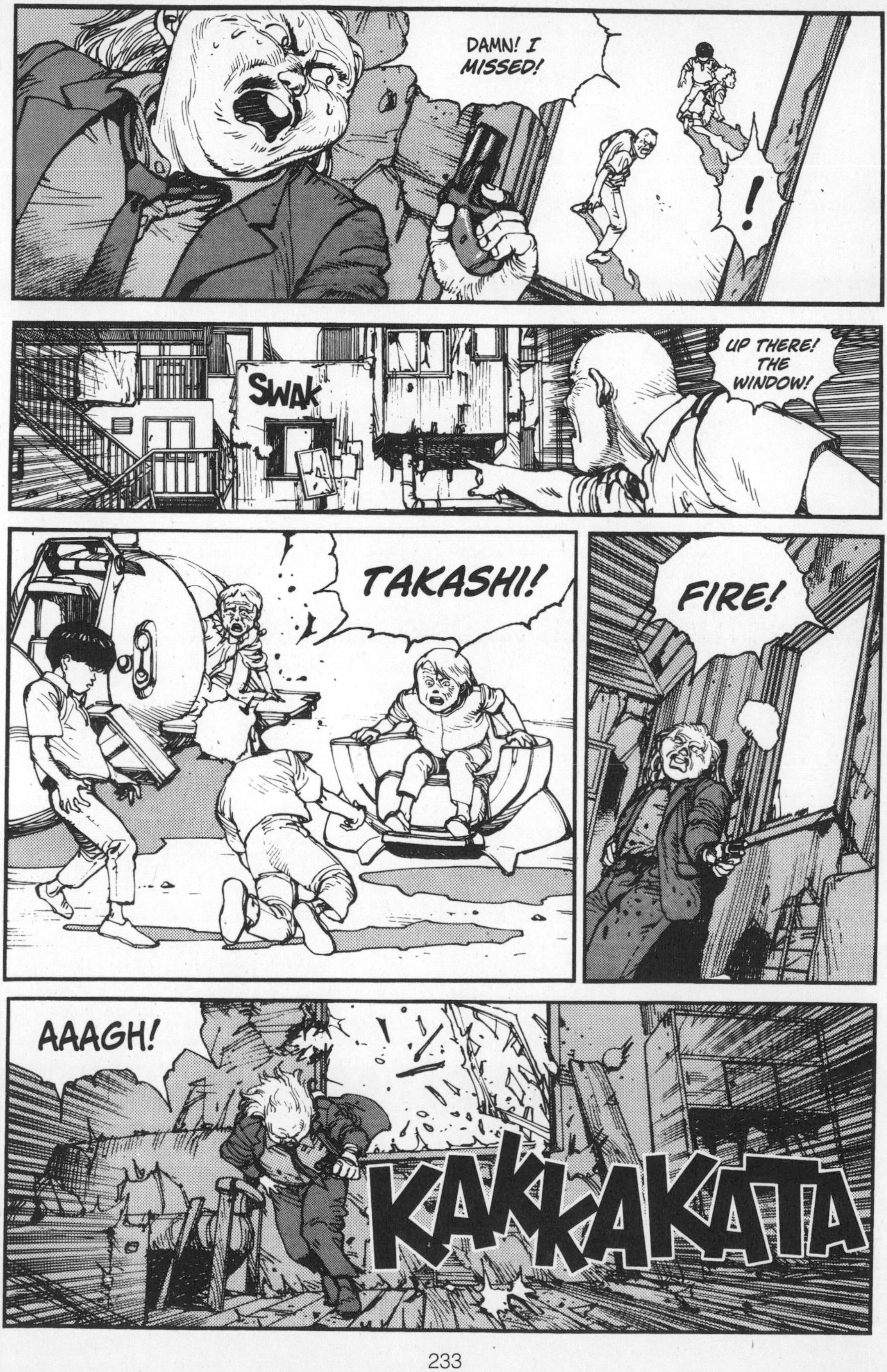

DAMN! I MISSED!
!
SWAK
UP THERE! THE WINDOW!
TAKASHI!
FIRE!
AAAGH!
KAKKAKATA

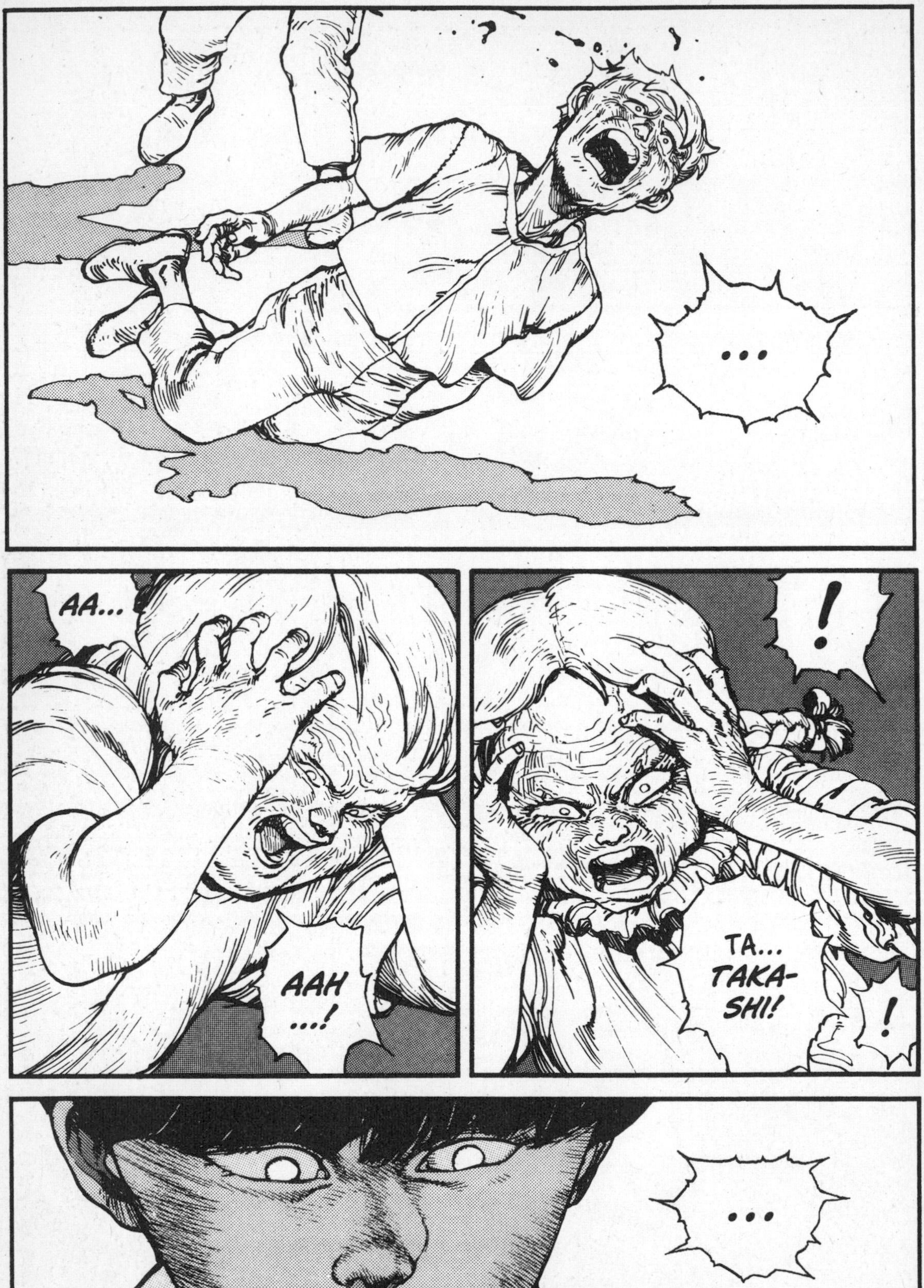
...
AA...
AAH ...!
!
TA... TAKA-SHI!
!
...

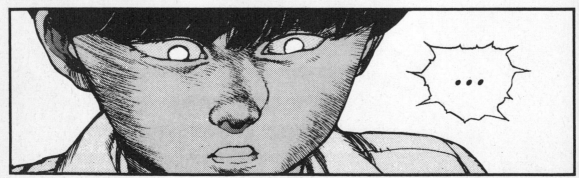

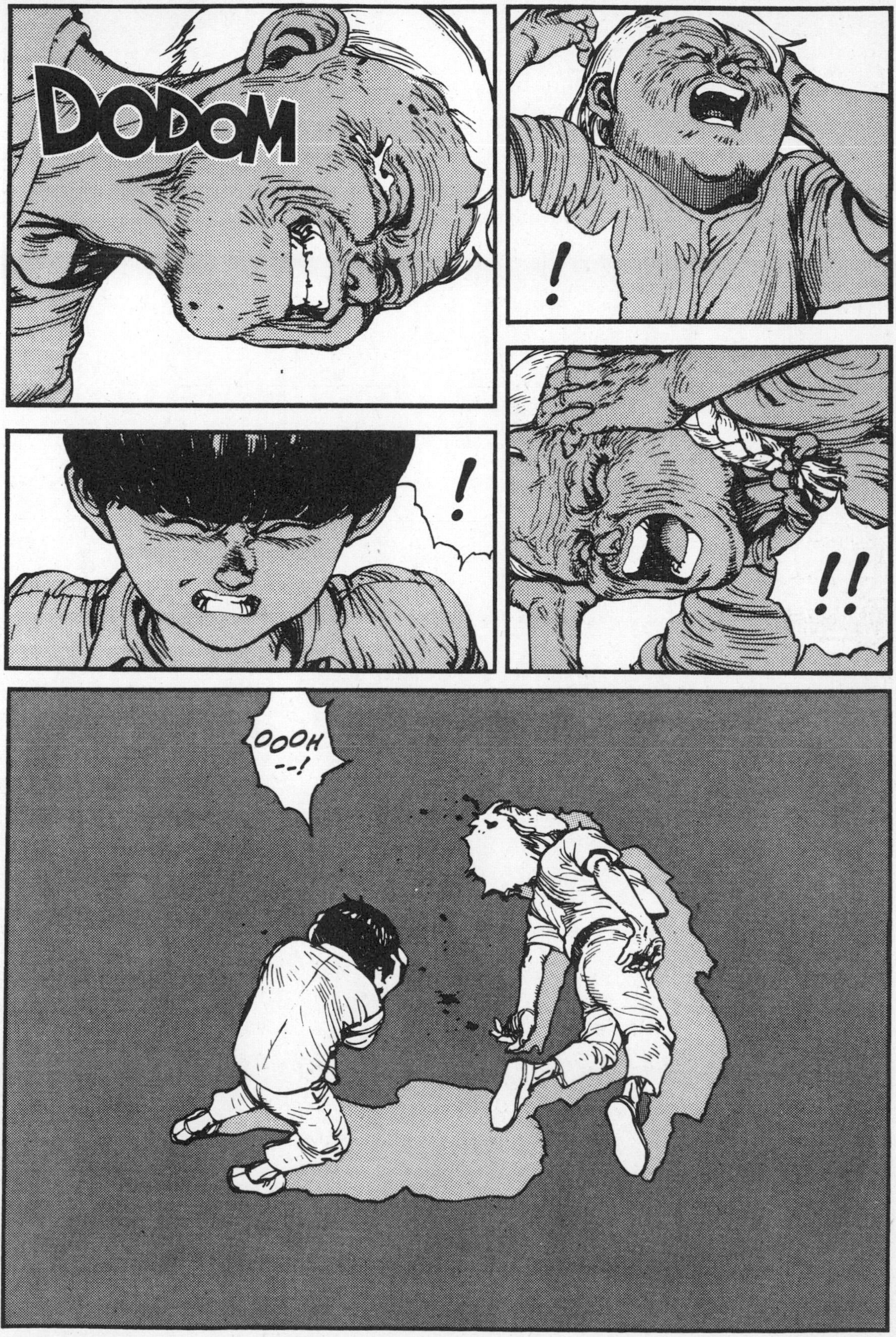
DODOM
!
!
!!
OOOH --!

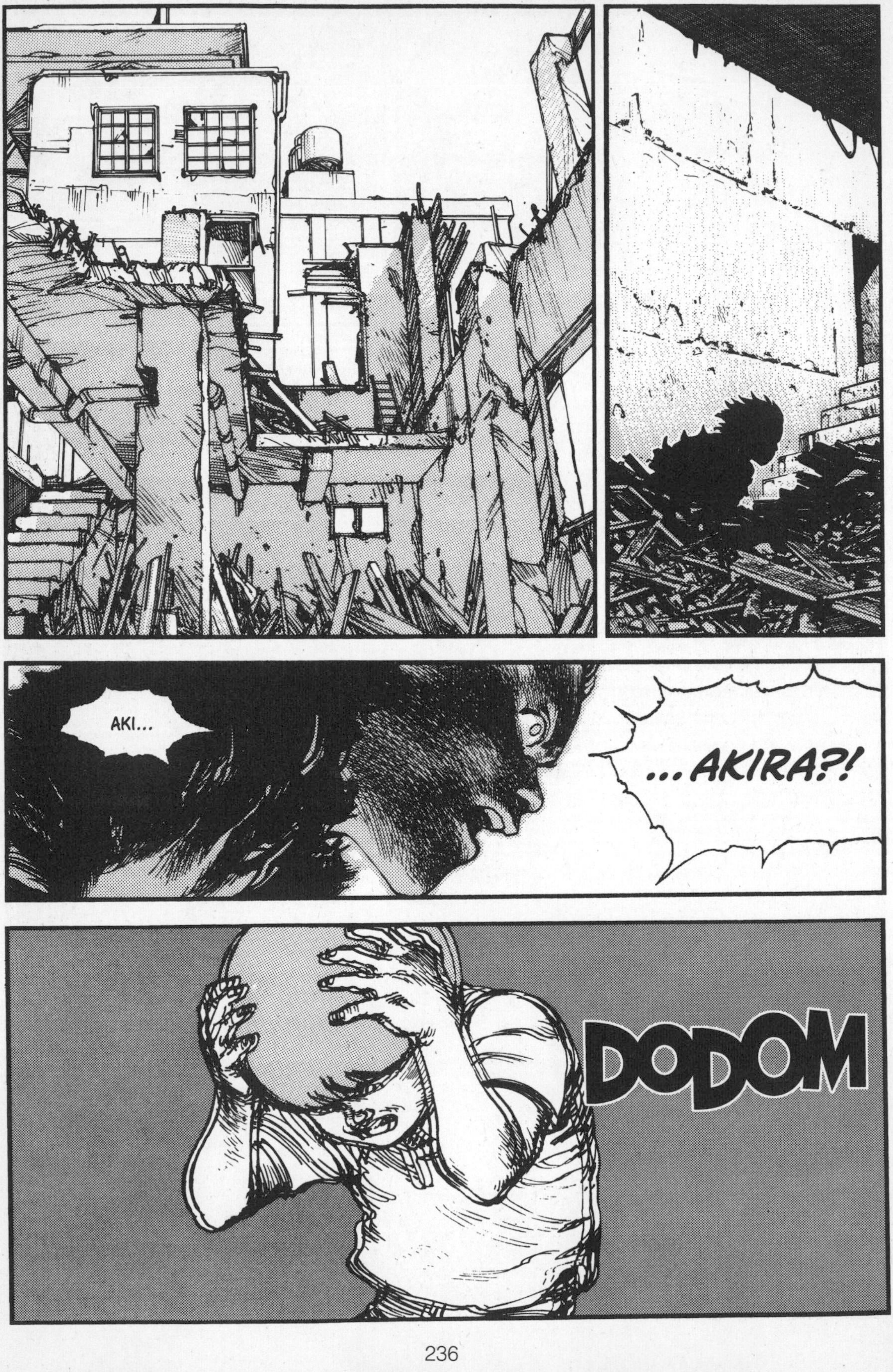
AKI...
...AKIRA?!
DODOM

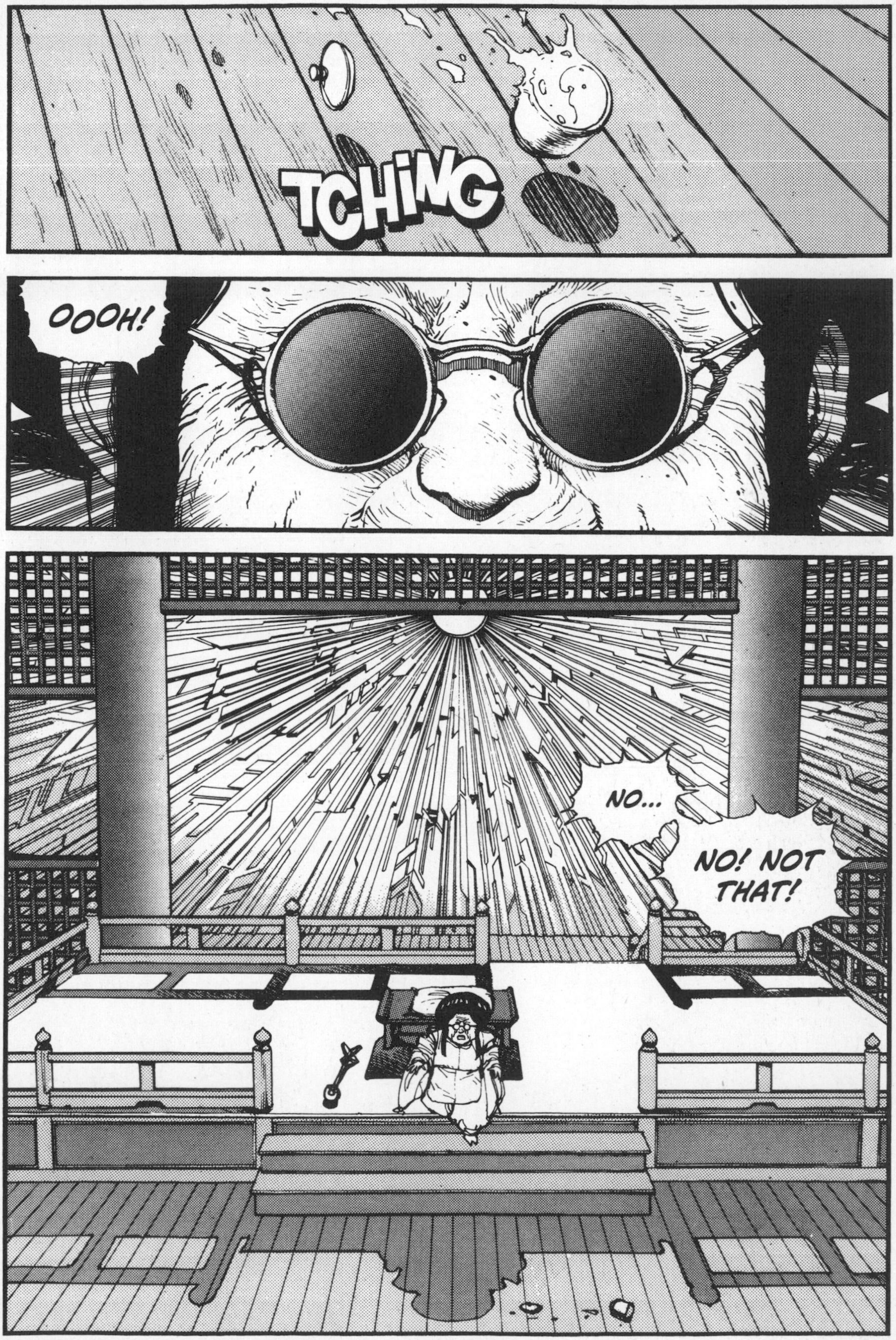
TCHiNG
OOOH!
NO...
NO! NOT THAT!

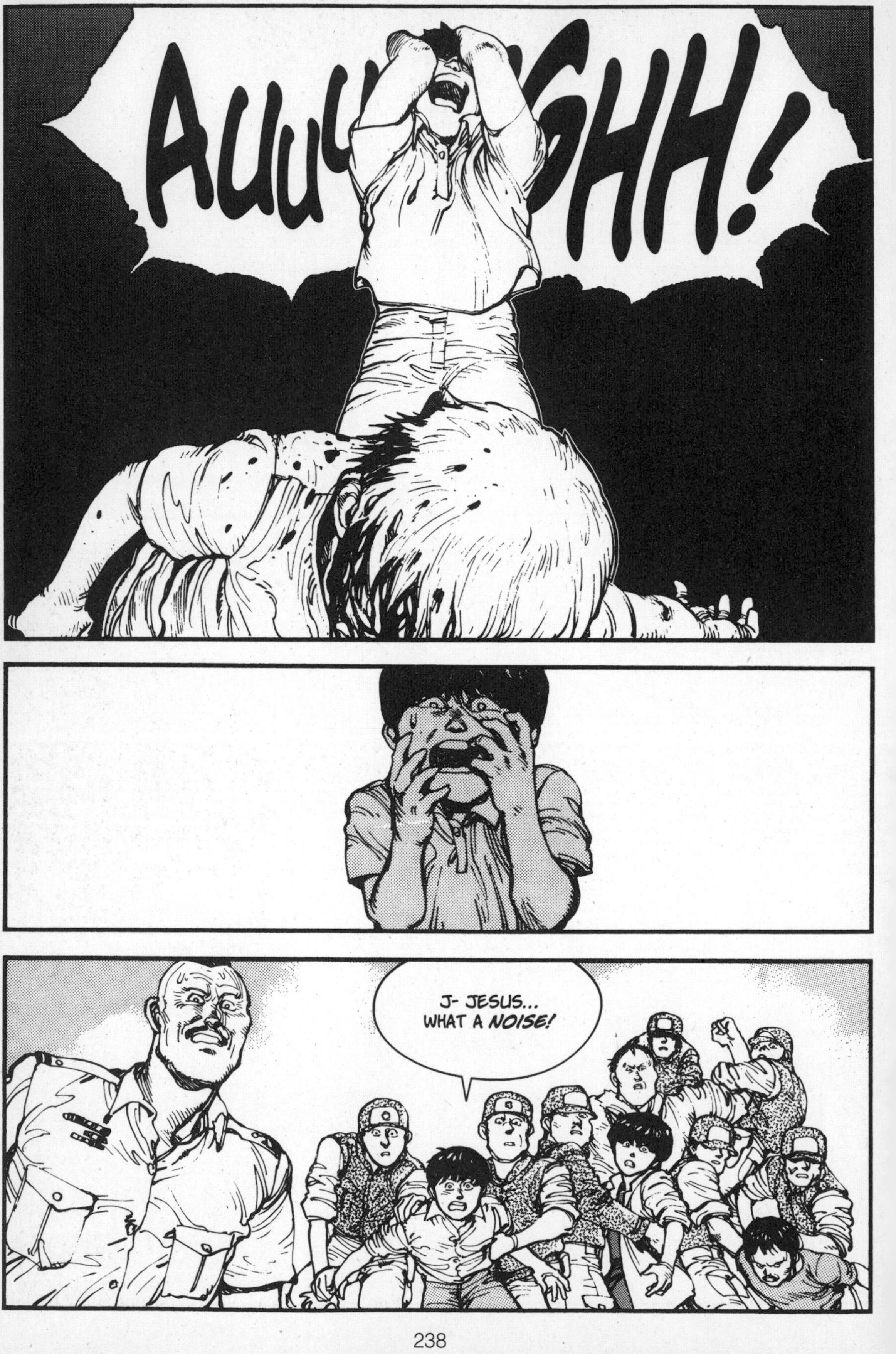
AUUUGHH!
J- JESUS... WHAT A *NOISE!*

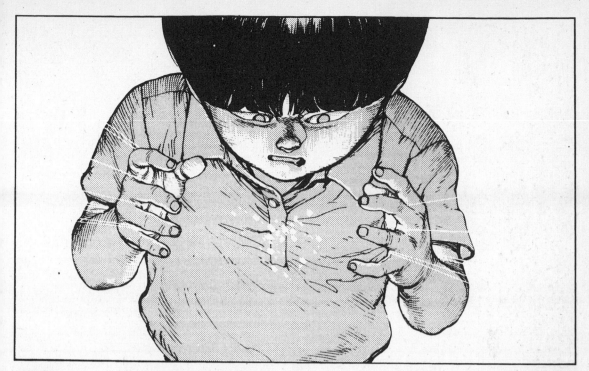

NO, AKIRA!

STOP IT!

YOU MUSTN'T!

INHALE, EXHALE! ONE AND TWO AND THREE...

...AND THREE...

BLOP BLOP BLOP BLOP

BLOP BLOP

WE INTERRUPT OUR REGULARLY SCHEDULED BROADCAST...

MICHIKO! HURRY UP OR YOU'LL BE LATE FOR SCHOOL!

...TO BRING YOU A MESSAGE FROM OUR NEW PROVISIONAL GOVERNMENT.

I CAN'T FIND MY SOCKS!

WAAH! I CAN'T FIND THEM!

THEREFORE ALL CITIZENS ARE ADVISED...

TURN THE TV OFF WHILE WE'RE EATING!

WOW! A TANK!

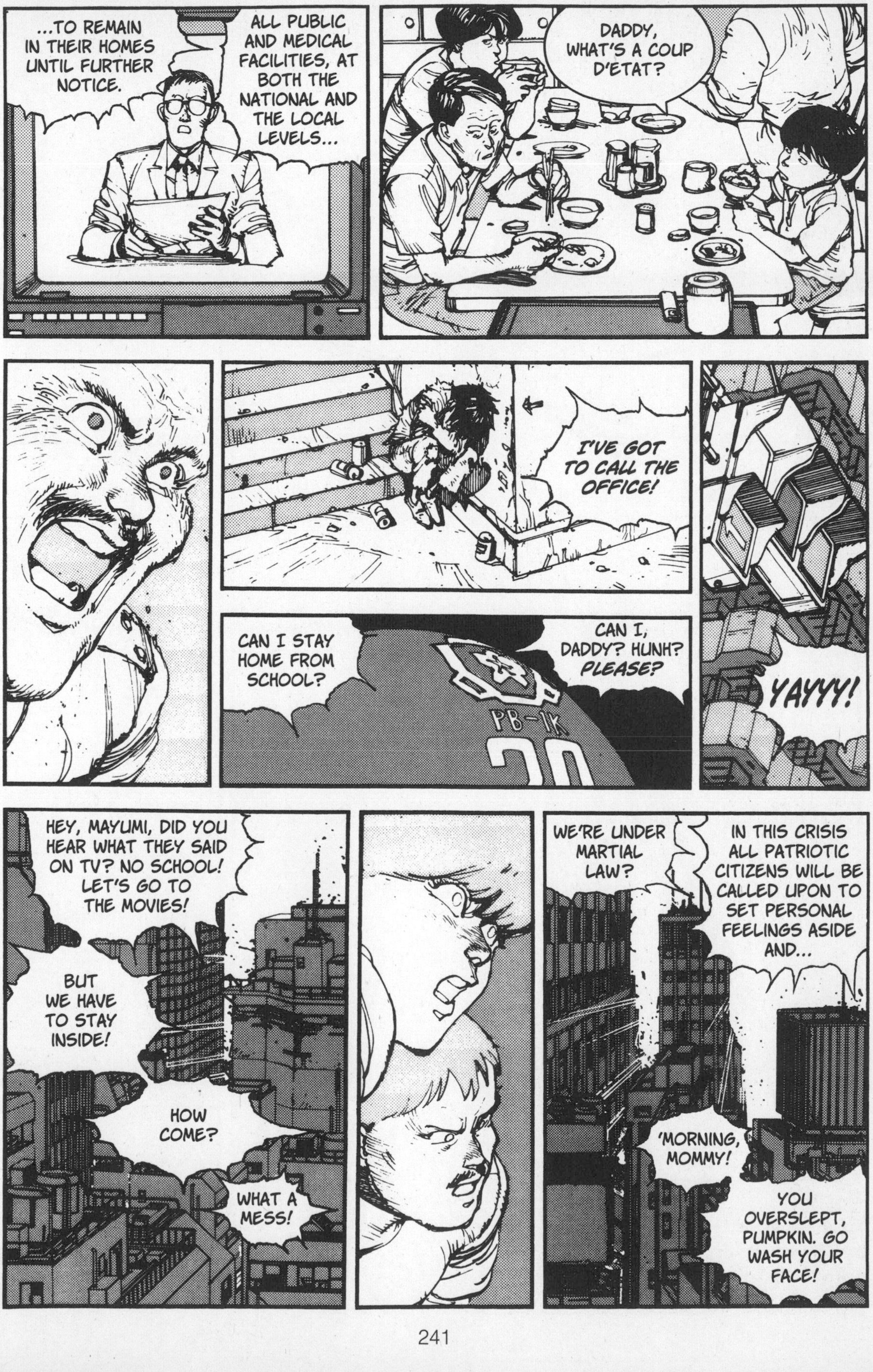
...TO REMAIN IN THEIR HOMES UNTIL FURTHER NOTICE.
ALL PUBLIC AND MEDICAL FACILITIES, AT BOTH THE NATIONAL AND THE LOCAL LEVELS...
DADDY, WHAT'S A COUP D'ETAT?
I'VE GOT TO CALL THE OFFICE!
CAN I STAY HOME FROM SCHOOL?
CAN I, DADDY? HUNH? PLEASE?
PB-1K
YAYYY!
HEY, MAYUMI, DID YOU HEAR WHAT THEY SAID ON TV? NO SCHOOL! LET'S GO TO THE MOVIES!
BUT WE HAVE TO STAY INSIDE!
HOW COME?
WHAT A MESS!
WE'RE UNDER MARTIAL LAW?
IN THIS CRISIS ALL PATRIOTIC CITIZENS WILL BE CALLED UPON TO SET PERSONAL FEELINGS ASIDE AND...
'MORNING, MOMMY!
YOU OVERSLEPT, PUMPKIN. GO WASH YOUR FACE!

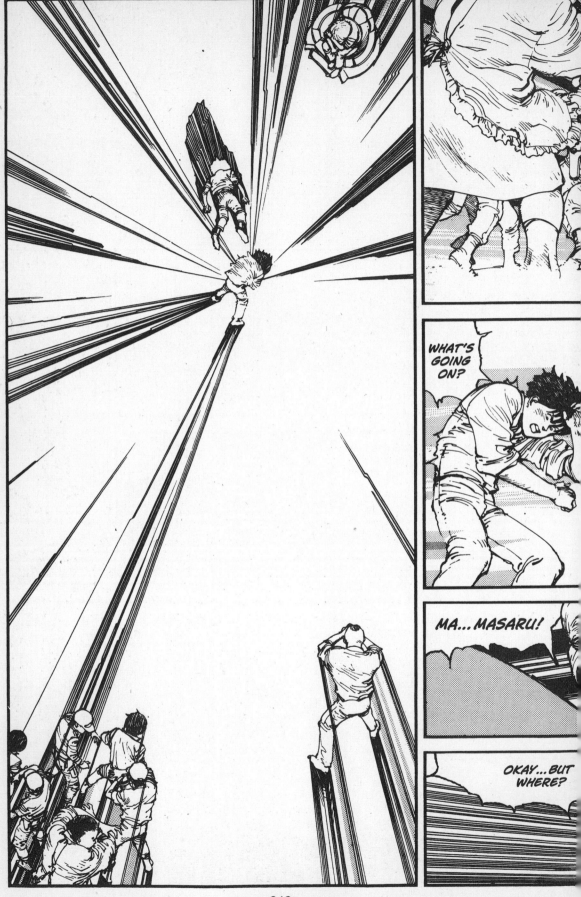

WHAT'S GOING ON?

MA... MASARU!

OKAY... BUT WHERE?

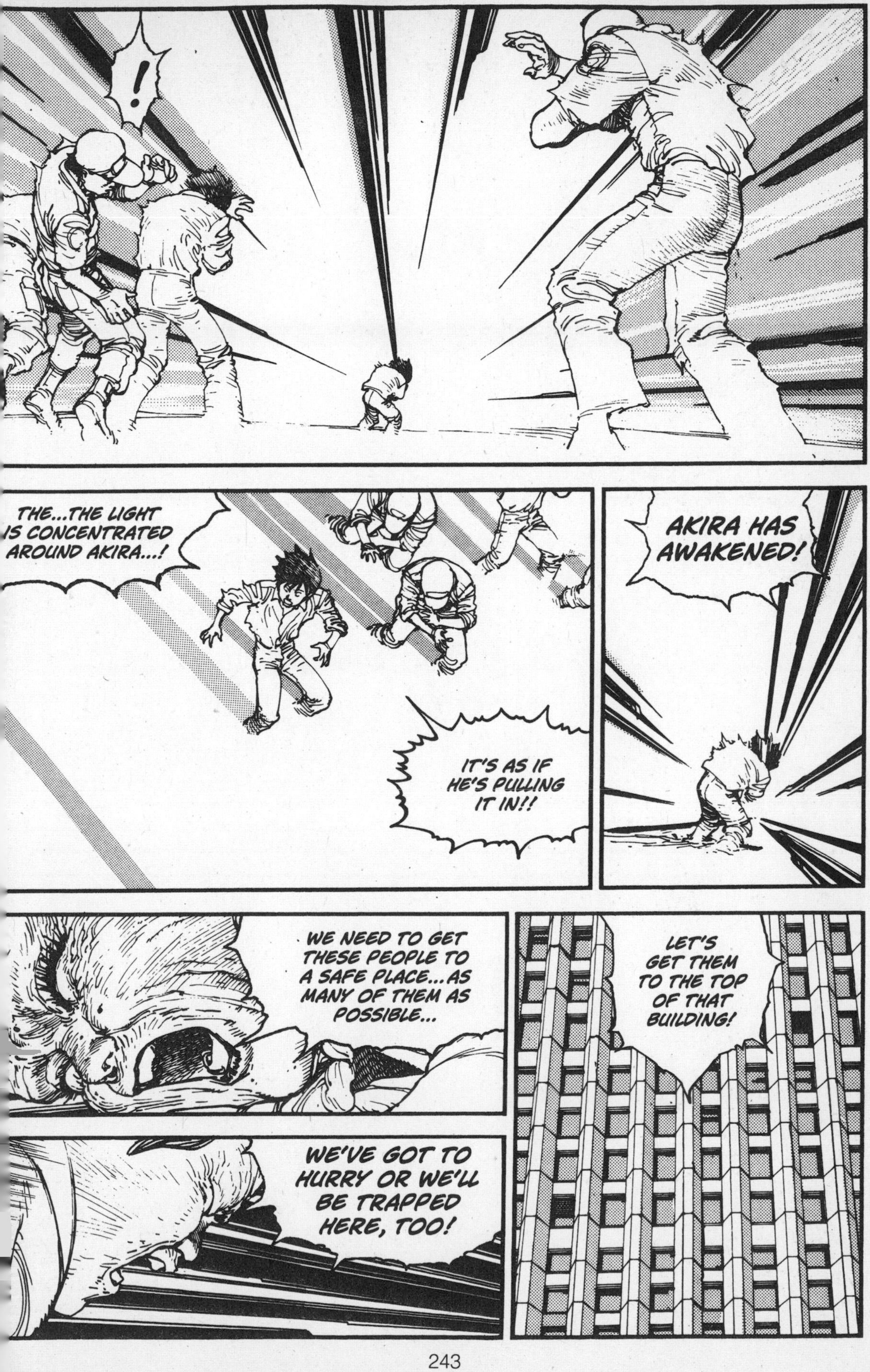
!
THE...THE LIGHT IS CONCENTRATED AROUND AKIRA...!
IT'S AS IF HE'S PULLING IT IN!!
AKIRA HAS AWAKENED!
WE NEED TO GET THESE PEOPLE TO A SAFE PLACE...AS MANY OF THEM AS POSSIBLE...
WE'VE GOT TO HURRY OR WE'LL BE TRAPPED HERE, TOO!
LET'S GET THEM TO THE TOP OF THAT BUILDING!

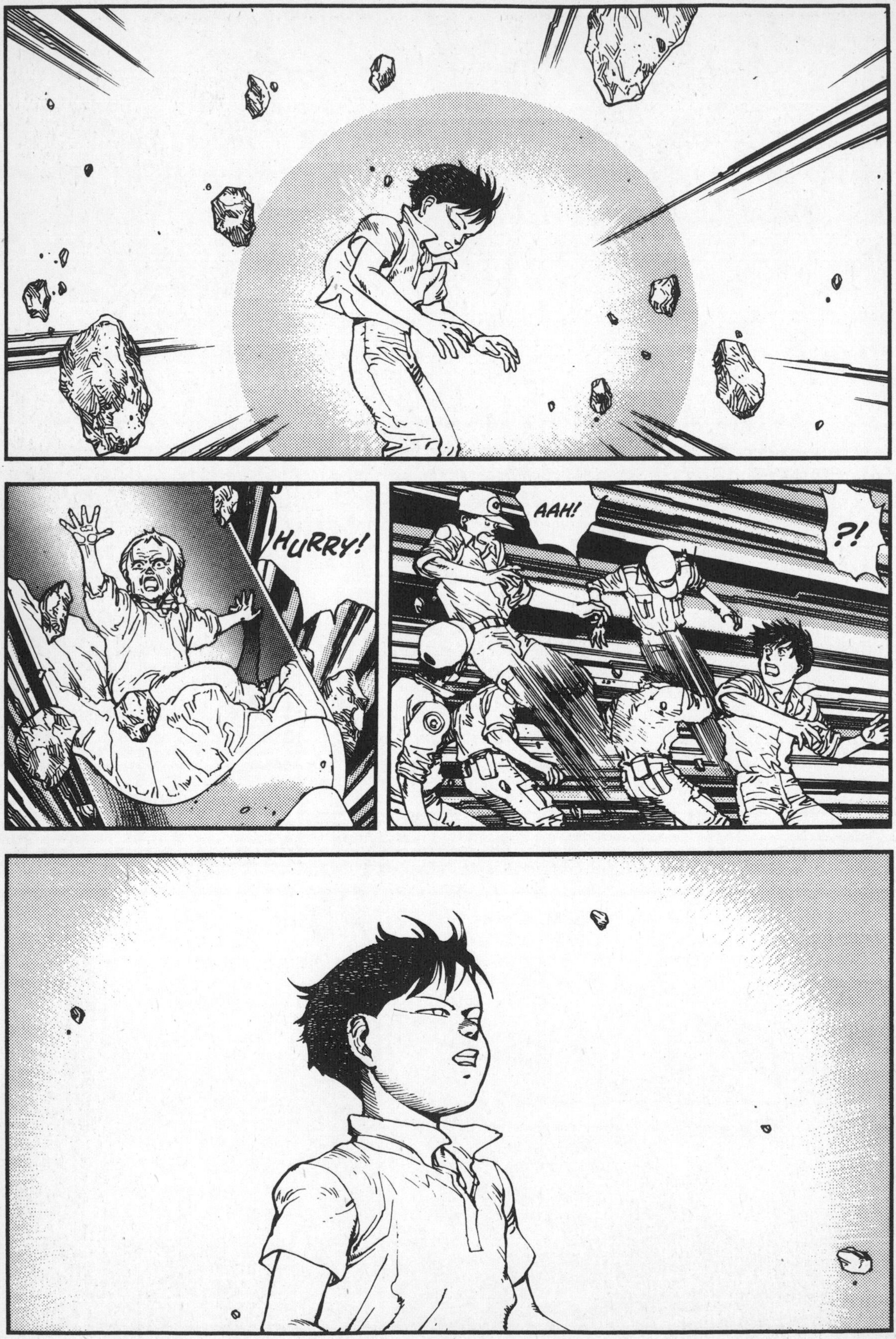
HURRY!
AAH!
?!

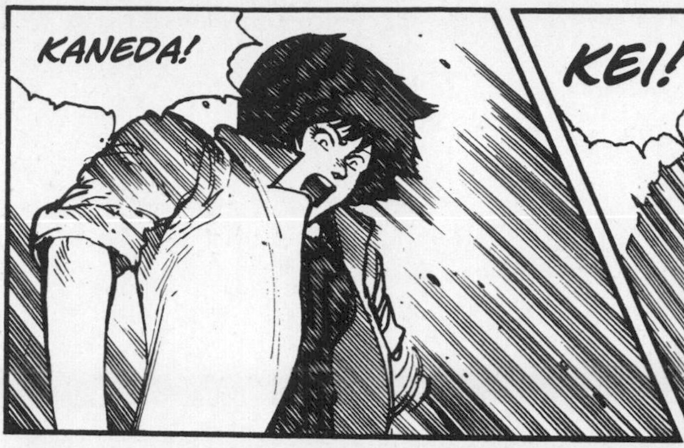
KANEDA!
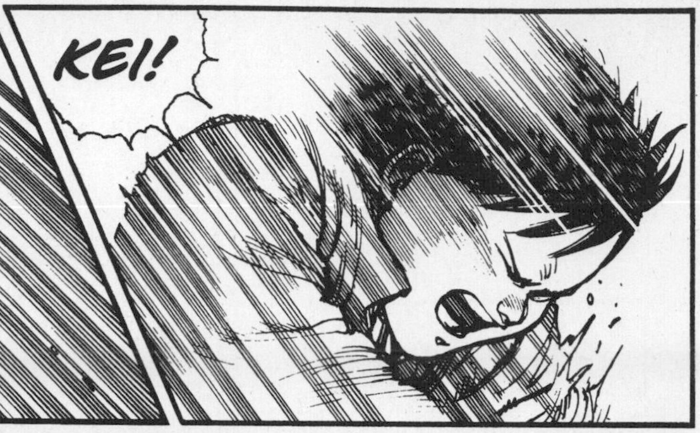
KEI!
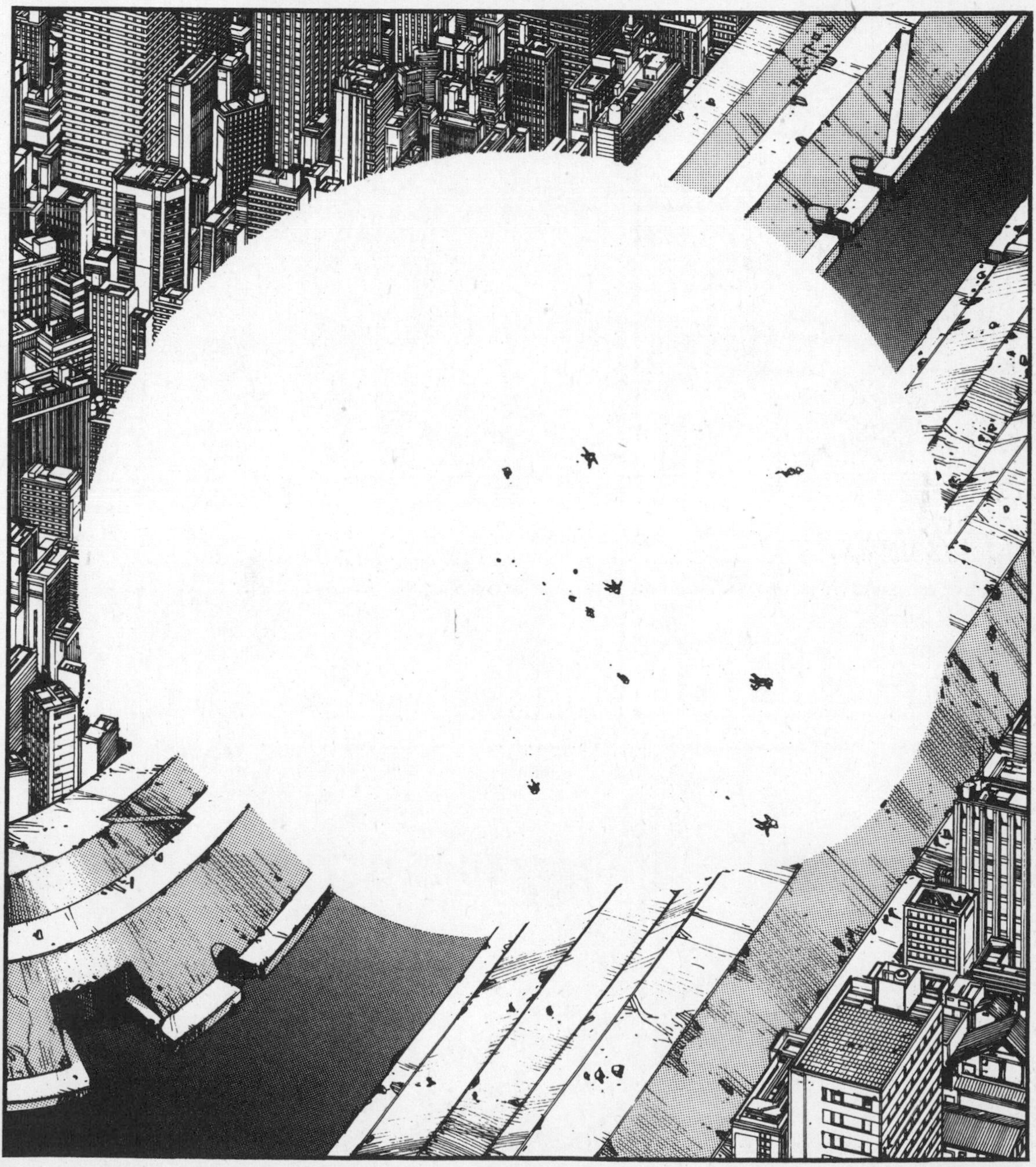

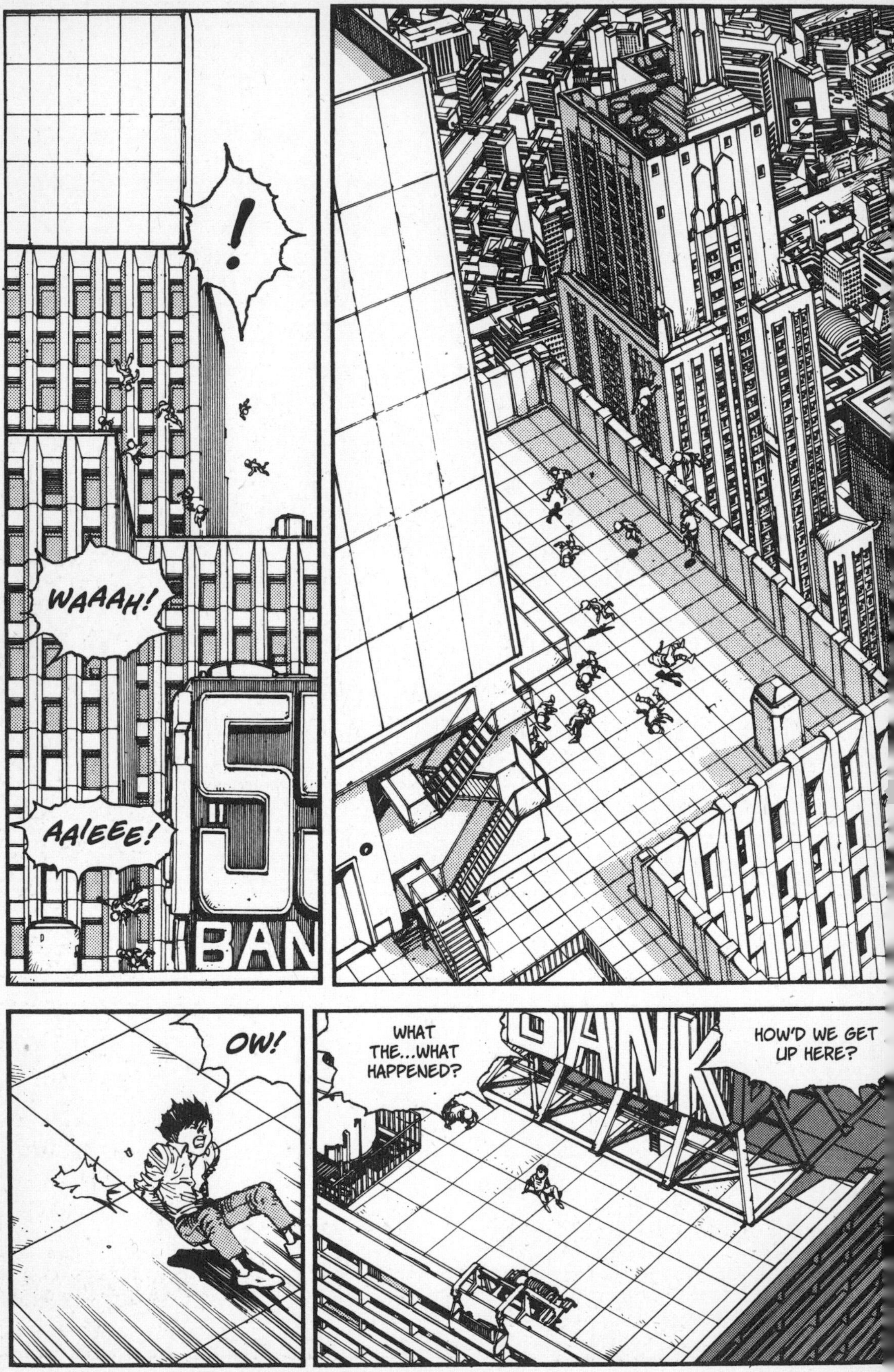
!
WAAAH!
AAIEEE!
5
BAN
OW!
WHAT THE...WHAT HAPPENED?
HOW'D WE GET UP HERE?

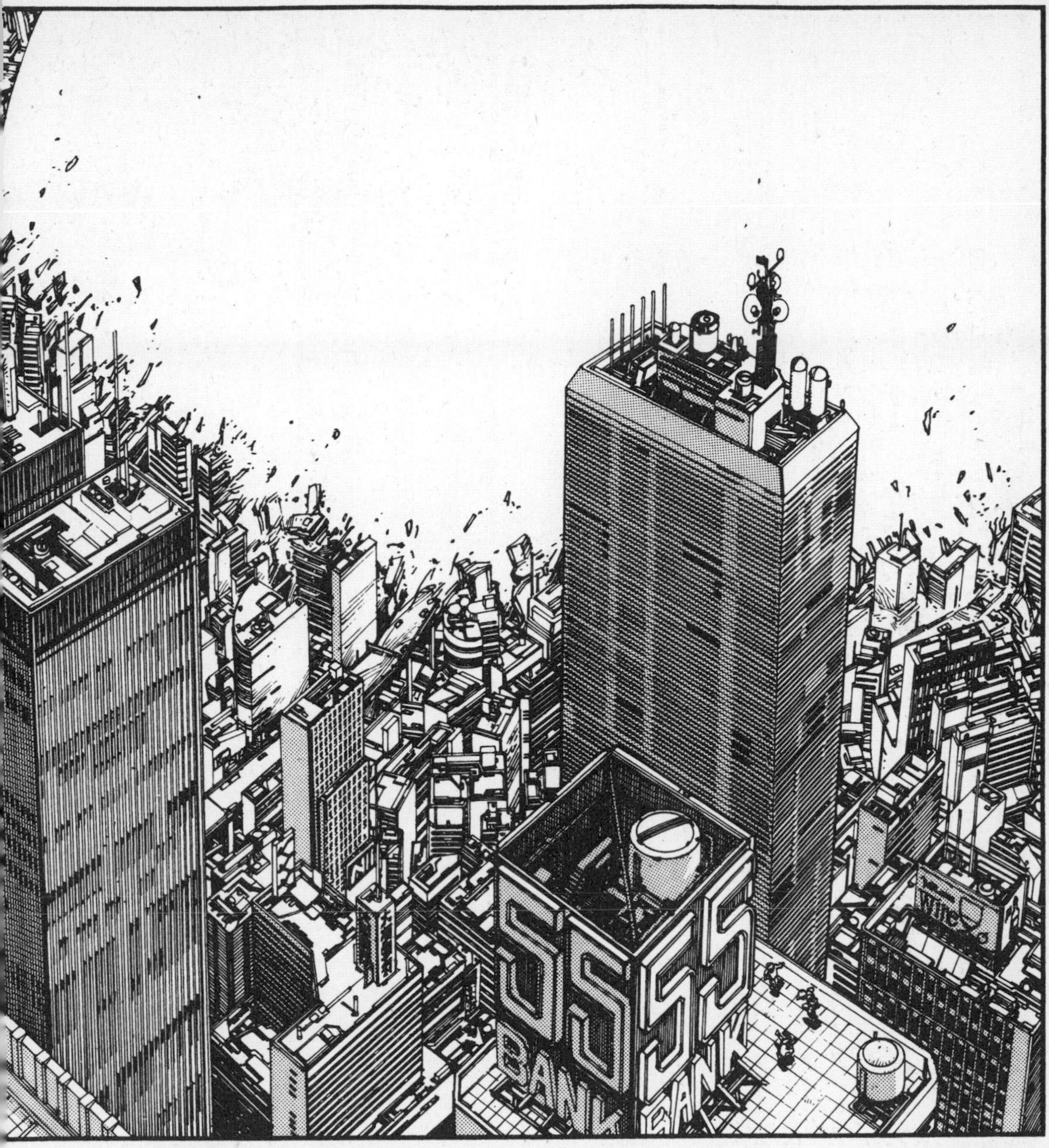
55
BANK
55
BANK

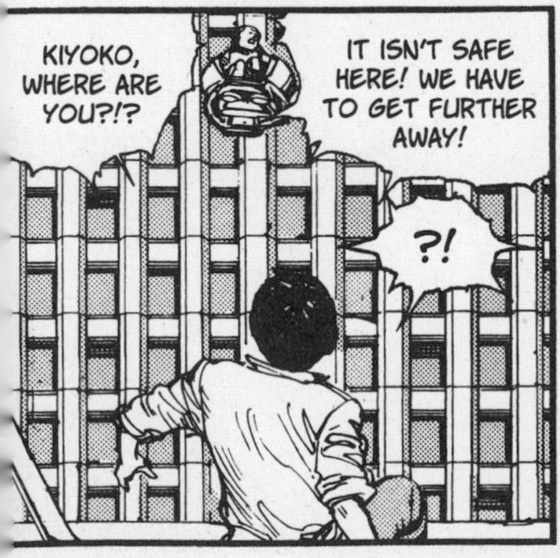
KIYOKO, WHERE ARE YOU?!?
IT ISN'T SAFE HERE! WE HAVE TO GET FURTHER AWAY!
?!

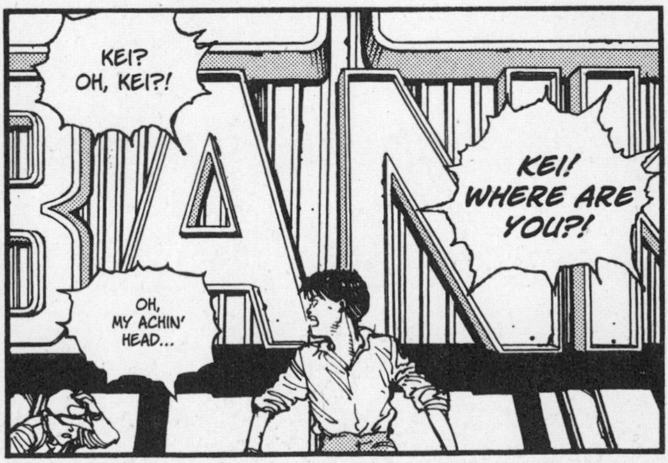
KEI? OH, KEI?!
KEI! WHERE ARE YOU?!
OH, MY ACHIN' HEAD...

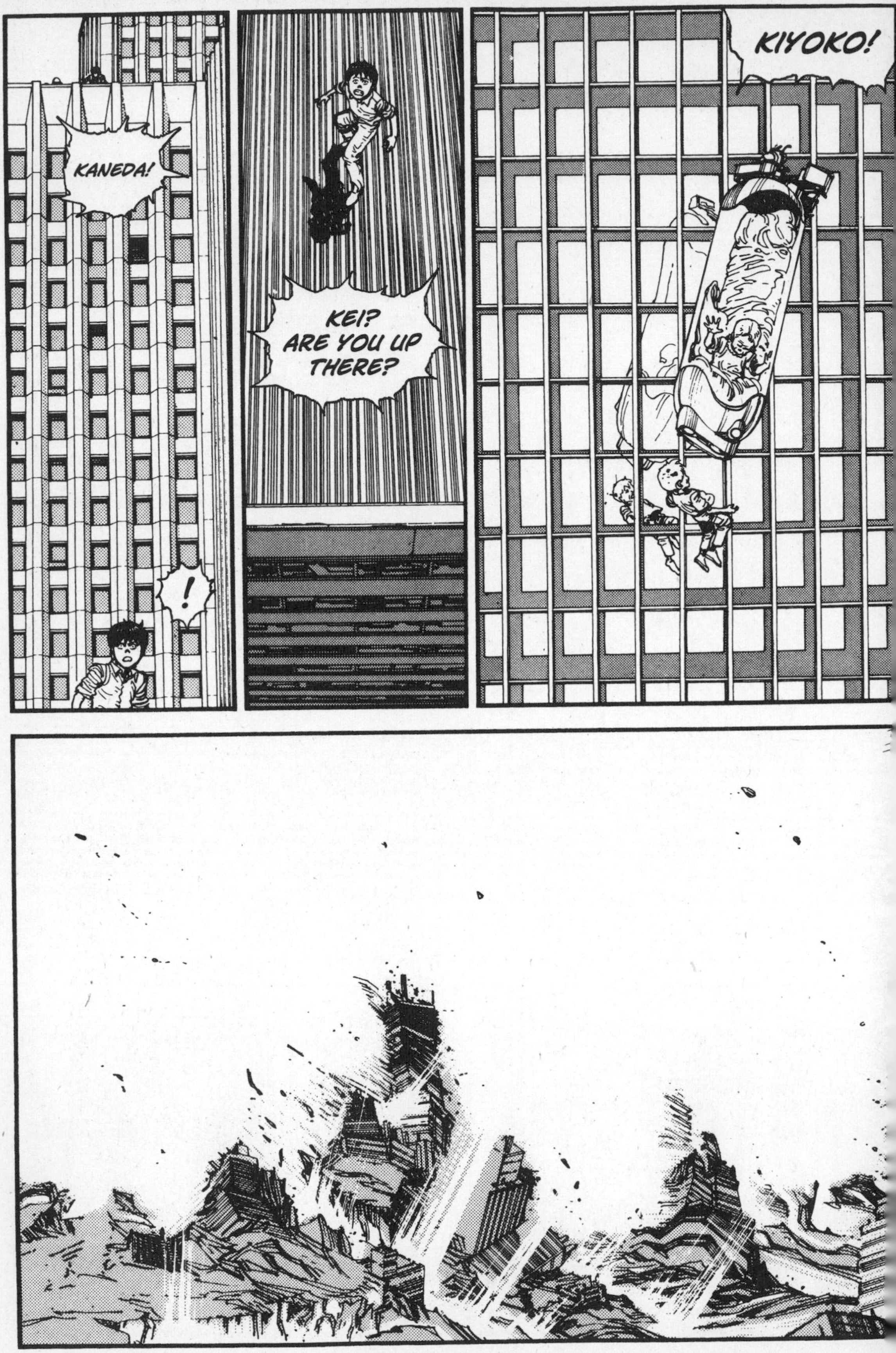
KANEDA!
!
KEI? ARE YOU UP THERE?
KIYOKO!

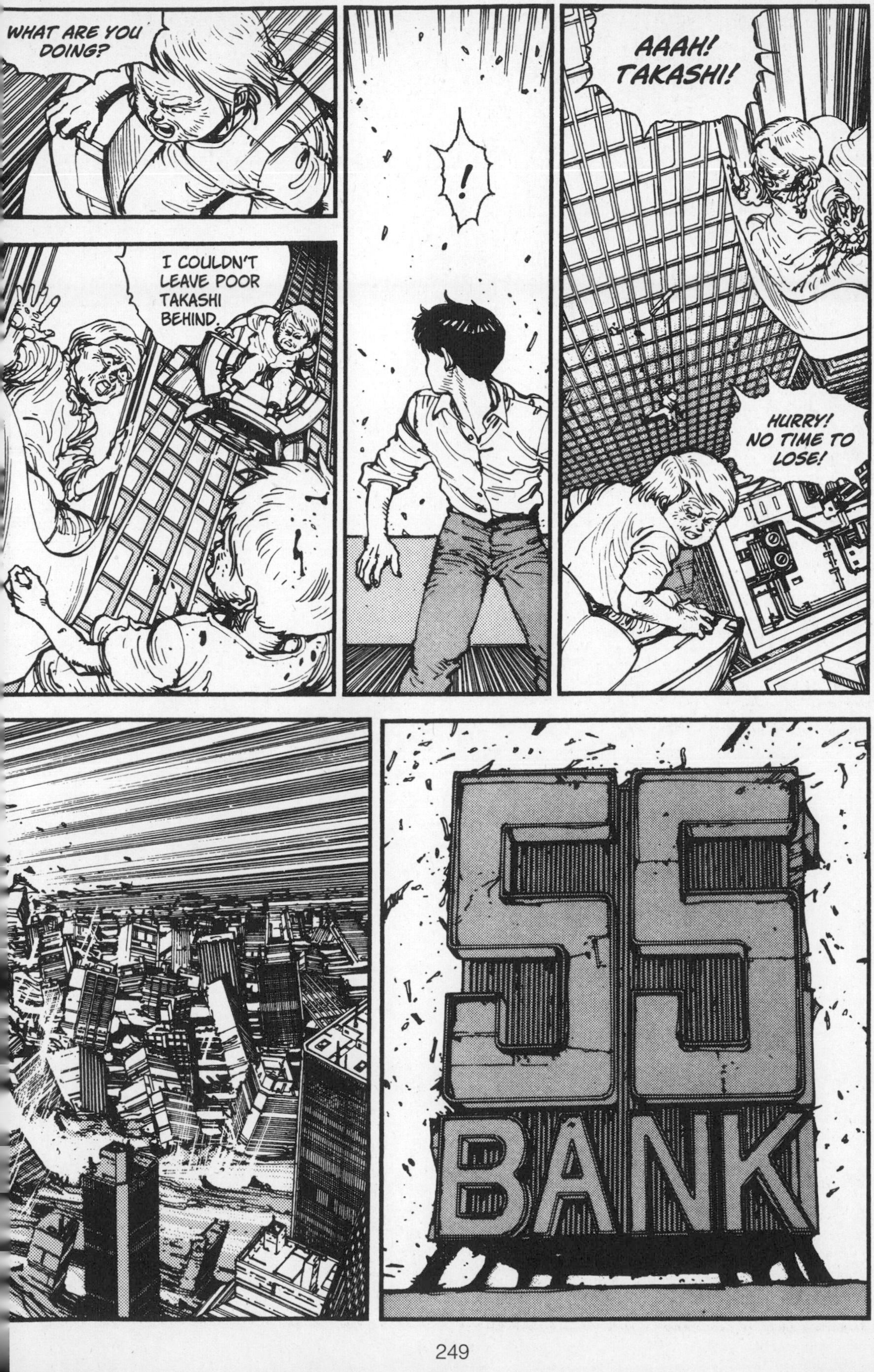
WHAT ARE YOU DOING?
I COULDN'T LEAVE POOR TAKASHI BEHIND.
!
AAAH! TAKASHI!
HURRY! NO TIME TO LOSE!
BANK

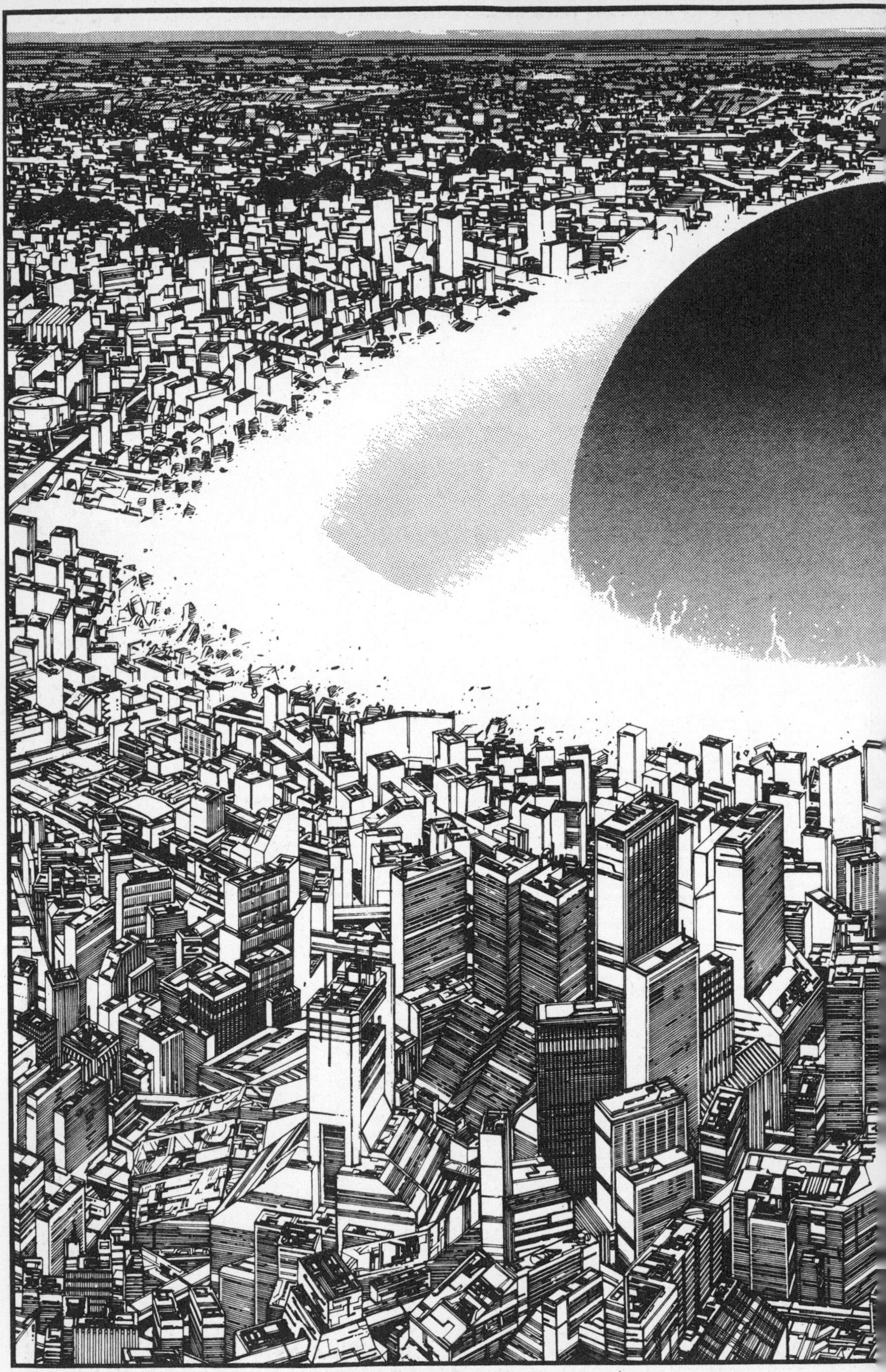

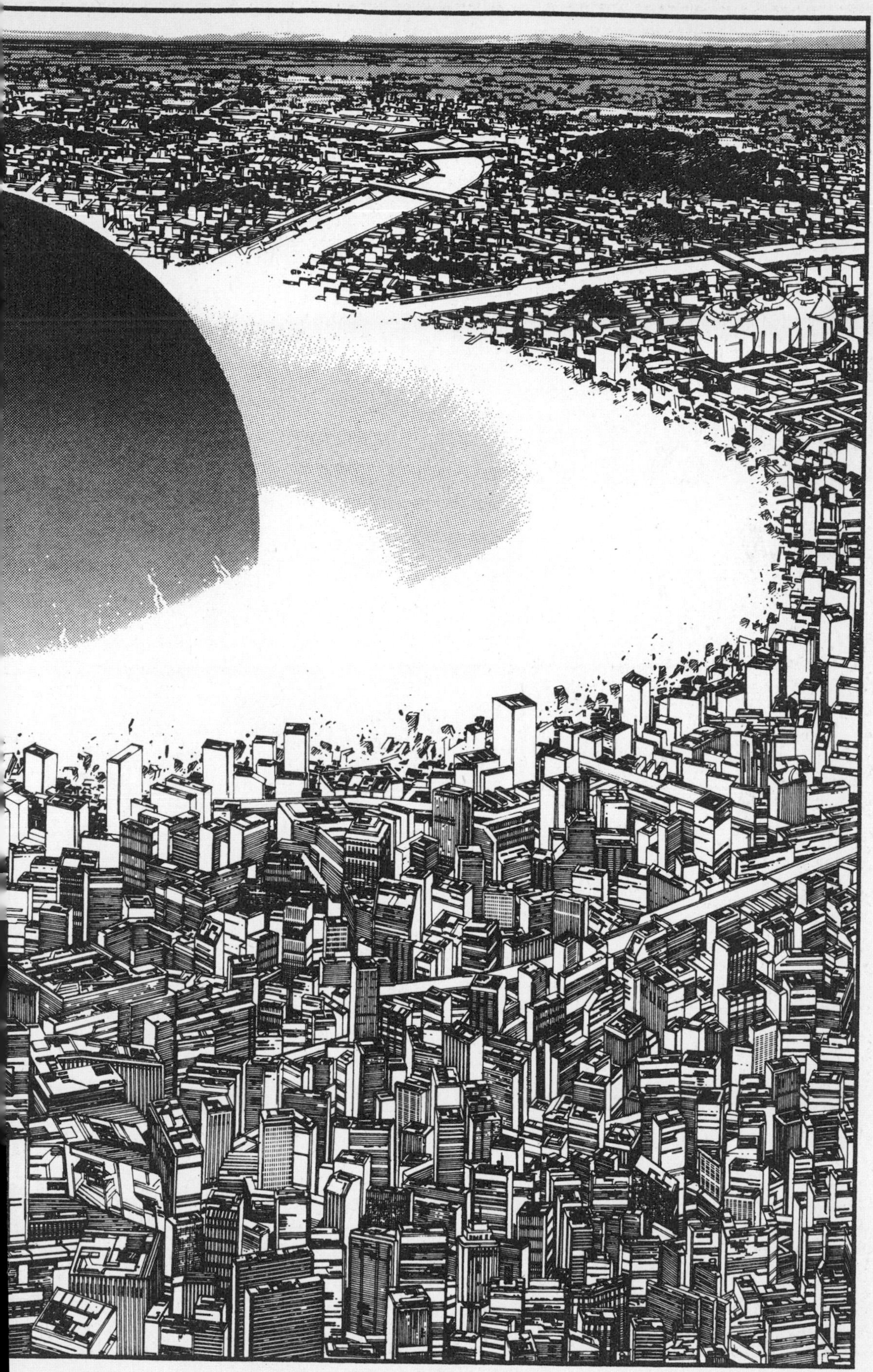

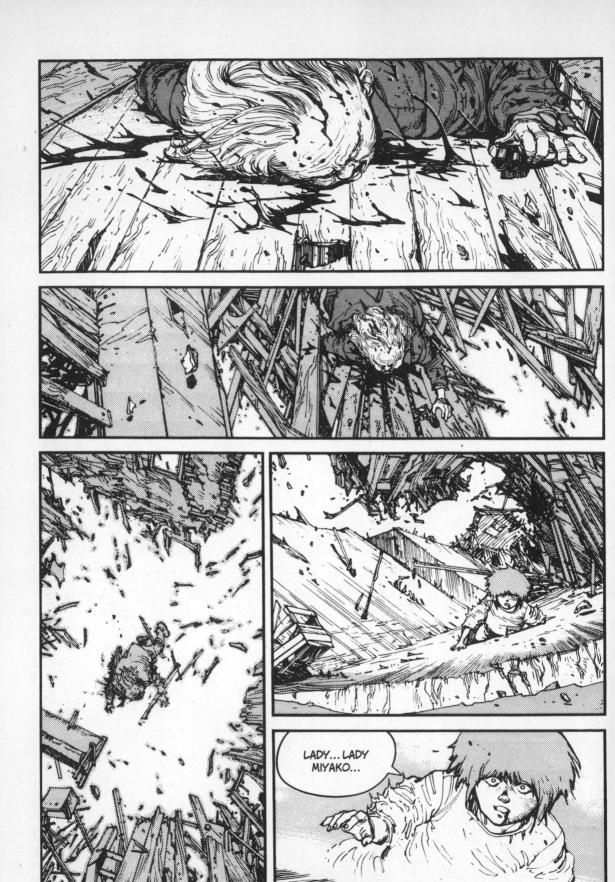

LADY... LADY MIYAKO...

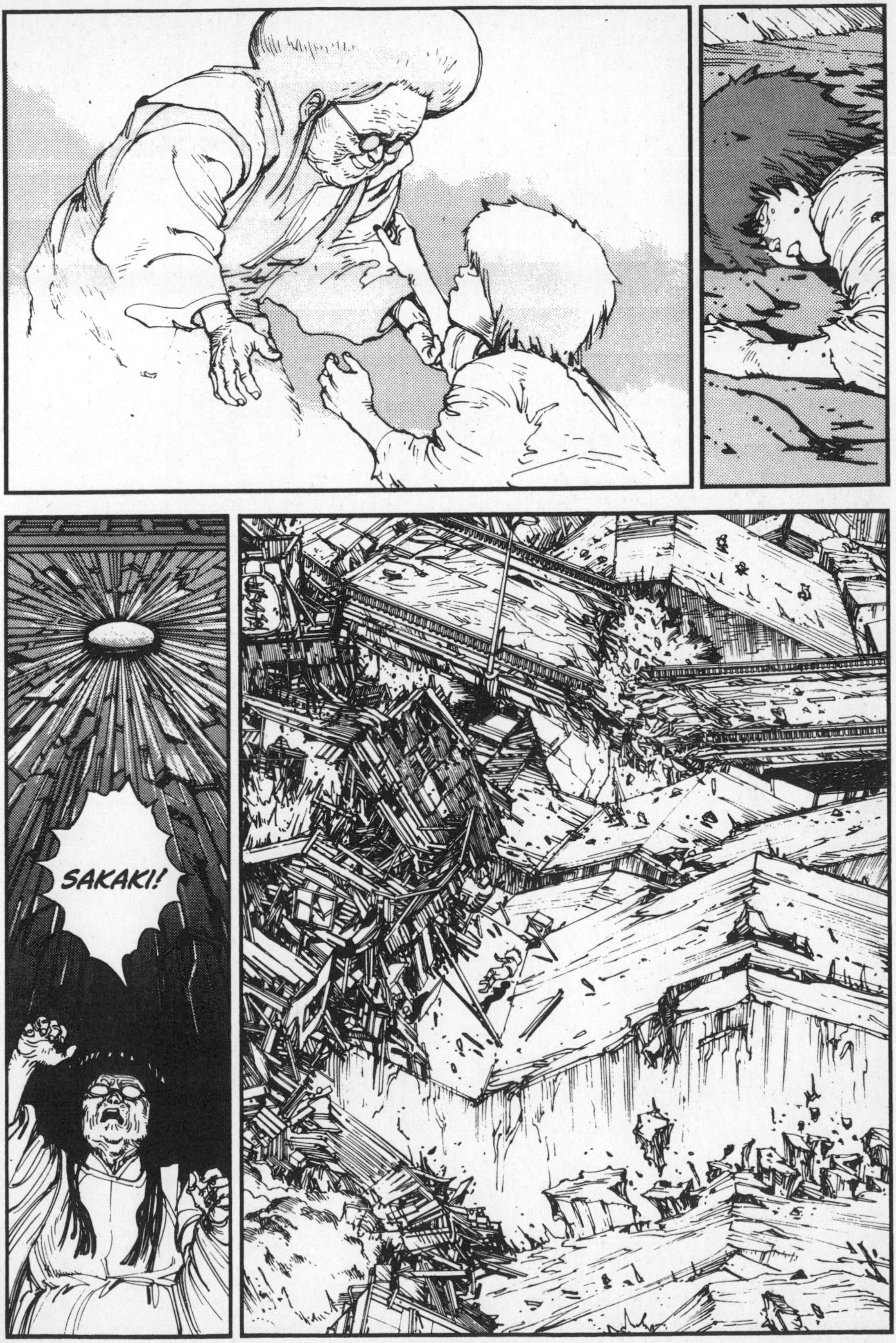
SAKAKI!

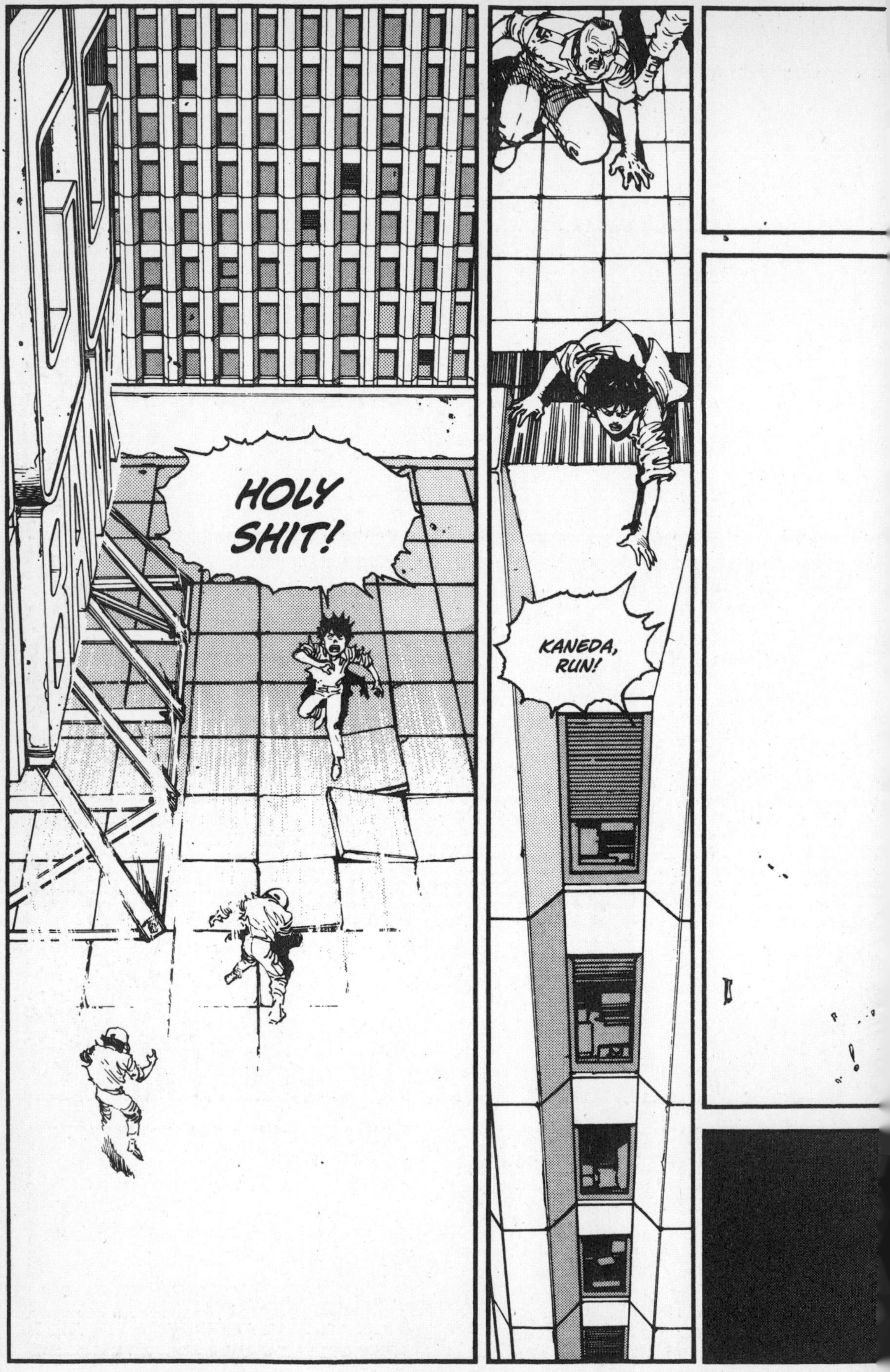
HOLY SHIT!
KANEDA, RUN!

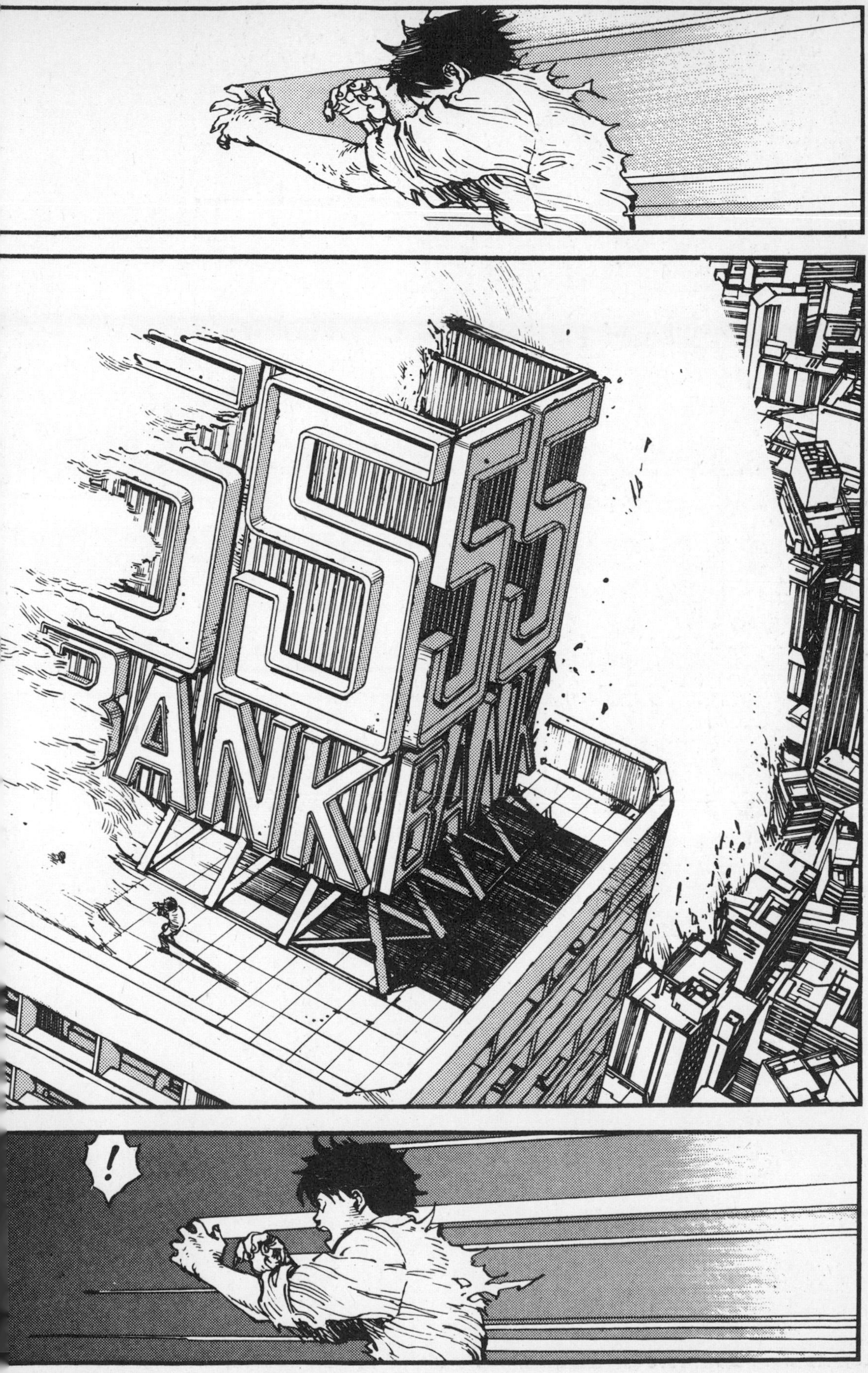
BANK
!

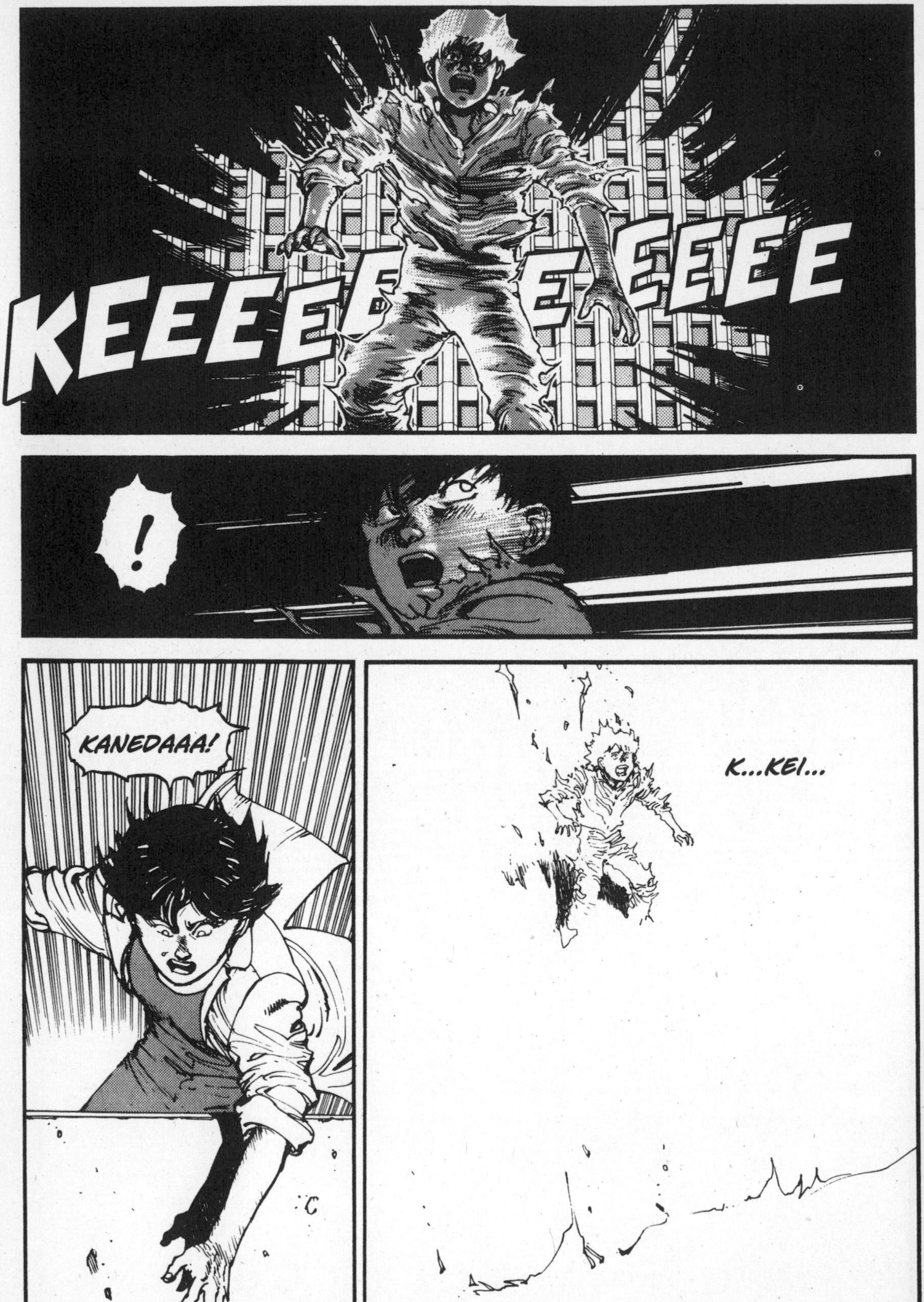
KEEEEEEEEEEE
!
KANEDAAA!
K...KEI...

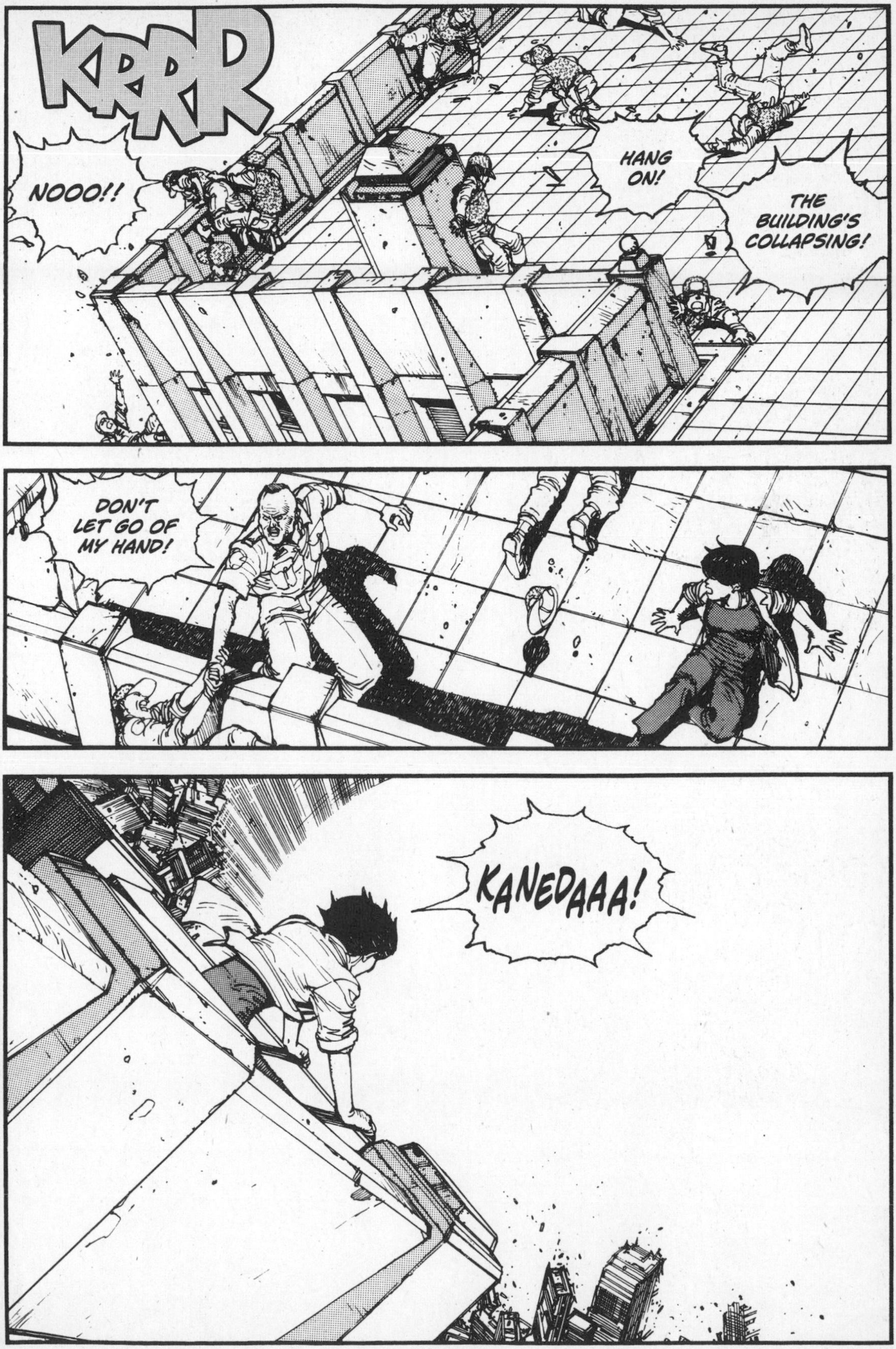
KRRR
NOOO!!
HANG ON!
THE BUILDING'S COLLAPSING!
DON'T LET GO OF MY HAND!
KANEDAAA!

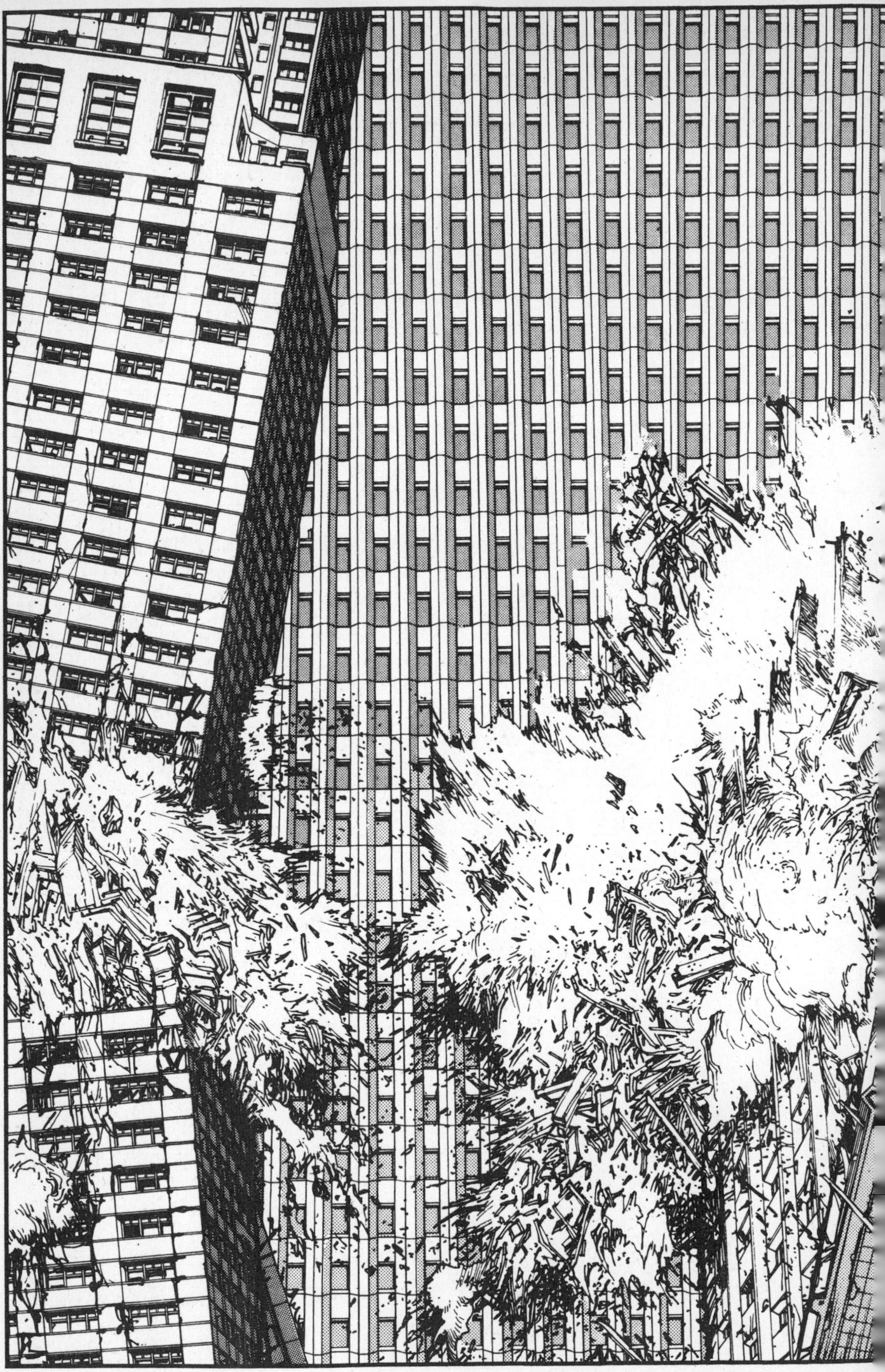

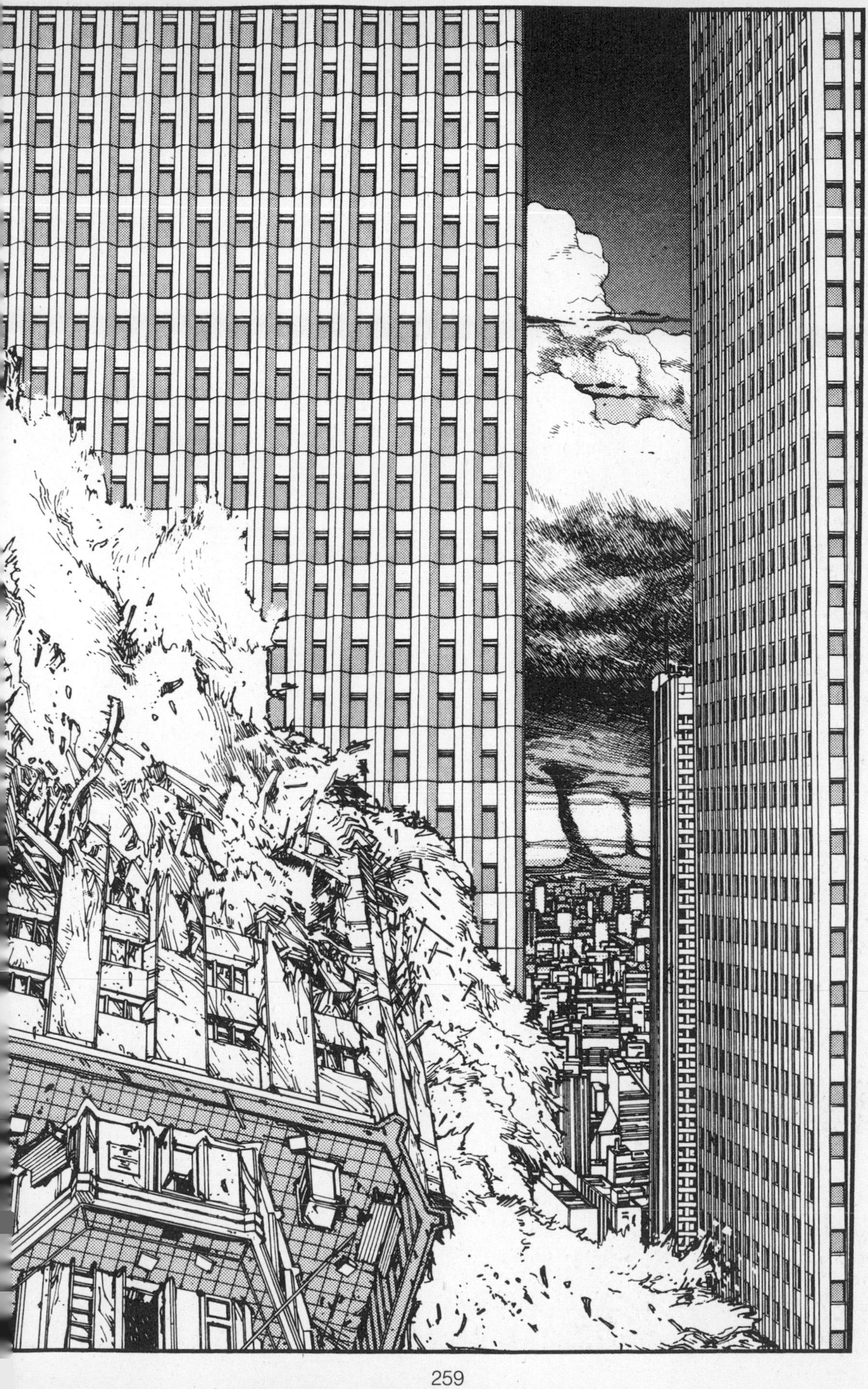

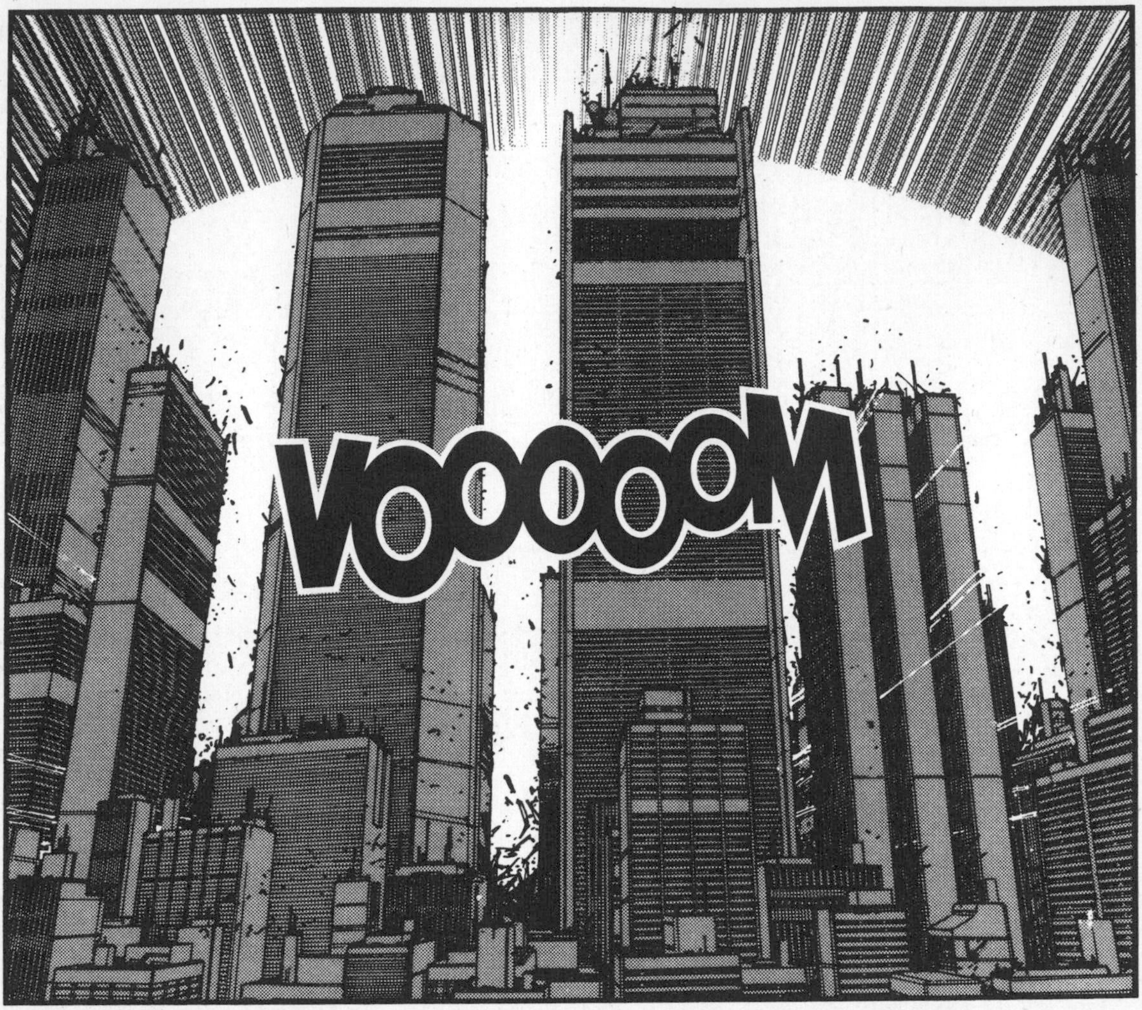
VOOOOOM
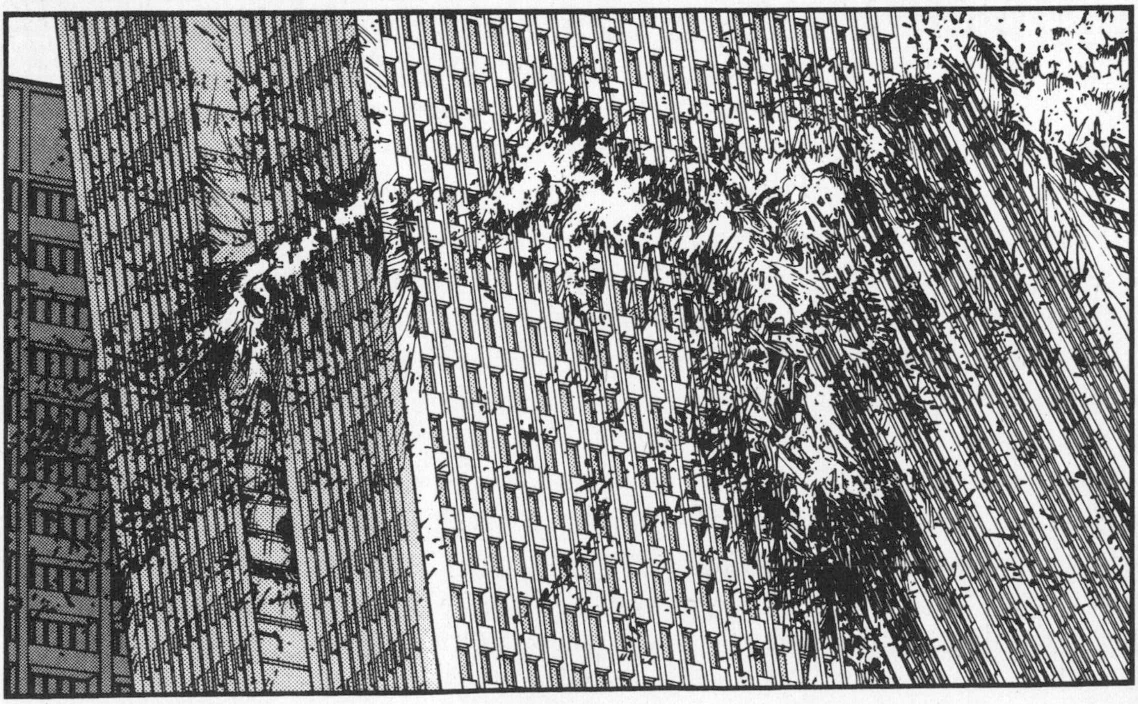

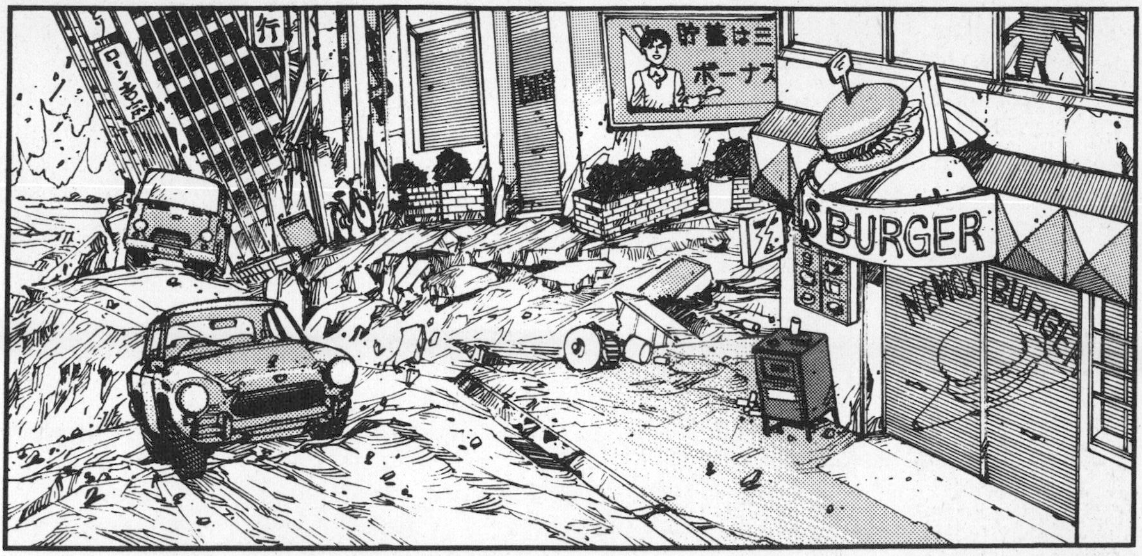
行
貯蓄は三
ボーナス
BURGER
NEWS BURGER
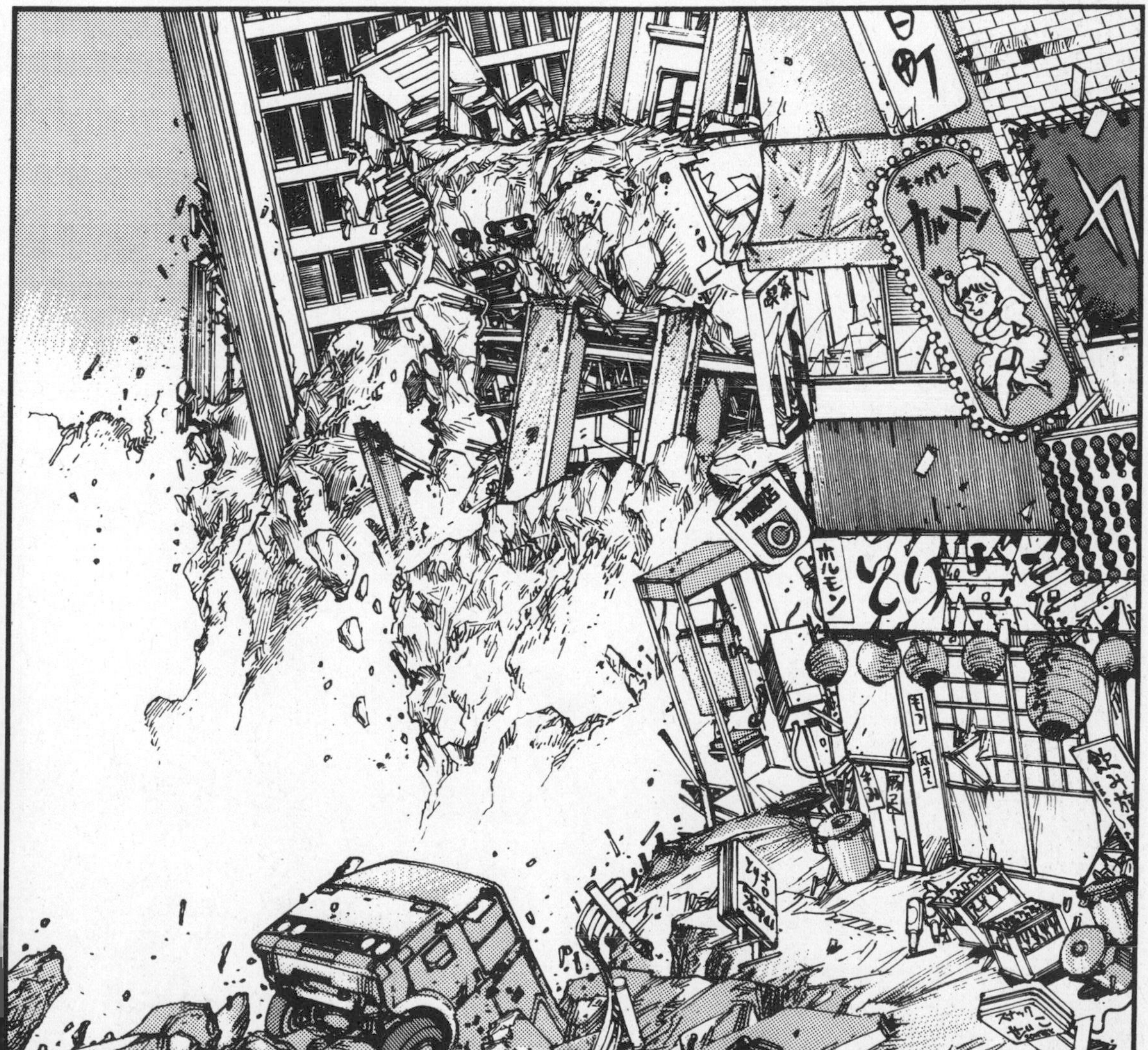
キャバレー
カルメン
ホルモン

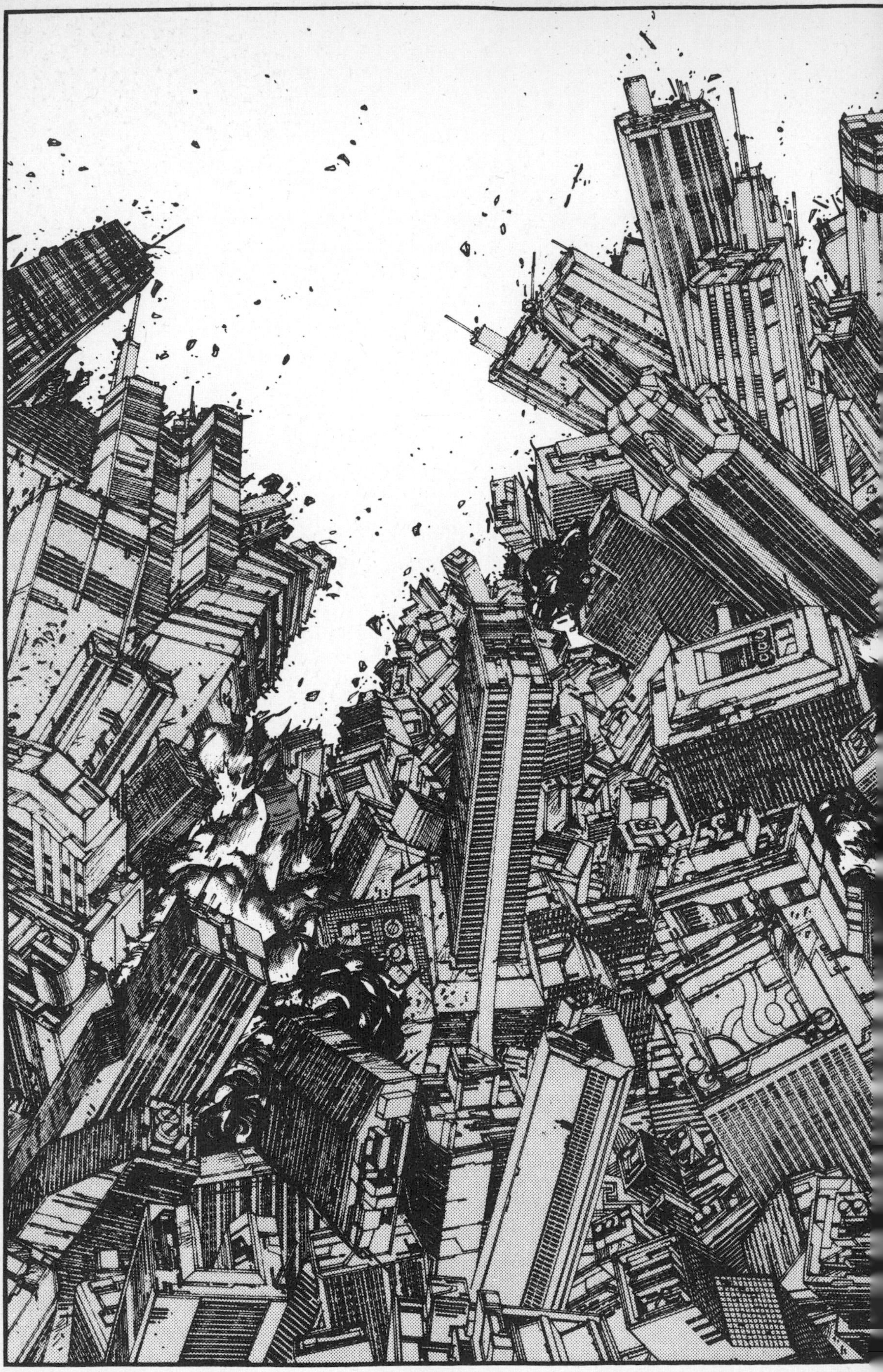

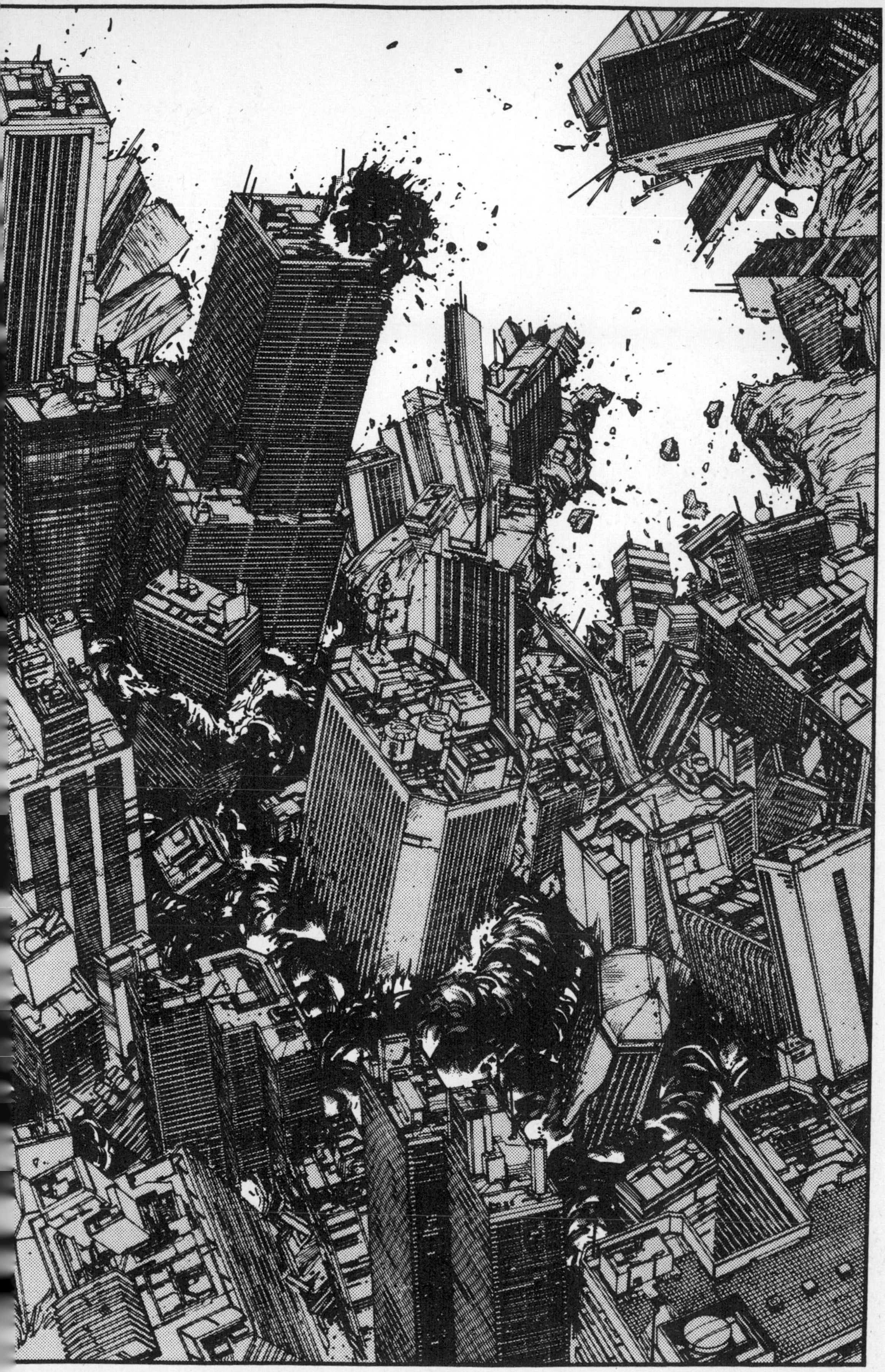

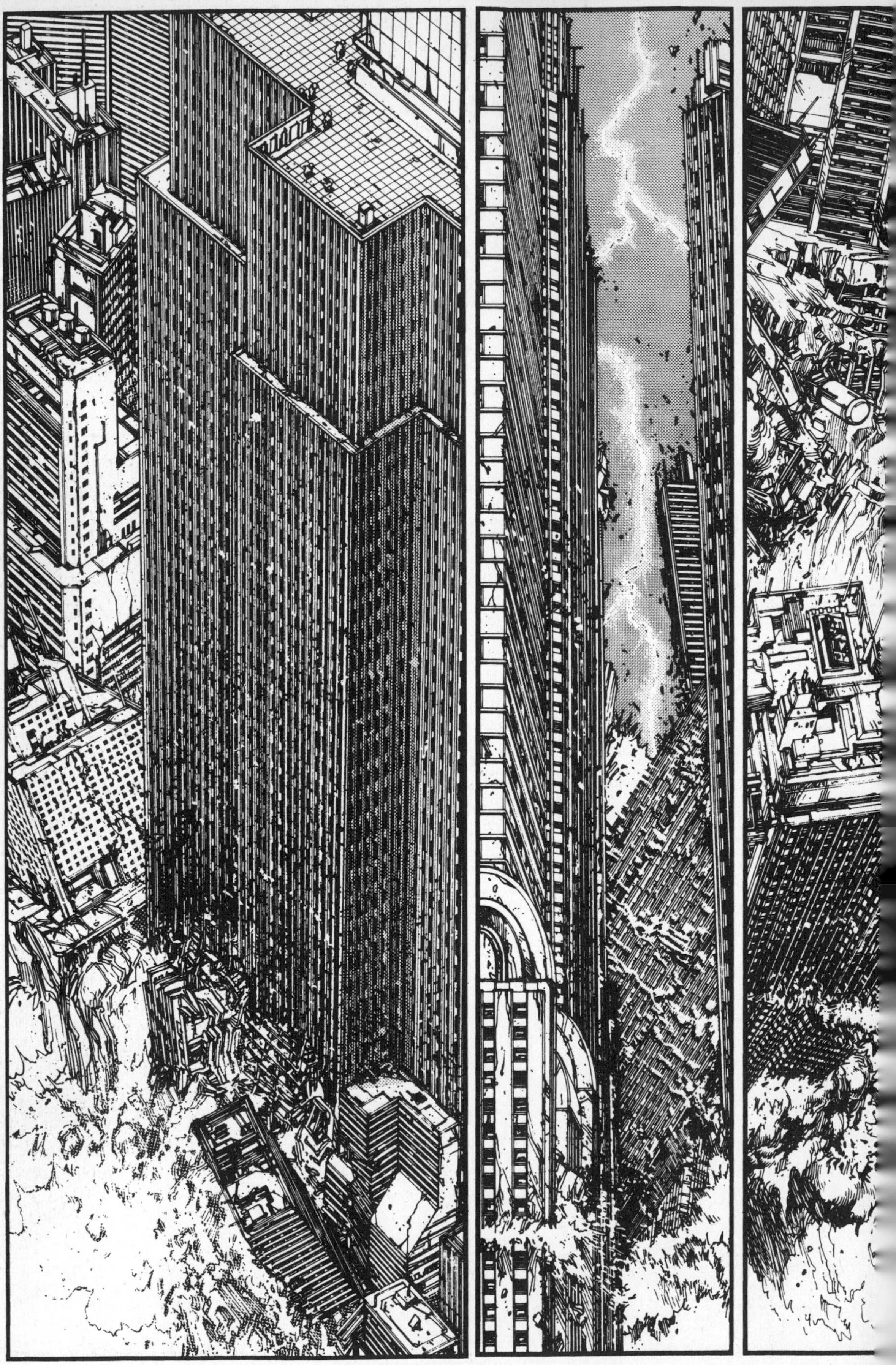

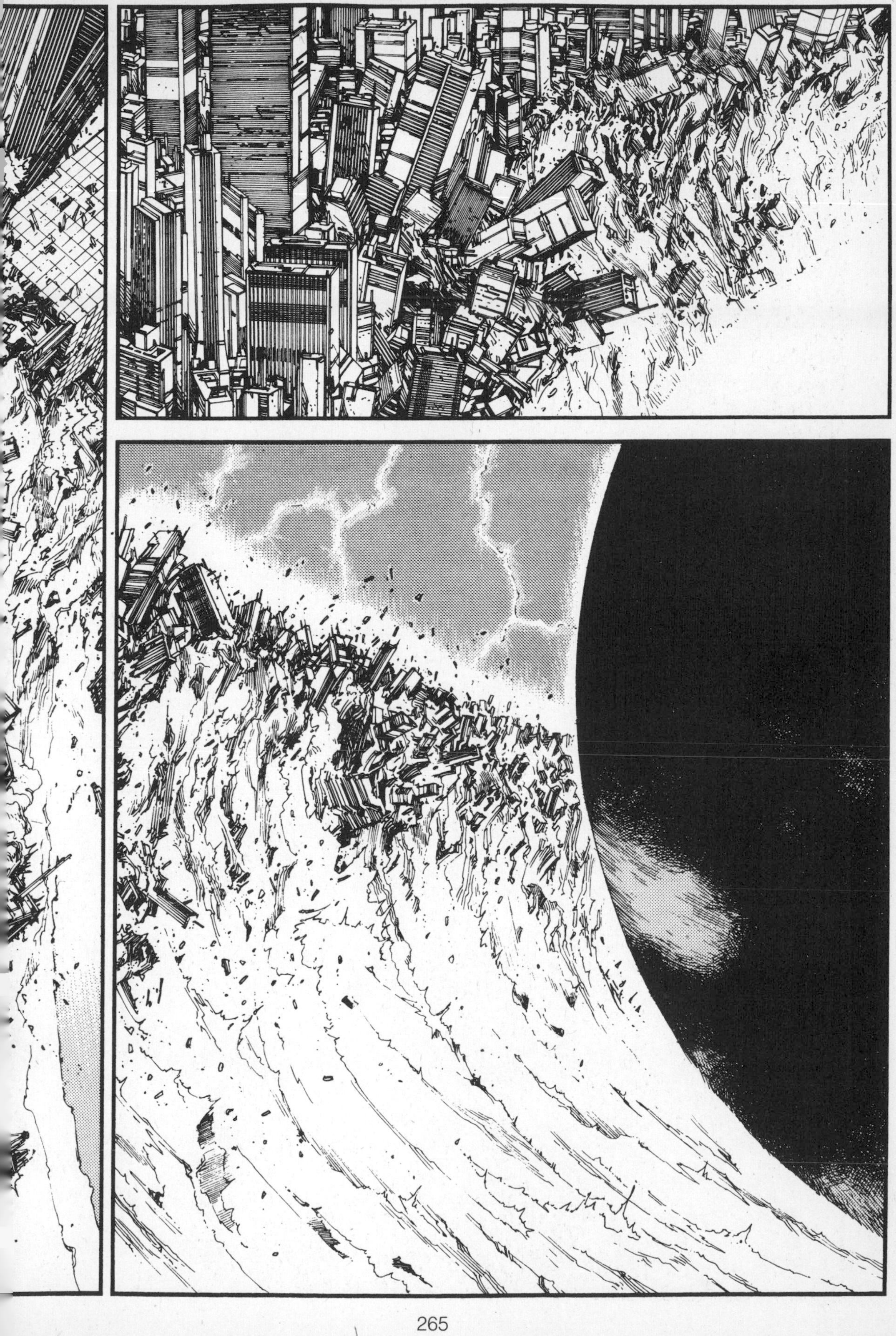

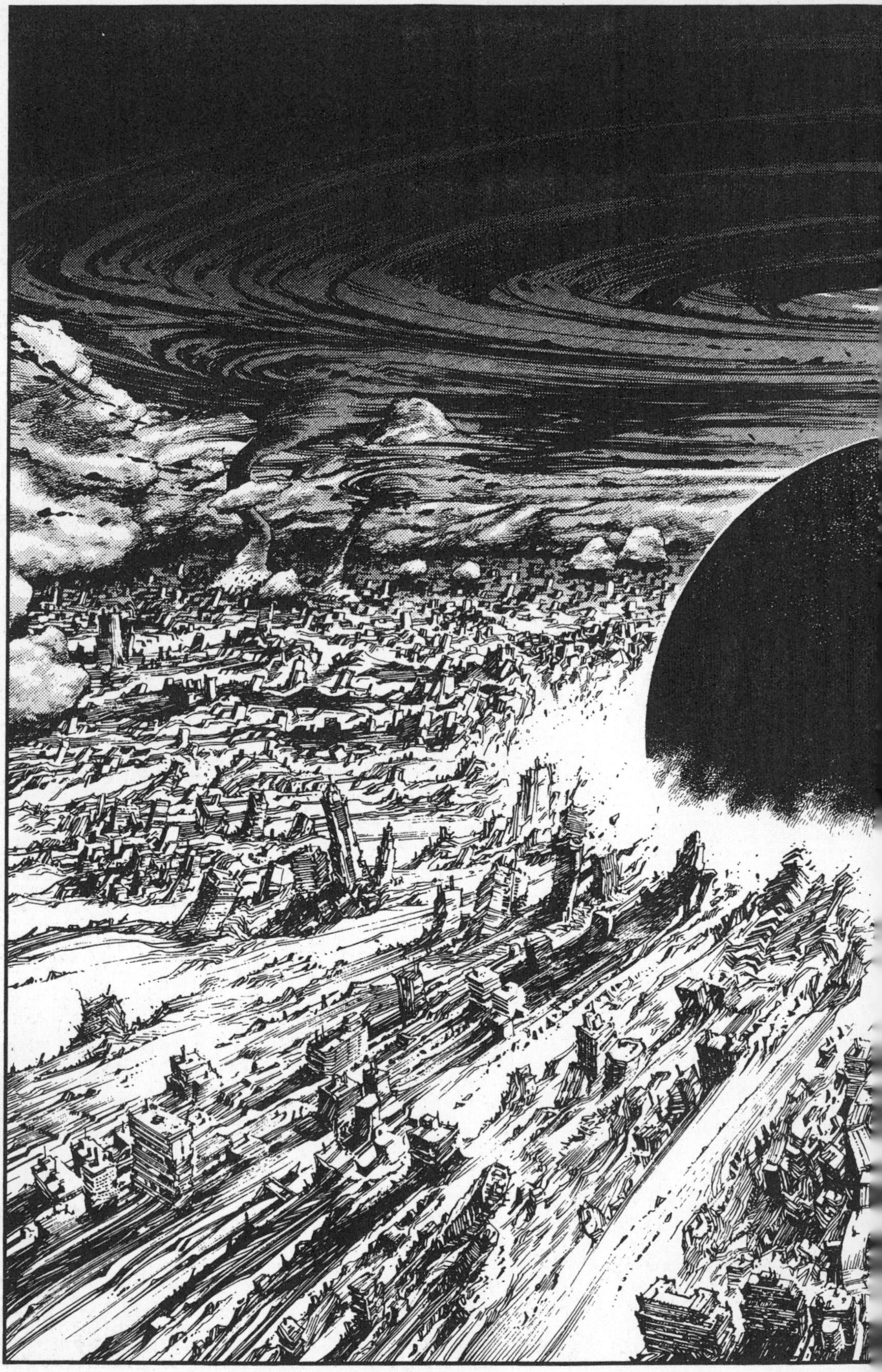

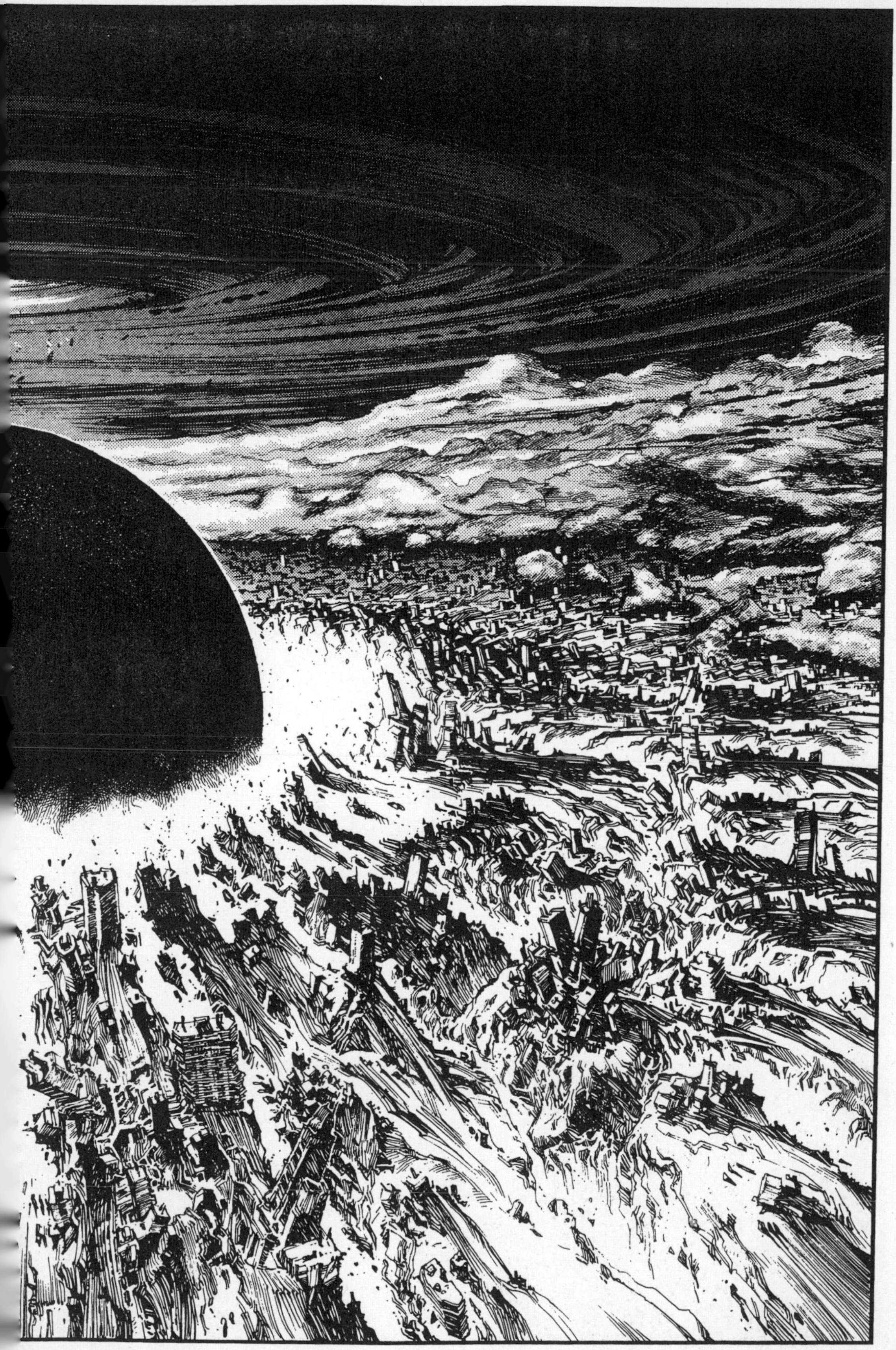

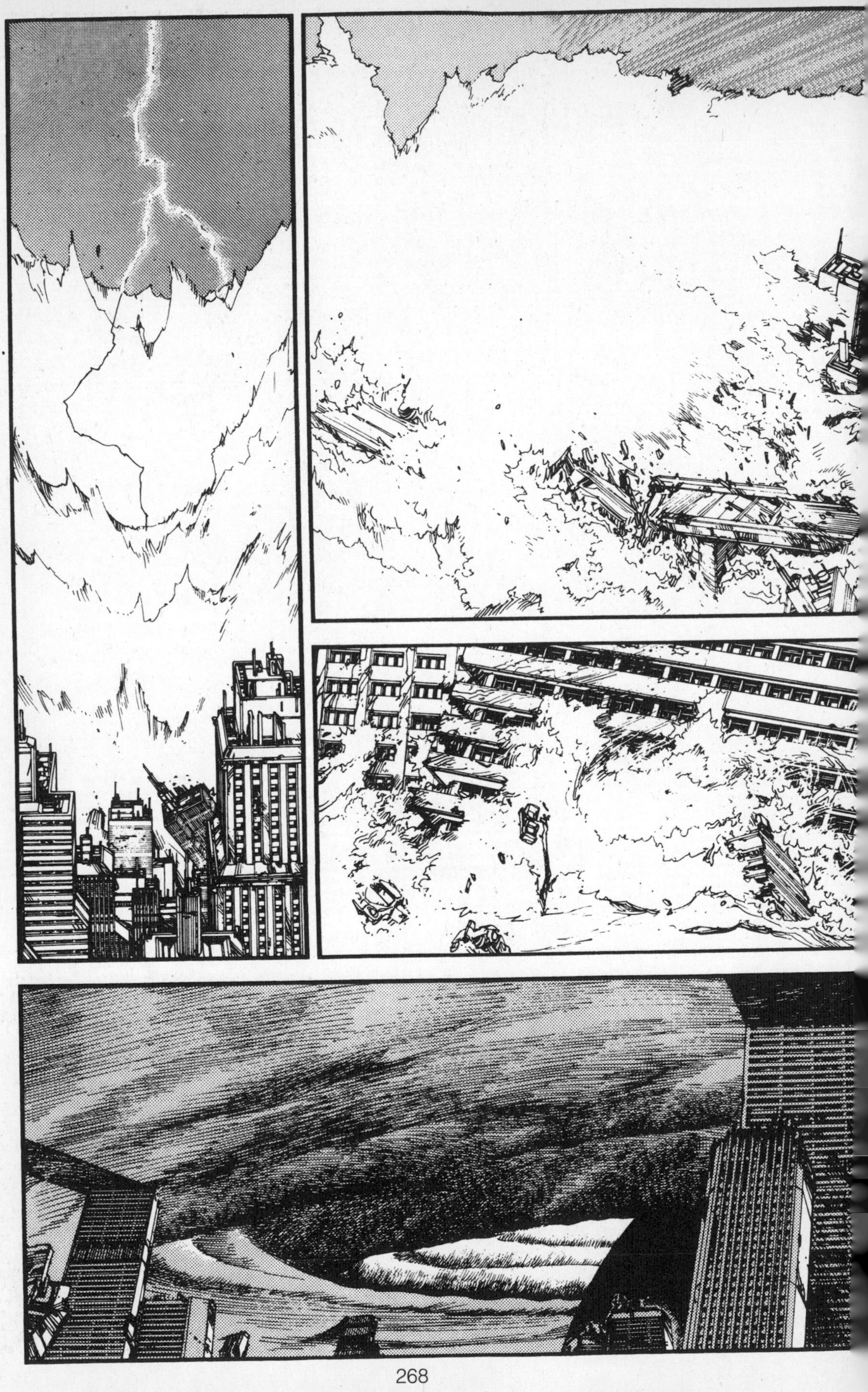

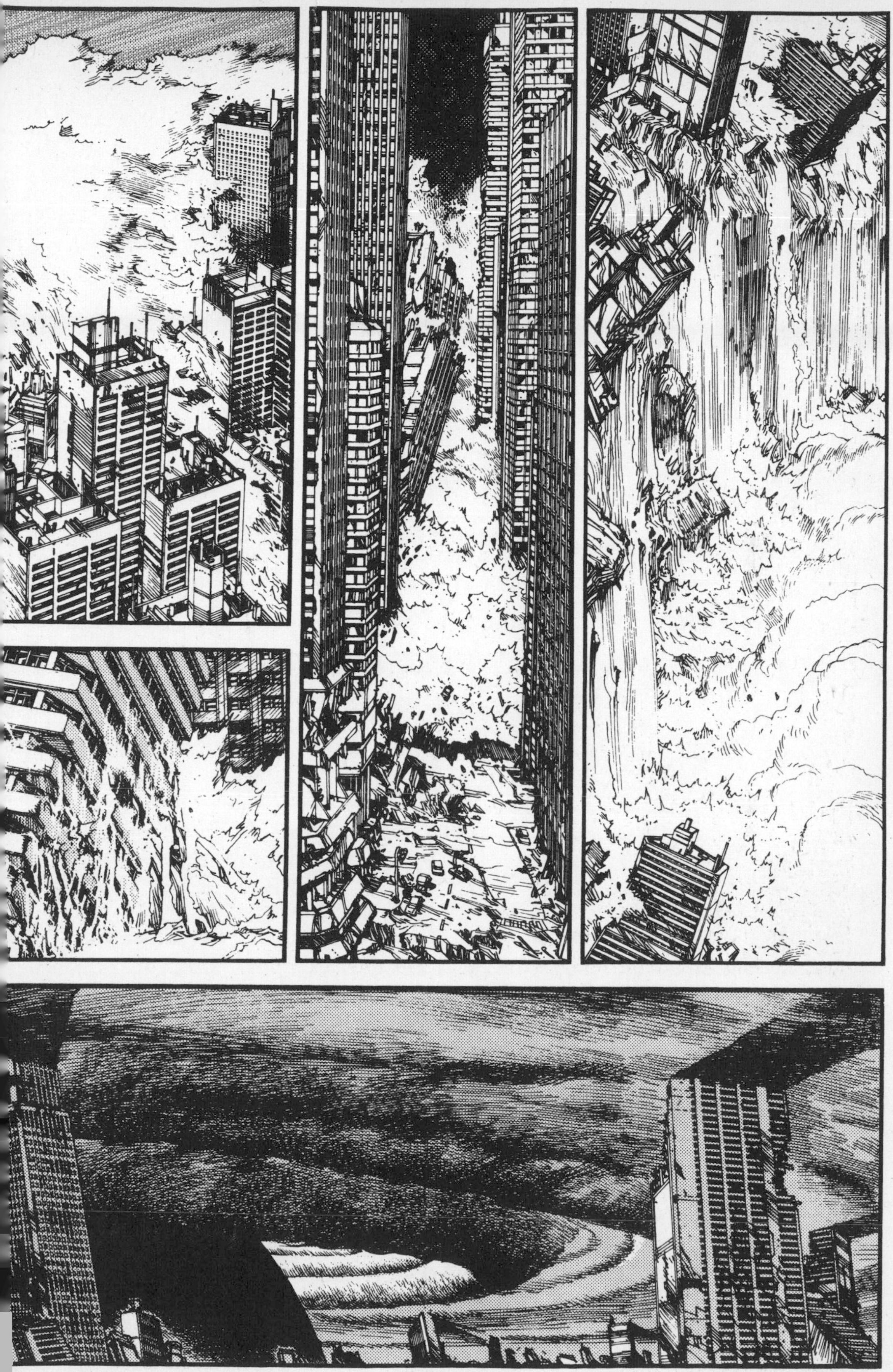

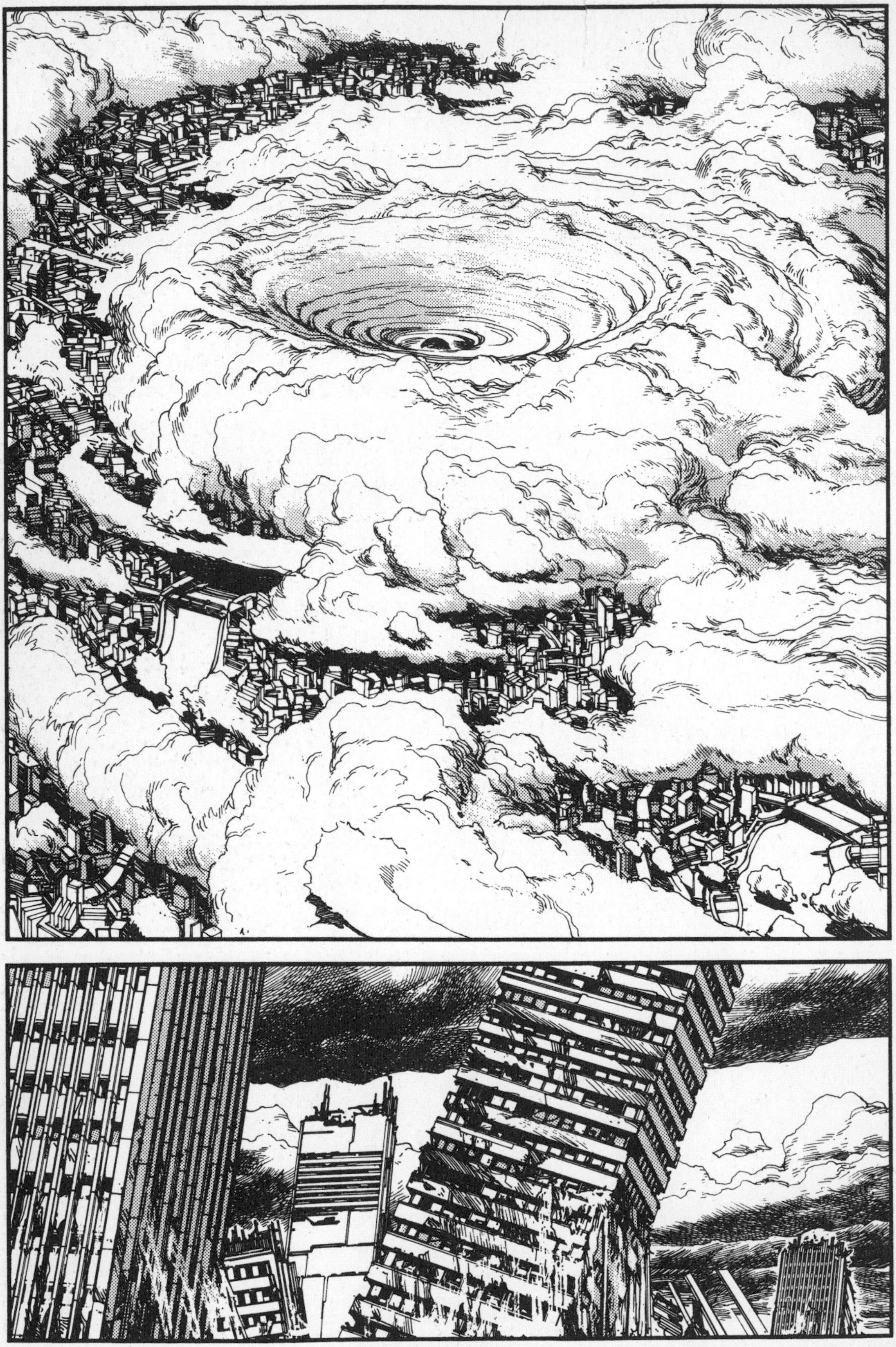

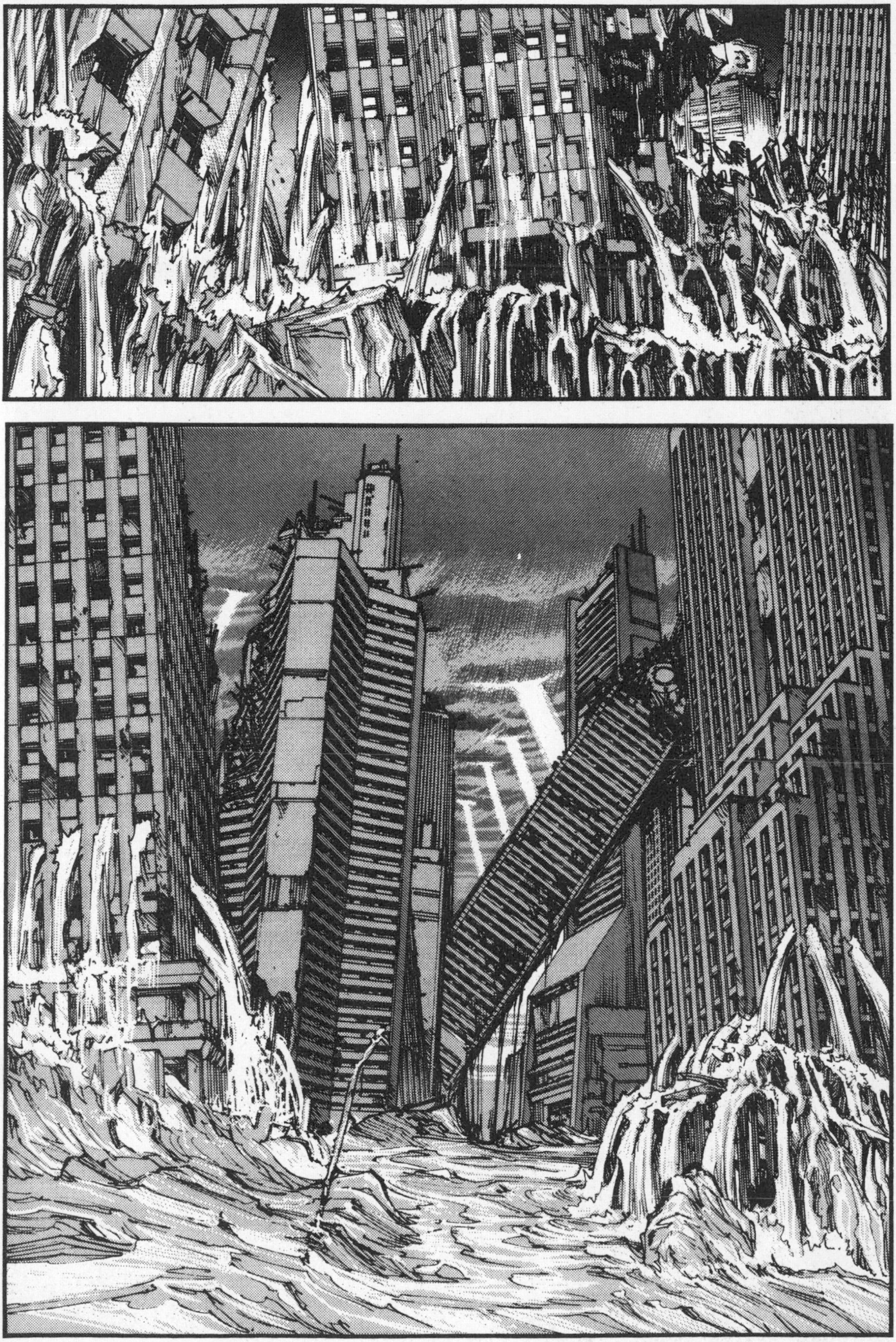

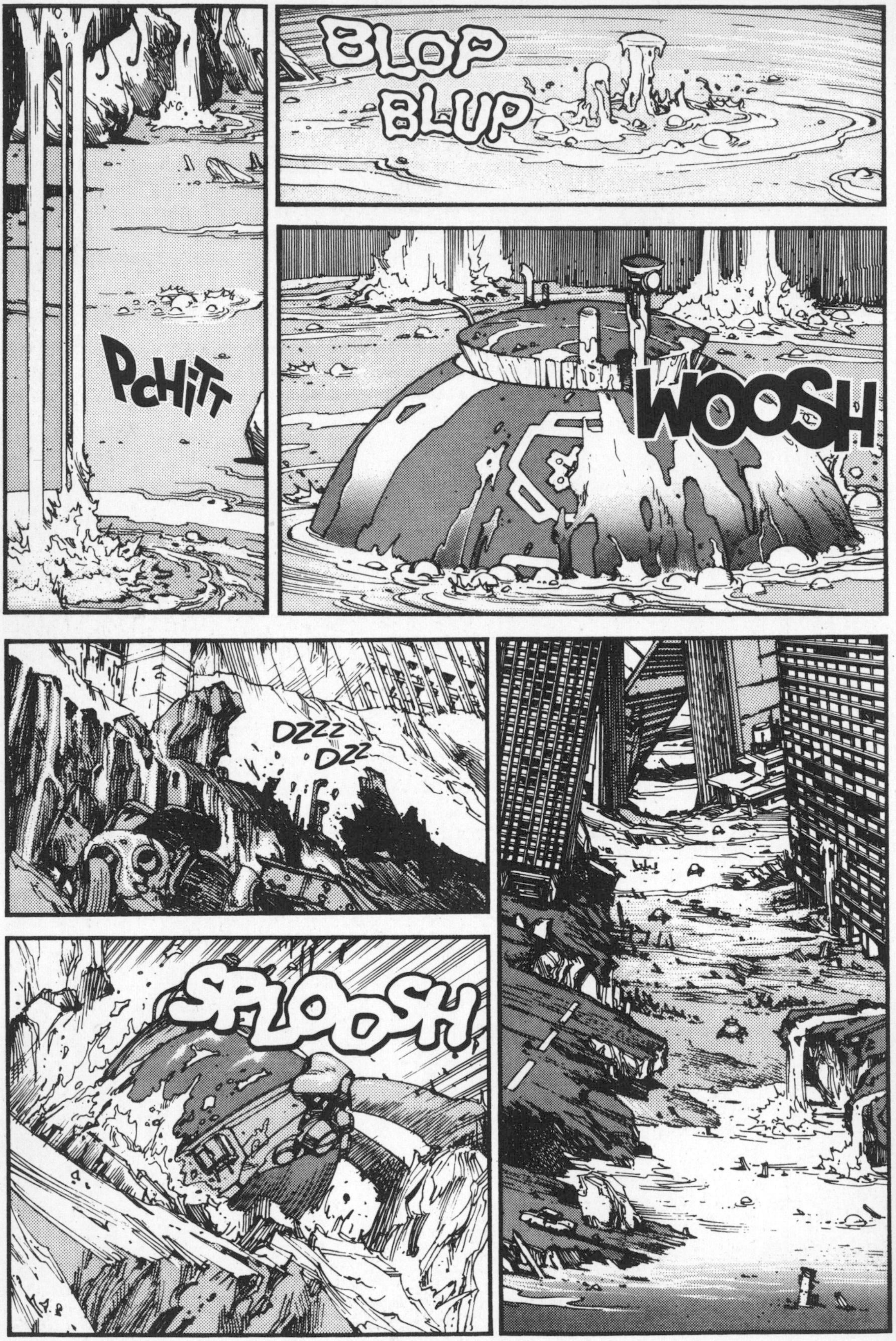
PCHITT
BLOP
BLUP
WOOSH
DZZZ
DZZ
SPLOOSH

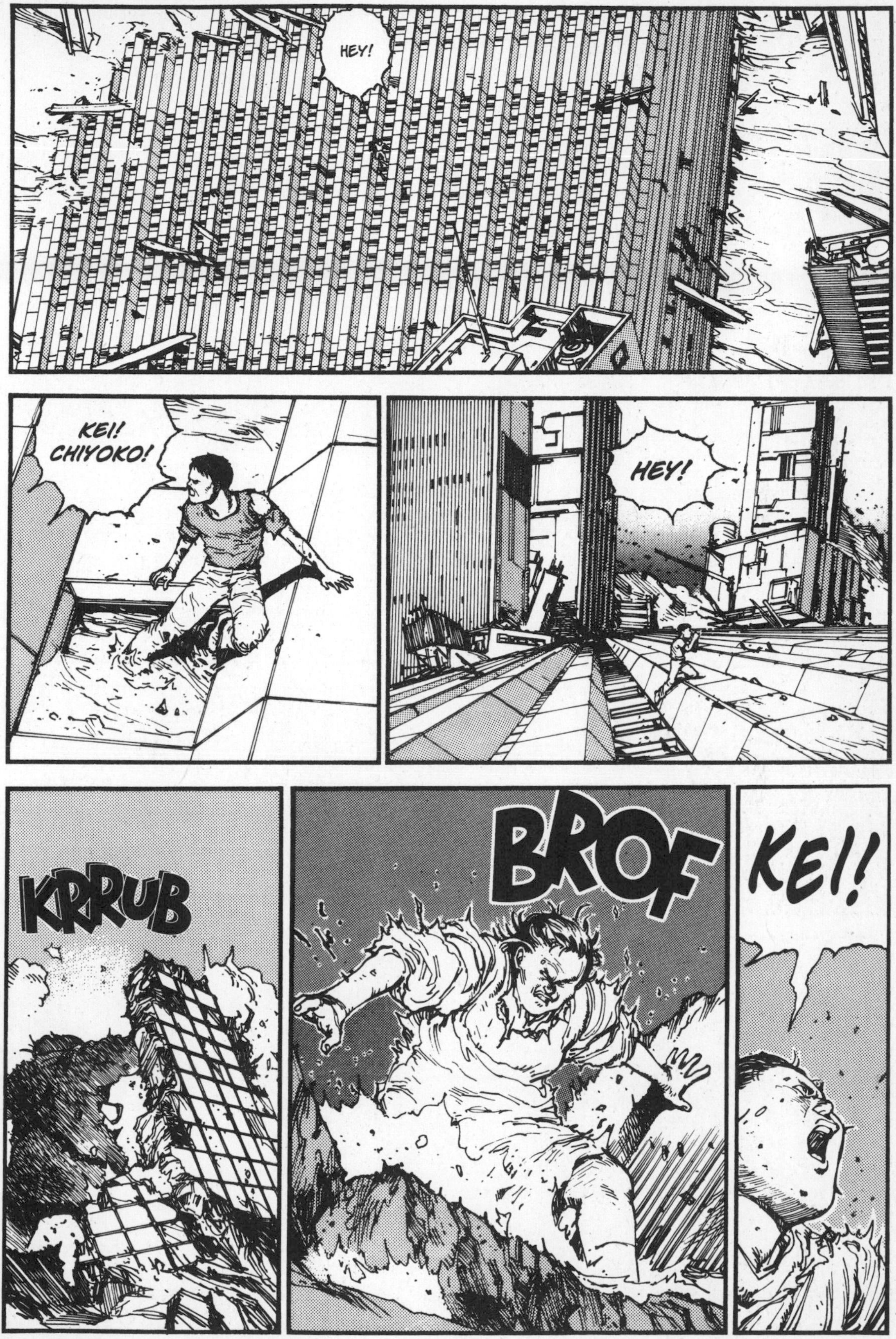
HEY!
KEI! CHIYOKO!
HEY!
KRRUB
BROF
KEI!

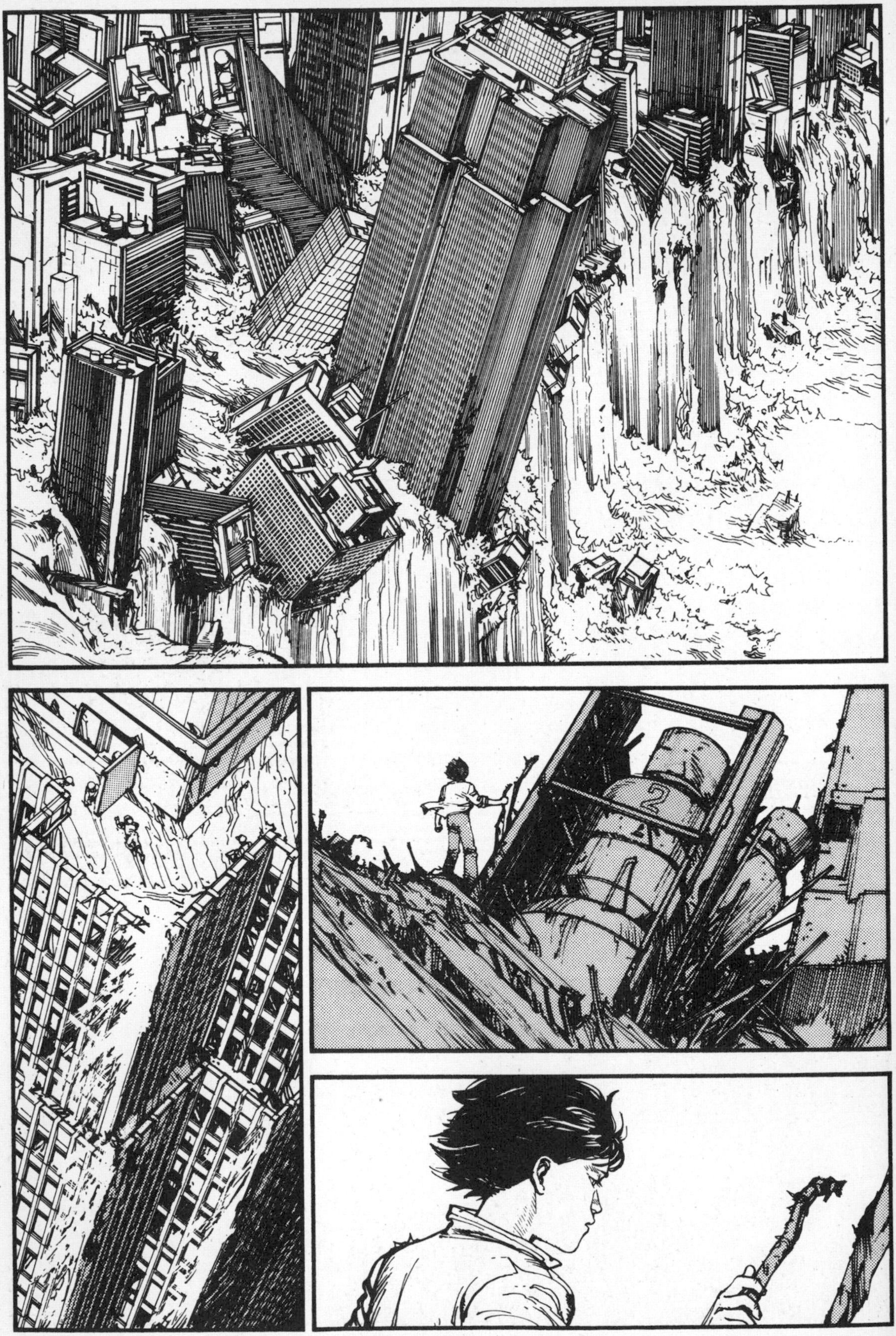
2

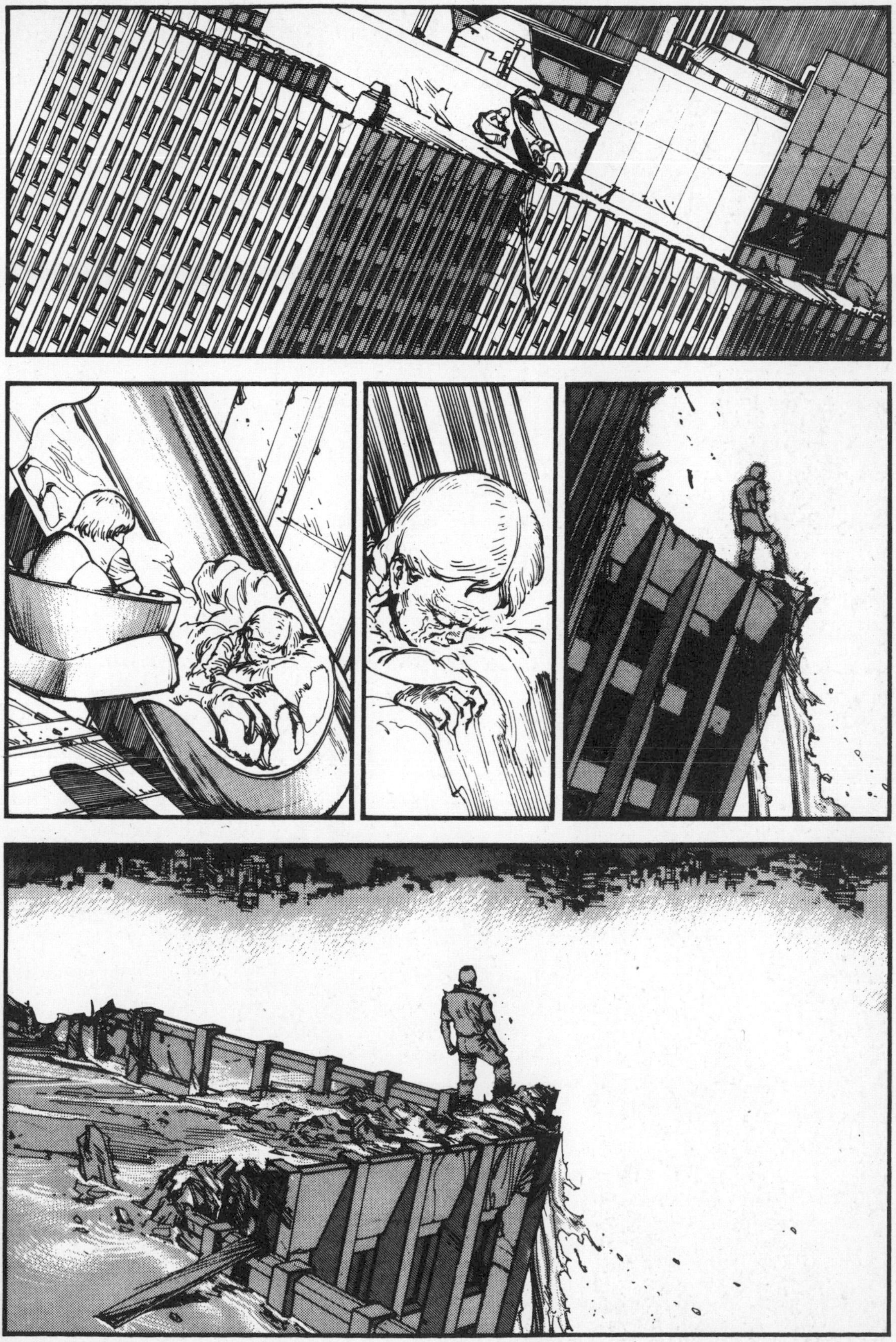

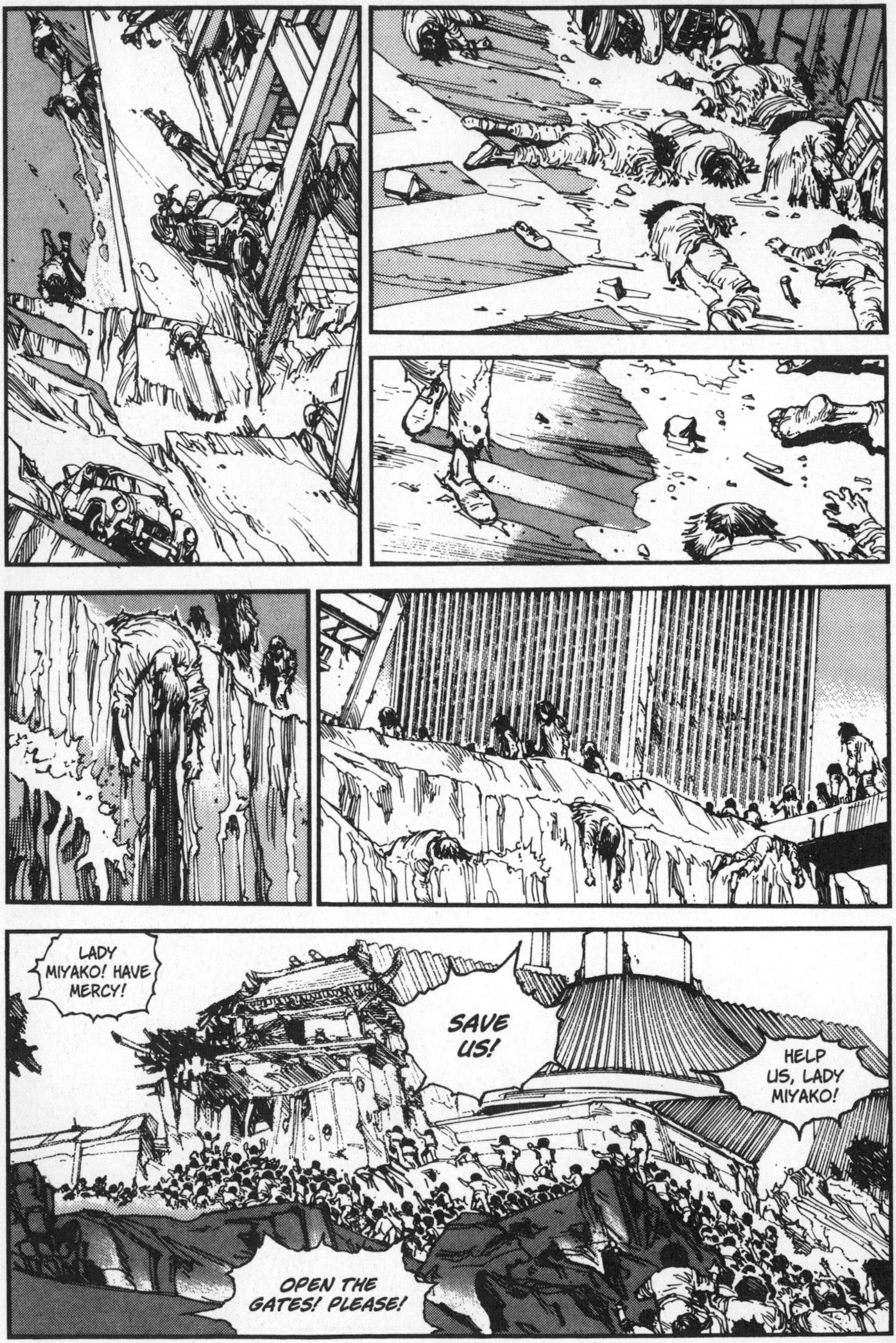
LADY MIYAKO! HAVE MERCY!
SAVE US!
HELP US, LADY MIYAKO!
OPEN THE GATES! PLEASE!

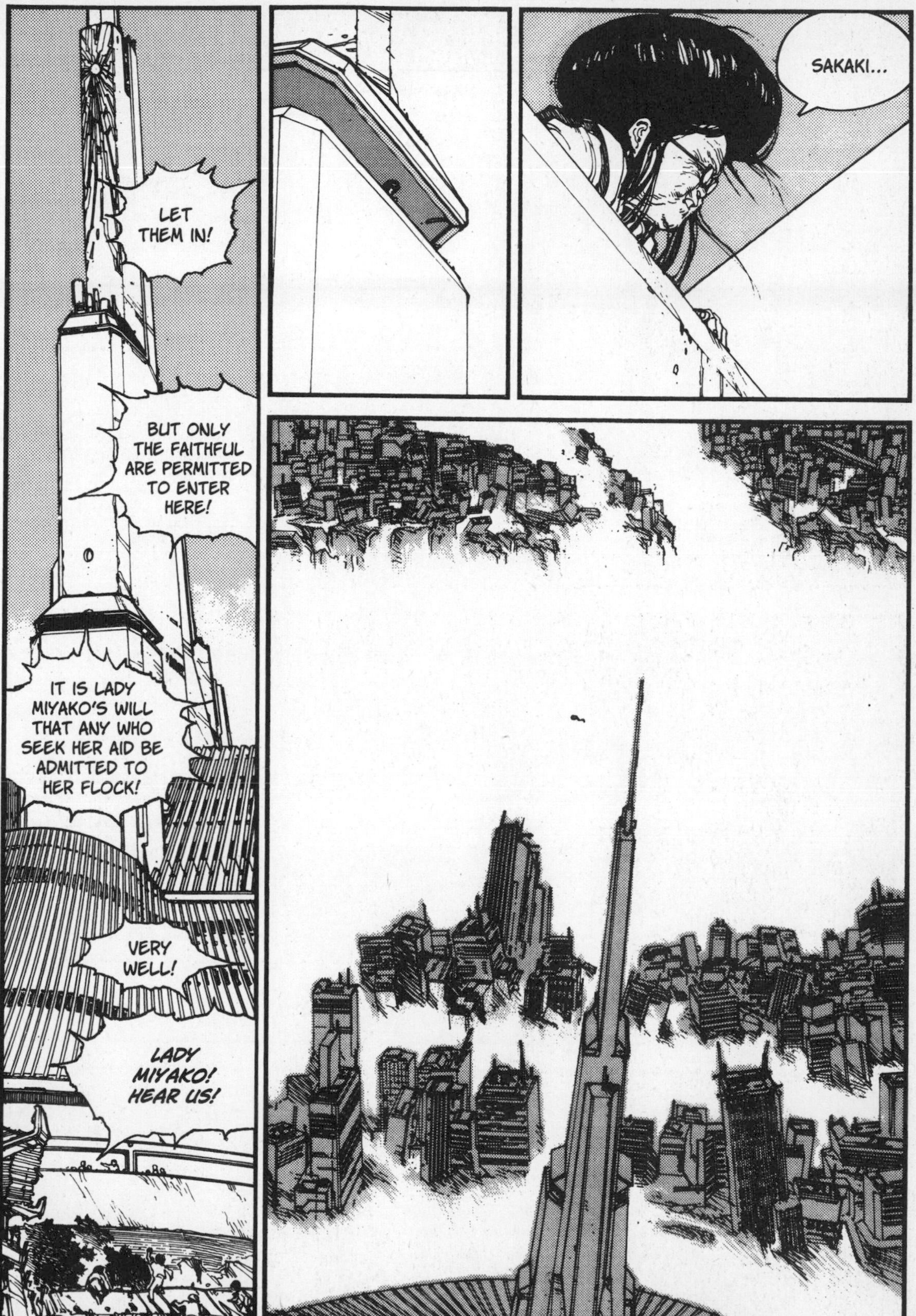
LET THEM IN!
BUT ONLY THE FAITHFUL ARE PERMITTED TO ENTER HERE!
IT IS LADY MIYAKO'S WILL THAT ANY WHO SEEK HER AID BE ADMITTED TO HER FLOCK!
VERY WELL!
LADY MIYAKO! HEAR US!
SAKAKI...

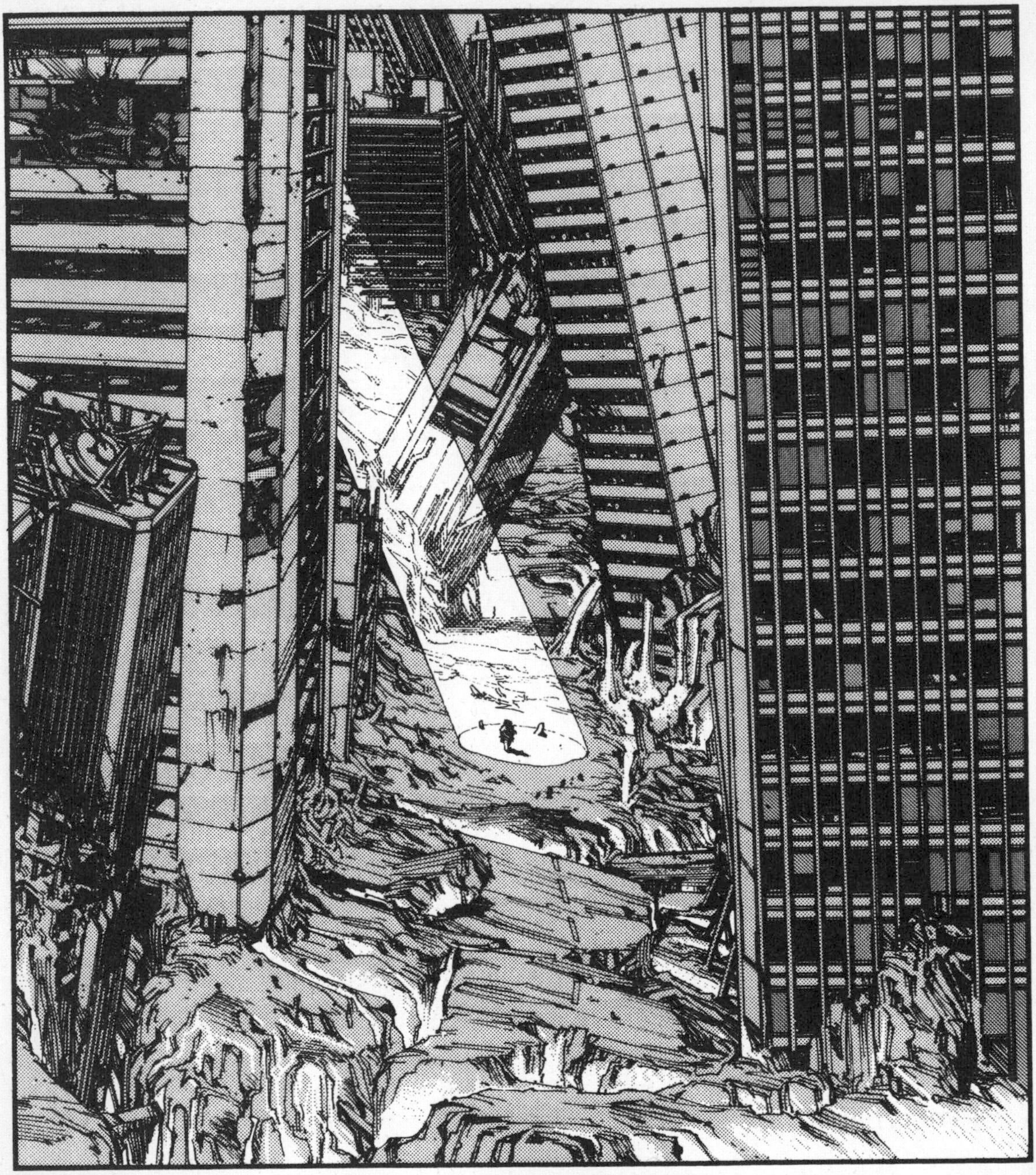

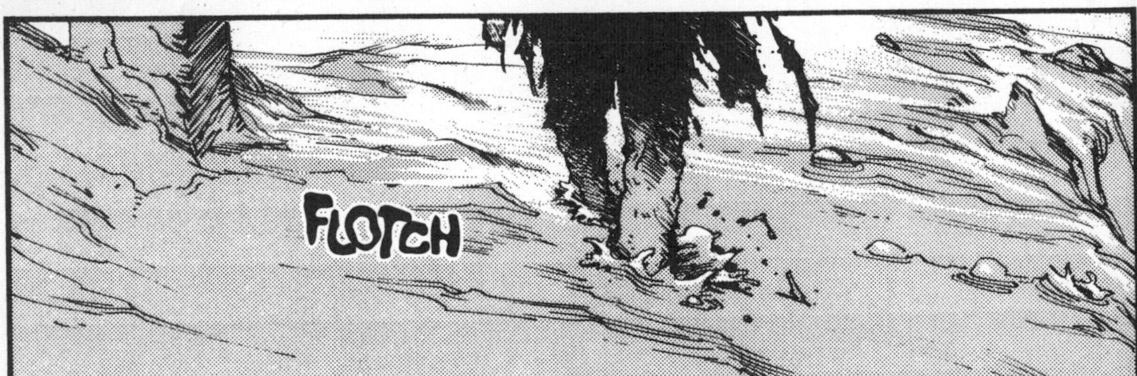
FLOTCH

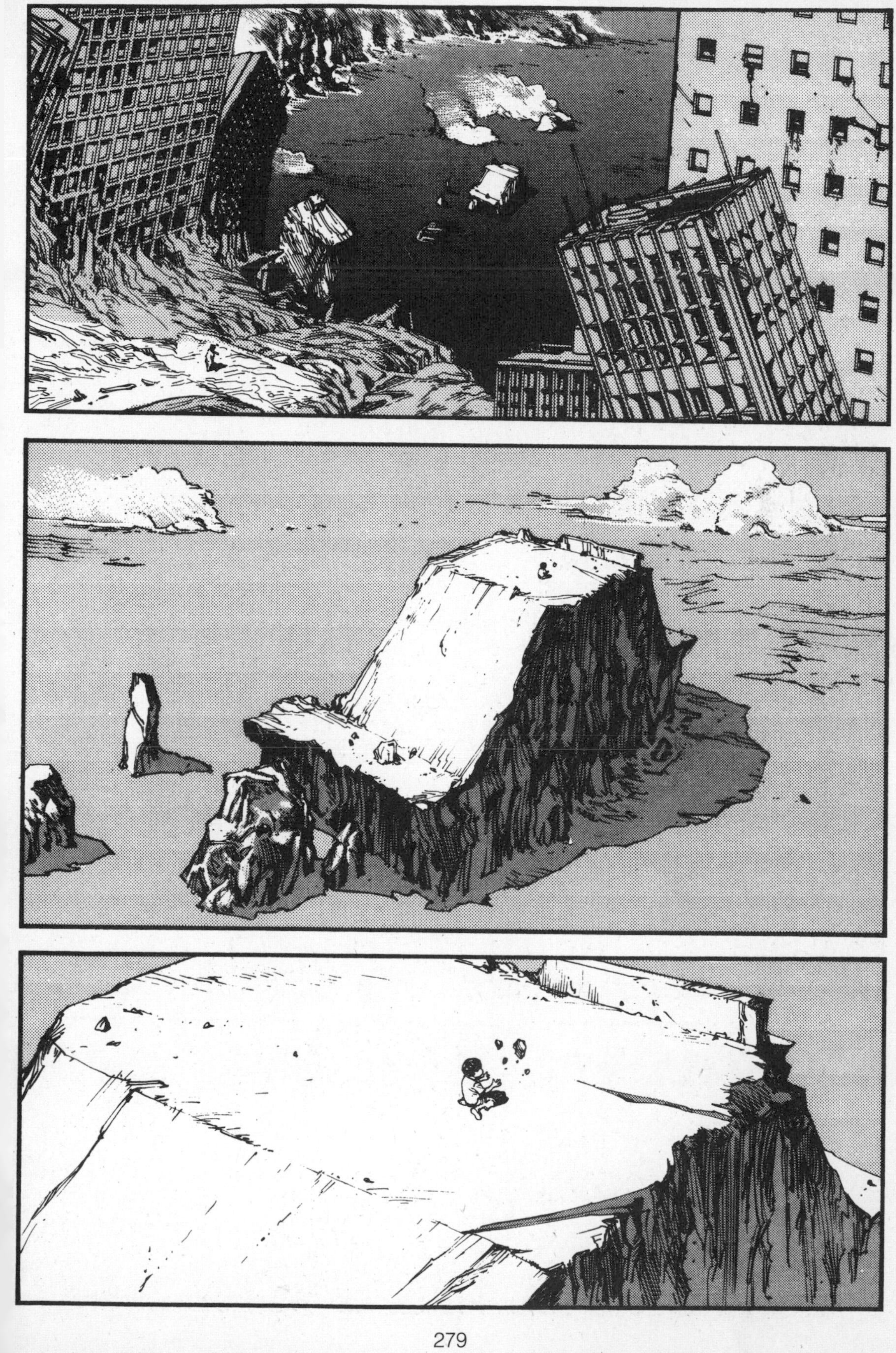

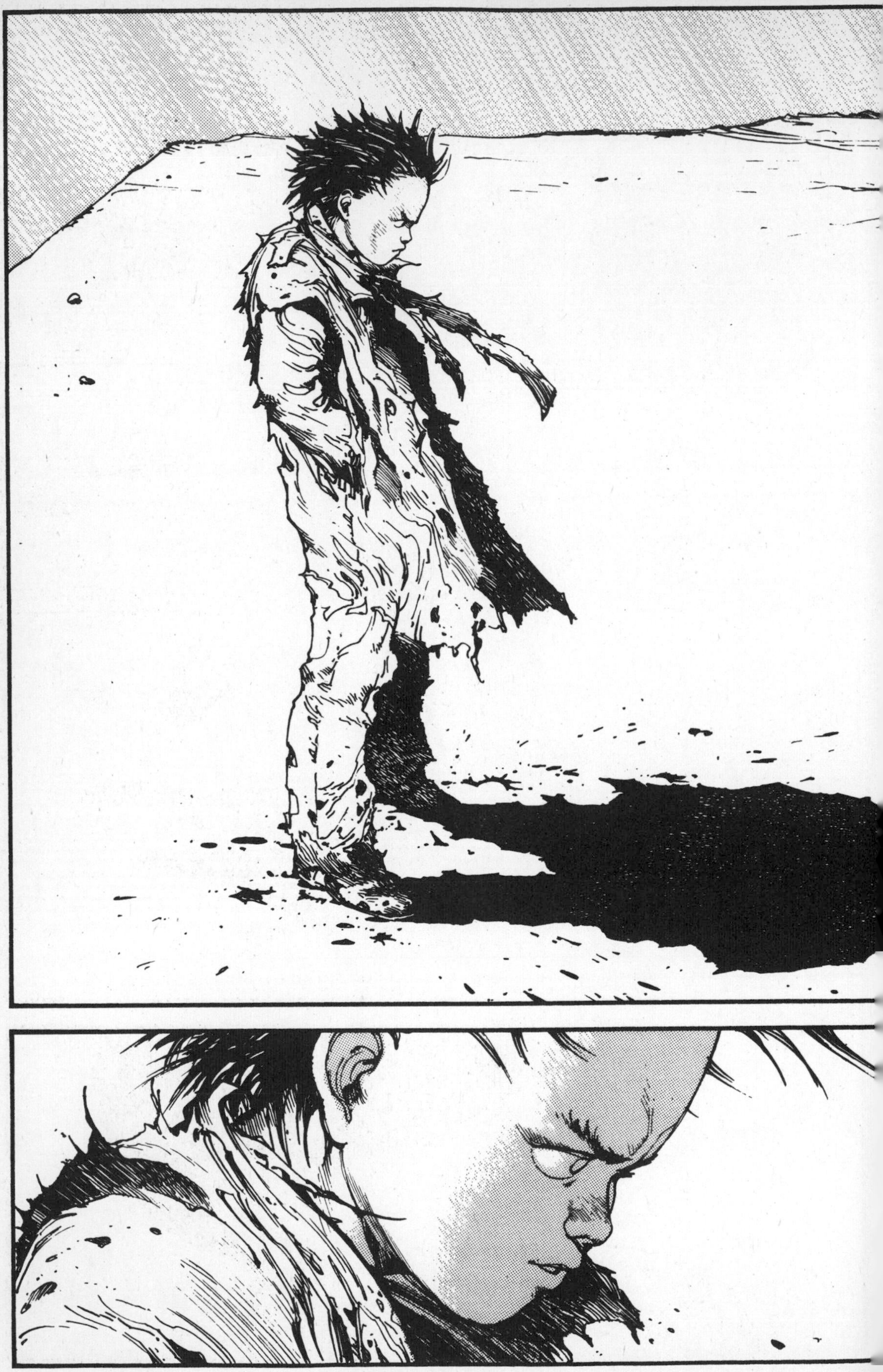

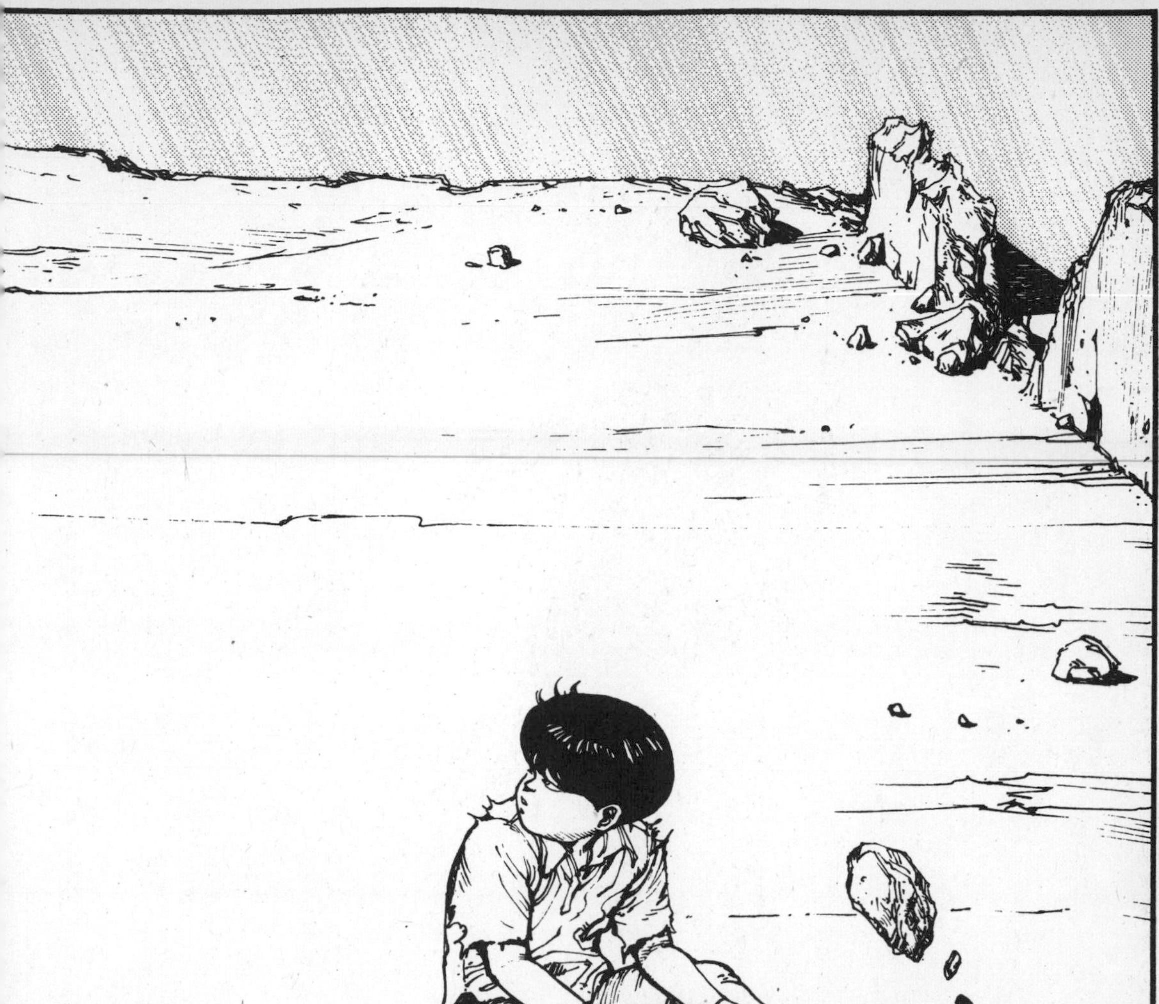

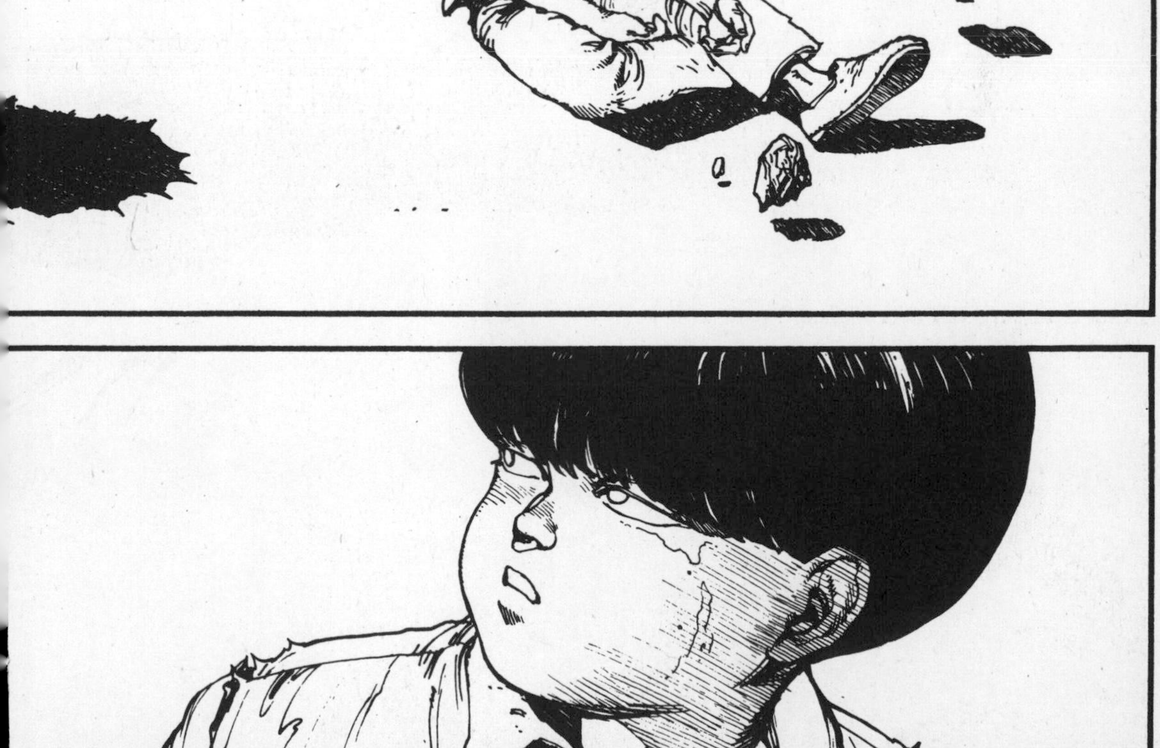

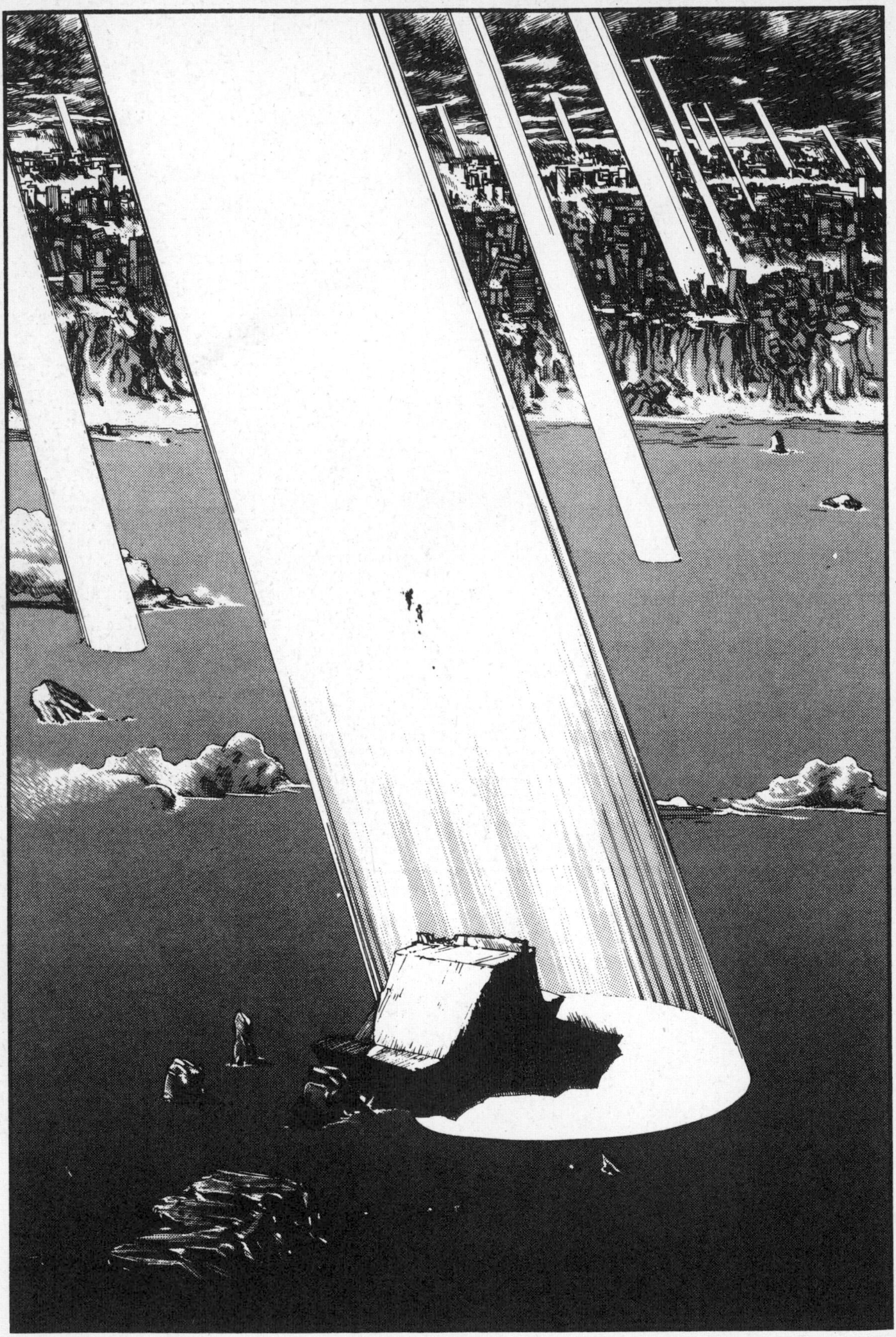

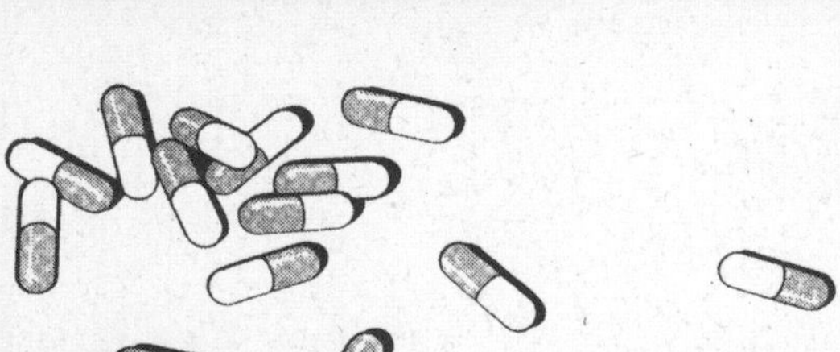

KATSUHIRO OTOMO

Katsuhiro Otomo was born in 1954 in Japan's Miyago Prefecture, a rural province some 300 miles northeast of Tokyo. While in high school, Otomo became, in his own words, "crazy about the movies." The young artist often traveled three hours by train just to see films, and the influence of cinema is a constant thread that runs through Otomo's work.

Soon after graduating high school, Otomo moved to Tokyo with the goal of becoming a comics artist. His first professional work was *Jyu-sei (A Gun Report)*, an adaptation of the Prosper Mérimée novella *Mateo Falcone*, which appeared in the weekly magazine *Action*. Otomo went on to create a series of short stories, usually twenty to thirty pages, challenging works that captured widespread critical acclaim in Japan. A 1980 review in the *Asahi* newspaper said, "Just as the New Cinema movement had demolished the old style of Hollywood filmmaking to usher in a fresh style of movie production in America, Katsuhiro Otomo…came to Tokyo to create a new comics style and shattered the conventions existing in manga."

In 1979, publication began on Otomo's first serialized work, *Fireball*, a story built around a "man versus computer" theme. Though the series was never completed, *Fireball* marked the beginning of Otomo's interest in science-fiction themes and was the forerunner of future work that would define his comics career and firmly establish him internationally as one of the acknowledged masters of the comics medium. *Domu*, first serialized in 1980 and collected in 1983, became a best seller and was the first manga to win the coveted Science Fiction Grand Prix Award, Japan's equivalent to America's Nebula Award. The media attention gained from this landmark achievement made Otomo one of the best-known comics authors in Japan. Critics raved about *Domu*, a story that combined terrifying paranormal genre elements with poignant observation of urban life in modern Japan. From the *Yomiuri* newspaper: "The weirdness that lurks in the seemingly peaceful living environment of a huge housing complex symbolizes the precariousness hidden at the bottom of today's living conditions in Japan."

Upon completion of *Domu*, Otomo began work on *Akira*, a two-thousand-plus-page epic of staggering illustrative virtuosity and gut-wrenching thematic power. Ten years in the making and eventually collected in six volumes, *Akira* went on to win every possible award and spawned video games, an animated feature film directed by Otomo himself — compared favorably by critics to science-fiction masterpieces such as *Blade Runner* and *A Clockwork Orange* — and a blizzard of merchandise. *Akira* has been published in virtually every language and stands not only as one of the crown jewels of manga, but is regarded by many as the finest work of graphic fiction ever created, anywhere. While the completion of *Akira* marked the beginning of Otomo's moving away from comics — his only major comics work since *Akira* has been the writing of *The Legend of Mother Sarah* — it began his odyssey as a filmmaker. After completion of the animated *Akira*, Otomo has gone on to work on a variety of animated films, including *Labyrinth Stories*, *Robot Carnival*, *Roujin Z*, *Spriggan*, and *Memories*, an anthology of adaptations of earlier Otomo comics stories. Otomo also directed the live-action *World Apartment Horror* as well as television commercials for Honda, Suntory, and Canon. Otomo lives and works in Tokyo.

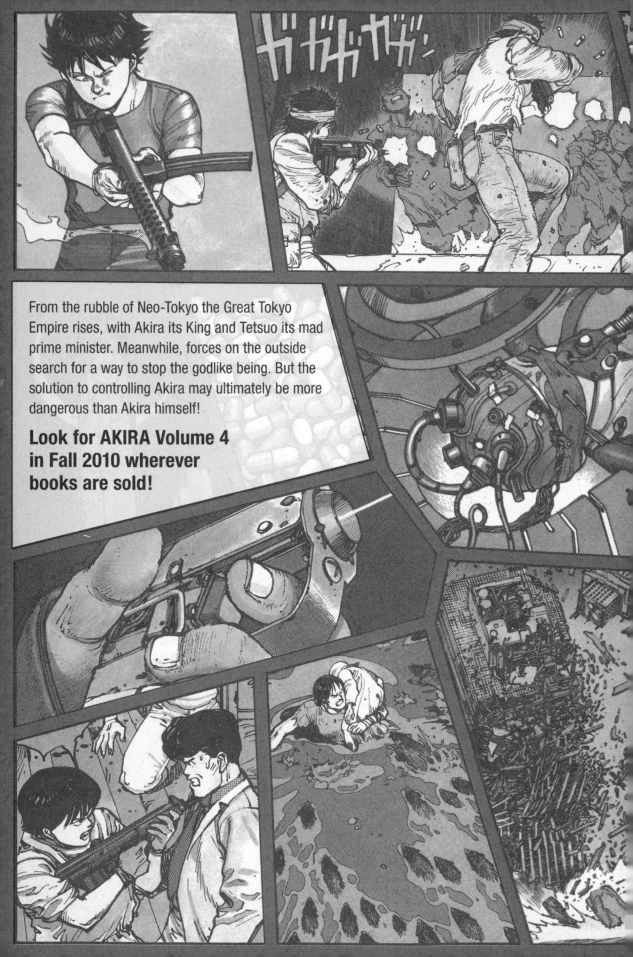

From the rubble of Neo-Tokyo the Great Tokyo Empire rises, with Akira its King and Tetsuo its mad prime minister. Meanwhile, forces on the outside search for a way to stop the godlike being. But the solution to controlling Akira may ultimately be more dangerous than Akira himself!

Look for AKIRA Volume 4 in Fall 2010 wherever books are sold!

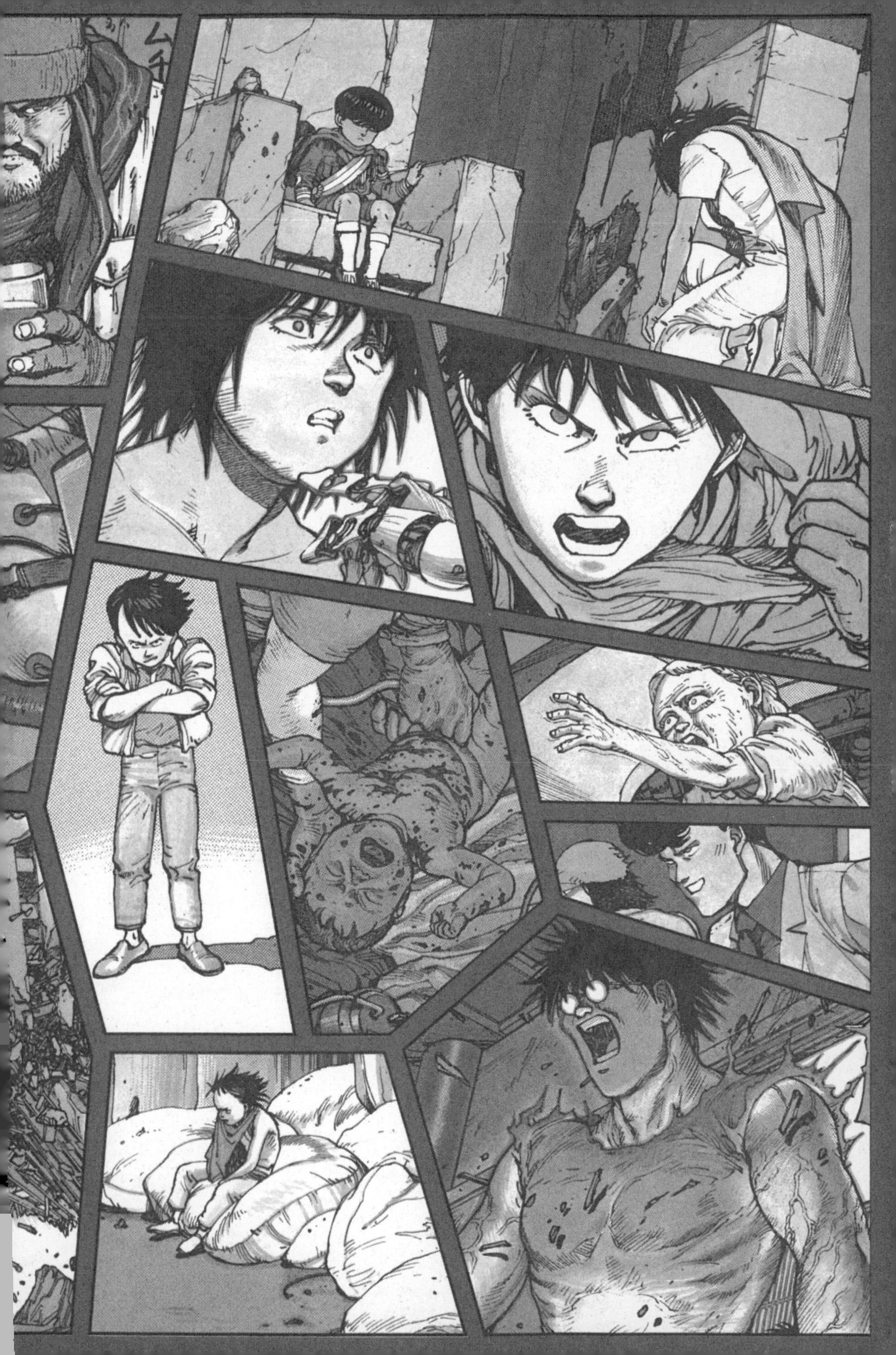

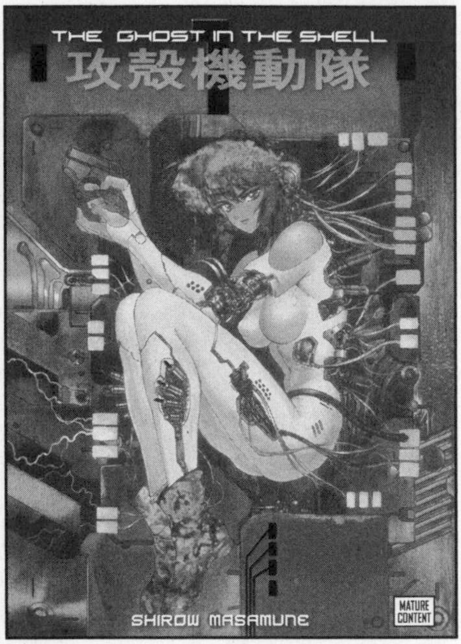
THE GHOST IN THE SHELL
攻殻機動隊
SHIROW MASAMUNE
MATURE CONTENT

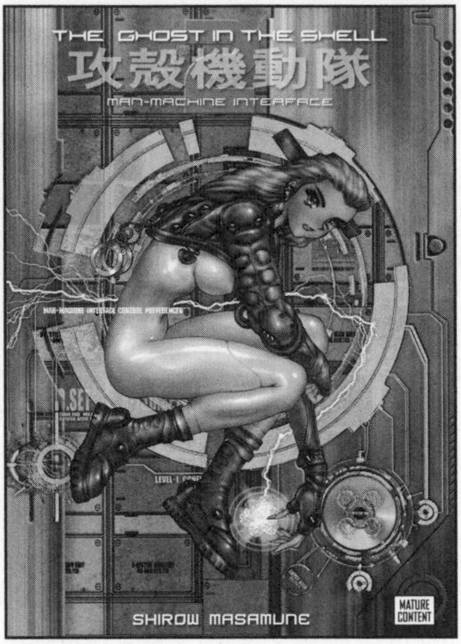
THE GHOST IN THE SHELL
攻殻機動隊
MAN-MACHINE INTERFACE
SHIROW MASAMUNE
MATURE CONTENT

The Ghost in the Shell series:

The Graphic Novels That Inspired a Generation of Filmmakers

In a futuristic world where society has become highly information intensive, and the human mind can dive directly into the computer network through neural devices, the thin line that defines the conscious self is referred to as one's "ghost." Major Motoko Kusanagi, leading Public Security Bureau Section 9, is human—but with an entirely cybernetic body. As her team solves one case after another of network crime and terrorism, she encounters a highly intelligent being that is not organic in origin.

#1 The Ghost in the Shell

#2 Man-Machine Interface

#1.5 Human Error Processor

KC KODANSHA COMICS